# PHP, MySQL® &
# JavaScript®

## ALL-IN-ONE

by Richard Blum

for
## dummies®
A Wiley Brand

## PHP, MySQL® & JavaScript® All-in-One For Dummies®

Published by: **John Wiley & Sons, Inc.**, 111 River Street, Hoboken, NJ 07030-5774, www.wiley.com

Copyright © 2018 by John Wiley & Sons, Inc., Hoboken, New Jersey

Published simultaneously in Canada

No part of this publication may be reproduced, stored in a retrieval system or transmitted in any form or by any means, electronic, mechanical, photocopying, recording, scanning or otherwise, except as permitted under Sections 107 or 108 of the 1976 United States Copyright Act, without the prior written permission of the Publisher. Requests to the Publisher for permission should be addressed to the Permissions Department, John Wiley & Sons, Inc., 111 River Street, Hoboken, NJ 07030, (201) 748-6011, fax (201) 748-6008, or online at http://www.wiley.com/go/permissions.

**Trademarks:** Wiley, For Dummies, the Dummies Man logo, Dummies.com, Making Everything Easier, and related trade dress are trademarks or registered trademarks of John Wiley & Sons, Inc. and may not be used without written permission. MySQL is a registered trademark of MySQL AB. JavaScript is a registered trademark of Oracle America, Inc. All other trademarks are the property of their respective owners. John Wiley & Sons, Inc. is not associated with any product or vendor mentioned in this book.

LIMIT OF LIABILITY/DISCLAIMER OF WARRANTY: THE PUBLISHER AND THE AUTHOR MAKE NO REPRESENTATIONS OR WARRANTIES WITH RESPECT TO THE ACCURACY OR COMPLETENESS OF THE CONTENTS OF THIS WORK AND SPECIFICALLY DISCLAIM ALL WARRANTIES, INCLUDING WITHOUT LIMITATION WARRANTIES OF FITNESS FOR A PARTICULAR PURPOSE. NO WARRANTY MAY BE CREATED OR EXTENDED BY SALES OR PROMOTIONAL MATERIALS. THE ADVICE AND STRATEGIES CONTAINED HEREIN MAY NOT BE SUITABLE FOR EVERY SITUATION. THIS WORK IS SOLD WITH THE UNDERSTANDING THAT THE PUBLISHER IS NOT ENGAGED IN RENDERING LEGAL, ACCOUNTING, OR OTHER PROFESSIONAL SERVICES. IF PROFESSIONAL ASSISTANCE IS REQUIRED, THE SERVICES OF A COMPETENT PROFESSIONAL PERSON SHOULD BE SOUGHT. NEITHER THE PUBLISHER NOR THE AUTHOR SHALL BE LIABLE FOR DAMAGES ARISING HEREFROM. THE FACT THAT AN ORGANIZATION OR WEBSITE IS REFERRED TO IN THIS WORK AS A CITATION AND/OR A POTENTIAL SOURCE OF FURTHER INFORMATION DOES NOT MEAN THAT THE AUTHOR OR THE PUBLISHER ENDORSES THE INFORMATION THE ORGANIZATION OR WEBSITE MAY PROVIDE OR RECOMMENDATIONS IT MAY MAKE. FURTHER, READERS SHOULD BE AWARE THAT INTERNET WEBSITES LISTED IN THIS WORK MAY HAVE CHANGED OR DISAPPEARED BETWEEN WHEN THIS WORK WAS WRITTEN AND WHEN IT IS READ.

For general information on our other products and services, please contact our Customer Care Department within the U.S. at 877-762-2974, outside the U.S. at 317-572-3993, or fax 317-572-4002. For technical support, please visit https://hub.wiley.com/community/support/dummies.

Wiley publishes in a variety of print and electronic formats and by print-on-demand. Some material included with standard print versions of this book may not be included in e-books or in print-on-demand. If this book refers to media such as a CD or DVD that is not included in the version you purchased, you may download this material at http://booksupport.wiley.com. For more information about Wiley products, visit www.wiley.com.

Library of Congress Control Number: 2018933793

ISBN 978-1-119-46838-7 (pbk); ISBN 978-1-119-46833-2 (ebk); ISBN 978-1-119-46837-0 (ebk)

Manufactured in the United States of America

10 9 8 7 6 5 4 3 2 1

# Contents at a Glance

**Introduction** . . . . . . . . . . . . . . . . . . . . . . . . . . . . . . . . . . . . . . . . . . . 1

**Book 1: Getting Started with Web Programming** . . . . . . . . . . . 5
CHAPTER 1:  Examining the Pieces of Web Programming . . . . . . . . . . . . . . . . . . . . . 7
CHAPTER 2:  Using a Web Server . . . . . . . . . . . . . . . . . . . . . . . . . . . . . . . . . . . . 27
CHAPTER 3:  Building a Development Environment . . . . . . . . . . . . . . . . . . . . . . . . . 51

**Book 2: HTML5 and CSS3** . . . . . . . . . . . . . . . . . . . . . . . . . . . . . . 71
CHAPTER 1:  The Basics of HTML5 . . . . . . . . . . . . . . . . . . . . . . . . . . . . . . . . . . . 73
CHAPTER 2:  The Basics of CSS3 . . . . . . . . . . . . . . . . . . . . . . . . . . . . . . . . . . . . 103
CHAPTER 3:  HTML5 Forms . . . . . . . . . . . . . . . . . . . . . . . . . . . . . . . . . . . . . . . 135
CHAPTER 4:  Advanced CSS3 . . . . . . . . . . . . . . . . . . . . . . . . . . . . . . . . . . . . . . 157
CHAPTER 5:  HTML5 and Multimedia . . . . . . . . . . . . . . . . . . . . . . . . . . . . . . . . . 177

**Book 3: JavaScript** . . . . . . . . . . . . . . . . . . . . . . . . . . . . . . . . . . . . 195
CHAPTER 1:  Introducing JavaScript . . . . . . . . . . . . . . . . . . . . . . . . . . . . . . . . . 197
CHAPTER 2:  Advanced JavaScript Coding . . . . . . . . . . . . . . . . . . . . . . . . . . . . . . 223
CHAPTER 3:  Using jQuery . . . . . . . . . . . . . . . . . . . . . . . . . . . . . . . . . . . . . . . . 243
CHAPTER 4:  Reacting to Events with JavaScript and jQuery . . . . . . . . . . . . . . . . . . 263
CHAPTER 5:  Troubleshooting JavaScript Programs . . . . . . . . . . . . . . . . . . . . . . . . 283

**Book 4: PHP** . . . . . . . . . . . . . . . . . . . . . . . . . . . . . . . . . . . . . . . . . . 301
CHAPTER 1:  Understanding PHP Basics . . . . . . . . . . . . . . . . . . . . . . . . . . . . . . . 303
CHAPTER 2:  PHP Flow Control . . . . . . . . . . . . . . . . . . . . . . . . . . . . . . . . . . . . . 325
CHAPTER 3:  PHP Libraries . . . . . . . . . . . . . . . . . . . . . . . . . . . . . . . . . . . . . . . 349
CHAPTER 4:  Considering PHP Security . . . . . . . . . . . . . . . . . . . . . . . . . . . . . . . . 375
CHAPTER 5:  Object-Oriented PHP Programming . . . . . . . . . . . . . . . . . . . . . . . . . 395
CHAPTER 6:  Sessions and Carts . . . . . . . . . . . . . . . . . . . . . . . . . . . . . . . . . . . . 419

**Book 5: MySQL** . . . . . . . . . . . . . . . . . . . . . . . . . . . . . . . . . . . . . . . 443
CHAPTER 1:  Introducing MySQL . . . . . . . . . . . . . . . . . . . . . . . . . . . . . . . . . . . . 445
CHAPTER 2:  Administering MySQL . . . . . . . . . . . . . . . . . . . . . . . . . . . . . . . . . . 465
CHAPTER 3:  Designing and Building a Database . . . . . . . . . . . . . . . . . . . . . . . . . . 489
CHAPTER 4:  Using the Database . . . . . . . . . . . . . . . . . . . . . . . . . . . . . . . . . . . . 513
CHAPTER 5:  Communicating with the Database from PHP Scripts . . . . . . . . . . . . . . 541

## Book 6: Creating Object-Oriented Programs ............... 561

CHAPTER 1: Designing an Object-Oriented Application ........................ 563

CHAPTER 2: Implementing an Object-Oriented Application ................... 593

CHAPTER 3: Using AJAX ..................................................... 619

CHAPTER 4: Extending WordPress .......................................... 651

## Book 7: Using PHP Frameworks ............................ 681

CHAPTER 1: The MVC Method ............................................... 683

CHAPTER 2: Selecting a Framework ........................................ 695

CHAPTER 3: Creating an Application Using Frameworks ..................... 715

## Index ........................................................ 735

# Table of Contents

**INTRODUCTION** . . . . . . . . . . . . . . . . . . . . . . . . . . . . . . . . . . . . . . . . . . . . . 1
  About This Book. . . . . . . . . . . . . . . . . . . . . . . . . . . . . . . . . . . . . . . . . . . . . 1
  Foolish Assumptions. . . . . . . . . . . . . . . . . . . . . . . . . . . . . . . . . . . . . . . . . 2
  Icons Used in This Book . . . . . . . . . . . . . . . . . . . . . . . . . . . . . . . . . . . . . . 3
  Beyond the Book . . . . . . . . . . . . . . . . . . . . . . . . . . . . . . . . . . . . . . . . . . . . 3
  Where to Go from Here . . . . . . . . . . . . . . . . . . . . . . . . . . . . . . . . . . . . . . . 3

**BOOK 1: GETTING STARTED WITH
WEB PROGRAMMING** . . . . . . . . . . . . . . . . . . . . . . . . . . . . . . . . . . . . . . . . . . 5

CHAPTER 1: **Examining the Pieces of Web Programming** . . . . . . . . 7
  Creating a Simple Web Page . . . . . . . . . . . . . . . . . . . . . . . . . . . . . . . . . . . 7
    Kicking things off with the World Wide Web . . . . . . . . . . . . . . . . . . . 8
    Making sense of markup languages. . . . . . . . . . . . . . . . . . . . . . . . . . 9
    Retrieving HTML documents . . . . . . . . . . . . . . . . . . . . . . . . . . . . . . .10
    Styling . . . . . . . . . . . . . . . . . . . . . . . . . . . . . . . . . . . . . . . . . . . . . . . . .14
  Creating a Dynamic Web Page . . . . . . . . . . . . . . . . . . . . . . . . . . . . . . . .17
    Client-side programming . . . . . . . . . . . . . . . . . . . . . . . . . . . . . . . . . .19
    Server-side programming . . . . . . . . . . . . . . . . . . . . . . . . . . . . . . . . . .21
    Combining client-side and server-side programming . . . . . . . . . .24
  Storing Content . . . . . . . . . . . . . . . . . . . . . . . . . . . . . . . . . . . . . . . . . . . .25

CHAPTER 2: **Using a Web Server** . . . . . . . . . . . . . . . . . . . . . . . . . . . . . . . . . . . . . 27
  Recognizing What's Required. . . . . . . . . . . . . . . . . . . . . . . . . . . . . . . . . .27
    The web server. . . . . . . . . . . . . . . . . . . . . . . . . . . . . . . . . . . . . . . . . . .28
    The PHP server. . . . . . . . . . . . . . . . . . . . . . . . . . . . . . . . . . . . . . . . . . .29
    The database server . . . . . . . . . . . . . . . . . . . . . . . . . . . . . . . . . . . . . .30
  Considering Your Server Options . . . . . . . . . . . . . . . . . . . . . . . . . . . . . .31
    Using a web-hosting company . . . . . . . . . . . . . . . . . . . . . . . . . . . . . .32
    Building your own server environment . . . . . . . . . . . . . . . . . . . . . . .33
    Using premade servers. . . . . . . . . . . . . . . . . . . . . . . . . . . . . . . . . . . . .37
  Tweaking the Servers . . . . . . . . . . . . . . . . . . . . . . . . . . . . . . . . . . . . . . . .41
    Customizing the Apache Server . . . . . . . . . . . . . . . . . . . . . . . . . . . . .41
    Customizing the MySQL server . . . . . . . . . . . . . . . . . . . . . . . . . . . . .44
    Customizing the PHP server. . . . . . . . . . . . . . . . . . . . . . . . . . . . . . . .46

CHAPTER 3: **Building a Development Environment** . . . . . . . . . . . . . . 51
  Knowing Which Tools to Avoid . . . . . . . . . . . . . . . . . . . . . . . . . . . . . . . .51
    Graphical desktop tools . . . . . . . . . . . . . . . . . . . . . . . . . . . . . . . . . . . .52
    Web-hosting sites . . . . . . . . . . . . . . . . . . . . . . . . . . . . . . . . . . . . . . . . .52
    Word processors . . . . . . . . . . . . . . . . . . . . . . . . . . . . . . . . . . . . . . . . . .53

Working with the Right Tools. . . . . . . . . . . . . . . . . . . . . . . . . . . . . . . . . . . .53
Text editors. . . . . . . . . . . . . . . . . . . . . . . . . . . . . . . . . . . . . . . . . . . . .53
Program editors. . . . . . . . . . . . . . . . . . . . . . . . . . . . . . . . . . . . . . . . .61
Integrated development environments. . . . . . . . . . . . . . . . . . . . . .64
Browser debuggers. . . . . . . . . . . . . . . . . . . . . . . . . . . . . . . . . . . . . .67

**BOOK 2: HTML5 AND CSS3** . . . . . . . . . . . . . . . . . . . . . . . . . . . . . . . . . .71

CHAPTER 1: **The Basics of HTML5** . . . . . . . . . . . . . . . . . . . . . . . . . . . . . .73
Diving into Document Structure. . . . . . . . . . . . . . . . . . . . . . . . . . . . . . .73
Elements, tags, and attributes. . . . . . . . . . . . . . . . . . . . . . . . . . . . .73
Document type. . . . . . . . . . . . . . . . . . . . . . . . . . . . . . . . . . . . . . . . .75
Page definition. . . . . . . . . . . . . . . . . . . . . . . . . . . . . . . . . . . . . . . . .76
Page sections. . . . . . . . . . . . . . . . . . . . . . . . . . . . . . . . . . . . . . . . . .78
Looking at the Basic HTML5 Elements. . . . . . . . . . . . . . . . . . . . . . . . . .81
Headings. . . . . . . . . . . . . . . . . . . . . . . . . . . . . . . . . . . . . . . . . . . . . .81
Text groupings. . . . . . . . . . . . . . . . . . . . . . . . . . . . . . . . . . . . . . . . .82
Breaks. . . . . . . . . . . . . . . . . . . . . . . . . . . . . . . . . . . . . . . . . . . . . . . .84
Marking Your Text. . . . . . . . . . . . . . . . . . . . . . . . . . . . . . . . . . . . . . . . . .85
Formatting text. . . . . . . . . . . . . . . . . . . . . . . . . . . . . . . . . . . . . . . . .85
Using hypertext. . . . . . . . . . . . . . . . . . . . . . . . . . . . . . . . . . . . . . . . .86
Working with Characters. . . . . . . . . . . . . . . . . . . . . . . . . . . . . . . . . . . .90
Character sets. . . . . . . . . . . . . . . . . . . . . . . . . . . . . . . . . . . . . . . . . .90
Special characters. . . . . . . . . . . . . . . . . . . . . . . . . . . . . . . . . . . . . . .91
Making a List (And Checking It Twice). . . . . . . . . . . . . . . . . . . . . . . . . .92
Unordered lists. . . . . . . . . . . . . . . . . . . . . . . . . . . . . . . . . . . . . . . . .92
Ordered lists. . . . . . . . . . . . . . . . . . . . . . . . . . . . . . . . . . . . . . . . . . .93
Description lists. . . . . . . . . . . . . . . . . . . . . . . . . . . . . . . . . . . . . . . . .95
Building Tables. . . . . . . . . . . . . . . . . . . . . . . . . . . . . . . . . . . . . . . . . . . .96
Defining a table. . . . . . . . . . . . . . . . . . . . . . . . . . . . . . . . . . . . . . . . .96
Defining the table's rows and columns. . . . . . . . . . . . . . . . . . . . . .97
Defining the table headings. . . . . . . . . . . . . . . . . . . . . . . . . . . . . . .99

CHAPTER 2: **The Basics of CSS3** . . . . . . . . . . . . . . . . . . . . . . . . . . . . . . .103
Understanding Styles. . . . . . . . . . . . . . . . . . . . . . . . . . . . . . . . . . . . . .103
Defining the rules of CSS3. . . . . . . . . . . . . . . . . . . . . . . . . . . . . . .104
Applying style rules. . . . . . . . . . . . . . . . . . . . . . . . . . . . . . . . . . . .110
Cascading style rules. . . . . . . . . . . . . . . . . . . . . . . . . . . . . . . . . . .111
Styling Text. . . . . . . . . . . . . . . . . . . . . . . . . . . . . . . . . . . . . . . . . . . . . .112
Setting the font. . . . . . . . . . . . . . . . . . . . . . . . . . . . . . . . . . . . . . . .112
Playing with color. . . . . . . . . . . . . . . . . . . . . . . . . . . . . . . . . . . . . .116
Working with the Box Model. . . . . . . . . . . . . . . . . . . . . . . . . . . . . . . .119
Styling Tables. . . . . . . . . . . . . . . . . . . . . . . . . . . . . . . . . . . . . . . . . . . .121
Table borders. . . . . . . . . . . . . . . . . . . . . . . . . . . . . . . . . . . . . . . . .122
Table data. . . . . . . . . . . . . . . . . . . . . . . . . . . . . . . . . . . . . . . . . . . .123

Positioning Elements . . . . . . . . . . . . . . . . . . . . . . . . . . . . . . . . . . . . .125
    Putting elements in a specific place . . . . . . . . . . . . . . . . . . . . . .128
    Floating elements . . . . . . . . . . . . . . . . . . . . . . . . . . . . . . . . . . . .130

CHAPTER 3: **HTML5 Forms** . . . . . . . . . . . . . . . . . . . . . . . . . . . . . . . . . . . . . . .135
Understanding HTML5 Forms . . . . . . . . . . . . . . . . . . . . . . . . . . . . . .135
    Defining a form . . . . . . . . . . . . . . . . . . . . . . . . . . . . . . . . . . . . . .136
    Working with form fields . . . . . . . . . . . . . . . . . . . . . . . . . . . . . . .137
Using Input Fields . . . . . . . . . . . . . . . . . . . . . . . . . . . . . . . . . . . . . . .138
    Text boxes . . . . . . . . . . . . . . . . . . . . . . . . . . . . . . . . . . . . . . . . .138
    Password entry . . . . . . . . . . . . . . . . . . . . . . . . . . . . . . . . . . . . . .140
    Check boxes . . . . . . . . . . . . . . . . . . . . . . . . . . . . . . . . . . . . . . . .141
    Radio buttons . . . . . . . . . . . . . . . . . . . . . . . . . . . . . . . . . . . . . . .142
    Hidden fields . . . . . . . . . . . . . . . . . . . . . . . . . . . . . . . . . . . . . . .143
    File upload . . . . . . . . . . . . . . . . . . . . . . . . . . . . . . . . . . . . . . . . .144
    Buttons . . . . . . . . . . . . . . . . . . . . . . . . . . . . . . . . . . . . . . . . . . .145
Adding a Text Area . . . . . . . . . . . . . . . . . . . . . . . . . . . . . . . . . . . . . .146
Using Drop-Down Lists . . . . . . . . . . . . . . . . . . . . . . . . . . . . . . . . . . .147
Enhancing HTML5 Forms . . . . . . . . . . . . . . . . . . . . . . . . . . . . . . . . . .149
    Data lists . . . . . . . . . . . . . . . . . . . . . . . . . . . . . . . . . . . . . . . . . .149
    Additional input fields . . . . . . . . . . . . . . . . . . . . . . . . . . . . . . . .150
Using HTML5 Data Validation . . . . . . . . . . . . . . . . . . . . . . . . . . . . . .154
    Holding your place . . . . . . . . . . . . . . . . . . . . . . . . . . . . . . . . . . .154
    Making certain data required . . . . . . . . . . . . . . . . . . . . . . . . . . .155
    Validating data types . . . . . . . . . . . . . . . . . . . . . . . . . . . . . . . . .155

CHAPTER 4: **Advanced CSS3** . . . . . . . . . . . . . . . . . . . . . . . . . . . . . . . . . . . . .157
Rounding Your Corners . . . . . . . . . . . . . . . . . . . . . . . . . . . . . . . . . . .157
Using Border Images . . . . . . . . . . . . . . . . . . . . . . . . . . . . . . . . . . . . .159
Looking at the CSS3 Colors . . . . . . . . . . . . . . . . . . . . . . . . . . . . . . . .162
Playing with Color Gradients . . . . . . . . . . . . . . . . . . . . . . . . . . . . . . .164
    Linear gradients . . . . . . . . . . . . . . . . . . . . . . . . . . . . . . . . . . . . .164
    Radial gradients . . . . . . . . . . . . . . . . . . . . . . . . . . . . . . . . . . . . .165
Adding Shadows . . . . . . . . . . . . . . . . . . . . . . . . . . . . . . . . . . . . . . . .166
    Text shadows . . . . . . . . . . . . . . . . . . . . . . . . . . . . . . . . . . . . . . .166
    Box shadows . . . . . . . . . . . . . . . . . . . . . . . . . . . . . . . . . . . . . . .167
Creating Fonts . . . . . . . . . . . . . . . . . . . . . . . . . . . . . . . . . . . . . . . . . .168
    Focusing on font files . . . . . . . . . . . . . . . . . . . . . . . . . . . . . . . . .169
    Working with web fonts . . . . . . . . . . . . . . . . . . . . . . . . . . . . . . .169
Handling Media Queries . . . . . . . . . . . . . . . . . . . . . . . . . . . . . . . . . .171
    Using the @media command . . . . . . . . . . . . . . . . . . . . . . . . . . .171
    Dealing with CSS3 media queries . . . . . . . . . . . . . . . . . . . . . . . .172
    Applying multiple style sheets . . . . . . . . . . . . . . . . . . . . . . . . . .175

CHAPTER 5: **HTML5 and Multimedia** . . . . . . . . . . . . . . . . . . . . . . . . . . . . . . 177
    Working with Images . . . . . . . . . . . . . . . . . . . . . . . . . . . . . . . . . . 177
        Placing images . . . . . . . . . . . . . . . . . . . . . . . . . . . . . . . 178
        Styling images . . . . . . . . . . . . . . . . . . . . . . . . . . . . . . . 179
        Linking images . . . . . . . . . . . . . . . . . . . . . . . . . . . . . . . 181
        Working with image maps . . . . . . . . . . . . . . . . . . . . . . . 182
        Using HTML5 image additions . . . . . . . . . . . . . . . . . . . . 183
    Playing Audio . . . . . . . . . . . . . . . . . . . . . . . . . . . . . . . . . . . . 185
        Embedded audio . . . . . . . . . . . . . . . . . . . . . . . . . . . . . . 185
        Digital audio formats . . . . . . . . . . . . . . . . . . . . . . . . . . 186
        Audio the HTML5 way . . . . . . . . . . . . . . . . . . . . . . . . . . 188
    Watching Videos . . . . . . . . . . . . . . . . . . . . . . . . . . . . . . . . . . 190
        Paying attention to video quality . . . . . . . . . . . . . . . . . . 190
        Looking at digital video formats . . . . . . . . . . . . . . . . . . 191
        Putting videos in your web page . . . . . . . . . . . . . . . . . . 192
    Getting Help from Streamers . . . . . . . . . . . . . . . . . . . . . . . . . 194

**BOOK 3: JAVASCRIPT** . . . . . . . . . . . . . . . . . . . . . . . . . . . . . . . . . . 195

CHAPTER 1: **Introducing JavaScript** . . . . . . . . . . . . . . . . . . . . . . . . . . . . 197
    Knowing Why You Should Use JavaScript . . . . . . . . . . . . . . . . 197
        Changing web page content . . . . . . . . . . . . . . . . . . . . . 198
        Changing web page styles . . . . . . . . . . . . . . . . . . . . . . . 198
    Seeing Where to Put Your JavaScript Code . . . . . . . . . . . . . . . 199
        Embedding JavaScript . . . . . . . . . . . . . . . . . . . . . . . . . . 199
        Using external JavaScript files . . . . . . . . . . . . . . . . . . . . 203
    The Basics of JavaScript . . . . . . . . . . . . . . . . . . . . . . . . . . . . 203
        Working with data . . . . . . . . . . . . . . . . . . . . . . . . . . . . 204
        Data types . . . . . . . . . . . . . . . . . . . . . . . . . . . . . . . . . . 205
        Arrays of data . . . . . . . . . . . . . . . . . . . . . . . . . . . . . . . 206
        Operators . . . . . . . . . . . . . . . . . . . . . . . . . . . . . . . . . . 207
    Controlling Program Flow . . . . . . . . . . . . . . . . . . . . . . . . . . 209
        Conditional statements . . . . . . . . . . . . . . . . . . . . . . . . 209
        Loops . . . . . . . . . . . . . . . . . . . . . . . . . . . . . . . . . . . . . 216
    Working with Functions . . . . . . . . . . . . . . . . . . . . . . . . . . . 220
        Creating a function . . . . . . . . . . . . . . . . . . . . . . . . . . . 221
        Using a function . . . . . . . . . . . . . . . . . . . . . . . . . . . . . 222

CHAPTER 2: **Advanced JavaScript Coding** . . . . . . . . . . . . . . . . . . . . . . . 223
    Understanding the Document Object Model . . . . . . . . . . . . . . 223
        The Document Object Model tree . . . . . . . . . . . . . . . . . 224
        JavaScript and the Document Object Model . . . . . . . . . . 226

Finding Your Elements .............................................233
  Getting to the point...........................................233
  Walking the tree...............................................235
Working with Document Object Model Form Data ..............238
  Text boxes ....................................................238
  Text areas.....................................................239
  Check boxes ...................................................240
  Radio buttons .................................................241

CHAPTER 3: **Using jQuery**.....................................243
Loading the jQuery Library .....................................244
  Option 1: Downloading the library file to your server .........245
  Option 2: Using a content delivery network ...................246
Using jQuery Functions..........................................246
Finding Elements ...............................................247
Replacing Data..................................................250
  Working with text .............................................250
  Working with HTML..............................................252
  Working with attributes .......................................253
  Working with form values ......................................253
Changing Styles ................................................254
  Playing with properties........................................254
  Using CSS objects .............................................256
  Using CSS classes..............................................257
Changing the Document Object Model .............................259
  Adding a node .................................................259
  Removing a node................................................260
Playing with Animation..........................................261

CHAPTER 4: **Reacting to Events with JavaScript and jQuery** ...263
Understanding Events ...........................................263
  Event-driven programming ......................................264
  Watching the mouse.............................................264
  Listening for keystrokes ......................................265
  Paying attention to the page itself ...........................266
Focusing on JavaScript and Events ..............................267
  Saying hello and goodbye ......................................267
  Listening for mouse events ....................................269
  Listening for keystrokes ......................................273
  Event listeners ...............................................275
Looking at jQuery and Events ...................................276
  jQuery event functions.........................................276
  The jQuery event handler.......................................280

CHAPTER 5: **Troubleshooting JavaScript Programs** . . . . . . . . . . . . . 283

Identifying Errors. . . . . . . . . . . . . . . . . . . . . . . . . . . . . . . . . . . . . . . .283
Working with Browser Developer Tools. . . . . . . . . . . . . . . . . . . . . .285
   The DOM Explorer. . . . . . . . . . . . . . . . . . . . . . . . . . . . . . . . . . . . .286
   The Console . . . . . . . . . . . . . . . . . . . . . . . . . . . . . . . . . . . . . . . . . .287
   The Debugger. . . . . . . . . . . . . . . . . . . . . . . . . . . . . . . . . . . . . . . . .290
Working Around Errors. . . . . . . . . . . . . . . . . . . . . . . . . . . . . . . . . . . .295

**BOOK 4: PHP** . . . . . . . . . . . . . . . . . . . . . . . . . . . . . . . . . . . . . . . . . . . .301

CHAPTER 1: **Understanding PHP Basics** . . . . . . . . . . . . . . . . . . . . . . .303

Seeing the Benefits of PHP. . . . . . . . . . . . . . . . . . . . . . . . . . . . . . . . .303
   A centralized programming language . . . . . . . . . . . . . . . . . . . . . .304
   Centralized data management . . . . . . . . . . . . . . . . . . . . . . . . . . . .304
Understanding How to Use PHP . . . . . . . . . . . . . . . . . . . . . . . . . . . .305
   Embedding PHP code . . . . . . . . . . . . . . . . . . . . . . . . . . . . . . . . . . .305
   Identifying PHP pages. . . . . . . . . . . . . . . . . . . . . . . . . . . . . . . . . . .306
   Displaying output . . . . . . . . . . . . . . . . . . . . . . . . . . . . . . . . . . . . . .307
   Handling new-line characters . . . . . . . . . . . . . . . . . . . . . . . . . . . .309
Working with PHP Variables. . . . . . . . . . . . . . . . . . . . . . . . . . . . . . . .310
   Declaring variables . . . . . . . . . . . . . . . . . . . . . . . . . . . . . . . . . . . . .311
   Seeing which data types PHP supports . . . . . . . . . . . . . . . . . . . . .312
   Grouping data values with array variables . . . . . . . . . . . . . . . . . .315
Using PHP Operators . . . . . . . . . . . . . . . . . . . . . . . . . . . . . . . . . . . . .317
   Arithmetic operators. . . . . . . . . . . . . . . . . . . . . . . . . . . . . . . . . . . .317
   Arithmetic shortcuts . . . . . . . . . . . . . . . . . . . . . . . . . . . . . . . . . . . .318
   Boolean operators. . . . . . . . . . . . . . . . . . . . . . . . . . . . . . . . . . . . . .319
   String operators. . . . . . . . . . . . . . . . . . . . . . . . . . . . . . . . . . . . . . . .320
Including Files . . . . . . . . . . . . . . . . . . . . . . . . . . . . . . . . . . . . . . . . . . .320
   The include() function . . . . . . . . . . . . . . . . . . . . . . . . . . . . . . . . . . .320
   The require() function. . . . . . . . . . . . . . . . . . . . . . . . . . . . . . . . . . .323

CHAPTER 2: **PHP Flow Control** . . . . . . . . . . . . . . . . . . . . . . . . . . . . . . . .325

Using Logic Control . . . . . . . . . . . . . . . . . . . . . . . . . . . . . . . . . . . . . .325
   The if statement. . . . . . . . . . . . . . . . . . . . . . . . . . . . . . . . . . . . . . . .326
   The else statement. . . . . . . . . . . . . . . . . . . . . . . . . . . . . . . . . . . . . .328
   The elseif statement . . . . . . . . . . . . . . . . . . . . . . . . . . . . . . . . . . . .328
   The switch statement. . . . . . . . . . . . . . . . . . . . . . . . . . . . . . . . . . . .330
Looping. . . . . . . . . . . . . . . . . . . . . . . . . . . . . . . . . . . . . . . . . . . . . . . . .331
   The while family. . . . . . . . . . . . . . . . . . . . . . . . . . . . . . . . . . . . . . . .331
   The for statement. . . . . . . . . . . . . . . . . . . . . . . . . . . . . . . . . . . . . . .333
   The foreach statement . . . . . . . . . . . . . . . . . . . . . . . . . . . . . . . . . .334
Building Your Own Functions . . . . . . . . . . . . . . . . . . . . . . . . . . . . . .336
Working with Event-Driven PHP . . . . . . . . . . . . . . . . . . . . . . . . . . . .339

Working with links . . . . . . . . . . . . . . . . . . . . . . . . . . . . . . . . .339

Processing form data . . . . . . . . . . . . . . . . . . . . . . . . . . . . . . .343

CHAPTER 3: **PHP Libraries** . . . . . . . . . . . . . . . . . . . . . . . . . . . . . . . . . . . . . 349

How PHP Uses Libraries . . . . . . . . . . . . . . . . . . . . . . . . . . . . . . . . . . .349

Exploring PHP extensions . . . . . . . . . . . . . . . . . . . . . . . . . . . . .350

Examining the PHP extensions . . . . . . . . . . . . . . . . . . . . . . . . .351

Including extensions . . . . . . . . . . . . . . . . . . . . . . . . . . . . . . . . .353

Adding additional extensions . . . . . . . . . . . . . . . . . . . . . . . . .354

Text Functions . . . . . . . . . . . . . . . . . . . . . . . . . . . . . . . . . . . . . . . . . .354

Altering string values. . . . . . . . . . . . . . . . . . . . . . . . . . . . . . . . .354

Splitting strings . . . . . . . . . . . . . . . . . . . . . . . . . . . . . . . . . . . . .356

Testing string values . . . . . . . . . . . . . . . . . . . . . . . . . . . . . . . . .359

Searching strings . . . . . . . . . . . . . . . . . . . . . . . . . . . . . . . . . . . .360

Math Functions . . . . . . . . . . . . . . . . . . . . . . . . . . . . . . . . . . . . . . . . .361

Number theory . . . . . . . . . . . . . . . . . . . . . . . . . . . . . . . . . . . . .361

Calculating logs and exponents. . . . . . . . . . . . . . . . . . . . . . . .362

Working the angles . . . . . . . . . . . . . . . . . . . . . . . . . . . . . . . . . .363

Hyperbolic functions . . . . . . . . . . . . . . . . . . . . . . . . . . . . . . . .364

Tracking statistics . . . . . . . . . . . . . . . . . . . . . . . . . . . . . . . . . . .364

Date and Time Functions . . . . . . . . . . . . . . . . . . . . . . . . . . . . . . . .365

Generating dates. . . . . . . . . . . . . . . . . . . . . . . . . . . . . . . . . . . .365

Using timestamps . . . . . . . . . . . . . . . . . . . . . . . . . . . . . . . . . . .367

Calculating dates . . . . . . . . . . . . . . . . . . . . . . . . . . . . . . . . . . .368

Image-Handling Functions . . . . . . . . . . . . . . . . . . . . . . . . . . . . . . .369

CHAPTER 4: **Considering PHP Security** . . . . . . . . . . . . . . . . . . . . . . . . .375

Exploring PHP Vulnerabilities . . . . . . . . . . . . . . . . . . . . . . . . . . . . .375

Cross-site scripting . . . . . . . . . . . . . . . . . . . . . . . . . . . . . . . . . .376

Data spoofing. . . . . . . . . . . . . . . . . . . . . . . . . . . . . . . . . . . . . . .379

Invalid data. . . . . . . . . . . . . . . . . . . . . . . . . . . . . . . . . . . . . . . . .380

Unauthorized file access. . . . . . . . . . . . . . . . . . . . . . . . . . . . . .382

PHP Vulnerability Solutions . . . . . . . . . . . . . . . . . . . . . . . . . . . . . . .384

Sanitizing data . . . . . . . . . . . . . . . . . . . . . . . . . . . . . . . . . . . . . .384

Validating data . . . . . . . . . . . . . . . . . . . . . . . . . . . . . . . . . . . . . .389

CHAPTER 5: **Object-Oriented PHP Programming**. . . . . . . . . . . . . . .395

Understanding the Basics of Object-Oriented Programming. . . . . .395

Defining a class . . . . . . . . . . . . . . . . . . . . . . . . . . . . . . . . . . . . .396

Creating an object instance . . . . . . . . . . . . . . . . . . . . . . . . . . .397

Using Magic Class Methods . . . . . . . . . . . . . . . . . . . . . . . . . . . . . . .401

Defining mutator magic methods. . . . . . . . . . . . . . . . . . . . . . .401

Defining accessor magic methods . . . . . . . . . . . . . . . . . . . . . .403

The constructor . . . . . . . . . . . . . . . . . . . . . . . . . . . . . . . . . . . . .406

The destructor . . . . . . . . . . . . . . . . . . . . . . . . . . . . . . . . . . . . . . . . . .407
Copying objects . . . . . . . . . . . . . . . . . . . . . . . . . . . . . . . . . . . . . . . . .408
Displaying objects . . . . . . . . . . . . . . . . . . . . . . . . . . . . . . . . . . . . . . .408
Loading Classes . . . . . . . . . . . . . . . . . . . . . . . . . . . . . . . . . . . . . . . . . . . . .409
Extending Classes . . . . . . . . . . . . . . . . . . . . . . . . . . . . . . . . . . . . . . . . . . .414

CHAPTER 6: **Sessions and Carts** . . . . . . . . . . . . . . . . . . . . . . . . . . . . . . . . . . . . . .419
Storing Persistent Data . . . . . . . . . . . . . . . . . . . . . . . . . . . . . . . . . . . . . . .419
The purpose of HTTP cookies . . . . . . . . . . . . . . . . . . . . . . . . . . . . . .420
Types of cookies . . . . . . . . . . . . . . . . . . . . . . . . . . . . . . . . . . . . . . . . .421
The anatomy of a cookie . . . . . . . . . . . . . . . . . . . . . . . . . . . . . . . . . .422
Cookie rules . . . . . . . . . . . . . . . . . . . . . . . . . . . . . . . . . . . . . . . . . . . . .424
PHP and Cookies . . . . . . . . . . . . . . . . . . . . . . . . . . . . . . . . . . . . . . . . . . . .424
Setting cookies . . . . . . . . . . . . . . . . . . . . . . . . . . . . . . . . . . . . . . . . . .424
Reading cookies . . . . . . . . . . . . . . . . . . . . . . . . . . . . . . . . . . . . . . . . .426
Modifying and deleting cookies . . . . . . . . . . . . . . . . . . . . . . . . . . . .428
PHP and Sessions . . . . . . . . . . . . . . . . . . . . . . . . . . . . . . . . . . . . . . . . . . .430
Starting a session . . . . . . . . . . . . . . . . . . . . . . . . . . . . . . . . . . . . . . . .431
Storing and retrieving session data . . . . . . . . . . . . . . . . . . . . . . . . .431
Removing session data . . . . . . . . . . . . . . . . . . . . . . . . . . . . . . . . . . .435
Shopping Carts . . . . . . . . . . . . . . . . . . . . . . . . . . . . . . . . . . . . . . . . . . . . .436
Creating a cart . . . . . . . . . . . . . . . . . . . . . . . . . . . . . . . . . . . . . . . . . .436
Placing items in the cart . . . . . . . . . . . . . . . . . . . . . . . . . . . . . . . . . .437
Retrieving items from a cart . . . . . . . . . . . . . . . . . . . . . . . . . . . . . . .437
Removing items from a cart . . . . . . . . . . . . . . . . . . . . . . . . . . . . . . .438
Putting it all together . . . . . . . . . . . . . . . . . . . . . . . . . . . . . . . . . . . .438

**BOOK 5: MYSQL** . . . . . . . . . . . . . . . . . . . . . . . . . . . . . . . . . . . . . . . . . . . . .443

CHAPTER 1: **Introducing MySQL** . . . . . . . . . . . . . . . . . . . . . . . . . . . . . . . . . . .445
Seeing the Purpose of a Database . . . . . . . . . . . . . . . . . . . . . . . . . . . . .445
How databases work . . . . . . . . . . . . . . . . . . . . . . . . . . . . . . . . . . . . .446
Relational databases . . . . . . . . . . . . . . . . . . . . . . . . . . . . . . . . . . . . .449
Database data types . . . . . . . . . . . . . . . . . . . . . . . . . . . . . . . . . . . . .451
Data constraints . . . . . . . . . . . . . . . . . . . . . . . . . . . . . . . . . . . . . . . . .451
Structured Query Language . . . . . . . . . . . . . . . . . . . . . . . . . . . . . . .452
Presenting MySQL . . . . . . . . . . . . . . . . . . . . . . . . . . . . . . . . . . . . . . . . . .454
MySQL features . . . . . . . . . . . . . . . . . . . . . . . . . . . . . . . . . . . . . . . . .454
Storage engines . . . . . . . . . . . . . . . . . . . . . . . . . . . . . . . . . . . . . . . . .456
Data permissions . . . . . . . . . . . . . . . . . . . . . . . . . . . . . . . . . . . . . . . .457
Advanced MySQL Features . . . . . . . . . . . . . . . . . . . . . . . . . . . . . . . . . . .458
Handling transactions . . . . . . . . . . . . . . . . . . . . . . . . . . . . . . . . . . . .458
Making sure your database is ACID compliant . . . . . . . . . . . . . . . .459
Examining the views . . . . . . . . . . . . . . . . . . . . . . . . . . . . . . . . . . . . . .461

Working with stored procedures. . . . . . . . . . . . . . . . . . . . . . . . . . . . .462
Pulling triggers . . . . . . . . . . . . . . . . . . . . . . . . . . . . . . . . . . . . . . . . . . .463
Working with blobs . . . . . . . . . . . . . . . . . . . . . . . . . . . . . . . . . . . . . . . .463

CHAPTER 2: **Administering MySQL** . . . . . . . . . . . . . . . . . . . . . . . . . . . . . . . . . . .465
MySQL Administration Tools . . . . . . . . . . . . . . . . . . . . . . . . . . . . . . . . . . .465
Working from the command line . . . . . . . . . . . . . . . . . . . . . . . . . . .466
Using MySQL Workbench. . . . . . . . . . . . . . . . . . . . . . . . . . . . . . . . . .470
Using the phpMyAdmin tool . . . . . . . . . . . . . . . . . . . . . . . . . . . . . . .475
Managing User Accounts . . . . . . . . . . . . . . . . . . . . . . . . . . . . . . . . . . . . .477
Creating a user account . . . . . . . . . . . . . . . . . . . . . . . . . . . . . . . . . .477
Managing user privileges . . . . . . . . . . . . . . . . . . . . . . . . . . . . . . . . .481

CHAPTER 3: **Designing and Building a Database** . . . . . . . . . . . . . . . . .489
Managing Your Data . . . . . . . . . . . . . . . . . . . . . . . . . . . . . . . . . . . . . . . .489
The first normal form . . . . . . . . . . . . . . . . . . . . . . . . . . . . . . . . . . . .490
The second normal form . . . . . . . . . . . . . . . . . . . . . . . . . . . . . . . . .491
The third normal form . . . . . . . . . . . . . . . . . . . . . . . . . . . . . . . . . . .491
Creating Databases. . . . . . . . . . . . . . . . . . . . . . . . . . . . . . . . . . . . . . . . .492
Using the MySQL command line. . . . . . . . . . . . . . . . . . . . . . . . . . . .492
Using MySQL Workbench. . . . . . . . . . . . . . . . . . . . . . . . . . . . . . . . . .495
Using phpMyAdmin. . . . . . . . . . . . . . . . . . . . . . . . . . . . . . . . . . . . . .497
Building Tables. . . . . . . . . . . . . . . . . . . . . . . . . . . . . . . . . . . . . . . . . . . . .500
Working with tables using the command-line interface . . . . . . . .500
Working with tables using Workbench. . . . . . . . . . . . . . . . . . . . . . .505
Working with tables in phpMyAdmin . . . . . . . . . . . . . . . . . . . . . . . .508

CHAPTER 4: **Using the Database** . . . . . . . . . . . . . . . . . . . . . . . . . . . . . . . . . . . . .513
Working with Data. . . . . . . . . . . . . . . . . . . . . . . . . . . . . . . . . . . . . . . . . .513
The MySQL command-line interface . . . . . . . . . . . . . . . . . . . . . . . .514
The MySQL Workbench tool . . . . . . . . . . . . . . . . . . . . . . . . . . . . . . .519
The phpMyAdmin tool . . . . . . . . . . . . . . . . . . . . . . . . . . . . . . . . . . .522
Searching for Data. . . . . . . . . . . . . . . . . . . . . . . . . . . . . . . . . . . . . . . . . .524
The basic SELECT format . . . . . . . . . . . . . . . . . . . . . . . . . . . . . . . . .525
More advanced queries . . . . . . . . . . . . . . . . . . . . . . . . . . . . . . . . . .527
Playing It Safe with Data. . . . . . . . . . . . . . . . . . . . . . . . . . . . . . . . . . . . .531
Performing data backups. . . . . . . . . . . . . . . . . . . . . . . . . . . . . . . . .532
Restoring your data. . . . . . . . . . . . . . . . . . . . . . . . . . . . . . . . . . . . . .538

CHAPTER 5: **Communicating with the Database from PHP
Scripts** . . . . . . . . . . . . . . . . . . . . . . . . . . . . . . . . . . . . . . . . . . . . . . . . . . .541
Database Support in PHP. . . . . . . . . . . . . . . . . . . . . . . . . . . . . . . . . . . . .541
Using the mysqli Library. . . . . . . . . . . . . . . . . . . . . . . . . . . . . . . . . . . . .543
Connecting to the database. . . . . . . . . . . . . . . . . . . . . . . . . . . . . . .544
Closing the connection . . . . . . . . . . . . . . . . . . . . . . . . . . . . . . . . . . .545

Submitting queries . . . . . . . . . . . . . . . . . . . . . . . . . . . . . . . . . . . .546
Retrieving data . . . . . . . . . . . . . . . . . . . . . . . . . . . . . . . . . . . . . . .547
Being prepared . . . . . . . . . . . . . . . . . . . . . . . . . . . . . . . . . . . . . .549
Checking for errors . . . . . . . . . . . . . . . . . . . . . . . . . . . . . . . . . . . .551
Miscellaneous functions . . . . . . . . . . . . . . . . . . . . . . . . . . . . . . . .553
Putting It All Together . . . . . . . . . . . . . . . . . . . . . . . . . . . . . . . . . . . . .554

## BOOK 6: CREATING OBJECT-ORIENTED PROGRAMS . . . . .561

CHAPTER 1: **Designing an Object-Oriented Application** . . . . . . . .563
Determining Application Requirements . . . . . . . . . . . . . . . . . . . . . . . .563
Creating the Application Database . . . . . . . . . . . . . . . . . . . . . . . . . . .565
Designing the database . . . . . . . . . . . . . . . . . . . . . . . . . . . . . . . .565
Creating the database . . . . . . . . . . . . . . . . . . . . . . . . . . . . . . . . .568
Designing the Application Objects . . . . . . . . . . . . . . . . . . . . . . . . . . .571
Designing objects . . . . . . . . . . . . . . . . . . . . . . . . . . . . . . . . . . . .571
Coding the objects in PHP . . . . . . . . . . . . . . . . . . . . . . . . . . . . . .573
Designing the Application Layout . . . . . . . . . . . . . . . . . . . . . . . . . . . .579
Designing web page layout . . . . . . . . . . . . . . . . . . . . . . . . . . . . . .580
The AuctionHelper page layout . . . . . . . . . . . . . . . . . . . . . . . . . . .581
Coding the Website Layout . . . . . . . . . . . . . . . . . . . . . . . . . . . . . . . .582
Creating the web page template . . . . . . . . . . . . . . . . . . . . . . . . . .582
Creating the support files . . . . . . . . . . . . . . . . . . . . . . . . . . . . . . .587

CHAPTER 2: **Implementing an Object-Oriented Application** . . .593
Working with Events . . . . . . . . . . . . . . . . . . . . . . . . . . . . . . . . . . . . . .593
Bidder Object Events . . . . . . . . . . . . . . . . . . . . . . . . . . . . . . . . . . . . .595
Listing bidders . . . . . . . . . . . . . . . . . . . . . . . . . . . . . . . . . . . . . . .595
Adding a new bidder . . . . . . . . . . . . . . . . . . . . . . . . . . . . . . . . . . .603
Searching for a bidder . . . . . . . . . . . . . . . . . . . . . . . . . . . . . . . . . .605
Item Object Events . . . . . . . . . . . . . . . . . . . . . . . . . . . . . . . . . . . . . . .605
Listing items . . . . . . . . . . . . . . . . . . . . . . . . . . . . . . . . . . . . . . . . .606
Adding a new item . . . . . . . . . . . . . . . . . . . . . . . . . . . . . . . . . . . . .611
Searching for an item . . . . . . . . . . . . . . . . . . . . . . . . . . . . . . . . . . .614
Logging Out of a Web Application . . . . . . . . . . . . . . . . . . . . . . . . . . . .614
Testing Web Applications . . . . . . . . . . . . . . . . . . . . . . . . . . . . . . . . . .616

CHAPTER 3: **Using AJAX** . . . . . . . . . . . . . . . . . . . . . . . . . . . . . . . . . . . . .619
Getting to Know AJAX . . . . . . . . . . . . . . . . . . . . . . . . . . . . . . . . . . . . .619
Communicating Using JavaScript . . . . . . . . . . . . . . . . . . . . . . . . . . . .621
Considering XMLHttpRequest class methods . . . . . . . . . . . . . . . . .622
Focusing on XMLHttpRequest class properties . . . . . . . . . . . . . . . .623
Trying out AJAX . . . . . . . . . . . . . . . . . . . . . . . . . . . . . . . . . . . . . . . .625

Using the jQuery AJAX Library . . . . . . . . . . . . . . . . . . . . . . . . . . . . . . . . .629
    The jQuery $.ajax() function . . . . . . . . . . . . . . . . . . . . . . . . . . . . . . . .629
    The jQuery $.get() function . . . . . . . . . . . . . . . . . . . . . . . . . . . . . . . . .633
Transferring Data in AJAX . . . . . . . . . . . . . . . . . . . . . . . . . . . . . . . . . . . . .635
    Looking at the XML standard . . . . . . . . . . . . . . . . . . . . . . . . . . . . . . . .635
    Using XML in PHP . . . . . . . . . . . . . . . . . . . . . . . . . . . . . . . . . . . . . . . .636
    Using XML in JavaScript . . . . . . . . . . . . . . . . . . . . . . . . . . . . . . . . . . . .640
Modifying the AuctionHelper Application . . . . . . . . . . . . . . . . . . . . . . . .643

CHAPTER 4:  **Extending WordPress** . . . . . . . . . . . . . . . . . . . . . . . . . . . . . . . . 651
Getting Acquainted with WordPress . . . . . . . . . . . . . . . . . . . . . . . . . . . .651
    What WordPress can do for you . . . . . . . . . . . . . . . . . . . . . . . . . . . . .652
    How to run WordPress . . . . . . . . . . . . . . . . . . . . . . . . . . . . . . . . . . . . .653
    Parts of a WordPress website . . . . . . . . . . . . . . . . . . . . . . . . . . . . . . .654
Installing WordPress . . . . . . . . . . . . . . . . . . . . . . . . . . . . . . . . . . . . . . . . .655
    Downloading the WordPress software . . . . . . . . . . . . . . . . . . . . . . . .655
    Creating the database objects . . . . . . . . . . . . . . . . . . . . . . . . . . . . . . .656
    Configuring WordPress . . . . . . . . . . . . . . . . . . . . . . . . . . . . . . . . . . . .658
Examining the Dashboard . . . . . . . . . . . . . . . . . . . . . . . . . . . . . . . . . . . .662
Using WordPress . . . . . . . . . . . . . . . . . . . . . . . . . . . . . . . . . . . . . . . . . . .664
Exploring the World of Plugins . . . . . . . . . . . . . . . . . . . . . . . . . . . . . . . .669
    WordPress APIs . . . . . . . . . . . . . . . . . . . . . . . . . . . . . . . . . . . . . . . . . .670
    Working with plugins and widgets . . . . . . . . . . . . . . . . . . . . . . . . . . .671
Creating Your Own Widget . . . . . . . . . . . . . . . . . . . . . . . . . . . . . . . . . . .674
    Coding the widget . . . . . . . . . . . . . . . . . . . . . . . . . . . . . . . . . . . . . . . .674
    Activating the widget plugin . . . . . . . . . . . . . . . . . . . . . . . . . . . . . . . .676
    Adding the widget . . . . . . . . . . . . . . . . . . . . . . . . . . . . . . . . . . . . . . . .677

**BOOK 7: USING PHP FRAMEWORKS** . . . . . . . . . . . . . . . . . . . . . . . . 681

CHAPTER 1:  **The MVC Method** . . . . . . . . . . . . . . . . . . . . . . . . . . . . . . . . . . . . 683
Getting Acquainted with MVC . . . . . . . . . . . . . . . . . . . . . . . . . . . . . . . . .683
    Exploring the MVC method . . . . . . . . . . . . . . . . . . . . . . . . . . . . . . . . .684
    Digging into the MVC components . . . . . . . . . . . . . . . . . . . . . . . . . . .686
    Communicating in MVC . . . . . . . . . . . . . . . . . . . . . . . . . . . . . . . . . . . .690
Comparing MVC to Other Web Models . . . . . . . . . . . . . . . . . . . . . . . . .691
    The MVP method . . . . . . . . . . . . . . . . . . . . . . . . . . . . . . . . . . . . . . . . .692
    The MVVM method . . . . . . . . . . . . . . . . . . . . . . . . . . . . . . . . . . . . . . .692
Seeing How MVC Fits into N-Tier Theory . . . . . . . . . . . . . . . . . . . . . . . .693
Implementing MVC . . . . . . . . . . . . . . . . . . . . . . . . . . . . . . . . . . . . . . . . .694

CHAPTER 2: **Selecting a Framework** . . . . . . . . . . . . . . . . . . . . . . . . . . . . 695

    Getting to Know PHP Frameworks . . . . . . . . . . . . . . . . . . . . . . . . . . . . . .695

        Convention over configuration . . . . . . . . . . . . . . . . . . . . . . . . . . . .696

        Scaffolding . . . . . . . . . . . . . . . . . . . . . . . . . . . . . . . . . . . . . . . . . . . .698

        Routing . . . . . . . . . . . . . . . . . . . . . . . . . . . . . . . . . . . . . . . . . . . . . .699

        Helper methods . . . . . . . . . . . . . . . . . . . . . . . . . . . . . . . . . . . . . . . .700

        Form validation . . . . . . . . . . . . . . . . . . . . . . . . . . . . . . . . . . . . . . .700

        Support for mobile devices . . . . . . . . . . . . . . . . . . . . . . . . . . . . . .700

        Templates . . . . . . . . . . . . . . . . . . . . . . . . . . . . . . . . . . . . . . . . . . . .701

        Unit testing . . . . . . . . . . . . . . . . . . . . . . . . . . . . . . . . . . . . . . . . . . .701

    Knowing Why You Should Use a Framework . . . . . . . . . . . . . . . . . . .702

    Focusing on Popular PHP Frameworks . . . . . . . . . . . . . . . . . . . . . . .704

        CakePHP . . . . . . . . . . . . . . . . . . . . . . . . . . . . . . . . . . . . . . . . . . . . .704

        CodeIgniter . . . . . . . . . . . . . . . . . . . . . . . . . . . . . . . . . . . . . . . . . . .705

        Laravel . . . . . . . . . . . . . . . . . . . . . . . . . . . . . . . . . . . . . . . . . . . . . . .707

        Symfony . . . . . . . . . . . . . . . . . . . . . . . . . . . . . . . . . . . . . . . . . . . . .708

        Zend Framework . . . . . . . . . . . . . . . . . . . . . . . . . . . . . . . . . . . . . . .709

    Looking At Micro Frameworks . . . . . . . . . . . . . . . . . . . . . . . . . . . . . .710

        Lumen . . . . . . . . . . . . . . . . . . . . . . . . . . . . . . . . . . . . . . . . . . . . . . .710

        Slim . . . . . . . . . . . . . . . . . . . . . . . . . . . . . . . . . . . . . . . . . . . . . . . . .711

        Yii . . . . . . . . . . . . . . . . . . . . . . . . . . . . . . . . . . . . . . . . . . . . . . . . . .713

CHAPTER 3: **Creating an Application Using Frameworks** . . . . . . .715

    Building the Template . . . . . . . . . . . . . . . . . . . . . . . . . . . . . . . . . . . . .715

        Initializing the application . . . . . . . . . . . . . . . . . . . . . . . . . . . . . . .716

        Exploring the files and folders . . . . . . . . . . . . . . . . . . . . . . . . . . . .718

        Defining the database environment . . . . . . . . . . . . . . . . . . . . . . . .719

    Creating an Application Scaffold . . . . . . . . . . . . . . . . . . . . . . . . . . . .721

        Installing the scaffolding . . . . . . . . . . . . . . . . . . . . . . . . . . . . . . . .721

        Exploring the scaffolding code . . . . . . . . . . . . . . . . . . . . . . . . . . . .724

    Modifying the Application Scaffold . . . . . . . . . . . . . . . . . . . . . . . . . .725

        Adding a new feature link . . . . . . . . . . . . . . . . . . . . . . . . . . . . . . . .726

        Creating the controller code . . . . . . . . . . . . . . . . . . . . . . . . . . . . . .728

        Modifying the model code . . . . . . . . . . . . . . . . . . . . . . . . . . . . . . . .730

        Painting a view . . . . . . . . . . . . . . . . . . . . . . . . . . . . . . . . . . . . . . . . .731

**INDEX** . . . . . . . . . . . . . . . . . . . . . . . . . . . . . . . . . . . . . . . . . . . . . . . . . . . . .735

# Introduction

The Internet has become an amazing place to shop, do your banking, look up homework assignments, and even keep track of your bowling league scores. Behind all those great applications are a bunch of different web technologies that must all work together to create the web experience you come to expect.

You may think that creating web applications is best left for the professionals, but you'd be surprised by just how well you can do with just a little knowledge and experience! That's the point of this book.

## About This Book

Think of this book as a reference book. Like the dictionary or an encyclopedia (remember those?), you don't have to read it from beginning to end. Instead, you can dip into the book to find the information you need and return to it again when you need more. That said, you won't be disappointed if you work through the book from beginning to end, and you may find it easier to follow along with some of the examples.

In this book, I walk you through all the different technologies involved with creating dynamic web applications that can track data and present it in an orderly and pleasing manner. I cover several key topics that you'll need to know to create a full-featured, dynamic web application:

>> **Creating the basic layout of a web page:** In this book, you see the program code behind placing content on a web page and reacting to your website visitors' mouse clicks.

>> **Styling the web page:** Just placing data on a web page is boring. In this book, you learn how to use CSS to help use color, images, and placement to help liven up your web applications.

>> **Adding dynamic features:** These days, having a static web page that just sits there doesn't get you many followers. This book shows you how to incorporate JavaScript to animate your web pages and provide dynamic features.

>> **Leveraging the power of the server:** The PHP programming language allows you to harness the power behind the web server to dynamically generate web pages "on the fly" as your website visitors make choices.

>> **Storing data for the future:** Just about every dynamic web application needs to store data, and in this book you learn exactly how to do that using the MySQL server, which is commonly available in just about every web platform.

>> **Creating full applications:** Many books throw a bunch of technology at you and expect you to put the pieces together yourself. This book not only shows you the technology, but also demonstrates how all the parts fit together to create a dynamic web application.

>> **Using helper programs:** No one is an island; everyone needs some help putting together those fancy web applications. There are plenty of tools to help you get the job done, and with this book you find out which tools will help you with which features of your application.

Throughout this book you see sidebars (text in gray boxes) and material marked with the Technical Stuff icon. All of these things are skippable. If you have time and are interested, by all means read them, but if you don't or aren't, don't.

Finally, within this book, you may note that some web addresses break across two lines of text. If you're reading this book in print and want to visit one of these web pages, simply key in the web address exactly as it's noted in the text, pretending as though the line break doesn't exist. If you're reading this as an e-book, you've got it easy — just click the web address to be taken directly to the web page.

# Foolish Assumptions

You don't need any level of programming experience to enjoy this book and start creating your own web applications. Each chapter walks through all the basics you need to know and doesn't assume you've ever coded before. As long as you're reasonably comfortable navigating your way around a standard desktop computer, you have all the experience you need!

That said, if you've already tried your hand at web programming and you just want to fill in a few holes, this book will work well for you, too!

This book doesn't expect you to run out and buy any expensive software packages to start your web development career. All the tools that are used in the book are freely available open-source software. I walk you through how to set up a complete development environment, whether you're working in Microsoft Windows, Apple macOS, or Linux.

# Icons Used in This Book

I use some icons throughout the book to help you identify useful information. Here's what the icons are and what I use them for:

**TIP**

Anything marked with the Tip icon provides some additional information about a topic to help you better understand what's going on behind the scenes or how to better use the feature discussed in the text.

**REMEMBER**

You don't have to commit this book to memory — there won't be a test. But every once in a while I tell you something so important that you should remember it. When I do, I mark it with the Remember icon.

**WARNING**

The Warning icon is there to point out potential pitfalls that can cause problems. If you want to save yourself a lot of time or trouble, heed these warnings.

**TECHNICAL STUFF**

When you see the Technical Stuff icon, be prepared to put your geek hat on. When I get into the weeds, I use the Technical Stuff icon. If you're not interested in these details, feel free to skip these sections — you won't miss anything essential about the topic at hand.

# Beyond the Book

In addition to the material in the print or e-book you're reading right now, you also get access to a free online Cheat Sheet filled with more tips and tricks on building a web application, including accessing any database from your PHP programs, filtering data your program receives from web forms to block unwanted or potentially dangerous data, quickly finding data in a MySQL database, and triggering JavaScript events at predetermined times in a browser. To access this resource go to www.dummies.com and enter **PHP, MySQL & JavaScript All-in-One For Dummies Cheat Sheet** in the search box.

# Where to Go from Here

This book doesn't have to be read from beginning to end, so you can dive in wherever you want! Use the Table of Contents and Index to find subjects that interest you. If you already know PHP and JavaScript and you're just interested in learning how to create a dynamic web application from scratch, start out with

Book 6, Chapter 1. If you're interested in learning how to use one of the framework packages available for PHP, check out Book 7, Chapter 1. Or, if you're interested in everything, start with Book 1, Chapter 1, and read until the very end.

With the information in this book, you'll be ready to start creating your own dynamic web applications. Web programming is one of those skills that takes time and practice to get good at, so the more coding you can do, the better you'll get at it. To get some practice, you may want to offer your services for free at first, to build up a reputation. Find a needy nonprofit organization that you're interested in supporting and offer to work on its website. They'll get a great website, and you'll get a project to add to your résumé!

Don't stop learning! There are always new things coming out in the web world, even if you just stick to using the same software packages to develop your web applications. Stay plugged in to the PHP world by visiting the official PHP website at www.php.net or by visiting (and even participating in) one or more of the many PHP forums. Just do some Googling to find them.

Enjoy your newfound skills in developing dynamic web applications!

# 1

# Getting Started with Web Programming

# Contents at a Glance

CHAPTER 1: **Examining the Pieces of Web Programming**...... 7

Creating a Simple Web Page ................................ 7

Creating a Dynamic Web Page ........................... 17

Storing Content ......................................... 25

CHAPTER 2: **Using a Web Server**................................ 27

Recognizing What's Required............................. 27

Considering Your Server Options ......................... 31

Tweaking the Servers ................................... 41

CHAPTER 3: **Building a Development Environment** ........... 51

Knowing Which Tools to Avoid ........................... 51

Working with the Right Tools........................... 53

IN THIS CHAPTER

» Understanding how simple web pages work

» Incorporating programming into your web page

» Storing content in a database

# Chapter **1**

# Examining the Pieces of Web Programming

A t first, diving into web programming can be somewhat overwhelming. You need to know all kinds of things in order to build a web application that not only looks enticing but also works correctly. The trick to learning web programming is to pull the individual pieces apart and tackle them one at a time.

This chapter gets you started on your web design journey by examining the different pieces involved in creating a simple web page. Then it kicks things up a notch and walks you through dynamic web pages. And finally, the chapter ends by explaining how to store your content for use on the web.

## Creating a Simple Web Page

Before you can run a marathon, you need to learn how to walk. Likewise, before you can create a fancy website, you need to know the basics of how web pages work.

Nowadays, sharing documents on the Internet is easy, but it wasn't always that way. Back in the early days of the Internet, documents were often created using proprietary word-processing packages and had to be downloaded using the cumbersome File Transfer Protocol (FTP). To retrieve a document, you had to know exactly what server contained the document, you had to know where it was stored on the server, and you had to be able to log into the server. After all that, you *still* needed to have the correct word-processing software on your computer to view the document. As you can imagine, it wasn't long before a new way of sharing content was required.

To get to where we are today, several different technologies had to be developed:

>> A method for linking related documents together

>> A way for the document reader to display formatted text the same way in any type of device

>> An Internet standard allowing clients to easily retrieve documents from any server

>> A standard method of styling and positioning content in documents

This section describes the technology that made viewing documents on the Internet work the way it does today.

## Kicking things off with the World Wide Web

In 1989, Tim Berners-Lee developed a method of interconnecting documents to make sharing research information on the Internet easier. His creation, the *World Wide Web*, defined a method for linking documents together in a web structure, so that a researcher could follow the path between related documents, no matter where they were located in the world. Clicking text in one document took you to another document automatically, without your having to manually find and download the related document.

The method Berners-Lee developed for linking documents is called *hypertext.* Hypertext embeds links that are hidden from view in the document, and directs the software being used to view the document (known as the *web browser*) to retrieve the referenced document. With hypertext, you just click the link, and the software (the web browser) does all the work of finding and retrieving the related document for you.

Because the document-viewing software does all the hard work, a new type of software had to be developed that was more than just a document viewer. That's where web browsers came into existence. Web browsers display a document on a computer screen and respond to the reader clicking hypertext links to retrieve other specified documents.

To implement hypertext in documents, Berners-Lee had to utilize a text-based document-formatting system. Fortunately for him, a lot of work had already been done on that.

# Making sense of markup languages

*Markup languages* were developed to replace proprietary word-processing packages with a standard way of formatting documents so that they could be read by any type of document viewer on any type of device. This goal is accomplished by embedding *tags* in the text. Each tag indicates a formatting feature, such as headings, bold or italic text, or special margins. What made markup languages different from word-processing packages is that these tags were common text codes instead of proprietary codes, making it generic enough that any device could read and process them.

The first popular markup language was the Generalized Markup Language (GML), developed by IBM in the 1960s. The International Organization for Standardization (ISO) took up the challenge of creating markup languages and produced the Standard Generalized Markup Language (SGML), mainly based on GML, in the 1980s. However, because SGML was developed to cover all types of document formatting on all types of devices, it's extremely complex and it wasn't readily adapted.

Berners-Lee used the ideas developed in SGML to create a simplified markup language that could support his hypertext idea. He called it *Hypertext Markup Language* (HTML). HTML uses the same concept of tags that SGML uses, but it defines fewer of them, making it easier to implement in software.

An example of an HTML tag is `<h1>`. You use this tag to define text that's used as a page heading. Just surround the text with an opening `<h1>` tag, and a corresponding closing `</h1>` tag, like this:

```
<h1>This is my heading</h1>
```

When the browser gets to the `<h1>` tag, it knows to format the text embedded in the opening and closing tags using a different style of formatting, such as a larger font or a bold typeface.

To define a hypertext link to another document, you use the `<a>` tag:

```
<a href="anotherdoc.html">Click here for more info</a>
```

When the reader clicks the *Click here for more info* text, the browser automatically tries to retrieve the document specified in the `<a>` tag. That document can be on the same server or on another server anywhere on the Internet.

HTML development has seen quite a few changes since Berners-Lee created it and turned it over to the World Wide Web Consortium (W3C) to maintain. Table 1-1 shows the path the language has taken.

**TABLE 1-1**

## HTML Versions

| Version | Description |
|---------|-------------|
| HTML 1.0 | Formally released in 1989 as the first public version of HTML |
| HTML 2.0 | Released in 1995 to add interactive elements |
| HTML 3.0 | Released in 1996 but never widely adopted |
| HTML 3.2 | Released in 1997, adding support for tables |
| HTML 4.01 | Released in 1999, widely adopted, and remains an often-used standard |
| XHTML 1.0 | Released in 2001, standardizing HTML around the XML document format |
| XHTML 1.1 | Released in 2002, making updates and corrections to XHTML 1.1 |
| HTML 5.0 | Released in 2014, adding multimedia features |

The HTML version 4.01 standard was the backbone of websites for many years, and it's still used by many websites today. However, HTML version 5.0 (called HTML5 for short) is the future of web development. It provides additional features for embedding multimedia content in web pages without the need for proprietary software plug-ins (such as Adobe Flash Player). Because multimedia is taking over the world (just ask YouTube), HTML5 has grown in popularity. This book focuses on HTML5; all the code included in this book use that standard.

## Retrieving HTML documents

Besides a document-formatting standard, Berners-Lee also developed a method of easily retrieving the HTML documents in a client–server environment. A *web server* software package runs in the background on a server, listening for connection requests from *web clients* (the browser). The browser sends requests to retrieve HTML documents from the server. The request can be sent anonymously (without using a login username), or the browser can send a username and password or certificate to identify the requestor.

These requests and responses are defined in the *Hypertext Transfer Protocol* (HTTP) standard. HTTP defines a set of requests the client can send to the server and a set of responses the server uses to reply back to the client.

This section walks you through the basics of how web servers and web clients use HTTP to interact with each other to move web pages across the Internet.

### Web clients

The web client sends requests to the web server on a standard network communication channel (known as TCP port 80), which is defined as the standard for

HTTP communication. HTTP uses standard text requests sent to the server, either requesting information from the server or sending information to the server. Table 1-2 shows the basic HTTP client requests available.

**TABLE 1-2**

## HTTP Client Requests

| Request | Description |
|---------|-------------|
| CONNECT | Converts the connection into a secure tunnel for sending data |
| DELETE | Deletes the specified resource |
| GET | Requests the specified resource |
| HEAD | Requests the title of the specified resource |
| OPTIONS | Retrieves the HTTP requests that the server supports |
| PATCH | Applies a modification to a resource |
| POST | Sends specified data to the server for processing |
| PUT | Stores specified data at a specified location |
| TRACE | Sends the received request back to the client |

As shown in Table 1-2, when you ask to view a web page from your client browser, the browser sends the HTTP GET request to the server, specifying the filename of the web page. The server then responds with a response code along with the requested data. If the client doesn't specify a filename in the GET request, most servers have a default file with which to respond.

## Web servers

With HTTP, the web server must respond to each client request received. If the client sends a request that the server can't process, the server must send some type of error code back to the client indicating that something went wrong.

The first part of the server response is a status code and text that the client uses to determine whether the submitted request was successful. The format of the HTTP response uses a three-digit status code, followed by an optional text message that the browser can display. The three-digit codes are broken down into five categories:

>> **1xx:** Informational messages

>> **2xx:** Success

>> **3xx:** Redirection

>> **4xx:** Client error

>> **5xx:** Server error

The three-digit status code is crucial to knowing what happened with the response. Many status codes are defined in the HTTP standards, providing some basic information on the status of client requests. Table 1-3 shows just a few of the standard HTTP response codes that you may run into.

**TABLE 1-3**     Common HTTP Server Response Status Codes

| Status Code | Text Message | Description |
|---|---|---|
| 100 | Continue | The client should send additional information. |
| 101 | Switching Protocols | The server is using a different protocol for the request. |
| 102 | Processing | The server is working on the response. |
| 200 | OK | The server accepted the request and has returned the response. |
| 201 | Created | The server created a new resource in response to the request. |
| 202 | Accepted | The data sent by the client has been accepted by the server but has not completed processing the data. |
| 206 | Partial Content | The response returned by the server is only part of the full data; more will come in another response. |
| 300 | Multiple Choices | The request matched multiple possible responses from the server. |
| 301 | Moved Permanently | The requested file was moved and is no longer at the requested location. |
| 302 | Found | The requested resource was found at a different location. |
| 303 | See Other | The requested resource is available at a different location. |
| 304 | Not Modified | The requested resource was not modified since the last time the client accessed it. |
| 307 | Temporary Redirect | The requested resource was temporarily moved to a different location. |
| 308 | Permanent Redirect | The requested resource was permanently moved to a different location. |
| 400 | Bad Request | The server cannot process the request. |
| 401 | Unauthorized | The resource requires authentication that the client did not provide. |

| Status Code | Text Message | Description |
|---|---|---|
| 402 | Payment Required | The requested resource is not freely available. |
| 403 | Forbidden | The resource requires authentication, and the client does not have the proper permission. |
| 404 | Not Found | The requested resource was not located on the server. |
| 414 | URI Too Long | The Uniform Resource Identifier (URI) describing the location of the resource was longer than the server is able to handle. |
| 415 | Unsupported Media Type | The server does not know how to process the requested resource file. |
| 429 | Too Many Requests | The client has sent too many requests within a specific amount of time. |
| 500 | Internal Server Error | An unexpected condition occurred on the server while trying to retrieve the requested resource. |
| 501 | Not Implemented | The server doesn't recognize the request. |
| 502 | Bad Gateway | The server was acting as a proxy to another server but received an invalid response from the other server. |
| 503 | Service Unavailable | The server is currently unavailable, often due to maintenance. |
| 505 | HTTP Version Not Supported | The server doesn't support the HTTP standard used by the client in the request. |
| 507 | Insufficient Storage | The server is unable to store the resource due to lack of storage space. |
| 511 | Network Authentication Required | The client is required to authenticate with a network resource to receive the response. |

As you can see from Table 1-3, a web server can return many possible responses. It's the client's job to parse the response and determine the next action to take.

If the response indicates the request was successful, the server will follow the response code with the data related to the request, such as the contents of an HTML file. The client must then read the returned data and decide what to do with it. For HTML files, the browser will display the requested file, applying the HTML formatting tags to the data.

**TIP**

Don't worry about trying to memorize all the HTTP status codes. Most of them you'll never run into in your web-programming career. Before long, you'll start to remember a few of the more common ones, and you can always look up any others you run into.

# Styling

The HTML standard defines how browsers perform basic formatting of text, but it doesn't really provide a way to tell a browser how to display the text. The `<h1>` tag indicates that the text should be a heading, but nothing tells the browser just how to display the heading to make it different from any other text on the page.

This is where styling comes into play. *Styling* allows you to tell the browser just what fonts, sizes, and colors to use for text, as well as how to position the text in the display. This section explains how styling affects how your web pages appear to your visitors.

## Style sheets

There are several ways to define styling for an HTML document. The most basic method is what the browser uses by default. When the browser sees an HTML formatting tag, such as the `<h1>` tag, it has a predefined font, size, and color that the developer of the browser felt was useful.

That's fine, but what if you want to make some headings black and others red? This is possible with *inline styling.* Inline styling allows you to define special styles that apply to only one specific tag in the document. For example, to make one heading red, you'd use the following HTML:

```
<h1 style="color: red">Warning, this is bad</h1>
```

The `style` term is called an *attribute* of the `<h1>` tag. There are a few different attributes you can apply directly to tags within HTML; each one modifies how the browser should handle the tag. The `style` attribute allows you to apply any type of styling to this specific `<h1>` tag in the document. In this example, I chose to change the color of the text.

Now, you're probably thinking that I've just opened another can of worms. What if you want to apply the red color to *all* the <h1> tags in your document? That's a lot of extra code to write! Don't worry, there's a solution for that.

Instead of inserting styles inline, you can create a style definition that applies to the entire document. This method is known as *internal styling.* It defines a set of styles at the top of the HTML document that are applied to the entire document. Internal styling looks like this:

```
<style>
h1 {color: red;}
</style>
```

Now the browser will display all the `<h1>` tags in the document using a red color. But wait, there's more!

Style listings can be somewhat lengthy for large web pages, and placing them at the top of a document can become cumbersome. Also, if you want to apply the same styles to all the web pages in a website, having to retype or copy all that text can be tiring. To solve that problem, you use an external style sheet.

An *external style sheet* allows you to define styles just as the internal method does, but in a separate file, called a *style sheet.* Any web page can reference the same style sheet, and you can apply multiple style sheets to a single web page. You reference the external style sheet using the `<link>` tag, like this:

```
<link rel="stylesheet" href="mystyles.css">
```

When the browser sees this tag, it downloads the external style sheet, and applies the styles you defined in it to the document.

This all sounds great, but things just got a lot more complicated! Now there are three different locations from which you can define styles for your HTML document, on top of what the browser itself does. How are you supposed to know which ones take precedence over the others?

The *Cascading Style Sheet* (CSS) standard defines a set of rules that determine just how browsers should apply styles to an HTML document. As the name implies, styles cascade down from a high level to a low level. Styles defined in a higher-level rule override styles defined in a lower-level rule.

The CSS standard defines nine separate levels, which I cover in greater detail in Book 2, Chapter 2, but for now, here are the four most common style levels, in order from highest priority to lowest:

» Styles defined within the element tags

» Styles defined in an internal style sheet

» Styles defined in an external style sheet

» Styles defined by the client's browser defaults

So, any style attributes you set in an element tag override any styles that you set in an internal style sheet, which overrides any styles you set in an external style sheet, which overrides any styles the client browser uses by default. This allows you to set an overall style for your web pages using an external style sheet, and then override those settings for individual situations using the standard element tags.

**TECHNICAL STUFF**

You may be wondering how assistive technology tools work to change the web page display for individuals who are sight impaired. Part of the nine rules that I cover in Book 2, Chapter 2, incorporate any rules defined in the browser for sight-impaired viewing.

### CSS standards

The CSS standard defines a core set of styles for basic rendering of an HTML document. The first version of CSS (called CSS1) was released in 1996, and it only defined some very rudimentary styles:

>> Font type, size, and color

>> Text alignment (such as margins)

>> Background colors or images

>> Borders

The second version of CSS, called — you guessed it! — CSS2, was released in 1998. It added only a few more styling features:

>> More-exact positioning of text

>> Styles for different output types (such as printers or screens)

>> The appearance of browser features such as the cursor and scrollbar

That's still not all that impressive of a list of styles. Needless to say, more was needed to help liven up web pages. To compensate for that, many browser developers started creating their own style definitions, apart from the CSS standards. These style definitions are called *extensions.* The browser extensions covered lots of different fancy styling features, such as applying rounded edges to borders and images, making a smoother layout in the web page.

As you might guess, having different extensions to apply different style features in different browsers just made things more complicated. Instead of coding a single style for an element in an HTML document, you needed to code the same feature several different ways so the web page would look the same in different browsers. This quickly became a nightmare.

When work was started on the CSS3 standard in 1999, one of the topics was to rein in the myriad browser extensions. However, things quickly became complicated because all the different browser developers wanted their own extensions included in the new standard.

To simplify the process, the CSS design committee split the CSS standards into separate modules. Each CSS module covers a specific area of styling, such as colors, media support, and backgrounds. Each module could be voted on and released under a different timeline. The downside to this approach is that now each module has been released as a recommended standard at a different time, making the CSS3 standard somewhat difficult to track and implement.

Quite possibly one of the most anticipated features of CSS3 is the ability to define fonts. Fonts have long been the bane of web programmers. When you define a specific font, that font must be installed on your website visitor's computer in order for the browser to use it. If the font isn't available, the browser picks a default font to use, which often becomes an ugly mess.

*Web fonts* allow you to define a font on your server so that every client browser can download the font and render text using it. This is a huge accomplishment! No longer are you reliant on your website visitors having specific fonts installed in their web browsers.

Yet another popular feature of CSS3 is the use of shadows and semitransparent colors in text and other web page elements, such as form objects. These features by themselves can transform an ugly HTML form into a masterpiece.

The combination of HTML5 and CSS3 has greatly revolutionized the web world, allowing developers to create some pretty amazing websites. However, one thing was still missing: the ability to easily change content on the web page.

# Creating a Dynamic Web Page

*Static web pages* contain information that doesn't change until the web designer or programmer manually changes it. In the early days of the Internet, simply jumping on the Internet bandwagon was important for corporations. It wasn't so important what companies posted on the web, as long as they had an Internet presence where customers could get basic information about the company and its products. Static web pages, consisting solely of HTML and CSS, easily accomplished this function.

But one of the big limitations of static web pages is how much effort it takes to update them. Changing a single element on a static web page requires rebuilding and reloading the entire page, or sometimes even a group of web pages. This process is way too cumbersome for an organization that frequently needs to post real-time information, such as events, awards, or closings. Also, during this process, a developer can accidentally change other items on the page, seriously messing up the information on the web page, or even the entire web page layout!

*Dynamic web pages* allow you to easily change your content in real time without even touching the coding of the page. That's right: Without manually making any changes to the page itself, the information on the page can change. This means you can keep the content on the page fresh so that what a visitor sees there now may be updated or replaced in a day, an hour, or a minute. The core layout of the web page can remain the same, but the data presented constantly changes.

To successfully create a dynamic web page, you have to know a method for automatically inserting real-time data into the HTML code that gets sent to the client browser. This is where web scripting languages come in.

A *web scripting language* allows you to insert program code inside your web page that dynamically generates HTML that the client browser reads. A processor reads the program code and dynamically generates HTML to display content on the web page, as shown in Figure 1-1.

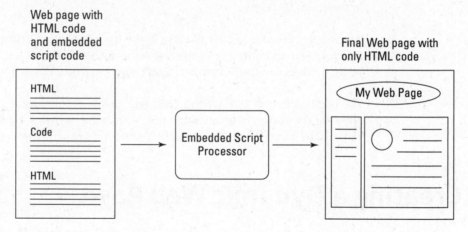

**FIGURE 1-1:**
Program code
embedded in a
web page.

Now, because programming code is embedded in the web page, something somewhere must run the code to produce the dynamic HTML for the new content. As it turns out, there are two places where the embedded program code can run:

» On the client's computer, after the web browser downloads the web page. This is known as *client-side programming.*

» On the web server before the web page is sent. This is known as *server-side programming.*

This section takes a look at how each of these types of programming differ in creating dynamic content for your website.

# Client-side programming

In client-side programming, you embed program code inside the HTML code that the server sends to the client browser with the HTML code. The browser must be able to detect the embedded program code and run it, either inside the browser or as a separate program outside the browser. Figure 1-2 demonstrates this process.

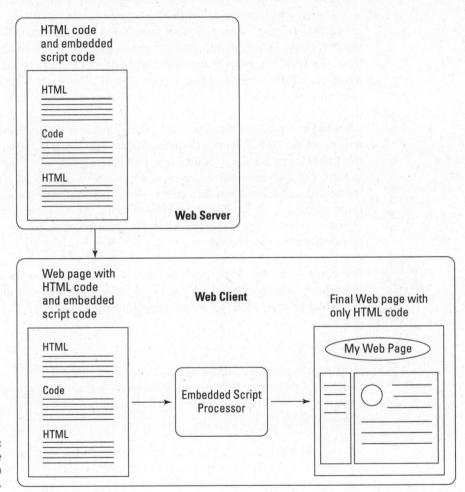

FIGURE 1-2:
Using client-side
code in a
web page.

## JavaScript

These days, the most popular client-side programming language is JavaScript. JavaScript is a scripting language that you embed inside the normal HTML code in your web page. It runs within the client browser and can utilize features of the browser that are not normally accessible from standard HTML code. JavaScript code is commonly used to produce pop-up messages and dialog boxes that people interact with as they view the page. These are elements that HTML code can't generate.

As shown in Figure 1-2, the entire web page with the embedded JavaScript code is downloaded to the client browser. The client browser detects the embedded JavaScript code and runs it accordingly. It does this while also processing the HTML tags within the document and applying any CSS styles defined. That's a lot for the browser to keep up with!

The downside of JavaScript is that, because it runs in the client browser, you're at the mercy of how the individual web browser interprets the code. Although the HTML language started out as a standard, JavaScript was a little different. In the early days of JavaScript, different browsers would implement different features of JavaScript using different methods. It was not uncommon to run across a web page that worked just fine for one type of browser, but didn't work at all in another type of browser — all because of JavaScript processing inconsistencies.

Eventually, work was done to standardize JavaScript. The JavaScript language was taken up by the Ecma International standards organization, which created the ECMAScript standard, which is what JavaScript is now based off of. As the ECMAScript standard evolved, more and more browser developers started seeing the benefits of using a standard client-side programming language and incorporated them in their JavaScript implementations. At the time of this writing, the eighth version of the standard, called ECMAScript 2017, has been finalized and implemented in most browsers.

**TECHNICAL STUFF**

The name JavaScript was chosen to capitalize on the popularity of the Java programming language for use in web applications. However, it doesn't have any resemblance or relation to the Java programming language.

## jQuery

JavaScript is popular, but one of its downsides is that it can be somewhat complicated to program. With so many different features incorporated by so many different developers, today a JavaScript program can quickly turn into a large endeavor to code.

To help solve this issue, a group of developers banded together to create a set of libraries to make client-side programming with JavaScript easier. Thus was born jQuery.

The jQuery software isn't a separate programming language; instead, it's a set of libraries of JavaScript code. The libraries are self-contained JavaScript functions that you can reference in your own JavaScript programming to perform common functions, such as finding a location in a web page to display text or retrieve a value entered into an HTML form field.

Instead of having to write lines and lines of JavaScript code, you can just reference one or two jQuery functions to do the work for you. That's a huge time-saver, as well as a great resource for implementing advanced features that you would never have been able to code yourself using just JavaScript.

## Server-side programming

The other side of web programming is server-side programming. Server-side programming languages solve the problem of different client code interpreters by running the code on the server. In server-side programming, the web server interprets the embedded programming code before sending the web page to the client's browser. The server then takes any HTML that the programming code generates and inserts it directly into the web page before sending it out to the client. The server does all the work running the scripting code, so you're guaranteed that every web page will run properly. Figure 1-3 illustrates this process.

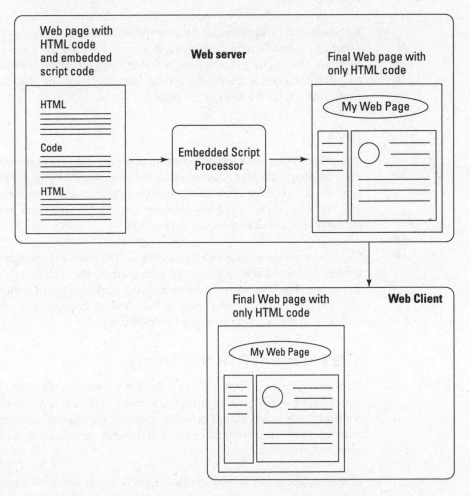

**FIGURE 1-3:**
Using server-side
programming
to create a web
page.

Unlike client-side programming, there are many popular server-side programming languages that are in use these days, each with its own set of pros and cons. This section takes a look at a few of the more popular programming languages.

## CGI scripting

One of the first attempts at server-side programming support was the Apache web server's Common Gateway Interface (CGI). The CGI provided an interface between the web server and the underlying server operating system (OS), which was often Unix-based.

This allowed programmers to embed scripting code commonly used in the Unix platform to dynamically generate HTML. Two of the most common scripting languages used in the Unix world and, thus, commonly used in CGI programming are Perl and Python.

Although CGI programming became popular in the early days of the web, it wasn't long before it was exploited. It was all too easy for a novice administrator to apply the wrong permissions to CGI scripts, allowing a resourceful attacker to gain privileged access to the server. Other methods of processing server-side programming code had to be developed.

## Java

One of the earlier attempts at a controlled server-side programming language was Java. Although the Java programming language became popular as a language for creating stand-alone applications that could run on any computer platform, it can also run as a server-side programming language in web applications. When used this way, it's called Java Server Pages (JSP).

The JSP language requires that you have a Java compiler embedded with your web server. The web server detects the Java code in the HTML code and then sends the code to the Java compiler for processing. Any output from the Java program is sent to the client browser as part of the HTML document. The most common JSP platform is the open-source Apache Tomcat server.

## The Microsoft ASP.NET family

Microsoft's first entry into the server-side programming world — Active Server Pages (ASP) — had a similar look and feel to JSP. ASP programs embedded ASP scripting code inside standard HTML code and required an ASP server to be incorporated with the standard Microsoft Internet Information Services (IIS) web server to process the code.

However, Microsoft developers determined that it wasn't necessary to maintain a separate programming language for server-side web programming, so they combined the server-side programming and Windows desktop programming environments into one technology. With the advent of the .NET family of programming languages, Microsoft released ASP.NET for the web environment, as an update to the old ASP environment.

With ASP.NET, you can embed any type of Microsoft .NET programming code inside your HTML documents to produce dynamic content. The .NET family of programming languages includes Visual Basic .NET, C#, J#, and even Delphi. NET. This allows you to leverage the same code you use to create Windows desktop applications as you do to create dynamic web pages. You can often use the same Windows features, such as buttons, slide bars, and scrollbars, inside your web applications that you see in Windows applications.

## JavaScript

Yes, you read that right. The same JavaScript language that's popular in the client-side programming world is now starting to make headway as a server-side programming language. The Node.js library allows you to interface JavaScript code inside HTML web pages for processing on the server.

The benefit to using Node.js is that you only need to learn one language for both client-side and server-side programming. Although it's still relatively new to the game, the Node.js language is becoming more popular.

## PHP

What started out as a simple exercise in tweaking CGI scripts turned into a new server-side programming language that took the world by storm. Rasmus Lerdorf wrote the Personal Home Page (PHP) programming language as a way to improve how his CGI scripts worked. After some encouragement and help, PHP morphed into its own programming language, and a new name, PHP: Hypertext Preprocessor (yes, it uses the acronym inside its name, which is called a *recursive acronym*).

The PHP language developers freely admit that they borrowed many features from other popular languages, such as Perl, Python, C, and even Unix shell scripting. However, PHP was developed specifically for server-side programming, and it has many features built in that aren't available in other scripting languages. You don't need to wrestle with strange setups or features to get PHP to work in a web environment. It has matured into a complete catalog of advanced features that cover everything from database access to drawing graphics on your web page.

Because of the dedication of the PHP developers to create a first-rate server-side programming language, and because it's free open-source software, PHP quickly became the darling of the Internet world. Many web-hosting companies include PHP as part of their basic hosting packages. If you already have space on a web-hosting server, it's possible that you already have access to PHP!

# Combining client-side and server-side programming

Client-side and server-side programming both have pros and cons. Instead of trying to choose one method of creating dynamic web pages, you can instead use both at the same time!

You can easily embed both client-side and server-side programming code into the same web page to run on the server, as shown in Figure 1-4.

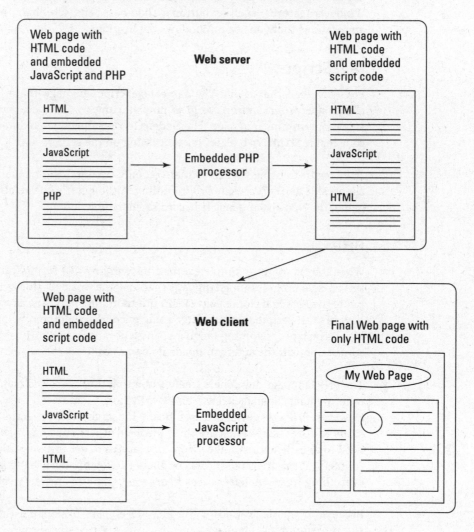

FIGURE 1-4: Combining client-side and server-side programming.

One common use for JavaScript and PHP coding is data validation. When you provide an HTML form for your website visitors to fill out, you have to be careful that they actually fill in the correct type of data for each field. With server-side programming, you can't validate the data until the site visitor completes and submits the form to the server. If a website visitor accidentally skips filling out a single field and the entire form needs to be filled out all over again, that can be a frustrating experience.

To solve that problem, you can embed JavaScript code into the form to check as the site visitor enters data into the form. If any form fields are empty when the Submit button is clicked, the JavaScript code can block the form submission and point out the empty field. Then, when all the data is completed and the form is successfully submitted, the PHP code on the server can process the data to ensure it's the correct data type and format.

# Storing Content

The last piece of the dynamic web application puzzle is the actual content. With static web pages, content is already built into the web page code. To change information on a static web page, you have to recode the page. Unfortunately, more often than not, when a web page is updated, the old version is lost.

With dynamic web applications, the content comes from somewhere outside of the web page. But where? The most common place is a database.

Databases are an easy way to store and retrieve data. They're quicker than storing data using standard files, and they provide a level of security to protect your data. By storing content in a database, you can also easily archive and reference old content and replace it with new content as needed.

Much like the server-side programming world, the database world has lots of different database software options. Here are some of the more popular ones:

>> **Oracle:** Oracle has set the gold standard for databases. It's found in many high-profile commercial environments. Although Oracle is very fast and supports lots of features, it can also be somewhat expensive.

>> **Microsoft SQL Server:** Microsoft's entry into the database server world, SQL Server is geared toward high-end database environments. It's often found in environments that utilize Microsoft Windows Servers.

» **PostgreSQL:** The PostgreSQL database server is an open-source project that attempts to implement many of the advanced features found in commercial databases. In its early days, PostgreSQL had a reputation for being somewhat slow, but it has made vast improvements. Unfortunately, old reputations are hard to shake, and PostgreSQL still struggles with overcoming them.

» **MySQL:** The MySQL database server is yet another open-source project. Unlike PostgreSQL, it doesn't attempt to match all the features of commercial packages. Instead, it focuses on speed. MySQL has a reputation for being very fast at simple data inserts and queries — perfect for the fast-paced web application world.

Mainly because of its speed, the MySQL database server has become a popular tool for storing data in dynamic web applications. It also helps that, because it's an open-source project, web-hosting companies can install it for free, which makes it a perfect combination with the PHP server-side programming language for dynamic web applications.

Chapter **2**

# Using a Web Server

<p>efore you can start developing dynamic web applications, you'll need a web server environment to work in. You have lots of different choices available to create your own development environment, but sometimes having more options just makes things more confusing. This chapter walks through the different options you have for creating your development environment.</p>

## Recognizing What's Required

Just like that famous furniture that needs assembly, you'll need to assemble some separate components to get your web application development environment up and running. There are three main parts that you need to assemble for your web development environment:

» A web server to process requests from browsers to interact with your application

» A PHP server to run the PHP server-side programming code in your application

» A database server to store the data required for your dynamic application

On the surface, this may seem fairly simple, but to make things more complicated, each of these parts has different options and versions available. That can lead to literally hundreds of different combinations to wade through!

This section helps you maintain your sanity by taking a closer look at each of these three requirements.

## The web server

The web server is what interacts with your website visitors. It passes their requests to your web application and passes your application responses back to them. The web server acts as a file server — it accepts requests for PHP and HTML files from client browsers and then retrieves those files and sends them back to the client browser. As I explain in the preceding chapter, the web server uses the HTTP standard to allow anonymous requests for access to the files on the server and respond to those requests.

There are quite a few different web server options around these days. Here are a few of the more popular ones that you'll run into:

>> **Apache:** The granddad of web servers, Apache was derived from the original web server developed at the University of Illinois. It's an open-source software project that has been and is currently the most commonly used web server on the Internet. It is very versatile and supports lots of different features, but with versatility comes complexity. Trying to wade through the configuration file for an Apache web server can be confusing. But for most web environments you just need to change a few of the default configuration settings.

>> **nginx:** The newer kid on the block, nginx is intended to ease some of the complexity of the Apache web server and provide improved performance. It's currently gaining in popularity, but it still has a long way to go to catch up with Apache.

>> **lighthttpd:** As its name suggests, lighthttpd is a lightweight web server that's significantly less versatile and complex than the Apache web server. It works great for small development environments and is becoming popular in embedded systems that need a web server with a small footprint. However, it doesn't hold up well in large-scale production Web server environments and probably isn't a good choice for a web development environment.

>> **IIS:** IIS is the official Microsoft Web server. It's popular in Microsoft Windows server environments, but there aren't versions for other operating systems. IIS focuses on supporting the Microsoft .NET family of server-side programming languages, such as C# .NET and Visual Basic .NET, but it can be interfaced with the PHP server. This configuration is not common, though, and you don't see very many PHP servers that utilize the IIS web server.

As you can tell from these descriptions, just about every web server is compared to the Apache web server. Apache has become the gold standard in Internet web servers. Unless you have a specific reason for not using the Apache web server, you should use it for your development environment, especially if you know that your production web server environment will use it.

## The PHP server

The PHP programming language began in 1995 as a personal project by Rasmus Lerdorf to help his web pages access data stored in a database. He released the first official version 1.0 to the open-source community on June 8, 1995.

Since then, the PHP language has taken on a life of its own, gaining in both features and popularity. The development of the PHP language is currently supported by Zend, which produces many PHP tools.

One of the most confusing aspects of the PHP server is that there are currently two different actively supported branches of the PHP language:

>> The version 5.x branch

>> The version 7.x branch

The first question that often comes to mind is: "What happened to version 6?" The short-lived version 6 of PHP had some unresolvable issues and was officially abandoned by the PHP developers, with the new features rolled back into version 5.

Now for the second question: "Why two active versions?" The version 5.x branch is still maintained mainly because of the great wealth of applications that continue to use features supported in version 5.x, but not in version 7.x. It will take some time before all the old 5.x applications will be migrated to version 7.x code. Unfortunately, version 7 of PHP breaks quite a few things that were popular in the 5.x version. However, the PHP developers are no longer performing bug fixes in the 5.x branch, only security patches. At the time of this writing, the current version in the 5.x branch is 5.4 and will be maintained until the end of 2018.

At the time of this writing, many popular web server packages support both the 5.x and 7.x version branches and will give you the choice of which one to use for your installation. If you're developing new dynamic web applications, it's best to use the 7.x version branch; at the time of this writing, the latest version is 7.2.

The PHP server contains its own built-in web server, but that's only intended for development and not for use as a live production web server. For large-scale use, you must interface the PHP server with a web server. As the web server receives requests for .php files, it must pass them to the PHP server for processing. You must set up this feature as part of the web server configuration file. This is discussed later in this chapter in the "Customizing the Apache Web Server" section.

**WARNING**

You may still run into some web-hosting companies that use PHP version 4. This was a very popular and long-running version, but it's no longer supported by PHP with security patches. It's best to stay away from any web host that only supports PHP version 4.

## The database server

As I describe in Chapter 1 of this minibook, there are many different types of database servers to handle data for your web applications. By far the most popular used in open-source web applications is the MySQL server.

Many websites and web packages use the term *MySQL Server*, but there are actually a few different versions of it. Because Oracle acquired the MySQL project in 2010, it has split the project into four versions:

>> **MySQL Standard Edition:** A commercial product that provides the minimal MySQL database features.

>> **MySQL Enterprise Edition:** A commercial product that provides extra support, monitoring, and maintenance features.

>> **MySQL Cluster Carrier Grade Edition:** A commercial product that in addition to the Enterprise Edition features, supports multi-server clustering.

>> **MySQL Community Edition:** The freely downloadable version of MySQL that supports the same features as the Standard Edition, but with no formal support.

As you can see from the list, the MySQL server has both commercial and open-source versions. The commercial versions support some advanced features that aren't available in the Open Source version, such as hot backups, database activity monitoring, and being able to implement a read/write database cluster on multiple servers. These advanced features can come in handy in large-scale database environments, but for most small to medium-size database applications, the MySQL Community Edition is just fine. That's what's usually included in most web server packages.

Just as with PHP, the MySQL project maintains multiple versions of the MySQL server software. At the time of this writing, the currently supported versions of MySQL are

>> Version 5.5

>> Version 5.6

>> Version 5.7

**TECHNICAL STUFF**

## MySQL AND MariaDB

The MySQL server project has had quite an interesting life. It was originally developed in 1994 as an open-source project by a Swedish company, MySQL AB. It gained in popularity and features, until MySQL AB was purchased by Sun Microsystems in 2008. However, Oracle purchased Sun Microsystems in 2010 and took control over the MySQL project.

When Oracle purchased the rights to MySQL from Sun Microsystems, the main MySQL developer and his team left to start their own separate open-source branch of MySQL, called MariaDB. With the terms of the open-source license, this move was completely legal, and the project has gained some respect and following in the open-source community. MariaDB is nearly 100 percent compatible with MySQL and is often used as a direct replacement for the MySQL Community Edition in some environments. Any PHP code that you write to interact with the MySQL server will also work with the MariaDB server. Don't be alarmed if the development environment you use switches to MariaDB!

Each version has some minor updates to the MySQL database engine, but for most dynamic web applications, the differences won't play a significant role in your application performance or functions, so it won't matter much which of these three versions your system uses.

Several cloud providers (including Oracle itself) provide the MySQL server as a cloud service. Instead of installing and running your own MySQL server you can rent space on their MySQL cloud server. The benefit of running MySQL in the cloud is that you're guaranteed perfect up-time for the database, because it's distributed among multiple servers in the cloud. The downside, though, is that this can get expensive and is only recommended for commercial web applications that require the extra server power provided by the cloud.

# Considering Your Server Options

Now that you know you'll need a web server, a PHP server, and a MySQL server for your development work, the next step is trying to find an environment that supports all three (and it would help if they were all integrated). You basically have three options for setting up a complete web programming development environment:

>> Purchase space on a commercial server from a web-hosting company.

>> Install the separate servers on your own workstation or server.

>> Install an all-in-one package that bundles all three servers for you.

The following sections walk you through each of these scenarios and the pros and cons of each.

## Using a web-hosting company

By far, the easiest method of setting up a PHP programming environment is to rent space on an existing server that has all the necessary components already installed. Plenty of companies offer PHP web development packages. Some of the more popular ones are

>> GoDaddy (www.godaddy.com)

>> HostGator (www.hostgator.com)

>> 1&1 (www.1and1.com)

>> 000webhost (www.000webhost.com)

These large web-hosting companies offer multiple levels of support for their services. Often, they'll offer several tiers of service based on the number of databases you can create, the amount of data that you can store, and the amount of network bandwidth your web applications are allowed to consume per month. That way, you can start out with a basic package for minimal cost and then upgrade to one of the more expensive packages as your Internet application takes off! It pays to shop around to check different pricing structures and support levels at the different web-hosting companies.

Besides these main competitors, you'll find many, many smaller web hosting companies willing to offer MySQL/PHP packages to host your applications. There's a good chance if you already have a web-hosting company you use to host your static web pages, it'll have some type of MySQL/PHP support. If you already have space on a web server for your website, check with them to see if they offer an upgrade to a MySQL/PHP package.

With the popularity of the new "cloud" environment where everything runs on shared server space, there are now a few more participants in the PHP server hosting game. The Wikipedia web page for cloud service providers lists more than 200 different providers! You'll probably recognize the more popular ones:

>> Amazon Web Services (AWS)

>> Google Cloud Platform

>> Oracle Cloud Platform

>> Microsoft Azure

Each of these cloud services provides some level of support for PHP program development. One of the main benefits of utilizing a cloud service is that your application is hosted on multiple servers that share the traffic load and are redundant for backup purposes. If a server in the cloud crashes, your application will still work on other servers. Of course, be prepared to pay a premium price for those features!

**WARNING**

Be careful with some of the smaller web-hosting companies. These days, just about anyone can install the PHP and MySQL server software onto a server and sell space, so many "mom-and-pop" web-hosting companies now provide this service. However, installing the server programs is different from maintaining the server programs. Often, you'll find these smaller web-hosting sites use outdated server versions that haven't been upgraded or patched with security updates, making them vulnerable to attacks.

# Building your own server environment

I wouldn't recommend it for a live production website, but for development work you can build your own web server environment. You don't even need to have a large server for a personal web development environment — you can build it using your existing Windows or Apple workstation or laptop.

The following sections walk you through the basics you need to know to get this working in either the Linux or Windows/Mac environments.

## Web servers in Linux

Linux desktops and servers are becoming more popular these days, especially for web development. You can download the Apache, MySQL, and PHP server source code packages and compile them on your Linux system, but unless you need the absolute latest version of things, that's not the recommended way to do it.

These days, most Linux distributions include packages for easily installing all the components you need for a complete web development environment. For Debian-based Linux distributions (such as Ubuntu and Linux Mint), you use the apt-get command-line tool to install software packages. For Red Hat–based Linux distributions (such as Red Hat, CentOS, and Fedora) you use the dnf command-line tool.

For Debian-based systems, such as Ubuntu, follow these steps to do that:

1. **From a command prompt, install the Apache web server using the following command:**

   ```
   sudo apt-get install apache2
   ```

2. **Install the MySQL server package using the following command:**

   ```
   sudo apt-get install mysql-server
   ```

   **WARNING**

   During the MySQL server installation, you'll be prompted for a password to use for the root user account. The root user account in MySQL has full privileges to all tables and objects. Make sure you remember what password you enter here!

3. **Install the PHP packages to install the PHP server and required extensions, the Apache modifications to run PHP, and the graphical phpMyAdmin tool:**

   ```
   sudo apt-get install php libapache2-mod-php
   sudo apt-get install php-mcrypt php-mysql
   sudo apt-get install phpmyadmin
   ```

   The first line installs the main PHP server, along with the Apache module to interface with the PHP server. The second line installs two PHP extensions that are required to interface with the MySQL server. The third line installs the web-based phpMyAdmin PHP program, which provides a web interface to the MySQL server.

4. **Open a browser and test things out by going to the following URL:**

   ```
   http://localhost/phpmyadmin
   ```

   You should be greeted by the phpMyAdmin administration window.

5. **Log in using the MySQL root user account and the password you supplied when you installed MySQL (you remember it, right?).**

   Figure 2-1 shows the main phpMyAdmin web page, which shows what versions of the Apache, PHP, and MySQL servers are running.

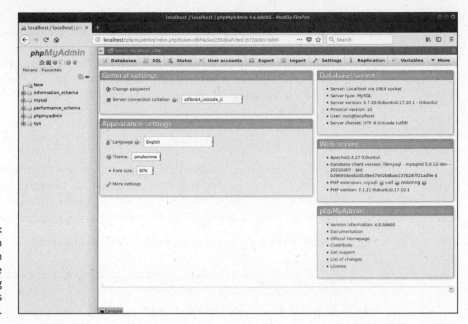

**FIGURE 2-1:**
The main
phpMyAdmin
web page
showing
everything that is
running.

For Red Hat–based systems, such as Fedora and CentOS, follow these steps to load LAMP:

1. **From a command prompt, install the Apache web server using the following commands:**

```
sudo dnf install httpd
sudo systemctl enable httpd
sudo systemsctl start httpd
```

The httpd package includes the Apache2 web server. The executable file for Apache is named httpd (thus, the name of the package). The package doesn't start the Apache web server by default, so the second two lines use the systemctl utility to enable the service so it starts automatically at boot time and then starts it.

2. **Install the MySQL server package using the following commands:**

```
sudo dnf install mariadb-server
sudo systemctl enable mariadb
sudo systemctl start mariadb
```

Notice that the Red Hat distribution (and thus CentOS and Fedora) has gone with the MariaDB replacement package for MySQL. When you install MariaDB, the package sets the root user account password to an empty string. This is not recommended if your server is on any type of a network. Fortunately, there's a quick utility that you can run to change the root user account's password:

```
mysql_secure_installation
```

When you run this script, it'll prompt you to answer a few questions, such as the new password for the root user account, whether to restrict the root user account to only logging in from the local host, whether to remove the anonymous users feature, and whether to remove the test database.

3. **Install the PHP packages using the following commands:**

```
sudo dnf install php php-mbstring php-mysql
sudo dnf install phpmyadmin
sudo systemctl restart httpd
```

The PHP server doesn't run as its own service — the Apache web server spawns it when needed. Because of that, you do need to use the systemctl utility to restart the Apache web server so it rereads the configuration file with the new PHP settings.

4. **Open a browser and test things out by going to the following URL:**

```
http://localhost/phpmyadmin
```

You should see the phpMyAdmin login page.

5. **Log in using the root user account in MySQL along with the password you defined when you installed MySQL.**

Figure 2-2 shows phpMyAdmin running on a CentOS 7 system.

TIP

By using the distribution software packages for each server, you're guaranteed that the server will run correctly in your Linux environment. An additional benefit is that the distribution software updates will include any security patches or bug fixes released for the servers automatically.

## Web servers in Windows and Mac

Installing and running the Apache, MySQL, and PHP servers in a Windows or Mac environment is very tricky, because there are lots of factors involved in how to install and configure them. For starters, both Windows and macOS come with a web server built in, so if you install the Apache web server you'll need to configure it to use an alternative TCP port.

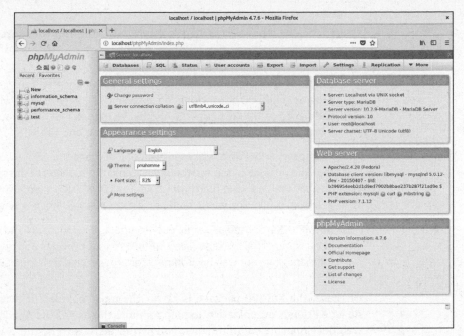

**FIGURE 2-2:**
Viewing the phpMyAdmin main web page on Fedora 27.

Likewise, macOS includes an older version of PHP by default, so if you install an updated version of PHP, things get tricky trying to make sure which version is active.

Because of these complexities, it's not recommended for beginners to install the Apache, MySQL, and PHP packages separately in the Windows and Mac environments. There's a much simpler way of getting that to work, which I'll describe in the next section.

## Using premade servers

Trying to get a working Apache, MySQL, and PHP server in Windows (called WAMP) or in the Mac environment (called MAMP) can be a complicated process. There's a lot of work downloading each of the individual server packages, configuring them, and getting things to work together.

Fortunately, some resourceful programmers have done that work for us! There are quite a few open-source packages that bundle the Apache web server, MySQL (or MariaDB) server, and PHP server together to install as a single package. This is by far the best way to go if you plan on using your Windows or Mac workstation or laptop as your web development environment.

There are quite a few pre-loaded packages available, but these are the most common ones:

>> **XAMPP:** An all-in-one package that supports PHP and Perl server-side programming and also includes an email and FTP server, along with a self-signed certificate to use the Apache web server in HTTPS mode. It has installation packages available for Windows, Mac, and Linux.

>> **Wampserver:** A Windows-based all-in-one package that allows you to install multiple versions of the Apache, MySQL, and PHP servers at the same time. You can then mix-and-match which versions of which server you have active at any time, allowing you to duplicate almost any web-hosting environment.

>> **MAMP:** A Mac-based all-in-one package that is easy to install and use. It also has a commercial package called MAMP Pro that provides additional features for managing your web environment for professional developers.

Of these, the XAMPP package is by far the most popular. It was created by the Apache Friends organization to help promote the use of the Apache web server in web development environments. Follow these steps to install XAMPP in a Windows or macOS environment:

1. **Open your browser and go to** www.apachefriends.org.

2. **Look for the Download section of the web page and click the link for the OS you're using.**

3. **After the download finishes, run the downloaded file in your OS environment.**

   This starts the XAMPP installation wizard.

4. **Click the Next button to go to the Select Components window, shown in Figure 2-3.**

   The Select Components window allows you to select which components in XAMPP you want installed. You won't use everything contained in XAMPP for this book, but feel free to install the entire package and explore on your own!

5. **Click the Next button to continue the installation.**

6. **Select the installation folder for XAMPP.**

   The default location for Windows is c:\xampp; for macOS, it's /Applications/XAMPP. Those will work just fine for both environments.

7. **Click the Next button to continue the installation.**

   The Apache Friends organization has teamed up with Bitnami, which has prepackaged many popular web applications specifically for use in XAMPP.

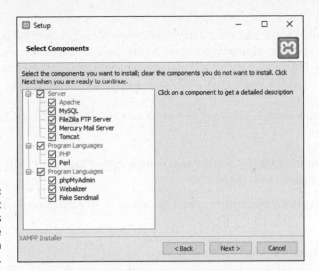

**FIGURE 2-3:**
The XAMPP Select
Components
window in the
installation
wizard.

8. **You can learn more about Bitnami by leaving the Learn More about Bitnami for XAMPP check box checked, or if you'd like to skip this step, remove the check mark from the check box, and then click the Next button to continue.**

9. **Click the Next button to begin the software installation.**

10. **You can keep the check mark in the check box to start XAMPP, and then click the Finish button to end the wizard.**

The XAMPP Control Panel provides easy access to start, stop, and configure each of the servers contained in the XAMPP package. Figure 2-4 shows the main Control Panel window.

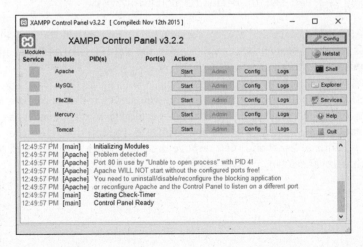

**FIGURE 2-4:**
The main XAMPP
Control Panel
window.

Using a Web Server

By default, XAMPP configures the Apache web server to use TCP port 80 for HTTP connections. Unfortunately, this port is often in use by web servers built into Windows and Mac workstations and servers. This will produce an error message when you first start the XAMPP Control Panel, as shown in Figure 2-4.

You can move the Apache web server to an alternative TCP port. Just follow these steps:

1.  **From the XAMPP Control Panel main window, click the Config button for the Apache web server.**

2.  **Select the menu option to edit the** `httpd.conf` **configuration file.**

    This opens the Apache web server configuration file in a text editor.

3.  **Look for the line:**

    ```
    Listen 80
    ```

4.  **Change the 80 in the line to 8080, a common alternative TCP port to use for HTTP communications.**

5.  **Save the updated configuration file in the editor, and then exit the editor window.**

6.  **Click the Start button for the Apache web server.**

    The Apache Web server should indicate that it has started and is using both TCP Ports 443 (for HTTPS) and 8080 (for HTTP).

7.  **Click the Start button for the MySQL database server.**

    The MariaDB database server should indicate that it has started and is using TCP Port 3306 (the default TCP port for MySQL).

After the Apache and MySQL servers start, you can exit the XAMPP Control Panel. If you need to stop the servers, reopen the XAMPP Control Panel and click the Stop buttons for both servers.

TIP

Although you've moved the Apache web server in the configuration file, XAMPP will still check to see if TCP Port 80 is available when you start the XAMPP Control Panel and complain that it's not available. To stop that, click the Config button in the Control Panel and then remove the check mark for the Check Default Ports on Startup check box.

# Tweaking the Servers

When you get the Apache, MySQL, and PHP servers installed in your development environment, you may need to do a little bit of tweaking to get them working just the way you want. Each of the servers uses a text configuration file to define just how the server behaves. The following sections walk you through how to find the configuration files and some of the settings that you may need to tweak for your development environment.

## Customizing the Apache Server

By default, the Apache Web server uses the `httpd.conf` configuration file to store its settings. For Linux and Mac systems, the file is usually stored in the `/etc` folder structure, often under either `/etc/httpd` or `/etc/apache2`.

TIP

The XAMPP package installs the Apache configuration file in the `c:\xampp\apache\conf` folder in Windows or `/Applications/XAMPP/apache/conf` in macOS.

The `httpd.conf` configuration file contains individual lines called *directives*. Each directive defines one configuration option, along with the value that you set.

The Apache web server is very versatile, with lots of different options and features. The downside to that is it can make the configuration seem complex at first, but the configuration file is organized such that you should be able to find what you're looking for relatively easily. In the following sections, I cover a few things that you'll want to pay attention to.

WARNING

Many systems break the Apache web server configurations into multiple files to help make the features more modular. Look for the `Include` directive lines in the main `httpd.conf` configuration file to see what other files contain Apache web server configuration settings.

### Defining the web folder location

The main job of the Apache web server is to serve files to remote clients. However, you don't want just anyone retrieving just any file on your system! To limit what files the Apache server serves, you must restrict it to a specific folder area in the system.

You set the folder where the Apache web server serves files using the `Document-Root` directive:

```
DocumentRoot c:/xampp/htdocs
```

The `htdocs` folder is the normal default used for the Apache web server in Windows and macOS environments (for macOS, it's located in `/Applciations/XAMPP/htdocs`). For Linux environments, it has become somewhat common to use `/var/www/html` as the `DocumentRoot` folder.

**WARNING**

If you choose to move the `DocumentRoot` folder to another folder location on the server, make sure the user account that runs the Apache web server has access to at least read files from the folder.

## Setting the default TCP port

The Apache web server listens for incoming connections from client browsers using two different default TCP network ports:

>> TCP port 80 for HTTP requests

>> TCP port 443 for HTTPS requests

HTTPS requests use encryption to secure the communication between the browser and the server. This method is quickly becoming a standard for all web servers on the Internet.

You set the ports the Apache web server accepts incoming requests on using the `Listen` directive:

```
Listen 80
Listen 443
```

You can use multiple `Listen` directives in the configuration file to listen on more than one TCP port.

## USING ENCRYPTION

To establish a secure HTTPS connection, your Apache web server must have a valid encryption certificate signed by a *certificate authority.* The certificate authority recognizes your website as valid and vouches for your authenticity. This enables your website visitors to trust that you are who you say you are and that your web server is what it says it is.

Unfortunately, signed certificates must be purchased and can be somewhat expensive. For development work, you can use a *self-signed certificate.* The self-signed certificate is what it says: You sign your own certificate. This doesn't instill any trust in your website visitors, so don't use a self-signed certificate on a production website — only use it for development. The XAMPP web server installs a self-signed certificate just for this purpose!

## Interacting with the PHP server

The Apache web server must know how to pass files that contain PHP code to the PHP server for processing. This is a two-step process.

First, you have to tell the Apache web server to load the PHP server module so that it can establish the link between the Apache and PHP servers. You do that using the LoadModule directive:

```
LoadModule php7_module "c:/xampp/php/apache2_4.dll"
```

After Apache loads the PHP module, you have to tell it what type of files to send to the PHP server. You do this using the AddHandler directive:

```
AddHandler application/x-httpd-php .php
```

This directive tells the Apache web server to forward all files with the .php file extension to the PHP module, which then forwards the files to the PHP server for processing.

**WARNING**

It may be tempting to just forward all .html files to the PHP server, because the PHP server will pass any HTML code directly to the client browser. However, this will add extra processing time to load your static web pages, causing a performance issue with your HTML pages.

## Tracking errors

When working in a development environment, it's always helpful to be able to track any errors that occur in your applications. The Apache web server supports eight different levels of error messages, shown in Table 2-1.

**TABLE 2-1**     Apache Web Server Error Levels

| Error Level | Description |
| --- | --- |
| emerg | A fatal error will halt the Apache web server. |
| alert | A severe error will have an adverse impact on your application and should be resolved immediately. |
| crit | A critical condition caused the operation to fail, such as a failure to access the network. |
| error | An error occurred in the session, such as an invalid HTTP header. |
| warn | A minor issue occurred in the session but didn't prevent it from continuing. |
| notice | Something out of the normal occurred. |
| debug | A low-level detailed message occurs for each step the server takes in processing a request. |

You define the level of error tracking using the LogLevel directive and the location of the error log using the ErrorLog directive:

```
LogLevel warn
ErrorLog logs/error.log
```

The debug log level can be useful for troubleshooting issues but is not recommended for normal activity, because it generates lots of output!

TIP

You can customize the appearance of the log messages using the LogFormat directive. Apache allows you to determine just what information appears in the log file, which can be handy when trying to troubleshoot specific problems. Consult the Apache server documentation for the different options you have available for customizing the logs.

## Customizing the MySQL server

The MySQL server uses two different filenames for its configuration settings:

>> my.cnf for Linux and Mac systems

>> my.ini for Windows systems

One of the more confusing features about the MySQL server is that there are three ways to specify configuration settings:

>> They can be compiled into the executable server program when built from source code.

>> They can be specified as command-line options when the server starts.

>> They can be set in the MySQL configuration file.

You can compile all the settings you need into the MySQL executable server program and run with no configuration file at all (that's the approach the MAMP all-in-one package takes). The downside to that is it's hard to determine just which settings are set to which values.

Most MySQL server installations use a combination of compiling some basic settings into the executable server program and creating a basic configuration file for the rest. The setting values set in the configuration file override anything compiled into the executable server program or set on the command line.

As with the Apache web server, the MySQL database server has lots of options you can change in the configuration file to fine-tune how things work. That said, there are only a few items that you'd ever really need to tweak in a normal setup. The following sections walk you through some of the settings you should become familiar with.

## The core server settings

The core server settings define the basics of how the MySQL server operates. These settings in the XAMPP for Windows setup look like this:

```
[mysqld]
port = 3306
socket = "C:/xampp/mysql/mysql.sock"
basedir = "C:/xampp/mysql"
tmpdir = "C:/xampp/mysql/tmp"
datadir = "C:/xampp/mysql/data"
log_error = "mysql_error.log"
```

The `port` setting defines the TCP port the MySQL server listens for incoming requests on. The `socket` setting defines the location of a socket file that local clients can use to communicate with the MySQL server without using the network.

The `basedir`, `tmpdir`, and `datadir` settings define the locations on the server that MySQL will use for storing its working files. The `datadir` setting defines where MySQL stores the actual database files.

## Working with the InnoDB storage engine

The InnoDB storage engine provides advanced database features for the MySQL server. It has its own set of configuration settings that control exactly how it operates and how it handles the data contained in tables that use that storage engine.

There are two main configuration settings that you may need to tweak for your specific MySQL server installation:

```
innodb_data_home_dir = "C:/xampp/mysql/data"
innodb_data_file_path = ibdata1:10M:autoextend
```

The `innodb_data_home_dir` setting defines the location where MySQL places files required to support the InnoDB storage engine. This allows you to separate those files from the normal MySQL database files if needed.

The `innodb_data_file_path` setting defines three pieces of information for the storage engine:

>> The filename MySQL uses for the main InnoDB storage file

>> The initial size of the storage file

>> What happens when the storage file fills up

To help speed up the data storage process, the InnoDB storage engine pre-allocates space on the system hard drive for the database storage file. That way, for each data record that's inserted into a table, the storage engine doesn't need to ask the operating system for more disk space to add to the database file — it's already there! This greatly speeds up the database performance. The second parameter defines the initial amount of disk space that the InnoDB storage engine allocates.

The third parameter is where things get interesting. It defines what the InnoDB storage engine does when the space allocated for the storage file becomes full. By default, the InnoDB storage engine will block new data inserts to the tables when it runs out of allocated storage space. You would have to manually extend the storage file size.

When you specify the `autoextend` setting, that allows the InnoDB storage engine to automatically allocate more space for the file. That's convenient, but it can also be dangerous in some environments. The InnoDB storage engine will keep allocating more storage space as needed until the server runs out of disk space!

WARNING

When you use the InnoDB storage engine for your MySQL applications, it's always a good idea to keep an eye on the storage space folder to make sure it's not taking up all the server disk space.

## Customizing the PHP server

The PHP server configuration file is named `php.ini`, but it can be located in several different areas. The locations that the PHP server checks are (in order):

>> The path set in the `PHPIniDir` directive in the Apache web server configuration file

>> The path set in a system environment variable named `PHPRC`

>> For Windows systems, the path set in the registry key named `IniFilePath` under the `HKEY_LOCAL_MACHINE/Software/PHP` registry hive

>> The folder where the PHP server executable file is stored

>> The default web server's folder

>> The OS system folder, which for Windows is the c:\winnt folder, and for Linux and Mac the /usr/local/lib folder

The XAMPP install process places the php.ini file in the c:\xampp\apache\bin folder.

If you're ever in doubt as to which php.ini configuration file the PHP server is using, run the phpinfo() function in a small PHP program. For your convenience, all the popular all-in-one packages provide a link to run the phpinfo() function from their main web pages. Figure 2-5 shows the output from the phpinfo() function in XAMPP running on a Windows system.

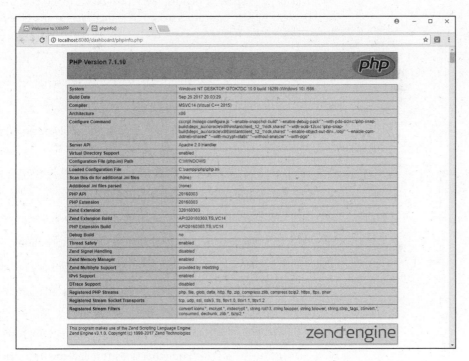

**FIGURE 2-5:**
The phpinfo() function output.

The phpinfo() function displays the system values for each of the configuration file settings and if any were overridden by a local setting. Look for the Loaded Configuration File entry that shows the path to the active php.ini file to see where that file is located for your PHP server.

As you can imagine, there are lots of settings available in the php.ini configuration file. Here are some of the php.ini settings (and the default values set in XAMPP) that you may need to tweak on your PHP server:

» date.timezone = Europe/Berlin: Defines the time zone of the PHP server. This must use a time zone value defined at http://php.net/manual/en/timezones.php.

» display_errors = On: Defines whether PHP error messages appear on the web page. This feature is extremely handy for development work but should be disabled for production servers.

» error_reporting = E_ALL & ~E_DEPRECATED: Sets the level of error reporting from the PHP server. PHP uses a complicated bit pattern to set which errors to display or not display. It uses labels to indicate the error level and Boolean bitwise operators to combine the levels — the tilde (~) indicates the NOT operator. The error levels are:

- E_ERROR: Fatal run-time errors

- E_WARNING: Run-time warnings that won't halt the script

- E_PARSE: Parsing syntax errors

- E_NOTICE: Script encountered something that could be an error and effect the results

- E_CORE_ERROR: Fatal error that prevents PHP from starting

- E_CORE_WARNING: Non-fatal errors during startup

- E_COMPILE_ERROR: Fatal error while compiling the PHP code

- E_COMPILE_WARNING: Non-fatal errors during compile time

- E_USER_ERROR: Fatal error message generated manually by your PHP code

- E_USER_WARNING: Non-fatal error message generated manually by your PHP code

- E_USER_NOTICE: Notice message generated manually by your PHP code

- E_STRICT: PHP detected code that doesn't follow the PHP strict rules

- E_RECOVERABLE_ERROR: A fatal error that you can catch with a try-catch block

- E_DEPRECATED: The PHP parser detected code that will no longer be supported

- E_USER_DEPRECATED: A deprecation error generated manually by your PHP code

- E_ALL: All errors and warnings except E_STRICT

» `variables_order = "GPCS"`: The order in which PHP populates the data from the HTTP session (G = GET, P = POST, C = Cookies, and S = System variables)

» `short_open_tag = Off`: Determines if you can use the `<?` tag to identify PHP code in your HTML documents

» `max_execution_time = 30`: Sets a time limit (in seconds) for a PHP program to run before the PHP server kills it (This is useful for stopping programs stuck in a loop!)

» `memory_limit = 128M`: Sets a limit on how much memory on the physical server the PHP server can allocate (This also helps prevent runaway programs from taking down the entire web server!)

# Chapter **3**

# Building a Development Environment

When you're ready to start coding your web application, you'll need some tools to help you out. Just as a carpenter needs a set of tools to do her job, web developers need tools as well. And just as the carpenter has a wide selection of tools to choose from, so do web developers. A carpenter can build an entire house using a hammer and hand saw (and possibly a tape measure), but most likely, she has a few more advanced tools to make her job easier. Likewise, you can build an entire web application using a standard text editor, but there are plenty of other tools around to make your job easier. The trick to becoming comfortable with web programming is to find the right tool, or combination of tools, for the task at hand. This chapter walks you through some of the tools that you can use to help make your programming job easier. But first, I start by telling you what *not* to use.

## Knowing Which Tools to Avoid

Before I get too far into the tool discussion, I need to tell you what tools *not* to use for serious web-programming jobs. These days, plenty of tools are available to help novice web designers create their own web pages without doing any coding at all. However, trying to develop dynamic web applications with these tools can create more problems than they're worth. Here are some of the tools you should avoid.

# Graphical desktop tools

Graphical desktop tools allow you to create a web page using a purely graphical interface, without having to do any coding. The most popular of these tools are the Microsoft Expression Web package and Adobe Dreamweaver.

Both of these tools use the *what you see is what you get* (WYSIWYG) method of creating web pages. Instead of an editor for writing code, the tool presents you with a graphical canvas that represents your web page. To add features to the web page, you drag and drop elements like text, menus, images, or multimedia clips onto the canvas. When you've created the web page layout, you click a button and the tool automatically generates all the HTML and CSS code required to build the web page. Click another button and the tool automatically uploads the files to your web-hosting server and you have a complete web page.

At first, tools like these may sound like a great idea, but they have some drawbacks:

>> **You have little control over the HTML and CSS code the tools automatically generate.** Because the tools need to generate code for all sorts of environments and applications, the code they generate is somewhat generic and can be bloated and unnecessarily complicated.

>> **Because of the code bloat, it's extremely difficult to add or modify any of the code that the tools generate.**

>> **When you use a graphical desktop tool to create your website, you're stuck using that tool forever.** Just like other desktop software packages, graphical desktop tools often change features as new versions come out. Old features are dropped and new features are added, sometimes forcing you to change the way you design your website. You're stuck in an endless loop of purchasing upgrades and learning new features just to maintain your website.

>> **The WYSIWYG principle isn't always accurate.** The layout you create in the canvas may not always represent what appears in web pages for all browsers and devices that people use to view your website.

# Web-hosting sites

Besides the graphical desktop tools, there are also web-hosting sites that mimic that type of web page design. Web-hosting sites such as Squarespace and Weebly are oriented toward novice non-programmers who want to build their own websites. These sites allow people with no experience to get a simple static website up and running in practically no time, and as you can imagine, they're becoming very popular.

These sites have all the same drawbacks as the desktop graphical tools. Plus, many of them don't even let you see the HTML and CSS code that they generate. With these template-based sites, you're completely at their mercy. You can never migrate your web application to a different host (which is exactly what they want).

## Word processors

Some word-processing software packages, such as Microsoft Word and Apple Pages, offer the ability to convert documents into web pages. This feature has the same drawbacks as the fancier WYSIWYG tools: You can't control the code they generate, and the code they do generate is often bloated. Stay away from creating web pages using word processors.

**WARNING**

Also stay away from the temptation to write your web application code using a word processor. Most word processors embed binary characters into the text, even if you save the document in a text mode. This causes all sorts of problems when you try to view the web page in a browser.

# Working with the Right Tools

Now that you know which tools to avoid, you're ready to look at the tools you can use to get the job done right. In this section, I fill you in on text editors, program editors, integrated development environments, and browser debuggers.

## Text editors

The hammer-and-saw equivalent for creating web applications is the standard text editor. You can build all the program code used in this book using the text editor that's already installed on your computer. You don't have to buy any fancy software packages or maintain any upgrades. This section explains how to use the standard text editors that are found on most computers, based on the operating system you're running.

### If you're running Microsoft Windows

If you're running Microsoft Windows, you have the trusty Notepad application for creating and viewing standard text files. Notepad provides a bare-bones interface for typing text and saving it. Figure 3-1 shows an example of writing HTML code in a Notepad window. Notepad is nothing fancy — just your code in black and white.

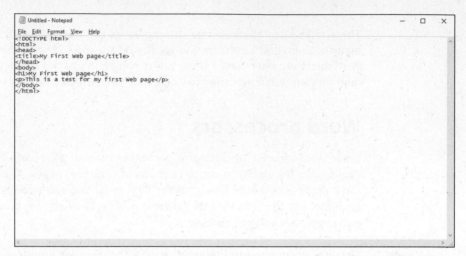

Notepad works fine as a programming tool, but you'll want to tweak a few of the settings before you start coding in Notepad, just to make things easier.

### DISABLING WORD WRAP

In Notepad, you can define the width of the document you want to create, and then Notepad automatically starts a new line when you've reached that limit. This feature is handy for typing memos, but it causes issues when coding.

Wrapping a line of code from one line to the next is generally not allowed in programming languages. All the code for a statement should be on the same line, unless you do some trickery to tell it otherwise.

Another issue with word wrap is that the GoTo option in the Edit menu becomes disabled when word wrap is turned on. Because Notepad doesn't show line numbers, the GoTo feature is all you have to hunt for specific line numbers that error messages point out. GoTo is a crucial tool to have in the Notepad editor.

To disable word wrap in Notepad, click the Format entry in the menu bar; then click the Word Wrap entry to ensure there is no check mark next to it.

### AVOIDING DEFAULT FILE EXTENSIONS

By default, Notepad assumes you're saving a text document and automatically appends a .txt file extension to the file. That doesn't work with programming code, because most programs use a specific file extension to identify themselves (such as .html for HTML files or .php for PHP files).

When you use the File ⇨ Save As menu option in Notepad, you'll need to be careful when saving your program file that the .txt file extension doesn't get appended to the end of the filename. To save a program file using Notepad, follow these steps:

**1.** **Choose File ⇨ Save As from the menu bar at the top of the editor.**

The Save As dialog box, shown in Figure 3-2, appears.

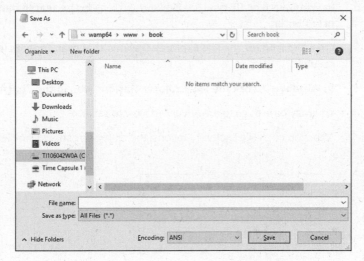

**FIGURE 3-2:**
The Microsoft
Notepad Save As
dialog box.

**2.** **In the drop-down list at the top of the Save As dialog box, navigate to the folder where you want to save the program file.**

**3.** **From the Save As Type text box near the bottom of the Save As dialog box, select All Files (\*.\*).**

This prevents Notepad from appending the .txt file extension to your filename.

**4.** **In the File Name field, enter the filename for your program file, including the file extension you want to use.**

**5.** **Click Save to save the program file.**

Your program file is properly saved in the correct format, with the correct filename, in the correct location.

## SEEING FILE EXTENSIONS

In Microsoft Windows you use File Explorer to navigate the storage devices on your system to open files. Unfortunately, the default setup in File Explorer is to hide the file extension part of the filename (the part after the period) so that it doesn't confuse novice computer users.

That can have the opposite effect for programmers, adding confusion when you're trying to look for a specific file. You may use the same filename for multiple files with different extensions. Fortunately, you can easily change this default setting in Windows. Just follow these steps:

1. **In Windows 8 or 10, open Settings. In Windows 7, open the Control Panel.**

2. **In Windows 8 or 10, type** File Explorer Options **in the search bar and press Enter.**

3. **Click the icon for the File Explorer Options tool that appears in the search results.**

4. **In Windows 7, click the File Explorer Options icon in the Control Panel.**

   You may have to go to the Advanced view to see it.

   After you open File Explorer Options, the dialog box should look like Figure 3-3.

**FIGURE 3-3:**
The File Explorer Options dialog box in Windows.

5. **Click the View tab.**

6. **Remove the check mark from the Hide Extensions for Known File Types check box, as shown in Figure 3-4.**

7. **Click OK.**

   Now you'll be able to see the full filename, including the extension, when you look for your programs using File Explorer.

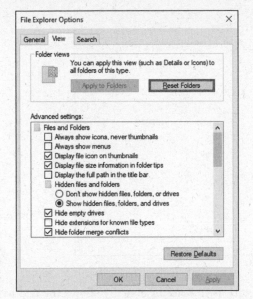

**FIGURE 3-4:**
Removing the
Hide Extensions
for Known File
Types check
mark.

### SETTING THE DEFAULT APPLICATION

Now that you can see the full filename of your program files in File Explorer, there's just one more hurdle to cross. If you want to open your program files using Notepad by default, you'll need to tell File Explorer to do that. Follow these steps:

**1.** **Navigate to the program file, and right-click the filename.**

**2.** **In the menu that appears, select Open.**

The Open dialog box appears.

**3.** **Select Notepad from the list of programs, and then select the check box to always open files of this type using the program.**

Now you'll be able to double-click your program files in File Explorer to automatically open them in Notepad.

## If you're running macOS

If you're running macOS (or one of the earlier Mac OS X versions), the text editor that comes standard is called TextEdit. The TextEdit application actually provides quite a lot of features for a standard text editor — it recognizes and allows you to edit a few different types of text files, including rich text files (`.rtf`) and HTML files.

The drawback to TextEdit is that sometimes it can be *too* smart. Trying to save and edit an HTML file in TextEdit can be more complicated than it should be. By default, TextEdit will try to display the HTML tags as their graphical equivalents in the editor window, as shown in Figure 3-5.

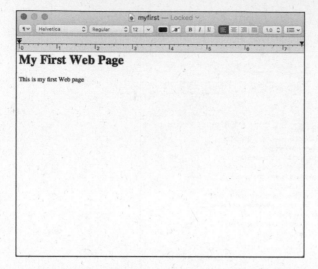

**FIGURE 3-5:**
Using the default
TextEdit settings
to edit an
HTML file.

As you can see in Figure 3-5, TextEdit actually shows the text as the HTML tags format it instead of the actual HTML code. This won't work for editing an HTML file, because you need to see the code text instead of what the code generates. There's an easy way to fix that — just follow these steps:

**1.** **Choose TextEdit ⇨ Preferences.**

The Preferences dialog box, shown in Figure 3-6, appears.

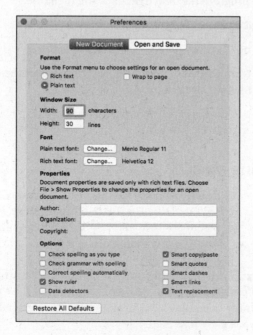

**FIGURE 3-6:**
The Preferences
dialog box in
TextEdit.

2. On the New Document tab, in the Format section, select the **Plain Text** radio button.

3. In the Options section, remove the check mark from the following check boxes:

   - Correct Spelling Automatically
   - Smart Quotes
   - Smart Dashes
   - Smart Links

4. Click the **Open and Save** tab (see Figure 3-7).

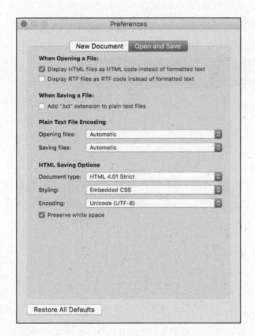

FIGURE 3-7:
The Open and Save tab of the Preferences dialog box.

5. In the When Opening a File section, check the **Display HTML Files as HTML Code Instead of Formatted Text** check box.

6. In the When Saving a File section, remove the check mark from the **Add ".txt" File Extension to Plain Text Files** check box.

7. Close the Preferences dialog box to save the settings.

Now you're all set to start editing your program code using TextEdit!

## If you're running Linux

The Linux environment was made by programmers, for programmers. Because of that, even the simple text editors installed by default in Linux distributions provide some basic features that come in handy when coding.

Which text editor comes with your Linux distribution usually depends on the desktop environment. Linux supports many different graphical desktop environments, but the two most common are GNOME and KDE. This section walks through the default text editors found in each.

### THE GNOME EDITOR

If you're working in a GNOME desktop environment, the default text editor is gedit, shown in Figure 3-8.

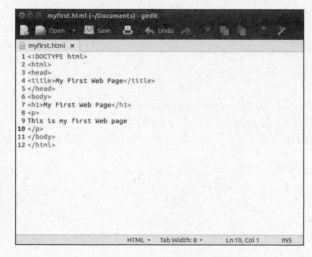

**FIGURE 3-8:**
The gedit editor used in Linux GNOME desktops.

The gedit editor automatically saves program files as plain text format and doesn't try to add a .txt file extension to filenames. There's nothing special you need to do to dive into coding your programs using gedit. Plus, it has some advanced features specifically for programming that you would find in program editors (see the "Program editors" section later in this chapter).

### THE KDE EDITOR

The default text editor used in the KDE graphical desktop environment is Kate, shown in Figure 3-9.

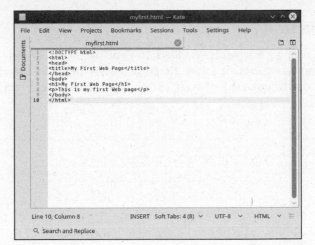

**FIGURE 3-9:**
The Kate editor
used in Linux KDE
desktops.

Just like gedit, the Kate editor contains lots of programmer-friendly features right out of the box. Again, no special configuration is required before you can start editing your program code in Kate.

## Program editors

The next step up from standard text editors is a family of tools called *program editors.* A program editor works just like a text editor, but it has a few additional built-in features that come in handy for programming. Here are some of the features that you'll find in program editors:

>> **Line numbering:** Providing the line numbers off to the side of the window is a lifesaver when coding. When an error message tells you there's a problem on line 1935, not having to count every line to get there helps!

>> **Syntax highlighting:** With syntax highlighting, the editor uses different colors for different parts of the program. Program keywords are displayed using different colors to help make them stand out from data in the code file.

>> **Syntax error marking:** Text that appears to be used as a keyword but that isn't found in the code statement dictionary is marked as an error. This feature can be a time-saver by helping you catch simple typos in your program code.

There are lots of commercial program editors, but some of the best program editors are actually free. This section discusses some of the better free ones available for HTML, CSS, JavaScript, and PHP coding.

## Notepad++

If you're running Microsoft Windows, the Notepad++ tool is a great place to start. As its name suggests, it's like Notepad, but better. You can download Notepad++ from www.notepad-plus-plus.org. The main editing window is shown in Figure 3-10.

The main interface for Notepad++ looks similar to Notepad, so there's nothing different to get used to. By default, it shows line numbers along the left margin, as well as the type of file and the column location of the cursor at the bottom.

Notepad++ recognizes the syntax for many different types of programming languages, including HTML, CSS, JavaScript, and PHP. It highlights the keywords and will even match up opening and closing block statements. If you miss a closing block, Notepad++ will point that out.

## Scintilla and SciTE

The Scintilla library (www.scintilla.org) is an open-source project to provide a programming text editor engine for use in any type of environment. Developers can embed the Scintilla editor into any type of application free of charge.

The SciTE package is a desktop text editor tool that implements the Scintilla library. The SciTE package is available for Windows, macOS, and Linux platforms. You can download it from the Scintilla website for the Windows and Linux platforms, and it's available in the Apple Store for the macOS platform. Figure 3-11 shows the basic SciTE editor window in action.

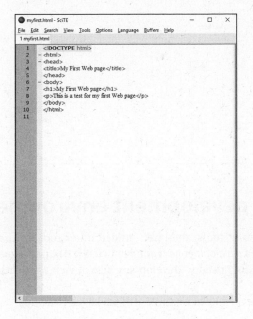

**FIGURE 3-11:**
SciTE.

SciTE provides all the program editing features mentioned earlier. It recognizes the syntax of many different programming languages and can help you organize your code by marking and collapsing code sections (this comes in handy if you write long if-then statement sections).

## jEdit

The jEdit program editor (www.jedit.org) is a little bit different from the other packages. It's written in Java code, so you can run it in any platform that supports Java. That means you can use the exact same editor interface in Windows, macOS, or Linux! jEdit supports all the common features you'd expect from a program editor. Figure 3-12 shows the basic jEdit editor window.

**WARNING**

Because jEdit is a Java application, your desktop platform must have either a Java Runtime Environment (JRE) or Java Development Kit (JDK) package installed in order for it to work. You can download and install one from Oracle at www.oracle. com/technetwork/java/javase/downloads. Also, because jEdit runs as a Java application, you may find it slower than some of the native desktop packages such as Notepad++ or SciTE.

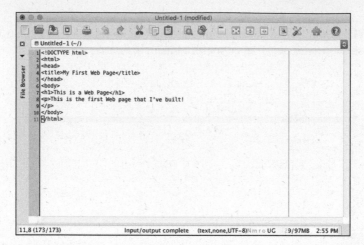

FIGURE 3-12:
jEdit.

# Integrated development environments

Moving up the ladder of tools, the laser–guided miter tool for program develop-ment is the *integrated development environment* (IDE). IDE packages provide every-thing you could possibly need to develop any size of web application.

Here are some of the advanced features IDE packages provide:

>> **Code completion:** Start typing a code statement, and the package will provide a pop-up list of statements that match what you're typing. It also shows what parameters are required and optional for the statement.

>> **Code formatting:** The IDE automatically indents code blocks to help make your code more readable.

>> **Program execution:** You can run your code directly from the editor window without having to jump out to a web browser.

>> **Debugging:** You can step through the program code line by line, watch how variables are set, and see whether any error messages are generated.

>> **Project and file management:** Most IDE packages allow you to group your application files into projects. This allows you to open a project and see just the files associated with that application. Some will even upload the project files to your web-hosting site for you, similar to what the graphical desktop tools do.

Using an IDE tool is not for the faint of heart. Because of all the fancy features, learning how to use the IDE interface can be almost as complicated as learning the programming language!

There are both commercial and open-source IDE packages available for the PHP environment. To give you a general idea of how IDE packages operate, this section walks through two of the more popular ones: Netbeans and Eclipse.

## Netbeans

The Netbeans IDE package was originally developed by Sun Microsystems and released as an open-source IDE for its Java programming language environment (thus the "beans" part of the name). When Oracle acquired Sun, it maintained support for Netbeans, and continued development of it with updated releases.

The Netbeans IDE now contains support for several different programming languages besides Java by using additional plug-in modules. As you can guess, the reason I'm mentioning it here is because there's a plug-in module for PHP.

You can download the Netbeans editor with the PHP module already installed, making it easy to install. Just go to www.netbeans.org/downloads and click the Download button under the PHP category.

When you start Netbeans, it will prompt you to start a new project, as shown in Figure 3-13.

FIGURE 3-13:
The Netbeans project dialog box.

Netbeans contains project templates for HTML and JavaScript applications, as well as PHP applications. When you start a new PHP project, Netbeans automatically creates an index.php file as the main program file for the project. It even builds a rough template for your code. As you would expect from an IDE, when you start typing a PHP function name, Netbeans opens a pop-up box that shows all the PHP functions that match what you're typing, as shown in Figure 3-14.

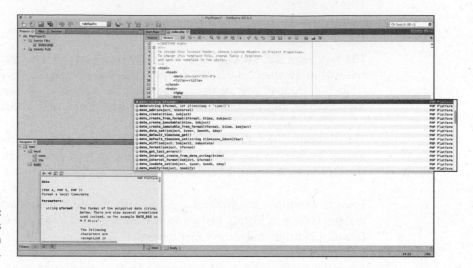

**FIGURE 3-14:** The Netbeans code completion dialog box.

Not only does it show the code completion list, as you can see in Figure 3-14, but it also shows you the PHP manual definition of the function! This is certainly a handy tool to have available if you plan on doing any large-scale PHP development.

## Eclipse

The other big name in PHP IDE packages is the Eclipse PHP Development Tool (usually just called Eclipse PDT). Eclipse was also originally designed as a Java application IDE. Many open-source proponents didn't trust Sun Microsystems maintaining the only IDE for Java, so they set out to develop their own. (The story goes that there was no intentional wordplay on the name Eclipse versus Sun Microsystems. If you can believe that, I may have a bridge to sell you.)

Just like the Netbeans IDE, Eclipse evolved from a Java-only IDE to support many different programming languages via the use of plug-in modules. You can download the Eclipse PDT as an all-in-one package at www.eclipse.org/pdt.

**WARNING**

Just like the jEdit editor, Eclipse PDT is written as a Java application and requires that you have a JRE or JDK installed on your workstation (see "jEdit," earlier in this chapter).

When you start Eclipse, a menu system appears, as shown in Figure 3-15.

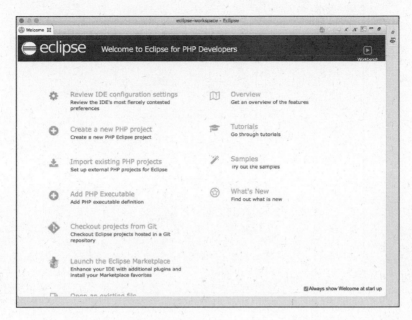

**FIGURE 3-15:**
The Eclipse
start menu.

This allows you to easily change the IDE configuration, start a new project, or open an existing project. Eclipse has all the same features that Netbeans offers. Plus, it has one additional feature: Eclipse PDT contains the advanced PHP Debugger tool developed by Zend, the company that sponsors PHP. The Debugger tool can help point out errors in your PHP code immediately as you type, or it can debug your code as you run it in the Eclipse editor window. Figure 3-16 demonstrates Eclipse pointing out a PHP coding error I made in my code.

Having an advanced PHP debugger at your fingertips can be a great time-saver when you're developing large applications!

## Browser debuggers

Before I finish this chapter, I want to mention one more tool that you have available when trying to troubleshoot web application issues. Most browsers today have a code-debugging feature either built in or easily installable. The browser debuggers can help you troubleshoot HTML, CSS, and JavaScript issues in the web page you send to the client. Figure 3-17 shows the debugging console in the Microsoft Edge web browser after you press F12 to activate it.

Building a Development Environment

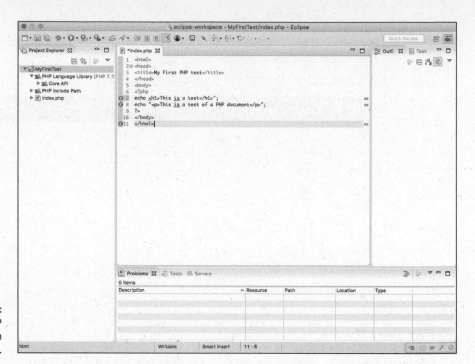

**FIGURE 3-16:**
The PHP
debugger in
action in Eclipse.

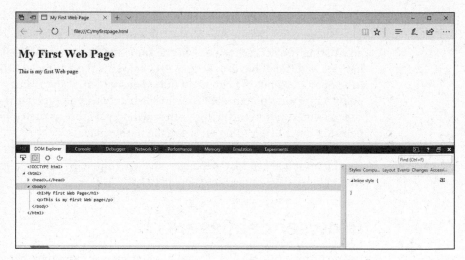

**FIGURE 3-17:**
The Microsoft
Edge
web browser
debugging a web
page.

Browser debuggers can show you exactly where something has gone wrong in the HTML or CSS code. They're also invaluable when working with JavaScript applications.

When you're developing web applications, it's crucial that you test, do some more testing, and then test again. Testing your application in every possible way your website visitors will use it is the only way to know just what to expect.

Things are getting better, but different browsers still may handle HTML, CSS, and even JavaScript code differently. Nowhere is this more evident than when errors occur.

When an error occurs in HTML or CSS code, the browser doesn't display any type of error message. Instead, it tries to fix the problem on its own so it can display the web page. Unfortunately, not all browsers fix code the same way. If you run into a situation where your web page looks different on two different browsers, most likely you have some type of HTML or CSS code issue that the browsers are interpreting differently.

# 2

# HTML5 and CSS3

# Contents at a Glance

**CHAPTER 1:** **The Basics of HTML5** ............................... 73

Diving into Document Structure ........................... 73

Looking at the Basic HTML5 Elements ...................... 81

Marking Your Text ...................................... 85

Working with Characters ................................ 90

Making a List (And Checking It Twice). ................... 92

Building Tables. ....................................... 96

**CHAPTER 2:** **The Basics of CSS3** ............................... 103

Understanding Styles ................................. 103

Styling Text ......................................... 112

Working with the Box Model ........................... 119

Styling Tables ....................................... 121

Positioning Elements ................................. 125

**CHAPTER 3:** **HTML5 Forms** ................................... 135

Understanding HTML5 Forms ........................... 135

Using Input Fields .................................... 138

Adding a Text Area ................................... 146

Using Drop-Down Lists ................................ 147

Enhancing HTML5 Forms ............................... 149

Using HTML5 Data Validation ........................... 154

**CHAPTER 4:** **Advanced CSS3** .................................. 157

Rounding Your Corners ................................ 157

Using Border Images. ................................. 159

Looking at the CSS3 Colors ............................ 162

Playing with Color Gradients .......................... 164

Adding Shadows ..................................... 166

Creating Fonts ....................................... 168

Handling Media Queries. .............................. 171

**CHAPTER 5:** **HTML5 and Multimedia** ........................... 177

Working with Images .................................. 177

Playing Audio ....................................... 185

Watching Videos ..................................... 190

Getting Help from Streamers ........................... 194

IN THIS CHAPTER

» **Looking at the HTML5 document structure**

» **Identifying the basic HTML5 elements**

» **Formatting text**

» **Using special characters**

» **Creating lists**

» **Working with tables**

Chapter **1**

# The Basics of HTML5

The core of your web application is the HTML5 code you create to present the content to your site visitors. You need an understanding of how HTML5 works and how to use it to best present your information. This chapter describes the basics of HTML5 and demonstrates how to use it to create web pages.

## Diving into Document Structure

The HTML5 standard defines a specific structure that you must follow when defining your web pages so that they appear the same way in all browsers. This structure includes not only the markups that you use to tell browsers how to display your web page content, but also some overhead information you need to provide to the browser. This section explains the overall structure of an HTML5 program, and tells you what you need to include to ensure your clients' browsers know how to work with your web pages correctly.

### Elements, tags, and attributes

An HTML5 document consists of one or more elements. An *element* is any object contained within your web page. That can be headings, paragraphs of text, form fields, or even multimedia clips. Your browser works with each element individually, positioning it in the browser window and styling it as directed.

You define elements in your web page by using tags. A *tag* identifies the type of element so the browser knows just how to handle the content it contains. The HTML5 specification defines two types of elements:

» **Two-sided elements:** Two-sided elements are the more common type of element. A two-sided element contains two parts: an *opening tag* and a *closing tag*. The syntax for a two-sided element looks like this:

```
<element>content</element>
```

The first element tag is the opening tag. It contains the element name, surrounded by the less-than symbol (<) and greater-than symbol (>), and defines the start of the element definition.

The second tag is the closing tag; it defines the end of the element definition. It points to the same element name, but the name is preceded by a forward slash (/). The browser should handle any content between the two tags as part of the element content. For example, the HTML5 h1 element defines a heading like this:

```
<h1>This is a heading</h1>
```

The element instructs the browser to display the text *This is a heading* using the font and size appropriate for a heading on the web page. It's up to the browser to determine just how to do that.

» **One-sided elements:** One-sided elements don't contain any content and usually define some type of directive for the browser to take in the web page. For example, the line break element instructs the browser to start a new line in the web page:

```
<br>
```

Because there's no content, there's no need for a closing tag.

**TIP**

The older XHTML standard requires that one-sided tags include a closing forward slash character at the end of the tag, such as <br/>. This isn't required by HTML5, but it's supported for backward compatibility. It's very common to still see that format used in HTML5 code.

Besides the basic element definition, many elements also allow you to define attributes to apply to the element. *Attributes* provide further instructions to the browser on how to handle the content contained within the element. When you define an attribute for an element, you must also assign it a *value*.

You include attributes and their values inside the opening tag of the element, like this:

```
<element attribute="value">content</element>
```

You can define more than one attribute/value pair for the element. Just separate them using a space in the opening tag:

```
<element attribute1="value1" attribute2="value2">
```

Attributes are commonly used to apply inline styles to elements:

```
<h1 style="color: red">Warning!!</h1>
```

The `style` attribute shown here defines additional styles the browser should apply to the content inside the element. In this example, the browser will change the font color of the text to red.

## Document type

Every web page must follow an HTML or XHTML document standard so the browser can parse it correctly. The very first element in the web page code is the markup language standard your document follows. This element, called the *document type,* is crucial, because the browser has to know what standard to follow when parsing the code in your web page.

You define the document type using the `<!DOCTYPE>` tag. It contains one or more attributes that define the markup language standard. Prior versions of HTML used a very complicated format for the document type definition, pointing the browser to a web page on the Internet that contained the standard definition.

Fortunately, the HTML5 standard reduced that complexity. To define an HTML5 document, you just need to include the following line:

```
<!DOCTYPE html>
```

When the browser sees this line at the start of your web page code, it knows to parse the elements using the HTML5 standard.

**WARNING**

If you omit the `<!DOCTYPE>` tag, the browser will still attempt to parse and process the markup code. However, because the browser won't know exactly which standard to follow, it follows a practice known as *quirks mode.* In quirks mode, the browser follows the original version of the HTML standard, so newer elements won't be rendered correctly.

# Page definition

To create an HTML5 web page, you just define the different elements that appear on the page. The elements fit together as part of a hierarchy of elements. Some elements define the different sections of the web page, and other elements contained within those sections define content.

The *html element* is at the top of the hierarchy. It defines the start of the entire web page. All the other elements contained within the web page should appear between the ‹html› opening and ‹/html› closing tags:

```
<!DOCTYPE html>
<html>
web page content
</html>
```

Most Web pages define at least two second-level elements, the head and the body:

```
<html>
<head>
head content
</head>
<body>
body content
</body>
</html>
```

The *head element* contains information about your web page for the browser. Content contained within the head element doesn't appear on the web page, but it directs things behind the scenes, such as any files the browser needs to load in order to properly display the web page or any programs the browser needs to run when it loads the web page.

One element that's commonly found in the head element content is the title, which defines the title of your web page:

```
<head>
<title>My First Web Page</title>
</head>
```

The web page title isn't part of the actual web page, but it usually appears in the browser's title bar at the top of the browser window or in the window tab if the browser supports tabbed browsing.

The *body element* contains the elements that appear in the web page. This is where you define the content that you want your site visitors to see. The body element should always appear after the head element in the page definition. It's also important to close the body element before closing out the html element.

Follow these steps to create and test your first web page:

**1.** **Open the editor, program editor, or integrated development environment (IDE) package of your choice.**

See Book 1, Chapter 3, for ideas on which tool to use.

**2.** **Enter the following code into the editor window:**

```
<!DOCTYPE html>
<html>
<head>
<title>My First Web Page</title>
</head>
<body>
This is text inside the web page.
</body>
</html>
```

**3.** **Save the code to the** DocumentRoot **folder of your web server, naming it** mytest.html.

If you're using the XAMPP server in Windows, the folder is c:\xampp\htdocs. For macOS, it's /Applications/xampp/htdocs.

**4.** **Start the XAMPP servers.**

**5.** **Open the browser of your choice, and enter the following URL:**

```
http://localhost:8080/mytest.html
```

Note that you may need to change the 8080 port number specified in the URL to match your XAMPP Apache server set up (see Book 1, Chapter 2). Figure 1-1 shows the web page that this code produces.

The head element defines the web page title, which as shown in Figure 1-1, appears in the web browser title bar. The body element contains a single line of text, which the browser renders inside the browser window area.

TIP

You may notice that other than the special <!DOCTYPE> tag, all the other HTML tags I used are in lowercase. HTML5 ignores the case of element tags, so you can use uppercase, lowercase, or any combination of the two for the element names in the tags. The older XHTML standard requires all lowercase tags, so many web developers have gotten into the habit of using lowercase for tags, and more often than not, you'll still see HTML5 code use all lowercase tag names.

**FIGURE 1-1:**
The output
for the sample
web page.

## Page sections

Web pages these days aren't just long pages of content. They contain some type of formatting that lays out the content in different sections, similar to how a newspaper presents articles. In a newspaper, usually there are two or more columns of content, with each column containing one or more separate articles.

In the old days, trying to create this type of layout using HTML was somewhat of a challenge. Fortunately, the HTML5 standard defines some basic elements that make it easier to break up our web pages into sections. Table 1-1 lists the HTML5 elements that you use to define sections of your web page.

**TABLE 1-1**     **HTML5 Section Elements**

| Element | Description |
|---------|-------------|
| article | A subsection of text contained within a section |
| aside | Content related to the main article, but placed alongside to provide additional information |
| div | A grouping of similarly styled content within an article |
| footer | Content that appears at the bottom of the web page |
| header | Content that appears at the top of the web page |
| nav | A navigation area allowing site visitors to easily find other pages or related websites |
| section | A top-level grouping of articles |

**REMEMBER**

Although HTML5 defines the sections, it doesn't define how the browser should place them in the web page. That part is left up to CSS styling, which I talk about in Chapter 2 of this minibook.

When you combine the HTML5 section elements with the appropriate CSS3 styling, you can create just about any look and feel for your web pages that you want. Although there's no one standard, there are some basic rules that you can follow when positioning sections in the web page. Figure 1-2 shows one common layout that I'm sure you've seen used in many websites.

```
body
  header

  nav      section          aside
             article


             article


           footer
```

**FIGURE 1-2:**
A basic web page layout using HTML5 section elements.

Just about every web page has a heading section at the top of the page that identifies it to site visitors. After that, a middle section is divided into three separate areas. On the left side is often a navigation section, providing links to other pages in the website. On the right side is often additional information or, in some cases, advertisements. In the middle of the middle section is the meat of the content you're presenting to your site visitors. Finally, at the bottom of the web page is a footer, often identifying the copyright information, as well as some basic contact information for the company.

The *div element* is a holdout from previous versions of HTML. If you need to work with older versions of HTML, instead of using the named section elements, you need to use the ‹div› tag, along with the id attribute to define a specific name for the section:

```
<div id="header">
content for the heading
</div>
```

The CSS styles refer to the id attribute value to define the styles and positioning required for the section. You can still use this method in HTML5. Designers often use the div element to define subsections within articles that need special styling.

## A WORD ABOUT WHITE SPACE

**TECHNICAL STUFF**

Quite possibly the most confusing feature in HTML is how it uses white space. The term *white space* refers to spaces, tabs, consecutive spaces, and line breaks within the HTML code.

By default, when a browser parses the HTML code, it ignores any white space between elements. So, these three formats all produce the same results:

```
<title>
My First Web Page
</title>

<title>My First Web Page
</title>

<title>My First Web Page</title>
```

It's completely up to you which format to use for your programs, but I recommend choosing a format and sticking to it. That'll make reading your code down the road easier, for you or anyone else.

## COMMENTING YOUR CODE

Every programming language allows you to embed comments inside the code to help with documenting what's going on. HTML is no different. HTML allows you to insert text inside the HTML document that will be ignored by the browser as it parses the text.

To start a comment section in HTML, you use the following symbol:

```
<!--
```

You can then enter as little or as much text as you need to properly document what's going on in your code. When the comment text is complete, you have to close the comment section using the following symbol:

```
-->
```

You can place anything between the opening and closing comment tags, including HTML code, and the browser will ignore it. However, be careful what you say in your comments, because they can be read by anyone who downloads your web page!

Now that you know how to define different sections of the web page, the next section discusses how to add content to them.

# Looking at the Basic HTML5 Elements

After you define one or more sections in your web page, you're ready to start defining content. Adding content to a web page is sort of like working on a car assembly line. You define each piece of the web page separately, element by element. It's up to the browser to assemble the pieces to create the finished web page.

This section covers the main elements that you'll use to define content in your web page.

## Headings

Normally, each new section of content in a web page will use some type of heading to make it stand out. Research shows that the first thing site visitors usually do when visiting a web page is to scan the main headings on the page. If you can't attract their attention with your section headings, you may quickly lose them.

HTML5 uses the *h element* to define text for a heading. It defines six different levels of headings. Each heading level has a separate tag:

```
<h1>A level 1 heading</h1>
<h2>A level 2 heading</h2>
<h3>A level 3 heading</h3>
<h4>A level 4 heading</h4>
<h5>A level 5 heading</h5>
<h6>A level 6 heading</h6>
```

Although there are six levels of headings in the HTML5 standard, most sites don't use more than two or three.

The client browser determines the font, style, and size of the text it uses for each heading level. Figure 1-3 shows how the Chrome web browser interprets the six levels of headings.

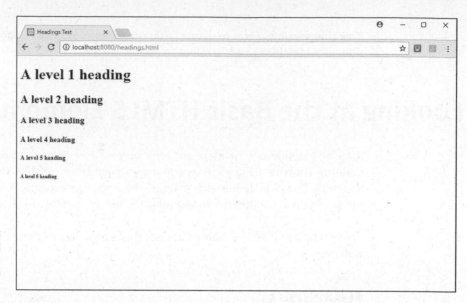

FIGURE 1-3:
Displaying all six
heading levels in
the Chrome web
browser.

The browser displays each heading level with a decreasing font size. By the time you get to the sixth heading level, it's pretty hard to tell the difference between the heading and normal text on the web page!

## Text groupings

There are several HTML5 elements that allow you to group text together into what are called *block-level elements*. The browser treats all of the content defined within the opening and closing tags of a block-level element as a single group. This allows you to use CSS to style or position the entire block of content as one piece, instead of having to style or position each element individually.

You can group headings together using a new feature in the HTML5 standard called a *heading group*, using the *hgroup* element:

```
<hgroup>
<h1>This is the main heading.</h1>
<h2>This is the subheading.</h2>
</hgroup>
```

The heading group doesn't change the h1 or h2 elements, but it provides a way for the browser to interpret the two headings as a single element for styling and positioning. This allows you to use CSS styles to format them as a single block so they blend together like a main heading and a subheading.

A web page consisting of sentences just strung together is boring to read and won't attract very many site visitors (or may just put them to sleep). In print, we group sentences of common thoughts together into paragraphs. You do the same thing in your web page content by using the *p element:*

```
<p>This is one paragraph of text. The paragraph contains two sentences of
    content.</p>
```

Notice that the p element uses an opening tag (`<p>`) and a closing tag (`</p>`) to mark the beginning and end of the grouped text. The browser treats all the text inside the p element as a single element. When you group the content together, you can apply styles and positioning to the entire block.

Be careful with the p element, though. The rules of white space that apply to HTML tags also apply to text inside the p element. The browser won't honor line breaks, tabs, or multiple spaces. So, if you have code like this:

```
<p>
This is one        line.
This is      another line.
</p>
```

It will appear in the web page like this:

```
This is one line. This is another line.
```

All the extra spaces and the line break are removed from the content. Also, notice that the web browser adds a space between the two sentences.

If you want to preserve the formatting of the text in the web page, use the *pre element.* The pre element allows you to group preformatted text. The idea behind preformatted text is that it appears in the web page exactly as you enter it in the code file:

```
<pre>
This is one        line.
This is      another line.
</pre>
```

The browser will display the text in the web page exactly as it appears in the HTML5 code.

Yet another method of grouping text is the *blockquote element.* The blockquote element is often used to quote references within a paragraph. The browser will indent the text contained within the blockquote separate from the normal paragraph text:

```
<p>The only poem that I learned as a child was:</p>
<blockquote>Roses are red, violets are blue. A face like yours, belongs in the
    zoo.</blockquote>
<p>But that's probably not considered classic poetry.</p>
```

This feature helps you embed any type of text within content, not just quotes.

## Breaks

Because HTML doesn't recognize the newline character in text, there's a way to tell the browser to start a new line in the web page when you need it. The single-sided *br element* forces a new line in the output:

```
<p>
This is one line.
<br>
This is a second line.
</p>
```

Now the output in the web page will appear as:

```
This is one line.
This is a second line.
```

Another handy break element is the *hr element.* It displays a horizontal line across the width of the web page section.

```
<h1>Section 1</h1>
<p>This is the content of section 1.</p>
<hr>
<h1>Section 2</h2>
<p>This is the content of section 2.</p>
```

The horizontal line spans the entire width of the web page block that contains it, as shown in Figure 1-4.

Sometimes that's a bit awkward, but you can control the width of the horizontal line a bit by enclosing it in a section and adding some CSS styling.

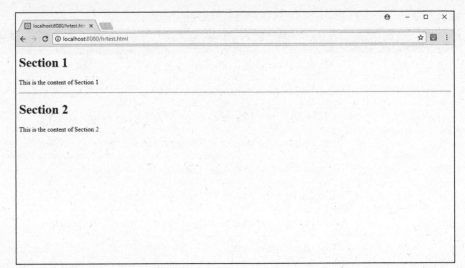

FIGURE 1-4:
Using the hr
element in a
web page.

# Marking Your Text

The opposite of block-level elements are *text-level elements.* Text-level elements allow you to apply styles to a section of content within a block. This section shows you the text-level elements you can apply to the content in your web page.

## Formatting text

The text-level elements apply predefined formats to text without the need for CSS styling. The most popular of the text-level elements are the *b* and *i elements,* which apply the bold and italic styles, respectively:

```
<p>I <i>wanted</i> the <b>large</b> drink size.</p>
```

Text-level elements are also called *inline,* because they appear in the same line as the content. You can embed text-level elements to apply more than one to the same text:

```
<p>I wanted the <b><i>large</i></b> drink size.</p>
```

REMEMBER

When applying two or more text-level elements to text, make sure you close the tags in the opposite order that you open them.

HTML5 supports lots of different text-level elements for using different styles of text directly, without the help of CSS. Table 1-2 lists the text-level elements available in HTML5.

**TABLE 1-2** **HTML5 Text-Level Elements**

| Element | Description |
|---------|-------------|
| abbr | Displays the text as an abbreviation |
| b | Displays the text as boldface |
| cite | Displays the text as a citation (often displayed as italic) |
| code | Displays the text as program code (often displayed with a fixed-width font) |
| del | Displays the text as deleted (often displayed with a strikethrough font) |
| dfn | Displays the text as a definition term (often displayed as italic) |
| em | Displays the text as emphasized (often displayed as italic) |
| i | Displays the text as italic |
| ins | Displays the text as inserted (often displayed with an underline font) |
| kbd | Displays the text as typed from a keyboard (often as a fixed-width font) |
| mark | Displays the text as marked (often using highlighting) |
| q | Displays the text as quoted (often using quotes) |
| samp | Displays the text as sample program code (often displayed with a fixed font) |
| small | Displays the text using a smaller font than normal |
| strong | Displays the text as strongly emphasized (often using boldface) |
| sub | Displays the text as subscripted |
| sup | Displays the text as superscripted |
| time | Displays the text as a date and time value |
| var | Displays the text as a program variable (often using italic) |

As you can see in Table 1-2, you have lots of options for formatting text without even having to write a single line of CSS code!

## Using hypertext

In Book 1, Chapter 1, I mention that hyperlinks are the key to web pages. Hyperlinks are what tie all the individual web pages in your website together, allowing site visitors to jump from one page to another.

The element that creates a hyperlink is the *anchor* text-level element. At first, that may sound somewhat counterintuitive — you'd think an anchor would keep you in one place instead of sending you someplace else. But think of it the other way around: The anchor element is what anchors another web page to your current web page. Following the anchor takes you to the other web page!

## Formatting a hyperlink

Because the anchor element is a text-level element, you use it to mark text inside a block. That text then becomes the hyperlink. You add an anchor element using the <a> tag. The anchor element is two-sided, so it has both an opening tag (<a>) and a closing tag (</a>). The text inside the opening and closing tags becomes the hyperlink text.

A few different attributes are available for the <a> tag, but the most important one is the href attribute. The href attribute specifies where the hyperlink takes your site visitors:

```
<a href="http://www.google.com">Click here to search.</a>
```

When a site visitor clicks the hyperlink, the browser automatically takes the visitor to the referenced web page in the same browser window. If you prefer, you can also specify the target attribute, which specifies how the browser should open the new web page. Here are your options for the target attribute:

>> _blank: Opens the specified page in a new tab or window.

>> _self: Opens the specified page in the current tab or window. This is the default behavior in HTML5, so it's not necessary to add it unless you want to for clarification in your code.

>> _parent: Opens the specified page in the parent window of a frame embedded within the window. Embedded frames aren't popular anymore in HTML5, so this option is seldom used.

>> _top: Opens the specified page in the main window that contains the frame embedded within other frames. This is seldom used.

You use the target attribute like this:

```
<a href="http://www.google.com" target="_blank">Click here to search.</a>
```

TIP

There's no set rule regarding how to handle opening new web pages, but generally it's a good idea to open other pages on your own website in the same browser tab or window, but open remote web pages in a new tab or window. That way your site visitors can easily get back to where they left off on your website if needed.

## Displaying a hyperlink

When you specify a hyperlink in the text, the browser tries to make it stand out from the rest of the text, as shown in Figure 1-5.

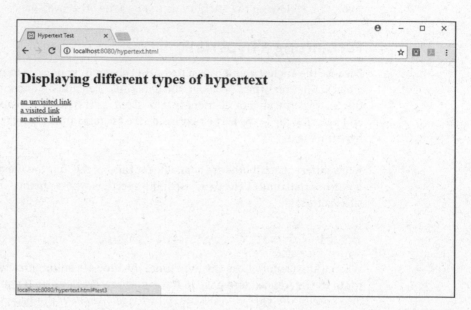

By default, browsers will display the anchor element text using a different format than the rest of the block text:

>> Unvisited links appear underlined in blue.

>> Visited links appear underlined in purple.

>> Active links are when you click an unvisited or visited link with your mouse. When you click your mouse, the link becomes active and appears underlined in red.

You can change these formats to your own liking using CSS styles, as I explain in the next chapter.

## Specifying a hyperlink

The href attribute defines the location of the web page that you want the browser to open for your site visitor, but there are a few different formats you can use to specify that location:

>> A different location on the same document

>> A separate web page in the same website

>> A web page in a remote website

You can use hyperlinks to force the browser to jump to a specific location inside the same web page. This is handy for long web pages that require lots of scrolling to get to sections at the bottom of the page. To use this method, you must first identify the locations in the web page by applying the id attribute to a block-level element, such as a heading or a paragraph element:

```
<h1 id="chicago">Chicago News</h1>
```

To create an anchor element to jump to that section, you use the id attribute value, preceded by a number sign or hash mark (#):

```
<a href="#chicago">See Chicago News</a>
```

When the site visitor clicks the link, the browser automatically scrolls to place the section in the viewing area of the window.

When jumping to another web page on the same server, you don't need to include the full http:// address in the href attribute. Instead, you can specify a *relative address.* The relative address isn't where your uncle lives; it's shorthand for finding another file on the same web server. If the file is in the same folder on the same server, you can just specify the filename:

```
<a href="store.html">Shop in our online store.</a>
```

You can also place files in a subfolder under the location of the current web page. To do that, specify the subfolder without a leading slash:

```
<a href="store/index.php">Shop in our online store.</a>
```

In both cases, the browser will send an HTTP request to retrieve the file to the same server where it downloads the original page from.

To specify a web page on a remote website, you'll need to use an *absolute address.* The absolute address specifies the location using the *Uniform Resource Locator* (URL), which defines the exact location of a file on the Internet using the following format:

```
protocol://host/filename
```

The Basics of HTML5

The *protocol* part specifies the network protocol the browser should use to download the file. For web pages, the protocol is either http (for unencrypted connections) or https (for encrypted connections). The *host* part specifies the host name, such as www.google.com for Google. The *filename* part specifies the exact folder path and filename to reach the file on the server. If you omit the filename, the remote web server will offer the default web page in the folder (usually, index.html).

TIP

You can also specify local filenames using an absolute path address. Just precede the folder name with a forward slash (/). The leading forward slash tells the server to look for the specified folder at the DocumentRoot location of the web server, instead of in a subfolder from the current location.

# Working with Characters

No, I'm not talking about Disneyland. I'm talking about the letters, numbers, and symbols that appear on your web pages. Humans prefer to see information as letters, words, and sentences, but computers prefer to work with numbers. To compensate for that, programmers developed a way to represent all characters as number codes so computers can handle them. The computer just needs a method of mapping the number codes to characters.

## Character sets

The character-to-number mapping scheme is called a *character set*. A character set assigns a unique number to every character the computer needs to represent. In the early days of computing in the United States, the American Standard Code for Information Interchange (ASCII) became the standard character set for mapping the English-language characters and symbols in computers.

As the computing world became global, most programs needed to support more than just the English language. The Latin-1 and ISSO 8859-1 character sets became popular, because they include characters for European languages. But that still didn't cover everything!

Because it's supported worldwide, the HTML5 standard required more than just European-language support. The Unicode character set supports characters from all languages of the world; plus, it has room for expansion. Because of its huge size, though, a subset of Unicode, called UTF-8, became more popular. UTF-8 also supports all languages, but with a smaller footprint; it has become the standard for HTML5.

Although the HTML5 standard specifies a default character set, it's a good idea to specify the character set in your web pages so that you're sure the client browser is using the same character set to interpret your content. You do that using the *meta element.* Because the meta element provides additional information about your web page, you have to place it inside the head element section of the HTML code.

The meta element uses the single-sided ‹meta› tag. To specify the character set in HTML5 you use the following format:

```
<meta charset="UTF-8">
```

If your HTML code requires a different character set, you specify it here.

**TIP**

The ‹meta› tag allows you to specify other features of your web page to the browser so that it knows how to process the body of the web page, and identify the content of the web page to servers that automatically scan your web pages for search engines. I talk some more about the ‹meta› tag in Book 4, Chapter 4.

## Special characters

The UTF-8 character set supports lots of fancy characters that you won't find on your keyboard, such as the copyright symbol (©), the cent symbol (¢), and the degree symbol (°). These are commonly referred to as *special characters.*

You can use special characters in your web page content because they're valid UTF-8 characters. You just need to use a different way of specifying them. Instead of typing these characters using your keyboard, you use a code to specify them.

HTML5 uses two types of codes to specify special characters:

>> **Numeric character reference:** The numeric character reference uses the UTF-8 numeric code assigned to the character. Place an ampersand (&) and a hash (#) in front of the character number, and a semicolon (;) after the character number. For example, to display the copyright symbol, use the following:

```
&#169;
```

>> **Character entity reference:** The character entity reference uses a short name to represent the character. Place an ampersand (&) in front of the character short name, and a semicolon (;) after the character short name:

```
&copy;
```

The Basics of HTML5

Both methods work equally well, so use whichever method you're most comfortable with. The list of special characters available in UTF-8 is pretty long, so I won't include them here. If you search the web for *UTF-8 characters,* you'll find plenty of websites that show the mappings between the UTF-8 numbers and character short names.

# Making a List (And Checking It Twice)

The world is full of lists — to-do lists, wish lists, grocery lists . . . the list just goes on and on. It's no surprise that the HTML5 developers created a way to easily present lists in web pages. There are three basic types of lists available for you to use in HTML5: unordered lists, ordered lists, and description lists. This section covers how to use each type of list in your web pages.

## Unordered lists

Some lists have no specific order to the items contained in them (like a grocery list). In the word-processing world, these are called *bulleted lists,* as each item in the list is preceded by a generic bullet icon. In HTML5, they're referred to as *unordered lists.*

The HTML5 standard uses the *ul element* to display an unordered list using bullets. The ul element is a two-sided element, so you use the <ul> tag to open the list and the </ul> tag to close the list.

You must identify each item in the list using the *li element.* The li element is also a two-sided element, so you use the <li> tag to open each item description and the </li> tag to close it. The overall structure for an unordered list looks like this:

```
<ul>
   <li>item1</li>
   <li>item2</li>
   <li>item3</li>
</ul>
```

Because HTML5 doesn't care about white space in code, it's common to indent the list items in the definition as shown here, to help make it easier to read the code. However, indenting isn't necessary.

Figure 1-6 shows the default way most browsers display unordered lists in the web page.

The bullet marks are fairly generic, similar to what you'd see in most word-processing documents. Fortunately, you can spice things up a little using CSS by defining different types of bullets to use.

## Ordered lists

Some lists have a specific order in which the items should appear and be processed. In word-processing, these lists are called *numbered lists.* In HTML5, they're called *ordered lists.*

The HTML5 standard uses the *ol element* to display an ordered list. The ordered list also uses the li element to mark the individual items contained in the list:

```
<ol>
    <li>Walk the dog.</li>
    <li>Eat breakfast.</li>
    <li>Read the paper.</li>
    <li>Get ready for work.</li>
</ol>
```

By default, browsers assign each item in the list a number, starting at 1, and increasing for each list item, as shown in Figure 1-7.

The Basics of HTML5

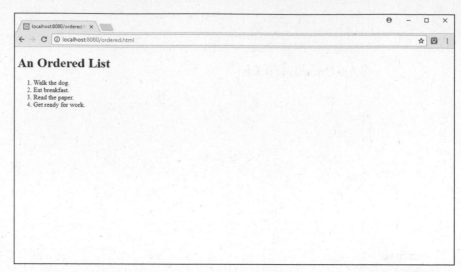

FIGURE 1-7:
The display
default for an
ordered list.

If you want the list to be in reverse order, add the `reversed` attribute:

```
<ol reversed>
```

If you'd like to start at a different number, add the `start` attribute, and specify the starting number as the value:

```
<ol start="10">
```

If you don't want to use numbers, there are a few other options available with the `type` attribute. Table 1-3 shows the different ordered list types available.

**TABLE 1-3**

## Ordered List Types

| Type | Description |
| --- | --- |
| 1 | Numerical list (the default) |
| A | Alphabetical list, using uppercase |
| a | Alphabetical list, using lowercase |
| I | Roman numerals, using uppercase |
| i | Roman numerals, using lowercase |

As you can probably guess, you can also embed lists within lists:

```
<ol type="I">
    <li>First item</li>
    <ol type="A">
        <li>Item 1, Subitem 1</li>
        <li>Item 1, Subitem 2</li>
    </ol>
    <li>Second item</li>
    <ol type="A">
        <li>Item 2, Subitem 1</li>
        <li>Item 2, Subitem 2</li>
    </ol>
</ol>
```

**WARNING**

When using embedded lists, it's very important to match up the opening and closing tags for each item in the list, as well as the lists themselves. Any mismatches will confuse the browser and will cause unpredictable results.

## Description lists

Another common use of lists is to provide descriptions for terms, such as a glossary. The HTML5 standard uses *description lists* to provide an easy way to do that.

Description lists use the *dl element* to define the list but use a slightly different method of defining the items in the list than the unordered and ordered lists. The description list breaks the items into terms and descriptions. You define a term using the *dt two-sided element* and the associated description using the *dd two-sided element.*

Because it's important to match the correct term with the correct description, be careful to alternate between the two in the list definition:

```
<dl>
<dt>Baseball</dt>
<dd>A game played with bats and balls</dd>
<dt>Basketball</dt>
<dd>A game played with balls and baskets</dd>
<dt>Football</dt>
<dd>A game played with balls and goals</dd>
</dl>
```

Figure 1-8 shows how this table is rendered in the browser.

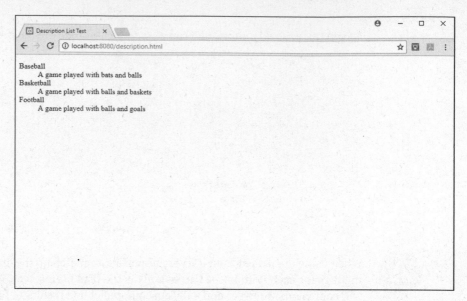

FIGURE 1-8:
Displaying a
description list.

The browser automatically separates the terms from the descriptions in the display, making it easier to tell which is which.

# Building Tables

No, don't get out your hammer and saw. I'm talking about data tables. The world is filled with data, and a very common use of web pages is to present that data to the world. This section describes the data table features built into HTML5 that you can use to easily present your data. The general process for creating a table involves three steps:

1. **Define the table element.**
2. **Define the table rows and columns.**
3. **Define the table headings.**

This section walks through each of these steps to show you how to create tables for your data.

## Defining a table

To add a table to your web page, you start out with the HTML5 *table element.* The table element is a two-sided element, so it opens with a `<table>` tag and closes with a `</table>` tag:

```
<table>
</table>
```

That creates the table, but it's not too exciting because there's nothing in it yet. The next step is to define cells for the data.

**WARNING**

Prior versions of HTML added attributes to the `<table>` tag to define the table appearance, such as the border type, cell spacing, and width. HTML5 has dropped all these attributes, so avoid using them if possible. You should now define those features using CSS styles instead.

## Defining the table's rows and columns

If you're familiar with standard spreadsheet software, such as Microsoft Excel or Apple Numbers, you're used to defining tables using cells, referenced by letters (for the columns) and numbers (for the columns). Unfortunately, HTML5 uses a different method for defining table cells.

To build the cells in a table you must define two separate elements:

>> **A row in the table:** You use the *tr element* to define the row inside the table. The tr element is a two-sided element, so you use the `<tr>` tag to open a row and the `</tr>` tag to close the row.

>> **The cell inside the row:** Inside the row you use the *td element* to define individual cells. Again, the td element is two-sided, so you use the `<td>` tag to open a cell and the `</td>` tag to close a cell.

So, with all that info, you can create your first table. Just follow these steps:

1. **Open your text editor, program editor, or IDE package and type the following code:**

```
<!DOCTYPE html>
<html>
<head>
<title>My First Table</title>
</head>
<body>
<h1>Bowling Scores</h1>
<table>
```

```
        <tr>
            <td>Bowler</td>
            <td>Game 1</td>
            <td>Game 2</td>
            <td>Game 3</td>
            <td>Average</td>
        </tr>
        <tr>
            <td>Rich</td>
            <td>100</td>
            <td>110</td>
            <td>95</td>
            <td>102</td>
        </tr>
        <tr>
            <td>Barbara</td>
            <td>110</td>
            <td>105</td>
            <td>103</td>
            <td>106</td>
        </tr>
        <tr>
            <td>Katie</td>
            <td>120</td>
            <td>125</td>
            <td>115</td>
            <td>120</td>
        </tr>
        <tr>
            <td>Jessica</td>
            <td>115</td>
            <td>120</td>
            <td>120</td>
            <td>118</td>
        </tr>
    </table>
</body>
</html>
```

**2.** Save the file in the **XAMPP** DocumentRoot **folder as** mytable.html.

**3.** Make sure the XAMPP servers are running.

**4.** Open your browser and enter the following URL:

```
http://localhost:8080/mytable.html
```

You may need to change the 8080 port number in the URL to match the Apache web server in your setup. When you display the web page it should look like Figure 1-9.

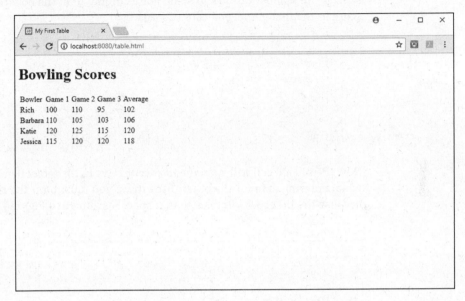

**Bowling Scores**

| Bowler | Game 1 | Game 2 | Game 3 | Average |
|--------|--------|--------|--------|---------|
| Rich | 100 | 110 | 95 | 102 |
| Barbara | 110 | 105 | 103 | 106 |
| Katie | 120 | 125 | 115 | 120 |
| Jessica | 115 | 120 | 120 | 118 |

**FIGURE 1-9:** Displaying the table in Chrome.

By default, the table doesn't contain any gridlines, but you can change that using CSS, as you see in the next chapter. Also, the table column headings appear just like the data rows. You fix that next.

## Defining the table headings

You can apply special formatting to table headings without the use of CSS by using the *th element* instead of the td element for the heading cells:

```
<tr>
   <th>Bowler</th>
   <th>Game 1</th>
   <th>Game 2</th>
   <th>Game 3</th>
   <th>Average</th>
</tr>
```

The th element causes the browser to display the heading cells using a bold font.

Often, in tables, you'll run into situations where a data cell must span two or more columns or rows. You can emulate that in your HTML5 tables using the rowspan and colspan attributes in the <td> tag.

To span two or more rows in a single data cell, just add the rowspan attribute, and specify the number of rows to span. For example, if all the bowlers had the same score in the first game, you could do this:

```
<tr>
    <td>Rich</td>
    <td rowspan=4>100</td>
    <td>110</td>
    <td>95</td>
    <td>102</td>
</tr>
```

Now the second cell will span the next four rows in the table. Remember, though, when entering data for the other three rows, you must omit the first cell of data, because the first row will take up that space, as shown in Figure 1-10.

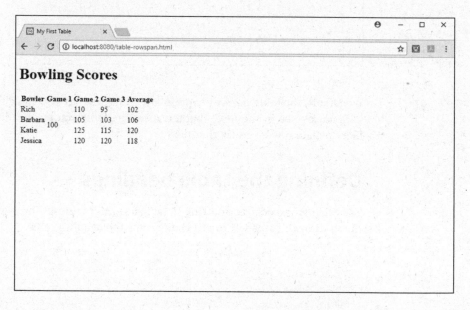

FIGURE 1-10:
Using the rowspan attribute in a table.

Likewise, if one of the bowlers had the same score in all three games, you could use the `colspan` attribute to combine all three columns into one cell:

```
<tr>
    <td>Katie</td>
    <td colspan=3>120</td>
</tr>
```

Now the second cell in the row will span all three data columns for that row, as shown in Figure 1-11.

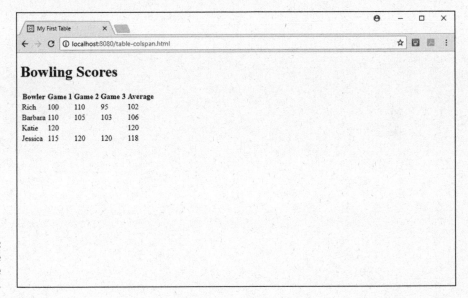

**FIGURE 1-11:**
Using the
`colspan` attribute
in a table.

The Basics of HTML5

IN THIS CHAPTER

» **Defining styles**

» **Formatting text**

» **Using the box model**

» **Sprucing up your tables**

» **Positioning elements where you want them**

# Chapter **2**

# The Basics of CSS3

In the last chapter, I explain how to use HTML5 to display content on your web page. However, when you just use HTML5, things look pretty boring! This chapter shows you how to incorporate style into your web pages to help liven things up (even if you're not an artist).

First, I explain how to use CSS style sheets to style elements contained in the web page. Then I show you how to work with styles to change the color and font of text, make fancier lists, and spruce up your tables within your web pages. Finally, I explain how to work with the CSS positioning features to arrange your content in an appealing manner on the page.

## Understanding Styles

When you specify an HTML5 element in your web page, the web browser decides just how that element should look. Browsers use a default styling to determine the difference between the text in an h1 element and the text in a blockquote element.

Fortunately, another standard is available to work with HTML5 that helps you make your web pages unique. Back in Book 1, Chapter 1, I explain how Cascading Style Sheets (CSS) work to style HTML5 content on the web page. That's the key to making your website stand out from the crowd!

The CSS standard specifies ways to define the color, size, and font type of text that appears on web pages. It also provides some styles for adding background colors and images and styling other types of elements on the web page.

TIP

The CSS standard has evolved some over the years. At the time of this writing, it's currently at version 3 — you'll often see it referred to as CSS3, and that's what I call it in this book.

Now you're ready to take a deeper dive into just how to use CSS3 in your web applications. This section walks through how CSS3 works and how you can use it to make your web pages look good.

## Defining the rules of CSS3

CSS3 uses *rules* to define how the browser should display content on the web page. Each rule consists of two parts: a *selector* that defines what elements the rule applies to and one or more *declarations* that define the style to apply.

The format of the CSS3 rule looks like this:

```
selector {declaration; declaration; ...}
```

In the rule definition, there are five ways to define the selector:

>> **Element type:** The rule applies to all elements of the specified type.

>> `id` **attribute:** The rule applies to the specific element with the specified id value.

>> `class` **attribute:** The rule applies to all elements with the specified class value.

>> **Pseudo-element:** The rule applies to a specific part within an element.

>> **Pseudo-class:** The rule applies to elements in a specific state.

Each declaration defines a CSS3 style property and its associated value. Each property sets a specific style (such as a color or a font) to the element the rule applies to. You must end each declaration with a semicolon, and you can list as many declarations as needed in the rule.

Here's the format of the property and its value as you list them in the declaration:

```
property: value
```

In the following sections, I explain in more detail the five ways to define a selector.

## Element type

You can apply the same styling to all elements of a specific type in your web page by specifying the element name as the selector:

```
h1 {color: red;}
```

This rule ensures that the browser displays all h1 elements in the web page using a red font color.

If you want to apply the same styles to multiple types of elements, you can either list them as separate rules or group the elements together in the selector by separating the element names with commas, like this:

```
h1, p {color: red;}
```

This rule instructs the browser to style all h1 and p elements using a red font color.

## id attribute

If you need to define a rule that applies to just a single element in the web page, use the id attribute as the selector. To specify an id attribute as the selector, place a pound sign (#) in front of the id name:

```
#warning {color: red;}
```

To use the rule in your HTML5 code, just apply the id attribute value to the element you need to style:

```
<h1 id="warning">This is a bad selection.</h1>
```

The browser will apply that rule to the specific element that uses the id attribute value.

## class attribute

If you need to define a rule that applies to multiple elements, but not necessarily all the elements of that type, use the class attribute as the selector. To specify a class attribute as the selector, place a period in front of the class name:

```
.warning {color: red;}
```

Then just apply that class attribute to whichever elements you need to style using that rule:

```
<h1 class="warning">This is a bad selection.</h1>
<p class="warning">Please make another selection.</p>
```

As you can see from this example, you can apply the same class attribute value to different element types, making this a very versatile way of styling sections of your web page!

If you decide you only need to apply a rule to one particular element type of the class, you can specify the element type in the selector before the class value:

```
p.warning {color: red;}
```

This rule will apply only to p elements with the class attribute value of warning.

## Pseudo-element

The CSS standard defines a handful of special cases where you can apply styles to a subsection of the element content, and not the entire content of an element. These rules are called *pseudo-elements.*

To use a pseudo-element rule, separate the rule from the selector it applies to using a double colon (::):

```
selector::pseudo-element
```

CSS3 supports a set of keywords for the pseudo-element names. For example, if you want to get fancy and style the first letter of a paragraph of text differently from the rest of the text, you can use the first-letter pseudo-element keyword:

```
p::first-letter {font-size: 20px}
```

The first-letter pseudo-element matches with only the first letter of the p element, as shown in Figure 2-1.

CSS3 defines only a handful of pseudo-elements. Table 2-1 lists them.

There aren't a lot of pseudo-elements available, but these few pseudo-elements can come in handy for trying special formatting of your web pages.

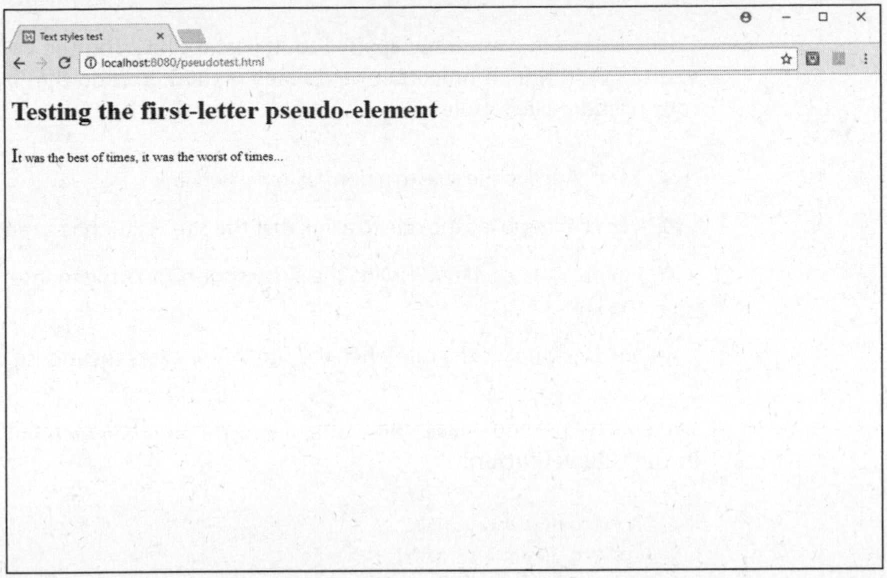

**FIGURE 2-1:**
Using the
first-letter
pseudo-element
on text.

**TABLE 2-1**

## CSS3 Pseudo-Elements

| Pseudo-Element | Description |
|---|---|
| after | Places an object before the selected element content |
| before | Places an object after the selected element content |
| first-letter | Applies the rule to the first letter of the selected element content |
| first-line | Applies the rule to the first line of the selected element content |
| selection | Applies the rule to the content area selected by the site visitor |

**TIP**

The after and before pseudo-elements may sound a bit strange, because there's no content to style before or after an element. They're most commonly used for placing images after or before the content in the element.

## Pseudo-class

A *pseudo-class* applies the defined styles to an element that is in a specific state on the web page. The state refers to how the element behaves, such as buttons that are disabled, check boxes that are checked, or input boxes that have the browser focus.

These rules are commonly applied to hypertext links on the web page to help site visitors distinguish links they've already visited. You do that by using a series of four pseudo-class style rules:

>> link: Applies the rule to a normal, unvisited link

>> visited: Applies the rule to a link that the site visitor has already visited

>> hover: Applies the rule when the site visitor hovers the mouse pointer over the link

>> active: Applies the rule when the site visitor clicks the mouse on the link

You specify pseudo-class rules using a single colon to separate it from the selector in the rule definition:

```
a: link {color: orange;}
a: visited {color: purple;}
a: hover {color: green;}
a: active {color: red;}
```

All these pseudo-class rules apply to all the anchor elements in the web page and apply different colors to the hyperlink text depending on the hyperlink state.

It's extremely important to list the anchor element pseudo-class rules in the order shown here, or they won't work!

**WARNING**

If you want to remove the underline that most browsers apply to hypertext links, add the following property to the pseudo-element style rule:

```
text-decoration:none;
```

**TIP**

There are lots of pseudo-classes that you can use to apply rules to specific elements in the your web pages. Table 2-2 shows the list of available pseudo-classes in CSS3.

Many of the pseudo-class style rules (such as first-child and last-child) work with the location of an element within the Document Object Model (DOM). Book 3, Chapter 2, discusses the DOM and how to use it to reference elements on the web page.

**TABLE 2-2**      **The CSS3 Pseudo-Classes**

| Pseudo-Class | Description |
|---|---|
| `active` | The rule applies to hypertext links while the site visitor clicks them. |
| `checked` | The rule applies to input check boxes and radio options that are selected (checked). |
| `disabled` | The rule applies to input elements that are disabled. |
| `empty` | The rule applies to elements that have no children. |
| `enabled` | The rule applies to input elements that are enabled. |
| `first-child` | The rule applies to the first child element of a parent element. |
| `first-of-type` | The rule applies to the first child element of the same type as the parent. |
| `focus` | The rule applies to elements that have the browser focus. |
| `hover` | The rule applies to elements that the mouse pointer is hovering over. |
| `in-range` | The rule applies to elements whose value is within the specified range. |
| `invalid` | The rule applies to elements whose value is invalid. |
| `lang(`*language*`)` | The rule applies to elements with the `lang` attribute specified. |
| `last-child` | The rule applies to the last child element of a parent element. |
| `last-of-type` | The rule applies to the last child element of the same type as the parent. |
| `link` | The rule applies to unvisited hypertext link elements. |
| `not(`*selector*`)` | The rule applies to all elements except the specified selector elements. |
| `nth-child(`*n*`)` | The rule applies to the *n*th child of the parent element. |
| `nth-last-child(`*n*`)` | The rule applies to the *n*th child of the parent element counting backward from the last element. |
| `nth-of-type(`*n*`)` | The rule applies to the *n*th child element with the same type as the parent. |
| `only-of-type` | The rule applies to every element that is the only element of the same type as the parent. |
| `only-child` | The rule applies to every element that is the same only child of a parent. |
| `optional` | The rule applies to input elements that do not have the `required` attribute. |
| `out-of-range` | The rule applies to elements with a value out of the specified range. |
| `read-only` | The rule applies to elements with a `readonly` attribute specified. |

*(continued)*

**TABLE 2-2** *(continued)*

| Pseudo-Class | Description |
|---|---|
| read-write | The rule applies to elements without a readonly attribute specified. |
| required | The rule applies to elements with a required attribute specified. |
| root | The rule applies to the document's root element. |
| target | The rule applies to the current active element specified. |
| valid | The rule applies to elements that have a valid value. |
| visited | The rule applies to hypertext links that the site visitor has already visited. |

## Applying style rules

In Book 1, Chapter 1, I discuss the different ways to apply CSS3 styles to an HTML5 document. To refresh your memory, there are three ways to do that:

» **Inline styles:** Place the style properties inside the HTML5 element opening tag, using the style attribute:

```
<h1 style="color: red;">Warning</h1>
```

» **Internal styles:** Use the <style> tag to define a set of styles that apply to the entire document:

```
<style>
h1 {color: red;}
</style>
```

» **External styles:** Use an external file to contain the style definitions, and then add the <link> tag in the HTML5 document to reference the external style sheet:

```
<link rel="stylesheet" href="mystyles.css">
```

Note that with the inline style definitions, you leave off the selector part of the rule. Because the rule applies only to the element that declares it, there's no need for the selector. With both the inline and external style sheet methods, you define the set of rules separately within the style sheet. The great benefit of using the external style sheet method is that you can then apply the same style sheet to all the pages of your website!

You can use any of these locations to define your style rules, or you can use them all at the same time! If two or more style rules apply to the same element on the web page, the cascading feature of CSS3 kicks in. CSS3 defines a specific process on how the browser applies conflicting rules to an element to ensure everything happens in order. The next section explains how that works.

## Cascading style rules

As the name suggests, if you define multiple style rules for a web page, the rules cascade down from the lower-priority rules, which are applied first, to the higher-priority rules, which are applied later.

TIP

Saying "down" from a lower to a higher priority may seem counterintuitive, but it's common jargon in CSS circles. Just remember that the higher-priority rules take precedence over the lower-priority rules.

The CSS3 standard defines a strict process for how browsers should apply style rules to each element. In Book 1, Chapter 1, I outline an abbreviated version of the cascading rules. There are actually ten different rule levels that the CSS3 standard defines for applying rules! However, most web designers don't use all ten levels to define rules, so things don't usually get that complicated.

Table 2-3 shows the official CSS3 cascading rules process.

**TABLE 2-3**  **The CSS3 Cascading Rules Process**

| Rule Type | Description | Priority Level |
|---|---|---|
| Importance | Rules contain the !important property and override all other rules | 1 |
| Inline | Rules defined using the style attribute in an element opening tag | 2 |
| Media | Rules defined for a specific media type | 3 |
| User defined | Accessibility features defined in the browser by the site visitor | 4 |
| Specific selector | A selector referring to an id, class, pseudo-element, or pseudo-class | 5 |
| Rule order | When multiple rules apply to an element, the last rule declared wins | 6 |
| Inheritance | Rules inherited from parent elements in the web page | 7 |
| Internal | Rules defined in internal style sheets | 8 |
| External | Rules defined in external style sheets | 9 |
| Browser default | The default styles built into the browser, the lowest priority | 10 |

**REMEMBER**

Notice that accessibility features have a special place in the cascading rule order. Many of your website visitors may have some type of viewing disability preventing them from viewing your content as you style it. Most browsers allow users to define their own style features, such as specifying foreground and background contrasting colors or changing the font size to make text more readable.

Now that you've seen how to define CSS3 rules and where to define them, the next step is to start learning some rules to apply to your web pages. The CSS3 standard defines a myriad of styles for you to use. Entire books have been written trying to cover all the different rules and features, such as *CSS3 For Dummies* by John Paul Mueller (Wiley). The remaining sections in this chapter walk you through some of the more commonly used rules that you'll want to keep in mind as you design your dynamic web applications.

# Styling Text

No place is styling more important than with the text that appears on your web page. You can transform a dull, boring website with just a few changes to the text styles. This section walks through the options you have available for styling text to help liven up your website.

## Setting the font

A *font* defines how a medium displays the characters in the content. Whether it's etching words into stone, setting text on paper using a printing press, or displaying pixels on a computer monitor, fonts help control how readers interpret the content.

When you place text on your web page using HTML5, the browser selects a default font style, size, and format based on the element type, and it uses that same setting for all the text in those elements on your web page. That not only makes for a boring web page, but can also confuse your site visitors if all the content blends together.

This section describes how you can change the font features the browser uses to display text in your web pages.

### Finding a family

The CSS3 standard defines the `font-family` style property to allow you to change the style of font. Here's the format for the `font-family` property:

```
font-family: fontlist;
```

The *fontlist* value is a comma-separated list of font names. There are two ways to specify a font in the list:

>> **Using a specific font name:** Specific font names require the browser to use that specific font to display the text, such as Times New Roman, Arial, or Helvetica. Browsers are limited to using only the fonts that are installed on the workstation, so specifying a specific font name can be a gamble. If that font isn't available on the site visitor's workstation, the browser will revert to the default font. It has become common practice to provide several options of font names in the font-family property. The browser will try to use the font presented first in the list, and if that's not available, it'll try the next font listed, and continue down the list. If no font is available, the browser reverts to the default font.

>> **Using a generic font group:** Generic font groups give the browser a little more leeway in selecting a font to use. Instead of looking for a specific font, the browser can use any font that's included in the font group. CSS3 defines the following font groups:

- cursive: A font that mimics handwritten text
- fantasy: An ornamental font used for special text
- monospace: A font that uses the same spacing for all characters
- sans-serif: A font without any ornamentation added to characters
- serif: A font that uses ornamentation at the tail of each character

It's common practice to list specific font names first in the font list and then, as a last resort, add a generic font group, like this:

```
font-family: Arial, 'Times New Roman', sans-serif;
```

With this rule, the browser will try to use the Arial font. If that's not available on the visitor's workstation, it will try to use the Times New Roman font. If Times New Roman is also not available, the browser will look for a font from the sans-serif font group.

REMEMBER

Note that for font names that contain spaces, you must enclose the name in single quotes.

TIP

The CSS3 standard defines an exciting new feature called *web fonts*. Web fonts allow you to define your own font on a server so that browsers can download them along with the web page. I dive into using web fonts in more detail in Chapter 4 of this minibook.

## Picking a size

After selecting a font style to use, the next step is to decide what size the font should be. Browsers have built-in sizes for separating out the different header levels, as well as standard text. However, you can change that by using the font-size property:

```
font-size: size;
```

You'd think specifying a font size would be easy, but CSS3 actually allows you to specify the size in one of five different methods:

» As an absolute unit of measurement

» As a relative unit of measurement

» As a percentage of the space assigned to the element

» Using a size keyword

» Using a size keyword relative to the space assigned to the element

You specify absolute units using a specific size value of measurement. To complicate things even more, CSS allows you to use six different units of measurements, shown in Table 2-4.

**TABLE 2-4** **CSS Font-Size Absolute Units of Measurement**

| Unit | Description |
| --- | --- |
| cm | Centimeters |
| in | Inches |
| mm | Millimeters |
| pc | Picas |
| pt | Points |
| px | Pixels |

The first three units of measurement shown in Table 2-4 are easily recognizable, but the last three aren't as common. There are 6 picas in an inch, and 72 points in an inch. The pixel unit originally matched up to pixels on a standard computer monitor, but with the advancement of monitor technology, that isn't the case anymore.

You can specify the size using either a whole number or a decimal value:

```
font-size: 0.25in;
font-size: 48pt;
```

The relative units of measurement set the size of the font relative to other elements on the web page. Table 2-5 shows the relative size units in CSS3.

**TABLE 2-5**

## CSS Font-Size Relative Units of Measurement

| Unit | Description |
| --- | --- |
| ch | Relative to the size of the zero character |
| em | Relative to the size of the normal font size of the elements |
| ex | Relative to the normal height of the font size currently used |
| rem | Relative to the height of the root element |
| vh | Relative to 1% of the browser window height |
| vw | Relative to 1% of the browser window width |
| vmax | Relative to 1% of the larger of the browser window width or height |
| vmin | Relative to 1% of the smaller of the browser window width or height |
| % | As a percentage of the normal element size |

The em relative unit size is the most popular. It sizes the element relative to the text in the web page. For example, here's a common rule that you'll see:

```
h1 {font-size: 2em;}
```

This tells the browser to size the h1 element twice the size of the text in the web page. By using relative units, you can easily change the size of headings based on the size of the text in the content. If you decide to change the font size of the text in the web page, the headings will automatically change size to stay in the same proportion.

To make things simpler, CSS also allows you to set the text size using a human-readable keyword. There are both absolute and relative keywords available:

>> **Absolute:** xx-small, x-small, small, medium, large, x-large, xx-large

>> **Relative:** smaller, larger

Using the keywords makes setting font sizes easier, but you're still a little at the mercy of the browser. It's up to the browser to determine just what is a small, medium, or large size font.

## Playing with color

By default, browsers display all text in black on a white background. Things don't get any more boring than that! One of the first steps in livening up your website is to change the text color scheme.

There are two CSS3 properties that you need to do that:

>> `color`: Selects the color the browser uses for the text font

>> `background-color`: Selects the color the browser uses for the background

You have a vast palette of colors to choose from for your color scheme. Usually, it's a good idea to pick a color scheme for your website and try to stick with that for most of the web pages contained in the website. Often, a corporation will set the color scheme of its website based on the colors used in the company logo. Occasionally, you may need some content to pop out at visitors, so you'll need to deviate some from the scheme.

The original CSS standard provided three ways to define colors used in styles:

>> **With color names:** You can choose a text value from a standard list of color names. CSS3 defines many different colors by name. If you plan on using a standard color, most likely you can call it just by its name:

```
p {color: red; background-color: white;}
```

>> **With RGB hexadecimal values:** If you want to fine-tune the colors your web page elements use, you can select the intensity of the red, green, and blue colors based on hexadecimal values from 00 to FF. If you're into hexadecimal numbers, define the color as three hexadecimal values preceded by a pound sign:

```
p {color: #ffa500;}
```

The `ffa500` value sets the red hue at full intensity, sets the green hue a little lower, and turns the blue hue off, producing the orange color.

>> **With the** `rgb()` **function:** You can select the color using decimal values from 0 to 255 for the red, green, and blue intensities. To specify the same color using the `rgb()` method, you'd use the following:

```
p {color: rgb(255, 165, 0);}
```

If you're not picky about the shade of red you want, the first method will work just fine. But odds are, you'll want to be more precise in your color selection (for example, matching the shade of red to the red in your company's logo), so you'll want to use one of the other two methods. Which of the other two methods you use is a matter of personal preference.

The updated CSS3 standard provides four new ways of working with colors in your web pages:

>> **RGBA:** Adds an opacity value to the standard RGB settings

>> **HSL:** Defines the color as a hue, saturation, and lightness percentage

>> **HSLA:** Defines the color as an HSL value, plus adds an opacity value

>> **Opacity:** Defines a transparency value to make the element more opaque

The main addition to the CSS3 color scheme is the opacity feature. The opacity feature provides the ability to make elements transparent, or faded. The opacity value ranges from 0.0 (fully transparent) to 1.0 (no transparency, also called opaque).

Here's an example to demonstrate just how changing colors in elements works:

1. **Open your favorite text editor, program editor, or integrated development environment (IDE) package.**

2. **Enter the following code into the editor window:**

```
<!DOCTYPE html>
<html>
<head>
<title>Testing colors in CSS3</title>
<style>
p {
    font-family: Arial, Helvetica, sans-serif;
    color: #ff0000;
    background-color: cyan;
}
```

```
h1 {
    color: rgb(255, 165, 0);
    background-color: green;
}
</style>
</head>
<body>
<h1>Testing the color scheme</h1>
<p>
The quick brown fox jumps over the lazy dog.
</p>
<h1>This is the end of the color test</h1>
</body>
</html>
```

3. **Save the program as** colortest.html **in the** DocumentRoot **folder of your web server.**

   If you're using XAMPP, it's c:\xampp\htdocs for Windows or /Applications/ XAMPP/htdocs for macOS.

4. **Start the web server.**

   If you're using XAMPP, launch the XAMPP Control Panel and then click the Start button for the Apache web server.

5. **Open your browser and go to the URL for the new file:**

   ```
   http://localhost:8080/colortest.html
   ```

   **Note:** You may need to change the port in the URL to what your web server uses.

6. **Stop the web server and close the browser.**

You should see in the output from your web page that the browser uses different colors for the h1 elements and the p elements. However, notice that there's some whitespace between the elements, as shown in Figure 2-2.

You didn't define any space between the p and h1 elements in the HTML5 code, so why is that there? You may be thinking that something has gone wrong with the browser, but actually, it's a feature of CSS that I cover next.

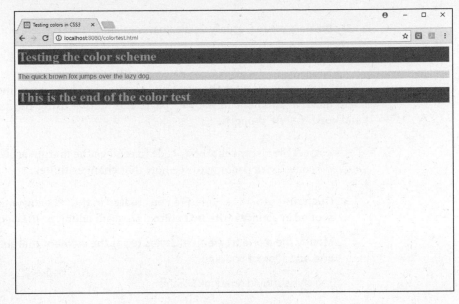

**FIGURE 2-2:**
Displaying
elements with
different colors
in CSS3

# Working with the Box Model

CSS3 handles all elements on the web page using the *box model*, which defines the area inside and around the element and provides a way for you to alter the style of those features. Figure 2-3 shows the box model defined in CSS3.

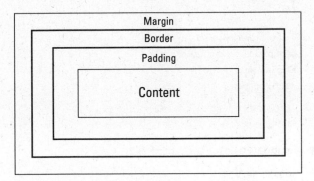

**FIGURE 2-3:**
The CSS3 box
model.

The box model defines four different sections in the element. Working from the inside out, they are as follows:

» **Content:** The text or image the element contains

» **Padding:** The space around the content

>> **Border:** An area, usually visible, that goes around the content and padding

>> **Margin:** The space outside of the element border, between elements

With CSS3, you can alter the padding, margin, and border around an element to help make it stand out in the web page. You do that using the `padding`, `margin`, and `border` style properties.

Let's correct the `colortest.html` code to remove the margin around the elements and add some extra padding to see how that changes things:

1. **Open the** `colortest.html` **file you created in the "Playing with color" section in your favorite text editor, program editor, or IDE package.**

2. **Modify the p and h1 element styles to set the element margins to 0px and add 10px of padding.**

   The styles should now look like this:

   ```
   <style>
   p {
       font-family: Arial, Helvetica, sans-serif;
       color: #ff0000;
       background-color: cyan;
       margin: 0px;
       padding: 10px;
   }

   h1 {
       color: rgb(255, 165, 0);
       background-color: green;
       margin: 0px;
       padding: 10px;
   }
   </style>
   ```

3. **Save the updated** `colortest.html` **file.**

4. **Start the web server.**

   If you're using XAMPP, launch the XAMPP Control Panel and then click the Start button for the Apache web server.

5. **Open your browser and go to the URL for the new file:**

   ```
   http://localhost:8080/colortest.html
   ```

*Note:* You may need to change the port in the URL to what your web server uses.

**6. Stop the web server and close the browser.**

Figure 2-4 shows the web page this code produces.

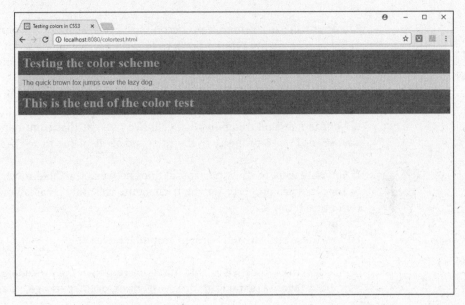

**FIGURE 2-4:**
The updated
`colortest.html`
file output.

Notice that the white space is gone and the background space around the text in the headings and paragraph is larger. Feel free to play around with the margin and padding numbers in the HTML5 code and watch how it changes the display results.

# Styling Tables

The previous chapter explains how to create tables using HTML5. Older versions of HTML defined attributes in the table element to help add some features, such as creating borders around the table cells and sizing the table cells. However, HTML5 removed all those attributes, so it's up to CSS to provide those features.

# Table borders

When you're presenting data in tables, you may want to create borders around the table and around the individual cells in the table. You do that with the CSS `border` property:

```
table {border: 1px solid black;}
```

The first value in the border property (`1px`) is the width of the border. The second value (`solid`) is the type of border; you can specify `dashed`, `dotted`, `double`, or `solid` for the border type. The third value (`black`) specifies the color of the border.

You can add borders around any of the table family of elements — table, th, tr, or td. However, if you specify the border property for all of them, you'll see double borders around the individual cells. To prevent that from happening, add the `border-collapse` property to the rule, and set its value to `collapse`.

TIP

If you only want to show horizontal lines between the table rows, you can use the `border-bottom` property for the tr element. This only creates borders at the bottom of each row.

Follow these steps to add borders around a table:

1. **Open the** `mytable.html` **file that you created in the preceding chapter in your favorite text editor, program editor, or IDE package.**

   If you haven't yet read Chapter 1 of this minibook, you'll have to turn back and at least work through the section on tables before proceeding with these steps. I'll wait for you!

2. **Add a style element to the head section of the document to define the table styling rule:**

   ```
   <style>
       table tr td {
           border: 1px solid black;
           border-collapse: collapse;
       }
   </style>
   ```

REMEMBER

   I included the `border-collapse` property to prevent double borders from appearing.

3. **Save the file.**

**4.** **Start your web server software, open your browser, and go to the following URL:**

```
http://localhost:8080/mytable.html
```

**5.** **Close the browser and stop your web server software.**

With the added stylings, you should see a single border line around each table cell and a single border line around the entire table, as shown in Figure 2-5.

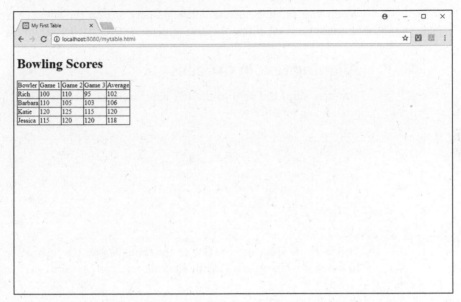

**FIGURE 2-5:**
Adding a border to the table.

Now that you have borders around each cell, it may seem a bit more obvious how cramped the data inside the table looks. You can do some more playing around with sizing and positioning the text inside each cell. I cover that in the next section.

## Table data

As you can see in Figure 2-5, by default, the browser creates the table cells just large enough to contain the largest data value in the cells. That can make for a somewhat cramped table. Fortunately, you can add a little more space around the data in the table cells using some additional CSS properties.

## Padding the cells

A padded cell sounds somewhat ominous, but adding the padding property to your table cells can make a huge difference in the appearance of the table data:

```
table tr td {
        border: 1px solid black;
        border-collapse: collapse;
        padding: 10px;
    }
```

When you provide some additional space inside the table cells, you have some more options on where the data appears within the table.

## Aligning text in the cells

You can align the data to the left side, center, or right side of the cell with the text-align property:

```
table th {
        border: 1px solid black;
        border-collapse: collapse;
        padding: 10px;
        text-align: center;
    }
```

This definition centers the text in the table header (th) elements. If you also want to move the text upward inside the cell, use the vertical-align property.

## Coloring tables

Just using the default black-and-white tables can quickly put your site visitors to sleep! Add the color and background-color properties to your table to make it stand out. You can apply the colors to the entire table, individual rows, or even individual cells.

To simulate the old mainframe printer report style using alternating row colors in the table, use the nth-child pseudo-class to style every other row in the table as a different color, like this:

```
tr: nth-child(even) {
    background-color: lightgreen;
}
```

If you're old enough to remember the mainframe computer report days, this should bring back memories!

Another feature that comes in handy is to use the hover pseudo-class to change the background color of an individual cell as your site visitor hovers the mouse pointer over it:

```
td: hover {
    background-color: yellow;
}
```

Now things are really starting to get fancy!

# Positioning Elements

By default, browsers place elements in the window following a set order. As the web page defines each element, the browser places it in the window starting at the upper-left corner of the window, proceeding from left to right, and top to bottom.

To demonstrate this, let's run a quick test. You'll create a web page that contains five sections:

>> A header to display at the top of the web page

>> A footer to display at the bottom of the web page

>> A navigation section to display on the left side of the middle section

>> An aside section to display on the right side of the middle section

>> A main content section to display in the middle of the middle section

This is a pretty standard web page layout structure, which I'm sure you've seen lots of times as you've browsed the web.

Follow these steps to run the test:

1. **Open your favorite text editor, program editor, or IDE package, and enter the following code:**

```
<!DOCTYPE html>
<html>
<head>
<title>Positioning Test</title>
<style>
```

```css
header {
    background-color: red;
    margin: 0px;
    padding: 10px;
    height: 25px;
    width: 600px;
}

nav {
    background-color: blue;
    margin: 0px;
    padding: 10px;
    height: 125px;
    width: 200px;
}

section {
    background-color: green;
    margin: 0px;
    padding: 10px;
    height: 125px;
    width: 200px;
}

aside {
    background-color: yellow;
    margin: 0px;
    padding: 10px;
    height: 125px;
    width: 200px;
}

footer {
    background-color: orange;
    margin: 0px;
    padding: 10px;
    height: 25px;
    width: 600px;
}
</style>
</head>
<body>
<header><p>This is the header</p></header>
<nav><p>Navigation</p></nav>
```

```
<section><p>Section</p></section>
<aside><p>Aside</p></aside>
<footer><p>This is the footer</p></footer>
</body>
</html>
```

2. **Save the file as** `positiontest.html` **in the** DocumentRoot **folder of your web server.**

3. **Start the web server, open your browser, and go to the following URL:**

```
http://localhost:8080/positiontest.html
```

4. **Close the browser and stop the web server.**

This test creates a web page that contains a header section, a navigation section, a main content section, an aside section, and a footer section. It uses the `height` and `width` style properties to define how large each section should be and sets a different background color for each section so you can tell them apart on the web page. However, when you display the web page, you'll probably be a bit disappointed with the results, which are shown in Figure 2-6.

The browser positioned each of the different sections in the order you defined them, each on top of the other. Ouch! That's not what we wanted at all!

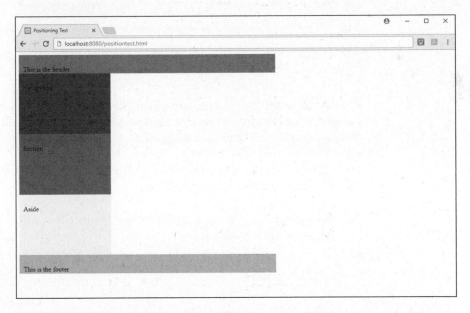

**FIGURE 2-6:**
Displaying the web page with no positioning.

To get the browser to place the different web page sections the way we want, we'll need to use some of the positioning properties available in CSS. The next sections walk you through how to do that.

## Putting elements in a specific place

Placing elements in specific locations on the web page requires using the *positioning properties* available in CSS. There are three main positioning properties that are normally used:

>> position: Sets the position method the browser should use to place the element

>> top: Defines the location for the top of the element

>> left: Defines the location for the left side of the element

The position property defines what method the browser uses to place the element in the web page. There are four different positioning methods:

>> absolute: Changes the element's position relative to the nearest positioned element that precedes it.

>> fixed: Places the element in a fixed location in the browser window. If the site visitor scrolls the window, the element stays in the same spot.

>> relative: Changes the element's position relative to the default position.

>> static: Places the element in its normal location in the web page following the default placement rules.

To use the absolute, fixed, and relative positioning methods, you need to define the location in the browser window where the element will be placed. You do that using the top and left properties.

Let's change the positiontest.html test file to use absolute positioning to place the sections. Just follow these steps:

**1.** **Open the** positiontest.html **file in your favorite text editor, program editor, or IDE package.**

**2.** **Modify the styles defined so they look like this:**

```
<style>

header {
    background-color: red;
    margin: 0px;
    padding: 10px;
    height: 25px;
    width: 600px;
    position: absolute;
    top: 0px;
    left: 0px;
}

nav {
    background-color: blue;
    margin: 0px;
    padding: 10px;
    height: 125px;
    width: 200px;
    position: absolute;
    top: 46px;
    left: 0px;
}

section {
    background-color: green;
    margin: 0px;
    padding: 10px;
    height: 125px;
    width: 200px;
    position: absolute;
    top: 46px;
    left: 201px;
}

aside {
    background-color: yellow;
    margin: 0px;
    padding: 10px;
    height: 125px;
    width: 200px;
```

```
        position: absolute;
        top: 46px;
        left: 402px;
    }

    footer {
        background-color: orange;
        margin: 0px;
        padding: 10px;
        height: 25px;
        width: 600px;
        position: absolute;
        top: 192px;
        left: 0px;
    }
    </style>
```

3. **Save the updated** positiontest.html **file as** positiontest2.html.

4. **Start your web server, open a browser, and go to the following URL:**

   ```
   http://localhost:8000/positiontest2.html
   ```

5. **Close the browser and stop the web server.**

The additional code sets the positioning method for the browser to use for each section to absolute, which means it will place the sections at exactly the place in the browser window you define using the top and left properties. When you display the web page, you should see the result as shown in Figure 2-7.

Now things are starting to look like a real web page!

## Floating elements

Absolute positioning has made a huge difference in how we can lay out elements in our web pages, but it doesn't solve all problems. You've probably already realized that trying to figure out the exact location for each element in a complicated web page would be somewhat difficult. Also, you'll notice as you resize the browser window that the sections stay in a fixed location and size — they don't expand or shrink with the browser window. Fortunately, there's a way you can avoid these problems.

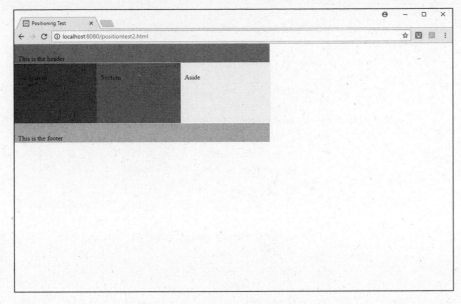

**FIGURE 2-7:**
Using absolute positioning to place sections in the web page.

CSS uses a feature called the `float` property to aid in positioning elements in the web page using a more dynamic method. The `float` property allows you to take an element out of the normal positioning flow in the web page and position it within the right or left edge of its parent container element. You don't need to calculate the exact position for the elements within the parent.

The format of the float property is pretty simple:

```
float: position
```

The position value can be `none`, `left`, or `right`.

The `float` property is most often used to create columns in a web page layout. Instead of using absolute positioning for the columns, you define a parent container element, and then just float the column elements inside the parent.

Let's give that a try with our `positiontest.html` example. You'll add a div element to use as the container for the middle three sections (nav, section, and aside) in the web page document. Follow these steps:

1.  **Open the original** `positiontest.html` **file in your favorite text editor, program editor, or IDE package.**

2. **Modify the styles defined so they look like this:**

```
<style>

header {
    background-color: red;
    margin: 0px;
    padding: 10px;
    height: 25px;
    width: 100%
}

nav {
    background-color: blue;
    margin: 0px;
    padding: 10px;
    height: 125px;
    width: 20%;
    float: left;
}

section {
    background-color: green;
    margin: 0px;
    padding: 10px;
    height: 125px;
    width: 55%;
    float: left;
}

aside {
    background-color: yellow;
    margin: 0px;
    padding: 10px;
    height: 125px;
    width: 20%;
    float: right;
}

footer {
    clear: both;
    background-color: orange;
    margin: 0px;
    padding: 10px;
```

```
      height: 25px;
      width: 100%;
  }
  </style>
```

3. **Modify the HTML code to add a div parent element around the nav, section, and aside elements.**

   That code should look like this:

```
<body>
<header><p>This is the header</p></header>
<div id="container">
<nav><p>Navigation</p></nav>
<section><p>Section</p></section>
<aside><p>Aside</p></aside>
</div>
<footer><p>This is the footer</p></footer>
</body>
```

4. **Save the updated** positiontest.html **file as** positiontest3.html.

5. **Start your web server, open your browser, and go to the following URL:**

```
http://localhost:8080/positiontest2.html
```

6. **Close the browser and stop the web server.**

   When you view the resulting web page, it should look similar to Figure 2-8.

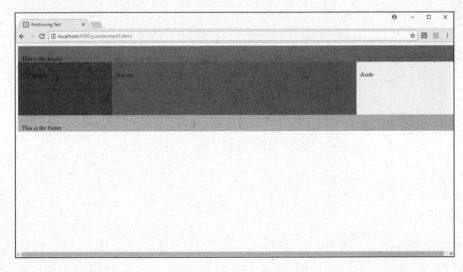

**FIGURE 2-8:**
Using float
positioning to
place sections in
the web page.

The float property in the nav, section, and aside elements causes them to float within the parent div element. I gave the parent element an id attribute value of container to help me remember its purpose. It's not necessary for it to have an id attribute defined because it isn't styled by itself.

Each of the inner sections appears side by side, as long as there's enough space for them in the browser window. By using a percentage value for the width, this creates what's called a *liquid layout*. With a liquid layout, if you resize the browser window, the individual section elements resize as well. If you resize the browser window too small, the browser automatically repositions the elements so that they all appear in the window.

# Chapter **3**

# HTML5 Forms

Quite possibly one of the most common ways that PHP programming helps is by processing data entered into an HTML5 form. There are plenty of applications that require data entry — from keeping track of your bowling team to filling out online job applications. HTML forms have been around for a long time, and with HTML5 it's sure to stick around for years to come. This chapter shows you how to create forms for your web applications using the HTML5 form features.

## Understanding HTML5 Forms

A dynamic web application requires some type of interaction with the site visitors who use it. That interaction is usually done with a form. Forms allow you to ask your site visitor for information using many of the same input interfaces that are commonly found in Windows and macOS systems, such as text boxes, drop-down lists, and radio buttons.

Before you can create a form for your web application, you need to do some house-keeping for HTML5. You need to define the form and how the browser should handle the data the site visitor enters into it. This section explains just how to do that.

# Defining a form

It's probably not too surprising that the HTML element you use to create a form is the *form element*. The form element has a simple enough format:

```
<form attributes>
    form elements
</form>
```

The `<form>` tag defines the start of the form area, which contains all the elements that create the form fields. The `</form>` tag defines the end of the form area.

The form element has lots of attributes that define just how the browser handles the data in the form. Table 3-1 shows all the attributes available.

**TABLE 3-1** **The Form Element Attributes**

| Attribute | Description |
|---|---|
| accept-charset | Specifies the character used in the form if it's different from the web page |
| action | Defines the URL where the browser should send the form data |
| autocomplete | Specifies whether the browser is allowed to use the autocomplete feature |
| enctype | Specifies the encoding the browser uses to submit the form data |
| method | Specifies the transfer method the browser should use to send the data |
| name | Defines a name assigned to the form |
| novalidate | Specifies that the browser shouldn't validate the data |
| target | Specifies the target window for the action URL |

Often, when you create a form, you don't need to worry about setting all the attributes shown in Table 3-1; you can use the standard default values. Here are the attributes you'll probably work with the most:

» action: You'll need to define the URL of the web page that will accept and process the form data. Usually, this is a page that contains server-side programming, such as PHP code.

» enctype: If your form contains binary data (such as an upload file), you'll need to set the encoding type so the server knows there's binary data involved with the form data.

>> method: You'll need to define how the browser sends the data to the server, using either the HTTP GET method or the HTTP PUT method.

- GET: The HTTP GET method sends the form data as part of the URL to the server. It embeds the form field names and data values together in the URL. Often, if you fill out a form on the Internet and click the Submit button, you'll see a URL that looks something like this:

```
http://myhost.com/index.php?content=store&id=100
```

This means the form used the GET method to send two form fields back to the server. Because the server needs to identify each value, the GET method associates the form field name with each value:

```
content=store
id=100
```

These values indicate that a form field named content is set to a value of store and a form field name id is set to a value of 100.

This method is a great way to quickly send small pieces of form data to the server, but it isn't recommended for larger forms. For forms that send lots of data, you're better off using the HTML PUT method.

- PUT: The PUT method sends the data behind the scenes in the HTTP request packets instead of using the URL. The data isn't seen in the address bar of the browser; instead, it's processed by the client browser and server as part of the HTTP communication behind the scenes.

**WARNING**

Just because the data isn't easily seen doesn't mean it's secure. The data sent by the PUT method is still sent in plain text in the HTTP request message. Any person with a network sniffer can still read that data. The only secure method of sending data is with an encrypted HTTPS session.

After you define the form and how it will send the form data, you're ready to start adding some form fields.

## Working with form fields

The original version of HTML didn't specify all that many form field elements for us to use. The list of form field elements that were available are shown in Table 3-2.

TABLE 3-2

## HTML Basic Form Field Elements

| Field | Description |
|---|---|
| button | A clickable area on the web page that triggers an action |
| input | Provides a single interface for one data value |
| select | A list of multiple objects in a drop-down list |
| submit | Signals to the browser to send the form data to the action URL |
| textarea | A larger multiline box for entering larger amounts of text |

HTML5 adds a couple more form field elements to the list:

» datalist: Provides a list of predefined options

» keygen: Creates a public/private key pair for authentication

» output: Creates an area to display results from a process

The following sections walk you through how to use each of these elements in your web forms.

# Using Input Fields

The *input element* is the most versatile of the form field elements. It provides for a few different types of interfaces to input data. You define the type of input field element to use by adding the type attribute to the tag:

```
<input type="type" attributes>
```

The HTML standard defines a handful of different input field types. If you've ever interacted with a Windows or macOS workstation (and who hasn't these days?), you're familiar with all these input types. The following sections explain how to use each one.

## Text boxes

The *text box* is the workhorse of the form. How many times have you filled out an online form that asked for your name, age, address, and so on? All these single-line form fields use the text box input type.

You create a text box input field by setting the `type` attribute value to `text`:

```
<input type="text" name="age" size=3>
```

The `name` attribute defines a unique identifier that allows you to retrieve the value entered into the field. It's important that you include that attribute. The `size` attribute allows you to set how large the form field appears on the web page. The default value is 20, which is a bit much for entering an age, so I've changed it to 3.

**TIP**

You can define a default value that appears in the form field using the `value` attribute. This feature is useful if you're trying to get your site visitor to update information that's already in your database. Just display the existing data as the default values for each form field.

**TIP**

The `disabled` attribute prevents you from entering data into the text field. It may sound weird to display a text field that you can't enter data into, but it has a purpose when you learn how to dynamically change the input fields using JavaScript later on in Book 3.

You can associate a label with a text box by using the *label element.* The input element should be enclosed in the label opening and closing tags:

```
<label>
   Last Name
   <input type="text" name="lastname">
</label>
```

With this format, you can use CSS to style and position both the label and the text box field at the same time.

Another feature is the ability to group input fields together into a *fieldset.* A fieldset creates a border area around the enclosed form fields to help separate them out in the web page. The format to use a fieldset is:

```
<fieldset>
   <legend>Enter your name</legend>
   <label>
      Last Name
      <input type="text" name="lastname">
   </label>
   <label>
      First Name
      <input type="text" name="firstname">
   </label>
</fieldset>
```

The legend element allows you to define text that appears in the fieldset border area. Figure 3-1 shows how this form looks.

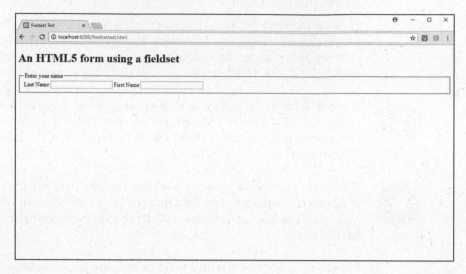

**FIGURE 3-1:**
Using a fieldset to group form fields.

The nice thing about the fieldset is that you can assign it an `id` attribute and then apply specific styles to the entire group in CSS3.

## Password entry

Many web applications require that site visitors enter sensitive information in the form, such as Social Security numbers (SSNs). The input element provides an easy way to hide that information from prying eyes trying to watch as visitors enter their data.

The `password` input field type instructs the browser to mask the characters as the site visitor enters them into the text box. Here's the format to create a password field:

```
<input type="password" name="ssn">
```

As your site visitor types data into the password form field, the browser masks the characters by displaying a neutral, nondescript character. Just how the characters are masked depends on the browser. Most browsers use bullet circles in the field.

# Check boxes

Check boxes provide a simple yes-or-no response form field. The checkbox input type creates a simple square box that the site visitor can click. The check box field toggles with each click — from showing a check mark in the box to not showing a check mark in the box.

To define a checkbox input type, use the following format:

```
<input type="checkbox" name="fishing">
```

The name attribute defines the name that's passed along to the action URL when the site visitor submits the form. The value sent is a Boolean true/false value — true if the check box is marked, and false if the check box is not marked.

Because the check box field is just a box, you'll most likely want to associate a label with the check box field so your site visitors know what they're selecting. Often, check boxes are used in groups, so you can use the fieldset element:

```
<fieldset>
    <legend>Please select which sports you like</legend>
    <label>
        Baseball
        <input type="checkbox" name="baseball"><br>
    </label>
    <label>
        Basketball
        <input type="checkbox" name="basketball"><br>
    </label>
    <label>
        Football
        <input type="checkbox" name="football"><br>
    </label>
    <label>
        Hockey
        <input type="checkbox" name="hockey"><br>
    </label>
</fieldset>
```

Figure 3-2 shows how this form looks in the browser window.

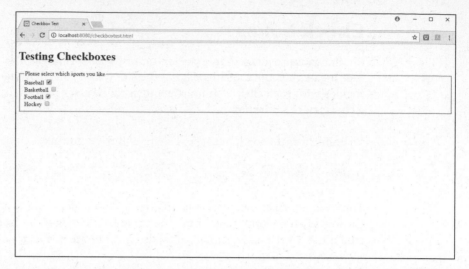

FIGURE 3-2:
Using check
boxes in a
fieldset.

You can also set a default state for the check box, but not by using the `value` attribute. Instead, you have to use the `checked` attribute:

```
<input type="checkbox" name="football" checked>
```

The `checked` attribute doesn't have a value associated with it. If it appears in the input element, the check box appears with a check mark in it.

## Radio buttons

A similar interface to check boxes are *radio buttons.* Radio buttons allow you to select only one out of a group of options. You create radio buttons by using the `radio` input type:

```
<input type="radio" name="sports">
```

To group options together, you have to assign them all the same name attribute. Then the browser will allow your site visitors to select only one option from the group. That code would look like this:

```
<fieldset>
    <legend>Please select your favorite sport</legend>
    <label>
       Baseball
       <input type="radio" name="sport"><br>
    </label>
```

```
      <label>
         Basketball
         <input type="radio" name="sport"><br>
      </label>
      <label>
         Football
         <input type="radio" name="sport" ><br>
      </label>
      <label>
         Hockey
         <input type="radio" name="sport"><br>
      </label>
</fieldset>
```

Figure 3-3 shows how the radio buttons appear on the web page.

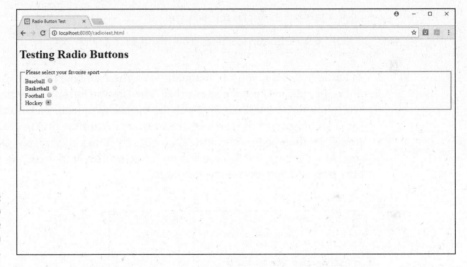

**FIGURE 3-3:**
Using radio
buttons to make
a selection from a
group.

As your site visitor selects each option, the previously selected option is reset. Only one value is sent back to the server from the form field.

If you'd like to set a default value for the radio button group, add the `checked` attribute to that radio button element.

**TIP**

## Hidden fields

Your application may need to pass data behind the scenes as part of the application control. Perhaps it's a product ID value related to an item the site visitor is purchasing or an employee ID number in a human resources application. Not all data that the form submits needs to be seen by the site visitor.

To accommodate that, HTML uses the `hidden` input type:

```
<input type="hidden" name="productid" value="121">
```

The hidden form field doesn't appear in the form itself, so you have to use the `value` attribute to assign a value to the form field that gets passed to the server. When the site visitor clicks the Submit button to submit the form data, any hidden form fields that are defined are sent along with the normal form field data.

## File upload

If your application requires that your site visitors upload files, you'll want to explore the `file` input type. The `file` input type produces an input field with two parts:

>> A text box to display the filename

>> A Browse button to launch a file manager

In some browsers, you can manually type the filename in the text box, but many of the popular browsers prevent that. The Browse button appears next to the text box, allowing site visitors to search for the file to upload. The interface that's used for searching depends on the OS the browser is running on. On Windows workstations, clicking the Browse button launches the File Explorer tool. On macOS workstations, clicking the Browse button launches the Finder tool. Figure 3-4 shows how the field appears on the web page.

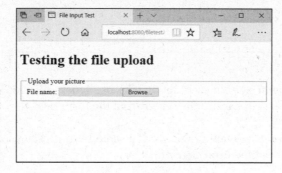

**FIGURE 3-4:**
The file input type interface as shown in the Microsoft Edge browser.

The format of the file input field is:

```
<input type="file" name="upload">
```

That's simple enough! However, you need to take care of one more thing when using the file input field. By default, the form sets the `enctype` attribute for encoding characters before they're uploaded. Most likely, your upload files will contain binary data, and encoding that data will corrupt it.

To solve that problem you need to set the `enctype` attribute in the `<form>` opening tag to use the `multipart/form-data` value:

```
<form method="POST" action="myhost.com/index.php" enctype="multipart/form-data">
```

This ensures that the binary data contained in the uploaded file is uploaded in binary format, but the data contained in the other form fields are properly encoded for upload.

# Buttons

Button, button, who's got the button? That's just a silly child's game, but buttons are a crucial part of your web forms. Buttons allow your site visitor to trigger actions on the web page, from launching JavaScript programs to uploading the form data to the server.

There are three types of button input types available to use: `button`, `reset`, and `submit`.

## Button

The `button` field type creates a generic button to trigger an event. When a site visitor clicks the button, nothing happens by default. The trick is to define an action using the `onclick` attribute:

```
<input type="button" name="launch" value="Click Me" onclick="myprogram()">
```

The `value` attribute defines what text appears in the button. The browser will automatically size the button to fit the text you specify. The `onclick` attribute defines a JavaScript function that the browser runs when you click the button.

## Reset

The `reset` field type resets any values in the form data fields back to their original values — either to empty if no default value is defined or to the default value if it's defined:

```
<input type="reset" name="reset" value="Reset fields">
```

## Submit

The submit input field type is a crucial part of most forms. It signals to the browser that it's time to upload the form field data values to the server:

```
<input type="submit">
```

By default, the button appears with *Submit* as the button label. You can change the button text using the value attribute. It's customary to place the Submit button at the bottom of a form, but that isn't required. You can place the Submit button anywhere between the opening <form> tag and the closing </form> tag.

# Adding a Text Area

Text boxes are extremely versatile, but there's a limit to what they can do. If you need to enter large amounts of text, the text box scrolls to allow you to enter the text, but you lose sight of the text you previously typed.

The textarea element provides a larger interface for entering text. To create a text area, you use the following opening and closing tags:

```
<textarea name="story"></textarea>
```

That, by itself, though, won't give you what you're looking for. There are a few attributes that you'll want to use to define the text area. Table 3-3 shows the attributes you can use.

**TABLE 3-3** **The textarea Attributes**

| Attribute | Description |
|-----------|-------------|
| cols | Specifies the width of the text area in the web page |
| disabled | Grays out the text area so nothing can be typed |
| name | Specifies the form field name associated with the field |
| readonly | Locks the text area so nothing can be typed, but default text can be displayed |
| rows | Specifies the height of the text area in the web page |

So, to create a text area that's 20 characters wide by 30 characters high, you'd use the following:

```
<textarea name="story" cols=20 rows=30></textarea>
```

Your site visitors can then type their text in the text area. If they type more than 30 rows of text, the browser will add a scrollbar to the right side of the text area and allow them to continue typing.

**TIP**

You'll notice that in my text area examples, there's nothing between the opening and closing textarea tags. That produces an empty text area. Any text that you place between the opening and closing tags appears as the default text in the text area.

## Using Drop-Down Lists

Often, you want to limit the choices your site visitors have for a specific data field. To do that, you use a drop-down list. The drop-down list appears in the form as a single line, similar to a text box, but with a down arrow. If you click the down arrow, a box drops down with all the options available in it. You can then select one or more options from the drop-down list.

In the HTML5 world, this feature is called a select element. The select element consists of two parts:

» The select opening and closing tags to define the select element

» One or more option elements that define the allowed options

Here's an example of a simple select element (see Figure 3-5):

```
<select name="sports">
<option value="baseball">Baseball</option>
<option value="basketball">Basketball</option>
<option value="football">Football</option>
<option value="hockey">Hockey</option>
</select>
```

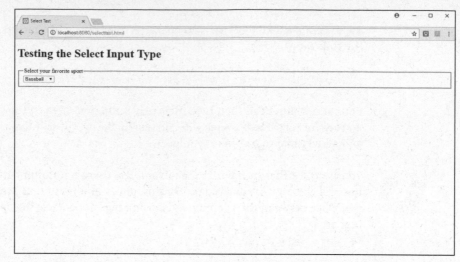

**FIGURE 3-5:**
Using the
`select` element.

With this format, the browser displays a single text box along with a down arrow indicating that there's a drop-down list to select from. When you click the arrow, you see the list.

If you prefer to have more of the options appear on the web page than just one, set the `size` attribute in the `<select>` tag:

```
<select name="sports" size="4">
```

This creates a list of options that you can scroll through, as shown in Figure 3-6.

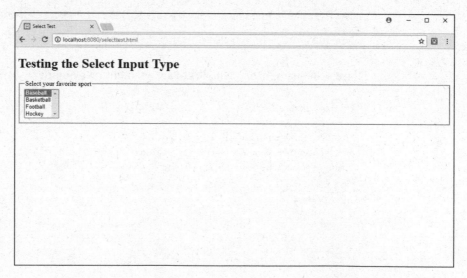

**FIGURE 3-6:**
Displaying
multiple options
in the select
element.

Each option element defines one item in the select list. The browser displays the text between the opening <option> and closing </option> tags, but it sends the value attribute of the item your site visitor selects to the server. This can come in handy if you want to use abbreviations or codes in your data, but you want to display the full text to the site visitors.

TIP

By default, the select element only allows the site visitor to select one value. You can change that behavior by setting the multiple attribute in the <select> opening tag.

# Enhancing HTML5 Forms

The original HTML standards were pretty bare-bones with the form field options. These days web developers gather all types of information from forms. To help with that, the HTML5 standard defines some fancier form types that you can use. This section walks you through what those are.

## Data lists

The datalist element is new to HTML5. It allows you to create an option list for drop-down lists that use the autocomplete feature, made popular by Google searching. As you start typing a value in the text box, the list that appears in the drop-down box narrows to only the values that match what you've typed.

The data list feature requires three parts:

>> An <input> tag that defines the data list

>> A datalist element that defines the list

>> One or more <option> tags that define the list values

A complete data list looks like this:

```
<input list="sports">
<datalist id="sports">
    <option value="Baseball">
    <option value="Basketball">
    <option value="Football">
    <option value="Hockey">
</datalist>
```

The list attribute in the `<input>` tag refers to the data list `id` attribute value for the data list to use. This allows you to define multiple data lists in your form. Figure 3-7 shows how the data list looks in action.

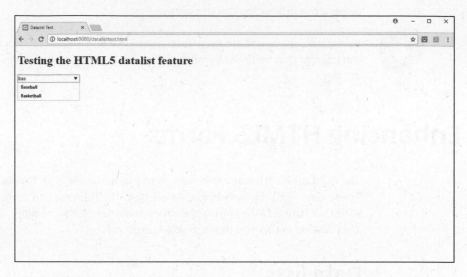

**FIGURE 3-7:**
Using a data list
in the web page.

In this example, as I typed the characters, the matching data list values appeared in the drop-down box, limiting my choices. Notice that the match is case insensitive and that the match is made anywhere in the text string of the option values.

## Additional input fields

One of the more exciting features in the HTML5 standard form additions are the additions to the `<input>` tag. HTML5 defines 13 additional input element types:

>> `color`: Produces a color palette for the site visitor to select a color. Returns the RGB color value associated with the selected color.

>> `date`: Produces a graphical month calendar to select a date. Returns the selected year, month, and day values.

>> `datetime`: Produces a graphical month calendar to select a date and a text box to select the time. Returns the selected year, month, date, hour, minute, second, and fraction-of-a-second values, along with the time zone.

>> `datetime-local`: Produces the same form field as the `datetime` input type, but doesn't return a time zone.

>> `email`: For inputting a single email address or a comma-separated list of email addresses.

>> `month`: Produces a graphical month calendar. Returns the year and month selected.

>> `number`: Produces a spin box for increasing or decreasing a numeric value in a text box. Returns the numeric value selected.

>> `range`: Produces a slider to select a value from a range. You define the range using the `min` and `max` attributes in the tag. Returns the numeric value selected.

>> `search`: Produces a text box that some browsers style like a search box (such as with a magnifying glass icon). Returns the value entered into the text box.

>> `tel`: Produces a standard text box for entering a telephone number. Some browsers may validate the format of the text entered to ensure it matches a telephone number format. Returns the value entered into the text box.

>> `time`: Produces a time selector that shows two numeric values, along with a spin box for increasing or decreasing the values. The numeric values indicate 1 through 12 for the hour and 0 through 59 for the minutes. Returns the values selected in a time format.

>> `url`: Produces a text box for entering a text URL. Some browsers may validate the URL format entered. Returns the text entered into the text box.

>> `week`: Produces a graphical calendar to select a week number for a specified year. Returns the year and the week number selected.

These produce some pretty amazing input fields in your web pages! The only downside is that different browsers may use different methods to produce these form fields. Let's walk through an example to create a test program so you can see how your browsers handle the new input fields:

1. **Open your favorite text editor, program editor, or integrated development environment (IDE) package.**

2. **Enter the following code:**

```
<!DOCTYPE html>
<html>
<head>
<title>HTML5 Input Types Test</title>
</head>
<body>
<h1>Testing the HTML5 Input Types</h1>
<fieldset>
<legend>HTML5 Input Fields</legend>
<label>
Color Selector
<input type="color" name="colortest">
</label><br>
```

```html
<label>
Date Selector
<input type="date" name="datetest">
</label><br>
<label>
DateTime Selector
<input type="datetime" name="datetimetest">
</label><br>
<label>
DateTime-Local Selector
<input type="datetime-local" name="datetimelocaltest">
</label><br>
<label>
Email Selector
<input type="email" name="emailtest">
</label><br>
<label>
Month Selector
<input type="month" name="monthtest">
</label><br>
<label>
Number Selector
<input type="number" name="numbertest">
</label><br>
<label>
Range Selector
<input type="range" min=0 max=100 name="rangetest">
</label><br>
<label>
Search Selector
<input type="search" name="searchtest">
</label><br>
<label>
Telephone Selector
<input type="tel" name="teltest">
</label><br>
<label>
Time Selector
<input type="time" name="timetest">
</label><br>
<label>
URL Selector
<input type="url" name="urltest">
</label><br>
```

```
<label>
Week Selector
<input type="week" name="weektest">
</label>
</body>
</html>
```

3. **Save the file as** `inputtypestest.html` **in the** `DocumentRoot` **folder for your web server (such as** `c:\xampp\htdocs` **for XAMPP in Windows, or** `/Application/XAMPP/htdocs` **for XAMPP in macOS).**

4. **Start your web server.**

5. **Open a browser and enter the following URL:**

```
http://localhost:8080/inputtypestest.html
```

6. **Close the browser window and shut down the web server.**

The `inputtypestest.html` file is a great way to see how the new HTML5 input types look in different browsers. Figure 3-8 shows how they look in the Google Chrome browser.

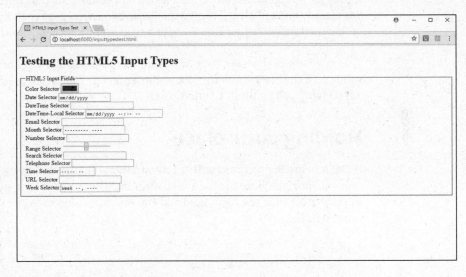

**FIGURE 3-8:** Viewing the `input typestest.html` output in the Google Chrome browser.

**TIP**

If you have a mobile device handy, try testing the `inputtypestest.html` web page on your mobile device. Mobile devices use virtual keyboards that appear on the screen when you click in an input form field. Most mobile devices will customize the keyboard depending on which type of input form field you click in. For example, in the `tel` input type, the mobile device may only display a numeric keypad for entering the phone number; for the `email` input type, the mobile device may display a keyboard with a .com button.

# Using HTML5 Data Validation

Accepting data from unknown website visitors is a dangerous thing. However, dynamic web applications must have user interaction to work. The conundrum is how to do both.

One method is to use *data validation*, which is the process of verifying that the data your site visitors enter into the form fields is correct. There are two ways to tackle that process:

>> On the server, with server-side programming code

>> In the client browser, using HTML, CSS, and JavaScript

In Book 4, Chapter 4, I cover all the bases on using server-side programming to validate form data. However, waiting until the browser has uploaded the data to the server to validate it can be somewhat cumbersome. By that time, the site visitor has already entered all the form data. Returning a web page making the site visitor re-enter all that data just because of one typo is not a good way to retain customers.

This is where client-side data validation comes in handy. The more data you can validate in the browser as the site visitor enters it, the better the chance you have of receiving valid data in the first place.

## Holding your place

HTML5 helps that process with a few additional features. One such feature is the `placeholder` attribute for the `input` element. The `placeholder` attribute appears as gray text inside the form field and can provide a suggested format for the data to enter:

```
<label>
Enter your daytime phone number:
<input type="tel" name="num" placeholder="(nnn)nnn-nnnn">
</label>
```

The browser displays the placeholder value inside the input form field, but as gray text, as shown in Figure 3-9.

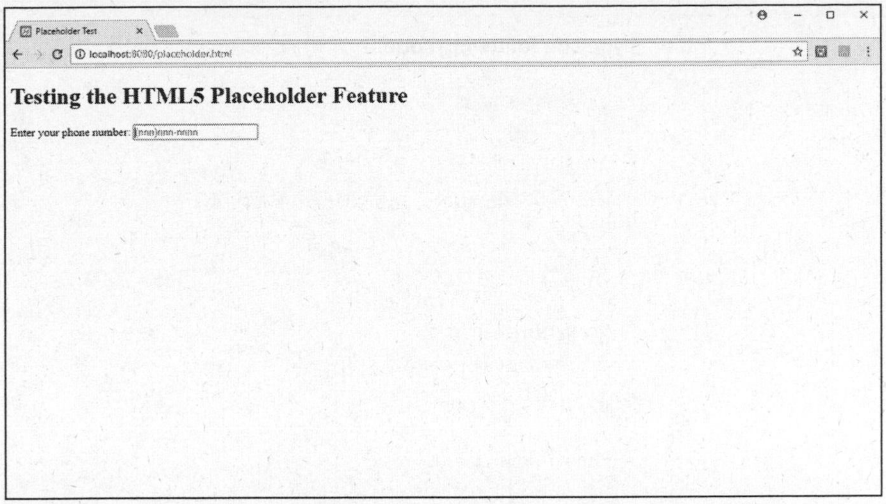

**FIGURE 3-9:**
Using the placeholder HTML5 attribute.

As you start typing text in the input field, the placeholder text disappears.

## Making certain data required

Another data validation attribute added by HTML5 is the `required` attribute:

```
<input type="text" name="lastname" required="required">
```

The `required` attribute marks the form field so that the browser won't upload the form if that field is empty. Some browsers will display an error message indicating which required form field(s) are empty.

## Validating data types

Not only do the additional HTML5 input types produce different types of input fields, but you can also use them to validate data. Browsers that support the new HTML5 data types will mark input form fields that contain data not in the proper format with the invalid state.

CSS provides pseudo-class rules to style elements based on their state (see Book 2, Chapter 2). You use the `invalid` and `valid` pseudo-class states to style input fields with invalid data differently from input fields with valid data. This helps make the fields with invalid data stand out in the form.

Here's a quick example you can try to test this feature:

**1.** Open your favorite text editor, program editor, or IDE package.

**2.** Type the following code:

```
<!DOCTYPE html>
<html>
<head>
<title>Testing for Invalid Data</title>
</head>
<style>

input:invalid {
    background-color: red;
}

input:valid {
    background-color: lightgreen;
}
</style>
<body>
<h1>Testing for invalid data</h1>
<fieldset>
<legend>You must be over 18 to participate</legend>
<label>
Age:
<input type="number" name="age" min="18">
</label>
</fieldset>
</body>
</html>
```

**3.** **Save the file as** `invaliddatatest.html` **in the** `DocumentRoot` **folder for your web server** (`c:\xampp\htdocs` **for XAMPP on Windows or** `/Applications/XAMPP/htdocs` **for XAMPP on macOS**).

**4.** **Start the Apache web server from XAMPP.**

**5.** **Open a browser and enter the following URL:**

```
http://localhost:8080/invaliddatatest.html
```

**6.** **Close the browser, and stop the XAMPP web server.**

When the invaliddatatest.html form first appears, the age data field will be empty and colored green. If you use the spinner icons on the right side of the text box, the numbers will start at 18, and the text box will stay green. However, if you try to manually enter an age less than 18, the text box immediately turns red.

IN THIS CHAPTER

» **Rounding corners**

» **Working with border images**

» **Exploring new colors**

» **Using gradients**

» **Lurking in the shadows**

» **Working with fonts**

» **Answering media queries**

# Chapter 4

# Advanced CSS3

The previous two chapters show you how to use the combination of HTML5 and CSS to create content and style it for your web pages. CSS3 provides some more advanced features, allowing you to do even *more* styling for your web pages. This chapter walks you through some of the more exciting features from CSS3 that you can use to liven up your site.

## Rounding Your Corners

In Book 2, Chapter 3, I explain how to build online forms using HTML5. However, by default, HTML forms are somewhat boring, even after adding some CSS styling.

The default styling used by browsers to display text boxes, buttons, and text areas in forms produces nothing but square boxes, which gets pretty boring. The original CSS standard didn't do anything to solve the problem, other than possibly adding some color to the square boxes. Cubism may be good for some styles of paintings, but that layout doesn't work in forms and can bore your website visitors.

One of the features that had been hotly sought after in the browser world has been the ability to use rounded corners for form elements. The simple act of rounding the square boxes just a bit can liven up the form. Many individual browsers added the rounded corners feature on their own, separate from the CSS standard. Unfortunately, as you may guess, different browsers used different methods for implementing rounded corners. Trying to write a style that would work across all browsers became both difficult and confusing. But because using rounded corners became so popular, that feature was finally added to CSS3 as a standard.

The new `border-radius` style property allows you to round off the sharp edges from elements on the web page. It does that by allowing you to define the radius of an imaginary circle used to create the rounded corners. You can just shave a little off the edge by using a small radius value, or you can create a full ellipse by completely rounding all four corners with a large radius value. Figure 4-1 shows an example of applying the `border-radius` property to a few form elements.

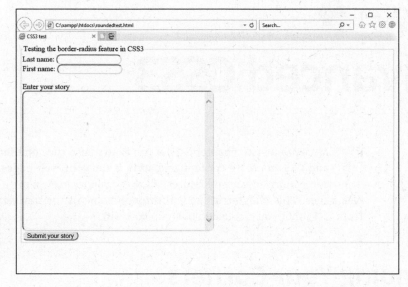

FIGURE 4-1:
Using the
`border-radius`
property to
create rounded
corners.

Notice that the input text boxes, the text area, and even the Submit button are rounded instead of the standard squares. That makes quite a difference in the appearance of the web form.

What can get confusing with the `border-radius` property, though, is that there are four different formats for using it — with one, two, three, or four parameters. The following single parameter sets the radius of all four corners to 10 pixels:

```
border-radius: 10px;
```

The following two parameters set the radius of the top-left and bottom-right corners to 10 pixels, but the top-right and bottom-left corners to 5 pixels:

```
border-radius: 10px 5px;
```

The following three parameters set the radius of the top-left corner to 10 pixels, the top-right and bottom-left corners to 5 pixels, and the bottom-right corner to 3 pixels:

```
border-radius: 10px 5px 3px;
```

The following four parameters set the radius of the top-left corner to 10 pixels, the top-right corner to 5 pixels, the bottom-right corner to 3 pixels, and the bottom-left corner to 1 pixel:

```
border-radius: 10px 5px 3px 1px;
```

When you're able to set the radius of each individual corner or pairs of corners, you can create quite a few different special effects, such as dialog bubbles or ellipses.

You can also set the individual corner radii values independently from one another with a few additional properties:

» `border-top-left-radius`

» `border-top-right-radius`

» `border-bottom-left-radius`

» `border-bottom-right-radius`

Each one sets the corresponding border radius value in the element.

The `border-radius` properties all use a size value to set the circle radius for the corner. You can specify the size using any of the standard CSS size unit measurements, such as inches, pixels, or em units.

# Using Border Images

The default border line that HTML5 places around objects is pretty dull. How about adding some more elaborate borders around objects? You can, thanks to another interesting feature added to CSS3. It provides the ability to use images for the border around elements instead of just a line. This feature allows you to use any type of image to create a flourish around your elements.

You apply a border image to an element by adding the `border-image` property:

```
border-image: url(file) slice repeat
```

The `url()` function defines the location of the image file used for the border. The path can be either an absolute value pointing directly to the image file or a relative path (relative to the location of the CSS script).

The `slice` value defines what parts of the border image to use for the border. This part can get somewhat complicated. By default, the browser slices the border image into nine sections, as shown in Figure 4-2. The nine border image sections are

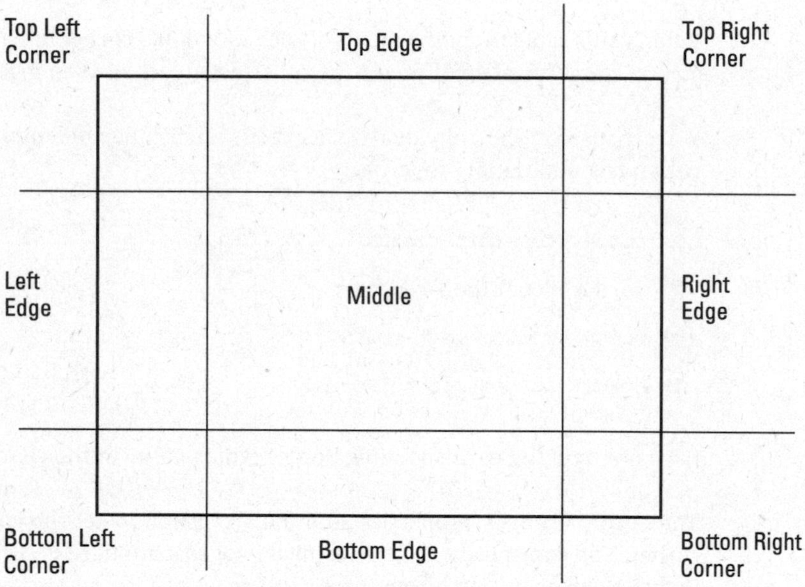

**FIGURE 4-2:**
Slicing a border image to retrieve the pieces.

Top Left Corner

Top Edge

Top Right Corner

Left Edge

Middle

Right Edge

Bottom Left Corner

Bottom Edge

Bottom Right Corner

>> The four corner pieces (top left, top right, bottom right, and bottom left)

>> The four edge pieces (top, right, bottom, and left)

>> The middle section

For the `slice` value, you specify the size of the image pieces to use for the individual border images. You can specify that as either a percentage of the entire image size, or a pixel value to represent how much of the image edges to use for the border edges. You have the option to specify the `slice` as one, two, or four separate values:

» **One value:** Cuts the same size of the image for the four corners and the four edges

» **Two values:** One size for the top and bottom, and another size for the left and right sides

» **Four values:** One size each for the top, right side, bottom, and left side

The `repeat` parameter defines how the browser should make the image fit the space required to create the border edges. There are four ways to do that:

» `repeat`: Repeats the image to fill the entire edge

» `round`: Repeats the image, but if the image doesn't fit the area as a whole number of repeats, rescales the image so it fits

» `space`: Repeats the image, but if the image doesn't fit the area as a whole number of repeats, adds spaces between the images so it fits

» `stretch`: Stretches the image to fill the edge

So, for example, to define a border image that uses 10-pixel slices from all the sides, and stretches them to fit the border area, you'd use the following:

```
border-image: url("myimage.jpg") 10 stretch;
```

Note that you don't use the units for the `slice` value. If you specify the value as a percentage of the entire image, add the percent sign, but if it's in pixels, leave off the `px`.

Instead of using one property statement for all the features, if you prefer, you can define these values in separate properties. There are five separate properties used to define the border image, and how the browser should use it (see Table 4-1).

**TABLE 4-1**    ## The CSS4 Border Image Properties

| Property | Description |
| --- | --- |
| border-image-outset | Specifies the amount the image extends beyond the normal border box area |
| border-image-repeat | Specifies how the image should be extended to fit the entire border area |
| border-image-slice | Specifies what piece of the image to use as the border |
| border-image-source | Specifies the path to the image used for the border |
| border-image-width | Specifies the widths of the border image sides |

Figure 4-3 shows what the border image looks like around an element. That's quite a bit better than the standard border line.

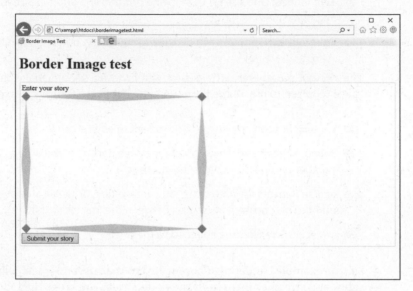

**FIGURE 4-3:**
Using a border image around an element.

TIP

The Mozilla Foundation developers' website includes a handy border image generator tool: `https://developer.mozilla.org/en-US/docs/Web/CSS/CSS_Background_and_Borders/Border-image_generator`. With this tool, you can upload an image or use one of their standard images, and the tool will automatically generate the CSS3 code necessary to extract the border image properties.

# Looking at the CSS3 Colors

In Book 2, Chapter 2, I show you the three formats that the original CSS standard defines for setting colors in the web page:

>> Using a color name

>> Using an RGB hexadecimal value

>> Using the `rgb()` function with decimal values

The CSS3 standard extends the options you have available for defining colors by adding the hue, saturation, and lightness (HSL) method. The HSL method of defining colors uses three values:

>> **Hue:** The degree of color on the color wheel. The color wheel concept has been around in the art world since the early 1800s. It places the colors around a circle with the primary colors — red, yellow, and blue — positioned on the wheel at 0, 60, and 240 degrees, respectively. The secondary colors — orange, green, and violet — are placed in between the primary colors, in locations based on their shades at 30, 120, and 260 degrees, respectively. From there, the different shades of color combinations are arranged appropriately on the wheel. To specify an individual color hue, you must know its location on the color wheel. Fortunately there are plenty of charts online to help out with that.

>> **Saturation:** The percentage of the color used. The saturation value is a percentage that specifies the grayness shade of the color, from 0 percent for no color (all gray) to 100 percent for full color saturation.

>> **Lightness:** The percentage of lightness added to the color. The lightness value is a percentage that specifies how dark (0 percent) or light (100 percent) the color should be. The 50 percent value creates the color at its normal shade. Larger percentages create darker shades of the color, while smaller percentages create lighter shades of the color.

To use the HSL method to specify a color, use the hsl() format. For example, the following property specifies the red color at position 0 of the color wheel, shown at 100 percent saturation, with 50 percent lightness:

```
color: hsl(0, 100%, 50%);
```

The CSS3 standard also adds the opacity feature to HSL, creating the *HSLA color method.* With HSLA, you add a fourth parameter to specify the opaqueness of the color, from 0 to 1. The following example uses the red color, but at 50 percent transparency:

```
color: hsla(0, 100%, 50%, 0.5)
```

**TIP**

The beauty of using the HSL values comes when you're choosing a color scheme for your website. If you want to use a single color for the website scheme, you can modify the saturation and lightness levels to make different shades of the color. If you want to create a two-color scheme, you may want to choose hues that are 180 degrees apart — those are considered complementary. For a three-color scheme, hues that are 120 degrees apart create a triad. In a four-color scheme, select hues that are 90 degrees apart to create a nice offset. By sticking with the color wheel rules, just about anyone can create a tasteful color scheme for a website.

Advanced CSS3

# Playing with Color Gradients

While using individual colors are a great way to liven up the website, even colors can get somewhat boring when you use them all the time. To help make things more interesting, the CSS3 standard adds color gradients to the mix. A *color gradient* slowly fades from one color into a second color, producing a warm transition effect. These transition colors are often used for backgrounds, creating an effect that helps the website visitor follow the content as the color gradient morphs into a different color.

There are two types of color gradients defined in the CSS3 standard:

>> **Linear gradients:** Fade using a side-to-side or top-to-bottom direction

>> **Radial gradients:** Use a center point and fade outward (radiate) from there, much like a tie-dyed T-shirt.

This section discusses how to use each of these methods in your web pages.

## Linear gradients

A linear gradient fades between two colors in a linear manner — that is, from side to side, or from top to bottom. Use the `linear-gradient()` function to define the direction of the fade and the transition colors:

```
linear-gradient(direction, color1, color2);
```

The `direction` parameter defines which way the gradient should go. If you omit the direction, the browser will create the gradient from top to bottom, a common effect for backgrounds. If you want to change the direction, specify it by the direction that the gradient should fade from *color1* to *color2*, like this:

```
linear-gradient(to right, black, white)
```

You can use `to top`, `to bottom`, or `to right` to specify the direction of the gradient. This example starts with the black color on the left side and fades to the white color on the right side, as shown in Figure 4-4.

To use the linear gradient, just add it anywhere you'd use a color value:

```
background: linear-gradient(red, orange);
```

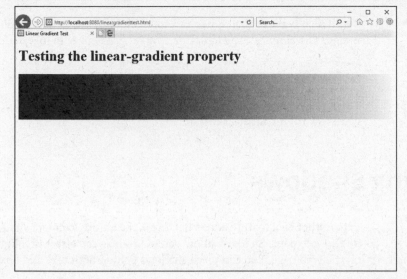

**FIGURE 4-4:**
A left-to-right
color gradient.

Linear gradients can create quite the stunning effect for web page backgrounds. If you want to get fancy, you can specify more colors in the `linear-gradient()` list as intermediate points between the two endpoints:

```
background: linear-gradient(red, orange, yellow);
```

This takes the color transition from a red to an orange first and then finally to the yellow destination.

## Radial gradients

The `radial-gradient()` does the same thing as the linear gradient, but in a circular pattern radiating from a central point. If you have fond memories of the days when tie-dyed T-shirts were popular, you may love the radial gradients!

Here's the format for the `radial-gradient()` function:

```
radial-gradient(shape size, color1, color2, ...)
```

The keys to creating the radial gradient are the *shape* parameter, which defines the shape of the gradient, and the *size* parameter. By default the radial gradient is drawn as an ellipse, but you can instead specify a circle. The size determines where the radial gradient stops. Usually this is a location, such as `closest-corner`, `closest-side`, `farthest-corner`, or `farthest-side`.

You'll also want to define two or more colors to create the gradient effect in the image. The simplest way to define a radial gradient is to just define the colors:

```
background: radial-gradient(red, orange, yellow);
```

This creates an elliptical radial gradient, centered in the element, radiating outward toward the farthest corner.

# Adding Shadows

Yet another cool feature added in CSS3 is the ability to create shadows of elements on the web page. Shadows allow you to produce the effect of a light shining down on the web page. You can place shadows behind both text and box elements.

## Text shadows

Placing shadows behind text on a web page can create a startling effect to draw attention to headings. Figure 4-5 shows how the text shadow effect can make the heading stand out on the web page.

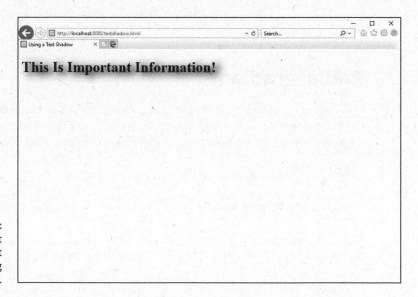

**FIGURE 4-5:**
Adding the text shadow effect to a heading element.

The CSS3 `text-shadow` style property allows you to define just how the shadow should look. Here's the format of the `text-shadow` style property:

```
text-shadow: color offsetx offsety blur;
```

The `color` parameter defines the color to use for the shadow. The `offsetx` and `offsety` parameters define the distance of the shadow from the text. You can use either positive or negative values to represent the offset values. Positive values move the shadow down and to the right of the text. Negative values move the shadow up and to the left of the text. The `blur` parameter defines the amount of space the shadow uses. The larger the space, the more stretched looking the shadow appears.

Here's an example of a CSS3 rule that sets a shadow for all h1 elements:

```
h1 {
    text-shadow: black, 10px, 5px, 15px;
}
```

This produces a black shadow to the right and below the text.

You can apply more than one shadow to a text element. Just list the different shadow definitions on the same `text-shadow` line, separated by commas:

```
text-shadow: shadow1, shadow2, ...;
```

The browser displays the shadows in the order you define them, with each shadow placed on top of the previous shadows.

# Box shadows

The box shadow helps the element stand out with almost a 3-D effect on the web page. Box shadows work the same way as text shadows, but you apply them to box elements, such as individual form input fields, text areas, or even entire div blocks. Figure 4-6 shows an example of applying a simple box shadow to a div section on the web page.

The format for the `box-shadow` property is similar to the `text-shadow` property, with a couple of added things:

```
box-shadow: [inset] color offsetx offsety blur [spread];
```

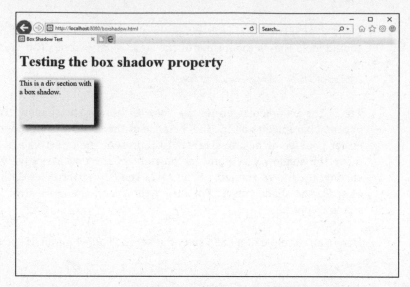

**FIGURE 4-6:**
Using a box
shadow on a div
element.

The inset keyword is optional. It determines whether the browser should display the shadow inside the element. By default, the size of the shadow is the same as the object; by adding the *spread* value, you can increase or decrease the size of the shadow.

# Creating Fonts

In Chapter 2 of this minibook, I mention the problem with fonts on a web page. In the past, browsers were only able to use fonts that were already installed on the workstation. Finding fonts that are available on all workstations is somewhat of a challenge.

The CSS3 standard has attempted to remedy this situation by providing a way for web designers to create their own fonts and deliver them to their site visitors as part of the web page download. The @font-face rule provides a way to specify a font file that the client browser must download as part of the style definitions. When the browser downloads the font file, your web application can use that font to style text in the web pages. These fonts are known as *web fonts*.

The following sections describe the different types of web fonts and how to use them in your web applications.

# Focusing on font files

The key to using web fonts is the ability to define a font in a file that every site visitor's browser can download and use. The *font files* contain detailed information on how the workstation should display individual characters and symbols.

The problem with font files, though, is that, over the years, lots of different font file formats have appeared. Table 4-2 shows the popular font file formats you may run into.

**TABLE 4-2**     ## Font File Formats

| Font | Description |
| --- | --- |
| TrueType | A font created in the 1980s by Microsoft and Apple. This font type is still commonly used by both operating systems. |
| OpenType | Created by Microsoft and built to extend TrueType fonts. The most common font type used. |
| Embedded OpenType | A font format created by Microsoft for use only in the Internet Explorer web browser. |
| Scalable Vector Graphics (SVG) | Primarily used for graphics on mobile devices, but can be used to display text. |
| Web Open Font Format (WOFF) | A font created by the W3C standards group, intended for web pages. |

The TrueType and WOFF font file formats are currently the only two supported by all browsers. It's best to stick with one of these types of fonts when creating your web fonts.

**WARNING**

Font files can often be found and downloaded from the Internet. However, beware of licensing restrictions on font files. Most font files are not free, or are free only for personal use.

# Working with web fonts

CSS3 allows you to define a web font file for client browsers to download using the @font-face rule. You may notice that the @font-face rule doesn't follow any of the standard style rule-naming conventions that I discuss in Chapter 2 of this minibook. There's a reason for that. The @font-face rule defines a *CSS command*. CSS commands are directives to the browser to perform some action while loading the styles. CSS commands start with the at symbol (@) and should be placed at the start of the CSS stylesheet area.

Here's the format of the @font-face rule:

```
@font-face {
    font-family: name;
    src: url(location);
    [descriptor:value];
}
```

The font-family property defines a unique name for the font in your stylesheet. The src property defines the location of the font file on your server, either as an absolute or relative path.

Following those two properties, you can add *descriptors* that indicate when the font should be used (such as for bold text or for text in italics).

An example of defining a web font would be:

```
@font-face {
    font-family: myfont;
    src: url(myfont.woff);
}
```

This defines a font family named myfont from the myfont.woff font file that the client workstation should download. Then, to use the new font in your web pages, just define the font-family name in a style rule:

```
div {
    font-family: myfont;
}
```

There are three descriptors that you can define for the web font:

>> font-stretch: Specifies how the font should be stretched to fill a space. The default is normal, but other values are condensed or expanded.

>> font-style: Specifies how the font should be styled. The values are normal, italic, or oblique.

>> font-weight: Specifies the boldness of the font. The values are normal, bold, or numeric values from 100 to 900.

By specifying different font-style and font-weight values, you can specify more than one font file, depending on how you use the font in the web page.

# Handling Media Queries

These days, it's likely that your web applications will be viewed by site visitors using a myriad of devices. Whether it's on a large monitor connected to a desktop workstation or a small mobile device that fits in the palm of your hand, your web application will need to be presentable to all your website visitors.

The CSS3 standard has some tricks that you can use to help determine just when you need to alter the style and layout of your web pages, based on how your site visitor is viewing the application. This section covers just how to use those tricks.

## Using the @media command

The CSS2 standard defined the @media CSS command to help you detect what type of device the web page is being viewed on. You can then create styles based on the media type. This allows you to style the web page one way when your site visitor is displaying it on a monitor screen and another way when the site visitor prints it out.

The CSS2 standard defined several different media types to use in the @media rule, as shown in Table 4-3.

**TABLE 4-3**     The CSS2 @media Types

| Type | Description |
| --- | --- |
| all | All types of output devices |
| braille | Devices that produce Braille |
| embossed | Braille printers |
| handheld | Mobile devices with small screens |
| print | Printers |
| projection | Large-screen projectors |
| screen | Standard computer monitors |
| speech | Text-to-speech readers |
| tty | Teletype terminals |
| tv | Television |

You use the @media command in your standard style sheet to define styles used for that specific type of device:

```
@media screen {
    body {
        font-family: sans-serif;
        font-size: 12pt;
    }
    h1 {
        font-family: sans-serif;
        font-size: 20pt;
    }
}

@media print {
    body {
        font-family: serif;
        font-size: 10pt;
    }
    h1 {
        font-family: serif;
        font-size: 18pt;
    }
}
```

These two @media commands define two sets of style rules — one for when the web page appears on a monitor, and one for when the web page is printed. It's up to the browser to determine which situation dictates which @media command set to use.

## Dealing with CSS3 media queries

The CSS2 @media command went a long way toward helping you determine what types of devices your site visitors are using to display your web application, but it didn't go quite far enough. For example, whether your site visitor is viewing your web application on a big monitor or a small mobile device, the device evaluates to the screen media type by the @media command.

The CSS3 standard solves that problem by adding *media queries* to the standard @media commands. Media queries allow you to query the features supported by the client browser and the device the browser is running on. You can add the media queries to the standard @media commands to produce a customized rule set for just about any type of circumstance.

Here's the format of the media query:

```
@media type and feature
```

The *type* parameter defines the media type, similar to the CSS2 media types, but now limits them to only four (all, print, screen, and speech). The *feature* parameter defines new features available to query. The CSS3 media features available are shown in Table 4-4.

**TABLE 4-4**   ## The CSS3 Media Features

| Feature | Description |
| --- | --- |
| any-hover | Whether the device supports hovering a pointer over elements |
| any-pointer | Whether the device supports a pointing device |
| aspect-ratio | The height and width ratio of the viewing device |
| color | The number of bits of color supported by the viewing device |
| color-index | The number of colors the device can display |
| grid | Whether the device supports a grid or a bitmap |
| height | The height of the viewing area of the device |
| hover | Whether the device supports hovering a pointer over elements |
| inverted-colors | Whether the browser is capable of inverting colors |
| light-level | The current ambient light level |
| max-aspect-ratio | The maximum ratio between the width and height of the viewing area |
| max-color | The maximum number of bits of color supported by the viewing area |
| max-color-index | The maximum number of colors the device supports |
| max-device-aspect-ratio | The maximum ratio between the width and height of the device |
| max-device-height | The maximum height of the device |
| max-device-width | The maximum width of the device |
| max-height | The maximum height of the device viewing area |
| max-monochrome | The maximum number of bits in a monochrome setting |
| max-resolution | The maximum resolution of the device |

*(continued)*

**TABLE 4-4** *(continued)*

| Feature | Description |
|---|---|
| max-width | The maximum width of the device |
| min-aspect-ratio | The minimum ratio between the width and height of the viewing area |
| min-color | The minimum number of bits of color supported by the viewing area |
| min-color-index | The minimum number of colors the device supports |
| min-device-aspect-ratio | The minimum ratio between the width and height of the device |
| min-device-height | The minimum height of the device |
| min-device-width | The minimum width of the device |
| min-height | The minimum height of the device viewing area |
| min-monochrome | The minimum number of bits in a monochrome setting |
| min-resolution | The minimum resolution of the device |
| min-width | The minimum width of the device |
| monochrome | The number of bits of color in a monochrome setting |
| orientation | The orientation (landscape or portrait) of the device |
| overflow-block | How the device handles overflowing block elements |
| overflow-inline | How the device handles overflowing inline elements |
| pointer | Whether the device supports a pointing device |
| resolution | The resolution of the device |
| scan | Whether the device uses progressive or interlaced scanning |
| scripting | Whether the device supports client-side scripting languages |
| update-frequency | How quickly the device can update the viewing area |
| width | The width of the device viewing area |

Table 4-4 shows lots of different device features you can test to customize the styles you apply to your web page. An example looks like this:

```
@media screen and (max-width: 1000px) {
    font-size: 12px;
}
```

```
@media screen and (max-width: 500px) {
    font-size: 10px;
}
```

The first rule only applies to devices that have a maximum viewing area width of 100 pixels. It uses the 12-pixel font size for the text on the web page. The second rule only applies to devices that have a maximum viewing area of 500 pixels (such as a mobile device). It uses the 10-pixel font size for the text on the web page to make it smaller.

## Applying multiple style sheets

You can also use the media types and features queries in the <link> tag to reference specific external style sheets depending on the media features. This allows you to apply entirely different style sheets to the web page based on the device your site visitor is using to view it. Here's the format for doing that:

```
<link rel="stylesheet" href="desktop.css" media="screen and (max-width:500px)">
```

Now the browser will apply the desktop.css external style sheet only if the device has a maximum viewing area width of 500 pixels.

**TIP**

It's always a good idea to have separate style sheets for mobile devices for your web application. Usually, you'll need to change the layout of navigation buttons to make them easily accessible on the mobile device, as well as limit the content that you display in the web page.

Advanced CSS3

# Chapter **5**

# HTML5 and Multimedia

Multimedia has taken over the Internet. Thanks to the popularity of websites like YouTube, these days if your website doesn't support some type of multimedia content, your visitors will consider it old school and may pass it by. This chapter examines the multimedia features available in HTML5 and shows you how to implement images, audio, and video in your dynamic web applications.

## Working with Images

The most basic type of multimedia to put on a web page is a picture. The old saying "a picture is worth a thousand words" is somewhat true, especially in the web world. Placing images on your web page can help break up the monotony of plain text, as well as help add to your content in an attractive manner. Often, the first thing a new website visitor will notice are the images.

The HTML standard has always supported placing images within web pages, but there are a few new tricks that you can try using HTML5 and CSS3 to make your images stand out. This section shows just how to do that.

# Placing images

The *img element* allows you to place an image file on the web page. The img element uses a one-sided tag, ⟨img⟩, that uses attributes to define the image and how the browser should display it.

Here's the basic format for the ⟨img⟩ tag:

```
<img src="location" alt="text" width="x" height="y">
```

The src attribute defines the location of the image file to display. You can specify the location as a relative or absolute file path for images stored on the same server as the web page, or you can use a URL to reference images stored on another server.

The alt attribute defines alternative text that appears if the browser can't display the image, such as if the image file is missing if the browser doesn't support displaying images (such as a text-based browser), if your site visitor is using a screen reader, or if your website is being read by a search engine. For all your images, it's a good idea to provide a good description of not only the image, but also any action that occurs in the image. You do this in the alternative text attribute.

By default, the browser displays the image at full size in the browser window. That may not always be what you want, or you may just want more control over how or where the image appears. To help control that you use the width and height attributes to define a specific viewing area for the image to fit into.

Alternatively, instead of using the width and height attributes, you can use the style attribute and define the width and height as style properties:

```
<img src="myimage.jpg" alt="My image" style="width: x; height: y;">
```

Either method is allowed in HTML5, although using an inline style will help prevent accidental styling of the image from an external style sheet.

**WARNING**

Browsers are able to display most image types these days, but some image types are more suited for web pages than others. The JPEG image type is commonly used on web pages because it compresses the image to a smaller file size, making it quicker to download to the client browser. Using image files that are too large may ruin the experience for some of your website visitors, especially those who are using mobile data connections. No one likes having to wait for an image to load on a web page.

# Styling images

The CSS3 standard defines some additional styles that you can apply to the images on your web page to make them stand out even more. In Book 2, Chapter 4, I demonstrate how you can use the CSS3 shadow effect on elements to help give them a 3D effect. You can use that effect on images on the web page, too. That adds a nice touch to help make the image pop out from the web page.

Another handy style added by the CSS3 standard is the `transform` property. The `transform` property allows you to alter how an image appears on the web page, such as scale it, rotate it, or even skew it! There are functions for both 2D and 3D manipulation of the images. Table 5-1 lists the 2D transform effects that are available.

**TABLE 5-1**  ## The CSS3 2D Transform Effects

| Effect | Description |
| --- | --- |
| `matrix(a,b,c,d,e,f)` | Combines the translation, scale, skew, and rotation effects in one property |
| `rotate(angle)` | Rotates the object clockwise by the specified angle |
| `scale(x,y)` | Resizes the object by a factor of $x$ horizontally and $y$ vertically |
| `scaleX(x)` | Resizes the object horizontally only by a factor of $x$ |
| `scaleY(y)` | Resizes the object vertically only by a factor of $y$ |
| `skew(x,y)` | Offsets the object horizontally by an angle of $x$ and horizontally by an angle of $y$ |
| `skewX(x)` | Offsets the object horizontally only by an angle of $x$ |
| `skewY(y)` | Offsets the object vertically only by an angle of $y$ |
| `translate(x,y)` | Moves the object $x$ pixels to the right and $y$ pixels down |
| `translateX(x)` | Moves the object $x$ pixels to the right |
| `translateY(y)` | Moves the object $y$ pixels down |

The `rotate()` function is one of my favorites. Just by adding the `rotate()` function to a standard image, you can help make it stand out from the text content on the web page. You can try that out yourself by following these steps:

1. **Open your favorite text editor, program editor, or integrated development environment (IDE) package.**

**2.** In the editor window, type the following code:

```html
<!DOCTYPE html>
<html>
<head>
<title>Image Rotation Test</title>
<style>
    #img1 {
        float: left;
        transform: rotate(30deg);
        box-shadow: black 10px 5px 15px;
    }

    #img2 {
        float: left;
        transform: rotate(-30deg);
        box-shadow: black 10px 5px 15px;
    }
</style>
</head>
<body>
<h1>Testing the image rotation feature</h1>
<header>
<h1>My vacation photos</h1>
</header>
<section>
<img id="img1" src="image1.jpg" width="50" height="50">
<img id="img2" src="image2.jpg" width="50" height="50">
</section>
</body>
</html>
```

**3.** Save the file as `imagetest.html` in the DocumentRoot **folder for your web server.**

For XAMPP on Windows, that's c:\xampp\htdocs. For XAMPP on macOS, that's /Applications/XAMPP/htdocs.

**4.** Find two of your favorite image files and copy them to the same folder as the `imagetest.html` file.

You'll need to either rename them as image1.jpg and image2.jpg or change the code in the imagetest.html file to match your image filenames.

**5.** Start the web server if necessary.

## 6. Open a browser and go to the URL for the file.

If you're using the XAMPP server set to TCP port 8080, use the following:

```
http://localhost:8080/imagetest.html
```

## 7. Close the browser and shut down the web server.

The code in the `imagetest.html` file places two images on the web page. The first image is rotated by a negative value so that it rotates counterclockwise; the second image is rotated by a positive value so that it rotates clockwise. Figure 5-1 shows the results using my test image.

**FIGURE 5-1:**
Rotating images on the web page.

That's a great start to a professional-looking website!

# Linking images

You can also use images as links to other web pages or locations. You do that by embedding the `<img>` tag inside an anchor element:

```
<a href="childrens.html">
<img src="children.jpg" alt="Children's clothes"
style="width: 50px; height: 50px; border: 0px;">
</a>
```

If the website visitor clicks anywhere on the image, the browser responds just as if the anchor element was a hypertext link, redirecting the browser to the destination defined by the `href` attribute.

**TIP**

It's also a good idea to add the `border` style property to the anchor style element and set it to 0 pixels to prevent the browser from drawing an ugly border around the image to indicate that it's a link.

## Working with image maps

Linked images are nice, but how about those fancy map images that allow you to click in different parts of the map to go to different locations? You do that by using image maps. An *image map* allows you to define sections of an image that act just like a hyperlink. You can define each section to redirect the visitor's browser to a different location.

Creating an image map requires that you first define the map and then apply it to your image. To define the map, you use the *map element:*

```
<map name="mapname">
    map area definitions
</map>
```

The `name` attribute is important, because you'll use that to reference the map from the image `<img>` tag in the `usemap` attribute:

```
<img src="location" usemap="#mapname">
```

After you define the map, you need to define one or more map areas. Each map area defines a specific location on the image to create a *hotspot* (clickable region). You define the map areas using the `<area>` tag:

```
<area shape="shape" cords="coordinates" href="location" alt="text">
```

The combination of the shape and coordinates defines the area in the image for the hotspot. Table 5-2 shows how to match those up.

**TABLE 5-2**    **Defining the Area Element Hotspots**

| Shape Value | Description |
| --- | --- |
| circle | Defines the *x* and *y* location of the circle center, as well as the radius value |
| poly | Defines multiple *x* and *y* locations for each point of the polygon |
| rect | Defines the *x* and *y* coordinates for the upper-left corner and the lower-right corner |
| default | No coordinates necessary; uses the remaining unmapped area of the image |

Defining an image map can be somewhat difficult. You'll need to know the exact size of the image on the web page and be able to define the exact location for each area hotspot. This is where a good image manipulation tool such as Photoshop or GIMP can come in handy. Anything that allows you to count pixels in the image will help you plot out the hotspots.

Here's an example of defining an image map for an image:

```
<map name="storemap">
<area shape="rect" coords="0, 0, 100, 500" href="books.html" alt="shop our
    books">
<area shape="rect" coords="101, 0, 200, 500" href="furniture.html" alt="shop our
    furniture">
<area shape="rect" coords="201, 0, 300, 500" href="clothes.html" alt="shop our
    clothes">
<area shape="rect" coords="301, 0, 400, 500" href="tools.html" alt="shop our
    selection of tools">
<area shape="rect" coords="401, 0, 500, 500" href="food.html" alt="shop for some
    groceries">
</map>
```

After you define the image map, you associate it to an image by adding the usemap attribute to the `<img>` tag:

```
<img src="store.html" alt="our store" usemap="#storemap">
```

The `#storemap` value references the `storemap name` attribute, so the browser applies that image map to the image on the web page. Clicking each individual section takes you to the associated `href` location defined for that area.

# Using HTML5 image additions

Besides the standard HTML image features, HTML5 adds a couple of new image features that you can use in your web pages.

## Figures and captions

It's common to want to place captions around images that you display on the web page. You can do that with standard HTML and CSS, but it takes some calculating to get the positioning correct, and if anything on the web page moves, the image and caption may get out of sync.

HTML5 adds the *figure element* to match images and captions together. The figure element encloses the image, along with a figcaption element, creating a single object that you can position and move around on the web page. Here's the general format for all that:

```
<figure>
<img src="image.jpg" alt="Figure 1">
<figcaption>Figure 1: Creating a web page</figcaption>
</figure>
```

You can now add styles for the figure element to position both the image and its associated caption on the web page together as a single object. In this example, the caption will appear under the image. If you prefer, you can place the `<figcaption>` tag above the image, too, by just listing it before the `<img>` tag.

**TIP**

You can use the figure element to link other objects with captions, too. For example, use the p element instead of the img element for embedding quotes inside a text section and linking them to the citation for the quote in the figcaption element.

## The picture element

The `<img>` tag, along with the transform CSS property, allows you to scale images to fit a specific area on the web page:

```
img {
    transform: scale(80,60);
}
```

This solution doesn't always produce the best-quality image for the device. With website visitors using a multitude of different devices, each with a different aspect ratio and screen size, it's hard to get one image to work in all situations.

The HTML5 standard has a solution for that problem. Instead of trying to scale one image to fit everywhere, you can define multiple versions of an image to display for different environments. You just need to define the environment parameters for the browser to test to know which image to display. You do that using the *picture element*.

The HTML5 picture element allows you to define one or more sources for the image, along with defining media rules to determine when each source should be used. I cover media rules in Book 2, Chapter 4, where I discuss how to use media rules to load different style sheets based on different properties of the website visitor's device. This is the same concept.

The picture element uses the `<picture>` tag, along with one or more source elements. Each source element defines a media rule and the image to use if the device meets the media rule criteria. The format for all that looks like this:

```
<picture>
<source media="(min-width: 1000px)" srcset="large.jpg">
<source media="(min-width: 500px)" srcset="small.jpg">
<img src="original.jpg" alt="My image">
</picture>
```

When the browser sees the picture element, it evaluates each of the source elements inside, from the first to the last. The first source element that matches the media environment is used to display the image defined in the `srcset` attribute. If none of the media tests defined in the source elements passes, the browser uses the image defined in the `<img>` tag.

# Playing Audio

The original HTML standard didn't account for playing audio clips in web pages. That created a free-for-all of methods developed to incorporate audio. Many different solutions were created along the way.

One such solution is to reference an audio file stored on the server using a standard anchor element:

```
<a href="myaudio.mp3">Click to play</a>
```

When the site visitor clicks the hypertext link, the browser downloads the audio file and opens an appropriate audio player from the workstation to play it. That's a pretty clunky way of trying to incorporate audio into a web page.

The following sections discuss better ways of playing audio files in your web pages.

## Embedded audio

The next step in the evolution of playing audio in web pages was the plugin. A *plugin* is a separate program that runs inside the browser to support additional features. Over the years, several different audio plugins had been developed, but the three most common were

>> **QuickTime:** A plugin developed by Apple, used mainly in the Safari web browser.

>> **RealAudio:** A vendor-neutral attempt to create an audio plugin. It only supports its own proprietary audio file format.

>> **Flash:** Developed by Adobe, Flash became a popular format for playing both audio and video files in browsers.

To play an audio file using a plugin, you had to use the *embed element*, which signals to the browser that some type of external file is embedded inside the web page and to find the appropriate plugin to handle the embedded file. The embed element uses the one-sided `<embed>` tag, with the following format:

```
<embed src="location" type="mime" width=x height=y>
```

The `src` attribute defines the location of the audio file, either as an absolute or relative path on the local server, or as a URL to point to an audio file stored on a remote server.

The `width` and `height` attributes are used if the plugin requires space on the web page to display an interface. Some audio plugins provide an interface to stop, start, and pause playing the audio file.

The `type` attribute defines the type of multimedia file. It uses the standard *Multimedia Internet Mail Extension* (MIME) type names to identify the audio file type. As the name suggests, MIME types were originally developed for sending binary files through email, but they're also used by web browsers for embedded binary files in web pages. The browser uses the MIME type to determine just what plugin to use to process the embedded file. Different audio file formats (such as QuickTime or RealAudio) require a different plugin to play. This is where it helps to know the different formats available for digital audio files.

## Digital audio formats

Since the transition from vinyl records to the digital world, many different methods had been used for converting analog sound to digital media. The process of converting sound to digital signals consists of three elements:

>> **Sampling rate:** How often the sound amplitude is measured and quantified to a digital value

>> **Sample resolution:** How many bits of data are used for each sample digital value

>> **Compression:** How the final digital data is compressed to make an audio file

The combination of the sampling rate and sample resolution result in the *bit rate* used for the digital recording. The larger the bit rate, the more accurately the digital playback will produce the original analog signal. However, the larger the bit rate, the more digital data that is generated and, thus, required to store the audio file.

A standard CD format for digital audio uses a bit rate of 1411 Kbps, which results in an extremely accurate reproduction, but also an extremely large file size (around 10MB) for each audio track. It's impractical to send a standard CD audio track across the Internet to play on client browsers.

This is where compression comes into play. Because the original audio files are too large to use on the web, we need to incorporate some type of compression scheme to make them more manageable. Unfortunately, over the years, many different companies have developed proprietary compression techniques, resulting in our current myriad of different audio file types. Table 5-3 lists the more common audio file types in use, along with their file extensions and MIME types.

**TABLE 5-3**  ## Audio File and MIME Types

| Audio | File | MIME | Description |
|---|---|---|---|
| AAC | .aac | audio/aac | Apple audio coding |
| AU | .au | audio/basic | Sun Microsystems standard for Unix systems |
| MIDI | .mid | audio/mid | Musical Instrument Digital Interface standard for recording instruments |
| MP3 | .mp3 | audio/mpeg | Motion Picture Experts Group standard |
| Ogg Vorbis | .ogg | audio/ogg | Open-source standard |
| RealAudio | .ra | audio/x-pn-realaudio | Real Media standard for streaming audio |
| SND | .snd | audio/basic | SouND format, developed by Apple based on the AU audio format |
| Shockwave Flash | .swf | audio/x-shockwave-flash | Adobe proprietary format |
| WAV | .wav | audio/wav | Waveform Audio format developed by Microsoft for uncompressed audio |

Each of these audio file formats has its own pros and cons to deal with. Different audiophiles have different opinions on which method is the best. To make matters more complicated, many of these audio file formats are proprietary and require a license to embed a player in a browser. The MP3 audio type has become the de facto standard over the years due to its high compression rate and high audio quality, but many developers don't like using MP3 because of its proprietary nature.

The Ogg Vorbis audio type is an open-source standard, free to use in any environment. However, it hasn't been widely adopted by all browsers yet (including Internet Explorer and Safari) due to its perceived lack of audio quality compared to other compression methods.

**TIP**

At the time of this writing, the only audio file type supported by all the major browsers is MP3. However, if your site visitor is using a Linux workstation, due to licensing restrictions, the MP3 codecs are often not loaded by default on all Linux distributions.

If you embed an audio file into your web page and a visitor doesn't have the appropriate plugin to handle it, the browser will react in one of three ways:

» Display an error message in place of the embedded audio file

» Display a pop-up message indicating the plugin required to play the audio file

» Redirect the web page to the web page for the required plugin

All three of these results are less than optimal for your web page. Fortunately, the HTML5 standard has produced a better way to incorporate sounds into web pages.

## Audio the HTML5 way

The key to embedding audio files into your web pages is similar to how you handle displaying images — it's best to have multiple versions available and let each site visitor's browser decide which one to use. The HTML5 standard provides a way for you to do that with the *audio element.*

The audio element works just like the picture element (see the "Using HTML5 image additions" section, earlier in this chapter). You use the ‹audio› tag to open a list of audio sources, defined using the ‹source› tag. Each source specifies a different audio file format for the browser to try. The first one in the list that the browser supports is what gets requested and played by the browser. That looks like this:

```
<audio>
<source src="myaudio.mp3" type="audio/ogg">
<source src="myaudio.ogg" type="audio/mpeg">
<source src="myaudio.wav" type="audio/wav">
</audio>
```

For the source elements, you use the `src` attribute to indicate the location of the audio file to play, as well as the `type` attribute to indicate the MIME type of the audio file. It's up to the browser to decide which one to use. In this example, the browser attempts to play the MP3 version first. Then for Linux workstations where that's not available, it automatically attempts to load and play the Ogg Vorbis version. If that's not available, it'll try to use the WAV version of the audio file.

**WARNING**

The HTML5 standard only supports the MP3, Ogg Vorbis, and WAV audio file types. Don't try to use the audio element to embed a QuickTime or RealAudio audio file. You'll need to use the embed element to do that.

You can also place a short message after the `<source>` tag list for the browser to display if it can't support any of the listed MIME types:

```
<audio>
<source src="myaudio.mp3" type="audio/ogg" controls>
<source src="myaudio.ogg" type="audio/mpeg" controls>
Sorry, your browser doesn't support MP3 or OGG audio
</audio>
```

The `<audio>` tag has a few attributes to help alter how the browser handles the audio file. Table 5-4 shows the available attributes.

**TABLE 5-4**    ## The <audio> Tag Attributes

| Attribute | Description |
|---|---|
| autoplay | The browser should start playing the file as soon as the web page loads. |
| controls | The browser should display a standard set of audio controls, such as Play, Stop, and Pause buttons. |
| loop | The browser should continually loop the audio file. |
| muted | The browser should mute the audio track immediately. |
| preload | Specifies whether the audio file should be loaded when the page loads or when the Play button is clicked. |
| src | Specifies the URL of an audio file when not using additional `<source>` tags. |

The `controls` attribute is recommended, because it provides an interface for the website visitor to have control over how or when the audio file plays. Each browser has its own way of displaying audio controls. Figure 5-2 shows how the controls appear in the Internet Explorer browser.

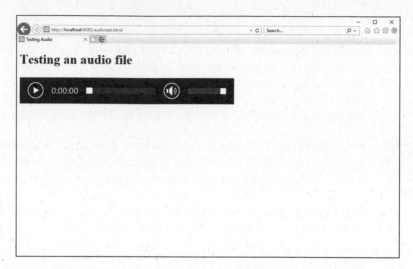

**FIGURE 5-2:**
The audio
controls in the
Internet Explorer
browser.

The audio controls shown by browser are fairly simplistic — a Play/Pause button, a Mute button, a slider to control the location in the audio file, and a sound level slider. Don't expect any fancy EQ settings to bump up the bass in your tunes!

**WARNING**

In the past, it was somewhat commonplace to embed an audio file in a web page and set it to automatically play with the loop feature enabled. This is a surefire way to annoy your site visitors, and it may even cause issues for visitors who use a screen reader to process your web page. I don't recommend using this method. Allow your site visitors the option of whether to play the audio embedded on your web pages.

# Watching Videos

These days, the world is full of video content. You can find videos on just about every topic under the sun, including how to make your own videos! This section walks through how you can embed videos in your web pages, but first, a quick look at the different types of video files you may have to deal with.

## Paying attention to video quality

Just like in the world of film, videos are composed of a series of individual images (called *frames*) played at a set rate of speed (called the *frame rate*). The higher the frame quality, the better the video quality. The higher the frame rate, usually the better the video quality (with exceptions, as noted in this section).

You can use any frame size for the video images, but there are standard frame sizes that are commonly used:

>> **160 x 120:** Low-quality video using the 3:4 aspect ratio

>> **320 x 240:** Higher-quality video, but still using the 3:4 aspect ratio

>> **640 x 480:** Highest-quality video using the 3:4 aspect ratio

>> **1280 x 720:** High-definition (HD) video using the 16:9 aspect ratio

>> **1920 x 1080:** HD-quality video using the 16:9 aspect ratio

As you can guess, a higher quality of frame images means a larger video file.

The frame rate used for television video is 60 frames per second (fps). That frame rate would create a huge video file. DVD-quality videos use 24fps as a compromise between video quality and file size.

A fast frame rate isn't necessarily a good thing with web video. As the video is sent from the server to the client browser, the network gets in the way. Usually, to help with a smooth playback, most browsers use a buffer to hold video data as it downloads. When the buffer area is filled enough that the browser feels it can play the video at the designated frame rate and keep up with the download, it plays the video.

However, if the download slows down and the buffer starts to catch up with the real-time data, video playback will appear choppy and reduce the viewing experience of your site visitors. This is why a high frame rate doesn't necessarily equate to a better video quality.

## Looking at digital video formats

Just as with audio files, many different companies have devised different methods of compressing videos for storage and playback. Unfortunately, this has resulted in a hodge-podge of different video formats that we have to work with. Table 5-5 lists the more popular video formats you'll most likely run into.

Just as with the audio files, each video file format has its own pros and cons, making it difficult to decide which one to use. Although the WebM video standard was developed by a consortium of browser developers, it's actually one of the lesser-used standards.

**TABLE 5-5**     **Common Video Formats**

| Format | File | MIME | Description |
|---|---|---|---|
| AVI | .avi | video/x-msvideo | Audio Video Interleave. Developed by Microsoft. |
| Flash | .flv | video/x-flv | Adobe Flash video. |
| MPEG | .mpg | video/mpg | The original Motion Pictures Expert Group standard for digital video. |
| MPEG-4 | .mp4 | video/mp4 | Updated MPEG standard, currently in use. |
| Ogg Theora | .ogg | video/ogg | Open-source video standard. |
| QuickTime | .mov | video/quicktime | Developed by Apple. |
| RealVideo | .rm | video/x-pn-realvideo | Developed by Real Media for video streaming. |
| WebM | .webm | video/webm | Developed by browser developers as a common video format. |
| WMV | .wmv | video/x-ms-wmv | Microsoft standard video format. |

## Putting videos in your web page

With the original version of HTML there was no standard way of embedding video content in your web pages. Proprietary methods became popular, and the Adobe Flash plugin became the de facto standard in web video.

However, HTML5 has changed that, by including a way to embed videos into your web pages without requiring the use of a separate plugin. The new *video element* is what does that.

As you can probably guess, the video element works the same way as the audio element does. It allows you to provide a list of source elements that define different videos using different MIME types. The basic format for that looks like this:

```
<video>
<source src="mymovie.mp4" type="video/mp4">
<source src="mymovie.ogg" type="video/ogg">
Sorry, your browser is unable to play the video
</video>
```

The browser attempts to play the first listed video, and if that fails, it tries the second listed video. Then if that fails, the browser will display the text specified.

**WARNING**

The HTML5 standard only defines support for the MP4, Ogg, and WebM video formats. If you need to play another video format you can try to use the embed element.

The `<video>` tag supports some attributes that allow you to control the viewing experience for your site visitors. Table 5-6 shows what attributes are available.

**TABLE 5-6**     **The &lt;video&gt; Tag Attributes**

| Attribute | Description |
|---|---|
| autoplay | Starts the video as soon as the web page loads |
| controls | Displays a set of icons for controlling the video (such as Play, Stop, and Pause) |
| height | Sets the height of the video display area in the web page |
| loop | Specifies that the browser should continually loop through the video |
| muted | Starts the video with muted audio |
| poster | Specifies an image URL to show while the video is downloading |
| preload | Loads the video when the web page loads instead of when the Play button is clicked |
| src | Specifies the location of the video file |
| width | Specifies the width of the video display area in the web page |

For videos, it's imperative that you specify the `height` and `width` attributes to maintain control of how the video appears in the web page. The browser will limit the video to display within the area you specify. Figure 5-3 shows playing a video with controls in the Internet Explorer web browser.

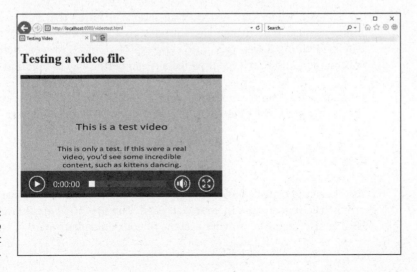

**FIGURE 5-3:** Playing a video in the Internet Explorer browser.

The video viewer in Internet Explorer provides a Play/Pause button, a status indicator showing the current position in the video file, a Mute button that also displays a volume control when you click it, and a button that allows you to switch to viewing the video in full-screen mode.

**WARNING**

The same warning that I gave you about automatically playing audio files applies to video files. Never assume that your site visitors will want to view the video as soon as the web page loads, even if you include the muted attribute. Playing videos takes a lot of processor power from the workstation; for site visitors using less powerful devices, that may cause issues.

# Getting Help from Streamers

Trying to provide your own videos in the correct format to display correctly in all browsers can be somewhat of a challenge. Sometimes it's best to cry "uncle," and let the professionals handle it. By "professionals," I mean the myriad of commercially available video-streaming services, such as YouTube, Vimeo, and LiveStream. Most of these services allow you to register for free trials, and some even allow you to host small videos for free in your own channel.

The beauty of using a streaming service is that usually you only need to upload your video in one format; then the streaming service takes care of reformatting the video to match other video formats or quality required by your website visitors. No more having to reformat videos yourself and worrying about how they'll appear in different browsers, at different bandwidth speeds.

To embed a video from a streaming service requires that you use the old HTML *iframe element.* The iframe element was popular in the early days of HTML as a way of dividing a web page into separate sections. However, the iframe method was clunky, and soon CSS provided a much better way of dividing web pages.

However, the iframe element has had something of a comeback as a container for displaying streaming videos. The format uses the two-sided `<iframe>` tag:

```
<iframe width=x height=y src="location">
</iframe>
```

As you would expect, the width and height attributes are necessary to control the size of the iframe area in your web page. The src attribute points to the custom URL your streaming provider assigns to your uploaded video.

# JavaScript

# Contents at a Glance

**CHAPTER 1: Introducing JavaScript** . . . . . . . . . . . . . . . . . . . . . . . . . . . . 197

Knowing Why You Should Use JavaScript . . . . . . . . . . . . . . . . . . . 197

Seeing Where to Put Your JavaScript Code . . . . . . . . . . . . . . . . . . 199

The Basics of JavaScript . . . . . . . . . . . . . . . . . . . . . . . . . . . . . . . . . 203

Controlling Program Flow . . . . . . . . . . . . . . . . . . . . . . . . . . . . . . . 209

Working with Functions . . . . . . . . . . . . . . . . . . . . . . . . . . . . . . . . . 220

**CHAPTER 2: Advanced JavaScript Coding** . . . . . . . . . . . . . . . . . . . . . . . 223

Understanding the Document Object Model . . . . . . . . . . . . . . . . 223

Finding Your Elements . . . . . . . . . . . . . . . . . . . . . . . . . . . . . . . . . . 233

Working with Document Object Model Form Data . . . . . . . . . . . 238

**CHAPTER 3: Using jQuery** . . . . . . . . . . . . . . . . . . . . . . . . . . . . . . . . . . . . 243

Loading the jQuery Library . . . . . . . . . . . . . . . . . . . . . . . . . . . . . . 244

Using jQuery Functions. . . . . . . . . . . . . . . . . . . . . . . . . . . . . . . . . . 246

Finding Elements. . . . . . . . . . . . . . . . . . . . . . . . . . . . . . . . . . . . . . . 247

Replacing Data. . . . . . . . . . . . . . . . . . . . . . . . . . . . . . . . . . . . . . . . . 250

Changing Styles . . . . . . . . . . . . . . . . . . . . . . . . . . . . . . . . . . . . . . . . 254

Changing the Document Object Model . . . . . . . . . . . . . . . . . . . . . 259

Playing with Animation. . . . . . . . . . . . . . . . . . . . . . . . . . . . . . . . . . 261

**CHAPTER 4: Reacting to Events with JavaScript and jQuery** . . . . . . . . . . . . . . . . . . . . . . . . . . . . . . . . . . . . . . . . 263

Understanding Events . . . . . . . . . . . . . . . . . . . . . . . . . . . . . . . . . . 263

Focusing on JavaScript and Events . . . . . . . . . . . . . . . . . . . . . . . . 267

Looking at jQuery and Events . . . . . . . . . . . . . . . . . . . . . . . . . . . . 276

**CHAPTER 5: Troubleshooting JavaScript Programs** . . . . . . . . . . . 283

Identifying Errors. . . . . . . . . . . . . . . . . . . . . . . . . . . . . . . . . . . . . . . 283

Working with Browser Developer Tools. . . . . . . . . . . . . . . . . . . . . 285

Working Around Errors. . . . . . . . . . . . . . . . . . . . . . . . . . . . . . . . . . 295

IN THIS CHAPTER

» **Defining JavaScript**

» **Adding JavaScript to your web pages**

» **Working with data**

» **Looking at JavaScript control structures**

» **Creating JavaScript functions**

# Chapter **1**

# Introducing JavaScript

The previous minibook shows you how to use HTML5 and CSS3 to create some pretty fancy-looking web pages. That's the first step to creating your dynamic web applications, but there are a few more parts to add. This minibook tackles the next piece you'll need to add to your web programs: client-side programming.

This chapter focuses on the JavaScript programming language, the most popular client-side programming language in use today. First, I cover the basics of how to add JavaScript code to your web pages. Then I explore some of the basics of the JavaScript language.

## Knowing Why You Should Use JavaScript

HTML5 and CSS3 work together to create web pages. The HTML5 code produces the content that appears on the web page, and the CSS3 code helps style it to change the format and location of the web page elements. So, what exactly does JavaScript do to help augment those languages?

JavaScript is program code that you embed into the HTML5 code. The web server sends the JavaScript program code to your site visitors' web browsers, which in turn detect and run the JavaScript code. The JavaScript code can alter features of the web page that the HTML5 and CSS3 code produce. This section explains what you can do with JavaScript code.

## Changing web page content

In your HTML5 code, you no doubt will have lots of text that appears in separate sections of your web page. For example, you may have a sidebar element that lists the day's news events related to your website topic, or you may have a header element that displays the current time and temperature for your city.

All that is great, but you need a way for that information to change dynamically, each time your site visitors load the web page. This is where JavaScript comes in.

JavaScript code allows you to alter the text that appears on your web page "on the fly," without requiring your site visitors to reload the web page. You can create JavaScript code that retrieves updated news articles even as your site visitors are viewing your web pages. The information will change right before their eyes — like magic!

## Changing web page styles

Book 2, Chapter 2, explains how you add CSS3 styles to your web pages to apply styles to text and elements, or to place elements in specific locations on the web page. The CSS3 code you create is placed inline in the HTML5 elements, internally in the head element of the web page, or as an external style sheet.

JavaScript code allows you to dynamically alter any style or position that you define for an HTML5 element in your CSS3 code. That's right — you can use JavaScript to turn blue backgrounds yellow, orange text green, or even move an entire section of text from one side of the web page to another! That's a lot of control to have at your fingertips.

One of the coolest features of JavaScript is the ability to dynamically make HTML5 elements appear out of nowhere! Each HTML5 element supports the `display` style property, which you use to determine how or if the element appears on the web page.

With JavaScript code you can dynamically alter the `display` style property for any element on the web page to make it appear as needed or disappear when not needed. That gives you the ability to dramatically alter the layout of a web page at any time while your site visitor is interacting with the web page. This helps hide sections that may be distracting to site visitors at times, then make them appear when the site visitor needs to interact with them.

# Seeing Where to Put Your JavaScript Code

Now that I've sold you on the benefits of using JavaScript code in your web pages, let's take a look at how you include JavaScript code in your HTML5 code. There are two ways of including JavaScript code in web pages:

» Embedding the JavaScript code directly into the HTML5 code for the web page

» Creating an external JavaScript file that the browser downloads and runs

This section walks through how to use both methods of working with JavaScript code in your HTML5 code.

## Embedding JavaScript

You embed JavaScript code directly into the HTML5 code for your web pages by using the *script element.* The script element is a two-sided element, so it has an opening and closing tag that surrounds your JavaScript code:

```
<script>
    JavaScript code
</script>
```

The script element informs the browser that there's code to run as part of the web page. Most browsers will recognize the JavaScript code that appears in the script element and run the code using an internal JavaScript interpreter. However, some programmers like to identify the type of code embedded in the script element using the type attribute:

```
<script type="text/javascript">
```

This isn't required in HTML5, but you're more than welcome to use this format if it helps you to remember that the embedded code is JavaScript. This can be especially helpful when you start embedding server-side programming languages, such as PHP, in your HTML5 code as well.

**TIP**

You can place script elements anywhere in the HTML5 code. The browser will process the JavaScript code as it parses the HTML5 code for the web page. However, that affects how the JavaScript code runs and how any output generated by the JavaScript code appears. The following sections demonstrate this.

## Embedding in the head element

If you place the script element inside the head element of the web page, the browser will run the JavaScript code before it processes the code to build the web page. Follow these steps to see how this works:

1. **Open your favorite text editor, program editor, or integrated development environment (IDE) package.**

2. **Enter the following code:**

```
<!DOCTYPE html>
<html>
<head>
<title>Testing JavaScript in the Head Section</title>
<script>
alert("This is the JavaScript program!");
</script>
</head>
<body>
<h1>This is the web page</h1>
</body>
<html>
```

3. **Save the code as** scriptheadtest.html **in the** DocumentRoot **folder for your web server.**

   That's c:\xampp\htdocs for XAMPP on Windows or /Applications/XAMPP/ htdocs for XAMPP on macOS.

4. **Start the XAMPP Control Panel and start the Apache web server.**

5. **Open your browser and enter the following URL:**

```
http://localhost:8080/scriptheadtest.html
```

   You may have to alter the TCP port to match your web server setup.

6. **Stop the Apache web server and exit from the XAMPP Control Panel.**

The scriptheadtest.html code embeds a script element inside the head element of the web page. Because this appears before the body section of the web page code, the browser processes the JavaScript code before the body element section. The script element contains a single line of JavaScript code:

```
alert("This is the JavaScript program!");
```

The alert() function displays text in a pop-up dialog box, separate from the main web page window of the browser.

When you run the program, you should see the alert dialog box pop-up, but no text appears on the web page, as shown in Figure 1-1. That's because the alert() function stops the browser from processing any more code until the site visitor clicks the OK button in the dialog box. The code is frozen in time, waiting for the browser to continue processing the rest of the code.

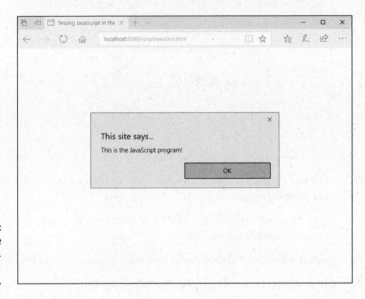

**FIGURE 1-1:** Testing the `script headtest.html` program file.

**WARNING**

When you run the test, your browser may not run the JavaScript code or it may prompt you to allow the code to run. Some browsers have built-in security features to block running JavaScript code embedded in a web page. You'll need to consult your browser documentation on how to enable JavaScript code, at least from the localhost address, so your test programs can run.

## Embedding in the body element

Alternatively, you can place the script element inside the body element section of the web page. When you do this, the browser runs the JavaScript code when it gets to the script element as it parses the HTML5 code to build the web page.

Follow these steps to test this out:

1. **Open your favorite text editor, program editor, or IDE package.**

2. **Enter the following code:**

```
<!DOCTYPE html>
<html>
<head>
<title>Testing JavaScript in the Body Section</title>
</head>
<body>
<h1>This is the web page</h1>
<script>
alert("This is the JavaScript program!");
</script>
<h1>This is the end of the web page</h1>
</body>
<html>
```

3. **Save the code as** `scriptbodytest.html` **in the** `DocumentRoot` **folder for your web server.**

   That's `c:\xampp\htdocs` for XAMPP on Windows or `/Applications/XAMPP/htdocs` for XAMPP on macOS.

4. **Start the XAMPP Control Panel and start the Apache web server.**

5. **Open your browser and enter the following URL:**

```
http://localhost:8080/scriptbodytest.html
```

   You may have to alter the TCP port to match your web server setup.

6. **Stop the Apache web server and exit from the XAMPP Control Panel.**

When you run the test, you should see the content from the first h1 element appear on the web page, and the `alert()` function dialog box, but not the content from the second h1 element. Figure 1-2 shows that result.

The browser processes the first h1 element in the body section and then stops to run the JavaScript `alert()` function. After you click the OK button in the alert dialog box, the browser displays the section h1 element content.

 Embedding JavaScript code inside the body element of a web page can slow down how the web page loads. If the code location is not crucial, it's best to place the script element at the end of the body element, after the normal HTML5 code.

TIP

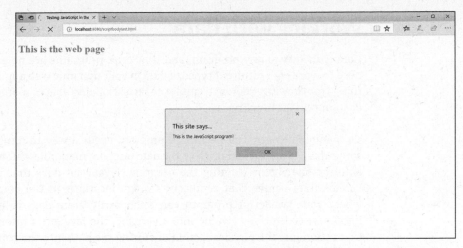

**FIGURE 1-2:**
Running JavaScript code in the body section.

## Using external JavaScript files

If you have JavaScript code that you need to embed in all of your web pages, having to retype the same code in each web page file can become tedious. And on top of that, if you need to change anything in the code, you have to revisit every single web page file that uses the code!

To solve that problem, you can use an external JavaScript file. The `<script>` opening tag supports the `src` attribute, which allows you to define an external location for the JavaScript code:

```
<script src="myjavascript.js"></script>
```

The `src` attribute can point to an absolute or relative file path on the local server, or you can use a full URL to point to a JavaScript file stored on a remote server. Note that although it's not mandatory, it's very common to use the `.js` file extension to identify JavaScript files.

**WARNING**

You place the JavaScript code inside the external file just as it would appear within the script element. Be careful though — don't include the `<script>` and `</script>` tags in the external JavaScript file.

# The Basics of JavaScript

Now that you've seen where to put your JavaScript code in your web pages, you can dive into coding using JavaScript. This section goes through the basics for getting started with JavaScript coding.

# Working with data

Data is the key to any program, and JavaScript programs are no exception. You'll need to work with different types of data in your dynamic web applications, everything from bowling scores to employee records. Being able to manipulate that data is an important function.

To manipulate data, the JavaScript program needs a way to temporarily store it somewhere so that it can retrieve the data later on, manipulate it, and then display it to the site visitor running the program. JavaScript does that using variables. *Variables* are names that represent storage locations in the computer memory where your JavaScript program can temporarily store data values. When your JavaScript code places a value into a variable, the JavaScript interpreter converts that action into the physical action of storing the data into the computer memory for future use.

**WARNING**

The downside to using variables to store data is that they only retain their values for the duration of the program. You can't save a data value to a variable in one web page and then retrieve it in another web page. After your site visitor leaves the web page, those values (and their data values) are gone forever. That's why we need some help from our MySQL database server — to have a place for storing data long term!

For all the JavaScript variables that you use in your programs, you must assign each one a unique name to represent the different memory locations. There are a few rules you'll need to remember when creating JavaScript variable names:

>> Variable names can contain letters, numbers, underscores, and dollar signs.

>> Variable names must begin with a letter, an underscore, or a dollar sign.

>> Variable names are case sensitive.

>> You can't use JavaScript keywords as variable names.

Before you can use a variable in your JavaScript code, you must first declare it as a variable using the var statement:

```
var test;
```

This format tells the JavaScript interpreter to set aside a place in memory for storing data and call that location test. For now, you haven't assigned a specific value to the test variable, so it contains what's called an *undefined value*.

You can then use the JavaScript *assignment operator* to assign a value to the variable:

```
test = 10;
```

If you prefer, you can both declare a variable and assign it a value in one statement:

```
var test = 10;
```

When you need to reference the value you stored in the variable later on in the program code, you just refer to it using the variable name:

```
alert(test);
```

The JavaScript interpreter retrieves the value stored in the location the variable represents and uses it just as if you had entered the value in the statement.

# Data types

JavaScript variables can hold different types of data. The two basic data types are

>> **Numbers:** Either integer values (such as 5) or floating point values (such as 3.1419)

>> **Strings:** A series of characters, strung together in memory one after the other (thus the term *strings*)

Declaring a number value is somewhat straightforward:

```
var age = 20;
```

This statement places the numeric value of 20 into the memory location pointed to by the age variable.

Declaring a string value is a little bit trickier:

```
var name = "Rich Blum";
```

You must enclose the string value in quotes. That delineates the start and end of the string value. If you forget the quotes, you'll get a JavaScript error message.

One interesting feature of JavaScript is that it uses *dynamic data typing*. With dynamic data typing, you don't need to tell JavaScript what type of data a variable contains ahead of time, like some other programming languages require. Instead, JavaScript will automatically try to figure out the type of data from the values you use.

With dynamic data typing, you can also use the same variable name to hold different data types at different times. For example, after declaring the age variable with a number, later in the program you could then do the following:

```
age = "really old";
```

JavaScript won't complain that you started out storing a number in the age variable and then shifted to storing a string value, it just happily changes the value stored in that variable.

**WARNING**

Although dynamic data types can come in handy, they can also cause problems if you're not careful. If you try to perform a mathematical operation on a variable that contains a string value, you won't get what you might have been expecting. Always keep track of what type of data you're storing in variables in your programs.

## Arrays of data

JavaScript allows you to store multiple values in a single variable. These variables are called *arrays*.

If you have an application that contains a list of items, it can often be somewhat clunky to specify each item as a separate variable:

```
var score1 = 100;
var score2 = 110;
var score3 = 105;
```

If you need to perform any type of operation on the variables, you need to know exactly how many variables are used to contain the list of items.

Arrays allow us to store an entire list of items into a single variable:

```
var scores = [100, 110, 105];
```

The scores array variable contains three items (called *elements*). You reference an individual element value by using an *index* value. You specify the index using brackets with the array variable:

```
scores[0]
```

This array variable contains the first element of the array (the value 100 in this example). Note that the first element of the array is at index 0, a very unfortunate fact that's important to remember when working with arrays in JavaScript!

You can change an individual array element value using the index in a standard assign statement:

```
scores[1] = 120;
```

This replaces the 110 value in the array with a value of 120.

JavaScript treats arrays as *objects.* An object has properties, as well as methods that you can run against the object. Properties return features for the array, such as the `length` property:

```
var games = scores.length
```

Methods are used to manipulate the values within the object:

```
scores.sort();
```

You can add new values to an existing array by using the `push()` method:

```
scores.push(115);
```

This allows you to dynamically store and retrieve data values from a single variable location in your program, without having to know exactly how many data values it will need to retain.

## Operators

JavaScript provides different *operators* for working with data. An operator performs some type of manipulation of the data provided. Table 1-1 shows the basic math operators that JavaScript uses.

**TABLE 1-1**    ### JavaScript Math Operators

| Operator | Description |
| --- | --- |
| + | Addition |
| – | Subtraction |
| * | Multiplication |
| / | Division |
| % | Modulus (the remainder of a division operation) |
| ++ | Increment (increases the value by 1) |
| –– | Decrement (decreases the value by 1) |

You use the math operators as part of an assignment statement:

```
result = 10 + 5;
```

The JavaScript interpreter performs the operation on the right side of the equal sign and then assigns the result to the variable declared on the left side. You can use variables with the operators as well:

```
var side1 = 10;
var side2 = 5;
var area = side1 * side2;
```

Again, JavaScript performs the operation on the right side of the assignment operator first and then assigns the result to the variable declared on the left side. In this example, JavaScript retrieves the value stored in both the side1 and side2 variables, performs the multiplication, and then stores the result in the area variable.

Don't think of the assignment as a mathematical equation. You can have an assignment statement that looks like this:

```
counter = counter + 1;
```

As a mathematical equation, this is impossible — you can't have a value equal to itself plus 1. What's happening here is that the interpreter adds 1 to the value stored in the counter variable and then stores the result back into the counter variable memory location.

**TIP**

JavaScript also provides the incrementor operator, ++. This adds 1 to the variable without all the extra text: counter++;.

Besides the math operators, JavaScript also supports logical Boolean operators, as shown in Table 1-2.

**TABLE 1-2**

## JavaScript Boolean Operators

| Operator | Description |
|----------|-------------|
| && | logical AND |
| \|\| | logical OR |
| ! | logical NOT |

Boolean operators are most commonly used in condition tests in control statements, as described a little later in the "Controlling Program Flow" section of this chapter.

There is also a string operator that you can use in JavaScript. Although it may seem odd, JavaScript supports the plus sign when working with string values:

```
var value1 = "test";
var value2 = "ing";
var value3 = value1 + value2;
```

The resulting `value3` variable will contain the string value *testing.* The plus sign concatenates the two separate string values into a single string value. This comes in handy when you want to display a string value stored in a variable along with some text, like this:

```
var display = "Welcome, " + name + " to the game!";
```

Notice the spaces at the end of the first string value, and at the beginning of the second string value. These are necessary because the concatenation doesn't add any spaces itself when it joins the variable value to the other strings.

# Controlling Program Flow

By default, JavaScript processes statements in a linear fashion, operating on one statement, and then moving on to the next statement in the program code. You may want to alter the behavior of the code based on some type of conditions, events, or variable values.

You can do that using *flow control statements.* Flow control statements alter the flow of the program to make the JavaScript interpreter jump over code to another statement, based on some type of condition. The following sections discuss two popular methods of flow control in JavaScript programming.

## Conditional statements

Life is full of conditions. How often do you get up in the morning and say "If it's raining today, I'd better bring my umbrella"? Your actions for the day depend on a specific condition (the weather). JavaScript programs provide the same type of condition checks for your code. These are called *conditional statements.* They process blocks of code depending on a condition that the program can test for.

There are a few different types of conditional statements:

- » `if` statements
- » `else` statements
- » `switch` statements

Each has its own set of nuances and formats that you'll need to become familiar with. This section walks through each type of conditional statement.

## `if` statements

The `if...else` statement checks a condition that you specify and runs specific code if that condition occurs or skips the code if the condition doesn't occur. Here's the basic format for an `if` statement:

```
if (condition) {
    code to process
}
```

The JavaScript interpreter evaluates the condition between the parentheses. If the condition evaluates to a `true` value, the interpreter runs the code inside the braces. If the condition evaluates to a `false` value, the interpreter skips all the code between the braces. Let's take a look at an example of this:

```
if (age > 17) {
    alert("You are allowed to play the game");
}
```

The condition in this `if` statement evaluates the value currently stored in the `age` variable. If the value is greater than 17, the interpreter runs the `alert()` function. If the value is not greater than 17, the interpreter skips the `alert()` function.

TIP

The greater-than symbol used in the condition is another type of JavaScript operator, called a *comparison operator*. Comparison operators compare two values to test their equality. Table 1-3 shows the JavaScript comparison operators to use in conditions.

The equal-to operator (==) is possibly the most forgotten operator in JavaScript, even for pros. If you want to check if a variable is equal to a specific value, you must use the equal-to operator:

```
if (counter == 20) {
```

**TABLE 1-3**

# The JavaScript Comparison Operators

| Operator | Description |
|----------|-------------|
| == | Equal to |
| === | Equal to and the same data type |
| != | Not equal to |
| !== | Not equal to the value or the type |
| > | Greater than |
| < | Less than |
| >= | Greater than or equal to |
| <= | Less than or equal to |
| ? | Ternary operator |

The equal-to operator compares the two values, and the interpreter processes the code in the code block only if they're equal. In coding, programmers often get in a hurry and write the following:

```
if (counter = 20) {
```

This uses the assignment operator (=) instead of the comparison operator (==). The assignment operator assigns the value of 20 to the counter variable and then returns a true value if the assignment was successful (which it usually is). This is *not* the same thing as the comparison operator, and it'll produce faulty results in your programs!

Most of the comparison operators are fairly self-explanatory. The ternary operator is somewhat different. It provides a shortcut way of combining an `if...else` statement and an assignment statement:

```
var display = (age > 21) ? "Too old":"Young enough";
```

The ternary operator performs the condition on the left side of the question mark. If the condition evaluates to a true value, it assigns the first value to the variable. If the condition evaluates to a false value, it assigns the second value to the variable.

## else **statements**

With the `if` statement, if the condition is not met, the interpreter just skips the code you specify in the code block. The `else` statement allows you to specify code to run if the condition evaluates to a false value. That looks like this:

```
if (age < 18) {
    display = "Sorry, you are not old enough to play";";
    status = "failed";
} else {
    display = "You may begin the game";
    status = "ok";
}
```

Now there are two separate code blocks — one associated with the `if` statement and another associated with the `else` statement. The two are linked. If the condition evaluates to a `true` value, the JavaScript interpreter runs the code in the `if` statement code block. If the condition evaluates to a `false` value, the JavaScript interpreter runs the code contained in the `else` statement code block. The interpreter runs the code in one block or the other. At no time will the interpreter run the code in both code blocks.

More often than not, you'll find yourself needing to test a variable for a range of values. Instead of having to write multiple `if...else` statements, JavaScript allows you to string them together into one long statement by using the `else if` statement. The `else if` statement strings together multiple `if` and `else` statements so that they become one long chain of condition tests:

```
if (age < 10) {
    display = "You are very young";
} else if (age < 20) {
    display = "You are between 10 and 19";
} else if (age < 30) {
    display = "You are between 20 and 29";
} else {
    display = "You are 30 or older";
}
```

When stringing together multiple `if` and `else` statements, the interpreter goes through the list in order from the first condition test to the last condition test. When the first condition evaluates to a true value, the interpreter runs the code in the code block and exits the statements.

# `switch` **statements**

Using the `else if` statement provides an easy way to check for a value within a range, but it's still somewhat clunky to code. JavaScript makes that test easier for us by providing the `switch` statement.

The `switch` statement performs a similar function to the `else if` statement, but using a cleaner format:

```
switch (expression) {
    case match1:
        statements
        break;
    case match2:
        statements
        break;
    default:
        statements
}
```

With the `switch` statement, the JavaScript interpreter evaluates the *expression* specified and then compares the result with one or more `case` statements. Each `case` statement specifies a different possible result of the expression. If the result matches, the interpreter runs the statements contained in that section. The `break` statement is used to force the interpreter to then skip over the remaining `case` statement sections to the end of the switch code block. If none of the case results matches, the interpreter runs the statements under the `default` statement.

This sounds complicated, but it actually makes your life much easier when coding to check for variable values. Here's an example of using a switch statement:

```
switch (counter) {
    case 0:
        alert("You have four lives left");
        break;
    case 1:
        alert("You have three lives left");
        break;
    case 2:
        alert("You have two lives left");
        break;
    case 3:
        alert("Careful, you only have one life left");
        break;
    case 4:
        alert("Sorry, you are out of lives");
}
```

The expression to evaluate is the value stored in the counter variable. Depending on the value, the program displays a different alert message and then breaks out of the switch statement code block.

Checking for a range of values is a little tricky, but doable with the switch statement. Follow these steps to experiment with using the switch statement in a JavaScript program:

1. **Open your favorite text editor, program editor, or IDE package.**

2. **Enter the following code:**

```
<!DOCTYPE html>
<html>
<head>
<title>Testing the switch statement</title>
<script>
var age = prompt("How old are you?");
</script>
</head>
<body>
<script>
switch (true) {
    case (age < 18):
        alert("Sorry, you are too young to play");
        break;
    case (age < 50):
        alert("Welcome to the game!");
        break;
    case (age >= 50):
        alert("Sorry, you are too old to play");
}
</script>
</body>
</html>
```

3. **Save the code as** switchtest.html **in the** DocumentRoot **folder of your web server.**

   That's c:\xampp\htdocs for XAMPP on Windows or /Applications/XAMPP/htdocs for XAMPP on Mac macOS.

4. **Open the XAMPP Control Panel and start the Apache web server.**

**5.** **Open your browser, and enter the following URL:**

```
http://localhost:8080/switchtest.html
```

You may need to change the TCP port based on your web server.

**6.** **Stop the Apache web server and close the XAMPP Control Panel.**

The `switchtest.html` code has two separate switch elements. The first one is in the head element of the web page. It uses the JavaScript `prompt()` function to prompt the site visitor for an age:

```
var age = prompt("How old are you?");
```

It stores the value in the `age` variable. Figure 1-3 shows what the prompt looks like using the Microsoft Edge browser.

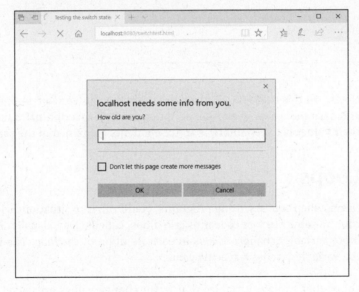

**FIGURE 1-3:**
The JavaScript
`prompt()`
function as
displayed by the
Microsoft Edge
browser.

Notice that the Edge browser provides some additional information in the prompt dialog box, such as the host that has produced the prompt. This can be helpful to prevent security issues with unwanted pop-up prompts from dangerous websites.

The second script element retrieves the `age` variable and uses it in a `switch` statement. The odd thing is that the switch statement just has a true value for the expression. This means the expression will always evaluate to a true condition, so the individual `case` statements test the condition.

The interpreter will run the first `case` statement that matches the age range. Figure 1-4 shows the `alert()` message that displays for entering an age of 15.

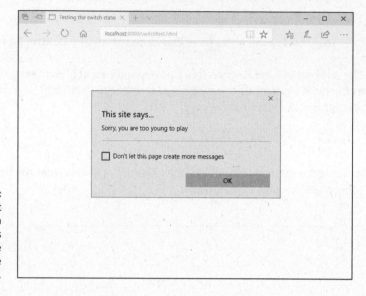

**FIGURE 1-4:**
The JavaScript `alert()` function response as displayed by the Microsoft Edge browser.

Notice, in this example, that the code sets the `age` variable in one script element and uses that value in another script element. JavaScript maintains variables and their values between multiple script elements contained in the same web page.

**TIP**

# Loops

Often, when you're writing programs, you'll run into situations where you need to run the same block of code multiple times, called a *loop.* Usually, in a loop, one or more variables changes values in each iteration of the loop. The loop exits when the variable reaches a specific value.

Loops that contain variables that never change values are called *endless loops.* If your program gets stuck in an endless loop, the browser will never show the web page as loading completely.

**WARNING**

JavaScript supports a few different types of loop statements, as shown in Table 1-4.

Each of these loop types is useful and comes in handy in different environments. The following sections walk through how to use each type of JavaScript loop statement.

**TABLE 1-4**  ## JavaScript Looping Statements

| Statement | Description |
|-----------|-------------|
| do..,while | Executes a block of statements and checks a condition at the end |
| for | Checks a condition, executes a block of statements, and then alters a specified variable |
| for...in | Executes a block of statements for each element contained in an array |
| while | Checks a condition and then executes a block of statements |

## The do...while loop

The do...while loop executes a block of statements and then at the end of the block tests a condition to determine if the block should be repeated:

```
var side1 = 1;
var side2 = 5;
do {
    area = side1 * side2;
    alert(side1 + "x" + side2 + " = " + area);
side1 = side1 + 1;
} while (side1 <= 10)
```

The do...while loop ensures that the code in the loop executes at least once before the condition is evaluated.

## The while loop

The while loop is the opposite of the do...while loop:

```
var side1 = 1;
var side2 = 5;
while (side1 <= 10) {
area = side1 * side2;
    alert(side1 + "x" + side2 + " = " + area);
side1 = side1 + 1;
}
```

Because the condition is checked before the interpreter executes the code in the code block, it's possible that the condition will fail before the first loop and none of the code will be executed.

# The for statement

The for statement is similar to the while loop, but it provides three features in one statement:

» It sets the initial values of one or more variables going into the loop.

» It defines the condition to evaluate before each iteration.

» It defines how a variable should be changed at the end of each iteration.

The basic format of the for statement is:

```
for(statement1; condition; statement2) {
    statements
}
```

The *statement1* statement is executed before the loop starts. The interpreter then evaluates the *condition* to determine whether to execute the statements in the code block. At the end of executing the statements in the code block, the interpreter executes the *statement2* statement.

This provides a compact way of creating loops for your programs. Try the following steps to test using the for statement to calculate the factorial of a value:

**1.** Open your favorite text editor, program editor, or IDE package.

**2.** Enter the following code:

```
<!DOCTYPE html>
<html>
<head>
<title>Calculating the Factorial</title>
<script>
var number = prompt("Please enter a number:");
</script>
</head>
<body>
<script>
var factorial = 1;
for (counter = 1; counter <= number; counter++) {
    factorial = factorial * counter;
}
```

```
var output = "The factorial of " + number + " is " + factorial;
alert(output);
</script>
</body>
</html>
```

**3.** **Save the file as** `factorial.html` **in the** DocumentRoot **folder for your web server.**

**4.** **Start the XAMPP Control panel and start the Apache web server.**

**5.** **Open your browser and enter the following URL:**

```
http://localhost:8080/factorial.html
```

You may need to change the TCP port to match your web server setup.

**6.** **Stop the Apache web server and close the XAMPP Control Panel.**

The `factorial.html` code uses the `prompt()` function to prompt for a value at the start of the program. This is shown in Figure 1-5.

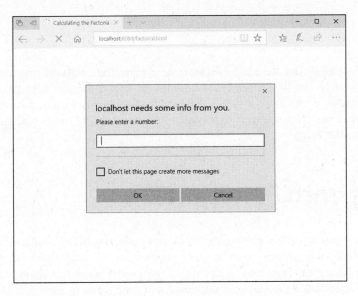

**FIGURE 1-5:**
Prompting for the factorial number.

You find the factorial of a number by multiplying the series of numbers up to and including the number you want. So the factorial of 5 is $1 \times 2 \times 3 \times 4 \times 5$, which is 120. To calculate the factorial, you set up a `for` statement to iterate through the numbers starting at 1, up to the number entered into the prompt dialog box:

```
for(counter = 1; counter <= number, counter++)
```

The counter variable keeps track of how many iterations of the for loop have taken place. After each iteration, you add 1 to the counter variable by using the incrementor operator (++). At the start of each new iteration, the interpreter checks the condition statement, which evaluates whether the counter variable value is less than or equal to the number value. If this is true, the interpreter continues with the next loop iteration.

### The for...in statement

The for...in statement comes in handy when you need to iterate through the data elements stored in an array variable. Often, you don't know how many values are stored in the array, so you can't just use a for loop to loop a specific number of times.

The for...in statement allows you to extract individual data values from the array and then stop when the array runs out of data elements. That code looks like this:

```
var scores = [100, 110, 105];
for (index in scores) {
    output = "One bowling score was " + scores[index];
    alert(output);
}
```

The first time the for...in statement runs, the index variable contains the value of 0, or the first index number from the array. For the next iteration, the index variable contains the value of 1, and for the final iteration, it contains the value 2. You can then use that index value to reference the individual data values stored in the array.

# Working with Functions

As you write more complex JavaScript code, you'll find yourself reusing parts of code that perform specific tasks. Sometimes it's something simple, such as displaying a prompt and retrieving a response from the site visitor. Other times it's a complicated calculation that's used multiple times in your program.

In each of these situations, writing the same blocks of code over and over again can get tiresome. It would be nice to just write the block of code once, and then be able to refer to that block of code in the other places it's needed.

JavaScript provides a feature that lets you do just that. Functions are blocks of code to which you assign names; then you can reuse them anywhere in your code. Any time you need to use the block of code in your program, you simply use the name you assigned to the function. This is referred to as *calling the function*. The following sections describe how to create and use functions in your JavaScript code.

## Creating a function

To create a function in JavaScript you use the `function` statement:

```
function name(parameter1, parameter2, ...) {
    function code
    return value;
}
```

The *name* that you assign to the function must be unique within your program code. The function can take parameters that the calling program passes to it. You can use the parameter variables within the function code.

**WARNING**

Functions are intended to be self-contained. The only data they work with are the values passed as the function parameters. This allows you to use the function in any program that requires that function task. Because of that, you can't directly access variables defined in the main program from inside the function code.

At the end of the function, you can opt to have it return a single value back to the calling program by including the `return` statement. If no data needs to be returned back to the calling program, you can leave out the `return` statement.

Here's an example of writing a function to calculate the factorial value of a number passed to the function:

```
function factorial(number) {
    var factorial = 1;
    for(counter = 1; counter <= number; counter++) {
        fact = fact * counter;
    }
    return fact;
}
```

The `factorial()` function requires a single parameter, assigned to the `number` variable. Inside the `factorial()` function the code uses the `number` variable to calculate the factorial. When the `for` loop completes, the answer is stored in the `fact` variable. The `return` statement returns the value of the `fact` variable back to the calling program.

# Using a function

To call a function from inside the JavaScript program, you just reference it by name, and include any parameters you need to pass. If the function returns a value, you can assign the output of the function to a variable:

```
var result = factorial(5);
```

The return value from the `factorial()` function is assigned to the `result` variable. You can use the `factorial()` function as many times as necessary in your program code.

**TIP**

Before you can use the function though, you must ensure that it gets defined. Because of this, it's common to define JavaScript functions at the start of the head element section of the web page.

IN THIS CHAPTER

» **Getting acquainted with the Document Object Model**

» **Working with the Document Object Model**

» **Reading data from your web page**

» **Writing to your web page**

Chapter **2**

# Advanced JavaScript Coding

In the previous chapter, I explain the basics of how to incorporate JavaScript code into a web page. If you read that chapter, you ran a couple of simple JavaScript programs, using the `prompt()` function for input and the `alert()` function for output. That was a great start, but the whole point of using JavaScript is to dynamically alter the data and/or appearance of web pages. This chapter explains how JavaScript interfaces with your web pages and shows you how to write JavaScript code to dynamically add, delete, or change content in your website.

## Understanding the Document Object Model

In order for JavaScript to have access to the elements in your web page, it needs to know how to find them. The Document Object Model (DOM) provides a standard way of accessing objects placed within a web page. It creates a tree structure that contains every element, attribute, content text, and even CSS3 style contained within the web page. It treats each of these items as objects that the browser (or your program code) can manipulate. Finding any of these items is just a matter of walking through the tree with your JavaScript code.

The browser defines every web page as a set of DOM objects that the web page contains. Just as your family has a family tree that you can trace back to find relatives, every web page has its own DOM tree of the objects contained within the web page. With JavaScript, you can peruse through the DOM tree and make modifications along the way.

## The Document Object Model tree

Every family tree has a head, and for the DOM tree, the head is the html element that starts out the web page. Just as parents have children, the html object in the DOM tree has two child objects: the head object and the body object, shown in Figure 2-1.

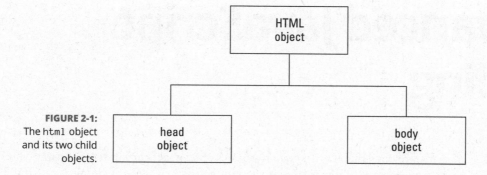

**FIGURE 2-1:** The html object and its two child objects.

The head and body elements in the HTML code are called *child objects* of the html object in the DOM tree. Because it comes first in the code, the head object is called the "first child object," while the body object is the "last child object." This terminology is important when working with DOM objects.

As you continue down the DOM tree, the browser places each object in the web page under its parent object. Let's take a look at a simple example of this principle. I'll use this sample web page for the demo:

```
<!DOCTYPE html>
<html>
<head>
<title>Sample DOM web page</title>
</head>
<body>
<h1>This is the heading of the web page</h1>
<p>This is sample text</p>
</body>
</html>
```

From this sample HTML5 code, the browser creates DOM objects from each element, and places them in a DOM tree layout it keeps in memory, as shown in Figure 2-2.

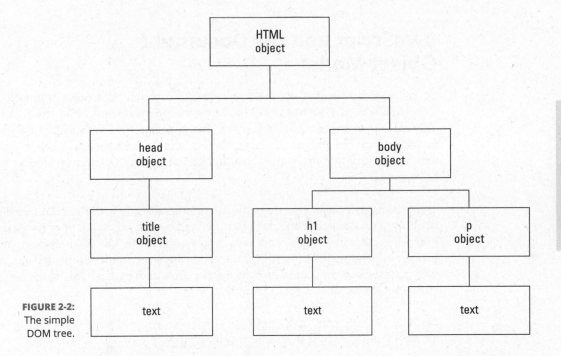

**FIGURE 2-2:** The simple DOM tree.

In the example shown in Figure 2-2, the html object contains the two child objects — head and body — but now each of those objects has child objects as well. The head object contains just one child object, the title object. The title object also has one child object, which may seem odd at first glance, because the title object doesn't contain any additional objects.

One of the more confusing features of the DOM tree is how it handles text inside elements. It treats the text inside an element as a separate DOM object that has its own features. So, in this example, the title object contains a single child object, which is the text object for the title text.

The body object has two child objects. The h1 object is the first child of the body object, and it, too, contains a text child object. The p object is the last child of the body object, and it has a text object in it as well.

This simple example shows the basics of DOM. Working out the DOM tree for a large web page with lots of different types of elements can be complicated, but it uses the same principle. Fortunately, JavaScript has some features that help make things a little easier for you.

# JavaScript and the Document Object Model

So far, you've seen that the browser breaks every web page down into a DOM tree of objects. The browser uses the DOM tree to keep track of all the HTML5 elements, their content, and the styles that appear on the web page. However, because JavaScript programs run in the browser (remember the whole client-side programming thing?), they have full access to the DOM tree created by the browser.

That means your JavaScript programs can interact directly with the DOM tree that the browser follows to create the web page. And not only that, but your JavaScript programs can add, change, and even remove objects in the DOM tree. As your JavaScript program modifies the DOM tree, the browser automatically updates the web page window with the new information. How cool is that? This is the key to client-side dynamic web programming.

Just like the DOM tree, JavaScript treats each element contained in a web page as an object. In JavaScript, objects have two features:

>> **Properties:** Properties define information about the object.

>> **Methods:** Methods are actions to take with the objects.

JavaScript assigns a special object named document to represent the entire web page DOM tree. You can reference many of the DOM objects directly from the document object, as well as add or remove objects. Table 2-1 lists some of the document properties available in JavaScript.

To reference a document property, you use the format *document.property*, like this:

```
var myurl = document.URL;
```

The same applies to using the document methods. Table 2-2 shows a list of the more popular document methods used in JavaScript.

**TABLE 2-1** JavaScript Document Properties

| Property | Description |
|----------|-------------|
| activeElement | Returns the element that currently has the focus of the web page window |
| anchors | Returns a list of all the anchor elements on the web page |
| body | Sets or retrieves the body element of the web page |
| cookie | Returns all cookie names and values set in the web page |
| characterSet | Returns the character set defined for the web page |
| documentElement | Returns the DOM object for the html element of the web page |
| documentMode | Returns the mode used by the browser to display the web page |
| domain | Returns the domain name of the server used to send the document |
| embeds | Returns a list of all the embed elements in the web page |
| forms | Returns a list of all the form elements in the web page |
| head | Returns the head element for the web page |
| images | Returns a list of all the img elements in the web page |
| lastModified | Returns the time and date the web page was last modified |
| links | Returns a list of all the anchor and area elements in the web page |
| title | Sets or retrieves the title of the web page |
| URL | Returns the full URL for the web page |

**TABLE 2-2** JavaScript Document Methods

| Method | Description |
|--------|-------------|
| createElement() | Adds a new element object |
| createTextNode() | Adds a new text object |
| getElementbyId(id) | Returns an element object with the specified id value |
| getElementsByClassName(class) | Returns a list of elements with the specified class name |
| getElementsByTagname(tag) | Returns a list of elements of the specified element type |
| hasFocus() | Returns a true value if the web page has the window focus |
| write(text) | Sends the specified text to the web page |
| writeln(text) | Sends the specified text to the web page, followed by a new line character |

Let's run a quick test to see how this works. Follow these steps to test using the `write()` method for a web page document:

1. **Open your favorite text editor, program editor, or integrated development environment (IDE) package.**

2. **Enter the following code:**

```
<!DOCTYPE html>
<html>
<head>
<title>DOM Test</title>
<script>
document.write("<h1>This is a test of the DOM</h1>");
</script>
</head>
<body>
</body>
</html>
```

3. **Save the file as** domtest.html **in the** DocumentRoot **folder for your web server.**

   If you're using XAMPP in Windows, that's the c:\xampp\htdocs folder; for XAMPP in macOS, it's /Applications/XAMPP/htdocs.

4. **Open the XAMPP Control Panel and then start the Apache Web server.**

5. **Open your browser and enter the following URL:**

```
http://localhost:8080/domtest.html
```

   You may need to change the TCP port in the URL to match your Apache web server.

6. **Close the browser.**

When you examine the code in the domtest.html file, you'll notice that there's nothing in the body element, so you may not expect to see anything on the resulting web page. However, when you run the program, you should see the output shown in Figure 2-3.

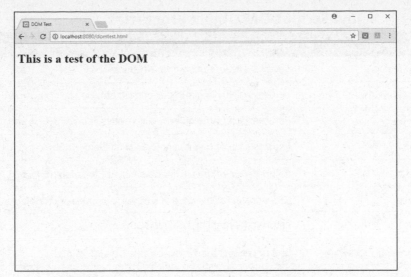

FIGURE 2-3:
The output from
the domtest.
html program.

The document.write() function runs the write() method from the document object to dynamically place the h1 element in the web page for us!

**WARNING**

The write() method is an easy way to dynamically place text in the web page, but it can be somewhat dangerous to use. The write() method overwrites everything that was originally in the web page. In this example, I ran it from the head element, so it placed the output at the top of the web page, before any elements defined in the body element. However, if you use the write() function from within the body element, it'll remove any elements that were previously on the web page. I'll show you some better methods for doing this later in this chapter.

Besides the document properties and methods, JavaScript also has properties and methods that apply to each element object in the document. The following sections detail how to use those properties and methods.

## JavaScript DOM object properties

Now that you have access to the objects contained in the web page, you can use JavaScript to manipulate them. Each DOM object contains one or more properties that define the actual object. There are lots of object properties JavaScript uses with objects. Table 2-3 shows a list of the more popular JavaScript DOM object properties you'll use.

**TABLE 2-3**      ## JavaScript DOM Object Properties

| Property | Description |
| --- | --- |
| attributes | Returns a list of the object's attributes |
| childElementCount | Returns a list of the number of child objects the object has |
| childNodes | Returns a list of the object's child nodes, including text and comments |
| children | Returns a list of only the object's child element object nodes |
| classList | Returns a list of the class name attributes of an object |
| className | Sets or returns the value of a class attribute of an object |
| firstChild | Returns the first child object for the object |
| id | Sets or returns the id value of the object |
| innerHTML | Sets or returns the HTML content of the object |
| lastChild | Returns the last child object for the object |
| nodeName | Returns the name of the object |
| nodeType | Returns the element type of the object |
| nodeValue | Sets or returns the value for the object |
| nextSibling | Returns the next object at the same level in the tree as the object |
| parentNode | Returns the parent object for the object |
| previousSibling | Returns the previous object at the same level in the tree as the object |
| style | Sets or returns the value of the style property for the object |

Besides these standard properties, each attribute that you assign to an HTML5 element and each CSS style property that you apply to an element becomes an object property of the DOM object as well.

Follow these steps to experiment with accessing the DOM object properties for our sample web page:

**1.** Open your favorite text editor, program editor, or IDE package.

**2.** Enter the following code:

```
<!DOCTYPE html>
<html>
<head>
<title>Testing DOM properties</title>
</head>
<body>
<body>
<h1>This is the heading of the web page</h1>
<p>This is sample text</p>
<br>
<button type="button" onclick="changeme('red')">Change background to
   red</button>
<button type="button" onclick="changeme('white')">Change background to
   white</button>
<script>
function changeme(color) {
    document.body.style.backgroundColor = color;
}
</script>
</body>
</html>
```

3. **Save the file as** domproperties.html **in the** DocumentRoot **folder for your web server.**

4. **Open the XAMPP Control Panel and start the Apache web server if it's not already running.**

5. **Open your browser and enter the following URL:**

   ```
   http://localhost:8080/domproperties.html
   ```

   You may need to change the TCP port to match your Apache web server.

6. **Click the buttons to change the background color of the web page.**

7. **Close the browser window.**

The domproperties.html code uses two buttons to trigger the changeme() function. (I talk more about how to do that in Book 3, Chapter 4.) The changeme() function uses the document.body object to reference the body element in the web page. It then uses the style object property to reference the CSS3 styles applied to the body element.

**TECHNICAL
STUFF**

You may be wondering why the backgroundColor style property isn't background-color, because that's how CSS3 defines that property. Unfortunately, the DOM standard doesn't like using dashes in property names. So, instead, wherever there's a dash in a CSS3 property name (such as in background-color), it removes the dash and capitalizes the first letter of the next word. That's how we get backgroundColor as the DOM property to change the background-color CSS3 property on the web page.

## JavaScript DOM object methods

Besides properties, JavaScript objects also contain methods. The methods provide actions to interact with the object. You've already seen a demonstration of using the write() method of a DOM object in JavaScript. There are plenty more object methods for you to use in your JavaScript programs to help you retrieve information about the DOM objects, modify existing DOM objects, or even add new DOM objects to your web page. Table 2-4 shows some of the more popular DOM object methods that you'll use.

**TABLE 2-4** JavaScript DOM Object Methods

| Method | Description |
|---|---|
| appendChild(object) | Adds a new child object to an existing object |
| blur() | Removes the page focus from an object |
| click() | Simulates a mouse click on the object |
| cloneNode | Duplicates an object in the DOM |
| contains(object) | Returns a true value if the object contains the specified object |
| focus() | Places the window focus on the object |
| getAttribute(attr) | Returns the value for the specified object attribute |
| getElementsByClassName(class) | Returns a list of objects with the specified class name |
| getElementsByTagName(tag) | Returns a list of objects with the specified tag name |
| hasAttribute(attr) | Returns true if the object contains the specified attribute |
| hasAttributes() | Returns true if the object contains any attributes |
| hasChildNodes() | Returns true of the object contains any child objects |
| insertBefore(object) | Inserts the specified object before the object |
| removeAttribute(attr) | Removes the specified attribute from the object |
| removeChild(object) | Removes the specified child object from the parent object |
| replaceChild(object) | Replaces the child object with the specified object |
| setAttribute(attr) | Sets the specified attribute of the object to the specified value |
| toString() | Converts the object to a string value |

As you can see, there are quite a few different methods available for you to use when you reference a specific element in the web page. However, part of the problem with using JavaScript to dynamically change elements is finding them in the first place. The next section covers how to do that.

# Finding Your Elements

As your web pages become more complicated, they'll contain dozens, hundreds, and possibly even thousands of different elements. Trying to find a specific element within that mess so you can dynamically change it can be a challenge.

There are basically two different ways to find a specific element buried within the HTML5 code in your web page:

>> Using a unique feature assigned to the element to jump directly to it

>> Walking the DOM tree to navigate your way down to the element's object from a specific point in the DOM tree

Both methods have their own pros and cons for using them. Obviously, if you can use a unique feature of an element (such as an id attribute) to reference a specific element that's the easiest way to go. However, that's not always possible, so it helps to know how to get there the hard way. The following sections describe how to use both methods for referencing element objects within the DOM tree.

## Getting to the point

The easiest way to uniquely identify an element in your web page is to assign it a unique id attribute value. When you assign the id attribute to elements, you can then reference them in your JavaScript code by using the getElementById() method.

The getElementById() method returns a pointer to the DOM object with the specified id value. When you have the pointer to the element object, you can use any of the DOM object properties or methods to work with the element.

Follow these steps to test this out:

**1.** Open your favorite text editor, program editor, or IDE package.

**2.** Enter the following code:

```html
<!DOCTYPE html>
<html>
<head>
<title>Finding an Element</title>
<script>
function changeit() {
    var answer = prompt("Enter some new text");
    var spot = document.getElementById("here");
    spot.innerHTML = answer;
}
</script>
</head>
<body>
<h1>Trying to find an element</h1>
<button type="button" onclick="changeit()">
Click to change
</button>
<p id="here">This is the original text</p>
</body>
</html>
```

**3.** Save the file as `findtest.html` in the DocumentRoot folder for your web server.

**4.** Start the Apache web server if it's not currently running.

**5.** Open your browser and enter the following URL:

```
http://localhost:8080/findtest.html
```

**6.** Note the text that appears in the web page below the button.

**7.** Click the button and then enter some new text at the prompt dialog box.

**8.** Click OK in the dialog box.

**9.** Note the text that now appears on the web page.

**10.** Close the browser window when you're done playing.

The `findtest.html` code defines the `changeit()` JavaScript function in the head section. The `changeit()` function uses a `prompt()` function to retrieve some text from the site visitor and then attempts to replace the text in the p DOM object with the new text.

To do that, it uses the getElementById() document method to create a pointer to the p object in the web page, identified by the id attribute value of here. After it retrieves the pointer to the p object, it uses the innerHTML object property to change the text that appears inside the p object.

When you run the program, you should see the heading, the same text, and a button. When you click the button, a prompt dialog box should appear, prompting you to enter some text (see Figure 2-4).

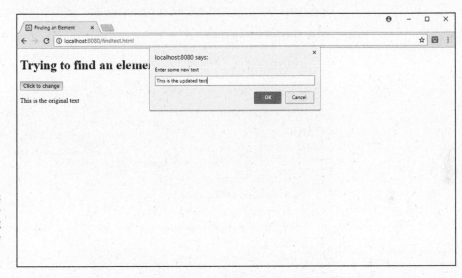

**FIGURE 2-4:**
The initial page
and dialog
box for the
findtest.html
web page.

Type some text and then click OK. The browser will automatically change the content of the p element to show the text you entered into the dialog box!

You can continue doing that for as long as you like. Each time you enter new text, it'll appear in the web page automatically!

## Walking the tree

Finding the DOM object for a specific HTML5 element in the DOM tree by using its id attribute is the preferred method, but that's not always available. Sometimes you need to find an element within the document to use as a base, and then use the element properties to find child and sibling objects:

» Use the firstChild property to find the first element in a group.

» Use the nextSibling property to find the related elements within the group.

You can then alternate between firstChild, lastChild, nextSibling, or previousSibling properties to work your way down to where you want to be in the DOM tree.

That can be tedious work, especially for large web pages. You need to be aware of exactly how all the elements appear and fit together in the web page.

Follow these steps to try this method out:

1. **Open your favorite text editor, program editor, or IDE package.**

2. **Enter the following code:**

```
<!DOCTYPE html>
<html>
<head>
<title>Walking Test</title>
<script>
function changeit() {
    var spot = document.getElementById("mylist");
    var item1 = spot.firstChild;
    var item2 = item1.nextSibling;
    var item3 = item2.nextSibling;
    var item4 = item3.nextSibling;
    item1.innerHTML = "Cake";
    item2.innerHTML = "Ice Cream";
    item3.innerHTML = "Cookies";
    item4.innerHTML = "Fudge";
}
</script>
</head>
<body>
<h1>Changing elements by walking</h1>
<h2>Here's a list of food to buy</h2>
<ul id="mylist"><li>Carrots</li><li>Brussel Sprouts</li><li>Eggplant
    </li><li>Tofu</li></ul>
<button type="button" onclick="changeit()">
Change the list
</button>
</body>
</html>
```

3. **Save the file as** walkingtest.html **in the** DocumentRoot **folder for your Apache web server.**

4. **Start the Apache web server if it's not already running.**

**5.** Open your browser and enter the following URL:

```
http://localhost:8080/walkingtest.html
```

**6.** Examine the items in the list.

**7.** Click the button.

**8.** Note the new items in the list.

**9.** Close the browser window when you're done.

The `walkingtest.html` code defines an `id` attribute for the unordered list element, but each of the items within the list isn't uniquely identified. In order to reference them, the code uses the `firstChild` and `nextSibling` object property values to walk its way through the list of items. When you click the button, all the items in the list are replaced, as shown in Figure 2-5.

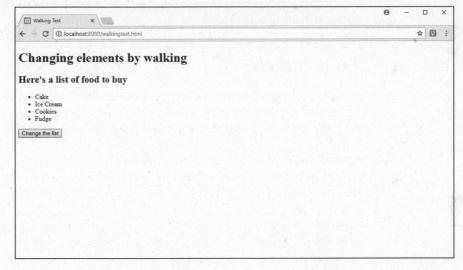

**FIGURE 2-5:**
The
walkingtest.
html results.

The code finds the `ul` object by using the `id` attribute value of the ul element. It assigns that object to the variable `spot`. Then the code can reference the individual list items based on that location in the DOM tree. The first child of the `ul` object is the first `li` object for the list. The `firstChild` property returns a pointer to that object, which the code stores in the `item1` variable. Next, the code uses the `nextSibling` property of the `item1` variable, which returns a pointer to the next item in the list and is stored in the `item2` variable. That continues on, using the `nextSibling` property for each item to find the next item in the list. After the code retrieves pointers to all the list items, it uses the `innerHTML` property to change the text for each item.

**WARNING**

Be careful how you create the list in the code. If you place each list item on a separate line, the code won't work! That's because the browser assigns any white space between elements as a text object in the DOM. So the `nextSibling` property will point to the new line character text object and not the next li object in the list! It's important to remember that when working with the positional properties of objects.

# Working with Document Object Model Form Data

When you use HTML5 forms in your web pages, you usually incorporate quite a few different elements — text boxes, text areas, check boxes, and radio buttons. Your JavaScript code can use the DOM tree objects to manipulate all these elements. The following sections show you how to use the DOM tree to work with different types of form elements.

## Text boxes

Handling data in a text input element is a little different from what I did with the p element. Because the input element is a one-sided tag, there's no `innerHTML` property to store the text that's inside the text box.

Instead, you need to use the `value` attribute of the object to read any text that may already be in the text box (whether placed there by the `value` attribute or typed by the site visitor). To do that, you use the `value` object property:

```
var textbox = document.getElementById("test");
var data = textbox.value;
```

You can also use the `value` property to write data to the text box. That code looks like this:

```
var textbox = document.getElementById("test");
var answer = prompt("Enter text to change");
textbox.value = answer;
```

This provides for an easy way to create a message area on your web page for displaying short messages, such as status messages. Just place a `textbox` input element near the bottom of the web page, and change the `value` property of it with any message you need to display.

There are also a few other DOM object properties associated with `textbox` objects that can come in handy. Table 2-5 shows the DOM `textbox` properties available.

**TABLE 2-5**      The `textbox` DOM Properties

| Property | Description |
|---|---|
| `autocomplete` | Sets or retrieves the value of the autocomplete attribute |
| `autofocus` | Sets or retrieves whether the text box gets the window focus when the web page loads |
| `defaultValue` | Sets or retrieves the default value assigned to the text box |
| `disabled` | Sets or retrieves whether the text box is disabled in the form |
| `form` | Retrieves the parent form the text box belongs to |
| `list` | Retrieves the data list associated with the text box |
| `maxLength` | Sets or retrieves the maximum length of the text box |
| `name` | Sets or retrieves the name attribute for the text box |
| `pattern` | Sets or retrieves the pattern attribute for the text box |
| `placeholder` | Sets or retrieves the placeholder attribute for the text box |
| `readOnly` | Sets or retrieves whether the text box is read only |
| `required` | Sets or retrieves whether the text box is a required field in the form |
| `size` | Sets or retrieves the value of the size attribute for the text box |
| `type` | Retrieves the type of element the text box is |
| `value` | Sets or retrieves the value attribute for the text box |

With these few properties, you have full control to dynamically modify any text box that appears on the web page.

## Text areas

The `textarea` DOM object works similar to the `textbox` object. Instead of the `innerHTML` property, you use the `value` attribute to retrieve any text from the text area or place any new text into the text area.

There are a few other properties that are unique to the `textarea` object:

>> `cols`: Sets or retrieves the number of columns assigned to the text area

>> `rows`: Sets or retrieves the number of rows assigned to the text area

>> `wrap`: Sets or retrieves whether text can auto-wrap within the text area

As you can tell, you can dynamically change the size of the text area in a web page using JavaScript and the DOM object properties. That can create quite an effect as your site visitor is filling out the form.

## Check boxes

The `checkbox` object is another oddity in the DOM. A check box in a form provides for a yes/no type of answer — either the visitor checks the check box or the box is unchecked. You can test for that condition using the DOM `checked` property:

```
var pizza = document.getElementById("pizzabox");
if (pizza.checked) {
    alert("your pizza will be delivered shortly");
}
```

You can also set whether the check box is checked by assigning the property a `true` or `false` value:

```
pizza.checked = true;
```

Table 2-6 shows all the DOM object properties that are supported when using check boxes.

**TABLE 2-6**     The `checkbox` DOM Properties

| Property | Description |
| --- | --- |
| autofocus | Sets or retrieves whether the check box gets the focus when the web page loads |
| checked | Sets or retrieves the state of the check box |
| defaultChecked | Retrieves the default state of the check box |
| defaultValue | Retrieves the default value assigned to the check box |
| disabled | Sets or retrieves whether the check box is disabled |

| Property | Description |
|---|---|
| form | Retrieves the parent form the check box belongs to |
| intermediate | Sets or retrieves the intermediate state of the check box |
| name | Sets or retrieves the name assigned to the check box element |
| required | Sets retrieves whether the check box must be checked before submitting the form |
| type | Retrieves the type of element the check box is |
| value | Sets or retrieves the value associated with the check box |

That gives you full control over how the check boxes behave in your web page.

## Radio buttons

Working with radio buttons is always a complicated matter. All the radio buttons in the same group use the same name property, so the browser can handle them as a group. Remember, only one radio button in the group can be selected at any time.

Handling data from a radio button requires using the checked and value object properties, just like the checkbox object. Because all the radio buttons use the same name, the value attribute is crucial in determining if you're working with the correct radio button in the form.

IN THIS CHAPTER

» **Loading the jQuery library**

» **Using jQuery in your web pages**

» **Finding elements**

» **Replacing data**

» **Changing styles**

» **Adding nodes**

» **Using animation**

Chapter **3**

# Using jQuery

A s you code dynamic web applications using JavaScript, you'll find yourself using the same statements and features over and over again to create dynamic effects on your web pages. As it turns out, JavaScript developers around the world use the same statements and features to implement the same effects on their web pages, too!

Because of that, lots of work has been done by developers in trying to create a standard JavaScript library of useful functions. Instead of having to write the same JavaScript statements over and over, you just run a simple function from a pre-built library. That makes life for the JavaScript programmer much easier!

By far the most common JavaScript library used around the world today is the jQuery library. The jQuery library was written to simplify five main functions that JavaScript is commonly used for:

» Finding content in an HTML5 document

» Changing content in an HTML5 document

» Creating animations using CSS

» Listening for web page events (see Book 3, Chapter 4)

» Communicating with remote servers (see Book 6, Chapter 3)

I cover how to use the first three features of jQuery in this chapter. In the next chapter, I show you how to use jQuery to simplify listening to actions your site visitors take while on your web pages. Then in Book 6, Chapter 3, I show how to use jQuery to simplify communicating with PHP programs running on the server from inside your web pages. But for now, let's examine how to use the basics of jQuery.

# Loading the jQuery Library

Before you can use the jQuery library functions in your web page, you need to load the library functions. The jQuery library is nothing more than a standard external JavaScript program that defines lots of handy functions for us. The project freely provides the JavaScript code library for use in any application, whether it's commercial or open source.

The main website for the jQuery project is `www.jquery.com`. From there, you can find documentation on jQuery, as well as the software download packages. There are two main versions of jQuery:

» The latest production version (at the time of this writing, 3.2.1)

» The latest development version (which isn't assigned a version number)

For all your website work, you'll want to use the latest production version of the jQuery library. The development package is for testing cutting-edge features and isn't guaranteed to work correctly at all times in all situations. This could lead to issues in your dynamic web application.

After you decide to use the latest production version of the jQuery library, there are actually four different versions of the library that you can use in your application:

» **Uncompressed:** The full jQuery library in an uncompressed file

» **Minified:** The full jQuery library in a compressed file

» **Slim:** Everything except support for animation and Ajax in an uncompressed file

» **Slim minified:** Everything except support for animation and Ajax in a compressed file

For most purposes, you'll be fine using the minified version of the file. This contains all the jQuery features, but in a compressed file so that it will load faster for your site visitors.

You've decided to use the minified version of the latest production version of the jQuery library software (because you trust me completely), but there's still one more decision for you to make. Because the jQuery file is a JavaScript library, your application needs to load it for each web page that contains jQuery code. This can get somewhat tedious for large applications.

You can either download the jQuery library file to your own server to host, making it easier for your website visitors to access it along with the rest of your application files, or you can point your site visitors' browsers to download the jQuery library file from a content delivery network (CDN) server. The following sections walk through how to use both options.

## Option 1: Downloading the library file to your server

Sometimes it's better to have your website visitors download all the files necessary for your dynamic web application from one place — your own server. To do that, you need to have the jQuery library file installed on your web server, in the DocumentRoot folder so that your site visitors can access it.

Downloading the file from the main jQuery web page and installing it on your web server is a fairly easy process. Just follow these steps:

1. **Open your web browser and go to** www.jquery.com/download.

2. **Click the link to the compressed production version of jQuery.**

   At the time of this writing, it's version 3.2.1.

   Your browser downloads the file to the default download folder. It should have a name something like jquery-3.2.1.min.js. (The numbers will be different if the version number has changed since this book was written.)

3. **Copy the file to the** DocumentRoot **folder for your web server.**

   If you're using XAMPP in Windows, that's c:\xampp\htdocs; for XAMPP in macOS, it's /Applications/XAMPP/htdocs.

To load the jQuery library in your web application, you'll need to include a <script> tag in the head element of your web page. The <script> tag should point to the jQuery library file that you downloaded:

```
<script src="jquery-3.2.1.min.js"></script>
```

**WARNING**

It's important that the browser loads the jQuery library file before you use any jQuery functions in your application. Place the ‹script› tag near the top of the head element section, after the ‹title› tag.

## Option 2: Using a content delivery network

One downside to hosting the jQuery library file on your own server is that all your site visitors will need to download it directly from your server, creating an additional load on your server. To prevent that, you can point the ‹script› tag to load the jQuery library file from a CDN.

A CDN provides content for applications from a common server or group of servers. Your website visitors can download the jQuery library file from the nearest CDN to their location, which may speed up the time it takes to load your web page.

The jQuery project runs its own CDN to host the latest jQuery library file and provides the ‹script› tag formats required for each of the different library file options. At the time of this writing, they host that at https://code.jquery.com. Here's the current ‹script› tag to use to load the jQuery library from the jQuery CDN website:

```
<script src="https://code.jquery.com/jquery-3.2.1.min.js" integrity="sha256-hwg4
    gsxgFZhOsEEamdOYGBf13FyQuiTwlAQgxVSNgt4=" crossorigin="anonymous"></script>
```

The integrity and crossorigin attributes are for the Subresource Integrity (SRI) feature, which helps the browser ensure the downloaded file hasn't been tampered with. This is a nice feature to add to ensure your site visitors aren't using a hacked library file.

**TIP**

Besides the jQuery CDN website, Google and Microsoft also host the jQuery library files on their own CDN websites. If your site visitors are geographically disbursed throughout the world, it may be faster for them to download the jQuery library file from a Google or Microsoft server. The https://code.jquery.com website provides instructions on how to use the Google and Microsoft CDN websites.

# Using jQuery Functions

After you have the jQuery library file downloaded to the site visitor's browser, you're ready to start using jQuery functions in your dynamic web application.

All jQuery functions must be embedded in the special jQuery() function. This signals to the browser that it must use the jQuery library to process the functions used in the code. The general format for embedding jQuery code into your web page thus looks like this:

```
<script>
    jQuery(code);
</script>
```

Because jQuery is still JavaScript code, you must surround the jQuery code using the standard script HTML5 element. The actual jQuery code itself must also be embedded within the jQuery() function.

**TIP**

If things are starting to look complicated, don't worry — this is a standard format. After you've written a few jQuery programs, you'll feel right at home using it. That said, there is a shortcut that can come in handy. Instead of using the jQuery() function name, you can use the $() shortcut function name.

# Finding Elements

One of the main features of jQuery is to help you find HTML5 elements in the web page to manipulate. In Book 3, Chapter 2, I show you how you need to use the JavaScript getElementById(), getElementByClassName(), or getElementBy TagName() functions to find elements in the web page. Needless to say, that gets fairly complicated when you start working with large web pages.

The jQuery library greatly simplifies this process. It incorporates the same selector method that CSS uses to apply styles to HTML5 elements. For example, to find the h1 element in a web page, you just use the jQuery code:

```
$("h1");
```

Now that's easy! If you want to find an element based on an id attribute value, you use the same format as in CSS:

```
$("#warning");
```

Likewise with class names:

```
$(".warning");
```

After you've found the HTML5 element that you're looking for, jQuery allows you to easily apply lots of different functions to modify the element — but more on that later in this chapter.

Follow these steps to experiment with retrieving text from an HTML5 p element using your new jQuery skills:

**1.** **Open your favorite text editor, program editor, or integrated development environment (IDE) package.**

**2.** **Type the following code:**

```
<!DOCTYPE html>
<html>
<head>
<title>Testing jQuery</title>
<script src="jquery-3.2.1.min.js"></script>
</head>
<body>
<h1>This is my heading</h1>
<p>This is some content on my web page</p>
<script>
    var data = $("p").text();
    alert(data);
</script>
</body>
</html>
```

**3.** **Save the file as** jquery1.html **in the** DocumentRoot **folder of your web server, where you also saved the jQuery library file.**

**4.** **Open the XAMPP Control Panel and start the Apache web server.**

**5.** **Open your browser and enter the following URL:**

```
http://localhost:8080/jquery1.html
```

You may need to modify the TCP port used in the URL to match your web server.

The jQuery code finds the p element in the web page, retrieves the text that it contains, and then stores it in the data JavaScript variable. You can then use that as any other JavaScript variable, including displaying it using an alert() function, as shown in the code. When you run the program, you should see the output shown in Figure 3-1.

**FIGURE 3-1:**
The output from the jquery1. html program.

Congratulations on running a successful jQuery program! However, one little issue remains: I placed the script element that contained the jQuery code at the very end of the body element section. There's a reason for that. The jQuery find feature can only find elements that have already been processed by the browser into the Document Object Model (DOM) tree. If you try to run a jQuery find operation before the browser completes building the DOM tree, it won't find the elements. That can be a huge problem with a dynamic web application, but there's a way around that: the .ready() function.

The .ready() function causes jQuery to wait until the browser has completely loaded the DOM tree, and all the HTML5 elements contained in the web page are available. After that's done, the .ready() function runs whatever jQuery code you place inside of it.

To do that, you need to embed your jQuery code into a code block that now looks like this:

```
<script>
jQuery(document).ready(function() {
     code
});
</script>
```

The .ready() function uses an anonymous function that it runs when the browser fully loads the DOM tree. You just embed your jQuery code inside the anonymous function, and you're guaranteed it won't run until the DOM tree is ready. When you use this method, you can place your jQuery script element anywhere in the web page code, including the head element section. That makes it much easier to spot the embedded jQuery code, instead of having to go hunting all around the web page code file for it.

Using jQuery

Using this method, the code that you created earlier would look like this:

```
<script>
    jQuery(document).ready(function() {
        var data = $("p").text();
        alert(data);
    });
</script>
```

Now you can place this script element block into the head element of the web page and it'll work just fine!

WARNING

Although you can now place your jQuery code anywhere in the head element section, you still need to place the script element that loads the jQuery library before any jQuery code.

# Replacing Data

After you find the HTML5 elements in your web page, the next step is to modify the content of the web page. Fortunately, jQuery makes that step easier, too. This section shows how jQuery allows you to change the text, HTML code, and even attributes of the HTML5 elements contained in your web pages.

## Working with text

As shown in the previous code example, adding the .text() function to the jQuery object retrieves the text contained in the object. You can use the same .text() function to replace that text. Just place the text you want to use as a parameter to the .text() function:

```
$("p").text("This has changed");
```

Follow these steps to test this out:

**1.** Open your favorite text editor, program editor, or IDE package.

**2.** Type the following code:

```
<!DOCTYPE html>
<html>
    <head>
```

```
<title>Testing jQuery Replacing Text</title>
<script src="jquery-3.2.1.min.js"></script>
<script>
    jQuery(document).ready(function() {
        $("button").click( function() {
            $("p").text("This has changed!");
        });
    });
</script>
</head>
<body>
<h1>This is my heading</h1>
<p>This is some content on my web page</p>
<button>Test button</button>
</body>
</html>
```

3. **Save the file as** jquery2.html **in the** DocumentRoot **folder of your web server.**

4. **Make sure the Apache web server is running, open your browser, and enter the following URL:**

```
http://localhost:8080/jquery2.html
```

5. **Click the button on the web page and watch the text on the page.**

There are a couple of new things I threw into this example, so let me explain a bit:

>> **I added a button element at the bottom of the web page.** Notice that I didn't need to add the onclick attribute for the button as I used in the preceding chapter with JavaScript. The jQuery library is kind enough to do that for us!

>> **In the jQuery code I added the following line:**

```
$("button").click( function() {
```

The first part you should recognize — it finds the first button element on the web page. The code then applies the .click() function to that object. The browser runs this function when it detects that the site visitor clicks the referenced button. In this case, when the button gets clicked, the code triggers another anonymous function. The code in the anonymous function is

```
$("p").text("This has changed!");
```

When you click the button, you should see the content of the p element change to the text you specify in the jQuery code, right before your eyes, as shown in Figure 3-2!

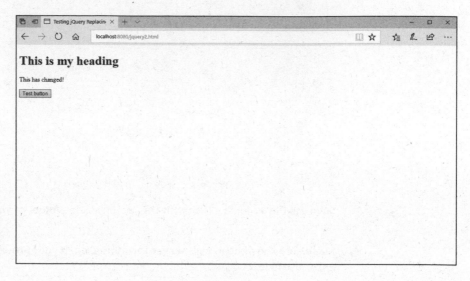

**FIGURE 3-2:**
The result of the
jquery2.html
program.

You use this method to change any type of text content in any type of block element.

## Working with HTML

The .text() function allows you to change the text contained within an element, but it doesn't change the HTML5 code for the element. You can do that by using the .html() function:

```
$("p").html("<h1>This changed to a heading</h1>");
```

Notice that you need to supply the full HTML5 element tags along with the text that you want to appear in the element.

If you replace the original .text() function in the example code with this line, when you click the button the p element turns into an h1 element, and the browser styles it accordingly, as shown in Figure 3-3!

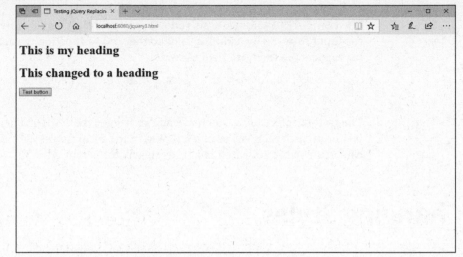

**FIGURE 3-3:**
Changing the
element using
the .html()
function.

## Working with attributes

Not only can you modify the text and HTML code in an element, but you can also retrieve and set attributes for the element using the .attr() function. To retrieve an attribute value, use the following format:

```
$(selector).attr("attribute");
```

To set a value associated with an attribute of the element, the format is as follows:

```
$(selector).attr("attribute", "value");
```

This allows you to change the appearance of an element by modifying the attributes as needed from your jQuery code.

## Working with form values

One of the greatest features of the jQuery library is the ability to dynamically read and modify data in HTML5 forms. This feature comes in handy if you need to validate form data as your site visitors are typing it into the form, before it even leaves their workstations!

The .val() function provides access to the value attribute for input elements:

```
var data = $("input").val();
```

Using jQuery

The `value` HTML5 attribute also allows you to set the default value that appears in the input form. So by adding a value to the `.val()` function, you can control what text appears in the form field as well:

```
$("input").val("Enter your last name");
```

The next chapter shows you how you can trigger the `.val()` function as your site visitor presses each key as she's typing in the form fields. With that feature, you can create dynamic search results as the visitor is typing!

# Changing Styles

The jQuery library can do more than just change the content that appears in the web page. It also contains functions that help you dynamically change the styles that the browser applies to elements on the web page.

This section discusses how you can access the CSS properties assigned to an object, as well as modify them on the fly as your site visitor interacts with the web page.

## Playing with properties

Book 2, Chapter 2, shows how you can apply CSS3 styles to elements to not only style them but also position them on the web page. Style rules defined in an internal or external style sheet determine just how the browser displays and positions the element on the web page.

The jQuery library provides some functions for you to use to help manipulate the CSS3 properties that the browser applies to elements. The first one I talk about is the `.css()` function.

The `.css()` function allows you to retrieve and set individual properties or a group of properties for any element in the web page. To retrieve the current value assigned to a CSS3 property, you use the following format, where *selector* is the CSS-style selector for finding the element and *property* is the CSS3 property name you want to retrieve:

```
$(selector).css(property);
```

For example, to determine the background color applied to a div element, you'd use the following:

```
var color = $("div").css("background-color");
```

When you use JavaScript to set CSS3 properties, you have to use different names, because JavaScript doesn't support the dash in the property names. Notice that with jQuery you use the actual CSS property name that you're already used to using — nothing new to learn!

Then, as you can probably guess by now, to set the CSS3 property for an element, you just add the value as the second parameter to the function call:

```
$("div").css("background-color", "red");
```

Follow these steps to test this out:

**1.** **Open your favorite text editor, program editor, or IDE package.**

**2.** **Type the following code:**

```
<!DOCTYPE html>
<html>
<head>
<title>Changing Properties with jQuery</title>
</head>
<style>
  div {
      background-color:yellow;
  }
</style>
<script src="jquery-3.2.1.min.js"></script>
<script>
    jQuery(document).ready(function() {
        $("button").click(function() {
            $("p").css("background-color", "red");
            $("p").css("font-size", "50px");
        });
    });
</script>
<body>
<div id="container">
<h1>This is my heading</h1>
<p>This is some content on my web page</p>
<button>Test button</button>
</div>
</body>
</html>
```

3. Save the file as jquery4.html in the DocumentRoot folder of your web server.

4. Make sure the Apache web server is running, and then open your browser and enter the following URL:

```
http://localhost:8080/jquery4.html
```

5. Click the button and watch the content from the p element on the web page.

This version of our example program uses a short CSS internal style sheet to set the background color of the div element around the elements on the web page. When jQuery detects the button click, it applies two new styles to the p element — changing the background color to red and increasing the font size to 50 pixels. Figure 3-4 shows what this looks like after you click the button.

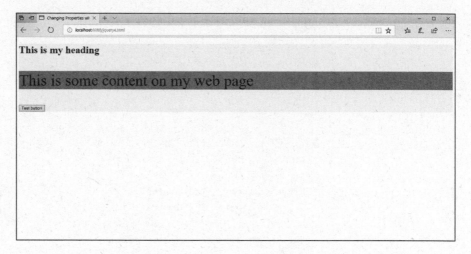

FIGURE 3-4:
The result of the jquery4.html program.

You can apply as many styles to as many elements as you need within the event trigger. However, the more styles you apply, the messier it gets. But fortunately, there are a couple of solutions to that problem.

## Using CSS objects

Instead of piling multiple .css() function lines on top of each other, trying to change lots of different style properties, you can create a *style object* in jQuery. The style object allows you to specify styles just as you do in the CSS3 style sheet and provide multiple styles in a single .css() function.

The style object has the following format:

```
{"property1":"value1", "property2":"value2"...}
```

Now things are really starting to look familiar — very similar to how CSS rules define properties and their values! Using this format, you can combine the two style changes in the `jquery4.html` example to one line:

```
$("p").css({"background-color":"red", "font-size":"50px"});
```

This is a great way to make dramatic changes to the web page layout and style dynamically in response to events that your site visitor triggers, such as changing the background color of text boxes as data is entered, or changing the location of important content that may be missed.

## Using CSS classes

Things are starting to get pretty fancy with your jQuery style coding, and you're starting to introduce another issue to your program. Now you're embedding styles inside your jQuery code, separate from the rest of the styles defined in the CSS3 style sheets. That can make things somewhat confusing when you're trying to troubleshoot a problem, or even if you're trying to go back over your own code several months later!

To solve that issue, the brilliant jQuery developers added another set of functions that interact with CSS3 class rules. With the jQuery class functions, you can add, remove, or even toggle a class to an element. Table 3-1 shows the classes available for you.

**TABLE 3-1**  **The jQuery Class Functions**

| Function | Description |
| --- | --- |
| `.addClass(class)` | Adds the specified class to the element |
| `.hasClass(class)` | Returns a true value if the element contains the specified class attribute |
| `.removeClass(class)` | Removes the specified class from the element |
| `.toggleClass(class)` | Alternately adds and removes the specified class each time it's called |

Now all you need to do is place the group of style properties you need into a class rule in your CSS style sheet definitions, and then add, remove, or even toggle the class for the element. The .hasClass() function allows you to check what class is currently assigned to the element.

Follow these steps to try this feature out:

1. Open the jquery4.html file from the previous example in your editor.

2. Modify the code so that it looks like this:

```html
<!DOCTYPE html>
<html>
<head>
<title>Changing Properties with jQuery</title>
</head>
<style>
   div {
       background-color:yellow;
   }

   .changeit {
       background-color:red;
       font-size:50px;
   }
</style>
<script src="jquery-3.2.1.min.js"></script>
<script>
   jQuery(document).ready(function() {
       $("button").click(function() {
           $("p").toggleClass("changeit");
       });
   });
</script>
<body>
<div id="container">
<h1>This is my heading</h1>
<p id="content">This is some content on my web page</p>
<button>Test button</button>
</div>
</body>
</html>
```

**3.** **Save the file as** jquery5.html **in the** DocumentRoot **folder of the Apache web server.**

**4.** **Ensure that the Apache web server is running, and then open your browser and enter the following URL:**

```
http://localhost:8080/jquery5.html
```

**5.** **Click the button multiple times to toggle the style effects on and off.**

In the updated code, I added a new class rule to the internal style sheet:

```
.changeit {
    background-color:red;
    font-size:50px;
}
```

And I used the .toggleClass() function to apply it to the p element:

```
$("p").toggleClass("changeit");
```

TIP

For even more fun, you can use the .show() and .hide() jQuery functions, which pretty much do what they say. They change the display CSS3 property of the element to block (for .show()) or none (for .hide()).

# Changing the Document Object Model

Not only can you use jQuery to modify content and styles of the existing elements in your Web page, you can also use it to add or remove entire elements! There are a handful of different jQuery functions available for manipulating the element nodes contained in the DOM tree.

## Adding a node

You can use jQuery to add a new node to the DOM tree to display additional content as needed. Table 3-2 shows the functions available for adding new nodes.

TABLE 3-2

## The jQuery Functions to add DOM Nodes

| Function | Description |
|----------|-------------|
| .after() | Adds a node after an existing node |
| .append() | Adds a node to the end of an existing node |
| .appendTo() | Adds a new node to the end of an existing node |
| .before() | Adds a node before an existing node |
| .insertAfter() | Adds a new node after an existing node |
| .insertBefore() | Adds a new node before an existing node |
| .prepend() | Adds a node to the beginning of an existing node |
| .prependTo() | Adds a new node to the beginning of an existing node |

Note the subtle difference between the .after() and .append() functions. The .append() function adds the new node to the end of the existing node, so it becomes a child node of the existing node in the DOM. The .after() function, on the other hand, adds a new sibling node after the existing node in the DOM. Likewise for the .before() and .prepend() functions.

For example, you can add a new p element to the existing p element in your example program by adding the following code:

```
$("p").after("<p>This is a new node</p>");
```

As you would expect, when you run one of these functions, the new node immediately appears in the web page.

## Removing a node

The jQuery library provides two functions for you to remove existing nodes from the DOM:

» .empty(): Removes all child nodes from the specified node

» .remove(): Removes the specified node

It's important to note that the .empty() function doesn't remove the specified node — it just removes any child nodes associated with the node.

# Playing with Animation

When you run the `jquery4.html` example code to change the background color and font size, the changes occur almost immediately after you click the button. That's a pretty stark effect, which can be toned down some.

One of the cooler features of jQuery is the ability to animate style changes. With the `.animate()` function, you can specify an endpoint style for the content, and jQuery will slowly work its way to that endpoint from the current style. This slow morphing process causes the web page to look like it's animated!

This is a hard feature to explain without actually viewing it, so follow these steps to try it out:

1. **Open the** `jquery4.html` **file in your editor.**

2. **Change the line that sets the** `font-size` **style property to use the** `.animate()` **function.**

   Look for the following line:

   ```
   $("p").css("font-size", "20px");
   ```

   And change it to this:

   ```
   $("p").animate({"font-size": "50px"});
   ```

3. **Save the new file as** `jquery6.html` **in the** `DocumentRoot` **folder for the web server.**

4. **Ensure the Apache web server is running and then open your browser and enter the following URL:**

   ```
   http://localhost:8080/jquery6.html
   ```

5. **Click the button and watch the animation.**

The `.animate()` function requires a CSS object, so even if you just specify one property to change, you must use the object format. When you click the button, instead of an instant change in font size, you see the text "grow" to get to the font size. You can change the rate of animation by adding a second parameter to the `.animate()` function — the milliseconds it takes to get to the final endpoint value. The default is 400 milliseconds (ms).

# Chapter **4**

# Reacting to Events with JavaScript and jQuery

I n the previous chapters in this minibook, I explain how to incorporate both JavaScript and jQuery into your HTML5 code to help create a dynamic web application. The trick to using JavaScript and jQuery, though, is knowing when to use them. How are you supposed to know when your site visitor is hovering the mouse pointer over a product in your catalog to pop up more information? Fortunately, your web page is talking to you, telling you what your website visitors are doing at all times. All you need to do is listen to your web page and direct your JavaScript or jQuery code accordingly. That's exactly what this chapter shows you how to do.

## Understanding Events

The world is full of events. There are birthday events, holiday events, school events, all types of events competing for your time. Your world is loaded with events, and it's your job to determine which events to participate in (your birth-day) and which ones to ignore (Talk Like a Pirate Day?).

The same is true with your web application. There are lots of events that your site visitor generates as she interacts with your web page. Each time your site visitor moves the mouse, that's an event. Each time she types text into a form field, that's an event. And of course, each time she clicks the mouse on a link or button, those are events, too. The key to successful dynamic web applications is to detect the events you need and ignore the ones you don't need.

## Event-driven programming

Most of the JavaScript code earlier in this minibook uses *procedural programming.* In procedural programming, the browser follows your JavaScript code line by line, processing each statement as it appears in the program.

There's another way to write programs, called *event-driven programming.* With event-driven programming, your program centers around events that occur in the web page. You must define a list of events to monitor, and if one of those events occurs, the browser runs the JavaScript function you've defined for the event.

With event-driven programming, you need to know what events to watch for. This section details the events that are generated by the browser on the different activities that occur while your site visitor views your web page.

## Watching the mouse

No, I'm not talking about Mickey. I'm talking about paying attention to what your site visitor is doing with the mouse device on his or her workstation. Believe it or not, your browser tracks every single move and action your mouse takes. You can tap into that wealth of information with your JavaScript or jQuery programs.

As you can imagine, there are many different events that the mouse generates as you move it around. Table 4-1 shows a list of the different mouse event names generated by the browser as defined in HTML5 and JavaScript. Later on, I show you the jQuery version of the event names.

As you can tell from the list in Table 4-1, you can watch exactly what your site visitors are doing while viewing your web page. (Scary!) Although this information can be useful, it can also result in information overload. The key to successful mouse watching is to only watch for the important events, such as when the site visitor clicks the primary mouse button on an object in the web page or when the mouse is hovering over an object.

**WARNING**

It's not a good idea to write code that watches the onmousemove event, because that event triggers for every pixel the mouse pointer moves to on the screen, generating thousands of events at a time!

**TABLE 4-1**     **Mouse Events**

| Event | Description |
| --- | --- |
| onclick | The primary mouse button has been clicked. |
| oncontextmenu | The secondary mouse button has been clicked. |
| ondblclick | The primary mouse button has been double-clicked. |
| onmousedown | The primary mouse button has been depressed. |
| onmouseenter | The mouse pointer has entered a specific area in the window. |
| onmouseleave | The mouse pointer has left a specific area in the window. |
| onmousemove | The mouse pointer is moving. |
| onmouseover | The mouse pointer is hovering over an object. |
| onmouseout | The mouse pointer has left a specific area in the window. |
| onmouseup | The primary mouse button has been released. |

## Listening for keystrokes

The keyboard talks to the browser, too. You can watch for key events in your JavaScript or jQuery programs just as you watch the mouse. Unlike the long list of mouse events, there are only three keyboard events for you to work with:

» onkeydown: A key is being pressed down.

» onkeypress: A key has been pressed and released.

» onkeyup: A key has been released.

Notice the subtle difference between the three events. The onkeydown event only triggers while the site visitor is pressing the key. Both the onkeypress and onkeyup events trigger when the site visitor releases the key. Granted, for most typing situations, the difference is very small, but for some applications (for example, games), it can be useful to know how long a key is being pressed, which you can only get from the onkeydown event.

**WARNING**

The term *keystroke* may be misleading. There are some keys on the standard keyboard that don't generate a keystroke themselves, such as the Shift, Alt, and Ctrl keys on a Windows keyboard. These keys are modifiers for other keys that generate the keystrokes.

# Paying attention to the page itself

Even the web page itself has events that your JavaScript and jQuery programs can listen for. Before HTML5, there were only a handful of page events that you could tap into. The newer HTML5 standard has defined a lot more page events to work with. Table 4-2 lists the more common HTML events that you may run into.

**TABLE 4-2**    **Page Events**

| Event | Description |
|---|---|
| onafterprint | Triggers after the site visitor prints the web page |
| onbeforeprint | Triggers before the site visitor prints the web page |
| onbeforeunload | Triggers just before the web page is removed from the browser window |
| onerror | Triggers when there is an error in loading a required file for the web page |
| onhaschange | Triggers when the server address of the URL has changed |
| onload | Triggers when the body of the web page loads |
| onmessage | Triggers when a message is sent to the browser window |
| onoffline | Triggers when the site visitor sets the browser to view the web page offline |
| ononline | Triggers when the site visitor sets the browser to view the web page online |
| onpagehide | Triggers when the site visitor navigates away from the web page |
| onpageshow | Triggers when the web page appears in the browser window |
| onpopstate | Triggers when the browser's history changes |
| onresize | Triggers when your site visitor resizes the browser window |
| onstorage | Triggers when a web storage area is updated |
| onscroll | Triggers when the site visitor moves the scrollbar in the browser window |
| onunload | Triggers when the web page is removed from the browser window |

The web page events allow you to track when your web page first appears in the site visitor's browser and when it leaves (and even just before it leaves). This gives you the opportunity to load things right up front when the page appears, or perform some operation as the page is about to disappear from the browser window.

# Focusing on JavaScript and Events

JavaScript and HTML5 team up to provide a way for your program to listen for events and perform some type of action when they occur. The HTML5 element code registers a JavaScript function for the browser to run when a specific element event occurs.

Different HTML5 elements generate different events based on how they interact with the site visitor on the web page. The following sections walk you through how to set up a JavaScript event monitor for different HTML5 elements.

## Saying hello and goodbye

The page events allow you to monitor when the web page loads and unloads from the site visitor's browser. You use these in the `<body>` tag of the web page to specify any `onload` or `onunload` event functions you need to run:

```
<body onload="welcome()">
```

In this example, the browser runs the `welcome()` JavaScript function when the web page first loads into the browser window, as shown in Figure 4-1.

**FIGURE 4-1:**
Running a function when the web page loads in the Chrome browser.

**WARNING**

There's some controversy as to just what the term *loads* means for the onload event. Some browsers trigger the onload event as the first thing before processing any of the HTML5 elements into the Document Object Model (DOM), while others wait until all the HTML5 elements have been processed before triggering the event. Because of this, it's not recommended to try to access any of the web page elements from a function triggered by the onload event — there's no guarantee that they'll be there yet.

You can test the onload event out in your own browsers by following these steps:

1. **Open your favorite text editor, program editor, or integrated development environment (IDE) package.**

2. **Type the following code into the editor window:**

```
<!DOCTYPE html>
<html>
<head>
<title>Testing the Page Events</title>
<script>
    function welcome() {
        alert("Welcome to my website!");
    }
</script>
</head>
<body onload="welcome()">
<h1>This is the main web page</h1>
<p>This is some content on the web page</p>
</body>
</html>
```

3. **Save the file as** loadtest.html **in the** DocumentRoot **folder of your web server.**

    For XAMPP on Windows, that's c:\xampp\htdocs; for XAMPP on macOS, that's /Applications/XAMPP/htdocs.

4. **Open the XAMPP Control Panel, and start the Apache web server.**

5. **Open your browser and enter the following URL:**

```
http://localhost:8080/loadtest.html
```

    You may need to change the TCP port to match your web server.

    You should see the welcome alert message, but you may or may not see the HTML code behind it on the web page.

**6.** Try different browsers to see if they behave any differently.

Figure 4-1 show the results from running the test using the Chrome browser. The alert() message appears from the onload event, but no content appears in the web page yet. Figure 4-2 shows running the same test using the Microsoft Edge browser.

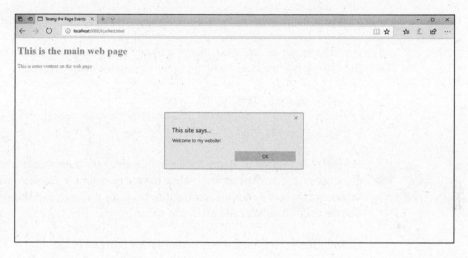

**FIGURE 4-2:**
Running the onload test using the Microsoft Edge browser.

The Edge browser displays the elements on the web page and then triggers the onload event to run the alert() function!

Using the onunload and onbeforeunload events can be even more problematic. Most browsers won't allow you to use the alert() function after the browser window has already closed, so don't try to use that in the onunload event. Usually you can still access the DOM tree objects during the unload process, but even that's not guaranteed. It's common practice to only use the onunload and onbeforeunload events to trigger functions that ensure any application data is safely stored before the application closes out the web page.

## Listening for mouse events

To trigger a JavaScript function for mouse events, you need to define the events as attributes in the HTML5 elements. This section shows you how to do that for a few different mouse events.

## Clicking the button

When your website visitor clicks the primary mouse button anywhere on your web page, that triggers an onclick event. To capture that event for individual elements, you must use add the onclick attribute to the element opening tag and specify the JavaScript function you want the browser to run when the event triggers. For example:

```
<button onclick="myfunction()">
```

If you have more than one button on your web page, you can pass a parameter to the JavaScript function identifying which button was selected:

```
<button onclick="func('buy')">Buy</button>
<button onclick="func('browse')">Browse</button>
<button onclick="func('help')">Help</button>
```

**TIP**

Notice that to pass a string value inside the attribute value you must use single quotes around the string value if you use double quotes around the HTML attribute. If you use double quotes, the browser will confuse them with the double quotes used to delimit the attribute value.

Follow these steps to test out listening for button clicks:

**1.** Open your favorite editor.

**2.** Type the following code:

```
<!DOCTYPE html>
<html>
<head>
<title>Testing Button Events</title>
<script>
    function clickme(name) {
        if (name == "help") {
            alert("Do you need some help?");
        } else if (name == "buy") {
            alert("What would you like to buy?");
        } else if (name == "browse") {
            alert("You can browse our catalog");
        }
    }
</script>
</head>
<body>
```

```
<h1>Store Menu</h1>
<p>Here are the current options:</p>
<button onclick="clickme('buy')">Buy a product</button>
<button onclick="clickme('browse')">Browse our catalog</button>
<button onclick="clickme('help')">Get Help</button>
</body>
</html>
```

3. **Save the file as** buttontest.html **in the** DocumentRoot **folder of your web server.**

4. **Ensure that the Apache web server is still running.**

5. **Open your browser and enter the following URL:**

```
http://localhost:8080/buttontest.html
```

6. **Click each of the buttons that appears on the web page.**

7. **Close the browser window when you're done testing.**

As you click each button, a different alert dialog box should appear, as shown in Figure 4-3.

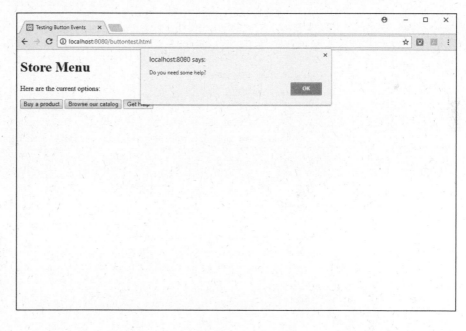

**FIGURE 4-3:**
The Help alert dialog box appearing from the buttontest.html application.

If you prefer, you can also use a unique ID attribute for each button to help identify it in the event function code.

## Hovering the pointer

It may seem odd, but the onmouseover and onmouseout events allow you to alter the appearance of many types of elements as your website visitors hover their mouse pointers over them. You're not limited to using these events on only buttons; you can work with the mouse events from inside any standard block element, such as paragraph and heading elements within your web page. Follow these steps to try that out:

**1.** **Open your editor.**

**2.** **Type the following code:**

```html
<!DOCTYPE html>
<html>
<head>
<title>Testing Mouse Events</title>
<style>
   #test {
      background-color: yellow;
      width:400px;
   }
</style>
<script>
   function changeit(state) {
      if (state == "in") {
         document.getElementById("test").style.backgroundColor="red";
      } else if (state == "out") {
         document.getElementById("test").style.backgroundColor="yellow";
}
   }
</script>
</head>
<body>
<h1>This is a test of the mouse events</h1>
<p id="test" onmouseover="changeit('in')" onmouseout="changeit('out')">
   This is some content that will change color!</p>
</body>
</html>
```

3. Save the file as `hovertest.html` in the `DocumentRoot` **folder of your web server.**

4. **Ensure that the Apache web server is running.**

5. **Open your browser and enter the following URL:**

```
http://localhost:8080/hovertest.html
```

6. **Move your mouse pointer around through the text in the paragraph and observe what happens.**

   The background color of the p element text should change when your mouse pointer hovers over it.

7. **Close your browser window when you're done testing.**

The `onmouseover` event triggers the `changeit()` JavaScript function, passing the text `in`, while the `onmouseout` event triggers the same `changeit()` JavaScript function, but passes the text `out`. The JavaScript code detects the value passed to the `changeit()` function and sets the `background-color` style property of the p element accordingly.

## Listening for keystrokes

Elements that accept data entry, such as text boxes and text areas, can trigger the keystroke events as your site visitors type. This allows you to monitor just what data your site visitors enter into the form fields as they type.

You'll often find yourself in situations where you need to count characters entered into a text box or text area in a form. You can use the `onkeyup` event to trigger a counter that counts the keystrokes.

Follow these steps to create a small program to demonstrate this feature using JavaScript and the `onkeyup` event:

1. **Open your favorite editor.**

2. **Type the following code:**

```
<!DOCTYPE html>
<html>
<head>
<title>Testing Keystroke Events</title>
```

```
<script>
    function gotkey() {
        var count =document.getElementById("text").value.length;
var output = "Character count: " + count;
        document.getElementById("status").innerHTML=output;
}
</script>
</head>
<body>
<h1>Testing for keystrokes</h1>
<p>Please enter some text into the text area</p>
<textarea id="text" cols="50" rows="20" onkeyup="gotkey()"></textarea><br>
<p id="status"></p>
</body>
</html>
```

3. **Save the file as** keytest.html **in the** DocumentRoot **folder of your web server.**

4. **Ensure that the Apache web server is running.**

5. **Open your browser and enter the following URL:**

   ```
   http://localhost:8080/keytest.html
   ```

6. **Start typing some text in the text area that appears on the page.**

   You should see the character count appear under the text area and be able to keep track of the characters that appear.

7. **Close the browser to exit the program.**

The gotkey() function uses the length property of the value attribute of the element. By stringing them all together into the same statement, you can easily return the number of characters that are currently in the text area:

```
var count = document.getElementById("text").value.length;
```

The p element after the text area starts out empty, but for each triggering of the gotkey() function, it changes the innerHTML property to the string that was stored in the output variable. Figure 4-4 shows what the result will look like as you type text into the text area.

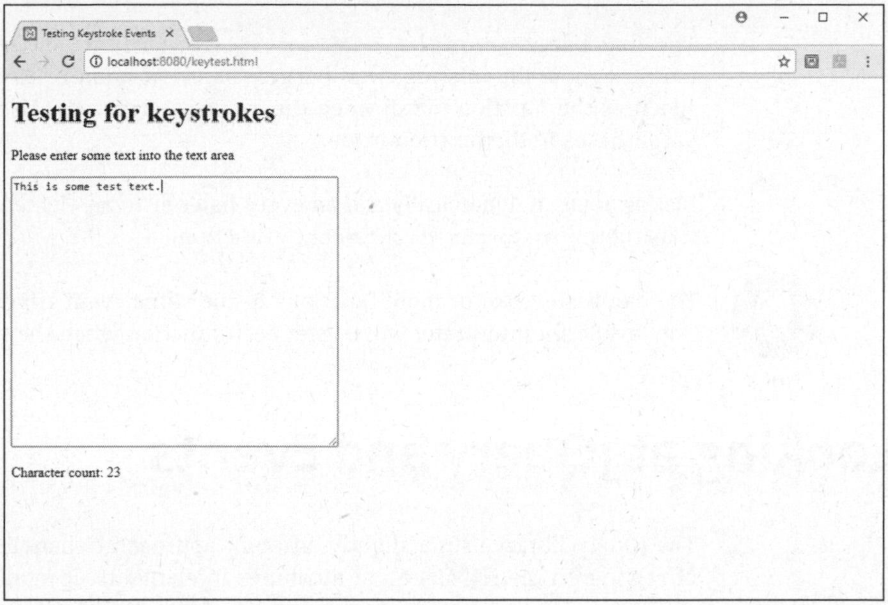

**FIGURE 4-4:**
Counting
keystrokes in the
`keytest.html`
program.

Now you can provide an interface that tells your site visitors how many characters they've typed into a text box or text area! You can take this feature one step further by disabling the text area if they've entered too many characters:

```javascript
function gotkey() {
    var count = document.getElementById("text").value.length;
    if (count > 20) {
        var output = "Sorry, that's too many characters";
        document.getElementById("text").disabled="disabled";
    } else {
        var output = "Character count: " + count;
    }
    document.getElementById("status").innerHTML=output;
}
```

Now things are really starting to get fancy!

## Event listeners

JavaScript provides one more way to assign events to elements. You use the `.addEventListener()` function to dynamically assign events to monitor the elements on your web page. That looks like this:

```javascript
document.getElementById("button1").addEventListener("click", clickbuy);
```

The first parameter of the .addEventListener() function defines the event to monitor (note the missing on as part of the event name). The second parameter specifies the function to call when the event is triggered. (Also note the missing parentheses in the function name.)

Just as you can dynamically add an event listener to an element, you can remove it using the .removeEventListener() function.

**TIP**

You can assign two or more functions to the same event trigger for an element. The JavaScript interpreter will trigger each function when the event occurs.

# Looking at jQuery and Events

The jQuery library uses a slightly different approach to handling events. Instead of relying on the HTML5 event attributes in elements, it monitors the events in the browser and allows you to tap into them directly. This helps simplify things, because you don't need to split the event code between the HTML5 code and the jQuery code. Everything you need is in the jQuery code.

## jQuery event functions

The jQuery library provides functions for handling all the HTML5 events that you've seen. The benefit of using the jQuery event model is that you don't need to specify the event attribute in the HTML5 code — the jQuery function does all the work for you!

For example, to monitor for the onclick event for a button, you just simply use the following:

```
$("button").click(function() {
    code
});
```

This creates an anonymous function to run whenever the site visitor clicks the button. The actual HTML5 button element would look like this:

```
<button>Click here</button>
```

And that's all you need! The benefit of this method is that you do all the event coding in the JavaScript code — there's nothing in the HTML5 code.

For the most part, the jQuery event functions mirror the HTML5 event attributes, but leave off the on part in the event name. There are, however, a couple of extra handy event functions available. Table 4-3 shows a list of the jQuery events that you're most likely to use.

**TABLE 4-3**      **The jQuery Event Functions**

| Event | Description |
|---|---|
| blur() | Triggers when the element loses the window focus |
| change() | Triggers when the element changes |
| click() | Triggers when the primary mouse button clicks on the element |
| dblclick() | Triggers when the primary mouse button is double-clicked on the event |
| focus() | Triggers when the element gains the window focus |
| focusin() | Triggers when the element or a child element gains the window focus |
| focusout() | Triggers when the element or a child element loses the window focus |
| hover() | Defines two functions — one for when the mouse pointer is over the element and another one for when it leaves |
| keydown() | Triggers when a key is held down |
| keypress() | Triggers when a key is pressed and released |
| keyup() | Triggers when a key is released |
| mousedown() | Triggers when the primary mouse button is held down |
| mouseenter() | Triggers when the mouse pointer enters the element area |
| mouseleave() | Triggers when the mouse pointer leaves the element area |
| mousemove() | Triggers when the mouse pointer moves |
| mouseout() | Triggers when the mouse pointer leaves the element area |
| mouseover() | Triggers when the mouse pointer is over the element area |
| mouseup() | Triggers when the primary mouse button is released |
| ready() | Triggers when the DOM tree is fully populated |
| resize() | Triggers when the browser window has been resized |
| scroll() | Triggers when the site visitor uses the scrollbar |
| select() | Triggers when an item is selected |
| submit() | Triggers when a submit button has been clicked |

An extremely handy addition is the hover() function. It allows you to define two separate functions at the same time — one for when the mouse is hovering over the element and another for when it's not. Follow these steps to test this feature out.

**1.** Open your favorite editor.

**2.** Type the following code into the editor window:

```html
<!DOCTYPE html>
<html>
<head>
<title>Testing Mouse Events</title>
<style>
    .yellow {
        background-color: yellow;
        width: 400px;
    }

    .red {
        background-color: red;
        width: 400px;
    }
</style>
<script src="jquery-3.2.1.min.js"></script>
<script>
    jQuery(document).ready( function() {
        $("p").hover( function() {
            $(this).addClass("red"); },
        function() {
            $(this).removeClass("red"); });
    });
</script>
</head>
<body>
<h1>This is a test of the mouse events</h1>
<p class="yellow">This is some content that will change color!</p>
<p>This is some content that will change color, too!</p>
</body>
</html>
```

3. **Save the file as** `jhovertest.html` **in the** DocumentRoot **folder for your web server.**

4. **Ensure that the Apache web server is running.**

5. **Open your browser and enter the following URL:**

```
http://localhost:8080/jhovertest.html
```

6. **Move the mouse pointer around to hover over the p element sections and watch what happens.**

   Each p element should get the red background only when you hover over it; the other p element should stay the same.

7. **Close out the browser to end the test.**

In the code for this example, everything happens in the jQuery code:

```
jQuery(document).ready( function() {
    $("p").hover( function() {
        $(this).addClass("red"); },
    function() {
        $(this).removeClass("red"); });
});
```

You should recognize the first line, which tells jQuery to wait until the browser loads the document before running the function code. The function code selects all p elements and then assigns the hover() event function to them. In this example, I created two p elements to show another neat feature in jQuery.

When you hover over each p element, only that p element changes background color! The key to that is the $(this) object in jQuery. The $(this) object represents the currently selected object. Using that, whichever p element triggered the event is the one that the addClass() function applies to, while the other p element is ignored. That saves us a whole lot of code from having to uniquely identify each p element on the web page! Figure 4-5 shows the result of the program in action.

This example shows just how easy it is to code events with jQuery. One of the primary goals of jQuery is to make coding for handling events easier, and I'd say they met their goals!

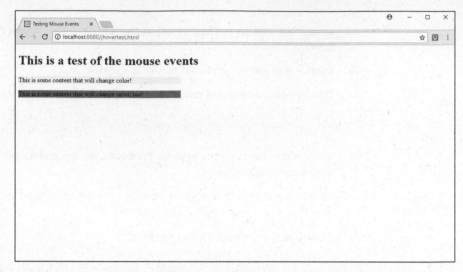

**FIGURE 4-5:**
The jhover.
html code test
only changes one
p element at
a time.

## The jQuery event handler

The jQuery library also provides a way for you to code event handlers. With jQuery, the event handler function is called on( ). Here's the format for the on( ) function:

```
$(selector).on("event", "filter", data, function() {
    code
});
```

The *selector* part you should be familiar with now. It determines which element(s) the event handler is attached to. The event parameter defines the jQuery event to attach to the element(s). The *filter* parameter is a little different. It defines a child selector to the main selector you specify. For example, if you only want to capture click events on buttons within an article element section, you'd use the following:

```
$("article").on("click", "button", function() {
```

To test this feature out, follow these steps to convert the keytest.html JavaScript code you worked on earlier to use jQuery instead:

1. **Open your favorite editor.**

2. **Type the following code into the editor window:**

```
<!DOCTYPE html>
<html>
<head>
<title>Testing jQuery Keystroke Events</title>
```

```
<script src="jquery-3.2.1.min.js"></script>
<script>
    jQuery(document).ready( function() {
        $("textarea").on("keyup", function() {
            var count = $(this).val().length;
            var output = "Character count: " + count;
            $("#status").text(output);
        });
    });
</script>
</head>
<body>
<h1>Testing for keystrokes</h1>
<p>Please enter some text into the text area</p>
<textarea cols="50" rows="20"></textarea><br>
<p id="status"></p>
</body>
</html>
```

3. **Save the file as** jkeytest.html **in the** DocumentRoot **folder of your web server.**

4. **Ensure that the web server is running.**

5. **Open your browser and enter the following URL:**

```
http://localhost:8080/jkeytest.html
```

6. **Start typing text in the text area.**

   You should see the count message appear in the status area, showing the accurate count of how many characters are in the text area.

7. **Close the browser window when you're finished.**

8. **Stop the web server.**

One thing you have to say about jQuery code: It's a lot cleaner looking than the JavaScript version! Notice that now you don't need to define an event attribute in the <textarea> tag. jQuery takes care of that for you.

Reacting to Events with
JavaScript and jQuery

The jQuery code itself is fairly clean and uncomplicated:

```
jQuery(document).ready( function() {
    $("textarea").on("keyup", function() {
        var count = $(this).val().length;
        var output = "Character count: " + count;
        $("#status").text(output);
    });
});
```

It starts out as usual, waiting for the document DOM to load and then assigns the event handler to the text area element on the web page. The event handler looks for the keyup event; when it's detected, the handler function retrieves the length of the text in the text area (again, using the $(this) selector) and then outputs it to the status p element area. Figure 4-6 shows how this looks.

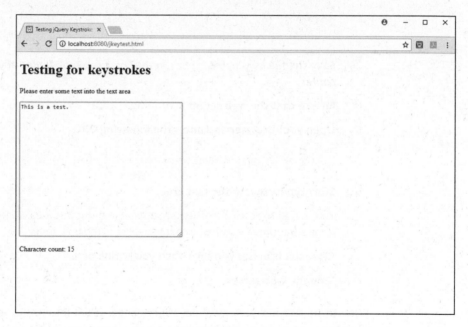

FIGURE 4-6:
The output of
the jkeytest.
html program in
action.

The results are the same as the JavaScript version, but with a lot less coding!

TIP

To define an event handler that only triggers once and goes away, use the one() function instead of the on() function. To remove an event handler that you've defined for a selector, use the off() function.

Chapter **5**

# Troubleshooting JavaScript Programs

A fact of life when working with any type of programming language is that there will always be errors as you develop your application code. Working with JavaScript is no different. There are plenty of opportunities for coding errors to cause all sorts of problems in your web applications. But don't worry — getting an error in your application isn't the end of the world. There are some simple tools at your disposal to help you find and fix those errors before your site visitors experience them. This chapter helps give you some ideas for what to do when errors occur as you develop your applications and offers tips for how to work your way through them.

## Identifying Errors

Your web application may run into an error and it's fairly obvious that something went wrong — something that was supposed to happen didn't. Other times, however, program errors can be a little more subtle, such as altering the data in a way that's not obvious until you analyze the output. These types of errors are dangerous, because often you don't even know they're present until it's too late. It helps to be able to watch your JavaScript program and observe when the subtle coding errors occur.

The old-fashioned way of doing that was to insert `alert()` statements at strategic places in your code to watch variables as your code processes things. Just stick in the variable you want to monitor inside the `alert()` function to get a quick display of the value the variable contains at that point in the program:

```
alert(lastName);
```

That generates a lot of pop-up messages as you walk through your application, but it's a great strategy for helping watch what's going on "behind the scenes" in the code. This method is especially helpful with logic errors in the code — to detect when something isn't working quite the way you thought it would.

Yet another code troubleshooting method often used in the past was commenting out sections of code. JavaScript supports adding comment lines in the code to help with documenting what's going on. There are two types of comments that you can use in JavaScript. This is a one-line comment:

```
// Comments are fun!
```

This is a comment that spans more than one line in the code:

```
/* Comments allow you to document what is happening with your code. Comments are
   useful, but calling them fun is a bit of a stretch. */
```

When JavaScript sees the comment tags, it skips any text that's within the comment. While this is mainly intended to add commentary to your programs so you (or anyone else reading your code) know what code does what, it was also common to use this method to temporarily remove lines or entire blocks of code from the program without actually deleting them. Just place the JavaScript comment tags around the code you want to skip, and then run the program to watch how it works.

These are good troubleshooting methods, and they still come in handy at times, but today we have more sophisticated troubleshooting techniques at our fingertips.

Fortunately, all the popular web browsers today support JavaScript debuggers. A *debugger* is a program that points out program errors as they occur while you run the web application in the browser. Most debuggers also allow you to step through your JavaScript code one line at a time. This provides the opportunity to watch as each variable changes value, to help you track exactly where things are going awry.

All the main web browsers in use today either have a JavaScript debugger built in or easily added as a plug-in. It has become somewhat of a standard to launch the debugger tools by hitting the F12 key while viewing a web page. Figure 5-1 shows the IE Developer Tools section that appears.

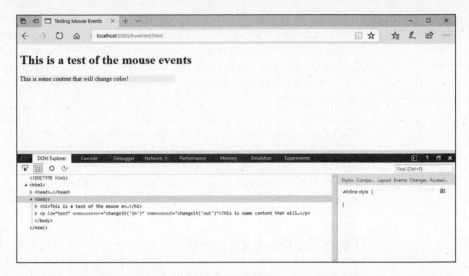

**FIGURE 5-1:**
The Microsoft
Edge Developer
Tools interface.

You can use the Developer Tools to help with your troubleshooting methods and quickly find (and fix) coding issues.

# Working with Browser Developer Tools

The Developer tools interface used by all the main web browsers has many of the same features across all browsers. The interface contains seven different tabs:

» **DOM Explorer:** Breaks down the web page elements into their Document Object Model (DOM) objects. This tool is great for exploring the DOM elements, especially if you need to isolate an element to reference in your JavaScript code.

» **Console:** Displays the JavaScript console, which logs error and warning messages caused by the JavaScript code in the web page, as well as any messages logged to the console directly from the JavaScript program.

» **Debugger:** A full-featured JavaScript debugger for troubleshooting JavaScript code line by line.

» **Network:** Displays network information about remote servers contacted to display the content on the web page.

» **Performance:** Profiles the central processing unit (CPU) utilization required while the JavaScript code in your web page runs.

» **Memory:** Profiles the memory utilization required while the JavaScript code in your web page runs.

>> **Emulation:** In addition to the standard developer tools, the Internet Explorer and Edge browsers allow you to change the version of browser emulation used to display a web page. This allows you to view the web page as it would be seen in an older version of Internet Explorer, a great tool for developing web pages.

The following sections walk through the first three tools as they work in the Microsoft Internet Explorer and Edge browsers. Other browsers offer similar features but may require slightly different methods for using them. When you've learned how to use the tools in one browser, it's fairly easy to figure out how to use them in the others.

# The DOM Explorer

The DOM Explorer disassembles the web page HTML5 code into the separate DOM elements that comprise the web page. It displays each element in a hierarchical tree structure, showing the general layout of the web page. Embedded elements are shown in the tree as child objects of the parent element, allowing you to collapse entire sections down to view a single level of the tree hierarchy at a time. Figure 5-2 demonstrates how this looks.

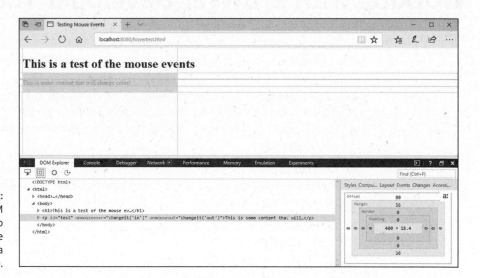

**FIGURE 5-2:** Using the DOM Explorer to examine the HTML in a web page.

In some browsers, when you hover the mouse pointer over a DOM element, the DOM Explorer highlights the area of the web page the DOM element generates. This helps you identify which area on the web page is created by which HTML5 code. Unfortunately, Internet Explorer doesn't support this feature, but Edge does.

Instead of highlighting the elements in the web page, Internet Explorer displays a layout diagram for the element to the right side of the DOM Explorer. The highlighted areas use separate colors to show the element text area, the padding area around the text, the border area around the element, and the margin area defined for the element.

Inside each area is a number showing how the area is sized in the HTML5 code. What's even cooler is that you can click the number of an area to edit it directly in the DOM tree and then see how the change affects the layout of the elements on the web page. This is a great way to help visualize and experiment with your web page layout.

TIP

For position values that are calculated by the browser (such as percentages and em units), the DOM Explorer displays both the configured value, as well as the calculated value in pixels. This is yet another great tool for experimenting with layout structures.

The DOM Explorer also allows you to make edits directly to the HTML5 code for an element and then view how the changes affect the web page in real time. There are three ways to do that:

>> Double-click directly on an element attribute in the DOM Explorer to change its value.

>> Right-click an element and select Add Attribute to add a new attribute.

>> Right-click an element and select Edit as HTML to edit the element manually.

The DOM Explorer also tracks event handlers that your JavaScript code attaches to HTML5 events, allowing you to detect when an event handler is misapplied or didn't get applied at all.

## The Console

The Console displays messages received by the browser from the loaded web page. There are three categories of messages that display in the Console:

>> **Errors:** Issues that cause the web page to not load or perform correctly, such as invalid JavaScript code

>> **Warnings:** Issues that allow the web page to load, but that may cause unexpected behavior

>> **Information:** Any noncritical information provided by the web page

When you click the Console tab, you see the interface shown in Figure 5-3.

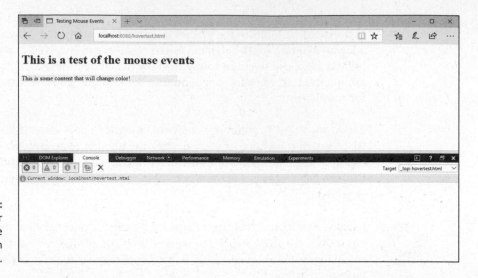

**FIGURE 5-3:**
The Developer
Tools Console
window in
Microsoft Edge.

The first three icons at the top allow you to filter the messages to hide or display the error (the red X), warning (the yellow triangle), or information (the blue circle) messages. They also show the count of each type of message generated since the last clear of the Console. You can clear out the messages by clicking the black X icon.

To watch the Console in action, let's work on an example with some bad JavaScript code and see what happens. Follow these steps:

1. **Open the** hover.html **file created in Book 3, Chapter 4.**

2. **In the** changeit() **function code, change the** getElementById() **functions to the incorrect** getElementByid() **name.**

   Note the lower-case *i* in the function name, a mistake that I make all too often on my own!

3. **Open the XAMPP Console and start the Apache web server.**

4. **Open Internet Explorer or Edge, and enter the following URL:**

   ```
   http://localhost:8080/hover.html
   ```

5. **Press F12.**

   The Developer Tools window appears.

6. **Click the Console tab.**

7. **Hover your mouse pointer over the p element content in the main web page, and watch the messages that appear in the Console area.**

While on the web page, all you see is that nothing happens, not much to help with why that was. However, the Console shows the error messages that identify exactly what went wrong. The misnamed `getElementByid()` functions generate an error in the Console each time the mouse events trigger. The error messages point you to the misnamed function and the line numbers they appear on in the code. This is a huge help in figuring out just what went wrong when a dynamic action doesn't work correctly in your web pages.

Besides watching the error and warning messages that the web page generates on its own, you can generate your own messages in the Console from your code. The `console.log()` JavaScript function allows you to send messages directly to the Console for viewing. Just add the line anywhere in your JavaScript code to display useful information to the Console.

For example, one method I often use when working with events is to add a `console.log()` function to identify each time an event is triggered in the JavaScript code:

```
function changeit(state) {
    if (state == "in") {
        console.log("mouseover triggered");
        document.getElementById("test").style.backgroundColor"red";
    } else if (state == "out") {
        console.log("mouseout triggered");
        document.getElementById("test").style.backgroundColor="yellow";
    }
}
```

As the HTML5 code triggers each mouse event and passes control over to the JavaScript `changeit()` function, the `console.log()` functions run based on just which event triggered. Then you can just watch the Console area to tell just what's going on "behind the scenes" in your application!

**WARNING**

Adding `console.log()` functions to the code is a great troubleshooting technique, but be sure to remove them before taking your application live for site visitors! You don't want to needlessly clutter up their Console logs with troubleshooting data.

Below the Console window is a command line interface (CLI) that allows you to enter JavaScript code to run inside the web page. Just type the JavaScript code you want at the CLI prompt and press Enter or Return. You can use this to quickly test variable values or override variable values to see how they affect the program operation.

If you need to enter a long JavaScript statement (such as defining a function), click the double up-arrow icon at the far-right side of the CLI. This expands the CLI pane to display more lines of code. When you're ready to submit the code, click the green arrow to run it.

**TIP**

The Console CLI also allows you to copy and paste code into it. You can use the CLI to insert new functions, or test out additional code as the program is running. As you enter new code, the browser interprets it on the fly, at the current point in the application. If the application is paused by the Debugger tool, the code is executed at that point in the program.

## The Debugger

The Debugger allows you to watch your JavaScript code in action. This tool is a powerful way to step through the JavaScript code in the application one statement at a time and observe exactly what's going on. The Debugger allows you to pause the JavaScript code at any point in the program and view the following:

» The path that caused the program to get where it is

» The values of any variables that have been set by the code

» How variables change at each statement after that point

To cause the JavaScript program to pause in the Debugger you need to set one or more breakpoints in the code. The breakpoint signals to the browser to stop processing code and enter the Debugger window.

When you open the Debugger tool window, you'll see different sections appear in the interface, as shown in Figure 5-4.

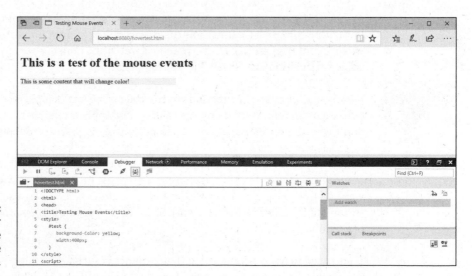

**FIGURE 5-4:**
The Debugger interface in the Microsoft Edge Developer Tools.

The Debugger interface has three main sections:

>> **Script pane:** The script pane (on the left side) shows the web page HTML5 and JavaScript code. It indicates whether there are any breakpoints and, if the program is paused, where in the code it's paused.

>> **Watch pane:** The watch pane (on the right side at the top) shows a list of variables that you're watching and their current values.

>> **Call Stack and Breakpoints pane:** The Call Stack and Breakpoints pane (on the right side at the bottom) displays the chain of function calls that led to the current location in the code (the call stack), as well as the list of breakpoints set in the program code.

Each pane provides information about the running JavaScript program and what's going on each time the Debugger pauses the program to examine the code in a breakpoint.

There are three ways to set a breakpoint in your JavaScript program:

>> Click next to the line number in the script pane of the statement where you want the program to pause.

>> Use the icons in the Breakpoints pane to add an XML or event breakpoint. Event breakpoints pause the program when a specified event is triggered (such as when you click the mouse button).

>> Add the debugger statement in your JavaScript code. Although this method is handy, it can also be very dangerous. If you use this method, don't forget to remove the debugger statements from your code before going live with site visitors.

TIP

Setting breakpoints inside the Debugger interface is the best method. Those breakpoints are only temporary — they go away when you close out your browser window.

When the Debugger pauses the program code at a breakpoint, you have a set of icons available above the script pane that control how the browser executes the code in debugger mode. Table 5-1 lists the icons that you can use.

**TABLE 5-1**     **Debugger Control Icons**

| Icon | Description |
|---|---|
| Continue | Removes the code pause and continues with the next statement. |
| Break | Exits from the Debugger mode after the next statement. |
| Step Into | Proceeds to the next line of code. If the next line is a function, the Debugger follows into the function code. |
| Step Over | Proceeds to the next line of code. If the next line is a function, the Debugger runs the function code, but not in debug mode. |
| Step Out | Exits from the called function back to the main program. |
| Break on New Worker | Exits the Debugger when a new web page is created. |
| Exception Control | Sets how to handle exceptions as they're thrown in the code. |
| Show Next Statement | Lets you skip lines of code to execute in the program. |
| Run to Cursor | Resumes execution of the code until the line in the code where the cursor is located. |
| Set Next Statement | Lets you skip statements in a function without running them. |

To go line-by-line through the JavaScript code, use the Step Into control icon. If you come to a JavaScript function in the code (such as the getElementById() function), clicking the Step Into control icon will follow the code into the JavaScript library that implements that function. This can get somewhat tedious at times, because some JavaScript functions require hundreds or even thousands of lines of code to implement, before you get back to your own code! To avoid that, use the Step Over control icon. The Step Over control feature runs through the JavaScript library code that implements the function, but then pauses again when control gets back to your code.

When you're done debugging the code, click the Continue control icon to return back to the normal operation of the program.

To watch the Debugger tool in action, follow these steps:

1. **Ensure that the Apache web server is running; if it isn't, start it from the XAMPP Console.**

2. **Open your Internet Explorer or Edge browser and enter the following URL:**

```
http://localhost:8080/hovertest.html
```

**3.** **Press F12.**

The Developer Tools window appears.

**4.** **Click the Debugger tab.**

**5.** **In the script pane, click the line number for the first statement in the**
changeit() **function.**

This should be the following line:

```
if (status == "in") {
```

**6.** **Observe what happens in the Breakpoint pane.**

A new breakpoint should be set, indicated by a red dot next to the line.

**7.** **Click Add Watch in the Watches pane.**

**8.** **In the text box that appears, type** state, **to watch the** state **variable that's
used in the** changeit() **function.**

**9.** **Reload the** hovertest.html **page in the browser window and then hover
the mouse pointer over the p element section on the web page.**

When you hover the mouse pointer over the p element, that triggers the
onmouseover event, which calls the changeit() JavaScript function. The
Debugger detects the breakpoint that you set and pauses the program
execution, as shown in Figure 5-5.

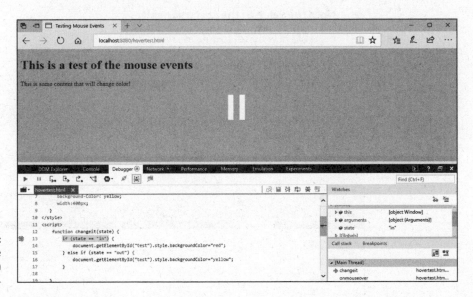

**FIGURE 5-5:**
Pausing the code
at a breakpoint in
the Debugger.

Notice the information you now have available at your fingertips. The orange arrow in the Script pane indicates the statement at which the debugger is paused. In the Watches pane, you can now see the state variable's value as the program enters into the changeit() function. In the Call Stack and Breakpoints pane, you can see just how the program got to the changeit() function. It shows that the main program thread triggered an onmouseout event, and it's currently at the changeit() function. In the Script pane, you see a pointer that shows just where in the code things stopped.

Follow these steps to continue on with the debugging process:

**1.** **Click the Step Into icon to move on to the next line of code.**

If you kept the console.log() statement in the code from the previous example, it'll take you into the JavaScript library to run that function. If you prefer to avoid doing that, click the Step Over icon.

**2.** **Continue clicking the Step Into icon to walk your way through the** changeit() **function code in the web page.**

Eventually the pointer will return to the p element defined in the hovertest.html file.

**3.** **Click the Continue icon in the controls.**

The Debugger will again stop at the changeit() function. This is because it detected that the mouse pointer is no longer in the p element section, so the onmouseout event triggered.

**4.** **Note the value of the** state **variable.**

It should now be set to out, as shown in Figure 5-6.

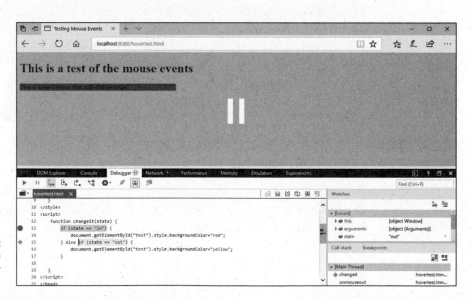

**FIGURE 5-6:**
Stopping the
Debugger later
on in the code.

5. **Click the Step Into icon, and watch how the** `if...else` **statement in the code evaluates the state variable and jumps to the** `else` **section of the code.**

6. **Click the Continue icon to return the program back to running normally.**

7. **Disable the breakpoint that you previously set by clicking the check box for the breakpoint in the Breakpoints pane.**

8. **Run the program again and watch what happens.**

   Now the Debugger won't stop at the breakpoint.

9. **Close the browser window to end the test.**

With just a few simple commands, you have a full-fledged method of debugging your dynamic web applications. That makes developing your web applications a much easier task.

# Working Around Errors

There may be times in your application where you don't want things to come to a grinding halt just because of some type of error in the program code. Often JavaScript programs rely on data supplied by the site visitor, and you wouldn't want an invalid data entry to cause your program to crash.

One method to prevent that is to intercept errors before they make it to the browser and cause problems. This process is called "catching the errors." With catching the errors, the program detects when something is amiss and provides some alternate code for the browser to run, bypassing the normal code that would have produced the fatal error.

You do this in JavaScript with the `try...catch` statement. The `try...catch` statement consists of two code blocks — the `try` code block to run and monitor for errors, and the `catch` code block to run in case any errors are detected in the `try` code block. Here's the format for the `try...catch` statement:

```
try {
    code to test
} catch (err) {
    code to run if test fails
}
```

The catch( ) function takes one parameter — a variable to place an Error object that JavaScript generates to describe the error that occurred. The Error object has two properties:

>> name: Returns the name of the error type

>> message: A string message describing the error in more detail

The error name identifies the type of error that occurred in the try code block. There are six different error types supported in JavaScript, shown in Table 5-2.

**TABLE 5-2**     ## JavaScript Error Types

| Error | Description |
|-------|-------------|
| EvalError | An eval( ) function has produced an error. |
| RangeError | A value out of range has occurred. |
| ReferenceError | An invalid location was referenced in the code. |
| SyntaxError | Invalid JavaScript code was detected. |
| TypeError | An invalid data type was used. |
| URIError | An error in the encodeURI( ) function was detected. |

Besides automatically detecting errors, you can create your own custom error checks and messages by using the throw statement inside the try code block:

```
try {
    if (value < 1000) throw "The value is too small";
    if (value > 10000) throw "The value is too large";
} catch (err) {
    alert(err);
}
```

The string assigned to the throw statement is displayed as part of the Error object. To demonstrate using the try...catch method to your JavaScript code, let's work out a simple exercise. Follow these steps to create the demo:

1. **Open your favorite text editor, program editor, or IDE package.**

2. **Type the following code:**

```
<!DOCTYPE html>
<html>
<head>
```

```
<title>Catching Errors Test</title>
<style>
    fieldset {
        width: 450px;
    }

    label, input {
        margin: 10px;
    }
</style>
<script>
function calculate() {
    var games, scores, array, total, average, output;
    games = document.getElementById("games").value;
    scores = document.getElementById("scores").value;
    array = scores.split(',');
    total = 0;
    for(i = 0; i < array.length; i++)  {
        total = total + parseInt(array[i]);
    }
    try {
      if (games == 0) {
        throw "Please enter a valid number of games";
      } else if (games == "") {
        throw "Please enter a valid number of games";
      } else if (isNaN(games)) {
        throw "Please enter a valid number of games";
      }
      average = total / games;
      output = "The average is " + average;
      document.getElementById("result").innerHTML = output;
    } catch (err) {
      document.getElementById("result").innerHTML = err;
    }
}
</script>
</head>
<body>
<fieldset>
<legend>Bowling Calculator</legend>
<label>Enter number of games bowled</label>
<input type="text" id="games" size="3"><br>
<label>Enter scores, separated by commas</label>
<input type="text" id="scores" size="20"><br>
<button onclick="calculate()">
```

```
Calculate average
</button>
<p id="result"></p>
</fieldset>
</body>
</html>
```

3. **Save the file as** `catchtest.html` **in the** `DocumentRoot` **folder of the Apache web server.**

   That's `c:\xampp\htdocs` for XAMPP on Windows, or `/Applications/XAMPP/htdocs` for XAMPP on macOS.

4. **Open the XAMPP Control Panel and start the Apache web server.**

5. **Open your browser, and enter the following URL:**

   ```
   http://localhost:8080/catchtest.html
   ```

   You may need to use a different port in the URL for your web server.

6. **Enter** 3 **for the number of games and** 100,105,100 **for the scores.**

7. **Click the Calculate Average button to view the results.**

8. **Change the number of games to an invalid value — enter** 0 **or some text, or just leave the field empty.**

9. **Click the Calculate Average button and see what happens.**

   You should see the text from the appropriate `throw` statement that caught the error appear.

10. **Close the browser, and shut down the Apache web server.**

When you enter an invalid value for the number of games, the `if...then` condition checks will detect it, and use the `throw` statement to intercept the error and trigger the `catch` code block, displaying the message defined in the `throw` statement (see Figure 5-7).

There's one more piece to the `try...catch` statement that you can use. The `finally` statement allows you to enter a block of code that gets executed no matter what happens in the try code block:

```
try {
    code to test
} catch (error) {
    code to run if errors
} finally {
    final code always runs
}
```

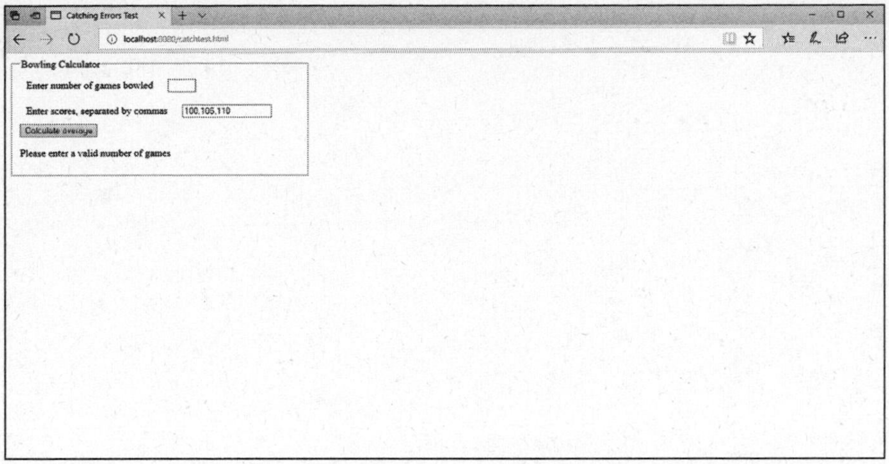

**FIGURE 5-7:**
Catching an invalid data entry using the try... catch statement.

Any code you place in the `finally` code block runs at all times. If the code in the `try` code block is successful, the JavaScript interpreter jumps to the `finally` code block and runs that code. If the code in the `try` code block fails, the JavaScript interpreter runs the code in the `catch` code block, and then runs the code in the `finally` code block. This is a good way to have "cleanup" code for the function.

PHP

# Contents at a Glance

**CHAPTER 1: Understanding PHP Basics** . . . . . . . . . . . . . . . . . . . . . . . 303

Seeing the Benefits of PHP. . . . . . . . . . . . . . . . . . . . . . . . . . . . . . . . . 303
Understanding How to Use PHP . . . . . . . . . . . . . . . . . . . . . . . . . . . . . 305
Working with PHP Variables. . . . . . . . . . . . . . . . . . . . . . . . . . . . . . . . 310
Using PHP Operators . . . . . . . . . . . . . . . . . . . . . . . . . . . . . . . . . . . . 317
Including Files . . . . . . . . . . . . . . . . . . . . . . . . . . . . . . . . . . . . . . . . . 320

**CHAPTER 2: PHP Flow Control** . . . . . . . . . . . . . . . . . . . . . . . . . . . . . . . 325

Using Logic Control . . . . . . . . . . . . . . . . . . . . . . . . . . . . . . . . . . . . . 325
Looping. . . . . . . . . . . . . . . . . . . . . . . . . . . . . . . . . . . . . . . . . . . . . . 331
Building Your Own Functions . . . . . . . . . . . . . . . . . . . . . . . . . . . . . . 336
Working with Event-Driven PHP . . . . . . . . . . . . . . . . . . . . . . . . . . . . 339

**CHAPTER 3: PHP Libraries** . . . . . . . . . . . . . . . . . . . . . . . . . . . . . . . . . . . 349

How PHP Uses Libraries . . . . . . . . . . . . . . . . . . . . . . . . . . . . . . . . . . 349
Text Functions . . . . . . . . . . . . . . . . . . . . . . . . . . . . . . . . . . . . . . . . . 354
Math Functions . . . . . . . . . . . . . . . . . . . . . . . . . . . . . . . . . . . . . . . . 361
Date and Time Functions . . . . . . . . . . . . . . . . . . . . . . . . . . . . . . . . . 365
Image-Handling Functions . . . . . . . . . . . . . . . . . . . . . . . . . . . . . . . . 369

**CHAPTER 4: Considering PHP Security** . . . . . . . . . . . . . . . . . . . . . . . 375

Exploring PHP Vulnerabilities . . . . . . . . . . . . . . . . . . . . . . . . . . . . . . 375
PHP Vulnerability Solutions . . . . . . . . . . . . . . . . . . . . . . . . . . . . . . . 384

**CHAPTER 5: Object-Oriented PHP Programming** . . . . . . . . . . . . 395

Understanding the Basics of Object-Oriented Programming. . . . 395
Using Magic Class Methods . . . . . . . . . . . . . . . . . . . . . . . . . . . . . . . 401
Loading Classes . . . . . . . . . . . . . . . . . . . . . . . . . . . . . . . . . . . . . . . . 409
Extending Classes . . . . . . . . . . . . . . . . . . . . . . . . . . . . . . . . . . . . . . 414

**CHAPTER 6: Sessions and Carts** . . . . . . . . . . . . . . . . . . . . . . . . . . . . . 419

Storing Persistent Data. . . . . . . . . . . . . . . . . . . . . . . . . . . . . . . . . . . 419
PHP and Cookies . . . . . . . . . . . . . . . . . . . . . . . . . . . . . . . . . . . . . . . 424
PHP and Sessions . . . . . . . . . . . . . . . . . . . . . . . . . . . . . . . . . . . . . . 430
Shopping Carts. . . . . . . . . . . . . . . . . . . . . . . . . . . . . . . . . . . . . . . . . 436

# Chapter **1**

# Understanding PHP Basics

W elcome to the PHP minibook! If you've been following along through the previous minibooks, you've seen how to create web page content using HTML5, how to style and position it using CSS3, and how to add some dynamic features to your web pages using JavaScript. This minibook examines the next piece to dynamic web applications — using a server-side programming language to make your web applications even more dynamic. As the title of the book suggests, the server-side programming language that I discuss is PHP, one of the most popular server-side programming languages in use on the Internet today!

## Seeing the Benefits of PHP

So far, you've already seen that JavaScript is a popular client-side programming language and that it has the ability to change the content and style of a web page dynamically. One question you may be asking is, "Why do I need a server-side programming language, too?" This section examines what your web applications will gain by adding PHP to the mix and what you can do when you incorporate PHP code in your applications.

# A centralized programming language

One of the downsides to using a client-side programming language is that your code is dependent on how each individual browser runs it. Great strides have been made in the standardization of JavaScript, but each browser still has its own set of quirks when running JavaScript code, as well as its own set of libraries that offers different features, making it impossible to know just how your JavaScript code will run in all situations.

Unlike that environment, server-side PHP programs run on the same server that hosts your web pages, so every site visitor who accesses your web pages runs the PHP code on the same server, using the same set of library features. You know exactly how your application code will run and exactly what it will produce for all your website visitors.

Another added benefit of using PHP code in your web pages is the ability to control the actual PHP server itself. Because all the PHP code in your web pages runs from the same location, you can customize the feature settings in the PHP server to your specific environment. This allows you to utilize just the libraries you need or set memory usage just how you want, giving you some control over the performance of your web applications.

**TIP**

Book 1, Chapter 2, shows some of the configuration settings available in the PHP server and how you can change them to customize your PHP environment.

# Centralized data management

These days, data rules the world. Just about every web application requires some type of data to run. Whether it's displaying news stories, posting blog entries, or just tracking your bowling team scores, you need some type of data to use in your dynamic web application.

When you use data, you need some method for storing it. A *content management system* (CMS) provides an interface to track data in a single repository, allowing you to create, read, update, and delete data records freely. The CMS package is often installed as part of the web server environment and often utilizes a database server that specializes in quickly storing and retrieving data records.

By using PHP, you can access the data in your CMS package directly from the server. That usually means faster response times, as opposed to your individual site visitors accessing the CMS server from their locations. It also means more control over how your application accesses and displays the data. The only data your site visitors can see is what your application presents to them. All your CMS access information stays hidden on the server — none of the code to access the data is downloaded to the client browsers. This is a also huge benefit for security reasons.

# Understanding How to Use PHP

After you decide to incorporate PHP into your web applications, you need to know just how to do that. This section walks through the basics of adding PHP code to your web pages and how to get output from your PHP programs to appear in your web pages as they display in your site visitors' browsers.

## Embedding PHP code

Just as with JavaScript, you embed PHP code directly into the HTML5 code that creates the web page. As you can probably guess, you need a way to identify the embedded PHP code, and that method is to use tags.

There are actually four different ways to tag PHP code in the HTML5 document. The most common method is to use the special `<?php` and `?>` tag combination. Just place the PHP code you need to embed between the opening `<?php` tag and the closing `?>` tag, like this:

```
<!DOCTYPE html>
<html>
<body>
<?php
    php code
?>
</body>
</html>
```

You can place the PHP tags anywhere in the HTML5 code — they don't need to be in the body element. You can have as many HTML5 elements that you need outside the PHP code area to provide supporting content on the web page, but you can't place HTML5 elements inside the PHP code area. Only PHP code can reside inside the PHP code area.

The `<?php` tag is the most common way to identify PHP code, but it's not the only way. Another method is to use the `<script>` HTML5 tag:

```
<!DOCTYPE html>
<html>
<body>
<script language="php">
    php code
</script>
</body>
</html>
```

This looks very similar to what you use to embed JavaScript code into HTML5 code, which could be good or bad. Just remember to include the `language` attribute in the tag and identify the code as PHP code. Using the same `<script>` tags to embed both JavaScript and PHP code can be a bit confusing, which is why the `<?php` tag has become so popular.

The third type of PHP tag is called the *short open tag*. It uses `<?` as the opening tag, instead of the full `<?php` tag. For this tag method to work, though, the PHP server must have the `short_open_tag` setting enabled in its configuration file. The short open tag saves some typing, but it can get confusing as you look through the program code.

Finally, the fourth type of PHP tag is the `<%` opening tag. This is called the *ASP style tag* because this is the same tag used when programming with the Microsoft ASP. NET family of server-side programming languages. If you're already comfortable with using ASP.NET programming, you can use this style of tag for PHP coding as well. Similar to the short open tag, you must enable the `asp_tags` setting in the PHP server configuration file to use this method.

## Identifying PHP pages

Because PHP is a server-side programming language, the PHP processor that runs the PHP code is located on the server — usually the same physical server as the web server. To process the embedded PHP code, your web page must pass your HTML5 document to the PHP server on its way to the site visitor who requested it.

The web server must be able to detect when a web page contains embedded PHP code and when it doesn't. If the web page contains PHP code, the web server must pass the entire HTML5 document to the PHP server for processing. We don't want the web server to pass all HTML5 documents to the PHP server, because that would slow down processing web pages that don't contain embedded PHP code. The web server must know when it has to send an HTML5 file to the PHP server for processing. You control that by using file extensions.

When the Apache web server has the PHP module installed, there's a directive in the main `httpd.conf` configuration file identifying PHP programs that need to be sent to the PHP server for processing. That directive looks like this:

```
AddHandler application/x-httpd-php .php
```

This tells the Apache web server to send any files that site visitors request that end with the `.php` file extension to the PHP server. This way, you can identify any web pages that contain embedded PHP code by using the `.php` file extension instead of the standard `.html` file extension. Figure 1-1 shows this process.

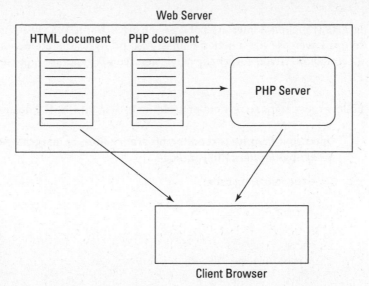

**FIGURE 1-1:**
Processing PHP
code in a
web page.

**WARNING**

Using the correct file extension for PHP files is crucial, because if you embed any PHP code into a file with an `.html` file extension, the PHP code won't get processed; instead, it will appear on the web page as text.

When working with PHP code, you must run the web page through the web server so that it gets processed by the PHP server. You can't just double-click a `.php` file to open it in your browser — you must open your browser and use the `http://` URL to access the file via the web server.

## Displaying output

As the PHP server reads the code in the file that the web server sends it, it passes any HTML5 code directly on to the client browser that requested the file and processes any PHP code embedded in the document. As it processes the PHP code, you'll want to be able to dynamically add content to the web page (after all, that's what you're here for). You do that using the `echo` statement.

The `echo` statement injects text into the HTML5 data stream that's sent to the client browser. The data appears to the client browser just as if it came from the HTML5 document — it has no idea that the PHP server dynamically generated the content.

To use the `echo` statement, you just specify the string value that you want to insert into the HTML5 output:

```
echo "this is my output";
```

In PHP, function names are not case sensitive, but it's fairly standard convention to use lowercase for function names. Also in PHP, all statements must end with a semicolon. If you forget the semicolon, you'll generate a parse error from the PHP processor.

Follow these steps to test out embedding PHP in an HTML5 document:

1. **Open your favorite text editor, program editor, or integrated development environment (IDE) package.**

2. **Type the following code:**

```
<!DOCTYPE html>
<html>
<body>
<h1>This is a test of PHP code</h1>
<?php
    echo "<p>This text was dynamically generated!</p>";
?>
<h1>This is the end of the test</h1>
</body>
</html>
```

3. **Save the file as** phptest.php **in the** DocumentRoot **folder of your web server.**

   For XAMPP on Windows, use the c:\xampp\htdocs folder; for XAMPP on macOS, use /Applications/XAMPP/htdocs.

4. **Open the XAMPP Control Panel and start the Apache web server.**

5. **Open your browser and enter the following URL:**

```
http://localhost:8080/phptest.php
```

   You may need to use a different TCP port based on your Apache web server setting.

6. **Close your browser when you're done.**

When you run the phptest.php file in your browser, the web page should appear as shown in Figure 1-2.

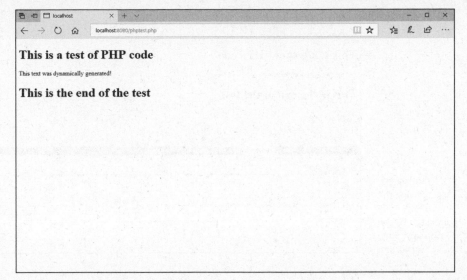

FIGURE 1-2:
Output generated
by the phptest.
php program.

The p element section appears just as if you had typed it directly in the HTML5 code. The PHP server injected it into the HTML5 code, and the browser added it to the Document Object Model (DOM) tree just as normal. It's also important to note that, in this demonstration, I embedded standard HTML5 tags into the output from the echo statement. Everything that's inside the string value is sent to the client browser, including any HTML5 elements that you specify.

**TIP**

If you see the PHP code appear in your web page, that means the PHP server didn't process the PHP code. Check to make sure you don't have a typo in the opening <?php tag (note that there are no spaces in the tag) and that the file uses the .php file extension.

## Handling new-line characters

There is one oddity that you may have noticed when running the phptest.php demo program. If you use the Developer Tools for your browser (see Book 3, Chapter 5) and look at the HTML5 code generated, it may look a little odd, as shown in Figure 1-3.

Instead of the p element being on a separate line in the code, it got pushed onto the same line as the second h1 element.

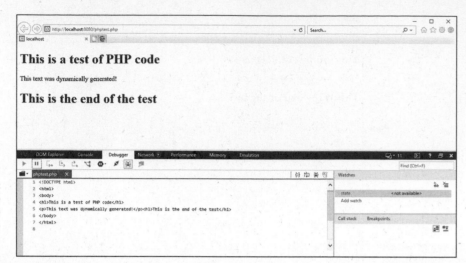

**FIGURE 1-3:**
Viewing the
HTML5 code
generated by the
phptest.php
program.

The echo statement in PHP doesn't add a new-line character at the end of the output. Because there aren't any new-line characters, any content that you display using the echo statement in PHP appears on the same line in the HTML5 code.

**REMEMBER**

The HTML5 standard ignores any white space between elements in the document, so the fact that the p element is on the same line as the h1 element doesn't effect the output that appears on the web page at all. However, having two elements on the same line can make troubleshooting HTML5 code generated by PHP somewhat complicated. That's especially true as you use PHP to create entire web pages!

**TIP**

To solve this problem, many PHP developers like to add their own new-line characters to the ends of all echo statements in the code, like this:

```
echo "<p>This text was dynamically generated!</p>\n";
```

The \n new-line character doesn't change the appearance of anything on the web page as it appears in the browser, but it does separate the p element from the following h1 element when you look at the HTML5 code using the browser Developer Tools features. It adds some extra typing to your development work, but it can save you lots of time trying to troubleshoot HTML5 code issues in your applications!

# Working with PHP Variables

The key to dynamic web applications is working with data. Just like any other programming language, PHP allows you to use variables to store data in your programs. *Variables* are placeholders that you assign values to throughout the duration of the program. When the program references the variable, it represents the actual value that the program last assigned to it.

This section walks through what you'll need to know to use variables in PHP.

## Declaring variables

In PHP, you identify variables with a leading dollar sign ($) in front of the variable name. You must start a variable name with either a letter or an underscore character (_), and it can contain only letters, numbers, and underscores (the variable name can't contain any spaces or other special characters). Here are some examples of valid PHP variable names:

```
$test
$Test1
$_another_test
```

Just as in JavaScript, PHP variable names are case-sensitive, so be careful when you reference variables in your code. The variable name $Test is different from $test. Case-sensitivity causes all sorts of headaches when trying to troubleshoot PHP code.

Unlike with JavaScript, with PHP, you don't declare variables with a var statement — you just use them. However, the first time you use a variable must be within an assign statement, assigning a value to the variable:

```
$test = "This is a test string";
```

The assignment statement assigns the value specified on the right side of the equal sign to the variable specified on the left side. As with all other PHP statements, don't forget the semicolon at the end of assignment statements!

After you assign a value to a variable, you can use it in your application:

```
$value1 = 10;
$value2 = 20;
$result = $value1 + $value2;
```

If you try using the third statement before assigning values to the $value1 or $value2 variables, you'll get a warning message from PHP about using a value with no assigned value. However, by default, PHP will assume the unassigned variables contain a value of 0.

As you can tell from these examples, PHP allows you to store different data types in variables. The next section takes a closer look at that.

## Seeing which data types PHP supports

Just as with JavaScript, PHP supports the following data types:

>> **Integer:** Stores whole-number values

>> **Float:** Also called floating-point or double; stores real numbers

>> **Boolean:** Stores a `true` or `false` value

>> **String:** Stores a *series* (string) of characters

>> **Array:** Stores multiple values referenced by the same variable name

>> **Object:** Stores instances of classes

>> **Reference:** Stores a pointer to a complex data type

**WARNING**

In PHP, just as in JavaScript, a single variable can hold any type of data at any time (PHP doesn't enforce strict data typing). Changing the data type stored in a variable can get confusing, and I strongly recommend sticking with one data type per variable name in your programs. Trust me, it'll make your life a lot easier!

Follow these steps to test out using different data types in PHP code:

**1.** **Open your editor and type the following code:**

```
<!DOCTYPE>
<html>
<head>
<title>Testing PHP Data Types</title>
</head>
<body>
<h1>PHP Data Type Test</h1>
<?php
$name = "Rich";
$age = 100;
$salary = 575.25;
echo "<h2>Information for $name</h2>\n";
echo "Age: $age<br>\n";
echo "Salary: $$salary\n";
?>
```

```
<h1>This is the end of the PHP test</h1>
</body>

</html>
```

2.  **Save the file as** phpdatatest.php **in the** DocumentRoot **folder for your web server.**

3.  **Ensure that the web server is running, open your browser, and enter the following URL:**

```
http://localhost:8080/phpdatatest.php
```

4.  **Close the browser window when you're done.**

When you run the phpdatatest.php program, you should see the output as shown in Figure 1-4.

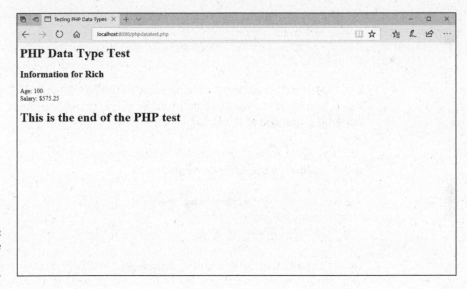

**FIGURE 1-4:**
Output from the
phpdatatest.
php program.

Let's look at exactly what's going on in this PHP program. First, the code assigns values for three variables:

```
$name = "Rich";
$age = 100;
$salary = 575.25;
```

## PHP AND QUOTES

You can use either single or double quotes to define a string value in PHP. They're interchangeable, but there are times when you'll want to use one over the other. Things can get somewhat confusing when you have to use quotes inside the string value itself. When you know you have to use one type of quote in the data, just use the other type to define the string value:

```
$test1 = "This'll work just fine in PHP";
$test2 = 'Rich says "this works, too" in PHP';
```

Where things get tricky is when you need to use both types of quotes inside the data value. To do that, you must escape the quote type that you use to define the string value. Use the backslash to identify the quotes in the data:

```
$test3 = "Rich says \"This'll work, too\" in PHP";
```

Be careful when working with quotes in data — it's easy to miss them and cause errors in your PHP code.

The first statement assigns a string value to the $name variable. To assign a string value, you must enclose the data in either single or double quotes. These mark the beginning and end of the string value.

After assigning the three variable values, the code then uses three echo statements to display the variable values:

```
echo "<h2>Information for $name</h2>\n";
echo "Age: $age<br>\n";
echo "Salary: $$salary\n";
```

Unlike many other programming languages, PHP allows you to just use a variable directly within a string value in the echo statement. However, how the echo statement handles the variable depends on the type of quotes you use to define the string (again with the quotes).

If you use double quotes to define the output string, PHP will display the variable value in the output. If you use single quotes to define the output string, PHP will display the variable name in the output:

```
echo "The variable value is $age";
echo 'The variable name is $age';
```

That's extremely versatile, but it can be somewhat confusing, and it takes some time getting used to as you code your PHP programs.

The last echo statement in the example code also does something rather odd: It uses two dollar signs in front of the $salary variable. That doesn't change anything for the variable — it just displays a dollar sign in front of the value contained in the $salary variable. This shows that PHP doesn't get confused when embedding variables inside the output string. You don't need to place spaces before the variable names. Again, though, this can get confusing, and you should take care when embedding variables in your output.

**WARNING**

There is one oddity with using single quotes for string values in PHP. For some reason, PHP doesn't recognize the \n newline character when you use single quotes. For that reason, I tend to stick with using double quotes for my string values.

## Grouping data values with array variables

Array variables allow you to group related data values together in a list using a single variable name. You can then either reference the values as a whole by referencing the variable name or handle each data value individually within the array by referencing its place in the list.

PHP supports two types of arrays: numeric and associative. The following sections cover these array types.

### Numeric

The standard type of array variable is the *numeric array.* With the numeric array, PHP indexes each value you store in the array with an integer value, starting at 0 for the first item in the array list.

The way to define an array is to use the PHP array() function in an assignment statement:

```
$myscores = array(100, 120, 115);
```

Just because the array is a numeric array, that doesn't mean you're restricted to storing only numeric values:

```
$myfamily = array("Rich", "Barbara", "Katie", "Jessica");
```

Starting in PHP version 5.4, you can also define an array using square brackets instead of the array() function:

```
$myscores = [110, 120, 115];
```

PHP references each value in the array using a positional number within square brackets after the variable name. The first element in the array is at position 0, the second at position 1, and so on.

For example, to retrieve the first value stored in the array, you'd use $myfamily[0], which would return the value Rich.

## Associative

The *associative array* variable is similar to what other programming languages call a "dictionary." Instead of using numeric indexes, it assigns a string key value to individual values in the list. You use the special => assignment operator to do that when you define the array:

```
$favs = array("fruit" => "banana", "veggie" => "carrot");
```

This array definition assigns the key value of fruit to the data value banana, and the key value veggie to the data value carrot. With associative arrays, to reference a data value you must specify the key value in the square brackets:

```
$favs["fruit"]
```

There is one thing to watch out for, though, when using associative array variables in your PHP code. For some reason, the echo statement has a hard time detecting associative array variables, so it needs some help from you.

When you use an associative array variable in an echo statement, it's a good idea to enclose it in braces, like this:

```
echo "My favorite fruit is {$favs['fruit']}\n";
```

This separates out the associative array variable from the string, so the echo statement can properly process it. Also, notice that the problem with quotes pops up when using associative array variables inside the echo statement. Because you want the output to show the value of the associative array variable, you need to use double quotes for the echo statement string. That means you must use single quotes around the associative array variable key.

# Using PHP Operators

Now that you know how to store data in variables and display those values on a web page, it's time to take a look at how to dynamically alter the values. The core of any programming language is the ability to let the computer system crunch your data and then display the results for you. To do that, you need data operators. This section covers the operators you'll run into when using arithmetic and string operations in your PHP code.

## Arithmetic operators

Arithmetic operators provide the basic mathematical functions that you're used to seeing on your calculator, directly within your PHP programs. You can perform all the standard calculations shown in Table 1-1 in your PHP programs.

**TABLE 1-1**    ## PHP Arithmetic Operators

| Operator | Description |
| --- | --- |
| + | Addition |
| – | Subtraction |
| * | Multiplication |
| / | Division |
| % | Modulus |

Arithmetic operators are normally used in an assignment statement to perform the calculations:

```
$value1 = 10;
$value2 = 20;
$result = $value1 + $value2;
echo "The result is $result\n";
```

The first two lines assign values to the two values used in the arithmetic operation. If you try to use a variable that hasn't been assigned a value in an arithmetic operation, you'll get a warning from PHP.

The third line is where you use the arithmetic operation on the two values. If you've never done programming before, this statement may look a little odd. Don't think of it as a mathematical equation. The equal sign is still acting to perform the assignment in PHP. The PHP server first evaluates the arithmetic operation on the right side of the equal sign and then assigns the result to the $result variable specified on the left side.

You can use both integer and float data type values in your arithmetic operations. However, float data type values need a little explaining here.

You can define a float value in one of three ways:

```
$float1 = 3.14159;
$float2 = 2.3e10;
$float3 = 5E-10;
```

The e and E symbols represent an exponential value applied to the value specified. You can use very large and very small float numbers, but be careful because the precision that PHP uses is somewhat limited, based on the server system. Don't be surprised if you store the value 3.0 in a variable and then later on retrieve it and it shows as 3.00001. Extra care is needed when working with float values.

## Arithmetic shortcuts

There are a few different shortcuts you can use when implementing arithmetic operators in your PHP code. A common function in programming code is to perform a mathematical operation on a value stored in a variable and then store the result back in the same variable, like this:

```
$counter = $counter + 1;
```

This code adds 1 to the value currently stored in the $counter variable and then saves the result back in the $counter variable. PHP provides a handy shortcut method for doing this:

```
$counter += 1;
```

This code accomplishes the exact same thing, but in a shorter form. You can use the same shortcut with any type of arithmetic operator:

```
$total *= 1.10;
```

This example multiplies the value stored in the $total variable by 1.10 and stores the result back in the $total variable. You can also use variables on the right side of the assignment operation:

```
$total *= $taxrate;
```

This is the same as typing the following:

```
$total = $total * $taxrate;
```

That can really save some typing for you!

Two other types of arithmetic shortcuts are the *incrementor* and *decrementor* operators. The incrementor operator adds 1 to a variable's value:

```
$counter++;
```

The decrementor operator subtracts 1 from the variable's value:

```
$counter--;
```

Now that's *really* saving some typing!

**WARNING**

The arithmetic shortcut operators assume there's already a value stored in the variable before the operation. If there isn't, PHP will generate a warning message, telling you that it assumes the initial value is 0. It's always a good idea to initialize a variable to a known value before trying to use it in any arithmetic operations.

# Boolean operators

Besides the standard arithmetic operators, PHP supports Boolean operators for logical operations with data. Boolean math allows you to work with TRUE and FALSE conditions in your programs. The Boolean operators test whether two values are both TRUE, both FALSE, or one is TRUE and the other is FALSE. Table 1-2 shows the Boolean operators supported by PHP.

**TABLE 1-2**

## PHP Boolean Operators

| Operator | Description |
|----------|-------------|
| and | logical AND |
| && | logical AND |
| or | logical OR |
| \|\| | logical OR |
| xor | logical XOR |
| ! | logical NOT |

Notice that PHP supports two forms for the AND and OR logical operations — both the symbols and the names. There's no preference as to which method to use, so feel free to use the method you're most comfortable with.

These operators come in handy when you need to evaluate two separate conditions at the same time:

```
if (($age > 50) and ($gender == "F"))
```

This can help to simplify the code in your programs!

## String operators

When you think of text string values, you don't necessarily think of arithmetic operations, but PHP does include a string operator that comes in handy when working with string values.

The *concatenation operator* allows you to "add" two string values together to create a single string value. Basically, the concatenation operator appends the second string to the end of the first string.

The concatenation operator in PHP is the period:

```
$string1 = "This is ";
$string2 = "a test";
$result = $string1 . $string2;
```

The result stored in the $result variable will be the string This is a test. Note that the concatenation operator doesn't add any spaces either before or after the text it concatenates, so it's up to you to do that if you need the space!

# Including Files

One feature of PHP that many web developers love is the ability to create and use *include files.* Include files (sometimes referred to as *server-side includes*) allow you to store HTML5 and PHP code in one file and then reference that file in another web page file. There are a couple of ways to do that in PHP.

## The include() function

The include() function allows you to include the contents of one web page within another web page simply by referencing a filename on the server. The PHP processor includes all the code contained within the included file, both HTML5 and PHP, directly into the PHP code of the main file, exactly where you place the include() function. It's just as if you had typed in all the lines of code from the include file yourself into the main file!

Developers often use the include() function to create standard header or footer sections on all the web pages in an application. Instead of having to add the same header or footer code to every web page in the application, you just save the header code in one file and the footer code in another file, and then use the include() function to include the header and footer files into each web page code.

The format of the include() function is simple:

```
include(filename);
```

You just replace *filename* with the actual name of the file you need to include in the program code.

Follow these steps to test out using an include file in a web page:

**1.** **Open your editor and type the following code:**

```
<h1>This is a test header</h1>
<?php
    echo "<p>This is the header text</p>\n";

?>
```

**2.** **Save the file as** myinclude.inc.php **in the** DocumentRoot **folder for your web server.**

**3.** **Open your editor to a new document and type the following code:**

```
<!DOCTYPE html>
<html>
<head>
<title>Testing PHP includes</title>
</head>
<body>
<header>
<?php include("myinclude.inc.php"); ?>
</header>
```

```
<section>
<br><br>
<h2>This is the body of the main web page</h2>
</section>
</body>
</html>
```

4. **Save the file as** `mymain.php` **in the** `DocumentRoot` **folder for your web server.**

5. **Ensure that the web server is running, and then open your browser and enter the following URL:**

```
http://localhost:8080/mymain.php
```

6. **Close the browser when you're done.**

You should see the output as shown in Figure 1-5.

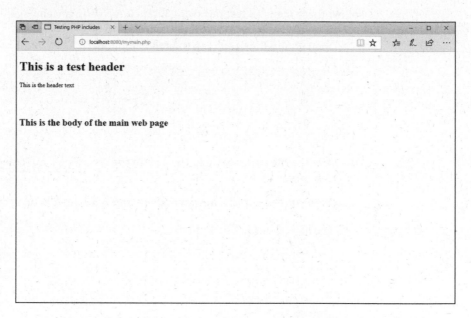

**FIGURE 1-5:**
The results of the `mymain.php` program.

If you view the HTML5 code in your browser's Developer Tools, the output appears as a single HTML5 document. The browser is unaware that the code came from two separate files on the server, and your site visitors will have no idea that you cheated when creating all your web pages!

**TIP**

The filename you specify in the `include()` function can use any file extension — it's not required to use `.php`, because the `include()` function includes it into the main file for processing. However, it's become common to use the `.inc.php` file extension to identify include files and to separate them out from main PHP files. You can also use either an absolute or relative path name to reference the filename. Because the PHP server is accessing the file as a file and not as a web document, you can't use the `http://` URL here — only a file path. Also, your web server must have access to read the file on the server.

## The require() function

There is one limitation to the `include()` function that may cause problems for you. If PHP is unable to find the file you reference, it'll produce a warning, but the PHP server will continue to process the rest of the program code. That may have detrimental effects on your program!

There may be times where you don't want the PHP server to continue on processing code if a crucial include file is missing from the server. Instead, you may want the program to stop immediately and produce an error message instead of just a warning. This is where the `require()` function comes in.

The `require()` function works exactly like the `include()` function, except for one difference: It forces the PHP server to stop processing code if the include file fails to load.

To test this out, follow these steps:

**1.** Open the `mymain.php` code from the previous example into your editor.

**2.** Change the `include()` function line to this:

```
require("mybadinclude.inc.php");
```

**3.** Save the file as `mybadmain.php` in the `DocumentRoot` folder for your web server.

**4.** Ensure that the web server is still running and then open your browser and go to the following URL:

```
http://localhost:8080/mybadmain.php
```

**5.** Close the browser and shut down the web server when you're done.

When you run the `mybadmain.php` program, you may or may not see an error message on your web page, as shown in Figure 1-6.

Understanding PHP Basics

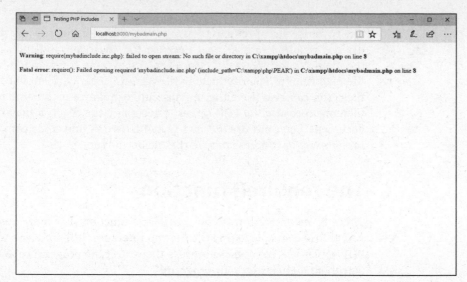

**FIGURE 1-6:**
The output from
the mybadmain.
php program.

If you have the `display_errors` setting enabled in your PHP server configuration file, you'll see the error message. None of the HTML5 code from the main program code appears on the web page, because the PHP server stopped processing code after the `require()` function failed.

# Chapter **2**

# PHP Flow Control

I n the preceding chapter, I cover the basics of creating and running PHP programs. I show you how to use variables to hold data, but you don't really do much with them to test the data and perform operations. In this chapter, I walk through how to use the PHP conditional tests to control how your program behaves, as well as show how to loop through code to perform multiple iterations. In case you have code that you find yourself using frequently, I show how you can convert them into functions to share among your programs. Finally, I cover how to use PHP code in your event-driven web applications to add to your dynamic web applications.

## Using Logic Control

Only having variables and echo statements in your PHP program would be pretty boring. You need to give your programs some intelligence so that they can make decisions based on what's happening in the application and display different sets of content based on those decisions.

Every programming language has methods for controlling the order the program handles statements, called the *program flow,* and PHP is no different. This section walks through the basics of controlling program flow in your PHP programs.

# The if statement

The `if` statement controls which statements PHP should run in the program based on conditions. You use `if` statements in your everyday life (for example, if it's raining, then you'll bring an umbrella). You apply the same logic to your PHP programs.

The basic format for the `if` statement is:

```
if (condition)
    PHP statement to run
```

PHP evaluates the condition defined inside the parentheses to determine whether it should run the specified PHP statement that appears immediately after the `if` statement. The condition uses a special PHP expression called the *comparison operator*, which it uses to compare two values. If the comparison evaluates to a Boolean `TRUE` value, PHP runs the statement listed after the `if` statement. If the comparison evaluates to a Boolean `FALSE` value, PHP skips the statement.

This may sound confusing, but it's not all that hard when you get used to the format. Here's an example of a simple `if` statement:

```
if ($age > 21)
    echo "Sorry, you are too old to play";
```

The condition inside the parentheses checks if the value stored in the variable named $age is greater than 21. If it is, the condition evaluates to a `TRUE` value and PHP runs the `echo` statement. If it isn't, the condition evaluates to a `FALSE` value and PHP skips the `echo` statement and moves on.

There are quite a few comparison operators that you have available to use in PHP. Table 2-1 shows the comparison operators available.

**WARNING**

Notice that the comparison operator used to check if two values are equal is the double equal sign, not a single equal sign. Forgetting that small detail causes all sorts of annoying errors in your PHP code because the equal sign performs an assignment operation, which always returns a `TRUE` value (been there, done that).

The triple equal sign not only compares the value of the variables, but also checks to make sure the variables contain the same data types. For example, a Boolean data type of `TRUE` will match against an integer data type of 1 using the double equal, but not the triple equal.

**TABLE 2-1**

## PHP Comparison Operators

| Operator | Description |
|----------|-------------|
| == | Equal to the same value |
| === | Equal to the same value, and they're the same data type |
| != | Not equal to the same value |
| <> | Not equal to the same value |
| !== | Not equal to the same value, or they aren't the same data type |
| < | Less than |
| <= | Less than or equal to |
| > | Greater than |
| >= | Greater than or equal to |

If you need to control more than just a single statement using the if condition, group the statements using braces:

```
if (condition) {
    statement1
    statement2
    statement3
}
```

You can have as many PHP statements contained within the group block as necessary — they'll all be controlled by the single condition in the if statement line. Here's an example:

```
if ($price > 50) {
    $tax = $price * .07;
    $shipping = 10;
    $total = $price + $tax + $shipping;
}
```

In this example, the entire group of statements will only be run by PHP if the $price variable value is greater than 50.

PHP Flow Control

# The else statement

The `if` statement has a cousin, called the `else` statement. The `else` statement allows you to provide an alternative group of statements to run if the condition in the `if` statement evaluates to a FALSE value:

```
if (condition) {
    PHP statements to run if TRUE
} else {
    PHP statements to run if FALSE
}
```

This gives you total control over what PHP statements are run in any condition!

# The elseif statement

You can string `if` and `else` statements together, but that uses a new statement in place of the `else` statement, called the `elseif` statement (yes, that's `else` and `if` as one word). An `elseif` statement looks like this:

```
if (condition1){
    PHP statements to run if condition1 is TRUE
} elseif (condition2) {
    PHP statements to run if condition2 is TRUE
}
```

You can string as many `elseif` statements into the code block as necessary to check for alternative conditions. Each `elseif` statement requires its own condition check.

Follow these steps to try out using `if`, `else`, and `elseif` statements:

1. **Open your favorite text editor, program editor, or integrated development environment (IDE) package.**

2. **Type the following code into the editor:**

```
<!DOCTYPE html>
<html>
<head>
<title>Testing PHP Program Control</title>
</head>
<body>
```

```
<h1>Random number test</h1>
<?php
    $number = rand(1, 100);
    if ($number > 50) {
        echo "<h2>The value $number is big!</h2>\n";
    } elseif ($number > 25) {
        echo "<h2>The value $number is medium</h2>\n";
    } else {
        echo "<h2>The value $number is small</h2>\n";
    }
?>
</body>
</html>
```

3. **Save the file as** `phpconditiontest.php` **in the** `DocumentRoot` **folder for your web server.**

   For XAMPP on Windows, use `c:\xampp\htdocs`; for XAMPP on macOS, use `/Applications/XAMPP/htdocs`.

4. **Open the XAMPP Control Panel and start the Apache web server.**

5. **Open your browser and enter the following URL:**

   ```
   http://localhost:8080/phpconditiontest.php
   ```

   You may need to change the TCP port used in the URL to match your web server.

6. **Click the Refresh button on your browser to reload the web page.**

   That should run the PHP program again, selecting a new random number.

7. **Close the browser when you're done.**

The program uses the PHP `rand()` function to select a random number from 1 to 100. The value is compared in two separate condition checks in the `if` and `elseif` statements. If both fail, the code falls through to the final `else` statement. PHP runs the appropriate `echo` statement based on which condition succeeds. Figure 2-1 shows an example of the output you should see in your web page.

Each time you click your browser's Refresh button, the browser makes a new request to the server to reload the web page. That triggers the server to reload the web page in the PHP server, which in turn reruns the program.

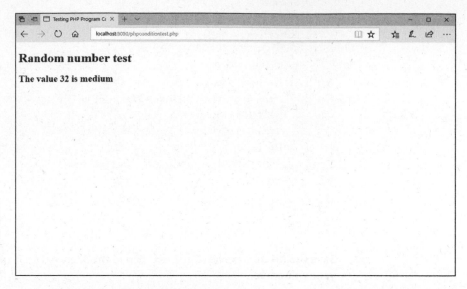

FIGURE 2-1:
The output
from the
phpcondition
test.php
program.

## The switch statement

Writing long if, elseif, and else statements to check for a long list of conditions can get tedious. To help out with that, PHP provides the switch statement. The switch statement allows you to perform one check, and then provide multiple values to compare the check against:

```
switch (condition) {
    case value1:
        statement1;
        break;
    case value2:
        statement2;
        break;
    default:
        statement3;
}
```

The switch statement evaluates the condition you specify against the different values presented in each case statement. If one of the values matches the result of the condition, PHP jumps to that section of the code to run the statements contained in that section.

It's important to note, though, that the case statements are labels and not code blocks. After PHP runs the statements in the case section it jumped to, it continues to run the statements in all the case sections after it! To prevent that from happening, use the break statement at the end of the case code section. That causes PHP to break out of the switch statement and skip any remaining case sections.

Also, you can place a `default` statement section at the end of the `switch` statement code block. If none of the `case` values matches the condition value, PHP jumps to the `default` section.

# Looping

Sometimes you'll find yourself needing to repeat the same operation multiple times, such as when you're displaying all the values in an array variable or database table. You could just write out all the PHP statements yourself, but that could get cumbersome:

```
$family = array("Rich", "Barbara", "Katie", "Jessica");
echo "One member of my family is $family[0]<br>\n";
echo "One member of my family is $family[1]<br>\n";
echo "One member of my family is $family[2]<br>\n";
echo "One member of my family is $family[3]<br>\n";
```

This code would certainly display all the elements contained within the array, but what if there were 100 elements in the array? That would require a lot of coding!

Notice that most of the code in the `echo` statements is the same — the only thing that differs is the index used in the array to reference the specific data element in the array. All that you need to do is iterate through the index numbers and use the same code. Well, that's exactly what you can do using the PHP looping functions.

PHP provides a family of looping functions available for you to use in your code. The following sections walk through the different ways to loop through code in PHP.

## The while family

The `while` statement allows you to create a simple loop of code based on a condition that you specify in the statement:

```
while (condition) {
    statements
}
```

In each iteration of the loop, PHP evaluates the condition you specify. If the condition evaluates to a TRUE value, PHP runs the statements contained in the while code block. As soon as the condition evaluates to a FALSE value, PHP breaks out of the loop and continues on with the next statement after the loop.

The while statement is tricky in that something inside the loop code must alter the value checked in the condition; otherwise, it will never end (called an *endless loop*). Usually, there's some type of variable that you must change inside the loop and then check in the condition.

Follow these steps to test using the while statement to create a loop:

1. **Open your editor and type the following code:**

```
<!DOCTYPE html>
<html>
<head>
<title>PHP While Test</title>
</head>
<body>
<h1>Presenting the Beatles</h1>
<?php
$group = array("John", "Paul", "George", "Ringo");
$count = 0;
while ($count < 4) {
   echo "One member of the Beatles is
            $group[$count]<br>\n";
   $count++;
}
?>
</body>
</html>
```

2. **Save the file as** phpwhiletest.php **in the** DocumentRoot **folder for your web server.**

3. **Ensure that the web server is running and then open your browser and enter the following URL:**

```
http://localhost:8080/phwhiletest.php
```

4. **Close the browser when you're done.**

When you run the program, you should see the output as shown in Figure 2-2.

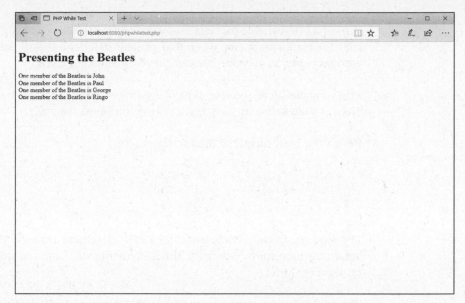

**FIGURE 2-2:**
The output of the
phpwhiletest.
php program.

Remember that array data indexes always start at 0, so you need to start the $count variable at 0 before entering the loop. In the while loop condition, you need to check to make sure the $count variable value hasn't gotten past the last index in the array. With four data elements in the array, the last index value is 3. So, as long as the $count variable value is less than 4, the program can continue iterating through the code in the loop. The code uses the $count variable as the $group array index to reference each individual data element in the echo statement. Finally, there's an incrementor statement to add 1 to the $count variable at the end of each loop iteration.

Similar to the while statement is the do...while statement. The do...while statement changes the order of when the condition check is performed:

```
do {
    statements
} while (condition)
```

With the do...while loop, PHP doesn't check the condition until after it runs the code inside the loop block. This ensures that the code will be run at least one time, even if the condition evaluates to a FALSE value.

## The for statement

The while loop statement is a great way to iterate through a bunch of data, but it can be a bit cumbersome to use. With the while statement, you need to make sure you set a PHP variable that changes value inside the loop code, and make sure you code the condition to stop when that variable reaches a specific value. Sometimes with large blocks of code, that can get complicated to track.

PHP provides an all-on-one type of looping statement called the `for` statement. The `for` statement can keep track of loop iterations for you.

Here's the basic format of the `for` statement:

```
for(statement1; condition; statement2) {
    PHP statements
}
```

The first parameter, `statement1`, is a PHP statement that the PHP server runs before the loop starts. Normally, this statement sets the initial value of the counter used in the loop.

The middle parameter, `condition`, is the standard PHP condition check that's evaluated after each loop iteration. The last parameter, `statement2`, is a PHP statement that's run at the end of each loop iteration. This is normally set to change the value of the counter used in the loop.

Here's the same code used to demonstrate the `while` loop, but using the `for` statement:

```php
<?php
$group = array("John", "Paul", "George", "Ringo");
for ($count = 0; $count < 4; $count++ ) {
  echo "One member of the Beatles is
          $group[$count]<br>\n";
}
?>
```

Because the `for` loop does everything for you, you don't need to worry about incrementing the counter value inside the code block. At the end of each iteration, PHP runs the incrementor specified in the for statement for you.

## The foreach statement

One problem that you may often run into with PHP is having to iterate through all the data elements contained within an associative array variable.

**REMEMBER**

An associative array uses text keys, not numbers, to track data values. There's no way you can increment through the keys in an associative array variable using the `for` statement.

Fortunately, the PHP developers have come to your rescue with the `foreach` statement. The `foreach` statement loops through each of the keys created in an associative array and allows you to retrieve both the key and its associated value.

Here's the format of the `foreach` statement:

```
foreach (array as $key => $value) {
    PHP statements
}
```

In each iteration, the `foreach` statement assigns the associative key to the *$key* variable, and its associated value to the *$value* variable. You can then use those variables in your PHP code inside the code block.

Follow these steps to try out the `foreach` statement with an associative array variable:

**1.** **Open your editor and type the following code:**

```
<!DOCTYPE html>
<html>
<head>
<title>PHP foreach Test</title>
</head>
<body>
<h1>My favorites</h1>
<?php
$favs = array("fruit"=>"banana","veggie"=>"carrot","meat"
    =>"roast beef");
foreach($favs as $food => $type) {
    echo "$food - $type<br>\n";
}
?>
</body>
</html>
```

**2.** **Save the file as** `foreachtest.php` **in the** DocumentRoot **folder of the web server.**

**3.** **Ensure that the web server is running, and then open your browser and enter the following URL:**

```
http://localhost:8080/foreachtest.php
```

**4.** **Close the browser when you're done.**

When you run the program, you should get the results shown in Figure 2-3.

**FIGURE 2-3:**
The output
from the
foreachtest.
php program.

The foreach statement iterates through each key contained in the $favs associative array variable, assigning the key to the $food variable and its value to the $type variable. The code then uses the echo statement to display the values on the web page.

# Building Your Own Functions

While you're coding in PHP, you'll often find yourself using the built-in functions available (such as the rand() function you used earlier in the example programs). *Functions* are nothing more than PHP code someone else wrote to accomplish a useful feature that you can use in any program. Instead of having to copy all the code into your application, you just use the function name.

PHP allows you to create your own functions to use in your programs and share with others. After you define a function, you can use it throughout your program. This saves typing if you use a common routine or block of code in lots of places in your application. All you need to do is write the code once in the function definition and then call the function everywhere else you need it.

The basic format for a function definition looks like this:

```
function name(parameters) {
    function code
    return value;
}
```

The *name* must uniquely identify the function. It can't be one of the existing PHP function names, and it can't start with a number (although numbers can appear anywhere else in the function name).

The *parameters* identify one or more variables that the calling program can pass to the function (or you can have a function that requires o parameters). If there is more than one variable in the parameter list, you must separate them with commas. You can then use the variables anywhere within the function code, but they only apply to inside the function code block. You can't access the passed parameter variables anywhere else in the program code.

Any variables you define inside the function code apply only to the function code. You can't use function variables in the PHP code outside the function definition.

The `return` statement allows you to pass a single value back to the calling program. It's the last statement in the function definition code, and it returns control of the program back to the main code section in your program.

Try out the following steps to experiment with creating a function and using it in your PHP program:

**1.** **Open your editor and type the following code:**

```
<!DOCTYPE html>
<html>
<head>
<title>PHP Function Test</title>
</head>
<body>
<?php
function factorial($value1) {
    $factorial = 1;
    $count = 1;
    while($count <= $value1) {
        $factorial *= $count;
    $count++;
    }
    return $factorial;
```

```
    }
    ?>
    <h1>Calculating factorials</h1>
    <?php
    echo "The factorial of 10 is " . factorial(10) . "<br>\n";
    echo "The factorial of 5 is " . factorial(5) . "<br>\n";
    ?>
    </body>
    </html>
```

2. **Save the file as** `factest.php` **in the** DocumentRoot **folder for your web server.**

3. **Open your browser and enter the following URL:**

    ```
    http://localhost:8080/factest.php
    ```

4. **Close your browser when you're done.**

When you run the `factest.php` program, the output should look like what's shown in Figure 2-4.

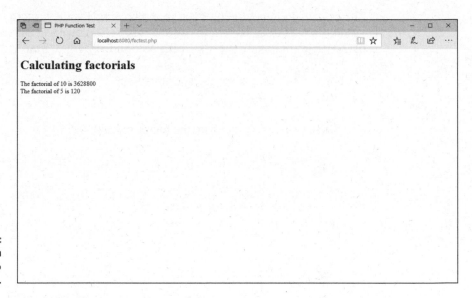

**FIGURE 2-4:**
The output from
the `factest.php`
program.

All the code required to calculate the function is contained within the `factorial()` function definition code block. When PHP uses the `factorial()` function, it passes a single value that the function assigns to the `$value1` variable. When the calculation is complete, the function code returns the results back to the main program.

The main program uses the `factorial()` function twice in the code, both embedded in `echo` statements:

```
echo "The factorial of 10 is " . factorial(10) . "<br>\n";
echo "The factorial of 5 is " . factorial(5) . "<br>\n";
```

You can embed variables inside the string values in `echo` statements, but you can't embed functions. To insert the output from the function into the `echo` statement output, the code uses the string concatenation operator (the period) to "glue" the output from the strings and the `factorial()` functions into a single string to display.

**TIP**

If you have lots of functions that you use in many of your programs, you can define them in a separate file. Then to use the functions in your programs just use the `include()` function to include the function file, and you can then use the functions inside your programs without having to retype them!

# Working with Event-Driven PHP

Because PHP is a server-side programming language, you can't associate it directly with events that occur within the browser. However, that said, you can link your PHP web pages to specific events in the web page so that the browser can request a specific web page based on an event.

There are basically two methods for doing that:

> » Creating a link to a PHP web page
> » Creating a form to pass data to a web page

The following sections describe how to use each of these event-driven methods to launch your PHP web pages.

## Working with links

In HTML5, you create hypertext links on the web page using the anchor element:

```
<a href="mypage.html">Click here</a>
```

The text Click Here appears on the web page, and when the site visitor clicks that link, the browser requests the `mypage.html` file from the web server.

You can use this method for passing small amounts of data to the PHP web pages in your web application. As part of the URL, you can embed variable/value pairs after the URL location that get passed to the web server:

```
<a href="mystore.php?content=store">Click to shop</a>
```

The browser sends the data combination of content and store to the web server as part of the GET request for the new web page. If you need to send more data, separate them with the ampersand sign:

```
href="mystore.php?content=buy&prodid=10"
```

This link sends two variable/value pairs to the web server using the GET method:

```
content=buy
prodid=10
```

To retrieve the data values passed using the GET method in your PHP code, use the special array variable $_GET[]. The PHP server populates the $_GET[] array variable with all the variable/value pairs passed in the GET method from the client browser. You can then access those array variables in your PHP program code.

Follow this example to test out using the GET method to pass data from a link click event to a PHP program:

**1.** **Open your editor and enter the following code:**

```
<!DOCTYPE html>
<html>
<head>
<title>Testing Link Events in PHP</title>
</head>
<body>
<h1>Please select one of the following links:</h1>
<a href="linktest2.php?content=buy">Buy products</a><br>
<a href="linktest2.php?content=browse">Browse for products</a><br>
<a href="linktest2.php?content=help">I need assistance</a><br>
</body>
</html>
```

**2.** **Save the file as** linktest.html **in the** DocumentRoot **folder for your web server.**

**3.** Open a new window in your editor and enter the following code:

```
<!DOCTYPE html>
<html>
<head>
<title>Testing link Events in PHP</title>
</head>
<body>
<h1>Thanks for visiting us!<h1>
<?php
$content = $_GET['content'];
echo "<h2>You are in the $content section</h2>\n";
?>
</body>
</html>
```

**4.** Save the file as linktest2.php in the DocumentRoot folder for your web server.

**5.** Ensure that the web server is running, and then open your browser and enter the following URL:

```
http://localhost:8080/linktest.html
```

**6.** Click one of the links on the web page, and observe what appears in the resulting web page.

**7.** Close the browser when you're done.

When you open the linktest.html web page, you'll see a series of links that simulate a navigation menu bar in a web page. Each link consists of a hyptertext link that points to the same web page (linktest2.php) but sets a different value for the content variable passed in the GET method. When you open the page, you should see the results, as shown in Figure 2-5.

When you click a link on the web page, the browser sends a GET request to the web server for the specified web page file, and passes the content variable setting assigned in the anchor element tag.

When the Apache web server receives the GET request from the client browser, it retrieves the linktest2.php file, and because it uses the .php file extension, it passes it to the PHP server to process the embedded PHP code. The PHP server detects the GET variable/value pair passed and assigns it to the $_GET[]

array variable. The code in the `linktest2.php` code retrieves that value from the `$_GET[]` array variable and assigns it to another variable:

```
$content = $_GET['content'];
```

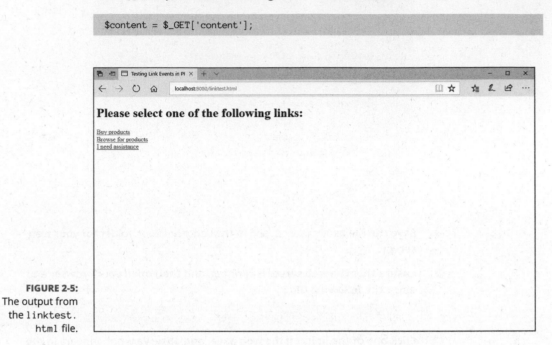

**FIGURE 2-5:**
The output from
the `linktest.`
`html` file.

The code then uses that variable in the echo statement to display on the web page. The result is shown in Figure 2-6.

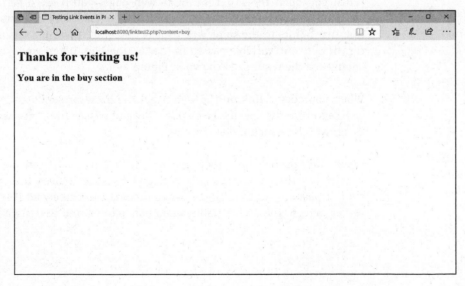

**FIGURE 2-6:**
The result of
clicking the Buy
a Product link on
the `linktest.`
`html` web page.

**WARNING**

Notice the URL that appears in the address bar in the `link2test.php` web page. It contains the content variable, along with the value that was set by the anchor element `href` attribute. Because the values set using the GET method appear in the URL, they aren't a secure method of sending data. You should limit using the GET method to passing data about web pages and not personal information.

## Processing form data

Book 2, Chapter 3, discusses how to build data entry forms using HTML5 code. To refresh your memory, the core of the HTML5 form is the `<form>` tag. This tag defines the beginning and end of the data fields that make up the form. The `<form>` tag uses three main attributes:

>> `name`: Specifies a unique name for the form

>> `method`: Specifies the HTTP method used to pass data

>> `action`: Specifies the web page to pass the form data to

Within the form element, you include HTML elements for text boxes, text areas, radio buttons, check boxes, and other HTML5 form data fields. Each element uses a unique name to identify it in the form data that the browser sends to the action web page.

Because PHP runs on the server, it has no way of knowing when the site visitor is done filling out the form data fields in the browser window. With PHP, it's imperative to have a Submit button in the form to indicate to the browser when to send the form data to the web page specified in the `action` attribute, using the method specified in the `method` attribute.

A simple HTML5 form to use with PHP would look like this:

```
<form name="myform" action="mypage.php" method="POST">
<label>First name</label>
<input type="text" name="fname" size="40"><br>
<label>Last name</label>
<input type="text" name="lname" size="40"><br>
<input type="submit">
</form>
```

After the site visitor fills in the form data, she needs to click the Submit button to send the data to the `mypage.php` file specified in the form `action` attribute. The browser sends the form data embedded behind the scenes in the HTTP communication with the web server.

In the receiving web server, it passes the data received by the POST method to the PHP server, which uses the special $_POST[] array variable to retrieve the form data. You can then access that data in your PHP code using the $_POST[] array variable, along with the form field names:

```
$firstname = $_POST['fname'];
$lastname = $_POST['lname'];
```

The same method works for retrieving data from a ‹textarea› form field.

To retrieve the value from a select element, the name attribute of the select element defines the field name, and the option element value attribute for the option selected in the field is the value passed in the POST data. Consider the following form field:

```
<select name="age">
<option value="young">18–35</option>
<option value="middleage'>36–55</option>
<option value="old">56+</option>
</select>
```

When the site visitor selects the option labeled 18–35 in the drop-down list, the form sends the value young in the POST data. The PHP code can then access the $_POST['age'] array variable to retrieve the selected value.

To retrieve the value from a radio button element, the name attribute for all the buttons in the same group is the same. The value attribute defines what data is sent to the server as part of the POST data:

```
<input type="radio" name="age" value="young">18–35
<input type="radio" name="age" value="middleage">36–55
<input type="radio" name="age" value="old">56+
```

The PHP code checks the $_POST['age'] variable for the data value passed by the selected radio button.

Working with check box data fields can be a little tricky. The check box doesn't pass any data — it just indicates whether the box is checked. If the box is checked, it sends the value specified by the value attribute assigned to the data field specified name attribute:

```
<input type="checkbox" name="age" value="old">
```

If the site visitor checks the box in the form, the form sends the data field age with a value of old, and your PHP code can retrieve the selection using the $_POST['age'] array variable.

The problem comes in if the site visitor doesn't select the check box. If the check box is not selected, the form doesn't send any data for the form field. In that case, if you try using the $_POST['age'] array variable, you get an error from PHP that it doesn't exist.

To determine if a check box form field has been selected, you use the isset() PHP function. The isset() function returns a TRUE value if the PHP variable exists and has a value assigned to it or a FALSE value if not. You can then write something like this:

```
if (isset($_POST['age'])) {
    $age = $_POST['age'];
} else
    $age = "not selected";
}
```

Now you're able to determine whether the site visitor selected the check box.

Working with forms and PHP can be a bit tricky, but the more you practice, the better you'll get at it. Try out this example to get a feel for how to work with forms and PHP:

**1.** Open your editor and type the following code:

```
<!DOCTYPE html>
<html>
<head>
<title>PHP Form Test</title>
<style>
    input, textarea {
        margin: 5px;
    }
</style>
</head>
<body>
<h1>Please fill in the form</h1>
<form action="formtest.php" method="post">
<fieldset>
<legend>My test form</legend>
<label>First name</label>
<input type="text" name="fname" size="40"><br>
<label>Last name</label>
<input type="text" name="lname" size="40"><br>
<fieldset>
<legend>Select your favorite sport</legend>
```

```
<input type="radio" name="sport" value="baseball">Baseball<br>
<input type="radio" name="sport" value="football">Football<br>
<input type="radio" name="sport" value="hockey">Hockey<br>
<input type="radio" name="sport" value="soccer">Soccer<br>
</fieldset>
<label>Please type your essay</label>
<textarea name="essay" cols="50" rows="10"></textarea><br>
<input type="submit" value="Submit your form">
</fieldset>
</body>
</html>
```

2. **Save the file as** formtest.html **in the** DocumentRoot **folder for your web server.**

3. **Open a new window in your editor and type the following code:**

```
<!DOCTYPE html>
<html>
<head>
<title>PHP Form Test</title>
</head>
<body>
<h1>Form results:</h1>
<?php
$fname = $_POST['fname'];
$lname = $_POST['lname'];
if (isset($_POST['sport'])) {
    $sport = $_POST['sport'];
} else {
    $sport = "not specified";
}
$essay = $_POST['essay'];

echo "<h2>First name: $fname</h2>\n";
echo "<h2>Last name: $lname</h2>\n";
echo "<h2>Favorite sport: $sport</h2>\n";
echo "<h2>Essay response:</h2>\n";
echo "<p>$essay</p>\n";
?>
</body>
</html>
```

4. **Save the file as** formtest.php **in the** DocumentRoot **folder for your web server.**

**5.** Ensure the web server is running and then open your browser and enter the following URL:

```
http://localhost:8080/formtest.html
```

**6.** Fill in the from data fields, selecting a radio button but leaving the check boxes all unchecked.

**7.** Click the Submit button when you're done filling in the form.

**8.** Close the browser and shut down the web server.

The `formtest.html` file displays a standard HTML5 form on the web page, as shown in Figure 2-7.

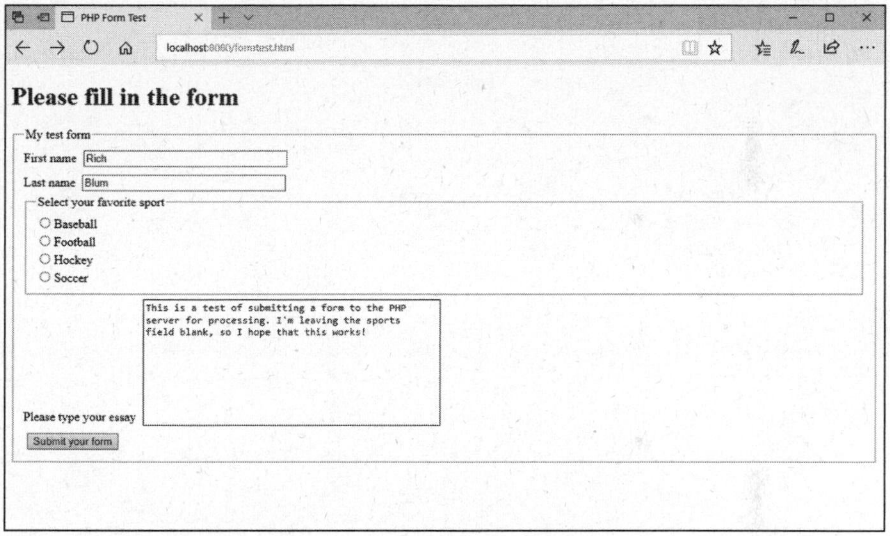

**FIGURE 2-7:**
The web form produced by the formtest. html file.

Enter your data in the form, but don't make a selection for your favorite sport. When you click the Submit button, the browser sends the form data as part of a POST method to the web server, which passes the form data to the `formtest.php` file as specified in the form `action` attribute.

The `formtest.php` code retrieves the form data and detects that none of the radio buttons was selected. By using the `isset()` function. It displays the data passed from the form, as shown in Figure 2-8.

Now you're ready to process any HTML5 form using your PHP server-side programming skills!

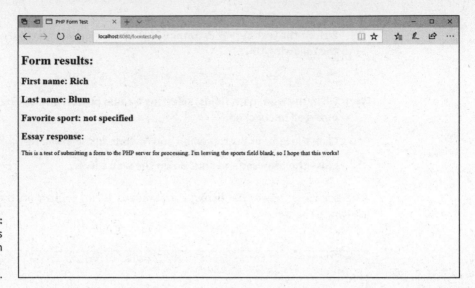

**FIGURE 2-8:**
The form results
as shown from
the formtest.
php file.

IN THIS CHAPTER

» **Getting familiar with PHP libraries**

» **Working with text functions**

» **Handling numbers**

» **Using dates**

» **Playing with images**

Chapter **3**

# PHP Libraries

s you start creating your dynamic web applications, you'll often find your-self wanting to perform certain functions that require quite a bit of coding, such as manipulating data or performing complex mathematical calculations. The true test of a robust programming language is in how much work it can save you by providing prebuilt code libraries that do most of the hard coding work for you. Fortunately, PHP has an extensive set of built-in libraries that can save you lots of development time as you build your web applications! This chapter dives into the basics of using the built-in libraries in PHP.

## How PHP Uses Libraries

All programming languages provide libraries of functions that help you with your coding. How many there are and how they do that differs somewhat between programming languages.

Some interpreted programming languages compile all the function libraries into a single monolithic executable program that loads into memory each time the web server runs a program that requires the interpreter. That can be a huge resource hog on your server!

PHP took a more modular approach to things. Instead of compiling all the function libraries in a single program, PHP provides them as separate loadable library files, called *extensions*. That way, you (or your web-hosting company) can opt to load only the extensions you need to use, saving memory on the server and hopefully improving the performance of the PHP server.

The downside to this approach is that you need to be more aware of just what PHP extensions are available and which ones you should load. This section shows you how PHP splits functions up into different extensions and how you can find the functions you need to do your work.

## Exploring PHP extensions

More than 150 extensions are available in the PHP package! There are extensions to cover functions as simple as manipulating string values or as complex as interacting with online search engines. The PHP developers have classified these extensions into 27 categories. Table 3-1 shows the different categories, along with a brief description of what each category contains.

**TABLE 3-1**     ## PHP Extension Categories

| Category | Description |
| --- | --- |
| PHP behavior | Functions that control how the PHP server operates |
| Audio formats | Functions that handle and manipulate audio files |
| Authentication | Functions that work with authentication services |
| Command line | Functions that interact with the server command-line environment |
| Compression | Functions that compress and archive files and folders |
| Credit card | Functions that process credit card transactions |
| Cryptography | Functions that encrypt and decrypt data |
| Database | Functions that interact with database servers |
| Date and time | Functions that handle dates and times |
| File system | Functions that interact with the server file system |
| GUI | Functions that work with user interface features |
| Human language | Functions that work with character sets |
| Image processing | Functions that create and manipulate images |
| Mail | Functions that interact with mail servers |
| Mathematical | Functions that perform complex mathematical operations |

| Category | Description |
|----------|-------------|
| Non-text MIME | Functions that handle binary data in MIME messages |
| Process control | Functions that interact with processes on the server |
| Other | Miscellaneous functions that manipulate data |
| Other services | Functions that interact with network services |
| Search engine | Functions that interact with online search engines |
| Session | Functions that handle browser sessions |
| Text | Functions that manipulate and process text |
| Variable | Functions that work with complex objects and data structures |
| Web services | Functions that interact with web service servers and clients |
| Windows | Functions that access Microsoft Windows features on Windows servers |
| XML | Functions that handle and manipulate data in XML format |

Each category contains multiple extensions that are available for you to load and use in your PHP programs. There are far too many PHP extensions to list them all individually here. For a full and current list of the PHP extensions, go to the PHP online documentation at www.php.net/manual/en/funcref.php.

## Examining the PHP extensions

You can view which extensions are actively installed in your specific PHP server environment by using the special phpinfo() function. Just include that as a single line in a PHP program. When you run the program, the phpinfo() function displays a table showing detailed information about the PHP server, including which PHP extensions are currently installed.

Follow these steps to determine which PHP extensions are installed in your PHP server environment.

1. **Open your favorite text editor, program editor, or integrated development environment (IDE) package.**

2. **Type the following code:**

```
<!DOCTYPE html>
<html>
<body>
```

```
<?php
phpinfo();
?>
</body>
</html>
```

3. **Save the file as** `extensions.php` **in the** `DocumentRoot` **folder for your web server.**

   For XAMPP on Windows, that's `c:\xampp\htdocs`; for XAMPP on macOS, it's `/Applications/XAMPP/htdocs`.

4. **Open the XAMPP Control Panel, and then start the Apache web server.**

5. **Open your browser, and enter the following URL:**

   ```
   http://localhost:8080/extensions.php
   ```

   You may need to change the TCP port in the URL to match your web server.

6. **Examine the output generated by the** `phpinfo()` **function, looking for which extensions are installed on your system.**

7. **Close the browser when you're done.**

Figure 3-1 shows the results from the XAMPP package running on a Windows workstation.

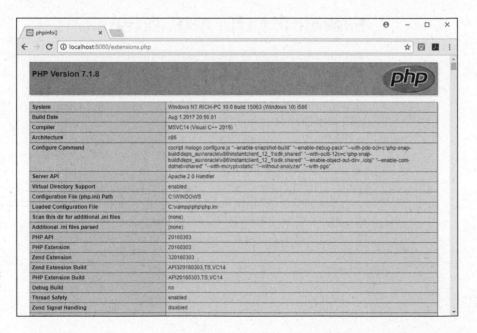

**FIGURE 3-1:**
The output from the `phpinfo()` function.

As you scroll through the listing generated by the phpinfo() function, you'll see separate sections devoted to the different extensions and the configuration settings that control how they operate. Most likely, your PHP server has quite a few (if not all) of the extensions already activated. If any are missing, you can usually activate them yourself. That's covered in the next section.

## Including extensions

Most PHP server environments include all the extension library files in the PHP server build, but they may not activate all of them to help save memory as the PHP server runs. If you find yourself needing to activate a specific PHP extension, you can easily do that from the PHP configuration file.

The first step is to find the php.ini configuration file for your PHP server environment. The easiest way to do that is from the output of the phpinfo() function.

If you followed the steps in the previous exercise, you can view the output of the phpinfo() function in your browser. In that output, look for the line in the top section for Loaded Configuration File. That shows the path to the configuration file the PHP server is using.

Using your system's file manager program (File Explorer for Windows, Finder for Mac), navigate to the folder where the php.ini file is stored, and then double-click the file to open it with a text editor.

Look for the section labeled Dynamic Extensions within the php.ini configuration file. This is where the configuration file defines the extensions to install. Each extension is referenced by a single line. For Windows systems, it looks like this:

```
extension=name.dll
```

For Mac and Unix/Linux systems, it looks like this:

```
extension=name.so
```

The extension names are in the format php_name where name is the unique name assigned to the extension. For example, the extension for interacting with MySQL servers is called php_mysqli (the i is added because it's an improved version from the original MySQL extension).

**WARNING**

Not all PHP server environments use extensions, so you may not see any entries for them in the `php.ini` configuration file. For example, the XAMPP for the macOS environment compiles all the extensions directly into the main PHP server executable.

### Adding additional extensions

As you can probably guess, you can create your own PHP extensions for your own custom functions. This has become quite popular in the PHP developer world, and a clearinghouse has been created for sharing custom-made extensions with other PHP developers.

The PHP Extension Community Library (PECL) hosts a library of custom extensions shared by developers from around the world. You can access PECL at `https://pecl.php.net`. There, you'll find extensions that add additional functionality to the standard PHP libraries, as well as add entirely new features, such as the `html_parse` extension, which provides functions to access a remote web page and parse the DOM tree elements to extract data!

Now that you know about PHP extensions, the following sections take a look at some of the more popular ones and the functions they contain that can help save you some time in your PHP coding.

## Text Functions

Just about every web application needs to work with text data. There's a wealth of text processing and manipulation functions available at your fingertips within the PHP extension library. This section walks through some of the more useful ones that may come in handy as you process data in your applications. There are so many text functions provided by PHP that trying to find just what you're looking for in the PHP online manual can be a bit overwhelming. This section breaks up the functions into categories to help simplify things a bit.

### Altering string values

PHP provides a handful of functions that manipulate either the text or the text format in string values. Table 3-2 shows the string functions that can be useful when you need to manipulate string values.

**TABLE 3-2**     **PHP String Manipulation Functions**

| Function | Description |
| --- | --- |
| addslashes | Adds an escape character (backslash) in front of single quote, double quote, backslash, and NULL characters. |
| chop | Removes all whitespace characters from the end of a string. |
| htmlentities | Converts HTML codes into HTML tags. |
| htmlspecialchars | Converts any HTML tags embedded in a string into HTML codes. |
| lcfirst | Changes the first character of the string to lowercase. |
| ltrim | Removes any whitespace characters from the start of a string. |
| money_format | Formats a monetary string value into a currency format. |
| nl2br | Converts newline characters to the `<br>` HTML tag. |
| number_format | Allows you to specify the format to display a number value. |
| rtrim | Removes all whitespace characters from the end of a string. |
| str_replace | Replaces the occurrences of a string with another string. |
| strip_tags | Removes all HTML and PHP tags from a string. |
| strtolower | Converts the string to lowercase. |
| strtoupper | Converts the string to uppercase. |
| trim | Removes all whitespace characters from the start and end of a string. |
| ucfirst | Converts the first character of the string to uppercase. |

The string manipulation functions don't change the value of the original string — they just return a new string value. If you want to use the result in your program, you have to assign it to another variable:

```
$newvalue = trim($data);
```

The `htmlspecialchars()` and `strip_tags()` functions are extremely helpful if you're creating a web application that accepts data from unknown site visitors. Unfortunately, it's all too common these days for an unseemly website to run robot scripts that scan the Internet looking for websites that allow site visitors to post comments without requiring a login. These robots then post advertisements as comments in the website, and these advertisements more often than not contain a hypertext link to a rogue website.

The htmlspecialchars() and strip_tags() functions can help block that silliness. They detect any HTML code embedded within a string value and either remove them completely (the strip_tags() function) or convert the greater-than and less-than symbols in the tag into the HTML &gt; and &lt; codes (the htmlspecialchars() function). This helps prevent your site visitors from accidentally clicking rogue hypertext links embedded within posts!

The nl2br() function comes in handy if your web application processes text files to display on the web page. If the text file contains new-line characters, those won't display on the web page, which may alter the layout of the text. If you pass the data through the nl2br() function, it converts any new-line characters in the text to HTML5 <br> tags, preserving the text layout on the web page.

Yet another useful string manipulation function you don't often see in other programming languages is the addslashes() function. This function is useful when you need to push data submitted by site visitors into a SQL database. It escapes any single or double quotes embedded within the string value, so that they don't conflict with any quotes needed to embed the string into a SQL statement to submit to the database. This little function can save you lots of trouble with handling data for your database!

## Splitting strings

Another common function in string manipulation is the ability to split strings into separate substrings. This comes in handy when you're trying to parse string values to look for words. Table 3-3 shows the PHP string splitting functions that are available.

**TABLE 3-3** **PHP String Splitting Functions**

| Function | Description |
| --- | --- |
| chunk_split | Splits a string value into smaller parts of a specified length. |
| explode | Splits a string value into an array based on one or more delimiter characters. |
| implode | Joins array elements into a single string value. |
| str_getcsv | Parses a comma-delimited string into an array. |
| str_split | Splits a string into an array based on a specified length. |

The str_getcsv() function is extremely useful when you need to parse comma-separated data entered by site visitors, such as search terms. Follow these steps to see a demonstration of how this works:

**1.** **Open your editor and type the following code:**

```
<!DOCTYPE html>
<html>
<head>
<title>String Parsing Test</title>
<style>
   input {
      margin: 5px;
   }
</style>
</head>
<body>
<h2>String parse test</h2>
<form action="parseoutput.php" method="post">
<p>Enter a list of search words, separated with commas</p>
<input type="text" name="search" size="40"><br>
<input type="submit" value="Search">
</form>
</body>
</html>
```

**2.** **Save the file as** parseinput.html **in the** DocumentRoot **folder for your web server.**

**3.** **Open a new tab or window in your editor and type the following code:**

```
<!DOCTYPE html>
<html>
<head>
<title>String Parse Test Results</title>
</head>
</body>
<h1>Search word results</h1>
<?php
$search = $_POST['search'];
$words = str_getcsv($search);
```

```
foreach ($words as $word) {
    $term = trim($word);
    echo "<p>Search term: '$term'</p>
\n";
}
?>
</body>
</html>
```

4. **Save the file as** parseoutput.php **in the** DocumentRoot **folder for your web server.**

5. **Ensure that your web server is still running, and then open your browser and enter the following URL:**

```
http://localhost:8080/parseinput.html
```

6. **In the text box, type a comma-separated list of words, and then click the Submit button.**

7. **Observe the results in the** parseoutput.php **page.**

8. **Close your browser window when you're done.**

The parseinput.html file creates a simple HTML form that contains a single text box for you to enter search words, as shown in Figure 3-2.

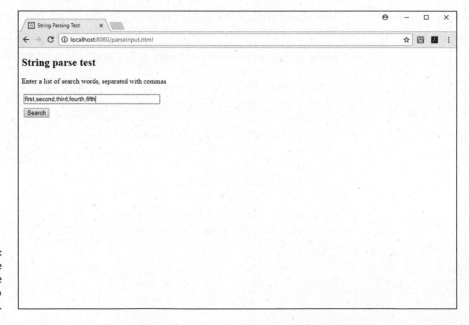

**FIGURE 3-2:**
The web page generated by the parseinput.php code.

Type a comma-separated list of words in the text box, and then click the Search button to send them to the `parseoutput.php` file. The `parseoutput.php` code retrieves the list of words using the standard `$_POST[]` array variable:

```
$search = $_POST['search'];
```

Then it uses the `str_getcsv()` function to parse the string and split the words into an array variable. It then uses the `foreach` statement to display the individual words in the web page, as shown in Figure 3-3.

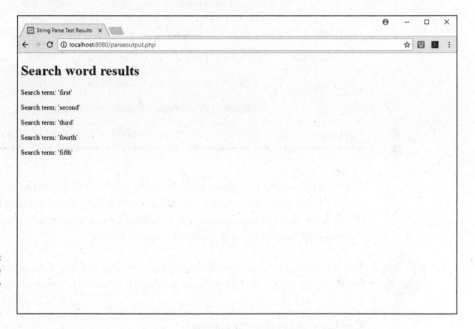

**FIGURE 3-3:** The web page result from the parseoutput. php code.

The `trim()` function is used to remove any extra spaces or tab characters that may have been added between the search terms in the form. These are handy little functions to have in your toolbox as you code your web applications!

## Testing string values

A vital function in string manipulation is the ability to test string values for specific conditions. PHP provides several string-testing functions that help with that, as shown in Table 3-4.

TABLE 3-4

## PHP String-Testing Functions

| Function | Description |
|---|---|
| is_bool | Returns a TRUE value if the string is a valid Boolean value. |
| is_float | Returns a TRUE value if the string is a valid float value. |
| is_int | Returns a TRUE value if the string is a valid integer value. |
| is_null | Returns a TRUE value if the string is a NULL value. |
| is_numeric | Returns a TRUE value if the string is a valid number or numeric string. |
| str_word_count | Returns the number of words in a string or an array of words. |
| strcasecmp | Performs a case-insensitive string comparison. |
| strcmp | Compares the binary values of two string values. |
| strlen | Returns the number of characters in a string. |
| strncmp | Compares the first *n* characters of two string values. |

The string-testing functions provide quite a bit of information about the data you receive from your site visitors, as well as performing simple string comparisons to check data. The strcmp() function is crucial in evaluating data entered into forms in response to questions in your web applications.

**TIP**

The is_numeric() function is handy to use when testing data submitted in HTML5 forms from unknown site visitors to ensure a numeric value was submitted.

## Searching strings

Yet another common string function is searching for a specific value within a string. If you just need to know if a substring value is contained within a string value, use the strpos() function. Here's the format of the strpos() function:

```
strpos(largestring, substring);
```

PHP will look for the string *substring* within the *largestring* string value. It returns the position where the substring is found inside the *largestring* (with position 0 being the first character of the string). If the substring is not found, it returns a FALSE value. Be careful though, because position 0 returns a numeric 0, which is different from a FALSE value! To properly test for the difference you must use the === comparison operator, which compares both the value and the data type.

# REGULAR EXPRESSIONS

Besides a simple string search, PHP supports more complex *regular expression* string searches. Regular expressions allow you to define a template to compare against the string value. If the string matches the template, it passes the regular expression test.

In the past, PHP supported two different types of regular expressions formats:

- Perl Compatible Regular Expressions (PCRE)

- POSIX Extended Regular Expressions

However, since PHP version 7, support for POSIX regular expressions has been dropped; only the PCRE regular expression format is supported today.

Using regular expressions to search for data is a powerful tool, but also a very complex tool. Entire books and websites have been devoted to explaining all the complexities of regular expression searching. In a nutshell, the key to regular expressions is defining a template that can filter out just the data you want. The template defines what character(s) to look for in a string, and you can even define in what positions the characters should appear within the string if needed. PHP matches the string value against the template, and if it matches, it returns a TRUE value. Check out the PHP online manual section on the PCRE regular expressions (www.php.net/manual/en/book.pcre.php) for more information on using regular expressions in your PHP code.

# Math Functions

Chapter 1 in this minibook shows the basic arithmetic operators that PHP supports. However, there are lots more advanced mathematical features that are available in the PHP extensions! This section discusses the different math functions you can add to your web applications to help save you from having to create complex code for your calculations.

## Number theory

Number theory functions provide handy mathematical features, such as finding the absolute value, square root, or factorial of a number. PHP has lots of different number theory functions built in and ready for you to use in your calculations. Table 3-5 lists some of the more common ones you'll use.

**TABLE 3-5**

## PHP Number Functions

| Function | Description |
|---|---|
| abs | Returns the absolute value of a number. |
| ceil | Rounds a value up to the next largest integer. |
| floor | Rounds a value down to the next lowest integer. |
| fmod | Returns the floating point remainder of the division. |
| intdiv | Performs an integer division. |
| is_finite | Returns TRUE if the value is a finite number. |
| is_infinite | Returns TRUE if the value is infinite. |
| is_nan | Returns TRUE if the value is not a proper float value. |
| max | Returns the largest value in an array. |
| min | Returns the smallest value in an array. |
| pi | Returns a float approximation of pi. |
| rand | Returns a random number. |
| sqrt | Returns the square root of a value. |

The rand() function is handy when you need to generate random numbers for applications (such as guessing games). Without any parameters, the rand() function returns a random integer value between 0 and the maximum integer value supported by the server (you can determine that using the getrandmax() function). If you need a value from a smaller range, you can specify the min and max range as parameters. The range values are inclusive, so if you specify the following, the rand() function will return a random number from 1 to 10:

```
$number = rand(1, 10);
```

**WARNING**

Despite what you might think from its name, the is_nan() function does not work to test input provided by site visitors to determine if the value is a number. The is_nan() function only works for float values to determine if the float is in the correct floating point notation. Use the is_numeric() string function instead.

## Calculating logs and exponents

PHP supports several logarithmic functions that can help with some of your more complex mathematical operations. Table 3-6 shows what tools you have available for that.

TABLE 3-6

## PHP Logarithmic Functions

| Function | Description |
|----------|-------------|
| exp | Calculates the exponent of *e*. |
| expm1 | Calculates the exponent of *e* minus 1. |
| log | Performs a standard natural logarithm. |
| log10 | Performs a base-10 logarithm. |
| log1p | Calculates a log(1 + number). |
| pow | Calculate the base raised to a power. |

Since version 5.6, PHP has included the $**$ operator to perform exponentiation as well as the pow( ) function. You can use either one in your mathematical calculations to get the same result.

## Working the angles

If trigonometry is your thing, you'll be glad to know that PHP includes all the standard trig functions in the math extension. These are shown in Table 3-7.

TABLE 3-7

## PHP Trigonometric Functions

| Function | Description |
|----------|-------------|
| acos | Calculates the arc cosine. |
| asin | Calculates the arc sine. |
| atan | Calculates the arc tangent. |
| cos | Calculates the cosine. |
| deg2rad | Returns the radian value of a degree. |
| hypot | Calculates the length of the hypotenuse of a right triangle. |
| rad2deg | Returns the degree value of a radian. |
| sin | Calculates the sine. |
| tan | Calculates the tangent. |

All the PHP trig functions require that you specify the angle values in radians instead of degrees. If your application is working with degree units, you'll need to use the deg2rad() function to convert the values to radians before using them in your calculations.

## Hyperbolic functions

Somewhat related to trigonometric functions are the hyperbolic functions. Whereas trigonometric functions are derived from circular calculations, hyperbolic functions are derived from a hyperbola calculation. Table 3-8 shows the hyperbolic functions that PHP supports.

**TABLE 3-8**

### PHP Hyperbolic Functions

| Function | Description |
|----------|-------------|
| acosh | Returns the inverse hyperbolic cosine. |
| asinh | Returns the inverse hyperbolic sine. |
| atanh | Returns the inverse hyperbolic tangent. |
| cosh | Returns the hyperbolic cosine. |
| sinh | Returns the hyperbolic sine. |
| tanh | Returns the hyperbolic tangent. |

Just as with the trigonometric functions, you must specify the hyperbolic function values in radian units instead of degrees.

## Tracking statistics

The PHP statistics extension contains functions commonly used for statistical calculations. It uses the open-source library of C routines for Cumulative Distributions Functions, Inverses, and Other parameters (DCDFLIB) created by Barry Brown and James Lavato.

The library contains about 70 functions for calculating statistical values from beta, chi-square, $f$, gamma, Laplace, logistic, normal, Poisson, $t$, and Weinbull distributions. If you understand any of those things, this is the extension for you! Check out the available statistical functions in the PHP online manual at www.php. net/manual/en/ref.stats.php.

# Date and Time Functions

Working with times and dates in web applications can be a tricky thing. If your application needs to perform date arithmetic (such as calculating when 60 days is from now), PHP has some useful functions for you! This section first walks through just how PHP handles time and dates, then shows you some functions that can help with your date calculations.

## Generating dates

PHP provides the date() function for generating human-readable dates and times. The date() function takes either one or two parameters:

```
date(format [, timestamp])
```

The *format* parameter is required. It specifies how you want PHP to display the date and/or time values. The *timestamp* parameter is optional. It represents the date and time you want to display as an integer timestamp value. The timestamp value represents the date and time as the number of seconds since midnight, January 1, 1970 (it's an old Unix standard). If you omit the timestamp value, PHP assumes the current date and time.

The *format* is a string value that uses a complicated code to indicate how you want the time and date to appear in the output. Table 3-9 shows the format codes that are available.

**TABLE 3-9** The PHP date() Function Format Codes

| Code | Description | Example |
|------|-------------|---------|
| a | Morning or evening as am or pm | am |
| A | Morning or evening as AM or PM | AM |
| B | The Swatch international time format | 952 (for 9:52 pm) |
| c | The date in ISO 8601 format | 2018-05-15T22:51:52+01:00 |
| d | The day of the month as a two-digit value with leading zero if necessary | 15 |
| D | The day of the week as a three-letter abbreviation | Mon |
| e | Time zone identifier | America/New_York |
| F | The month of the year in full text | January |

*(continued)*

**TABLE 3-9** *(continued)*

| Code | Description | Example |
|------|-------------|---------|
| g | The hour of the day in 12-hour format | 4 |
| G | The hour of the day in 24-hour format | 16 |
| h | The hour of the day in 12-hour format with leading zero | 04 |
| H | The hour of the day in 24-hour format with leading zero | 16 |
| i | Minutes past the hour with leading zero | 05 |
| I | Whether the time zone is using daylight saving time | 0 (for not using daylight savings time) |
| j | The day of the month as a number without leading zeroes | 5 |
| l | The day of the week in full text | Monday |
| L | Whether the year is a leap year | 0 (for non-leap years) |
| m | The month of the year as a two-digit number with leading zero | 01 |
| M | The month of the year as a three-letter abbreviation | Jan |
| n | The month of the year as a number without leading zero | 1 |
| o | The year in ISO 8601 format | 2018 |
| O | The difference between the current time zone and GMT | -0500 |
| r | The date and time in RFC822 format | Mon, 15 Jan 2018 22:56:35 +0100 |
| s | Seconds past the minute in two-digit format with leading zero | 05 |
| S | Ordinal suffix of the date in two-letter format | th (for 15) |
| t | The total number of days in the date's month | 31 |
| T | The time zone setting of the server | EST |
| U | The date and time in Unix timestamp format | 1516053508 |
| w | The day of the week as a single digit | 1 |
| W | The week number in the year | 03 |
| y | The year in two-digit format with leading zero | 18 |
| Y | The year in four-digit format | 2018 |
| z | The day of the year as a number | 78 |
| Z | Offset for the current time zone in seconds | -18000 |

As you can see from the list of codes in Table 3-9, the `date()` function output is very flexible! For example, if you use the following format:

```
$today = date("l, F jS, Y");
```

The `$today` variable would display the current date as:

```
Thursday, January 4th, 2018
```

Or if you prefer, you can just use:

```
$today = date("m/d/Y");
```

To display the date as:

```
01/04/2018
```

With the `date()` function codes, you can display the date and time in any format you need!

**WARNING**

Displaying dates in a website that can be seen internationally can be somewhat tricky. Keep in mind the differences in how the United States represents dates and how the rest of the world represents dates. To accommodate that difference, the Organization of International Standards (ISO) has created the ISO 8601 standard for displaying dates. It follows none of the common date formats, but instead, uses its own style: 2018-01-04, which represents January 4, 2018. Later in the book, when you work with dates in the MySQL server, you need to use this format to store dates in the database.

## Using timestamps

The second parameter of the `date()` function allows you to specify a different date/time to display using a timestamp value. The problem, though, is that you most likely don't know what the timestamp value for a date is! No worries — you have the handy `strtotime()` function to help you out.

The `strtotime()` function converts a date/time string value in just about any format into a timestamp value. For example, if you want to find out what day of the week the Fourth of July is in the year 2020, just use the following code:

```
$timestamp = strtotime("07/04/2020");
$holiday = date("l", $timestamp);
```

The strtotime() function returns the value 1593820800, which is the timestamp representation for midnight on that day. You then use that as the second parameter in the date() function, and use the l (lowercase letter *L*) code format for the output. The output will be the day of the week, Saturday.

**WARNING**

There is a looming problem with using timestamp values in your PHP code. Because the timestamp format is an old format, to remain backward-compatible, systems store the value as a 32-bit integer data type. As you can guess, at some point in the future, that value will overflow the storage capability of the integer data type. That date happens to be January 14, 2038. If your application needs to work with dates past then, you have to use some other way to handle dates.

## Calculating dates

You have a couple of different ways to handle date calculations at your disposal in PHP. One method is to work with timestamp values. If you know the timestamp for the current date/time, you can add the number of seconds needed to represent another date/time.

For example, to calculate the time ten minutes from now, you'd use the following code:

```
$start = strtotime("07/04/2020 10:00:00");
$end = $start + (60 * 10);
$duedate = $date("H:i:s", $end);
```

The first line returns the timestamp value for the start date. The second line adds the number of seconds for 10 minutes (60 seconds × 10 minutes) to the date timestamp. Finally, the third line returns the resulting time.

With timestamp values, you can perform all types of calculations, adding and subtracting values from any start point. Just remember that you're working with seconds, so you need to convert the values into the appropriate timestamp values, and add or subtract the appropriate number of seconds.

The other method for performing date calculations is to use the strtotime() function itself. The strtotime() function is extremely versatile and can recognize all sorts of common date representations. For example, if you want to find out yesterday's date, you use the following:

```
$yesterday = strtotime("yesterday");
```

And the `strtotime()` function will return the timestamp value for yesterday! You can also use some basic calendar math:

```
$duedate = strtotime("today + 120 days");
```

PHP will calculate that for you automatically! That saves you from having to do the calculations yourself using timestamp values.

# Image-Handling Functions

These days, it's a common requirement to work with images in your web pages. Whether vacation pictures on a blog or an online catalog of products, images have become a crucial part of most web applications.

PHP doesn't disappoint here. The php_gd2 extension is a complete graphical manipulation library for processing images directly in your PHP applications. Instead of having to rely on an external image manipulation program such as Photoshop or GIMP, you can edit images directly in your application as you or your site visitors upload them!

Not only can you manipulate uploaded images, but the php_gd2 extension also has functions that allow you to create new images on the fly in your PHP code! To create a new image, use the `imagecreatetruecolor()` function. This function takes two parameters: the width and height of the new image, specified in pixels. It returns a resource variable value that you use to reference the new image as you add components to the image.

For example, to create a new image that is 80 pixels wide by 60 pixels high, use this code:

```
$myimage = imagecreatetruecolor(80, 60);
```

After creating the new image, you'll probably want to draw something in it. First, you must allocate colors to use for the background and foreground objects:

```
$bg = imagecolorallocate($myimage, 255, 255, 255);
$fg = imagecolorallocate($myimage, 0, 0, 0);
```

The `imagecolorallocate()` function takes four parameters. The first parameter is the image resource value returned when you create the image. The next three parameters are the color, defined by the RGB value, just as you do with CSS style colors. The value 255, 255, 255 represents white, while the 0, 0, 0 value represents black.

After allocating the colors you need, you're ready to start drawing on your canvas. Table 3-10 covers the functions you have available for drawing lines, shapes, and even text.

**TABLE 3-10**     **The GD2 Library Drawing Functions**

| Function | Description |
|---|---|
| imageline | Draws a line between two specified points, using a defined color. |
| imagechar | Draws an alphanumeric character using a specified font, color, and location. |
| imagerectangle | Draws a rectangle outline between four points using a defined color. |
| imagefilledrectangle | Draws a solid rectangle between four points using a defined color. |
| imagestring | Draws a string of characters using a specified font, color, and location. |

So, to create a new image file with the words *Test Image*, you'd use this code:

```
$image = imagecreatetruecolor(80, 60);
$bc = imagecolorallocate($image, 255, 255, 255);
$fc = imagecolorallocate($image, 0, 0, 0);
imagefilledrectangle($image, 0, 0, 80, 60, $bc);
imagestring($image, 5, 20, 5, "Test", $fc);
imagestring($image, 5, 10, 20, "Image", $fc);
imagejpeg($image, "myimage.jpg");
imagedestroy($image);
```

You should recognize most of these image functions. The imagestring() function defines a font size followed by the X and Y coordinates of where to start the string, followed by the string, followed by the color.

The imagejpeg() function converts the referenced image object in memory to either an image on the web page or saves it to a file. I specified a filename to save the image to. The imagedestroy() function removes the image from memory to free up space. This is especially necessary when working with large images.

One of the biggest problems I often run into when using images in web applications is that they're too big to fit nicely in the spaces I allocate on the web page. If you run a web application that allows site visitors to upload their own images for posting, you never know quite what to expect. Some visitors upload tiny picture files, while others upload mega-sized images. The trick to a good web page is to standardize all the images to make them fit nicely on the web page.

Sure, you can do that by manually downloading all the images, opening them in Photoshop, resizing them, and then uploading the new images back to the web server. That works, but it's extremely time consuming and awkward. Fortunately, the php_gd2 library has just the tool for you!

The `imagecopyresampled()` function allows you to resample an existing image to a new image. Resampling rebuilds the image pixel by pixel, at a different resolution, using special algorithms to maintain the picture clarity.

By resampling the image, you can make it larger or smaller. The php_gd2 extension library takes care of all the mathematical routines required to do that. Follow these steps to try that out:

**1.** **Open your editor and enter the following code:**

```html
<!DOCTYPE html>
<html>
<head>
<title>Image Manipulation Test</title>
<style>
    input {
        margin: 5px;
    }
</style>
</head>
<body>
<h2>Please select an image to upload</h2>
<form action="imageconvert.php" method="post"
    enctype="multipart/form-data">
<input type="file" name="picture"><br>
<input type="submit" value="Submit">
</form>
</body>
</html>
```

**2.** **Save the file as** `imageupload.html` **in the** `DocumentRoot` **folder for your web server.**

**3.** **Open a new tab or window in your editor and enter the following code:**

```html
<!DOCTYPE html>
<html>
<head>
<title>Image Manipulation Test</title>
</head>
```

```
<body>
<h1>The uploaded image:</h1>
<?php
$file = $_FILES['picture']['tmp_name'];
$picture = file_get_contents($file);
$sourceImage = imagecreatefromstring($picture);

$width = imageSX($sourceImage);
$height = imageSY($sourceImage);

$newheight = 400;
$newwidth = $newheight * ($width / $height);

$newImage = imagecreatetruecolor($newwidth, $newheight);
$result = imagecopyresampled($newImage, $sourceImage,
        0, 0, 0, 0,
         $newwidth, $newheight, $width, $height);
imagejpeg($newImage, "newimage.jpg");
?>
<img src="newimage.jpg">
</body>
</html>
```

4. Save the file as imageconvert.php in the DocumentRoot folder for your web server.

5. Have an image file handy that you want to copy and convert to a different sized image.

6. Ensure the web server is running, and then open your browser to the URL:

```
http://localhost:8080/imageupload.html
```

7. Click the file chooser button for the file upload text box as it appears in your browser, navigate to your image file, select it, and then click the Open button to select the name.

8. Click the Submit button to upload the image file for converting.

9. You should see the resized image appear on the resulting web page.

10. Close your browser and shut down the web server when you're done.

The imageupload.html file creates a simple HMTL5 form using the file data input type. The browser will provide a method for you to select a local file to enter into the file input field, as shown in Figure 3-4 for the Chrome browser.

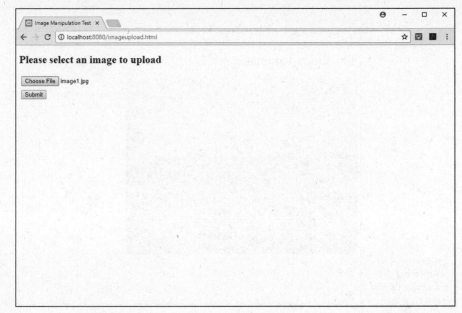

**FIGURE 3-4:**
The output
from the
`imageupload.`
`html` program.

The `imageconvert.php` code retrieves the uploaded image from the PHP server using the special `$_FILES[]` array variable. The `$_FILES[]` array provides information about files uploaded to the server within an HTML5 form. The `tmp_name` array element contains the name of the temporary file the server creates to store the uploaded file.

After retrieving the uploaded file, the code converts it to an editable php_gd2 library object using the `imagecreatefromstring()` function.

Using the uploaded image object, the code calculates the width and height of the original image using the `imageSX()` and `imageSY()` functions. Then with a little bit of algebra, the code sets the new image height to a set height, and calculates the new width required to keep the original aspect ratio of the image. This ensures that all images that appear on the web page use the same height.

With the new width and height values calculated, the code then uses the `image copyresampled()` function to copy and resample the original image to the resized image object. The `imagejpeg()` function saves the new image as the file `newimage.jpg` in the `DocumentRoot` folder of the web server. Finally, the code displays the new image on the web page using a standard `<img>` HTML5 tag, as shown in Figure 3-5.

Now you can resize uploaded image files on the fly, without any intervention required on your part!

**FIGURE 3-5:**
Displaying the
resampled and
resized image.

IN THIS CHAPTER

» **Identifying PHP attacks**

» **Stopping cross-site scripts**

» **Hiding your files**

» **Watching for data spoofing**

» **Handling data safely**

Chapter **4**

# Considering PHP Security

Web application security is a hot topic these days, and for good reason! It seems that almost every day there's a news story about some company being attacked and having important data stolen. These breaches are costly — both for the company and for the thousands of customers who have personal information stolen.

As a web application developer, your job is to put security first in all your design and coding work. You're the front line in the battle of data security! This chapter helps with that job, by giving you an idea of the types of attacks you need to watch out for and then walking you through how to avoid those attacks with your PHP code.

## Exploring PHP Vulnerabilities

To avoid attacks, you first need to know where they'll come from. It doesn't do any good to barricade the front door, if you leave the windows wide open. The majority of attacks against your web applications are avoidable by following some basic PHP coding rules.

There are thousands of different ways for an attacker to break into your PHP program, but most of them boil down into four general categories:

» Cross-site scripting

» Data spoofing

» Invalid data

» Unauthorized file access

Each of these attacks has different causes and results, as well as different methods for you to use to block them. The following sections examine each of these attacks in depth.

## Cross-site scripting

*Cross-site scripting* (known as XSS) is quite possibly the most dangerous type of attack made on dynamic web applications. The main idea of an XSS attack is to embed malicious JavaScript code in data that the attacker submits to the web application as part of the normal data input process. When the web application tries to display the data in a client browser, the JavaScript is pushed to the client browser that's viewing the website and runs.

Follow these steps to watch an XSS exploit in action:

1. **Open your favorite text editor, program editor, or integrated development environment (IDE) package.**

2. **Type the following code into the editor window:**

```
<!DOCTYPE html>
<html>
<head>
<title>XSS Test</title>
<style>
   input {
       margin: 5px;
    }
</style>
</head>
<body>
<h2>Please enter your first name:</h2>
<form action="xsstest.php" method="post">
<input type="text" name="fname"><br>
```

```
<input type="submit" value="Submit name">
</form>
</body>
</html>
```

**3.** **Save the file as** `xssform.html` **in the** `DocumentRoot` **folder for your web server.**

For XAMPP on Windows, that's `c:\xampp\htdocs`; for XAMPP on macOS, that's `/Applications/XAMPP/htdocs`.

**4.** **Open a new tab or window in your browser, and type the following code:**

```
<!DOCTYPE html>
<html>
<head>
<title>XSS Test</title>
</head>
<body>
<h1>XSS Test</h1>
<?php
    $fname = $_POST['fname'];
    echo "<p>Welcome, $fname</p>\n";
?>
<h2>This is the end of the test</h2>
</body>
</html>
```

**5.** **Save the file as** `xsstest.php` **in the** `DocumentRoot` **folder for your web server.**

**6.** **Open the XAMPP Control Panel, and then start the Apache web server.**

**7.** **Open your browser, and enter the following URL:**

```
http://localhost:8080/xssform.html
```

You may need to change the TCP port used to match your web server.

**8.** **In the form, type the following code in the Name text box:**

```
<script>alert("Hello!");</script>
```

**9.** **Click the Submit button to continue.**

**10.** **Close the browser window when you're done with the test.**

When you submit the form with the embedded JavaScript code, you should get the output as shown in Figure 4-1.

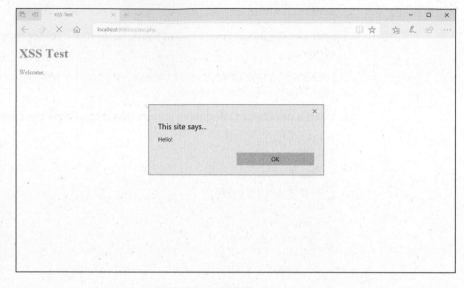

FIGURE 4-1:
The output from entering embedded JavaScript in a form.

The PHP code sent the JavaScript to the browser as part of the echo statement output, and the browser dutifully ran the JavaScript code. This example is harmless, because it just displays a simple alert message, but a real attacker would embed much more malicious code.

**TIP**

Some browsers, such as Safari and Chrome, have built-in XSS attack detection, which may trigger on this test and block the JavaScript code from running. If you don't see the alert() pop-up box, open the developer tools for your browser and see if there's a notice that the browser blocked a potential XSS attempt.

The "cross-site" part of the XSS name comes from where the <script> tag sends the browser to retrieve the JavaScript code file. In the previous example, I just submitted embedded JavaScript code directly within the script element. *Remember:* The <script> HTML5 tag can also reference an external JavaScript file, which the browser will load and run. An attacker can specify the src attribute in the <script> tag to redirect the browser to run JavaScript located on a rogue server anywhere in the world.

There are two different methods of carrying out an XSS attack:

>> **Reflected attack:** The attacker places the rogue script as a link in the submitted data. Victims must actively click the link to launch the XSS attack.

>> **Persistent attack:** The attacker places the rogue script as data that the browser displays when the web page loads (as in the previous example).

Persistent attacks are very dangerous. The malicious script runs as soon as an unsuspecting website visitor opens the web page that contains the script as part of the content, without any actions required by the victim. For example, if an attacker posts a blog comment that contains malicious JavaScript code, every time the web application displays that blog comment on a client browser, the malicious script is run.

## Data spoofing

Our dynamic web applications use all types of data to produce content. All too often, though, we assume the values stored in a particular variable are placed there by our program and are correct. However, that may not always be the case.

Another popular form of attack is *data spoofing* (externally inserting fraudulent data into a PHP program code). The biggest culprit of this attack is the register_ globals setting in the php.ini configuration file for the PHP server (see Book 1, Chapter 2).

The register_globals setting was originally intended to make life easier for PHP developers. When that setting is enabled, PHP automatically converts any data passed via the GET or POST methods into a PHP variable.

For example, let's say you build a form that contains the following input element:

```
<input type="text" name="fname">
```

When the PHP server receives the form data, it automatically creates a PHP variable named $fname, and assigns it the value passed from the form data field with that name. This feature certainly makes your coding life easier, but it adds a new problem.

Suppose your application uses an authentication method to validate the administrators of your website. When an administrator logs in, you set a variable indicating that the session is an administrative session and then check that variable whenever the user attempts to do some admin work. The code for that would look something like this:

```
if ($admin == 1) {
    do some admin functions
} else {
    echo "Sorry, you do not have permission";
}
```

The application assumes the $admin variable is set to a value of 1 when the user is an authenticated administrator.

Now, consider what would happen if an attacker figured this out and the register_globals setting in PHP were enabled. All the attacker would need to do is spoof the $admin variable with a phony value. And all that attack requires is to use this URL:

```
http://yourhost.com/index.php?admin=1
```

The register_globals setting allows the PHP server to retrieve the value set in the GET method, create the variable $admin, and set it to a value of 1. This will then allow the attacker to perform the admin function in the application without having to log in!

**WARNING**

Newer versions of PHP disable the register_globals setting by default, but that setting is still present. It's never a good idea to enable the register_globals setting. Just retrieve any data you need using the standard $_GET[] and $_POST[] array variables. It's worth the effort!

# Invalid data

Invalid data comes in all shapes and sizes. Often invalid data is just the result of a site visitor not paying close enough attention to the form fields and entering the wrong data into the wrong field, such as typing a zip code into a city name data field. Other times there may be some malicious intent to the invalid data, such as entering an invalid email address into a contact form on purpose to remain anonymous. It's your job as the application developer to anticipate invalid data and try to prevent it before it becomes a problem in the application.

There are two schools of thought on data validation:

>> Client-side data validation

>> Server-side data validation

The following sections dig a little deeper into just how these two methods differ.

## Client-side data validation

As you can probably guess, *client-side data validation* requires adding some Java-Script code to your web-page form to ensure site visitors enter the proper data into the proper data fields. Book 3, Chapter 4, details how to watch for form events and trigger JavaScript code to check as the site visitor types the data. If any invalid data is entered, the JavaScript can block sending the form data to the server.

**WARNING**

Don't rely on JavaScript data validation alone, though. Your website visitors can disable JavaScript in their browsers to get around it!

You can also use the HTML5 data-filtering elements and attributes that limit the range of possible values for a form field — for example, by using the new phone or email input element types instead of just a standard text input element. The browser won't accept data that doesn't match the format defined by the filters.

A combination of JavaScript, HTML5, and CSS produces a three-pronged approach to client-side data validation. That combination allows you to monitor the data your site visitors type into the data fields and then change the styles applied to the data field accordingly. A common feature is to use the background color style to indicate invalid data in a data field. When the site visitor enters invalid data, JavaScript changes the data field background color to red.

## Server-side data validation

Because the focus of this chapter is PHP, I talk more about *server-side data validation.* Server-side data validation is a little trickier in that you must wait for the site visitor to submit the form before you can validate the data in your PHP code. You can't detect invalid data in real time, but you do have a few more tools available for validating the data in your PHP code.

When the client browser sends the form data to the server, your PHP code retrieves it from the $_GET[] or $_POST[] array variables and then can work on determining which data is valid and which is invalid. Usually, there's a set process that you can undertake to validate data, such as making sure numeric values are really numbers or that text values don't contain any extraneous characters that shouldn't be there (such as the semicolon character discussed in the SQL injection sidebar).

One common method used in PHP development is to create an array to contain the "clean" data values retrieved from the table. As the code validates each data field value, that value is placed into the array with the corresponding variable name used as the key. The application doesn't use any of the data retrieved directly from the form; instead, it only accesses data values from the array of cleaned data values. That ensures that you won't make any mistakes by accidentally using a data value that hasn't been validated.

There are a few PHP functions to help out with the data validation process, which I discuss later in this chapter.

## SQL INJECTION

Possibly the most dangerous attack involving invalid data is the SQL injection attack. With SQL injection, an attacker embeds a SQL statement inside form field data, hoping that the application will forward the data to a database server without validating it and that the database server will run the SQL statement. The embedded SQL statement usually performs some type of malicious action, such as deleting a table, or at least all the data within the table.

If your application uses a database, it's important to block SQL injection attempts within form data. SQL injections usually involve embedding a semicolon to separate out the SQL statement. Always validate input data looking for embedded semicolons to block these types of attacks.

## Unauthorized file access

The PHP code that you write for your web applications may contain lots of privileged information, whether it's database user accounts for accessing a database or admin passwords that it checks to validate admin login attempts. Being able to properly protect your PHP files from unauthorized viewing is a must.

By default, any `.php` files accessed via the web server are passed to the PHP server and processed, so if attackers try to access a `.php` file directly, they only see the output from the file, not the actual code. However, if an attacker manages to break into the DocumentRoot folder using some attack, your PHP code will be wide open. Your job as a PHP developer is to try to hide your code from these types of attacks.

One method of doing that is to utilize the `include()` function. Chapter 1 of this minibook covers how to use the `include()` function to access PHP and HTML5 code located in a separate file from within a program file. The `include()` function isn't bound by the web server DocumentRoot setting folder location; it can retrieve data from anywhere on the server that it has read access to.

You can leverage that feature by storing all your application PHP code as include files outside the DocumentRoot boundaries. Then you only need to place the main `index.php` template file into the DocumentRoot folder for site visitors to access.

The main template file defines the different sections of the web page, and calls the appropriate include files for each one:

```
<body>
<header>
<?php include("/secretlocation/header.inc.php"); ?>
</header>
<nav>
<?php include("/secretlocation/navigation.inc.php");?>
</nav>
<main>
<?php
$content = $_GET['content'];
switch ($content) {
    case "initial":
        include("/secretlocation/initial.inc.php");
        break;
    case "registration":
        include("/secretlocation/registration.inc.php");
        break;
    case "query":
        include("/secretlocation/query.inc.php");
        break;
    case "newdata":
        include("/secretlocation/newdata.inc.php");
        break;
    default:
        echo "<p>Sorry, invalid page location</p>\n";
}
?>
</main>
<aside>
<?php include("/secretlocation/aside.inc.php"); ?>
</aside>
<footer>
<?php include("/secretlocation/footer.inc.php"); ?>
</footer>
</body>
```

Each section of the web page uses a separate include file to load the content for the section. A GET variable controls what content displays in the main section of each web page. The content HTML variable contains the name of the include file to use for each feature of the application. If an attacker tries to set the content HTML variable to some other value, an error message displays.

Now all the actual PHP code is safely stored away in include files located outside the DocumentRoot folder area of the web server. This method isn't foolproof, but it does provide an extra layer of security for your data.

# PHP Vulnerability Solutions

Fortunately, the PHP programming language provides several features that you can utilize to help you avoid all these types of attacks. This section walks through the different tools that you have at your disposal, showing you how best to use them to protect your website data and code.

## Sanitizing data

Just like sanitizing your kitchen is a good idea to help protect you from nasty bugs and viruses, sanitizing your PHP data helps render any harmful code injected into the data harmless. The idea is to detect any embedded HTML code and make it harmless by removing the HTML5 tags that trigger actions in the browser. This stops any type of XSS attack dead in its tracks.

The best defense against XSS attacks is to block any types of HTML code from the data your site visitors enter, both as they try to input it and as your application tries to output it. Two functions are good for this:

» `htmlspecialchars()`

» `filter_var()`

The following sections takes a closer look at how to use these functions to help make your web application safer.

### Using htmlspecialchars()

The `htmlspecialchars()` function detects HTML5 tags embedded in a data string and converts the greater-than and less-than symbols in the tags to the HTML5 entity codes `&gt;` and `&lt;`. This doesn't remove the tags from the data; instead, it turns them to ordinary text that displays as normal content.

Here's the format for the `htmlspecialchars()` function:

```
htmlspecialchars(string [, flags [,encoding [,double]]])
```

By default, the `htmlspecialchars()` function encodes the following characters that it finds in the data string:

» Ampersand (&)

» Double quote (")

>> Single quote (')

>> Less than (<)

>> Greater than (>)

You can pick and choose which of these items the htmlspecialchars() function converts and which ones it allows through by specifying one or more flags. Table 4-1 shows the flags that are available to choose from.

**TABLE 4-1** **htmlspecialchars Flags**

| Flag | Description |
|---|---|
| ENT_COMPAT | Converts only double quotes. |
| ENT_QUOTES | Converts both single and double quotes. |
| ENT_NOQUOTES | Doesn't convert either single or double quotes. |
| ENT_IGNORE | Doesn't convert anything. |
| ENT_SUBSTITUTE | Replaces invalid code with Unicode replacement characters instead of returning an empty string. |
| ENT_DISALLOWED | Replaces invalid code with Unicode replacement characters instead of leaving them as is. |
| ENT_HTML401 | Handles the code as HTML version 4.01. |
| ENT_XML1 | Handles the code as XML version 1. |
| ENT_XHTML | Handles the code as XHTML. |
| ENT_HTML5 | Handles the code as HTML5. |

The *encoding* parameter allows you to define what character set encoding the data uses, and the *double* parameter allows PHP to double-encode the data, also looking for HTML5 entity codes embedded in the data and converting them as well.

The best way to get a handle on what htmlspecialchars() does is to watch it in action. Follow these steps to test this out:

**1.** Open the xsstest.php file in your editor, program editor, or IDE package.

**2.** Change the line of code that retrieves the $_POST['fname'] array variable to make it look like the following:

```
$fname = htmlspecialchars($_POST['fname']);
```

3. **Save the file as** xsstest.php **in the** DocumentRoot **folder of your web server.**

4. **Ensure that the web server is running and then open your browser and enter the following URL:**

   ```
   http://localhost:8080/xssform.html
   ```

5. **Enter the following text in the text box:**

   ```
   <script>alert("Hello!");</script>
   ```

6. **Click the Submit button to submit the text.**

7. **Observe the output in the** xsstest.php **web page and then close the browser window.**

With the simple addition of the htmlspecialchars() function, you should now see the output shown in Figure 4-2.

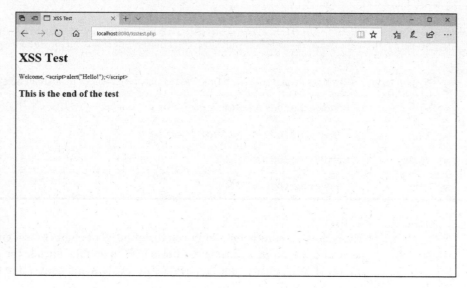

**FIGURE 4-2:**
The output from adding the html specialchars() function.

The htmlspecialchars() function converted the script element tags into plain text and displayed the JavaScript code as regular text in the output. That's not ideal, but it did block the XSS attack from hitting the browser.

## Using filter_var()

The filter_var() function is the Swiss Army knife of functions for protecting data in your PHP applications. It provides a host of customized filters for finding and sanitizing different types of data that could potentially cause harm in your PHP application.

You control the behavior of the filter_var() function by specifying both options and flags as parameters:

```
filter_var(string [, filter] [, flags])
```

The *filter* and *flags* parameters are optional, but almost always you'll at least specify the filter to use. The *filter* defines what class of characters the filter_var() function should look for, and the *flags* parameter fine-tunes subsets of characters within the filter class.

What makes the filter_var() function so versatile is that it can both sanitize (remove) and validate (test) string data. Table 4-2 shows the data-sanitizing options that you can use.

**TABLE 4-2**      ## The filter_var Data-Sanitizing Options

| Option | Description |
| --- | --- |
| FILTER_SANITIZE_EMAIL | Removes invalid characters from an email address. |
| FILTER_SANITIZE_ENCODED | Encodes a string to make a valid URL. |
| FILTER_SANITIZE_MAGIC_QUOTES | Escapes embedded quotes. |
| FILTER_SANITIZE_NUMBER_FLOAT | Removes all characters except digits and float symbols. |
| FILTER_SANITIZE_NUMBER_INT | Removes all characters except digits and integer symbols. |
| FILTER_SANITIZE_SPECIAL_CHARS | Removes quotes, as well as greater-than, less-than, and ampersand characters. |
| FILTER_SANITIZE_FULL_SPECIAL_CHARS | Converts the greater-than and less-than symbols in HTML5 tags to entity codes (the same as htmlspecialchars()). |
| FILTER_SANITIZE_STRING | Removes all HTML5 tags. |
| FILTER_SANITIZE_STRIPPED | Removes all HTML5 tags. |
| FILTER_SANITIZE_URL | Removes all invalid URL characters. |
| FILTER_UNSAFE_RAW | Does nothing, the default action. |

The `filter_var()` function allows you to customize just what data gets sanitized from the input data and what data is allowed to pass through. Follow these steps to test this out:

1. **Open the** `xsstest.php` **file in your editor.**

2. **Change the line that assigns the** `$fname` **variable to this:**

   ```
   $fname = filter_var($_POST['fname'], FILTER_SANITIZE_STRING);
   ```

3. **Save the file as** `xsstest.php` **in the** DocumentRoot **folder for your web server.**

4. **Ensure that your web server is running, and then open your browser and type the following URL:**

   ```
   http://localhost:8080/xsstest.php
   ```

5. **Enter the following text into the text box:**

   ```
   http://localhost:8080/xssform.html
   ```

6. **Click the Submit button.**

7. **Observe the output from the** `xsstest.php` **program and then close the browser window.**

The `filter_var()` function not only disables the script element in the text, but also completely removes the opening and closing tags, as shown in Figure 4-3.

The embedded JavaScript code is still visible, but at least the ‹script› tags are completely removed from the data, rendering the attack useless.

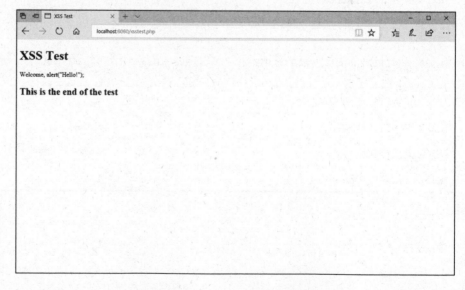

**FIGURE 4-3:**
The output from adding the `filter_var()` function.

**TIP**

The `filter_var()` function is also a great way to extract numeric data from a string, using the `FILTER_SANITIZE_NUMBER_INT` option.

# Validating data

Detecting all types of invalid data can be impossible, but PHP provides a few ways for you to at least detect some types of invalid data to help make things at least a little bit easier. This section describes the PHP functions available for helping detect when a site visitor has attempted to input invalid data into a form data field.

## Validating data types

One primary goal for catching invalid data is to at least determine that the input data is the correct data type. PHP provides a series of functions to do that (see Table 4-3).

**TABLE 4-3**

### PHP Data Validation Functions

| Function | Description |
|----------|-------------|
| `is_bool()` | Returns TRUE if the value is a Boolean data type. |
| `is_float()` | Returns TRUE if the value is in valid float format. |
| `is_int()` | Returns TRUE if the value is an integer value. |
| `is_null()` | Returns TRUE if the value is NULL. |
| `is_numeric()` | Returns TRUE if the value is in a valid numeric format. |
| `is_string()` | Returns TRUE if the value is a string as opposed to a number. |

Of these, the `is_numeric()` function is the most useful. It comes in handy to validate simple numeric data that your site visitors enter into forms, such as ages or quantities.

To test this out, follow these steps:

**1.** **Open your editor and type the following code:**

```
<!DOCTYPE html>
<html>
<head>
<title>Data Type Test</title>
<style>
    input {
```

```
        margin: 5px;
    }
</style>
</head>
<body>
<h1>Please enter data into the form fields</h1>
<form action="typetest.php" method="post">
<label>Last Name</label>
<input type="text" name="name"><br>
<label>Email address</label>
<input type="text" name="email"><br>
<label>Age</label>
<input type="text" name="age"><br>
<input type="submit" value="Submit form">
</form>
</body>
</html>
```

2. **Save the file as** typetest.html **in the** DocumentRoot **folder for your web server.**

3. **Open a new tab or window in your editor, and type the following code:**

```
<!DOCTYPE html>
<html>
<head>
<title>Data Type Test</title>
<style>
    .warning {
        color:red;
    }
</style>
</head>
<body>
<h1>Form results:</h1>
<?php
$name = htmlspecialchars($_POST['name']);
$email = htmlspecialchars($_POST['email']);
$age = htmlspecialchars($_POST['age']);

echo "<p>Name: $name</p>\n";
echo "<p>Email: $email</p>\n";
if (is_numeric($age)) {
```

```
    echo "<p>Age: $age</p>\n";
} else {
    echo "<p class='warning'>Please enter a valid age</p>\n";
}
?>
<br>
<a href="typetest.html">Return to form</a>
</body>
</html>
```

4. **Save the file as** typetest.php **in the** DocumentRoot **folder for your web server.**

5. **Ensure that the web server is running and then open your browser and enter the following URL:**

```
http://localhost:8080/typetest.html
```

6. **Enter your name and numeric age into the form and click the Submit button.**

7. **Observe the results on the** typetest.php **page output and then click the Return to Form link.**

8. **This time, enter your name and a text value for the age and then click the Submit button.**

9. **Observe the results in the** typetest.php **page output.**

10. **Close your browser window when you're done.**

In this example, the is_numeric() function detects when the site visitor enters an invalid value for the age and displays a warning message, as shown in Figure 4-4.

The is_numeric() function can't stop site visitors from lying about their ages, but at least it can prevent someone from entering text into the age data field.

## Validating data format

Testing for valid data types is fine when you're working with numeric values, but it doesn't help all that much for text values such as names, home addresses, and email addresses. The is_string() function can tell you that the value is a valid string value, but not the format of the data contained within the string.

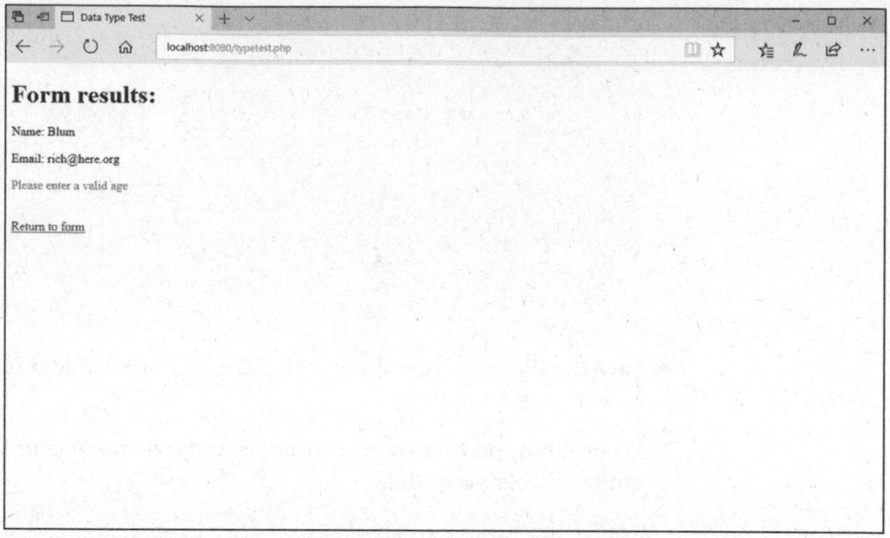

FIGURE 4-4:
The result
from entering
an invalid age
value into the
typetest.html
form.

This is another time where the filter_var() function can come in handy. Not only can the filter_var() function sanitize data, but it can also validate data formats for us! Table 4-4 shows the data validation options that are available for the filter_var() function.

**TABLE 4-4** The filter_var() Data Validation Options

| Option | Description |
|---|---|
| FILTER_VALIDATE_BOOLEAN | Returns TRUE if the value is a valid Boolean value. |
| FILTER_VALIDATE_EMAIL | Returns TRUE if the value is in a valid email address format. |
| FILTER_VALIDATE_FLOAT | Returns TRUE if the value is in a valid float format. |
| FILTER_VALIDATE_INT | Returns TRUE if the value is in a valid integer format. |
| FILTER_VALIDATE_IP | Returns TRUE if the value is in a valid IP address format. |
| FILTER_VALIDATE_MAC | Returns TRUE if the value is in a valid MAC address format. |
| FILTER_VALIDATE_REGEXP | Returns TRUE if the value matches the specified regular expression. |
| FILTER_VALIDATE_URL | Returns TRUE if the value is in a valid URL format. |

The email address check in filter_vars() comes in handy when you need to validate email addresses entered into contact forms. Follow these steps to test that out:

1. **Open the** typetest.php **file in your editor.**

2. **Modify the code so that it looks like the following:**

```
<!DOCTYPE html>
<html>
<head>
<title>Data Type Test</title>
<style>
    .warning {
        color:red;
    }
</style>
</head>
<body>
<h1>Form results:</h1>
<?php
$name = htmlspecialchars($_POST['name']);
$emal = htmlspecialchars($_POST['email']);
$age = htmlspecialchars($_POST['age']);

echo "<p>Name: $name</p>\n";
if (filter_var($email, FILTER_VALIDATE_EMAIL)) {
    echo "<p>Email: $email</p>\n";
} else {
    echo "<p class='warning'>Please enter a valid
            email address</p>\n";
}
if (is_numeric($age)) {
    echo "<p>Age: $age</p>\n";
} else {
    echo "<p class='warning'>Please enter a valid
            age</p>\n";
}
?>
<br>
<a href="typetest.html">Return to form</a>
</body>
</html>
```

3. **Save the file as** typetest.php **in the** DocumentRoot **folder of your web server.**

4. **Ensure that the web server is running and then open your browser and enter the following URL:**

```
http://localhost:8080/typetest.html
```

5. **Enter a valid name and age, but enter an email address in an invalid format.**

6. **Click the Submit button to submit the form data.**

7. **Observe the output.**

8. **Click the link to return to the form and try out different email address formats to see what gets caught by the data validation and what doesn't.**

9. **Close your browser window when you're done.**

The added `filter_var()` validation check looks for the email address to be in the proper format of name@hostname. If it is, the `filter_var()` function returns a TRUE value, which triggers the `if...else` statement to display the data. If it isn't, the `else` code block triggers and displays a warning, as shown in Figure 4-5.

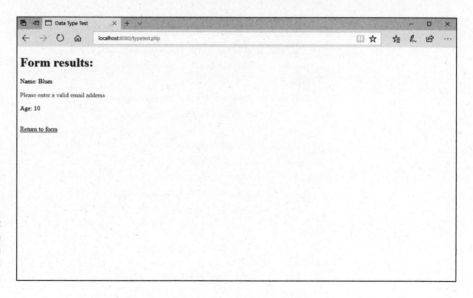

**FIGURE 4-5:**
The result from entering an invalid email address.

Again, this check is not foolproof — it can only check the format of an email address. It doesn't test the account to make sure it's a live account. But at least this is a start!

# Chapter **5**

# Object-Oriented PHP Programming

So far, all the PHP scripts presented in this minibook have followed the procedural style of programming. With procedural programming, you create variables and functions within your code to perform certain procedures, such as storing values in variables, and then checking them with conditional statements. The data you use and the functions you create are completely separate entities, with no specific relationship to one another. With object-oriented programming, on the other hand, variables and functions are grouped into common objects that you can use in any program. In this chapter, you learn what object-oriented programming is and how to use it in your web applications.

## Understanding the Basics of Object-Oriented Programming

Before you can start working on object-oriented programming (OOP), you need to know how it works. OOP uses a completely different paradigm from coding than what I cover earlier in this minibook. OOP requires that you think differently about how your programs work and how you code them.

With OOP, everything is related to objects. (I guess that's why they call it object-oriented programming!) Objects are the data you use in your applications, grouped together into a single entity.

For example, if you're writing a program that uses cars, you can create a Car object that contains information on the car's weight, size, color, engine, and number of doors. If you're writing a program that tracks people, you might create a person object that contains information about each person's name, date of birth, height, weight, and gender.

OOP uses classes to define objects. A *class* is the written definition in the program code that contains all the characteristics of the object, using variables and functions. The benefit of OOP is that after you create a class for an object, you can use that same class in any other application. Just plug in the class definition code and put it to use!

An OOP class contains *members.* There are two types of members:

>> **Properties:** Class *properties* (also called *attributes*) denote features of the object, such as the car's weight or the person's name. A class can contain many properties, with each property describing a different feature of the object.

>> **Methods:** Class *methods* are similar to the standard PHP functions that you've been using. A method performs an operation using the properties in a class. For instance, you could create class methods to retrieve a specific person from a database, or change the address property for an existing person. Each method should be contained within the class and perform operations only in that class. The methods for one class shouldn't deal with properties in other classes.

## Defining a class

Defining a class in PHP isn't too different from defining a function. To define a new class, you use the class keyword, along with the name of the class, followed by any statements contained in the class.

Here's an example of a simple class definition:

```
class Product {
    public $description;
    public $price;
    public $inventory;
    public $onsale;
```

```
    public function buyProduct($amount) {
        $this->inventory -= $amount;
    }
}
```

**TIP**

The class name you choose must be unique within your program. Class names follow the same rules as PHP variable names. Although it's not required, programmers often start class names with an uppercase letter to help distinguish them in program code.

This example defines four property members and one method member. Each member is defined using one of three *visibility* classifications. The visibility of the member determines where you can use or reference that member. There are three visibility keywords used in PHP:

>> public: The member can be accessed from outside the class code.

>> private: The member can only be accessed from inside the class code.

>> protected: The member can only be accessed from a child class. (I talk about that a little later in the "Extending Classes" section.)

The Product class example declares all the members to be public, so you can reference them anywhere in your PHP code.

The buyProduct() method uses an odd variable name in the function:

```
$this->inventory
```

The $this variable is a special identifier that references the current object of the class. In this example, it points to the $inventory property of the object. Notice the removal of the dollar sign from the inventory property when referencing it this way. This helps PHP know that you're referencing the $inventory property from within the class object and not the class itself.

This code defines the makeup of the class, but it doesn't actually do anything with it. The next section shows you how to actually use your class template to create objects.

## Creating an object instance

To use a class, you have to *instantiate* it. When you instantiate a class, you create what's called an *instance* of the class in your program. Each instance represents one occurrence of the object within the program. To instantiate an object in PHP code, you use the following format:

```
$prod1 = new Product();
```

This creates the object called $prod1 using the Product class. When you instantiate an object, you can access the public members of that class directly from your program code:

```
$prod1->description = "carrot";
$prod1->price = 1.50;
$prod1->inventory = 10;
$prod1->onsale = false;
```

This code sets values for each of the properties for the object. Notice the -> symbol in use again. It tells PHP that you're referencing the properties and methods specifically for the $prod1 object.

The $prod1 variable now contains these values set for the object properties, and you can use it anywhere in your PHP code to reference the properties. The same applies when you need to use a public method of an object:

```
$prod1->buyProduct(4);
```

This calls the buyProduct() method for the class object, passing the value of 4. Because the buyProduct() method alters the $inventory property of the object, the next time you reference the $prod1->inventory property in your code, it'll have the value of 6.

You can instantiate as many instances of a class as you need within your program. Just make sure that each instance uses a different variable name:

```
$prod2 = new Product();
$prod2->description = "eggplant";
$prod2->price = 2.00;
$prod2->inventory = 5;
$prod2->onsale = true;
```

PHP will keep the two instances of the Product class completely separate, maintaining the property values for each one.

Follow these steps to test out creating and using classes in PHP:

1. **Open your favorite text editor, program editor, or integrated development environment (IDE) package.**

2. **Type the following code into the editor window:**

```
<!DOCTYPE html>
<html>
<head>
<title>PHP OOP Test</title>
</head>
<body>
<h1>Testing PHP OOP code</h1>
<?php
class Product {
    public $description;
    public $price;
    public $inventory;
    public $onsale;

    public function buyProduct($amount) {
        $this->inventory -= $amount;
    }
}

$prod1 = new Product();
$prod1->description = "Carrots";
$prod1->price = 1.50;
$prod1->inventory = 10;
$prod1->onsale = false;
echo "<p>Just added $prod1->description<p>\n";


$prod2 = new Product();
$prod2->description = "Eggplants";
$prod2->price = 2.00;
$prod2->inventory = 5;
$prod2->onsale = true;
echo "<p>Just added $prod2->description<p>\n";

echo "<p>Now buying 4 carrots...<p>\n";
$prod1->buyProduct(4);
```

```
echo "<p>Inventory of $prod1->description is now
        $prod1->inventory</p>\n";
echo "<p>Inventory of $prod2->description is still
        $prod2->inventory</p>\n";
?>
</body>
</html>
```

3. **Save the file as** ooptest1.php **in the** DocumentRoot **folder for your web server.**

   For XAMPP on Windows, that's c:\xampp\htdocs; for XAMPP on macOS, that's /Applications/XAMPP/htdocs.

4. **Open the XAMPP Control Panel and then start the Apache web server.**

5. **Open your browser, and enter the following URL:**

```
http://localhost:8080/ooptest1.php
```

   You may need to change the TCP port to match your web server.

6. **Close the browser window when you're done.**

When you run the ooptest1.php file, you should see the output shown in Figure 5-1.

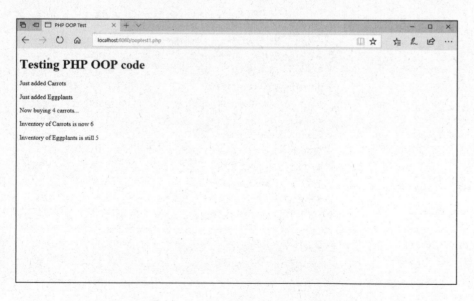

**FIGURE 5-1:**
The output from the ooptest1.php program.

The example code defines the Product class, which contains the four properties and one method that has already been discussed. After the Product class definition, the code creates two instances of the Product class: $prod1 and $prod2. When using classes, you need to define the class first in the code before you create an instance of it.

After creating the two instances, the code uses the buyProduct() method for the $prod1 instance to reduce the inventory by 4. Then it uses two echo statements to display the inventory properties for the two instances. Notice that the buyProduct() method reduced the inventory of the $prod1 instance, but not the $prod2 instance, showing that the two instances are, indeed, separate objects in the program.

# Using Magic Class Methods

No, you won't be learning any new tricks involving smoke and mirrors. *Magic class methods* are built-in method names in PHP that apply to all class objects. You can redefine them in your code to provide additional functionality to your PHP classes. This process is called *overloading* or *overriding.* In overloading, you define a method in your class code with the same name as an existing method. PHP uses the newly defined method when you call it from your program code in the class object.

Magic class methods are most often used to help provide common functionality for classes, such as creating a new class object, copying an existing class object, or displaying class objects as text. The PHP developers identify magic class methods by using a double underscore at the start of the method name.

The following sections walk through how to use some of the more common magic class methods in your own classes.

## Defining mutator magic methods

*Mutator magic methods* are methods that change the value of a property that you set with the private visibility. These are also commonly called *setters.*

The class example in the previous section used the public visibility feature for the class properties, but that's not always a good thing to do. That means that any application can directly access the properties and change them to whatever values it wants. That could be dangerous, and it's somewhat frowned upon in OOP circles.

The preferred way to handle class properties is to make them private so external programs can't change them directly. Instead, to manipulate the data, external programs are forced to use mutator magic class methods that interface with the properties.

The mutator magic method in PHP is __set() (note the leading double underscores). You use the mutator magic method to set all the values of the properties in the class with a single method definition:

```
public function __set($name, $value) {
    $this->$name = $value;
}
```

The mutator uses two parameters: the name of the property to set and the value to assign to the property. Where the magic comes into play is with how PHP uses the mutator. In your PHP application code, you don't actually have to call the __set() mutator method. You can define the $description property just by using a simple assignment statement:

```
$prod1->description = "Carrots";
```

PHP automatically knows to look for the __set() mutator method defined for the class and runs it, passing the appropriate property name and value.

Even though the $description property is set to the private visibility, by defining the mutator magic method you can allow external programs to assign a value to the property. The benefit of using mutators, though, is that you can control how external programs use the properties you define for the class.

With the mutator definition, you can place any code you need to control property features, such as ranges of values allowed or the allowed settings applied to the property. For example, you could so something like this:

```
public function __set($name,$value) {
    if ($name == "price" && $value < 0) {
        $this->price = 0;
    } else {
        $this->$name = $value;
    }
}
```

This example checks if the property being set is the $price property. If it is, it checks if the value is less than 0. If the value is less than 0, the price is set to 0 instead of the supplied price value. This gives you a way to control the value that is set for the price from external programs that use the class object.

# Defining accessor magic methods

*Accessor magic methods* are methods you use to access the private property values you define in the class. Creating special methods to retrieve the current property values helps create a standard for how other programs use your class objects. These methods are often called *getters* because they retrieve (get) the value of the property.

You define the accessor using the special __get() method:

```
public function __get($name) {
    return $this->$name;
}
```

That's all there is to it! Accessor methods aren't overly complicated; they just return the current value of the property. To use them you just reference the property name as normal:

```
echo "<p>Product: $prod1->description</p>\n";
```

PHP automatically looks for the accessor method to retrieve the property value. Follow these steps to try creating and using a class definition with mutators and accessors:

**1.** **Open your editor and type the following code:**

```
<!DOCTYPE html>
<html>
<head>
<title>PHP OOP Test</title>
</head>
<body>
<h1>Testing PHP OOP setters and getters</h1>
<?php
class Product {
    private $description;
    private $price;
    private $inventory;
    private $onsale;

    public function __set($name, $value) {
        if ($name == "price" && $value < 0) {
            echo "<p>Invalid price set<p>\n";
            $this->price = 0;
        } elseif ($name == "inventory" && $value < 0) {
```

```php
            echo "<p>Invalid inventory set: $value</p>\n";
        } else {
            $this->$name = $value;
        }
    }


    public function __get($name) {
        return $this->$name;
    }


    public function buyProduct($amount) {
        if ($this->inventory >= $amount) {
            $this->inventory -= $amount;
        } else {
            echo "<p>Sorry, invalid inventory requested:
                $amount</p>\n";
            echo "<p>There are only $this->inventory
                left</p>\n";
        }
    }
}


$prod1 = new Product();
$prod1->description = "Carrots";
$prod1->price = 1.50;
$prod1->inventory = 5;
$prod1->onsale = false;

echo "<p>Just added $prod1->inventory $prod1->description</p>\n";

echo "<p>Now buying 4 carrots...<p>\n";
$prod1->buyProduct(4);
echo "<p>Inventory of $prod1->description is now $prod1->inventory</p>\n";

echo "<p>Trying to set carrot inventory to -1:</p>\n";
$prod1->inventory = -1;

echo "<p>Now trying to buy 10 carrots...</p>\n";
$prod1->buyProduct(10);
echo "<p>Inventory of $prod1->description is now $prod1->inventory</p>\n";
?>
</body>
</html>
```

2. **Save the file as** ooptest2.php **in the** DocumentRoot **folder for your web server.**

3. **Ensure that the web server is running, and then open your browser and enter the following URL:**

```
http://localhost:8080/ooptest2.php
```

4. **Close the browser window when you're done.**

Figure 5-2 shows the output that you should see when you run the program in your browser.

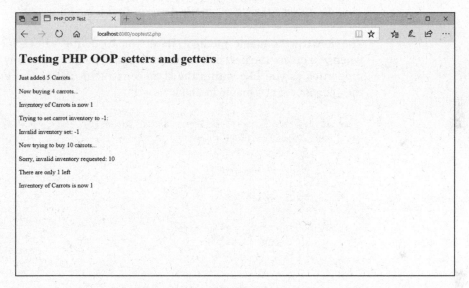

**FIGURE 5-2:**
The output from the ooptest2. php program.

There's a lot going on in this example, so hang in there with me! First, the PHP code defines the Product class, using the four properties, but this time it defines them with private visibility. Following that, the mutator and accessor magic methods are defined. The mutator checks to ensure the price and inventory properties can't be set to a negative value.

After the class definition, the code creates an instance of the Product class, and experiments with the inventory values. First, it uses the buyProduct() method to purchase four carrots. That works just fine.

Next, it uses the mutator to set the inventory property for the carrot object to a negative value. The mutator code intercepts that request and prevents the inventory from being set, instead producing an error message.

Finally, the code tries to use the buyProduct() method to purchase more carrots than what's set in inventory. The added code in the buyProduct() method prevents that from happening.

Now the class definition is starting to do some useful functions for the application. But wait, there are more magic methods available for you to use!

## The constructor

Having to set property values using the mutator methods each time you instantiate a new object can get old, especially if you have lots of properties in the class. The *constructor* magic class method makes that job a lot easier.

The constructor magic method allows you to define values for the properties when you create the new object instance. You can define as many or as few of the properties as you like within the class constructor definition. You do that with the __construct() magic method:

```
public function __construct($name, $cost, $quantity) {
    $this->description = $name;
    if ($price > 0) {
        $this->price = $cost;
    } else {
        $this->price = 0;
    }
    $this->inventory = $quantity;
    $this->onsale = false;
}
```

This constructor for the Product class uses three parameters to assign values to three of the class properties when you instantiate the class. It also automatically sets the $onsale property to a false value for each new class instance. To use the constructor, you just provide the three property values as parameters to the class:

```
$prod1 = new Product("Carrot", 1.50, 10);
```

**WARNING**

When you define a constructor, you have to make sure that the property values are provided in the correct order and data type when you instantiate a new object. If you provide too few arguments to the constructor, PHP will produce an error message. If you provide the right number of arguments but in the wrong order, you may not run into a problem until PHP tries to use the properties in the code.

# The destructor

Handling memory management in PHP programs is normally a lot easier than with some other programming languages. By default, PHP recognizes when a class instance is no longer in use and automatically removes it from memory. However, sometimes a program might need to do some type of "cleanup" work for the class object before PHP removes it from memory.

You can specify a magic class method that PHP automatically attempts to run just before it removes the instance from memory. These methods are called *destructors.*

Destructors come in handy with a class that works with files or databases to ensure that the files or database connections are properly closed before the system removes the class instance. This helps prevent any corruption in the data from an improperly closed session being stopped.

You use the __destruct() magic class method to define any final statements to process before PHP removes the class instance from memory:

```
public function __destruct() {
    statements
}
```

The __destruct() method doesn't allow you to pass any parameters into the method. All the statements you specify in the method need to be self-contained and must not rely on any data from the main program. They can, however, rely on properties within the class, because those should be available when the class object is removed.

You can also manually remove an instance of an object from memory using the unset() function:

```
unset($prod1);
```

When you run this command, PHP will process the destructor for the Product class for the instance.

**WARNING**

Although PHP will normally attempt to process a class destructor any time it removes a class instance from memory, it may not always be successful. If the program crashes or stops due to a fatal error, there's no guarantee that PHP will be able to run the destructor method code. If your application relies on closing open files or database connections, it's a good idea to use the unset() function to manually remove the object from memory when you're done using it!

## Copying objects

You can copy objects within PHP, but not using the standard assignment statement. Instead you need to use the `clone` keyword:

```
$prod1 = new Product("Carrot", 1.50, 100);
$prod2 = clone $prod1;
```

Now the $prod2 variable contains a second object instance of the Product class, with the same property values as the $prod1 instance.

You may however have a situation where you don't want the copy of the object to have all the same property values as the original. To do that, you can override the __clone() magic method in your class code:

```
public function __clone() {
    $this->price = 0;
    $this->inventory = 0;
    $this->onsale = false;
}
```

With this code, when you clone an object only the `description` property will copy over; all the other property values will be reset.

## Displaying objects

Most likely, at some point in your application, you'll want to display the properties of your objects in the web page. However, if you try to use the `echo` statement to display the object instance, you'll get a somewhat ugly error message from PHP:

```
Recoverable fatal error: Object of class Product could not be converted to
    string
```

You can solve that problem by defining the __toString() magic class method in the class definition.

The __toString() magic method defines how you want PHP to handle the properties when you try to use the object as a string value, such as in the `echo` statement. You just build the string value from the properties and store the output in a variable. Then use the `return` statement to return the output variable back to the main program. That code looks like this:

```
public function __toString() {
    $output = "<p>Product: " . $this->description . "<br>\n";
```

```
    $output .= "Price: $" . number_format($this->price,2) . "<br>\n";
    $output .= "Inventory: " . $this->inventory . "<br>\n";
    $output .= "On sale: ";
    if ($this->onsale) {
        $output .= "Yes</p>\n";
    } else {
        $output .= "No</p>\n";
    }
    return $output;
}
```

With the __toString() magic method defined, you can now use an instance of the Product class in an echo statement just like any variable:

```
echo $prod1;
```

And you'll get the following output in your web page:

```
Product: Carrots
Price: 1.50
Inventory: 10
On sale: No
```

With the __tostring() magic method, displaying your class objects in the web page is as easy as any other type of variable value!

# Loading Classes

At the beginning of this chapter, I mention that OOP helps make it easy to reuse program code in multiple applications. After you create the Product class for one application, you can use the same code to use the Product class in any other application that uses products.

However, having to retype the entire Product class code definition in each application that uses it can be somewhat tedious, especially for complicated classes. To solve that problem you can use our friend the include() function.

Just save your class definitions in separate PHP code files; then use the include() function to include the files in any code that uses the class definitions. This enables you to include only the files for the classes the application uses, without having to retype the entire class code definition! That's good, but there may still be a downside to that.

Complex applications may use dozens or possibly even hundreds of separate class objects to manage and manipulate data in the application. Having to list each of the class include files can still be somewhat tedious, as well as be prone to typing mistakes that will cause errors. To solve that problem, the PHP developers created the *autoload feature,* which determines when a class is being instantiated in the program and then tries to load the appropriate include file that defines that class. You implement that using the spl_autoload_register() function.

With the spl_autoload_register() function, you define the location for all of the class include files based on the class name. With a little bit of programming magic, you can make that task a breeze:

```php
spl_autoload_register(function($class) {
    include $class . ".inc.php";
});
```

The anonymous function provided to the spl_autoload_register() function defines the include file to load whenever a class is instantiated in the PHP code. The anonymous function attempts to load the include file with the same name as the class name, with an .inc.php file extension. Using this method, you must be careful to save the class definition files using the class name as the filename, plus the .inc.php file extension.

Follow these steps to try out using the autoload feature in PHP:

**1.** **Open your editor and type the following code:**

```php
<?php

class Product {
    private $description;
    private $price;
    private $inventory;
    private $onsale;

    public function __construct($name, $cost, $quantity, $sale) {
        $this->description = $name;
        $this->onsale = $sale;
        if ($cost < 0) {
            $this->price = 0;
        } else {
            $this->price = $cost;
        }
        if ($quantity < 0) {
```

```php
            $this->inventory = 0;
        } else {
            $this->inventory = $quantity;
        }
    }

    public function __set($name, $value) {
        if ($name == "price" && $value < 0) {
            echo "<p>Invalid price set<p>\n";
            $this->price = 0;
        } elseif ($name == "inventory" && $value < 0) {
            echo "<p>Invalid inventory set: $value</p>\n";
        } else {
            $this->$name = $value;
        }
    }

    public function __get($name) {
        return $this->$name;
    }

    public function __clone() {
        $this->price = 0;
        $this->inventory = 0;
        $this->onsale = false;
    }

    public function __toString() {
        $output = "<p>Product: " . $this->description . "<br>\n";
        $output .= "Price: $" . number_format($this->price,2) . "<br>\n";
        $output .= "Inventory: " . $this->inventory . "<br>\n";
        $output .= "On sale: ";
        if ($this->onsale) {
            $output .= "Yes</p>\n";
        } else {
            $output .= "No</p>\n";
        }
        return $output;
    }

    public function buyProduct($amount) {
        if ($this->inventory >= $amount) {
            $this->inventory -= $amount;
```

```
        } else {
            echo "<p>Sorry, invalid inventory requested:
                $amount</p>\n";
            echo "<p>There are only $this->inventory
                left</p>\n";
        }
    }

    public function putonsale() {
        $this->onsale = true;
    }
    public function takeoffsale() {
        $this->onsale = false;
    }
}
?>
```

2. **Save the file as** Product.inc.php **(note the capitalization) in the** DocumentRoot **folder for your web server.**

3. **Open a new tab or window in your editor and type the following code:**

```
<!DOCTYPE html>
<html>
<head>
<title>PHP Total OOP Test</title>
</head>
<body>
<h1>Testing the PHP class</h1>
<?php

spl_autoload_register(function($class) {
    include $class . ".inc.php";
});

$prod1 = new Product("Carrots", 4.00, 10, false);
echo "<p>Creating one product:</p>\n";
echo $prod1;

$prod2 = new Product("Eggplant", 2.00, 5, true);
echo "<p>Creating one product:</p>\n";
echo $prod2;
```

```
echo "<p>Putting $prod1->description on sale:</p>\n";
$prod1->price = 3.00;
$prod1->putonsale();
echo "<p>New product status:</p>\n";
echo $prod1;
?>
</body>
</html>
```

4. **Save the file as** ooptest3.php **in the** DocumentRoot **folder for your web server.**

5. **Ensure that the web server is running and then open your browser and enter the following URL:**

   ```
   http://localhost:8080/ooptest3.php
   ```

6. **Close the browser window when you're done.**

When you run the ooptest3.php file, you should see the output shown in Figure 5-3.

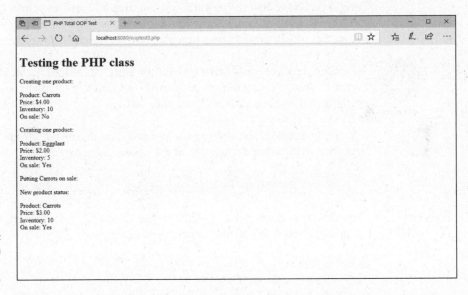

**FIGURE 5-3:**
The output from
the ooptest3.
php program.

The code saves the Product class definition code in the Product.inc.php file and then uses the autoloader feature to load the Product class include file when needed. It instantiates two Product class objects using the constructor and displays them on the web page.

CHAPTER 5 **Object-Oriented PHP Programming** 413

Following that, the code changes the price for the $prod1 object using the class mutator and uses the putonsale() method to place the product on sale. The code finishes with an echo statement so you can see the changes made to the class object. Now things are really starting to get fancy!

**WARNING**

Be very careful when naming class include files. If you're using a server that's case-sensitive with filenames (such as Linux or macOS), then the include filename must match the case of the class name.

# Extending Classes

No, I'm not talking about making you stay after school! OOP provides a way to extend an existing class by adding additional members to an existing class. That's the whole beauty of OOP: You can take classes and use them as is, or you can modify just the pieces you need to fit your particular application.

Defining a new class that's an extension of another class is called *inheritance.* The new class (called the *child*) inherits all the public or protected members from the original class (called the *parent*). You can then add new members to the child class and even override members of the parent class. If you use the overridden members, the child members take precedence over the parent members.

**WARNING**

Members marked with private visibility aren't inherited by child classes. If you want a child class to inherit properties but don't want them visible to external programs, use the protected visibility setting.

To create a child class, you use the normal class definition format, along with the extends keyword and the name of the class you're extending:

```
class Soda extends Product {
```

For the new class, Soda, to inherit the Product class properties, you need to change the visibility of the properties to protected:

```
class Product {
    protected $description;
    protected $price;
    protected $inventory;
    protected $onsale;
    ...
```

With the properties set to protected visibility, the Soda child class will automatically inherit the description, price, inventory, and onsale properties from the Product class, along with all the public class methods.

In the child class definition, you can add additional properties and methods that are unique to the child class:

```
private ounces;

public function restock($amount) {
    $this->inventory += $amount;
}
```

Notice that the restock() method uses the inventory property that was inherited from the Product parent class. When you define a method in a child class, it's only available for objects that are instantiated from the child class. Objects instantiated from the parent class won't see that method.

Because the Soda child class contains an additional property, you need to override the __construct() method from the parent class to add the new property. That code looks like this:

```
public function __construct($name, $value, $amount, $sale,
                           $size) {
    parent::__construct($name, $value, $amount,
                        $sale);
    $this->ounces = $size;
}
```

The new constructor for the Soda child class requires five parameters. Note the first line in the constructor code:

```
parent::__construct($name, $value, $amount, $sale);
```

The parent:: keyword tells PHP to run the constructor from the parent object. This assigns values to those properties inherited from the parent. The property unique to the child class is assigned a separate value from the parameters.

To instantiate a new child object you'd then just use the following:

```
$rootbeer = new Soda("Root Beer", 1.50, 10, false, 18);
```

Inside the child class definition, you can override any or all of the parent methods. Any methods that don't override the child class objects can use the parent methods.

Follow these steps to test out using inheritance in your OOP PHP code.

**1.** **Open the** Product.inc.php **file in your editor.**

**2.** **Change the** private **visibility keyword to** protected.

Look for these four lines:

```
private $description;
private $price;
private $inventory;
private $onsale;
```

And change them to the following:

```
protected $description;
protected $price;
protected $inventory;
protected $onsale;
```

**3.** **Save the file as** Product.inc.php **in the** DocumentRoot **folder for your web server.**

**4.** **Open a new tab or window in your editor, and type the following code:**

```
<?php

include("Product.inc.php");

class Soda extends Product {
    private $ounces;

    public function __construct($name, $value, $amount, $sale, $size) {
        parent::__construct($name, $value, $amount, $sale);
        $this->ounces = $size;
    }

    public function __toString() {
        $output = "<p>Product: " . $this->description . "<br>\n";
        $output .= "Price: $" . number_format($this->price,2) . "<br>\n";
        $output .= "Inventory: " . $this->inventory . "<br>\n";
        $output .= "On sale: ";
        if ($this->onsale) {
            $output .= "Yes<br>\n";
        } else {
            $output .= "No<br>\n";
```

```
        }
        $output .= "Ounces: " . $this->ounces . "</p>\n";
        return $output;
    }


    public function restock($amount) {
        $this->inventory += $amount;
    }
}
?>
```

5. **Save the file as** `Soda.inc.php` **in the** `DocumentRoot` **folder for your web server.**

6. **Open yet another new tab or window in your editor, and type the following code:**

```php
<!DOCTYPE html>
<html>
<head>
<title>Testing PHP Inheritance</title>
</head>
<body>
<h1>Testing inheritance in PHP OOP</h1>
<?php

spl_autoload_register(function($class) {
    include $class . ".inc.php";
});

$prod1 = new Soda("Root Beer", 1.25, 10, false, 18);
echo $prod1;

echo "<p>Buying 6 bottles:</p>\n";
$prod1->buyProduct(6);
echo $prod1;

echo "<p>Restocking 4 bottles:</p>\n";
$prod1->restock(4);
echo $prod1;

?>
</body>
</html>
```

**7.** Save this file as ooptest4.php in the DocumentRoot folder for your web server.

**8.** Ensure that the web server is running, and then open your browser and enter the following URL:

```
http://localhost:8080/ooptest4.php
```

**9.** Close the browser, and stop the web server.

When you run the ooptest4.php code, you should see the output as shown in Figure 5-4.

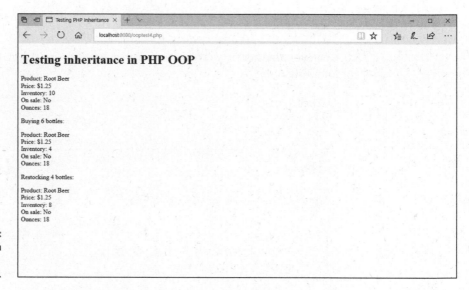

The Soda class code overrides both the constructor and the __toString() methods of the Product parent class to accommodate the additional $ounces property. The ooptest4.php code creates an instance of the Soda class, uses the buyProduct() method from the parent class to buy bottles, and then uses the restock() method from the child class to restock them. Notice that the child class object has access to the public buyProduct() method from the parent class.

# Chapter **6**

# Sessions and Carts

I n the previous chapters of this minibook, I show you how to use the HTTP GET and POST methods to send data from one web page to another. Although they work fine for clicking links and submitting forms, they're somewhat impractical to use for sharing data between all the web pages in an application. To do that requires some other form of persistent data, someplace where you can temporarily store it so that your PHP programs can access the data at any time from any page. This is where sessions and carts help out. This chapter explains how they work, why you shouldn't be afraid of them, and how to use them as another piece of your dynamic web applications.

## Storing Persistent Data

Most dynamic web applications require some way of temporarily storing data while site visitors work their way through the application web pages. I'm not talking about long-term storage of data (I cover that in the next minibook). I'm talking about short-term storage of data that one web page can store and another web page retrieves, such as passing an authenticated user's info through the website. This helps your application track the site visitors and what they're doing within the application.

This is where HTTP cookies come into play. Cookies have received somewhat of a bum rap in the web world, mainly because of a misunderstanding of how companies use them. A company can't track all of your browsing history using cookies, but it can track which of its advertisements you've visited. This helps the marketing gurus target advertising to your browser based on which of the company's links you've already visited. Cookies do have a valid place in the assembly line of dynamic web application tools, playing a crucial function in being able to keep track of individual site visitors in your application. It's crucial that you know how they work and how to use them.

This section walks through the basics of cookies, why you need them, and how to safely (and responsibly) use them in your dynamic web applications.

## The purpose of HTTP cookies

In the mainframe computer world, people who need to access programs running on the system must first log in to the system. This usually requires entering some type of data that uniquely identifies you, such as typing a user ID, placing your finger on a scanner, or inserting a smart ID card that includes a unique encrypted key. When the system authenticates that you are who you say you are, it allows you access to the system and your data. This process starts what's called a *session*.

The mainframe tracks every transaction you perform within the session. A system administrator can look through the log file and identify the user who performed each transaction on the system.

When you've finished entering transactions, you must log off of the system to stop the session. If you forget to log out, another user can come in and enter new transactions that the mainframe credits to your session.

On a mainframe system, keeping track of sessions is easy, because each user logs in from a specific device (either a directly connected terminal or a persistent network connection), performs transactions, and then logs out. Unfortunately, it's not that easy in our dynamic web applications.

The HTTP standard was intended to retrieve data from a remote server in an anonymous, stateless manner. This means not having to deal with the formalities of a session. In essence, a web session consists of a single transaction, and it doesn't even require an ID to identify the user.

Dynamic web applications are somewhat of a hybrid of these two environments. You want to maintain the ease of an HTTP anonymous session, but you need to track users and their transactions like a mainframe session. This is where cookies come to save the day.

*Cookies* are data that a server can temporarily store in the browser of each site visitor. When the browser stores the cookie data, the server can retrieve that information in later transactions with the site visitor. This allows the server (and, thus, the server-side application) to identify individual site visitors and keep track of what they're doing within the application. This is the beginning of a true web session.

## Types of cookies

Before you start thinking chocolate chip and oatmeal raisin, let me start out by saying we're not talking about those types of cookies here. There are several different characteristics of HTTP cookies, each one defining a different way to use the cookie. Table 6-1 lists the different HTTP cookie types you can use.

**TABLE 6-1**     **Types of HTTP Cookies**

| Type | Description |
| --- | --- |
| HttpOnly | Can only be accessed via HTTP, not via JavaScript |
| Persistent | Expires at a specific date/time or after a specific length of time |
| SameSite | Can only be sent in requests from the same origin as the target domain |
| Secure | Can only be sent in HTTPS connections |
| Session | Expires when the client browser window closes |
| Supercookie | Uses a top-level domain as the origin, allowing multiple websites access |
| Third-party | Uses a domain that doesn't match the URL domain for the web page |

The standard type of cookie is the *persistent cookie.* Persistent cookies are sent by the web server to be stored in the client browser for a specific amount of time. Your application can store data in a persistent cookie and then access that data any time in the future until the cookie expires.

As opposed to persistent cookies, *session cookies* only last for as long as the client browser window stays open. When the site visitor closes the browser window, the session cookies (and the data they contain) go away.

*Third-party cookies* are what gave cookies a bad name. With persistent and session cookies, a web server can only retrieve and read the cookies that it sets — it doesn't have access to cookies set by other servers. This helps protect the privacy of site visitors by preventing a single server from determining all the websites a site visitor has visited. Third-party cookies use a loophole to get around that.

These days it's very common for a web page to contain embedded advertisements from other websites. Those embedded advertisements run code created by the remote website and can set cookies from the remote website, storing the location of the main website the advertisement is embedded in. This allows a company to purchase advertising space on multiple common websites and then determine which site visitors have visited which website by tracking the cookies that it sets in the advertisements. Now that's sneaky!

**TIP**

Most modern browsers allow you to block third-party cookies separate from session or persistent cookies, allowing you to use cookies for normal operations but block third-party cookies trying to track your website history.

## The anatomy of a cookie

The HTTP standard defines how web servers set and retrieve cookies within the HTTP session with a client browser. When a client browser requests to view a web page on a server, it sends an HTTP `GET` request:

```
GET /index.php
Host: www.myserver.com
```

The request specifies the web page to retrieve and the host from where to retrieve it (usually the same server the request is sent to). The host server returns an HTTP response, which includes the status code for the request, along with any cookies that it wants to set using the `Set-Cookie` statement and then the HTML for the requested web page:

```
HTTP/1.0 GET OK
Content-type: text/html
Set-Cookie: name1=value1; attributes
Set-Cookie: name2=value2; attributes
    Web page HTML content
```

The cookie information appears before the HTML from the requested web page. The server assigns each cookie a unique name and a value, and possibly adds optional attributes that define the cookie type. The client browser stores each cookie as a separate temporary file on the client workstation.

The `Set-Cookie` statement can list one or more optional attributes for the cookie. Table 6-2 lists the cookie attributes that you can set.

**TABLE 6-2**     ## HTTP Cookie Attributes

| Attribute | Description |
|---|---|
| Domain=*site* | Specifies the domain the cookie applies to. If omitted the server is the default location. |
| Expires=*datetime* | Specifies the expiration date for the cookie as an HTTP timestamp value. |
| HttpOnly | Specifies that the cookie can only be retrieved in an HTTP session. |
| Max-Age=*number* | Specifies the expiration time for the cookie in seconds. |
| Path=*path* | Indicates the path in the URL that must exist in the requested resource. |
| SameSite-*setting* | Specifies if the cookie can only be accessed from the same site that set it. Values are Strict or Lax. |
| Secure | Specifies that the cookie can only be sent in an HTTPS secure session. |

If either the Expires or Max-Age attributes are set, the cookie is a persistent cookie. It will remain available until the expiration date and/or time. If no attributes are specified, the cookie is a session cookie and will be deleted when the client browser window closes.

The Expires attribute specifies an exact date and time the cookie will expire:

```
Set-Cookie: id=25; Expires=Mon 12 May 2025 13:30:00 GMT;
```

The Max-Age attribute sets a time duration (in seconds) that the cookie should remain valid:

```
Set-Cookie: id=25; Max-Age=3600
```

After the server sets a cookie, the next time the client browser requests a web page from the same destination, it sends all the cookies set from that destination in the HTTP request using a single Cookie statement:

```
GET /index.php
Host: www.myserver.com
Cookie: name1=value1; name2=value2
```

The Cookie statement just sends the name/value pair for all the cookies set by that server. It doesn't send any attributes that the server had set for the cookies. The server can then extract the separate cookie names and values and pass them to any server-side programming language (such as your PHP programs).

## Cookie rules

Overall, the implementation of cookies in browsers is somewhat nonstandard. No two client browsers may handle cookies the same way. There are however a few minimum requirements that the HTTP standard specifies:

» The browser must support cookies up to 4,096 bytes in size.

» The browser must support at least 50 cookies per website.

» The browser must be able to store at least 3,000 cookies total.

Most browsers exceed these requirements, but it's best not to test the limits in your applications. If you need to store large amounts of data for an application, it's best to use some other type of persistent data storage, such as a database. You can store a key identifying the site visitor as a cookie, and then use that key to reference the larger amounts of data stored in the database associated with that site visitor.

**WARNING**

Be careful when using session cookies. There is still some controversy in the browser world over how to handle session cookies, especially now that tabbed browsers have become all the rage. Most browsers consider all the web page tabs within the same browser window as a single session. To close the session, your site visitor must close the entire browser window, not just the tab for the web page. Also, many browsers now have a feature that allows for the option of saving sessions by storing session cookie data rather than removing it when the browser window closes. This somewhat circumvents the whole idea of session cookies!

# PHP and Cookies

PHP allows you to fully interact with cookies in your web applications. You can set cookies from one web page, retrieve and read them in another web page, and remove them from yet another web page. This section walks through the code you need to use to implement cookies in your PHP applications.

## Setting cookies

PHP uses the `setcookie()` function to set new cookies and update existing cookies. Here's the basic format of the `setcookie()` function:

```
setcookie(name [, value] [, expire] [, path] [, domain] [, secure] [, httponly])
```

The only required parameter is the name of the cookie, although you'll almost always want to include a cookie value, too. Leaving off the value sets the cookie value to NULL.

The optional *expire* parameter allows you to specify the expiration date and time as a Unix timestamp value, making it a persistent cookie. The Unix timestamp format is an integer value of the number of seconds since midnight on January 1, 1970. The last four parameters allow you to specify the URL paths and domains allowed to access the cookie, and whether the cookie should be set as Secure or HttpOnly.

Be careful with the expire parameter. Even though the HTTP message sends the expire attribute as a full date and time, with the setcookie() function you set it using a timestamp value, not a standard date and time. The way most PHP developers do that is by adding the number of seconds to the current date and time retrieved from the time() function:

```
setcookie("test", "Testing", time() + (60*60*24*10));
```

This sets the cookie named test to expire ten days from the time the web page is accessed by the site visitor.

**WARNING**

Because the cookie is part of the HTTP message and not part of the HTML data, you must set the cookie before you send any HTML content, including the opening <!DOCTYPE> tag. There is an exception to this, though. If the PHP output_buffer setting is enabled, the PHP server sends all output from the program to a buffer first. Then, either when the buffer is full or the program ends, it rearranges the data in the buffer to place the HTTP messages first and then sends the data to the client browser.

Follow these steps to test setting a persistent cookie from a PHP application:

**1.** Open your favorite text editor, program editor, or integrated development environment (IDE) package.

**2.** Type the following code into the editor window:

```
<?php
setcookie("test1", "This is a test cookie", time() + 600);
?>
<!DOCTYPE html>
<html>
<head>
<title>PHP Cookie Test</title>
</head>
```

```
<body>
<h1>Trying to set a cookie</h1>
</body>
</html>
```

3. **Save the file as** `cookietest1.php` **in the** `DocumentRoot` **folder for the web server.**

   For XAMPP in Windows, that's `c:\xampp\htdocs`; for XAMPP in macOS, that's `/Applications/XAMPP/htdocs`.

4. **Start the XAMPP Control Panel and then start the Apache web server.**

5. **Open your browser and enter the following URL:**

```
http://localhost:8080/cookietest1.php
```

   You may need to change the TCP port number to match your web server.

6. **Using your browser's Developer Tools, check the cookies that are set from the web page and their expiration date and time.**

   You should see the `test1` cookie created. It should be set to expire in ten minutes.

7. **Close the browser window when you're done.**

The Developer Tools allow you to see the `test1` cookie that was set by the program. For the Microsoft Edge browser, look in the Debugger section for the cookies, as shown in Figure 6-1.

The cookie is set, along with the value, and the expiration time is set to ten minutes (600 seconds) in the future.

You have to place the `setcookie()` function lines before the `<html>` section of the web page. Otherwise, you'll get an error message. The web server must send any cookie data in the HTTP session before any HTML content.

## Reading cookies

PHP makes reading cookies that your application sets a breeze. The PHP server automatically places all cookies passed from the client in the `$_COOKIE[]` special array variable. The cookie name that you assigned in the `setcookie()` statement becomes the associative array key:

```
$_COOKIE['name']
```

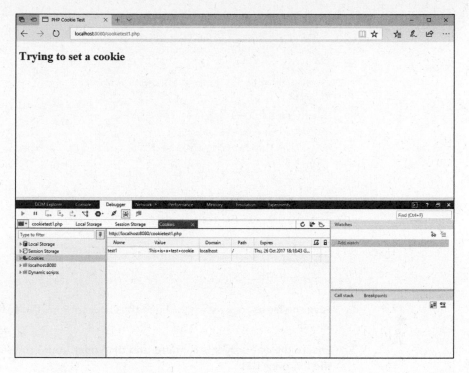

**FIGURE 6-1:**
Displaying the cookie in the Microsoft Edge Developer Tools window.

If a cookie has expired, you'll get an error message when trying to access it using the $_COOKIE[] array variable. It's a good idea to always check that the cookie exists first, using the isset() function:

```
if (isset($_COOKIE['test'])) {
    $data = $_COOKIE['test'];
} else {
    $data = 0;
}
```

This code will set the value of the $data variable used in the program to 0 if the cookie doesn't exist. You can then check for the 0 condition in the variable to determine if the cookie is missing.

Follow these steps to test reading the cookie you set in the cookietest1.php program:

**1.** Open your editor, and type the following code:

```
<!DOCTYPE html>
<html>
<head>
```

```
<title>PHP Cookie Test</title>
</head>
<body>
<h1>Retrieving the test cookie</h1>
<?php
if (isset($_COOKIE['test1'])) {
    $data = $_COOKIE['test1'];
      echo "<p>The cookie was set: $data</p>
\n";
} else {
      echo "<p>Sorry, I couldn't find the cookie</p>
\n";
}
?>
</body>
</html>
```

2. **Save the file as** `cookietest2.php` **in the** `DocumentRoot` **folder for your web server.**

3. **Ensure the web server is running, and then open your browser and enter the following URL:**

```
http://localhost:8080/cookietest2.php
```

4. **Close the browser when you're done testing.**

If you run the `cookietest2.php` program within ten minutes of the `cookietest1.php` program, you should see the data stored in the cookie appear on the web page and in the browser Developer Tools, as shown in Figure 6-2.

If you wait longer than the ten-minute expiration time of the cookie, you'll get the message that the program couldn't find the cookie.

## Modifying and deleting cookies

You can easily modify an existing cookie just by resending the cookie with the updated value:

```
setcookie("test1", "New data", time() + 600);
```

When you resend the cookie, the browser overwrites the original cookie information with the new information, including the updated expiration time. If you specify a time relative to the current time, that will change the expiration time of the cookie.

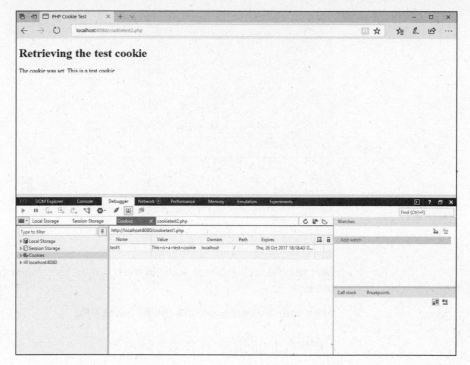

**FIGURE 6-2:**
The result of the
cookietest2.
php code
displaying the
cookie data.

To delete a cookie, just set the expiration time to a time value in the past:

```
setcookie("test1", "", time() - 1);
```

When you set the expiration time to one second earlier than the current time, the browser will immediately expire the cookie.

Follow these steps to test setting and removing a cookie:

**1.** **Open your editor and type the following code:**

```
<?php
if (!isset($_COOKIE['test1'])) {
    setcookie("test1", "This is a test cookie", time() + 600);
} else {
    setcookie("test1", "", time() - 1);
}
?>
<!DOCTYPE html>
<html>
<head>
<title>Deleting a Cookie</title>
```

```
</head>
<body>
<h1>Cookie status:</h1>
<?php
    if (isset($_COOKIE['test1'])) {
        $data = $_COOKIE['test1'];
        echo "<p>Cookie set: $data<p>\n";
    } else {
        echo "<p>Cookie not set</p>\n";
    }
?>
<a href="cookietest3.php">Click to try again</a>
</body>
</html>
```

**2.** **Save the file as** cookietest3.php **in the** DocumentRoot **folder for your web server.**

**3.** **Open your browser and enter the following URL:**

```
http://localhost:8080/cookietest3.php
```

**4.** **Note if the cookie has been set or not, then click the Click to Try Again link in the web page to reload the page.**

You can continue clicking the link to toggle the cookie on and off.

**5.** **Close the browser window when you're done testing.**

In the cookietest3.php code, each time you visit the page the PHP code checks if the cookie exists. If the cookie exists, the code deletes it by setting the expiration time back one second. If the cookie doesn't exist, it creates the cookie. You can continue going back and forth by clicking the link to reload the page each time.

# PHP and Sessions

PHP handles sessions and session cookies a little differently from persistent cookies. Instead of storing session cookies in the client browser as separate data files, PHP assigns a unique session ID to each site visitor session and stores that as a session cookie in the client browser.

PHP then stores any data associated with the session in a temporary file located on the actual PHP server. This helps protect the session data, because it's not being stored in the client browser at any time. When the session ends, PHP automatically deletes the temporary session file on the server.

This feature alone makes using sessions to store data more attractive than using persistent cookies. The only data sent between the client browser and the server is the session ID value assigned to the session. All the data stays local on the server.

The following sections describe how to use sessions in your PHP applications.

## Starting a session

Before you can set or read any session data, you must start the session. PHP provides an easy way for you to declare sessions in your web pages. The PHP session_start() function automatically sends the required HTTP code to the remote client browser to create a session cookie. PHP assigns the session cookie a unique ID value to identify the session.

In the PHP file (the code for your web page), the session_start() function must come before any HTML code, including the <!DOCTYPE> tag. The session PHP code then looks like this:

```
<?php
session_start();
?>
<!DOCTYPE html>
<html>
```

You must add the session_start() function at the start of every web page that needs to access the session data. If the session_start() function is not present, PHP doesn't look for the session ID, and your application can't access any of the session data.

**WARNING**

Don't place any HTML comment lines, blank lines, or even a space before the opening <?php tag when using the session_start() function. Any text that appears before the opening <?php tag will be sent as HTML code to the client browser. Then you'll get an error message for trying to send the session data.

## Storing and retrieving session data

After you initialize the session using the session_start() function, you can use the $_SESSION[] array variable to both set and retrieve session data in your application. To set a new value, just define it in an assignment statement:

```
$_SESSION['item'] = "computer";
```

Use the session cookie name as the associative array key. When you set a session cookie name/value pair, you can access it at any time in any web page that's part of the same session:

```
echo "You purchased a " . $_SESSION['item'];
```

Follow these steps to test out setting and reading session cookie data:

**1.** **Open your editor and type the following code:**

```
<?php
session_start();
?>
<!DOCTYPE html>
<html>
<head>
<title>Testing Session Cookies</title>
</head>
<body>
<h1>Setting a session cookie</h1>
<?php
    $_SESSION['test2'] = "Second test cookie";
?>
<a href="sessiontest2.php">Click to continue</a>
</body>
</html>
```

**2.** **Save the file as** sessiontest1.php **in the** DocumentRoot **folder for your web server.**

**3.** **Open a new tab or window in your editor and type the following code:**

```
<?php
session_start();
?>
<!DOCTYPE html>
<html>
<head>
<title>Testing Session Cookies</title>
</head>
<body>
<h1>Retrieving the session cookie</h1>
<?php
```

```
    if (isset($_SESSION['test2'])) {
        $data = $_SESSION['test2'];
        echo "<p>Session cookie: $data</p>\n";
    } else {
        echo "<p>Error accessing the session
                cookie</p>\n";
    }
?>
<a href="sessiontest1.php">Go back to start</a>
</body>
</html>
```

**4.** **Save the file as** sessiontest2.php **in the** DocumentRoot **folder for your web server.**

**5.** **Ensure that the web server is started, and then open your browser and enter the following URL:**

```
http://localhost:8080/sessiontest1.php
```

**6.** **Click the Click to Continue link to go to the second test page.**

**7.** **Close your browser window.**

**8.** **Open your browser window, and go directly to the following URL:**

```
http://localhost:8080/sessiontest2.php
```

**9.** **Close the browser at the end of the test.**

When you open the sessiontest1.php web page, the PHP code starts a session and then saves the test session cookie and value. If you use the Developer Tools in your browser, you can see that the web page doesn't create a test2 cookie, but instead creates a cookie named PHPSESSID with a long hexadecimal value, as shown in Figure 6-3.

This is the unique session ID that the PHP server assigned to the browser session.

When you click the link, the browser requests the sessiontest2.php web page from the server, passing the session ID cookie that was set in the sessiontest1.php web page code. This tells PHP that the second page is part of the same browsing session and allows the PHP code access to any session cookie data set in that session. Figure 6-4 shows the output that you should see from the sessiontest2.php file, along with the PHPSESSID cookie value shown in the Developer Tools.

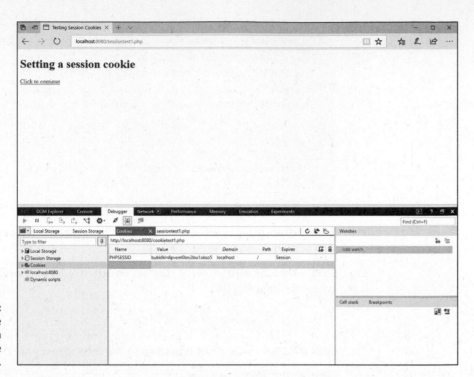

**FIGURE 6-3:**
Looking for the PHP session cookie using the Developer Tools.

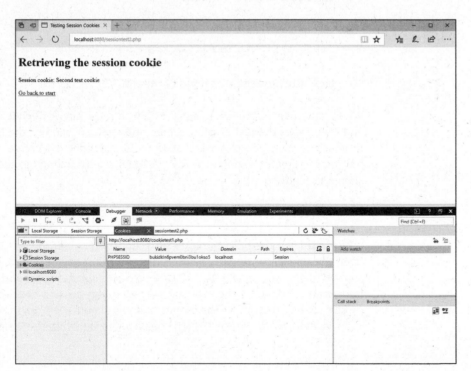

**FIGURE 6-4:**
The output from the sessiontest2.php file.

When you close the browser window, that deletes the session ID session cookie. When you reopen the browser window and attempt to go directly to the sessiontest2.php file, the original session ID is not present, so PHP creates a new session for the connection. That new session doesn't have access to the data set in the original session, so you'll get an error message, as shown in Figure 6-5.

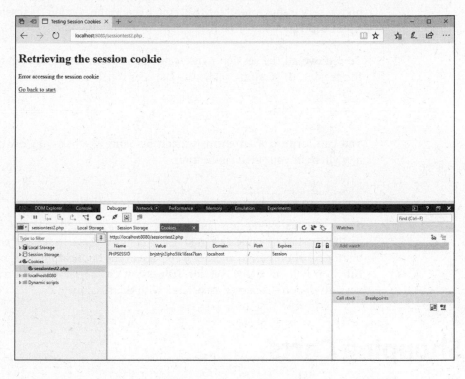

**FIGURE 6-5:**
The error message generated from trying to access data in an expired session.

If you take a look at the PHPSESSID value using the Developer Tools, it has a different value than before, because the new browser window is a new session.

## Removing session data

There are three ways to remove session cookie data:

» Remove individual session values.

» Remove all session values but keep the session active.

» Remove the original session ID session cookie, which deletes the session.

To remove individual session values, use the `unset()` function, along with the session array variable to remove:

```
unset($_SESSION['item']);
```

This removes the session name/value pair from the session data in the temp file on the server, but maintains the temp file and the session ID session cookie in the client browser.

To remove all the session name/value pairs from the session data, but maintain the session ID session cookie, use the `session_unset()` function:

```
session_unset();
```

You can terminate an entire session by using the `session_destroy()` function anywhere in your PHP application:

```
session_destroy();
```

This removes all session name/value pairs associated with the session, as well as the session ID value assigned to the client browser's session cookie. If the site visitor continues on to another web page in the application, the `session_start()` function will set a new session ID session cookie, along with a new temporary session file on the server associated with the session.

# Shopping Carts

Quite possibly one of the most common uses of session cookies is the ability to track items customers intend to purchase while browsing through an online store. Just like old-fashioned shopping carts, the online shopping cart should allow customers to place one or more of an item into the cart, view the cart contents at any time, and remove any item from the cart — all with the benefit of not having to listen to a squeaky cart wheel!

This section shows you how to use session cookies to implement simple shopping carts in your own dynamic web applications.

## Creating a cart

To create an online shopping cart, you just need to use two PHP features: session cookies and arrays. The idea is to create a session cookie as an empty array variable.

As shoppers place new items into the cart, the code adds a new element to the array, setting the quantity of the item selected as the array value.

You do that by creating a multidimensional array session cookie. That sounds like a mouthful, but it's actually very easy to create:

```
$_SESSION['cart'] = array();
```

This single line of code creates a session cookie named cart and defines it as an array variable. That's the start to your shopping cart.

## Placing items in the cart

When you create the shopping cart session cookie, you're ready to start placing items into it. To place an item into the cart, you'll create a new array element and pair it with a value. The array element key will be the name of the product placed in the cart, and the array element value will be the quantity of the product to purchase. That looks like this:

```
$_SESSION['cart']['apples'] = 10;
```

This statement creates an array element in the $_SESSION['cart'] session cookie with the name apples and assigns it a value of 10.

You can create as many array elements as you want to add into the session cookie array variable.

## Retrieving items from a cart

Now that you have a multidimensional session cookie array that contains the products you placed in the cart, all you need to do is extract the values stored in the array to see what's there. However, that can be a little tricky.

Because the array is an associative array, you can't just loop through the array element using a simple for or while statement because you don't know what key names are in the array. This is where the foreach statement comes in handy! It allows you to iterate through all the array keys without having to know what they are:

```
foreach($_SESSION['cart'] as $key => $value) {
    echo "<p>$key - $value</p>\n";
}
```

The `foreach` statement iterates through the array, extracting each key and value pair in each iteration. You can then use the individual key and value pairs in your code to list the items and their quantities.

## Removing items from a cart

Because each product in the cart is a separate array element of the session cookie, you can handle each product individually, as long as you know the product name that you used for the array key. To remove an individual product, just specify it in the `unset()` function:

```
unset($_SESSION['cart']['apples']);
```

This statement removes just the `apples` array key and its value from the array, leaving any other items still in the array. If you want to remove the entire shopping cart, you'd use the following:

```
session_unset($_SESSION['cart']);
```

This statement removes the entire `cart` session cookie. To start a new cart, your code would need to create a new cart session cookie and make it an array variable.

**WARNING**

Be careful when unsetting the individual shopping cart items or the entire session cookie, because there's no going back. When you remove a session cookie, it's gone and can't be recovered!

## Putting it all together

As you can tell, working with a shopping cart is a multistep process, and it can get somewhat complicated. Let's take a look at an example of using a shopping cart on a web page. Listing 6-1 shows the code.

---

**LISTING 6-1:** **The carttest.php Program**

```php
<?php
session_start();
?>
<!DOCTYPE html>
<html>
<head>
<title>Shopping Cart Test</title>
</head>
<body>
```

```
<h1>Items available</h1>
<form action="carttest.php" method="post">
<table>
<tr><th>Item</th><th>Quantity</th></tr>
<tr><td>Apples</td><td><input type="text" name="apples" size="2"></td></tr>
<tr><td>Bananas</td><td><input type="text" name="bananas" size="2"></td></tr>
</table>
<input type="submit" value="Click to add to cart">
</form>
<br>
<?php
    if (isset($_POST['apples'])) {
        if (is_numeric($_POST['apples'])) {
            $_SESSION['cart']['apples'] = $_POST['apples'];
        } elseif ($_POST['apples'] == "Remove") {
            unset($_SESSION['cart']['apples']);
        }
    }

    if (isset($_POST['bananas'])) {
        if (is_numeric($_POST['bananas'])) {
            $_SESSION['cart']['bananas'] = $_POST['bananas'];
        } elseif ($_POST['bananas'] == "Remove") {
            unset($_SESSION['cart']['bananas']);
        }
    }
?>
<fieldset style="width:300px">
<legend>Your Shopping Cart</legend>
<?php
    if (!isset($_SESSION['cart'])) {
        $_SESSION['cart'] = array();
        echo "Your shopping cart is empty\n";
    } else {
        echo "<form action=\"carttest.php\" method=\"post\">\n";
        echo "<table>\n";
        echo "<tr><th>Item</th><th>Quantity</th><th/></tr>\n";
        foreach($_SESSION['cart'] as $key => $value) {
            echo "<tr><td>$key</td><td>$value</td>\n";
            echo "<td><input type=\"submit\" name=\"$key\" value=\"Remove\"></
  td></tr>\n";
        }
        echo "</table>\n";
        echo "</form>\n";
    }
?>
</fieldset>
</body>
</html>
```

Listing 6-1 shows the carttest.php program, which I'll walk through to demonstrate using a shopping cart. The first part of the program creates a simple form for selecting the products to purchase. The code lists two products — apples and bananas — and provides a text box to indicate the quantity of each you want to place in the shopping cart.

The next section uses PHP code to check whether the form has already been submitted. If the site visitor has submitted the form, the PHP code checks to see which (if any) of the products had been selected for purchase. If either one had been selected, the PHP code stores the new quantity number in the cart session cookie for that product:

```php
if (isset($_POST['apples'])) {
    if (is_numeric($_POST['apples'])) {
        $_SESSION['cart']['apples'] = $_POST['apples'];
```

Next, the code shows the shopping cart status. If there isn't a shopping cart session cookie, one is created:

```php
$_SESSION['cart'] = array();
```

If a shopping cart session cookie exists, the program creates a form containing the shopping cart items, along with a Remove button. The foreach statement is used to iterate through each of the items in the shopping cart:

```php
foreach($_SESSION['cart'] as $key => $value) {
    echo "<tr><td>$key</td><td>$value</td>\n";
    echo "<td><input type=\"submit\" name=\"$key\"
    value=\"Remove\"></td></tr>\n";
}
```

Because there are two forms on the web page, you need to add some more code to check if a Remove button has been clicked by the shopper. That was added to the code that checks for the other form data:

```php
} elseif ($_POST['apples'] == "Remove") {
    unset($_SESSION['cart']['apples']);
}
```

Follow these steps to test the carttest.php program:

1. **Open your editor and enter the code from Listing 6-1.**
2. **Save the file as** carttest.php **in the** DocumentRoot **folder for your web server.**

   It's important that you use this exact filename because the forms use that as the action attribute.

3. **Ensure that the Apache web server is running, and then open your browser and enter the following URL:**

```
http://localhost:8080/carttest.php
```

4. **Enter a quantity to purchase for one of the items, and then click the Click to Add to Cart button.**

5. **Enter a quantity to purchase for the other item, and then click the Click to Add to Cart button.**

6. **Click the Remove button for one of the items.**

7. **Repeat the process to add or remove products in the shopping cart.**

8. **Close your browser and close the Apache web server when you're done.**

When you first open the `carttest.php` file, the shopping cart should show that it's empty, as shown in Figure 6-6.

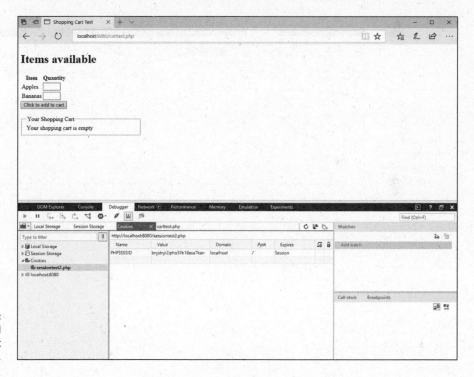

**FIGURE 6-6:**
The initial shopping cart web page.

When you enter a quantity for a product and then click the button to submit it, the product and quantity appear in the shopping cart, as shown in Figure 6-7.

Click the Remove button to remove a product from the shopping cart, or add more quantity of a product to change the value shown in the shopping cart. Congratulations! You've just created a simple shopping cart!

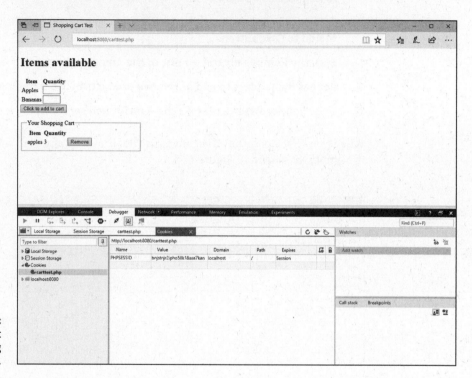

**FIGURE 6-7:**
The shopping cart after selecting products.

**MySQL**

# Contents at a Glance

CHAPTER 1: **Introducing MySQL** . . . . . . . . . . . . . . . . . . . . . . . . . . . . . . . 445

Seeing the Purpose of a Database . . . . . . . . . . . . . . . . . . . . . . . . . . 445
Presenting MySQL . . . . . . . . . . . . . . . . . . . . . . . . . . . . . . . . . . . . . . 454
Advanced MySQL Features . . . . . . . . . . . . . . . . . . . . . . . . . . . . . . . 458

CHAPTER 2: **Administering MySQL** . . . . . . . . . . . . . . . . . . . . . . . . . . . . . 465

MySQL Administration Tools . . . . . . . . . . . . . . . . . . . . . . . . . . . . . . 465
Managing User Accounts . . . . . . . . . . . . . . . . . . . . . . . . . . . . . . . . 477

CHAPTER 3: **Designing and Building a Database** . . . . . . . . . . . . . 489

Managing Your Data . . . . . . . . . . . . . . . . . . . . . . . . . . . . . . . . . . . . 489
Creating Databases . . . . . . . . . . . . . . . . . . . . . . . . . . . . . . . . . . . . . 492
Building Tables . . . . . . . . . . . . . . . . . . . . . . . . . . . . . . . . . . . . . . . . 500

CHAPTER 4: **Using the Database** . . . . . . . . . . . . . . . . . . . . . . . . . . . . . . . 513

Working with Data . . . . . . . . . . . . . . . . . . . . . . . . . . . . . . . . . . . . . 513
Searching for Data . . . . . . . . . . . . . . . . . . . . . . . . . . . . . . . . . . . . . 524
Playing It Safe with Data . . . . . . . . . . . . . . . . . . . . . . . . . . . . . . . . 531

CHAPTER 5: **Communicating with the Database from
PHP Scripts** . . . . . . . . . . . . . . . . . . . . . . . . . . . . . . . . . . . . . 541

Database Support in PHP . . . . . . . . . . . . . . . . . . . . . . . . . . . . . . . . 541
Using the mysqli Library . . . . . . . . . . . . . . . . . . . . . . . . . . . . . . . . 543
Putting It All Together . . . . . . . . . . . . . . . . . . . . . . . . . . . . . . . . . . 554

Chapter **1**

# Introducing MySQL

Computers are all about storing information. However, unlike that junk drawer in your kitchen that contains multiple shards of paper with names and phone numbers scribbled on them, you want to store your dynamic web application data in an orderly fashion. After all, you wouldn't want to mix up the data from your astrophysics experiments with your bowling league scores!

The MySQL database server provides a user-friendly platform for you to organize your application data, making it simple to identify which data belongs to which application and easy for the application to access the data, all while maintaining security so the right people can only get to the right data. This chapter describes just why you need a database for your dynamic web applications, and why you should choose the MySQL database server.

## Seeing the Purpose of a Database

With PHP, you have a few different options for storing persistent data in your application to retrieve at a later time. One method is to use the PHP file system functions to create a standard text file on the server to store the application data, and then read the data back as necessary.

One downside to using standard text files to store your application data is that it's hard to find a specific data item buried in the text file. Standard text files are often called "flat files" because you can't create any type of relationships in the data to make searching for specific information easier. Your application must open the text file and read each line until it finds the data it needs. That's fine for small amounts of data, but for large amounts of data that can be slow, especially if there are thousands of site visitors all trying to access their data from the same file at the same time.

To solve that problem, most web developers have turned to using databases. Databases organize data in a manner making it easier for the database server to insert, find, modify, and delete data. There are lots of different database types available, but one of the most popular is the relational database system. This section describes how relational databases work with data to help speed up your web application.

## How databases work

Microsoft Access is by far the most popular end-user database tool developed for commercial use. Many Windows users, from professional accounts to bowling league secretaries, use Access to track data. It provides an easy, intuitive user interface, allowing novice computer users to quickly produce queries and reports with little effort.

However, despite its user-friendliness, Access has its limitations. To fully understand how MySQL differs from Access, you must first understand how database systems are organized.

There is more to a database than just a bunch of data files. Most databases incorporate several layers of files, programs, and utilities, which all interact to provide the database experience. The whole package is referred to as a *database management system* (DBMS).

There are different types of DBMS packages, but they all basically contain the following parts:

>> A database engine

>> One or more database files

>> An internal data dictionary

>> A query language interface

The *database engine* is the heart and brains of the DBMS. It controls all access to the data, which is stored in the database files. Any application (including the DBMS itself) that requires access to data must go through the database engine (see Figure 1-1).

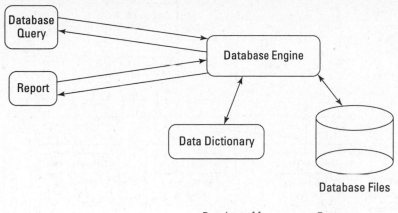

**FIGURE 1-1:**
A simple
database
management
system.

Database Files

Database Management System

The database engine uses an internal *data dictionary* to define how the database operates, the type of data that can be stored in the database files, and the structure of the database. It basically defines the rules used for the DBMS. Each DBMS has its own data dictionary.

If you're a user running a simple database on Access, you probably don't even realize you're using a database engine. Access keeps much of the DBMS work under the hood and away from users. When you start Access, the database engine starts, and when you stop Access, the database engine stops.

In MySQL, the database engine runs as a service that is always running in the background on the server. Users run separate application programs that interface with the database engine while it's running. Each application can send queries to the database engine and process the results returned. When the application stops, the MySQL database engine continues to run, waiting for commands from other applications.

Both Access and MySQL require one or more database files to be present to hold data. If you work with Access, you've seen the .mdb database files. These files contain the data defined in tables created in the Access database. Each database has its own .mdb file.

In the Access environment, if two or more applications want to share a database, the database file must be located on a shared network drive available to all the applications. Each application has a copy of the Access database engine program running on the local workstation, which points to the common database file, as shown in Figure 1-2.

Introducing MySQL

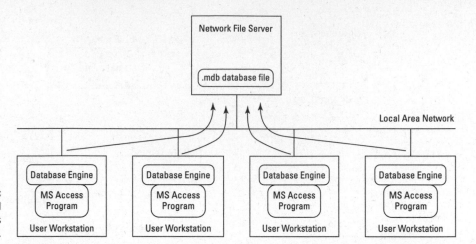

FIGURE 1-2:
A shared
Microsoft Access
environment.

Where this model falls apart is that there are multiple database engines, all trying to access the database files across a network environment. This generates large amounts of data on the network and slows down the performance of the individual database engines.

In the MySQL model, the database engine and database files are always on the same computer. Queries and reports run from separate applications, but they all send requests to the common database engine, as shown in Figure 1-3.

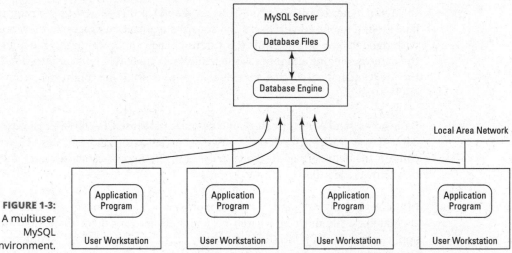

FIGURE 1-3:
A multiuser
MySQL
environment.

As you can see from Figure 1-3, the MySQL database engine accepts data requests from multiple users across the network. All the database access is performed on the local system running the MySQL server, so the data interaction with the database files stays on the local system. The database engine only sends the query or report results across the network to the applications.

This feature alone makes using MySQL a better database choice in multiuser database projects.

# Relational databases

Databases are all about arranging data to make finding information faster. *Relational database theory* arranges data in three levels: databases, tables, and data fields.

## Databases

A *database* groups related data into a single container. The database is the highest level or grouping of data on the relational database server. The server allows you to create multiple databases, all accessible from the same server service running on the server.

**TIP**

To help keep things organized, it's a good idea to create a separate database for each application you're hosting on the server. This helps to separate data elements and eliminates accidents caused by accessing the wrong data from the wrong application.

**REMEMBER**

Each database you create must have a unique name on the server. To help with the organization process, it's usually a good idea to somehow relate the database name to the name of the application.

## Table

The *table* is a subset of data within the database, which contains a grouping of similar data items. For example, if a company wants to track data on employees, customers, and products, instead of having just one group of mixed-up data elements, the company would create four separate tables to hold the data:

>> An Employees table to hold data related to employees

>> A Customers table to hold data related to customers

>> A Products table to hold data related to products

>> An Orders table to track which products are in individual customer orders

The process of grouping application data into tables is called *data normalization.* Grouping similar data into its own table gives you more control over the data. For example, if you have a program that interfaces only with customer orders, you can give it permissions to only the Customers, Products, and Orders tables, leaving the Employees table safe from accidental exposure.

## Data fields

You use *data fields* to hold individual data elements within a table. For example, the Employees table might contain data fields for an employee ID number, first name, last name, home address, salary, and employment start date. The data fields are the core of the application because they're where the application actually stores data.

The table groups data fields into *data records.* Each data record is a single occurrence of values for each of the data fields. Figure 1-4 shows a diagram of how the Employees table might look.

| employeeid | lastname | firstname | address | salary | startdate |
|---|---|---|---|---|---|
| 143 | Smith | John | 123 Main St.; Chicago, IL | 45000 | 4/30/1986 |
| 219 | Jones | Fred | 33 Oak Road; New York, NY | 37500 | 1/4/1990 |
| 312 | Brown | Sara | 221 Pine St.; Miami, FL | 67000 | 4/13/1993 |
|  |  |  |  |  |  |

**FIGURE 1-4:**
An example of an Employees table layout.

Figure 1-4 shows the data fields as table headings. Each data record appears as a single line of data in the table (in this case, the information for a single employee). Because data is often displayed this way in a table, you'll often hear the word *row* used to reference a single data record.

# Database data types

Just as with variables in programming languages, databases need to identify the type of data stored in each data field so that it knows how much space to reserve to store the data, and how to handle the data. Table 1-1 shows the basic data types found in most relational database systems.

**TABLE 1-1**  **Standard Database Data Types**

| Data Type | Description |
|---|---|
| int | A whole number between –2,147,483,648 and 2,147,483,647 |
| float | A floating point number between –3.40283466E+38 and +3.40283466E+38 |
| bool | A Boolean true or false value |
| date | A day value in the YYYY-MM-DD format |
| datetime | A day and time value displayed in YYYY-MM-DD HH:MM:SS format |
| char($x$) | A fixed-length character string with $x$ characters |
| varchar($x$) | A variable-length character string with $x$ or fewer characters |
| text | A variable-length character string of up to 65,536 characters stored as a binary value |

Many relational database servers provide variations of these standard data types, such as small integer values or large text values, to help you customize exactly how much space to reserve for each data field. Unfortunately, these customized data types aren't necessarily standardized between relational databases.

# Data constraints

Besides the data field name and value, a data field can be marked with special *data constraints.* Relational databases use data constraints to control how you place data into a data field. The most popular data constraint is the *primary key.*

A primary key defines the table data field(s) that uniquely identify each individual data record in the table. For example, if you're retrieving an employee data record and your company has two employees named John Smith, you'll run into a problem trying to get the correct data for the correct employee. To solve this problem, relational databases allow you to add a special data field to tell you which John Smith each data record refers to.

To do this, you must create an employee ID data field and assign a unique ID number to each employee. Because the new employee ID data field uniquely identifies each employee record, you can specify it as the primary key for the Employees table. The database server creates a separate hidden table relating the primary key values to data record numbers, and then uses it as an index to quickly retrieve the correct data record based on the primary key value.

Another popular data constraint you'll run across is the is null restriction. If you set a data field with the is null data constraint, the database server will prevent you from entering a data record without a value in that data field.

## Structured Query Language

The Structured Query Language (SQL) is a language for interacting with relational database systems that been around since the early 1970s. Over the years, other database vendors have tried to mimic or replace SQL with their own query languages. But despite their attempts, SQL still provides the easiest interface for both users and administrators to interact with any type of relational database system.

In 1986, the American National Standards Institute (ANSI) created the first SQL standards. The U.S. government adopted them as a federal standard and named it ANSI SQL89. Most commercial database vendors now use this SQL standard to interface with their products.

TIP

The SQL standard has been evolving over the years, with new standards being released to support new advanced database features. At the time of this writing, the most current standard is SQL:2016.

The SQL language specifies a format that you use to send commands to the database server. The SQL command format consists of:

>> **A keyword:** *SQL keywords* define the action the database server takes based on the SQL statement. The SQL standard defines lots of different keywords for performing lots of different actions. However, you'll find yourself just using a few standard keywords in your database programming, so it's not all that hard to remember them. Table 1-2 lists the popular ones you'll get to know.

**TABLE 1-2**

## SQL Keywords

| Keyword | Description |
|---------|-------------|
| DELETE | Removes a data record from a table |
| DROP | Removes a table or database |
| INSERT | Adds a new data record to a table |
| SELECT | Retrieves data records from a table |
| UPDATE | Modifies data within an existing data record in a table |

>> **An identifier:** The SQL command *identifier* defines the database object used in a command. This is most often a database name, table name, or the names of data fields. The SQL identifiers help you select which data elements to retrieve from the database and which table to select them from.

>> **One or more literals (optional):** SQL command *literals* define specific data values referenced by the keyword. Literals are constant values, such as data values to insert into a table or data values used to search within the table data. You must enclose string literals in quotes (either single or double quotes), but you can use numerical values without quotes.

The most common SQL command you'll use in your web applications is the *query*. A query is a SQL SELECT statement that searches the database for specific data records. Here's the basic format of a SELECT statement:

```
SELECT datafields FROM table
```

The *datafields* parameter is a comma-separated list of the data field names you want the query to return. If you want to retrieve all the data field values for the data records, you use an asterisk as a wildcard character.

You must also specify the specific *table* you want the query to search. To get meaningful results, you must match your query data fields with the proper table.

**TIP**

SQL keywords are often identified with all capital letters in a SQL statement. MySQL allows you to use either uppercase or lowercase for keywords. I use all capitals in this book to help you identify the keywords within the SQL statements.

By default, the SELECT statement returns all the data records in the specified table. You can use one or more *modifiers* to define how MySQL returns the data requested by the query. Table 1-3 shows the more popular modifiers you'll run into with SQL queries.

Introducing MySQL

TABLE 1-3

**SQL Query Modifiers**

| Modifier | Description |
|---|---|
| LIMIT | Displays only a subset of the returned data records |
| ORDER BY | Displays data records in a specified order |
| WHERE | Displays a subset of data records that meet a specified condition |

The WHERE clause is the most common SELECT statement modifier. It allows you to specify conditions to filter data from the table. For example:

```
SELECT lastname FROM Employees WHERE salary > 100000;
```

This SELECT statement only returns the last name of the employees with a salary of over $100,000.

TIP

Having to use SQL to interact with a database server can seem a bit overwhelming at first — you have to learn an entirely new programming language besides the languages you're learning to build your dynamic web application. Don't fret, though. There are really only a handful of SQL statements that you'll regularly use during the course of your application development. You'll start remembering them in no time.

# Presenting MySQL

The specific relational database server that I discuss in this book is the MySQL database server. The MySQL server is the most popular database server used in web applications — and for good reason. The following sections describe the features of the MySQL server that make it so popular.

## MySQL features

The MySQL database server was created by David Axmark, Allan Larsson, and Michael Widenius as an upgrade to the mSQL database server and was first released for general use in 1996. It's now owned and supported by Oracle but released as open-source software.

MySQL was originally created to incorporate indexing data to speed up data queries in the mSQL database server, by using the indexed sequential access method (ISAM). It did this by incorporating a special data management algorithm called the MyISAM storage engine. This proved to be a huge success.

MySQL was initially recognized for its speed of accessing data. The MyISAM data storage and indexing method proved to be a game changer in speeding up data access from other types of DBMS packages. It wasn't long before the Internet world took notice, and MySQL became the DBMS package of choice for high-volume web applications.

These days, MySQL has evolved to do more than just fast data queries. Development is continually ongoing to add new features to MySQL. A short list of features includes the following:

>> It was written in C and C++ and has been compiled to run on many different platforms.

>> It incorporates a modular design approach to create a multi-layer server design.

>> It supports multi-threading, making it easily scalable to incorporate multiple CPUs if available.

>> It uses a thread-based memory allocation system.

>> It implements hash tables in memory to increase performance.

>> It supports client/server and embedded server environments.

>> It supports multiple data storage engines.

>> It implements all SQL functions using a class library.

>> It includes support for all standard SQL data types.

>> It offers a security system that supports both user-based and host-based verification.

>> It includes support for large databases using more than 5 billion rows of data.

>> It provides application programming interfaces (APIs) for many common programming languages (including PHP).

>> It incorporates many different character sets, allowing it to support many different languages.

>> It provides both command line and graphical tools for common database management.

Of these features, let's take a closer look at two specific features to demonstrate the versatility of MySQL. The following sections dive into the ability for MySQL to support different database storage types, as well as how MySQL handles user authentication.

# Storage engines

As shown in the preceding section, the MySQL server uses a modular approach to building the database server. One of those modules is how it stores and accesses database data. This is called the *storage engine.*

The storage engine is the gatekeeper to your data and all requests to your data go through it. The MySQL server incorporates several different types of storage engines, shown in Table 1-4.

**TABLE 1-4**     **The MySQL Storage Engines**

| Storage Engine | Description |
|---|---|
| Archive | Produces a special-purpose table for inserting and retrieving data, but not updating or deleting it. |
| Blackhole | Accepts data but does not store it. Used for development testing. |
| CSV | Stores data in a comma-separated file format. |
| Federated | Allows data access from a remote server without using replication. |
| Example | A storage engine that does nothing. Used as a template for storage engine developers. |
| InnoDB | An advanced storage engine that balances high reliability and high performance. |
| Memory | Stores all data in memory for fast performance, but it doesn't retain the data. |
| MyISAM | The initial MySQL storage engine, known for being fast with few advanced features. |

The MyISAM storage engine is what made MySQL famous, but it's no longer being developed by Oracle. The default and recommended storage engine for MySQL is now the InnoDB storage engine.

The InnoDB storage engine supports many advanced database features found in commercial databases, but initially it was known for not being all that fast. Developers had to decide which was more important to their application: performance or fancy database features.

However, work has been done by the MySQL developers to increase the performance of the InnoDB storage engine so that it comes close to the performance of the MyISAM storage engine. This gives you the best of both worlds — advanced database features and a high-performance storage engine, all as open-source software!

# Data permissions

The MySQL database server handles access to database data using a two-tiered approach:

>> The user account assigned to a user

>> The location from where the user connects to the server

MySQL considers your identity from both the user account you use to log into the system, as well as the host from which you connect. That means you can control access to your data not only to specific user accounts, but from where the users happen to be when they log into the database server. For example, you can give a user account full access to a database when she logs in from the local server but restricted read-only access to the database when she logs in from a remote server.

MySQL does this by using an *access control list* (ACL) to define permissions to databases, tables, and special features based on the identities. When you create an identity in MySQL, you not only create a user account, but also specify the location from which the access control applies. You can use wildcards to allow users to have the same permissions from multiple locations.

MySQL uses a two-stage approach to verifying your database connection. First, MySQL accepts or rejects the connection request based on the user ID/password combination provided and whether the account is locked on the system. Then, if the connection is granted, MySQL accepts or rejects the access request based on database and table permissions.

A user account can have access to the database server, but not every database on the server. You can create separate user accounts for each application database that you create on the MySQL server. If your application requires more control, you can even create separate user accounts that have access to only certain tables within the same database!

As the database administrator you also have the ability to grant system-level privileges to user accounts, such as the ability to create new databases or even new user accounts.

**WARNING**

The MySQL server has a single main administration user account named *root*. If you forget the password to the root user account that may or may not be recoverable, depending on your server setup and environment. It's always a good idea to keep track of the root user account's password, but also to protect it so that no one else can use it. If your system requires multiple administrators, give them each a separate user account and grant those user accounts elevated privileges on the database server so they can create databases and user accounts as needed.

# Advanced MySQL Features

When you use the default InnoDB storage engine in MySQL, you have a wealth of advanced database feature available for your applications to utilize. This section walks through the more advanced features that the InnoDB storage engine brings to the MySQL world.

## Handling transactions

All database servers allow users to enter database commands to query and manipulate data. What separates good database servers from bad ones is the way they handle commands.

The database engine processes commands as a single unit, called a *transaction*. A transaction represents a single data operation on the database. Most simplistic database servers treat each command received — such as adding a new record to a table or modifying an existing record in a table — as a separate transaction. Groups of commands create groups of transactions.

However, some advanced database servers (such as the MySQL with the InnoDB storage engine) allow you to perform more complicated transactions. In some instances, it's necessary for an application to perform multiple commands as a result of a single action.

**REMEMBER**

In a relational database, tables can be related to one another. This means that one table can contain data that is related to the data in another table. In the store example, the Orders table relied on data in both the Customers and Products tables. Although this makes organizing data easier, it makes managing transactions more difficult. A single action may require the database server to update several data values in several different tables.

In the store example, if a new customer comes into the store and purchases a laptop computer, the database server must modify three tables:

» Add a new data record to the Customers table

» Add a new data record to the Orders table

» Modify the Products table to subtract one from the laptop inventory value

For the action to be complete, all three of these actions must succeed. If any one of the actions fails, the data will become corrupt. In an advanced database server, you can combine all these actions into a single transaction. If any one of the actions fails, the database server rolls back the other two actions to return the database to the previous condition. This feature is crucial to have available for your web applications!

# Making sure your database is ACID compliant

Over the years, database experts have devised rules for how databases should handle transactions. The benchmark for all professional database systems is the ACID test. No, we're not throwing the server into an acid bath; the ACID test is actually an acronym for a set of database features defining how the database server should support transactions:

- >> Atomicity
- >> Consistency
- >> Isolation
- >> Durability

The following sections examine these four features and discuss how MySQL implements them.

## Atomicity

The atomicity feature states that for a transaction to be considered successful, all steps within the transaction must complete successfully. Either all the steps should be applied to the database, or none of them should. A transaction should not be allowed to complete partway.

To support atomicity, MySQL uses a system called *commit and rollback.* Database actions are only temporarily performed during a transaction. When it appears that all the actions in a transaction would complete successfully, the transaction is committed (the server applies all the actions to the database). If it appears that any one of the actions would fail, the entire transaction is rolled back (any previous steps that were successful are reversed). This ensures that the transaction is completed as a whole.

MySQL uses the two-phase commit approach to committing transactions. The two-phase commit performs the transaction using two steps (or phases):

- >> **Prepare phase:** A transaction is analyzed to determine if the database is able to commit the entire transaction.
- >> **Commit phase:** The transaction is physically committed to the database.

The two-phase commit approach allows MySQL to test all transaction commands during the prepare phase without having to modify any data in the actual tables. Table data is not changed until the commit phase is complete.

## Consistency

The concept of consistency is a little more difficult than atomicity. The consistency feature states that every transaction should leave the database in a valid state. The tricky part here is what is considered a "valid state."

Often, this feature is applied to how a database server handles unexpected crashes. If the database takes a power hit in the middle of the commit phase of a multi-action transaction, can it leave the tables in a state where the data makes sense?

MySQL utilizes two features to accomplish consistency:

>> **Double-write buffering:** With double-write buffering, before MySQL writes data to the actual tables, it stores the data in a buffer area. Only after all the transaction data is written to the buffer area will MySQL write the buffer area data to the actual table data files.

>> **Crash recovery:** If there is a system crash before the buffer area is completely written to the table files, MySQL can recover the buffer area using the crash recovery feature, which recovers submitted transactions from a transaction log file.

## Isolation

The isolation feature is required for multiuser databases. When there is more than one person modifying data in a database, odd things can happen. If two people try to modify the same data value at the same time, who's to say which value is the final value?

When more than one person tries to access the same data, the DBMS must act as the traffic cop, directing who gets access to the data first. Isolation ensures that each transaction in progress is invisible to any other transaction in progress. The DBMS must allow each transaction to complete and then decide which transaction value is the final value for the data. It accomplishes this task using a feature called *locking*.

Locking does what it says: It locks data while a transaction is being committed to the database. While the data is locked, other users can't access the data, not even for queries. This prevents multiple users from querying or modifying the data while it's in a locked mode.

There are two basic levels of locking that MySQL uses to support isolation:

>> **Table-level locking:** With table-level locking, any time a user requires a modification to a data record in a table, the DBMS locks the entire table, preventing other users from even viewing data in the table. As you can guess, this has an adverse effect on database performance, especially in environments where there is a lot of change to the data in the database. Early DBMS implementations used table-level locking exclusively.

>> **Row-level locking:** To solve the problems of table-level locking, many DBMS implementations (including the MySQL InnoDB storage engine) now incorporate row-level locking. With row-level locking, the DBMS locks only the data record that's being modified. The rest of the table is available for other users to access.

## Durability

The durability feature states that when a transaction is committed to the database, it must not be lost. This sounds like a simple concept, but in reality durability is often harder to ensure than it sounds.

Durability means being able to withstand both hardware and software failures. A database is useless if a power outage or server crash compromises the data stored in the database.

MySQL supports durability by incorporating multiple layers of protection. The same double-write buffer and crash recovery features mentioned for the consistency feature also apply to the durability feature. MySQL writes all transactions to a log file, writes the changes to the double-write buffer area, and then writes them to the actual database files. If the system crashes during this process, most of the time MySQL can recover the transaction within the process.

TIP

The onus of durability also rests on the database administrator. Having a good uninterruptable power supply (UPS) for your database server, as well as performing regular database backups, is crucial to ensuring your database tables are safe.

## Examining the views

The SQL programming language provides developers with the ability to create some pretty complex queries, retrieving data from multiple tables in a single SQL statement. However, for queries that span more than a couple of tables, the SQL statement can become overly complex.

To help simplify complex query statements, some DBMS packages (including MySQL) allow administrators to create views. A *view* allows you to see (or view) data contained in separate database tables as if it were in a single table. Instead of having to write a sub-select query to grab data from multiple places, all the data is available in a single table view.

To a query, the view looks like any other database table. The DBMS can query views just like normal tables. A view does not use any disk space in the database files, because the DBMS generates the data in the view "on the fly" when a query tries to access the data. When the query is complete, the view data disappears. Figure 1-5 shows a sample view that you could create from the store database example.

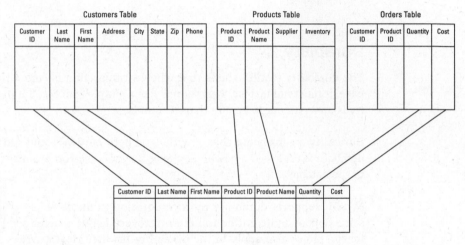

**FIGURE 1-5:**
A view of customer order information.

The view shown in Figure 1-5 incorporates some of the customer data from the Customers table, product data from the Products table, and order data from the Orders table. Queries can access all the fields in the view as if they belonged to a single table.

**WARNING**

You can always use a view to read data, but you may or may not be able to use the view to insert new data or update existing data. It depends on the relationship between the data fields in the view. Data fields related in a one-to-one relationship can be inserted or updated, but data fields related in a one-to-many relationship can't.

## Working with stored procedures

A *stored procedure* is a set of SQL statements that are commonly used by applications. Instead of each application needing to submit the multiple SQL statements, you can create a stored procedure that contains the SQL statements and each application just needs to run the stored procedure.

Stored procedures can also help with the performance of the application, because less information needs to be sent between the client and the server (especially for long procedures). Stored procedures also allows you to create your own library of common functions in the database server to share among multiple applications. This helps you performance-tune queries and ensure all the applications use the same procedure to retrieve the data.

## Pulling triggers

A *trigger* is a set of instructions that the DBMS performs on data based on an event in the table that contains the data. Events that can trigger the instructions are inserts, updates, or deletions of data contained in one or more tables. Here are the most common triggers you'll see:

>> AFTER DELETE: Perform the set of instructions after a data record has been deleted from the table.

>> BEFORE DELETE: Perform the set of instructions before a data record is deleted from the table.

>> AFTER INSERT: Perform the set of instructions after a data record has been inserted into the table.

>> BEFORE INSERT: Perform the set of instructions before a data record is inserted into a table.

>> AFTER UPDATE: Perform the set of instructions after a data record is updated in the table.

>> BEFORE UPDATE: Perform the set of instructions before a data record is updated in the table.

Triggers help you maintain data integrity within your database tables by monitoring when data is changed and having the ability to change related data at the same time.

## Working with blobs

Most database users are familiar with the common data types that you can store in a database. These include integers, floating point numbers, Boolean values, fixed-length character strings, and variable-length character strings. However, in the modern programming world, support for lots of other data types is necessary. It's not uncommon to see web applications that are used to store and index pictures, audio clips, and even short videos. This type of data storage has forced many professional databases to devise a plan to store different types of data.

MySQL uses a special data type called the binary large object (BLOB) to store any type of binary data. You can enter a BLOB into a table the same as any other data type. This allows you to include support for any type of multimedia storage within applications and still use all the fast retrieval and indexing methods of the database.

**WARNING**

Just because you can save large binary files in your tables doesn't mean that it's necessarily a good idea to do it. Large binary files can quickly fill a database disk space and slow down normal database queries. You'll need to analyze your particular application requirements to determine if it's better to store binary data inside the database or store the binary data outside as standard files, with just a pointer to the filename stored in the database.

IN THIS CHAPTER

» **Working from the command line**

» **Using MySQL Workbench**

» **Administering the server from the web**

» **Creating user accounts**

» **Assigning database privileges to users**

Chapter **2**

# Administering MySQL

As you can tell from the previous chapter, the MySQL database server is a crucial component in your dynamic web applications. It's important that you know how to interact with the MySQL database server to create the database objects and user accounts required for your application. This chapter examines the different methods you have available for interacting directly with the MySQL database server in your application environment.

## MySQL Administration Tools

There are lots of different tools available for interacting with a MySQL server to help manage your database environment. Over the years, three particular tools have risen to the top to be the most popular:

» The MySQL command-line utilities

» The MySQL Workbench graphical tool

» The phpMyAdmin web-based tool

All these methods allow you to create, modify, and remove database objects in the server, manage user accounts and privileges, and perform standard database maintenance tasks such as backups and restores. They just all happen to use different environments to do that.

This section walks through the basics of these tools, showing you how to use them to perform basic administration functions on the MySQL database server.

# Working from the command line

Just about everything these days uses some type of graphical interface, but the MySQL project still provides a method for interacting with the database directly from a text command line in the Windows, Mac, and Linux environments. That may seem old-fashioned, but the command line can often provide a handy interface for quickly entering commands. It's also great to use in emergencies — you never know when you'll find yourself working in a situation where the command line is all you have to work with!

This section walks through how to perform standard database administration functions with the MySQL server using just the command line.

## Command-line tools

MySQL offers many scripts and programs that provide different ways for you to interact with the MySQL server in a command-line environment. Table 2-1 lists the command-line tools you'll find in your MySQL server installation.

**TABLE 2-1**      **MySQL Command-Line Tools**

| Tool | Description |
|------|-------------|
| innochecksum | Checks for damaged MyISAM storage engine files |
| l4z_decompress | Expands a mysqlpump archive file |
| myisam_ftdump | Displays information about full text indexes in MyISAM files |
| myisamchk | Repairs corrupt MyISAM storage engine files |
| myisamlog | Displays the contents of the MyISAM log file |
| myisampack | Compresses MyISAM storage engine table files |
| mysql | Provides an interactive command-line interface to the MySQL server |
| mysqld | The main MySQL database server program |
| mysqld_multi | Manages multiple mysqld server processes on a server |
| mysqld_safe | MySQL server startup script for Linux and Unix systems |
| mysql.server | MySQL server startup script for Mac systems |
| mysqladmin | Command-line administration tool |

| Tool | Description |
| --- | --- |
| `mysqlbinlog` | Parses binary log files |
| `mysqlcheck` | Analyzes, optimizes, and repairs MySQL tables |
| `mysqldump` | Performs a database backup |
| `mysqldumpslow` | Parses the MySQL slow query log |
| `mysqlimport` | Loads data from a file into a database |
| `mysqlpump` | Generates a SQL file to migrate a database to another SQL server |
| `mysqlsh` | A MySQL shell for creating scripts |
| `mysqlshow` | Displays database, table, and data field information |
| `mysqlslap` | Emulates client load on a MySQL server |
| `perror` | Displays a text description from a MySQL error code number |
| `zlib_decompress` | Expands compressed output from the `mysqlpump` command |

As you can see in Table 2-1, there are quite a few command-line utilities that MySQL provides to help you out as a database administrator. Most likely, you'll never use most of them, but it's good to know they're there (and what they do) in case you ever need them.

For most normal interactions with the MySQL server, you'll use the `mysql` command-line program, which is discussed in the next section.

## Exploring the MySQL client tool

The `mysql` command provides a text-based interactive interface (commonly called a *command-line interface*, or CLI) to the MySQL server. When you start the command, you'll get an interactive prompt:

```
C:\xampp\mysql\bin>mysql --user=root --password
Enter password:
Welcome to the MariaDB monitor.  Commands end with ; or \g.
Your MariaDB connection id is 4
Server version: 10.1.28-MariaDB mariadb.org binary distribution

Copyright (c) 2000, 2017, Oracle, MariaDB Corporation Ab and others.

Type 'help;' or '\h' for help. Type '\c' to clear the current input statement.

MariaDB [(none)]>
```

From the > prompt, you can submit SQL statements directly to the server to interact with the databases contained on the server. There are also some built-in commands available in the CLI to help manage your database objects.

The mysql command provides a lot of command-line parameters that allow you to customize what it does when you start it. You can use the -? parameter to display all the available parameters and what they do. There are lots of parameters that provide a lot of features that, again, you'll most likely never use. Usually the only parameters you'll need to worry about are --user and --password.

These parameters allow you to specify the user ID and password to use when connecting to the MySQL server (by default the mysql command attempts to connect to the MySQL server using the user account of the currently logged-in user). These days it's not a good idea to enter your password in plain text on the command line. If you use the --password parameter by itself (without a specified value), the mysql command prompts you to enter your password as a hidden entry, as I did in the preceding example.

Occasionally, you may find yourself in an environment where you need to connect to a remote MySQL server. If that's the case, add the --host parameter to specify the host name or address of the remote server.

Besides standard SQL statements, the mysql command has quite a few special internal commands of its own. These commands help you set features within the CLI that regulate how it behaves. Each command has a full-name version and a shortcut-character version. If you want to use the shortcut, precede the shortcut character with a backslash. Table 2-2 lists the commands and their shortcuts that are currently available.

**TABLE 2-2**    **The mysql Commands**

| Command | Shortcut | Description |
|---------|----------|-------------|
| charset | \C | Switch to another character set for the output |
| connect | \r | Reconnect to the server with a specified database |
| delimiter | \d | Set the delimiter used between SQL statements (the default is a semicolon) |
| edit | \e | Edit the command using the default editor |
| ego | \G | Send command to the MySQL server and display results |
| exit | \q | Exit the command-line interface |
| go | \g | Send the command to the MySQL server |
| help | \h | Display available commands |

| Command | Shortcut | Description |
|---------|----------|-------------|
| nopager | \n | Disable the pager and send output to the standard output |
| notee | \t | Don't redirect output to an output file |
| nowarning | \w | Don't display MySQL warning messages |
| pager | \P | Define a program to use to page output (such as more) |
| print | \p | Print the current command |
| prompt | \R | Change the command-line prompt |
| quit | \q | Quit the command-line interface |
| rehash | \# | Rebuild the command-line completion hash |
| source | \. | Execute the specified SQL script file |
| status | \s | Retrieve status information from the MySQL server |
| tee | \T | Redirect output to specified output file as well as the display |
| use | \u | Use another database as the default database |
| warnings | \W | Display MySQL warnings after each command |

After you enter the command, the mysql program processes it and displays the results within the CLI environment. Figure 2-1 demonstrates the output from using the status command.

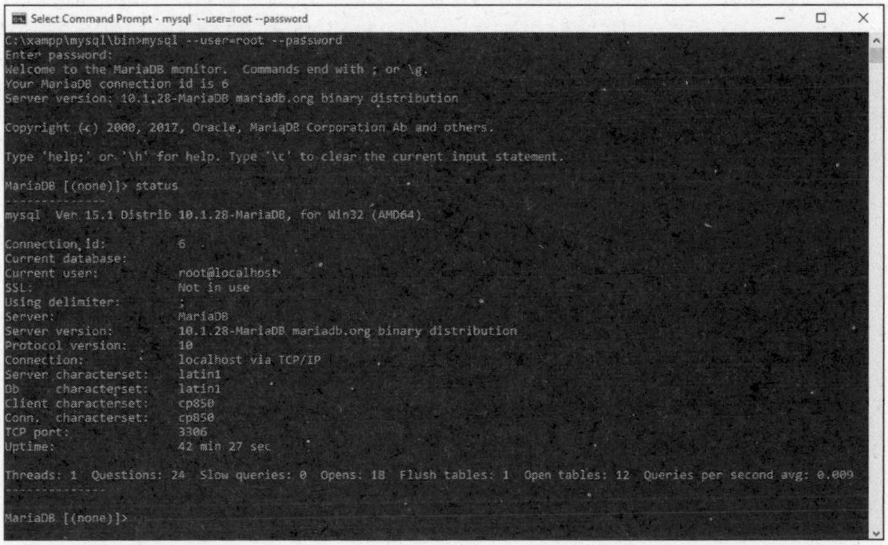

**FIGURE 2-1:** The status command output.

To exit the `mysql` command prompt environment, just type **exit**.

**TIP**

As you can see from my examples, some all-in-one Apache/MySQL/PHP packages (such as XAMPP) use the MySQL sister application, MariaDB, instead of the original MySQL server package. The MariaDB package is a spinoff from the original MySQL package done by the original developers after Oracle took over development of the MySQL package. They created MariaDB to be a complete replacement for the MySQL server. To maintain complete compatibility between the two packages, the MariaDB developers use the same `mysql` commands, but insert the MariaDB signature in the command output, as you can see in Figure 2-1.

# Using MySQL Workbench

Working from the command line can make you feel like a hard-core administrator, but relying on a graphical interface doesn't make you any less of a true administrator. Many administrators prefer to work with graphical tools, especially if they're already working in a graphical desktop environment.

The MySQL project includes a great graphical administration tool called Workbench. It's not often installed by default in most MySQL setups, but it's not hard to download and install yourself. This section walks through that process and shows you some of the features available in the graphical interface.

## Installing the Workbench package

You can get the Workbench tool directly from the MySQL website (https://dev.mysql.com/downloads/workbench). The Download page is shown in Figure 2-2.

Scroll to the bottom of the page to see the section for downloading the program installation package. Just follow these steps to download and install Workbench:

1. **Select the OS where you plan to run Workbench.**

   Because it's a binary program, you need to download a separate package for each OS environment where you plan to use it.

2. **Click the Download button to start the download.**

   **WARNING**

   If you're a Windows user, be careful — there are two download options available. One option downloads the complete MySQL server along with Workbench. If you already have an all-in-one package installed, you don't need to download the MySQL server, only the Workbench client.

3. **When the download completes, run the download package and follow the step-by-step instructions on installing Workbench on your workstation.**

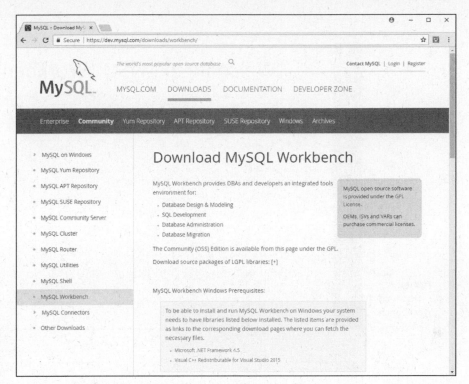

**FIGURE 2-2:**
The MySQL
Workbench
download
web page.

**WARNING**

If you're using Workbench on a Windows workstation, you'll need to have both the Microsoft .NET 4.5 and Visual C++ 2015 Redistributable libraries installed. You can find both of these library packages on the Microsoft developer website. The Workbench installation provides the URLs that you need to get them.

## Exploring the Workbench options

After you install Workbench on your workstation and launch it, you'll be greeted by the main window, shown in Figure 2-3.

Before you can get started with your database administration, you'll need to tell Workbench how to find and log into your MySQL server. To do that, follow these steps:

**1.** **Click the Plus sign next to the MySQL Connections heading to add a new connection.**

This opens the Setup New Connection dialog box, show in Figure 2-4.

FIGURE 2-3:
The main
Workbench
window.

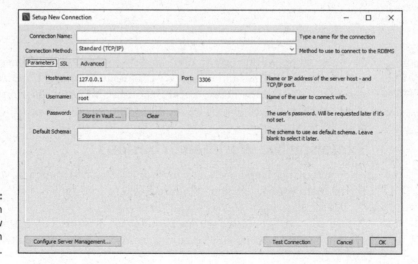

FIGURE 2-4:
The Workbench
Setup New
Connection
dialog box.

2. **Enter a unique name for the connection in the Connection Name text box.**

3. **Enter the IP address or hostname for the MySQL server in the Hostname textbox.**

   If you're running MySQL server on your workstation (such as if you're using the XAMPP package), keep the default IP address of 127.0.0.1.

**4.** **Enter the user account you use to log into the MySQL server in the Username textbox.**

For full administration privileges, use the root user account.

**5.** **Click OK to save the connection information.**

After you create the connection, it appears as an option in the main Workbench window. Click that entry to start the connection to the database.

**WARNING**

The MySQL Workbench tool assumes you're working with the latest version of MySQL server. If your MySQL installation isn't the latest version (as is usually the case with all-in-one packages), Workbench will display a warning message when you connect, informing you that not all the features will be supported. Just click the Continue Anyway button to continue with the connection.

When Workbench establishes the connection, it produces the main administration window, as shown in Figure 2-5.

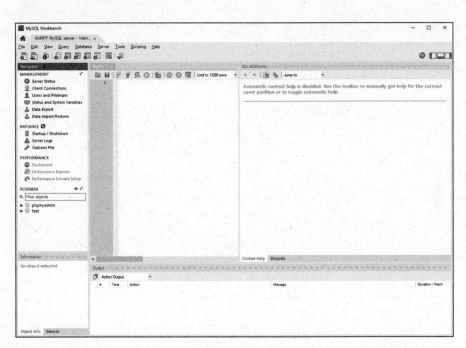

**FIGURE 2-5:**
The Workbench administration window.

The main administration window consists of five sections:

>> **Navigation:** Provides links to start and stop the server, monitor client connections, administer user accounts, export and import data, watch the

performance of the databases and tables, and add, modify, or remove databases and tables from the system schema.

» **Query1:** Submit SQL queries directly to the server for testing.

» **SQL Additions:** Provides online help with SQL statements, showing the context help for the SQL statements you enter into the Query1 panel.

» **Information:** Displays information on the connection session or an individual object that you select from the Query1 panel.

» **Action Output:** Displays the status of any actions you submit to the server, such as queries.

When you submit a query (or group of queries) from the Query1 panel, a new panel appears under the Query1 panel, showing the results from the transaction. If the transaction was a SELECT statement, the data records from the result set appear in a grid, as shown in Figure 2-6.

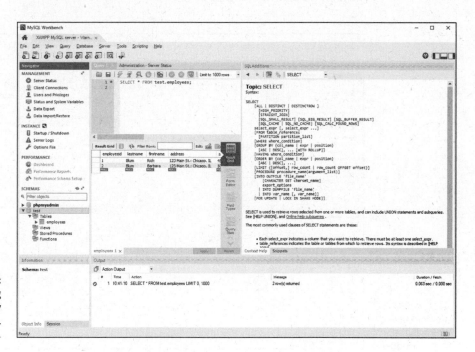

**FIGURE 2-6:** Submitting a query using MySQL Workbench.

From the Workbench interface, you can perform all the same functions that you can from the MySQL command-line interface but with a fancy graphical twist, making it a snap to manage your MySQL server!

# Using the phpMyAdmin tool

Quite possibly the most popular graphical tool for working with MySQL servers is the web-based phpMyAdmin tool. As the name suggests, the phpMyAdmin tool is a PHP web application that interfaces with a MySQL server to provide a wealth of administration functions, all as a website that you can access from any browser!

The phpMyAdmin tool has become so popular that it's usually installed by default in many Apache/MySQL/PHP packages, such as XAMPP, MAMP, and LAMP, as well as supported by most commercial web hosting companies.

Since it's a website, to launch the phpMyAdmin application you need to open your browser and enter the URL that points to the package on your server. For most installations that's just `http://localhost/phpmyadmin`.

If you had to move the Apache web server to an alternative TCP port in your installation, you need to include that port in the URL: `http://localhost:8080/phpmyadmin`.

Depending on your particular environment, the phpMyAdmin package may be configured by default to automatically log into the MySQL server when you start it (such as in XAMPP and MAMP). If not, you'll be greeted by a login form to enter a MySQL user account and password. For full access privileges, log in using the `root` user account.

When you're logged into phpMyAdmin, you'll see the main window, as shown in Figure 2-7.

The main phpMyAdmin window displays the existing databases on the server on the left-hand side of the window. At the top is the navigation area, allowing you to select from 12 different options:

- **Databases:** Create and manage databases.
- **SQL:** Submit SQL statements directly to the server.
- **Status:** Displays the status of connections, server processes, and database queries.
- **User accounts:** Create and manage user accounts.
- **Export:** Create a backup of one or more databases.
- **Import:** Restore one or more databases.

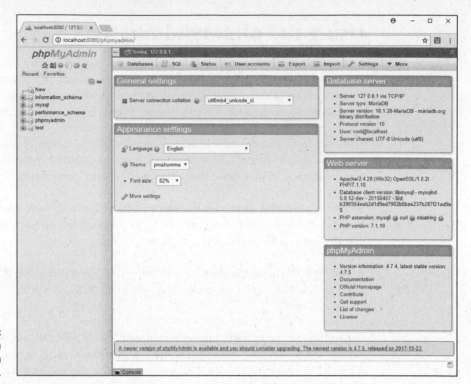

FIGURE 2-7:
The main
phpMyAdmin
window.

>> **Settings:** Manage settings for phpMyAdmin.

>> **Replication:** Control the master and slave replicas if created.

>> **Variables:** Manage the MySQL server configuration settings.

>> **Charsets:** Display the character sets available for the server.

>> **Engines:** Display the storage engines available for the server.

>> **Plugins:** Display plugins installed for phpMyAdmin.

As you can tell, phpMyAdmin also gives you full access to all the server features that you'd need to manage as the MySQL server administrator, all from a simple web interface!

Now that you've seen the three most popular administrator interfaces used for working with a MySQL server, the next sections take a look at doing some basic database administration work using each interface.

# Managing User Accounts

One of the basic administration functions you need to perform in your MySQL server is creating and maintaining user accounts. By default, the MySQL server installs with a single user account, root, which has full access to everything on the database server. It's not a good idea to use this user account in web applications to access the databases. If your application should become compromised, the attacker would have full access to the database server, which would definitely cause a bad day for you.

This section walks through how to create and manage MySQL user accounts using each of the three popular MySQL tools.

## Creating a user account

It's usually a good idea to create a separate user account for each web application that uses the MySQL server. That way you can restrict each user account to only access the single database used for the application, helping to prevent accidental data access and modification.

Just how you do that depends on the interface you've chosen to use to interact with the MySQL server.

### From the MySQL command line

Managing user accounts from the MySQL CLI requires that you know a few SQL statements. To create a new user account, you use the CREATE USER statement. Here's the basic format for that:

```
CREATE USER username@location IDENTIFIED BY password;
```

As noted in Chapter 1 of this minibook, the MySQL server tracks user privileges based on a username and the location from where the user logs into the server. The CREATE USER statement lists both of these items in the definition. You can create separate user@location combinations if you desire to grant different privileges to applications depending on where they're running.

To create a new MySQL server user account, follow these steps:

1. **Open a command-line interface in your OS environment.**

   For Windows, that's the Command Prompt tool. For macOS, that's the Terminal utility.

## 2. Navigate to the folder that contains the MySQL server programs.

If you're using the XAMPP package on Windows, the command is

```
cd \xampp\mysql\bin
```

For the macOS environment, the command is

```
cd /Applications/XAMPP/mysql/bin
```

## 3. Enter the mysql command to start the CLI, specifying the root user account and prompting for the password:

```
mysql --user root --password
```

For the macOS and Linux environments, you may have to precede the mysql command with the ./ symbol to tell the OS that the program is located in the current folder.

## 4. Enter the root user account password at the prompt.

For XAMPP, the password is empty, so just press Enter.

## 5. At the > prompt, type the CREATE USER command to create a new user account:

```
MariaDB [(none)]> CREATE USER user1@localhost IDENTIFIED BY
    'MyL0ngP@ssword';
Query OK, 0 rows affected (0.08 sec)


MariaDB [(none)]>
```

## 6. Type exit to leave the MySQL CLI.

## 7. Type exit at the command-line prompt to exit the Command Prompt or Terminal session.

Now you have a new user account named user1 that can log into the MySQL server.

## Using Workbench

Since the MySQL Workbench is a graphical tool, you don't need to know any SQL statements to create user accounts. You can create new accounts from the graphical interface by simply filling out a form. Follow these steps to do that:

## 1. Launch the MySQL Workbench tool from your workstation environment.

## 2. Select the option to connect to your MySQL server.

3. **From the main Workbench window, click the Users and Privileges link in the Management section under the Navigation pane.**

The Users and Privileges window, shown in Figure 2-8, appears.

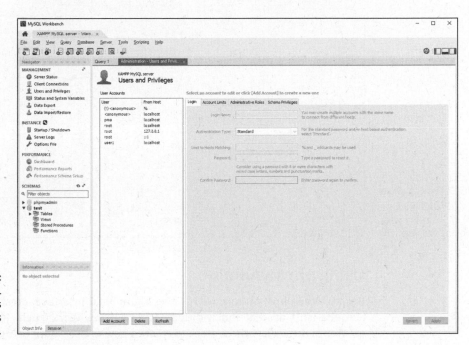

FIGURE 2-8:
The MySQL Workbench Users and Privileges window.

Notice that the window displays a complete list of the user accounts already available for the server. You should see the user1 account you created from the command line, as well as the entry for the root user account.

4. **To add a new user account, click the Add Account button, located toward the bottom of the window.**

5. **Fill in the form to specify a new user's login name of user2, the host location of localhost, and a password of MyL0ngP@ssword.**

Figure 2-9 shows this process.

6. **Click Apply at the bottom of the window to create the user account.**

7. **Close the MySQL Workbench tool when complete.**

That's all there is to creating a new user account from Workbench.

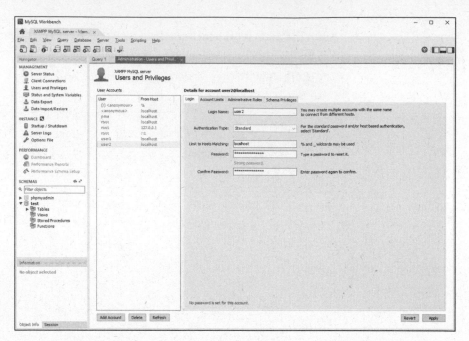

FIGURE 2-9:
Creating a new
user account
using Workbench.

## Using phpMyAdmin

Because the phpMyAdmin tool is also a graphical interface, creating a new user account isn't all that much different from using Workbench, just from a web environment. Follow these steps to create a new user account using phpMyAdmin:

1. **Open your browser and enter the URL to get to the phpMyAdmin tool for your environment.**

   If you're using XAMPP, enter the following URL:

   ```
   http://localhost:8080/phpmyadmin
   ```

   You may need to use a different TCP port depending on your web server.

2. **Click the User Accounts button at the top of the main phpMyAdmin web page.**

   This produces the User Accounts Overview page, shown in Figure 2-10.

3. **To create a new user account, click the Add User Account link in the New section.**

   The Add User Account page appears.

4. **For the username, type** user3.

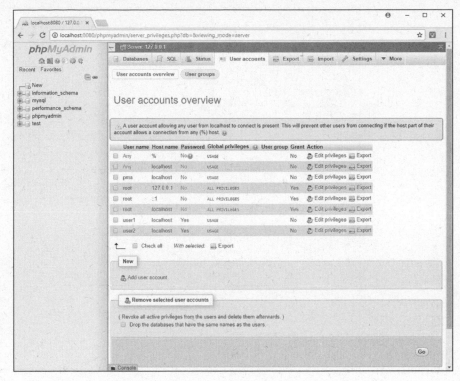

**FIGURE 2-10:**
The User
Accounts
Overview
window in
phpMyAdmin.

5. **From the Host Name drop-down list, choose Local.**

6. **For the password form fields, type** MyL0ngP@ssword.

   Figure 2-11 shows what these entries should look like.

7. **Scroll to the bottom of the web page and click the Go button.**

8. **Click the User Accounts button at the top of the web page to view the user account list to verify the new user account.**

9. **Click the Exit icon on the left side of the web page to close the session, and then close your browser window.**

As you can see, creating user accounts in the phpMyAdmin environment isn't all that different from the Workbench environment, because they both use similar graphical interfaces to build and submit the CREATE USER SQL statement for you!

## Managing user privileges

After you create a user account for your web application, you'll need to grant it privileges to use the database that supports the application. As part of a security feature, MySQL only grants new user accounts the ability to log into the server — they don't have access to any data on the server by default.

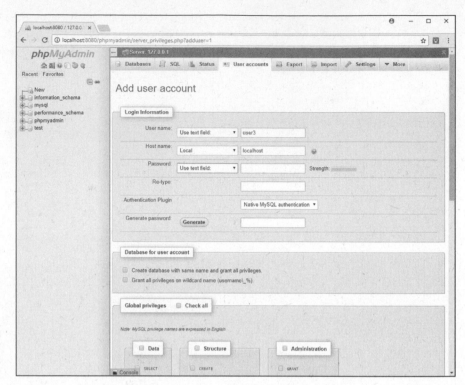

To solve that, you need to use the GRANT SQL statement, using either the MySQL
CLI or one of the fancy graphical tools you've just learned how to use. The basic
format of the GRANT statement is:

```
GRANT privileges ON objects TO user;
```

The `privileges` list controls just what access the user account has on the database objects defined in the `objects` list. MySQL allows you to grant as many or
as few privileges to a user account as you need, providing very fine control over
database access. Table 2-3 lists the privileges that you can use.

**TABLE 2-3**      ## MySQL Privileges

| Privilege | Description |
|---|---|
| ALL | All privileges |
| ALTER | The ability to change a database or table definition |
| ALTER ROUTINE | The ability to change or remove a stored routine |
| CREATE | The ability to create a new database or table within a database |

| Privilege | Description |
| --- | --- |
| CREATE ROUTINE | The ability to create a new stored routine |
| CREATE TABLESPACE | The ability to create a new database storage area |
| CREATE TEMPORARY TABLES | The ability to create temporary tables in a database |
| CREATE USER | The ability to create, rename, or remove user accounts on the server |
| CREATE VIEW | The ability to create or change a database view |
| DELETE | The ability to remove data from tables |
| DROP | The ability to remove databases or tables |
| EVENT | The ability to use events in the event scheduler |
| EXECUTE | The ability to run stored routines |
| FILE | The ability to cause the server to read or write to files |
| GRANT OPTION | The ability to add or remove privileges to other users |
| INDEX | The ability to create or remove table indexes |
| INSERT | The ability to add new data to tables |
| LOCK TABLES | The ability to lock tables for data access |
| PROCESS | The ability to see all the database processes |
| PROXY | The ability to use proxying |
| REFERENCES | The ability to create and remove foreign key relationships |
| RELOAD | The ability to force database writes to files |
| REPLICATION CLIENT | The ability to list replication servers and clients |
| REPLICATION SLAVE | The ability to enable replication slaves to contact the server |
| SELECT | The ability to query databases and tables |
| SHOW DATABASES | The ability to list all the databases on the server |
| SHOW VIEW | The ability to list all the views on the server |
| SHUTDOWN | The ability to stop the MySQL server |
| SUPER | The ability to have administrative control of the MySQL server |
| TRIGGER | The ability to create and remove triggers |
| UPDATE | The ability to modify existing data in tables |
| USAGE | The ability to log into the MySQL server, but no data access |

There are two levels of privileges in MySQL:

>> **Global privileges:** Apply to all database objects

>> **Local privileges:** Apply to a specific database or table

To see what global privileges an existing user account has from the CLI, use the SHOW GRANTS statement, as shown in Figure 2-12.

The output shows that the user1 user account only has USAGE global privileges, so it can log into the database server, but not access any data.

To grant privileges to a specific database, you must list the privileges in the GRANT statement, along with the specific database:

```
GRANT SELECT ON phpmyadmin.* TO user1@localhost;
Query OK, 0 rows affected (0.00 sec)

MariaDB [(none)]>
```

The wildcard character used in the database object list indicates that the privileges apply to all the tables contained in the phpmyadmin database. If needed, you could apply specific privileges to individual tables within your application.

Now you can log in using the user1 user account and access the phpmyadmin database:

```
C:\xampp\mysql\bin>mysql --user=user1 --password
Enter password: **************
Welcome to the MariaDB monitor.  Commands end with ; or \g.
Your MariaDB connection id is 35
Server version: 10.1.28-MariaDB mariadb.org binary distribution

Copyright (c) 2000, 2017, Oracle, MariaDB Corporation Ab and others.

Type 'help;' or '\h' for help. Type '\c' to clear the current input statement.

MariaDB [(none)]> use phpmyadmin;
Database changed
MariaDB [phpmyadmin]>
```

Doing the same thing from one of the graphical interfaces is similar, but just using a graphical form. Follow these steps to grant database privileges to a user account using Workbench:

1. **Start the Workbench application and then click the connection icon to connect to your MySQL server.**

2. **Click the Users and Privileges link in the Navigation section on the right side of the window.**

   This displays the Users and Privileges window, as shown in Figure 2-13.

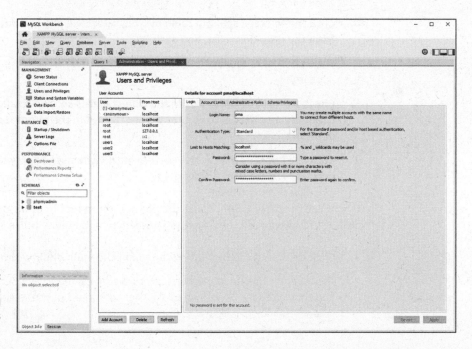

**FIGURE 2-13:** The Workbench Users and Privileges window.

3. **Click the** user2 **user account in the list.**

4. **Click the Schema Privileges tab at the top of the display section.**

   The current global and database privileges granted to the user account appear.

5. **Click the Add Entry button.**

   The New Schema Privilege Definition form, shown in Figure 2-14, appears.

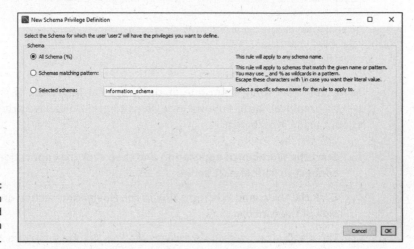

**FIGURE 2-14:**
The Workbench
form to add
schema
privileges.

6. **Click the Selected schema radio button, select the phpmyadmin database from the drop-down list, and click OK.**

   The Details for Account user2@localhost window, shown in Figure 2-15, appears.

7. **Check the SELECT check box in the Object Rights section to allow the user2 account access to view and query tables in the phpmyadmin database.**

8. **Click the Apply button at the bottom of the window to apply the new privileges to the user account.**

As you can probably guess, using the phpMyAdmin tool to grant privileges is very similar to how you did it using the Workbench tool. Follow these steps:

1. **Click the User Accounts tab at the top of the main phpMyAdmin web page.**

   The list of the user accounts currently configured in the MySQL server appears. You should see the user1 and user2 user accounts that you've already created, as shown in Figure 2-16.

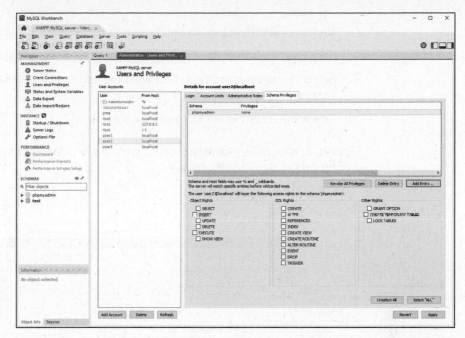

**FIGURE 2-15:**
Adding schema
privileges using
Workbench.

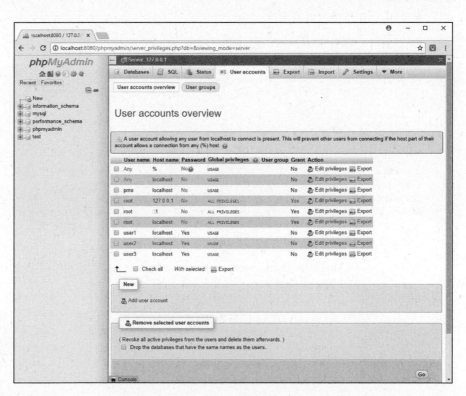

**FIGURE 2-16:**
Using the
phpMyAdmin
tool to display
user accounts.

**2.** Click the Edit Privileges link for the user3 user account.

**3.** Click the Database button at the top of the Edit Privileges page.

**4.** Select the phpmyadmin database from the list and then click the Go button.

**5.** Check the SELECT check box and then click Go.

Figure 2-17 shows the web page for displaying the privileges set for the `user3` user account on the `phpmyadmin` database.

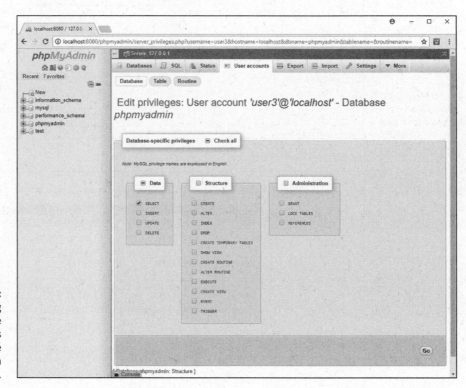

FIGURE 2-17:
Setting
database
privileges
using the
phpMyAdmin
tool.

All three methods produce the exact same results, so feel free to use whichever tool you prefer!

# Chapter **3**

# Designing and Building a Database

n the preceding chapter, you learned your way around the MySQL server interface tools. The next step in the process of building a dynamic web application is to create a database and tables for the data required for your application.

In this chapter, I show you how to determine just what data is required for an application and how to divide it into tables to manage the data. Then I show you how to create databases using the popular MySQL server interface tools. Finally, I explain how to create the tables by using each of the tools, so that you can manage the data in your applications.

## Managing Your Data

When you start out a new dynamic web application, your first decision, before you even start any coding, is how to handle the application data. Often you're faced with a myriad of data elements you need to track, such as employee, customer, and product information for a store. The trick to successfully managing all that information is in how to sort it all out.

The process of structuring application data into tables is called *database normalization.* The key to database normalization is to build your database so that your application can quickly and easily add, modify, delete, and search for data contained in the tables, and do it with a minimum amount of server overhead. For large applications, that can be easier said than done!

Fortunately, many very smart people have worked out some standard rules you can follow for organizing the data in your applications. These rules are called *normal forms.* Each normal form defines a set of standards to follow to organize and protect the data in your application. Each normal form builds on the other normal forms to provide a tiered approach to organizing data. Although there are many different normal forms, for most applications you just need to follow three: the first, second, and third normal forms. These are described in the following sections.

## The first normal form

In the *first normal form,* the idea is to organize the application data to find related data elements and group them into tables, identify the unique data elements with a key to make them easier to find, and eliminate any redundant data stored in tables.

The first part of the rule specifies to group related data into separate tables. In the store example from Chapter 1 of this minibook, you create three tables for a store application by grouping employee information into an Employees table, customer information into a Customers table, and product information into a Products table. That covers the first part of the first normal form!

The second part of the rule specifies that you should provide a way to uniquely identify each individual data record in each of the tables. You do that by defining a *primary key* data field for each table. Sometimes that can be done using existing data elements; other times it requires that you add new data elements.

In the Employees table, you can't necessarily use one of the existing data values to point to a specific employee — there could be multiple John Smiths working at the company, or there could be multiple employees with the same address. It's even possible to have multiple employees with the same birth date.

The solution is to create a separate data field that assigns a unique value to each employee. The application assigns a unique `employeeid` to each employee that it can use to find individual employees. This data field is designated at the *primary key* for the Employees table. The primary key guarantees that you'll retrieve the information for a single employee based on a unique `employeeid` value. You then do the same thing for the Customers and Products tables.

The last part of the rule specifies that you should eliminate any redundant data contained in the table. For example, if an employee has multiple phone numbers, it may not be a good idea to have multiple phone data fields in the Employees table. How many should you create? What if you create home and cellphone number data fields, but then need to add an employee's summer house number? You can't just continue adding new data fields to the table all the time.

The solution is to create a separate table with the phone number information. The phone number table can have multiple data records with the same `employeeid` data values, but each with a different phone number. To find all the phone numbers for an employee, just query the Phone Numbers table with that `employeeid`. Now you can accommodate as many or as few phone numbers for each employee without wasting data field space in the Employees table.

## The second normal form

The *second normal form* specifies that you should create separate tables for data fields that could apply to multiple tables. In the store example, this would apply to how you track customer orders.

In this application, customers place orders, so the `orderid` value could be tracked by `customerid`. However, orders contain one or more products, so the order could be tracked by `productid`. This presents a problem.

Adding the order information directly in the Customers table would be bad. Hopefully, your customers will have multiple orders, so each order data record would need to duplicate the customer's information. That would violate the data redundancy rule. Plus, it wouldn't work putting order information in the Products table, because multiple products could also be in the same order.

The solution is to create a separate Orders table, and relate that table to both the Customers and Products tables. Each order data record would use the `customerid` and `productid` primary key values from the Customers and Products tables so that it could relate the order item back to a customer and the products it contains.

## The third normal form

The third normal form defines how to work with data fields that don't necessarily depend on the primary key in a table but need to be searched. This level of normalization depends heavily on just how your application uses the data that it stores.

An example of this would be the `startdate` data field in the Employees table. If your application needs to perform a lot of queries to find employees who've worked at the company for a specific number of years, it could help the application performance to create a separate table with the startdate values, separate from the Employees table. This helps speed up the query process by reading a smaller table with the one value instead of the entire Employees table. This is often referred to as an *index table*.

The index table contains data that is commonly queried in the application but is separate from the primary key of the table. If your application needs to query the startdate of employees as a primary function, it will help increase the performance of those queries by creating a separate index table of the startdate values contained in the Employees table.

However, index tables come with drawbacks. As you insert each new employee data record, the database system must now make two entries: one in the Employees table and another in the startdate index table. That will slow down the performance of adding new employee data records!

As you can see, this produces a trade-off. If your application queries the startdate of employees a lot, it would help to implement the third normal form rule and create the separate index table. If not, it would be best to ignore the third normal form rule and not create the separate table. It all comes down to knowing how your application and your application users work!

# Creating Databases

After you determine the structure required to support your application data, you can start creating it in the MySQL server. The first step in that process is to create a database for the application. This section walks through the different ways to create a new database using the different MySQL tools covered in the previous chapter.

## Using the MySQL command line

To create a new database from the MySQL command line interface (CLI) you use the CREATE DATABASE SQL statement. Depending on your needs and environment, this command can be either very simple or very complex. If you just want to create a database that uses the server default character set settings, just specify the name of the database in the command:

```
MariaDB [(none)]> CREATE DATABASE dbtest1;
Query OK, 1 row affected (0.00 sec)

MariaDB [(none)]>
```

You now have a new database!

On Mac, Linux, and Unix systems, the database names are case sensitive; on Windows systems, they're case-insensitive. This can cause all sorts of problems if you migrate your database from one environment to another, so be careful with using mixed-case database names! Your best bet is to stick with the same case for all characters in the database name.

To make sure the database was actually created, use the SHOW DATABASES statement at the CLI to display the databases contained on the server:

```
MariaDB [(none)]> SHOW DATABASES;
+--------------------+
| Database           |
+--------------------+
| dbtest1            |
| information_schema |
| mysql              |
| performance_schema |
| phpmyadmin         |
| test               |
+--------------------+
6 rows in set (0.00 sec)

MariaDB [(none)]>
```

The database you created should appear in the list of databases. If you'd like to see a little more detail about the new database, use the SHOW CREATE DATABASE statement:

```
MariaDB [(none)]> SHOW CREATE DATABASE dbtest1;
+----------+----------------------------------------------------------------+
| Database | Create Database                                                |
+----------+----------------------------------------------------------------+
| dbtest1  | CREATE DATABASE `dbtest1` /*!40100 DEFAULT CHARACTER SET latin1*/|
+----------+----------------------------------------------------------------+
1 row in set (0.00 sec)

MariaDB [(none)]>
```

The output from the SHOW CREATE DATABASE statement indicates that the database is using the latin1 character set. The character set defined for your database may be different, depending on the default settings in your MySQL server. If you need to create a database using a specific character set, you can specify that in the CREATE DATABASE statement:

```
MariaDB [(none)]> CREATE DATABASE dbtest1
    -> CHARACTER SET latin1
    -> COLLATE latin1_general_cs;
Query OK, 1 row affected (0.00 sec)
MariaDB [(none)]>
```

This statement creates the dbtest1 database using the latin1 character set, and the latin1_general_cs collation.

## CHARACTER SETS AND COLLATIONS

MySQL supports different character sets and collations for storing data. The *character set* defines the binary code MySQL uses to store character text, while the *collation* defines the algorithms used to compare text values. MySQL uses a cascading method of assigning character sets and collations. If you define a default character set and collation for the server, they'll be used when you create new data objects that don't specify a character set or collation. If you define a default character set and/or collation for a database, those will override the server defaults. If you then create a new table, it will use the character set and collation defined for the database by default. If you define a character set and/or collation for a table, those will override any database or server defaults.

The latin1 character set supports Western European languages. If your application needs to support text from other languages, use the utf8 character set. Likewise, the latin1_general_ci collation compares text based on the latin1 character set. The ci part of the collation name indicates that comparisons are made in case-insensitive mode, so uppercase and lowercase letters will match. If your application needs to support case-sensitive comparisons, you'll want to specify a collation that ends with cs, such as the latin1_general_cs collation.

You can see what character sets your particular MySQL server supports by using the SHOW CHARACTER SET statement. This lists the character sets and the default collation that MySQL will use with that character set. To see the collations that are available, use the SHOW COLLATION statement.

If you need to remove a database from the MySQL server, you use the DROP statement:

```
MariaDB [(none)]> DROP DATABASE dbtest1;
Query OK, 0 rows affected (0.00 sec)

MariaDB [(none)]> SHOW DATABASES;
+--------------------+
| Database           |
+--------------------+
| information_schema |
| mysql              |
| performance_schema |
| phpmyadmin         |
| test               |
+--------------------+
5 rows in set (0.00 sec)

MariaDB [(none)]>
```

**WARNING**

Be careful using the DROP and DELETE SQL statements! The DROP statement removes the entire object, while the DELETE statement removes the data but keeps the object.

## Using MySQL Workbench

The MySQL Workbench tool provides a nice graphical environment for you to easily create databases. The Schemas section of the Navigator pane displays the current databases created on the server. (*Remember:* Workbench refers to databases as schemas.)

To create a new database using Workbench, follow these steps:

1. **Right-click in the Schemas section and select Create schema from the pop-up menu.**

   A New schema form opens in the left-hand section of the window, as shown in Figure 3-1.

2. **Enter the name of the database in the Name text box.**

3. **Select a character set and appropriate collation from the Collation drop-down menu.**

   You can leave the Server Default value to use the default character set and collation settings for the server.

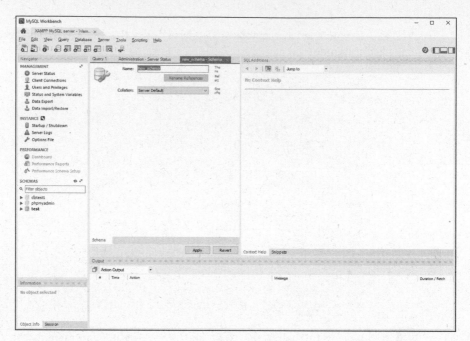

FIGURE 3-1:
Creating a new
database using
Workbench.

## 4. Click Apply.

The Workbench Create Database Wizard appears, which walks you through the
database creation process. First, the CREATE DATABASE statement generated
by the information you entered into the form appears, as shown in Figure 3-2.

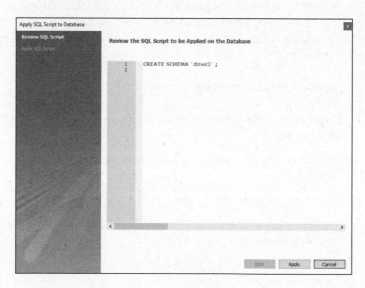

FIGURE 3-2:
The Workbench
Create Database
Wizard.

5.  **Click Apply to submit the generated SQL statement to the MySQL server to create the database.**

6.  **When the MySQL server runs the statement, the wizard displays the results, as shown in Figure 3-3.**

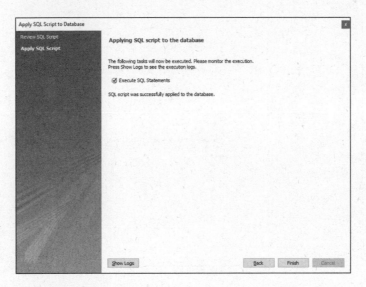

**FIGURE 3-3:**
The results of the Workbench Create Database Wizard.

If the SQL submission was successful, the new database will appear under the Schemas section in the left-hand section of the window.

If you need to remove a database using Workbench, simply right-click the database entry in the Schemas list and then select the Drop schema menu entry. Simple!

## Using phpMyAdmin

As you might guess, creating a database in the phpMyAdmin web-based graphical tool is similar to using Workbench. Here are the steps to do that:

1.  **After you open the phpMyAdmin tool in your browser, click the Databases button in the top Navigation bar.**

    Figure 3-4 shows the form that appears.

    The Databases page displays the existing databases on the MySQL server, along with a form to create a new database.

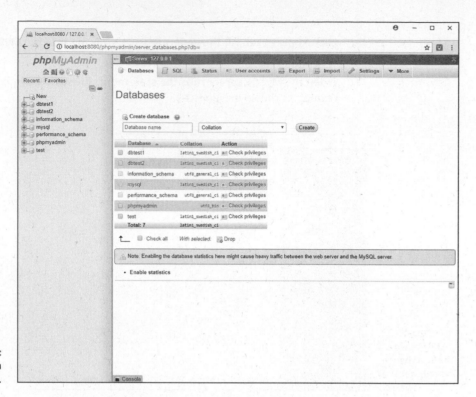

**FIGURE 3-4:**
The phpMyAdmin
Databases page.

2. **Enter the name of the new database in the Database name text box.**

3. **Select the character set and collation from the Collation drop-down menu.**

   If you want to use the server default values, just leave the drop-down box empty.

4. **Click the Create button to submit the SQL to create the database.**

If the database creation was successful, phpMyAdmin automatically takes you to the database interface web page, prompting you to create a new table in the database, as shown in Figure 3-5.

Removing a database using phpMyAdmin is a little more complex than in Workbench. Here are the steps to remove an existing database:

1. **Click the database you want to remove in the left-hand list of databases.**

2. **Click the Operations tab at the top of the database web page.**

   The database operations web page, shown in Figure 3-6, appears. On the operations web page, you can rename the database, copy the database, create tables in the database, and of course, remove the database.

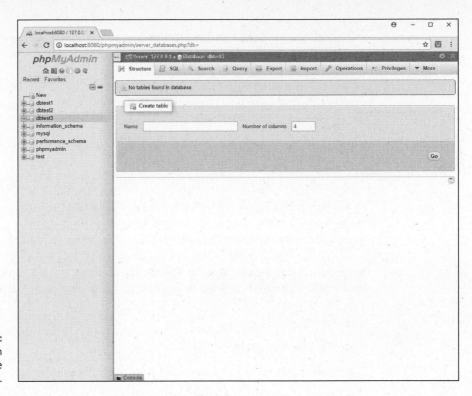

**FIGURE 3-5:**
The phpMyAdmin
database
web page.

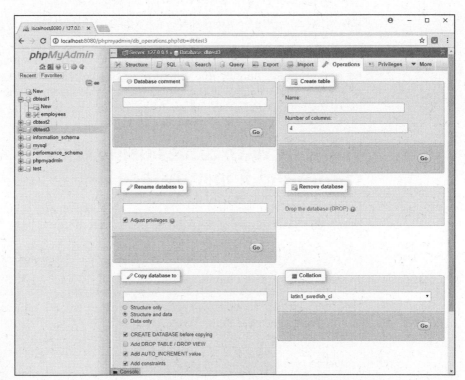

**FIGURE 3-6:**
The phpMyAdmin
database
operations
web page.

CHAPTER 3  **Designing and Building a Database**     499

3. **Click the Drop the Database (DROP) link that appears on the right-hand side of the page (in red font) to remove the database.**

After you've created your application database, you can move onto the next step: creating the tables to hold the application data.

# Building Tables

In a relational database model, tables are what hold all the actual application data. As mentioned at the start of this chapter, it's important that you take time to plan your table layout and structure before you try creating any tables.

Each data table definition must specify the individual data elements contained in the table, along with all the properties for those data elements. That includes

>> The data field name

>> The data field data type

>> Any indexes required for the data field (such as the primary key)

>> Whether any foreign keys need to be defined for the table

>> Any data constraints required for the data field

All this information can make creating a table from the command line require a lot of typing! Fortunately, the graphical tools available make the process a little easier, but before you get to the easy stuff, let's take a look at how to create tables using the command line so you can learn the SQL format for the statements.

## Working with tables using the command-line interface

In the MySQL CLI, you use the CREATE TABLE statement to build a new table. Here's the basic format of the CREATE TABLE statement:

```
CREATE TABLE name (field1 datatype constraints, field2 datatype constraints...);
```

You must define each individual data field, specifying the data field name, data type, and any data constraints applied to the data field. For tables with lots of data fields, this can become quite a long statement!

Instead of trying to include all the information required to create a table in one CREATE statement, database administrators often utilize the ALTER TABLE statement. This statement alters the definition of an existing table, allowing you to add, modify, or remove data fields, data field types, and of course, data field constraints. So, you can build a base definition of the table using the CREATE TABLE statement and then add additional elements using ALTER TABLE statements.

The following sections go through the process of creating a table and adding additional elements to the base table.

## Defining the base table

For the basic table definition, just define the table name and the individual data fields and their required data types. For tables with lots of data fields, even just this primary information can make for a long CREATE TABLE statement! To help keep your sanity, you can use the command completion feature of the MySQL CLI. Just press Enter in the middle of the statement, and you'll get a prompt to complete the statement. By default, the MySQL CLI won't process the statement until it sees a semicolon.

Follow these steps to create a simple base table:

1. **Open the MySQL CLI and log into the MySQL server.**

2. **Use the** dbtest1 **database as the default database by entering the** USE **command:**

   ```
   MariaDB [(none)]> use dbtest1;
   Database changed
   MariaDB [dbtest1]>
   ```

   The CLI prompt shows the default database selected.

3. **Enter the start of the** CREATE TABLE **statement defining the Employees table, along with the opening parenthesis to start the data field definition:**

   ```
   MariaDB [dbtest1]> CREATE TABLE employees (
       ->
   ```

   The CLI prompt changes, indicating that it's waiting for the completion of the SQL statement.

4. **Enter the individual data fields and their data types, with a comma at the end of each line, and press Enter at the end of each data field entry; after**

**the last data field, add the closing parenthesis and the semicolon to complete the statement:**

```
    -> employeeid int,
    -> lastname varchar(50),
    -> firstname varchar(50),
    -> departmentcode char(5),
    -> startdate date,
    -> salary float);
Query OK, 0 rows affected (0.22 sec)

MariaDB [dbtest1]>
```

This creates the basic table defining the table name and the data fields but omits any data constraints and indexes. You can double-check that the table was created by using the SHOW TABLES statement:

```
MariaDB [dbtest1]> SHOW TABLES;
+-------------------+
| Tables_in_dbtest1 |
+-------------------+
| employees         |
+-------------------+
1 row in set (0.00 sec)

MariaDB [dbtest1]>
```

If you'd like to see the data fields contained in the table, use the SHOW CREATE TABLE statement:

```
MariaDB [dbtest1]> SHOW CREATE TABLE employees;
+-----------+------------------------------------+
| Table     | Create Table                       |
+-----------+------------------------------------+
| employees | CREATE TABLE `employees` (
  `employeeid` int(11) DEFAULT NULL,
  `lastname` varchar(50) DEFAULT NULL,
  `firstname` varchar(50) DEFAULT NULL,
  `departmentcode` char(5) DEFAULT NULL,
  `startdate` date DEFAULT NULL,
  `salary` float DEFAULT NULL
) ENGINE=InnoDB DEFAULT CHARSET=latin1 |
+-----------+------------------------------------+
1 row in set (0.00 sec)

MariaDB [dbtest1]>
```

Now that the basic table exists, you can add any required data constraints and indexes.

## Adding more table features

After you create a table, you can add, modify, or remove data fields using the ALTER TABLE statement. Here's the format of the ALTER TABLE statement:

```
ALTER TABLE tablename action
```

The *action* parameter can be one or more SQL commands used to modify the table. MySQL defines lots of actions that you can take on an existing table. Table 3-1 lists and describes the more common commands that you'll probably want to use.

**TABLE 3-1**

### ALTER TABLE Actions

| Action | Description |
|---|---|
| ADD COLUMN *name* | Add a new column (data field) to the table. |
| DROP COLUMN *name* | Remove an existing column from the table. |
| ALTER COLUMN *name* MODIFY *action* | Change the definition of an existing column based on the specified action. |
| ADD *constraint* | Add a new data constraint to the table. |
| DROP *constraint* | Remove an existing data constraint from the table. |
| RENAME COLUMN *old* TO *new* | Change the name of a table column. |
| RENAME TO *new* | Change the table name. |

As you can tell from Table 3-1, there are lots of changes you can make to an existing table in MySQL using the ALTER TABLE statement! Follow these steps to try out a few of them:

1. **Open the MySQL CLI and log in using the root user account.**

2. **Use the** dbtest1 **database as the default by entering the** USE **command:**

```
MariaDB [(none)]> use dbtest1;
Database changed
MariaDB [dbtest1]>
```

Designing and Building a Database

**3.** **Submit an** ALTER TABLE **statement to add the primary key data constraint to the** employeeid **data field:**

```
MariaDB [dbtest1]> ALTER TABLE employees add primary key (employeeid);
Query OK, 0 rows affected (0.57 sec)
Records: 0  Duplicates: 0  Warnings: 0

MariaDB [dbtest1]>
```

**4.** **Submit an** ALTER TABLE **statement to add the** NOT NULL **data constraint to the** lastname **data field:**

```
MariaDB [dbtest1]> ALTER TABLE employees MODIFY lastname varchar(50) NOT
   NULL;
Query OK, 0 rows affected (0.58 sec)
Records: 0  Duplicates: 0  Warnings: 0

MariaDB [dbtest1]>
```

**5.** **Enter an** ALTER TABLE **statement to add a new data field named** birthdate, **using the** date **data type:**

```
MariaDB [dbtest1]> ALTER TABLE employees ADD COLUMN birthdate date;
Query OK, 0 rows affected (0.30 sec)
Records: 0  Duplicates: 0  Warnings: 0

MariaDB [dbtest1]>
```

To make sure the table changes actually took effect, use the SHOW CREATE TABLE statement again:

```
MariaDB [dbtest1]> SHOW CREATE TABLE employees;
+-----------+--------------------------------+
| Table     | Create Table
   |
+-----------+--------------------------------+
| employees | CREATE TABLE `employees` (
 `employeeid` int(11) NOT NULL,
 `lastname` varchar(50) NOT NULL,
 `firstname` varchar(50) DEFAULT NULL,
 `departmentcode` char(5) DEFAULT NULL,
 `startdate` date DEFAULT NULL,
 `salary` float DEFAULT NULL,
 `birthdate` date DEFAULT NULL,
```

```
   PRIMARY KEY (`employeeid`)
) ENGINE=InnoDB DEFAULT CHARSET=latin1      |
+------------+-----------------------------+
1 row in set (0.00 sec)

MariaDB [dbtest1]>
```

The table definition now shows the updates made to the table — the primary key assigned to the employeeid data field, the new NOT NULL constraint for the last-name data field, and the new birthdate data field.

Removing a table using the MySQL CLI requires that you use the DROP TABLE statement:

```
DROP TABLE employees;
```

The DROP statement removes the entire table structure. If you just need to remove data records, use the DELETE statement instead.

## Working with tables using Workbench

The graphical environment in Workbench makes creating tables much simpler than the MySQL CLI environment. As you would expect, it's just a matter of filling in a form!

Here are the steps to create a table using the MySQL Workbench tool:

1. **Click the arrow icon next to the** dbtest2 **database entry in the Schemas section of the Navigator pane.**

2. **Right-click the Tables menu item, and select Create Table.**

   The New Table form appears, as shown in Figure 3-7.

3. **Enter the table name of** employees **in the Table Name text box.**

4. **Click in the text area that shows the Column Name field.**

   An empty text box appears for the Column Name and Datatype.

5. **Enter employeeid for the Column Name, and select INT from the Datatype drop-down box.**

   Notice that Workbench automatically selects the Primary Key and Not Null constraint check boxes in the form for the first data field you enter. Keep those checked.

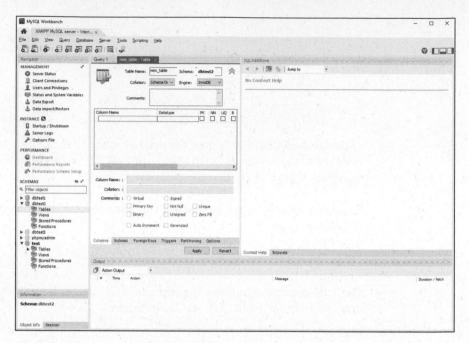

**FIGURE 3-7:**
Creating a new
table using
Workbench.

6. **Click the empty line under the** `employeeid` **data field in the form.**

   A new data field name of `employeescol` appears.

7. **Double-click the new** `employeescol` **name to change it to** `lastname`.

   A default data type of `varchar(45)` appears in the DataType column.

8. **Change** `varchar(45)` **to** `varchar(50)`.

9. **Check the Not Null check box in the form.**

10. **Repeat steps 4 through 9 to add the remainder of the table data fields:**

```
lastname varchar(50) Not Null
firstname varchar(50)
departmentcode char(5)
startdate date
birthdate date
salary float
```

When you complete the form, it should look like what's shown in Figure 3-8.

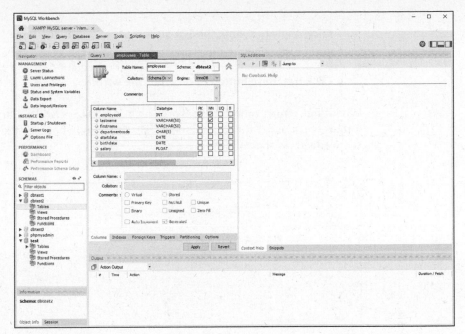

**FIGURE 3-8:**
The completed
New Table
form for the
Employees
table.

## 11. Click Apply.

A wizard appears, showing the SQL code generated from the information you
entered into the form, as shown in Figure 3-9.

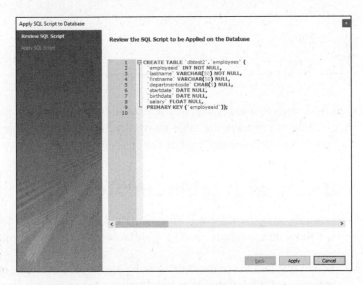

**FIGURE 3-9:**
The CREATE
TABLE statement
generated by
Workbench.

Notice that the CREATE TABLE statement generated by Workbench to create
the table looks just like what you did manually using the MySQL CLI.

**12.** **Click Apply to submit the SQL statement to create the table.**

The status of the submitted SQL statement appears.

**13.** **Click the Finish button to close out the wizard.**

When you return to the main Workbench interface, click the arrow next to the Tables entry under the `dbtest2` database. You should now see the new Employees table added, as shown in Figure 3-10.

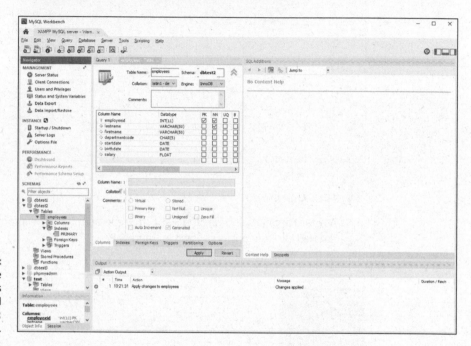

**FIGURE 3-10:**
Viewing the Employees table created in the `dbtest2` database.

From here you can modify any of the data field names, data types, or data constraints. You can remove the table by right-clicking on the table name and then selecting the Drop Table entry from the pop-up menu.

## Working with tables in phpMyAdmin

phpMyAdmin also provides a pretty fancy graphical interface for creating your tables. Follow these steps to create a new table using phpMyAdmin:

**1.** **After you open the phpMyAdmin web page in your browser, click the `dbtest3` database entry from the database list on the left-hand side of the main page.**

This takes you to the database structure page, shown in Figure 3-11.

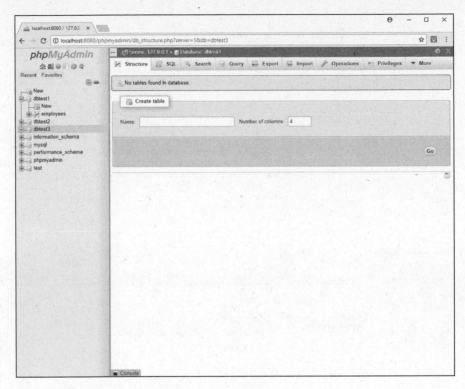

**FIGURE 3-11:**
The database
structure page in
phpMyAdmin.

2. **Enter** employees **in the Name text box.**

3. **Change the number of columns to 7.**

4. **Click Go.**

   This produces the table data field form, shown in Figure 3-12.

5. **Fill in the top form field with the** employeeid **data field information.**

6. **Click the Index drop-down box and select PRIMARY.**

   A pop-up window appears, prompting you for additional information on the
   index key, as shown in Figure 3-13.

7. **Click Go to accept the default values.**

**WARNING**

Be careful with the NOT NULL data constraint when using phpMyAdmin. Notice
that it provides a Null check box. If you select the check box, that means the
data field can have a Null value. Keep the check box empty to apply the NOT
NULL data constraint.

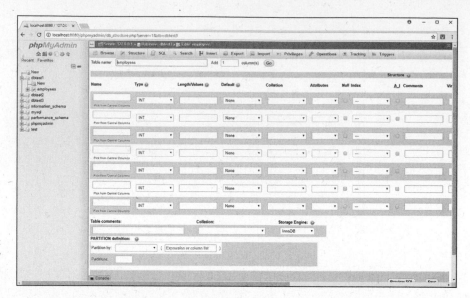

**FIGURE 3-12:**
The empty new table form in phpMyAdmin.

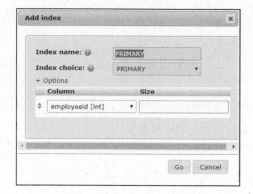

**FIGURE 3-13:**
The Index dialog box in phpMyAdmin.

8. **Complete the form for the rest of the Employees table fields, as shown in Figure 3-14.**

9. **If you'd like to see the** SQL CREATE TABLE **statement that the form information would generate ahead of time, click the Preview SQL button at the bottom of the form page.**

10. **Click the Save button to create the table.**

After phpMyAdmin submits the SQL to create the table, it automatically redirects you to the structure page for the new table, as shown in Figure 3-15.

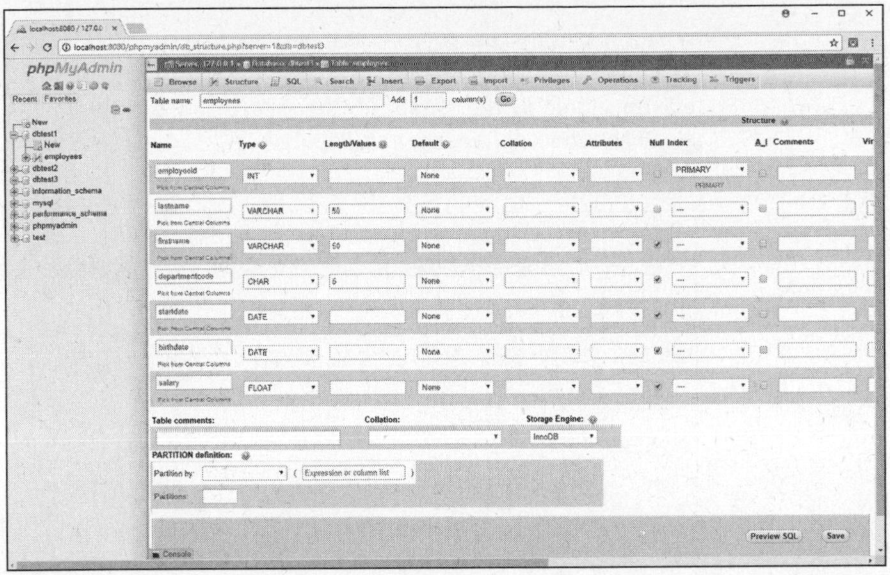

**FIGURE 3-14:**
The completed
new table form in
phpMyAdmin.

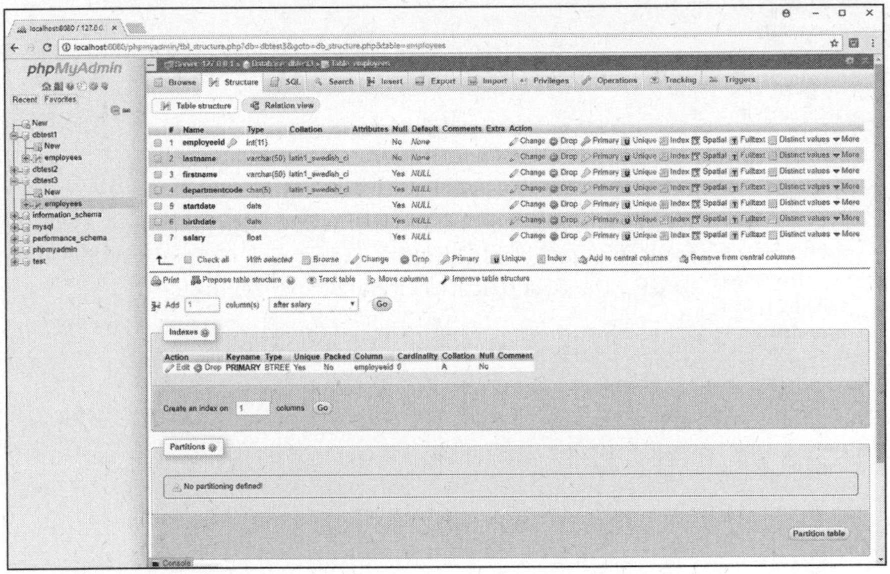

**FIGURE 3-15:**
The phpMyAdmin
table structure
page.

The table structure page is a very busy web page! It shows the data fields for the table, along with a series of action icons for each data field. From here, you can change any of the data field properties, along with adding a new data field or removing an existing data field.

If you click the dbtest3 database link on the left side of the web page, phpMyAdmin will take you back to the database Structure page. This time, because you have an existing table in the database, the Structure page shows the table, along with some action icons, as shown in Figure 3-16.

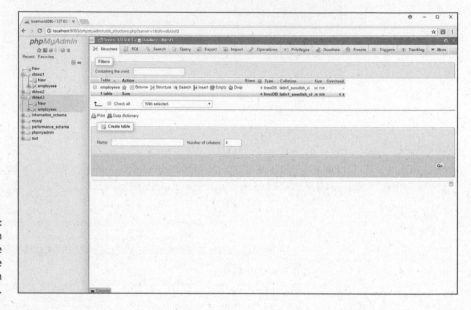

**FIGURE 3-16:**
The phpMyAdmin database structure page with an existing table.

From here you can remove the table by clicking the Drop link or delete the data from the table by clicking the Empty link. To get back to the table structure page to view the data fields, click the Structure link.

# Chapter **4**

# Using the Database

The preceding chapter covers how to create databases and tables for your dynamic web application. That's all well and good, but databases and tables don't really do anything until you start placing data in them.

This chapter explores the different methods you have available for adding, changing, and removing data in your application tables. After that, it walks through possibly the most important feature of any database: how to quickly retrieve the data that your application needs. The chapter closes by discussing the important jobs of backing up and restoring database data.

## Working with Data

The ability to easily manage application data is the whole reason dynamic web applications use databases. So it stands to reason that the SQL language has quite a few options for working with data. There are four basic functions that we need to do with the data in our application:

» Add new data records to tables.

» Modify existing data records in tables.

» Remove unwanted data records from tables.

» Query existing data for specific information.

This section walks through how to accomplish the first three items in this list using the three different MySQL interfaces I cover earlier in this minibook — the MySQL command-line interface (CLI), the graphical MySQL Workbench tool, and the web-based phpMyAdmin tool. Querying data is a complex topic, so I save that for its own section. Let's get started and look at managing the data in your tables.

## The MySQL command-line interface

The MySQL CLI uses standard SQL statements to interact with the MySQL server. There are just three basic SQL statements that you need to know to manage data in your database tables:

>> INSERT: To add new data records to a table

>> UPDATE: To modify existing data records in a table

>> DELETE: To remove existing data records from a table

The following sections describe these three statements and show how to use them in your application.

### Adding new data

You use the INSERT SQL statement to add one or more new data records to a table in the database. A data record consists of a single instance of data values for each data field.

TIP

In some MySQL documentation, you'll often see the terms *column* used to refer to a single data field and *tuple* used to refer to an entire data record. I'll use the more generic terms *data field* and *data record* in this book.

Here's the basic format of the INSERT statement:

```
INSERT INTO table [(fieldlist)] VALUES (valuelist)
```

The `fieldlist` parameter is optional. By default, the INSERT statement tries to load comma-separated values from the `valuelist` into each data field in the table, in the order the data fields appear in the table definition. Chapter 3 of this minibook explains how can you use the SHOW CREATE TABLE statement to list the data fields in the table. Another method is to use the DESCRIBE SQL statement:

```
MariaDB [dbtest1]> DESCRIBE employees;
+------------------+-------------+------+-----+---------+-------+
| Field            | Type        | Null | Key | Default | Extra |
```

```
+----------------+--------------+------+-----+---------+-------+
| employeeid     | int(11)      | NO   | PRI | NULL    |       |
| lastname       | varchar(50)  | NO   |     | NULL    |       |
| firstname      | varchar(50)  | YES  |     | NULL    |       |
| departmentcode | char(5)      | YES  |     | NULL    |       |
| startdate      | date         | YES  |     | NULL    |       |
| salary         | float        | YES  |     | NULL    |       |
| birthdate      | date         | YES  |     | NULL    |       |
+----------------+--------------+------+-----+---------+-------+
7 rows in set (0.01 sec)

MariaDB [dbtest1]>
```

It doesn't show the exact SQL statement used to create the table, but it produces a quick summary of the data fields contained in the table. That's all you need to see what order the data fields appear in the table for the INSERT statement.

Follow these steps to enter a data record into the employees table that you created back in Chapter 3 of this minibook. (If you skipped that part, or haven't read it yet, just jump back there and run the CREATE statements to do that. I'll wait.)

1. **Ensure that the MySQL server is started, and then open the MySQL CLI program.**

2. **Log in as the root user account.**

3. **Specify the dbtest1 database from Chapter 3 as the default database by entering the USE statement:**

```
MariaDB [(none)]> USE dbtest1;
Database changed
MariaDB [dbtest1]>
```

4. **Add a new data record by entering the INSERT statement:**

```
MariaDB [dbtest1]> INSERT INTO employees VALUES
    -> (123, 'Blum', 'Rich', 5, '2020-01-01', 10000, '2000-05-01');
Query OK, 1 row affected (0.12 sec)

MariaDB [dbtest1]>
```

TIP

In the INSERT statement, text and date values must be enclosed in quotes to delineate the start and end of the text value. Numeric values don't need to use quotes. Notice that I split the INSERT statement into two parts here. That's not necessary, but it can come in handy when you don't want too long of a line for the INSERT statement.

The INSERT statement returns a status message indicating how many data record rows were successfully added to the table. (If you need to, you can specify more than one group of data values in the *valuelist*, surrounding each with the parentheses.)

5. **Check to ensure the data was added correctly by using the** SELECT **statement:**

```
MariaDB [dbtest1]> SELECT * FROM employees;
+------------+----------+-----------+-------+------------+--------+
------+
| employeeid | lastname | firstname | dcode | startdate  | salary |
  birthdate |
+------------+----------+-----------+-------+------------+--------+
------+
|        123 | Blum     | Rich      | 5     | 2020-01-01 | 10000  |
  2000-05-01 |
+------------+----------+-----------+-------+------------+--------+
------+
1 row in set (0.00 sec)

MariaDB [dbtest1]>
```

The SELECT statement shows the data fields in the table (I truncated the departmentcode data field name in this output so it would fit the width of the book page), and then shows the data records contained in the table.

If you don't want to assign values to all the data fields in the data record, you must include the *fieldlist* parameter. This specifies the data fields (and the order) that the data values will be placed in:

```
MariaDB [dbtest1]> INSERT INTO employees (employeeid, lastname, firstname)
    -> VALUES (124, 'Blum', 'Barbara');
Query OK, 1 row affected (0.10 sec)

MariaDB [dbtest1]>
```

**WARNING**

Be careful when skipping data fields when adding a new data record. If a data field that uses the NOT NULL data constraint isn't assigned a data value, the server may reject the INSERT statement. I say "may" because it depends on the configuration of the MySQL server. To maintain backward compatibility with older versions of MySQL, by default MySQL won't enforce some data constraints, such as the NOT NULL constraint by default. To enforce it, you must change the sql_mode setting, either in the MySQL server configuration, or by setting it in the MySQL connection session. The sql_mode setting value of STRICT_ALL_TABLES tells MySQL to enforce all data constraints on all tables. When you do that, you'll get an error message if you don't supply a value for any data field that uses the NOT NULL constraint:

```
MariaDB [dbtest1]> set sql_mode=STRICT_ALL_TABLES;
Query OK, 0 rows affected (0.00 sec)

MariaDB [dbtest1]> INSERT INTO employees (employeeid, firstname) VALUES
    -> (126, 'Katie');
ERROR 1364 (HY000): Field 'lastname' doesn't have a default value
MariaDB [dbtest1]>
```

## Modifying existing data

If you need to change data that you've already entered into the table, don't worry — all is not lost. You can modify any existing data records in the table, as long as the privileges assigned to your MySQL user account contains the UPDATE privilege.

You use the UPDATE SQL statement for updating one or more data records contained in the table. The UPDATE statement is another of those SQL statements that, though simple in concept, can easily get complex. Here's the basic format for the UPDATE statement:

```
UPDATE table SET datafield = value [WHERE condition]
```

The basic format of this statement specifies a *datafield* in the *table* to change the data value of that data field to the *value* specified. The WHERE clause specifies the condition that a data record must meet to have the change applied to it. However, notice that it's optional, which can cause lots of problems.

Here's the way the scenario often plays out: Suppose you need to go back into the Employees table to change the NULL startdate value for Barbara that wasn't supplied when the data record was created. If you just use the basic format for the UPDATE statement, you'll get a surprise:

```
MariaDB [dbtest1]> UPDATE employees SET startdate = '2020-01-02';
Query OK, 2 rows affected (0.10 sec)
Rows matched: 2  Changed: 2  Warnings: 0

MariaDB [dbtest1]>
```

Your first clue that something bad happened would be the output returned from the MySQL server. The Rows matched and the Changed fields indicate that two data records were updated — but you just wanted to change one data record. Running a SELECT statement will verify your mistake:

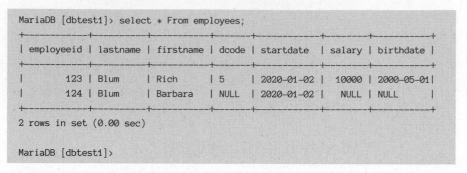

```
MariaDB [dbtest1]> select * From employees;
+------------+----------+-----------+-------+------------+--------+-----------+
| employeeid | lastname | firstname | dcode | startdate  | salary | birthdate |
+------------+----------+-----------+-------+------------+--------+-----------+
|        123 | Blum     | Rich      | 5     | 2020-01-02 |  10000 | 2000-05-01|
|        124 | Blum     | Barbara   | NULL  | 2020-01-02 |   NULL | NULL      |
+------------+----------+-----------+-------+------------+--------+-----------+
2 rows in set (0.00 sec)

MariaDB [dbtest1]>
```

The basic UPDATE statement changed the startdate data field value for all of the data records in the table! This is an all-too-common mistake made by even the most experienced database administrators and programmers when in a hurry. By default, MySQL applies the update to all the table data records.

To solve that problem, you just need to add the WHERE clause to specify exactly which data record(s) you intend the change to apply to:

```
UPDATE employees SET startdate = '2020-01-01' WHERE employeeid = 123;
```

TIP

It's a good practice to get in the habit of always including a WHERE clause in your UPDATE statements, even if you really do want the update to apply to all the data records. That way, you know the update will always be applied to the correct data records and avoid costly mistakes.

## Deleting existing data

The DELETE statement allows you to remove data from a table but keep the actual table intact (unlike the DROP statement, which removes the table and the data). Here's the format for the DELETE statement:

```
DELETE FROM table [WHERE condition]
```

This statement works similar to the UPDATE statement. Any data records matching the condition listed in the WHERE clause are deleted. And just like the UPDATE statement, if you leave off the WHERE clause, the DELETE function applies to all the data in the table. Make sure you really mean that before using it!

Here are a couple of examples of using the `DELETE` statement:

```
MariaDB [dbtest1]> DELETE FROM employees WHERE employeeid = 124;
Query OK, 1 row affected (0.08 sec)

MariaDB [dbtest1]> DELETE FROM employees WHERE employeeid = 124;
Query OK, 0 rows affected (0.00 sec)

MariaDB [dbtest1]>
```

In the second example, I tried to delete a data record that I had already deleted. Notice that when the `DELETE` statement fails to find any data records to delete, it does not produce an error message; instead, it just indicates in the return status that the number of data records deleted was zero.

## The MySQL Workbench tool

Thanks to its graphical interface, working with table data using MySQL Workbench is a breeze. You don't need to memorize any SQL statements — just fill out a form and apply it to the database. Much like ordering a pizza!

Follow these steps to experiment with the data management features in Workbench:

1. **Ensure that the MySQL database server is running, and then open the MySQL Workbench tool.**

2. **Double-click the** `dbtest2` **database link in the Navigator pane, under the Schemas section.**

3. **Double-click the Tables link under the dbtest2 link.**

4. **Hover the mouse pointer over the Employees table entry.**

   Three icons appear:

   - An *i* icon, which displays information about the table

   - A wrench icon, which allows you to modify the table structure

   - A spreadsheet table icon, which allows you to manage data in the table

5. **Click the spreadsheet table icon next to the Employees table entry.**

   The Result Grid pane appears under the Query1 pane, as shown in Figure 4-1.

   The Result Grid pane shows the existing table data (if any) in a grid layout. Each row in the grid is a data record in the table.

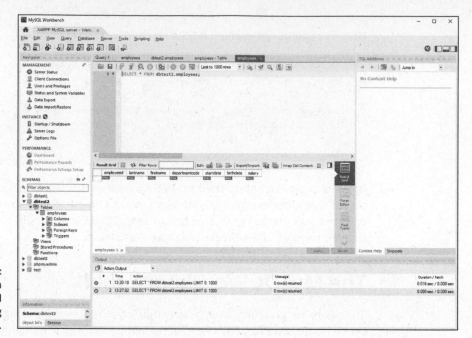

FIGURE 4-1:
The Workbench
Result Grid
for displaying
table data.

TIP

Depending on the size of the Workbench window, the Result Grid area may be truncated on the right-hand side. If that happens, grab the margin line at the right-hand edge of the Result Grid area and drag it to the right to expand the pane.

6. **To enter a new data record, either double-click in the empty grid row at the bottom of the table or, if your grid is very long, click the Insert Row icon at the top of the grid to jump to the empty grid row.**

7. **To modify an existing single data value in a data record, single-click the value in the grid and replace the existing value with the new value.**

8. **To remove an existing data record, highlight the grid row by clicking the empty cell at the left-hand side of the row, and then click the Delete selected rows icon at the top of the Result Grid pane.**

9. **To apply the changes to the table, click the Apply button at the bottom of the pane.**

   The Apply SQL Wizard appears, as shown in Figure 4-2.

   The wizard shows the SQL statements generated to add, modify, or delete the data records based on the changes you made in the data grid.

10. **Click the Apply button to apply the SQL statements to the table.**

11. **Click the Finish button to close the wizard.**

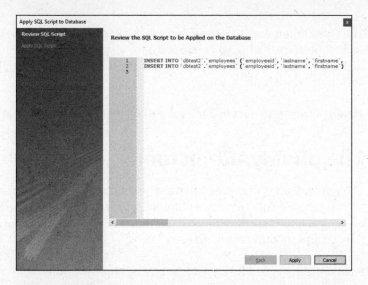

FIGURE 4-2:
The Apply
SQL Wizard in
Workbench.

**WARNING**

The Result Grid can be a bit misleading. Just making the changes in the grid display doesn't commit them to the table. You have to click the Apply button to run the wizard to commit the changes, or else they'll be gone when you close out the grid!

If you feel a bit restricted by the small area of the result grid, click the Form Editor button on the right-hand side of the pane. That displays a single data record in the table using a form format, as shown in Figure 4-3.

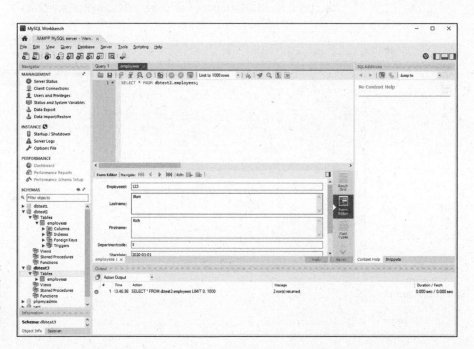

FIGURE 4-3:
Using the
Form Editor in
Workbench to
manage data
records.

The Form Editor does the same thing as the Result Grid but provides a single data record interface, giving you more room for viewing long data fields. Again, if you make any changes in the Form Editor, make sure to click the Apply button at the bottom to commit the changes.

Making changes to data in a table doesn't get any easier than that!

## The phpMyAdmin tool

The phpMyAdmin web-based tool also provides a graphical interface for working with your table data, but it's a little more complicated than Workbench. Instead of using a single interface for all data management, phpMyAdmin breaks them up into a couple of different interfaces.

Follow these steps to insert new data using phpMyAdmin:

**1.** **Ensure that the MySQL server is running, and then open your browser and go to the phpMyAdmin URL for your system.**

For XAMPP it's http://localhost:8080/phpmyadmin/. Note that the TCP port may be different for your server environment.

**2.** **Click the dbtest3 database link on the left-hand side of the main phpMy-Admin web page.**

This produces the Database web page, as shown in Figure 4-4.

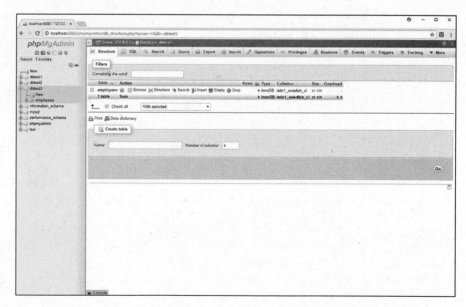

**FIGURE 4-4:**
The phpMyAdmin Database web page.

**3. To add a new data record, click the Insert link in the Actions section.**

This produces a form to insert one or two new data records, as shown in Figure 4-5.

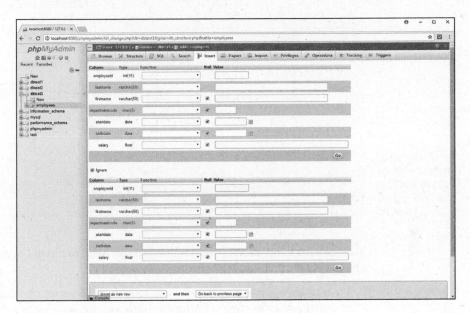

**FIGURE 4-5:**
The INSERT form in phpMyAdmin.

**4. Enter data values in the appropriate data fields, and then click the Go button to add the data record.**

When you click the Go button, phpMyAdmin generates the INSERT statement and submits the data record to the table. It then takes you back to the Database web page, showing the status for the completed statement.

Managing existing data in a table uses a different interface in phpMyAdmin. Follow these steps to manage the existing data records in the table:

**1. Open your browser and enter the following phpMyAdmin URL:**

```
http://localhost:8080/phpmyadmin/
```

**2. Click the dbtest3 database link on the left-hand side of the main phpMyAdmin web page.**

**3. Click the Browse icon in the employee table actions section of the Database web page.**

This produces a list of all the data records contained in the table, as shown in Figure 4-6.

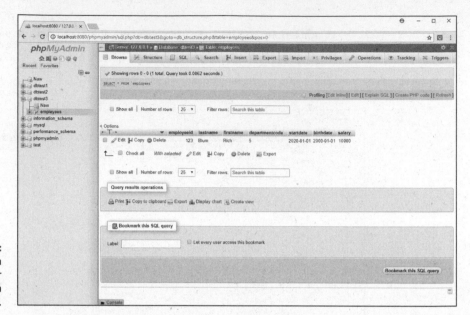

FIGURE 4-6:
The phpMyAdmin window for browsing data records.

**4.** **Click the Edit icon for the data record you need to modify or the Delete icon for the data record you need to delete.**

To delete multiple data records, select the check boxes for those data records, and then click the Delete icon at the bottom of the data record list.

**5.** **Click the Go button to confirm editing or deleting the selected data record.**

Thanks to the graphical interface in phpMyAdmin, entering and managing data is still a simple process. However, finding specific data records in an application can be somewhat tricky, even when using a graphical interface. The next section tackles that topic.

# Searching for Data

Quite possibly the most important function you'll perform in your dynamic web applications is to query existing data in the database. Many web developers spend a great deal of time concentrating on the design layout of the web pages, but the real heart of the application is the behind-the-scenes SQL used to query data to produce the website content. If this code is inefficient, it can cause huge performance problems, and possibly even make the web application virtually useless to customers — no matter how fancy the web pages look.

As a good database application developer, it's essential that you understand how to write good SQL query statements. The SQL statement used for queries is SELECT. Because of its importance, a lot of work has been done on the format of the SELECT statement, to make it as versatile as possible. Unfortunately, with versatility comes complexity.

Because of the versatility of the SELECT statement, the statement format has become somewhat unwieldy and intimidating for the beginner. To try and keep things simple, in this section I walk through the different features of the SELECT statement one piece at a time. The next few sections demonstrate how to use these features of the SELECT statement.

## The basic SELECT format

The basic format for the SELECT statement seems simple enough:

```
SELECT fieldlist FROM table
```

The *fieldlist* parameter specifies the data fields that should appear in the output from the *table* you specify. The *fieldlist* can be a comma-separated list of specific data fields in the table, or the wildcard character (the asterisk) to specify all data fields, as shown in the SELECT example I use earlier in this chapter:

```
SELECT * FROM employees;
```

This statement returns all the data field values for all the data records contained in the Employees table. If that's all you need for your application, you don't need to know anything more about the SELECT statement (lucky you)!

However, more than likely, you'll need to customize just what data fields (and data records) need to appear in the output. That's where things start getting complicated. The following sections show some more features that you may need to use in your SELECT statements.

### Sorting output data

The output from a SELECT statement is called a *result set.* The result set contains only the data fields specified in the SELECT statement. The result set is only temporary and, by default, is not stored in any tables in the database.

By default, the data records displayed in the result set are not displayed in any particular order. As records are added or removed from the table, MySQL may place new data records anywhere within the table order. Even if you enter data in a particular order using INSERT statements, there is still no guarantee that the records will display in the same order in the result set.

If you need to specify the order in which the data records appear in your output, you must add the ORDER BY clause to the SELECT statement:

```
> SELECT employeeid, lastname, firstname FROM employees ORDER BY firstname;
+------------+----------+-----------+
| employeeid | lastname | firstname |
+------------+----------+-----------+
|        124 | Blum     | Barbara   |
|        126 | Blum     | Jessica   |
|        125 | Blum     | Katie     |
|        123 | Blum     | Rich      |
+------------+----------+-----------+
4 rows in set (0.00 sec)

>
```

In this example, only the data fields specified in the SELECT statement are displayed, ordered by the firstname data field. The default order used by the ORDER BY clause is ascending order, based on the data type and collation you select when creating the table. You can change the order to descending by adding the DESC keyword at the end of the ORDER BY clause:

```
ORDER BY firstname DESC;
```

This gives you complete control over how the data records appear in the result set output.

## Filtering output data

By default, the SELECT statement places all the data records in the table in the result set output. The power of the database query comes from displaying only a subset of the data that meets a specific condition.

You add the WHERE clause to the SELECT statement to determine which data records to display in the result set output. Now we're getting to the heart of the SELECT statement!

For example, you can check for all the employees who work in the department identified by departmentcode 5 by using the following query:

```
MariaDB [dbtest1]> SELECT * FROM employees WHERE departmentcode = 5;
+-----+-------+-------+----------------+------------+--------+------------+
| id  | lname | fname | departmentcode | startdate  | salary | birthdate  |
+-----+-------+-------+----------------+------------+--------+------------+
| 123 | Blum  | Rich  | 5              | 2020-01-02 | 10000  | 2000-05-01 |
```

```
| 125| Blum  | Katie | 5                | 2020-02-25 |  14000 | 2004-01-01 |
+----+-------+-------+------------------+------------+--------+------------+
2 rows in set (0.00 sec)

MariaDB [dbtest1]>
```

The result set only contains the data records from the table that match the WHERE clause condition you specified. In this example, the data field was an integer type, but if the data field you use is a text or date value, you must place quotes around the value to delineate the start and end of the value:

```
SELECT * FROM employees WHERE startdate < "2020-03-01";
```

**WARNING**

In the WHERE clause condition, the collation you define for the data field is important. MySQL evaluates the specified condition based on the collation defined. If you use a case-insensitive collation, MySQL can't tell the difference between the values Rich and rich. Be very careful in selecting the collation you use for tables, because that plays an important role in just how your application can handle the data contained in the tables.

## More advanced queries

Now that you've seen the basics (and the power) of the SELECT statement, let's dive into some more complex topics. The following sections help add to your SELECT querying skills by showing you how to do some pretty complex searches in your database!

### Querying from multiple tables

In a relational database, data is split into several tables in an attempt to keep data duplication to a minimum. In Chapter 3 of this minibook, I show you how to apply the second normal form rule of database design to create separate Customers and Orders tables so that the customer information didn't need to be duplicated for every order data record. Although this helps reduce data redundancy, it produces a small problem for your application queries.

When your application needs to generate a report for an order, it most likely will need the customer's address information to place on the report. That means now your program needs to retrieve the order information from the Orders table, and the customer information from the Customers table.

You can do that with two separate queries:

1. **Query the Orders table with the** `orderid` **value to retrieve the** `customerid`.

2. **Query the Customers table with the** `customerid` **to retrieve the customer address information for that order.**

However, the two separate queries do take some extra processing time, both in your PHP application code and in the MySQL server. A more efficient way of retrieving that information is to submit a single SELECT statement that retrieves the data from both tables.

To query data from multiple tables in a single SELECT statement, you must specify both tables in the FROM clause. Also, because you're referencing data fields from both tables in the data field list, you must indicate which table each data field comes from. That looks like this:

```
MariaDB [dbtest1]> SELECT orders.orderid, customers.name, customers.address
    -> FROM orders, customers
    -> WHERE orderid = 1000 AND orders.customerid = customers.customerid;
+---------+------------+-------------------------+
| orderid | name       | address                 |
+---------+------------+-------------------------+
|    1000 | Acme Paper | 134 Main St.; Miami, FL |
+---------+------------+-------------------------+
1 row in set (0.00 sec)

MariaDB [dbtest1]>
```

As you can see from this example, it doesn't take long for a seemingly simple SELECT statement to get complex! Let's walk through just what this statement does.

The first line in the query defines the data fields you want to see in the result set output. Because you're using data fields from two tables, you must precede each data field name with the table it comes from.

In the second line, you have to define which tables the data fields come from in the FROM clause. You can list the tables in any order here.

Finally, in the WHERE clause, you have to define the condition that filters out the records you want to display. In this example, there are two conditions that must be met:

>> You need the Orders table data record that meets the specific orderid value you're looking for.

>> You need the Customers table data record that matches the customerid value for that specific order.

You use the logical AND operator to combine the two conditions. The result set contains the data record values that meets both of those conditions.

## Using joins

In the previous example, you had to write a lot of code in the WHERE clause to match the appropriate data record from the Customers table to the Orders table data record information. In a relational database, this is a common thing to do. To help programmers, the SQL designers came up with an alternative way to perform this function.

A database *join* matches related data records in relational database tables without your having to perform all the associated checks in your code. Here's the format for using the join in a SELECT statement:

```
SELECT fieldlist FROM table1 jointype JOIN table2 ON condition
```

The *fieldlist* parameter lists the data fields from the tables to display in the output as usual. The *table1* and *table2* parameters define the two tables to perform the join on. The *jointype* parameter determines the type of join for MySQL to perform. There are three types of joins available in MySQL:

>> INNER JOIN: Only displays data records found in both tables.

>> LEFT JOIN: Displays all records in table1 and the matching data records in table2.

>> RIGHT JOIN: Displays all records in table2 and the matching data records in table1.

The LEFT and RIGHT join types are also commonly referred to as *outer joins.* The order in which you specify the tables and the join type that you use are very important to the join operation.

Finally, the ON condition clause defines the data field relation to use for the join operation.

It's common practice to use the same data field name for data fields in separate tables that contain the same information (such as the customerid data field in the Customers and Orders tables). You can add the NATURAL keyword before the join type to tell MySQL to join using the common data field name. Here's an example of querying the customer information for all the orders using a NATURAL INNER JOIN:

```
MariaDB [dbtest1]> SELECT orders.orderid, customers.name, customers.address
    -> FROM orders NATURAL INNER JOIN customers;
+---------+---------------+------------------------------+
| orderid | name          | address                      |
+---------+---------------+------------------------------+
|    1000 | Acme Paper    | 134 Main St.; Miami, FL      |
|    1001 | Acme Paper    | 134 Main St.; Miami, FL      |
|    1002 | Acme Machines | 264 Oak St.; Los Angeles, CA |
+---------+---------------+------------------------------+
3 rows in set (0.00 sec)

MariaDB [dbtest1]>
```

Now that's a lot less typing to mess with! The result set shows all the data records in the Orders table that have matching customerid data records in the Customers table.

Another way of doing this is to add the USING clause to a JOIN statement:

```
MariaDB [dbtest1]> SELECT orders.orderid, customers.name, customers.address
    -> FROM orders LEFT JOIN customers USING (customerid);
+---------+---------------+------------------------------+
| orderid | name          | address                      |
+---------+---------------+------------------------------+
|    1000 | Acme Paper    | 134 Main St.; Miami, FL      |
|    1001 | Acme Paper    | 134 Main St.; Miami, FL      |
|    1002 | Acme Machines | 264 Oak St.; Los Angeles, CA |
+---------+---------------+------------------------------+
3 rows in set (0.00 sec)

MariaDB [dbtest1]>
```

The USING keyword works with the LEFT and RIGHT joins to specify the data field for the join operation.

WARNING

Using joins the wrong way can cause severe performance issues on your MySQL server, especially when working with large amounts of data (joining all the data records in tables with millions of data records can take quite a long time). I strongly suggest testing out your SELECT statements first before coding them into your web application. That will help give you a feel for any performance issues that may occur. In some situations, it's better to submit multiple smaller SELECT statements than to submit a single complex SELECT statement.

### Using aliases

Having to specify the table and data field names in SELECT statements can get somewhat cumbersome. To help out, you can use the *table alias* feature, which defines a name that represents the full table name within the SELECT statement. Here's the format for using aliases:

```
SELECT fieldlist FROM table AS alias
```

When you define an alias for a table, you can use the alias anywhere within the SELECT statement to reference the full table name. This is especially handy in the long WHERE clauses when you're working with multiple tables:

```
MariaDB [dbtest1]> SELECT t1.orderid, t2.name, t2.address
    -> FROM orders as t1, customers as t2
    -> WHERE t1.orderid = 1000 AND t1.customerid = t2.customerid;
+---------+------------+-------------------------+
| orderid | name       | address                 |
+---------+------------+-------------------------+
|    1000 | Acme Paper | 134 Main St.; Miami, FL |
+---------+------------+-------------------------+
1 row in set (0.00 sec)

MariaDB [dbtest1]>
```

The t1 alias represents the Orders table, and the t2 alias represents the Customers table. Notice that you can use the aliases anywhere in the SELECT statement, even in the data field list!

# Playing It Safe with Data

You've worked hard managing the data contained in the database (or at least your application has!). It would be a tragedy if something happened that corrupted the database so that you couldn't access that data. You never know when a catastrophic event will occur in the computer world, so it's always a good idea to have a duplicate copy of your data handy at all times.

The MySQL server provides a few different methods for backing up and restoring database data. This section walks through how to back up and restore database data in the MySQL server environments.

# Performing data backups

When backing up a MySQL database server, you have a few different options available:

>> Copy the physical files the MySQL server uses to store data and database information.

>> Use MySQL utilities to extract database and table structure information.

>> Use MySQL utilities to extract table data.

>> Use MySQL utilities to extract both the table structure and data.

If you choose to copy the physical file structure of the MySQL server, you'll need to be careful. MySQL uses file locking to protect data as the server is running, so you may not be able to copy all the files required for the server operation at any given time.

Before you try to manually copy the MySQL server files, it's best to stop the MySQL server process from running to ensure all the data files are available and that you can safely copy them. This is called a *cold backup.*

In a cold backup, because you've stopped the MySQL server, web applications can't access the application data, so your website users won't be able to properly interact with your application. If your application has certain downtimes where website visitors won't use it (such as outside of business hours), this is fine, but for most web applications, your website visitors need access 24 hours a day, seven days a week! In those situations a cold backup just won't work.

The alternative is to perform a *hot backup,* which copies database information while the MySQL server is running and the web applications are still in use. Because the server is still running, the backup process can't lock the data tables, so the MySQL server can still process SQL statements, altering the data contained in the databases.

Because of this, the hot backup methods can't copy any of the files associated with the server operations. Instead, all they can do is take snapshots of the data contained within the database at specific moments in time. This type of backup is called a *data export.*

In a data export hot backup, the backup program exports the table structure and any data contained in the table into a text file that you can then copy to a safe location. The text file formats can differ, from placing data in a comma-separated spreadsheet format, to generating SQL statements that you can feed into the MySQL server to re-create the tables.

Each of the MySQL interfaces that you've been working with support data export hot backups. The following sections describe how to use these options within each of the interfaces.

## From the command-line interface

The `mysqldump` command-line utility allows you to quickly and easily export a table structure and data from the command line. The `mysqldump` program is usually included with the other binary programs in MySQL, and you should find it in the same folder as the other MySQL command-line utility files (for XAMPP, that's the `c:\xampp\mysql\bin` folder in Windows, or `/Applications/XAMPP/mysql/bin` in macOS).

Here's the format for the `mysqldump` utility:

```
mysqldump [options] database [tablelist]
```

There are lots of options available for you to customize just how to perform the export. Here are some of the more common ones you may run into:

>> `--add-drop-database`: Add a DROP DATABASE statement in the output to replace any existing databases with the same name.

>> `--add-drop-table`: Add a DROP TABLE statement in the output to replace any existing tables with the same name.

>> `--all-databases`: Backup all the tables from all the databases on the server.

>> `--databases`: List multiple databases to export.

>> `--lock-tables`: Lock the tables during the export.

>> `--password`: Specify the user password, or if empty, prompt for a password.

>> `--tab`: Produce a tab-separated output for the data instead of SQL statements.

>> `--user`: Specify the user account to log into the MySQL server for the export.

Follow these steps to back up the `dbtest1` database tables using the `mysqldump` utility:

**1.** **Open a command line in Windows or a Terminal session in Linux or macOS.**

**2.** **Change to the MySQL folder that contains the MySQL utilities for your installation environment.**

For XAMPP on Windows, that's:

```
cd \xampp\mysql\bin
```

**3.** Run the `mysqldump` utility to export the table data from the `dbtest1` database.

By default, the `mysqldump` utility will output the database contents to the screen. To save it to a file, you must redirect the output to a file. Enter this command:

```
C:\xampp\mysql\bin>mysqldump --user=root --password dbtest1 > dbtest1.sql
Enter password:


C:\xampp\mysql\bin>
```

**4.** View the generated `dbtest1.sql` file using your favorite text editor.

Figure 4-7 shows the results from my database.

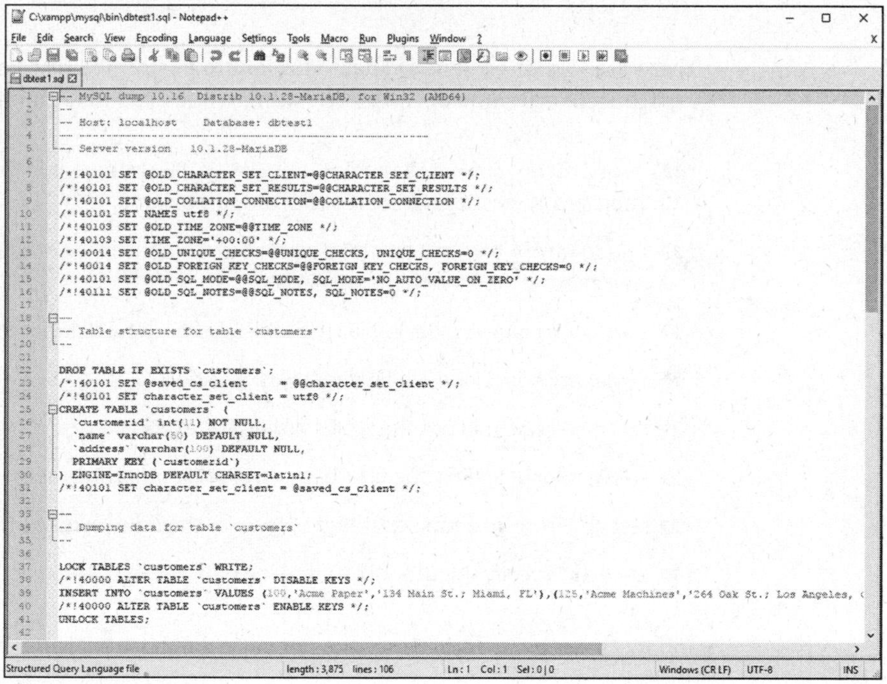

**FIGURE 4-7:**
The output from
the `mysqldump`
utility.

As you peruse through the `dbtest1.sql` file that the `mysqldump` utility generated, you'll probably recognize the SQL statements that it uses. For each table in the database, it generates a CREATE TABLE statement to rebuild the table structure; then it generates an INSERT statement to add each data record from the original table.

## Using Workbench

The MySQL Workbench graphical program provides a nice form for you to use to pick out the mysqldump options for the export. Follow these steps to generate an export file using Workbench:

1. **Ensure that the MySQL server is running, and then start the Workbench tool.**

2. **Click the Data Export link from the Management section in the Navigator window pane.**

   Figure 4-8 shows what the Data Export interface looks like.

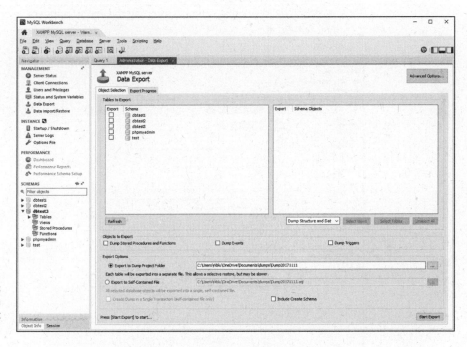

**FIGURE 4-8:**
The Workbench
Data Export
window.

3. **Single-click the dbtest2 database entry in the left-hand window of the Tables to Export section of the main window.**

   The tables contained in the dbtest2 database appear in the right-hand side window.

4. **Select the check box for the dbtest2 database in the left-hand window.**

   This automatically selects the check boxes for the tables it contains.

**5.** Under the right-hand side window, ensure that the drop-down box has the Dump Structure and Data option selected.

**6.** In the Export Options section, select the Export to Self-Contained File radio button and specify the location and name of the .sql file that will contain the export.

The default will create a file in your Documents folder under the dump folder.

Alternatively, you can opt to save the export as a project, which generates multiple files for each table. This allows you some more flexibility when restoring the data, but it's more difficult to manage the exported files.

**7.** Click the Advanced Options button at the top of the window.

A complete list of options for customizing the export appears, as shown in Figure 4-9.

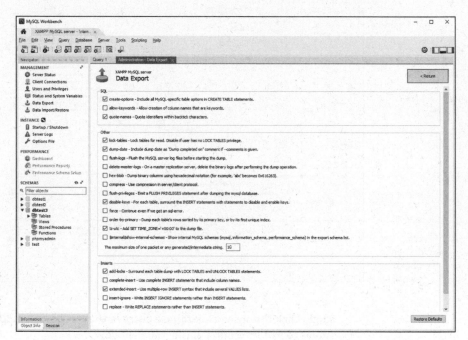

**FIGURE 4-9:**
The Workbench Data Export advanced options window.

**8.** Click the Return button to return to the main Data Export interface window.

**9.** Click the Start Export button at the bottom of the window.

A dialog box appears, prompting you for the root user account password.

**10.** **For XAMPP, leave it empty and click the OK button.**

The Export Progress window appears, showing the progress of the export.

**11.** **Use your favorite text editor to view the** `.sql` **file that was generated by the export.**

Using a graphical interface certainly makes the data export process much simpler!

## Using phpMyAdmin

The phpMyAdmin tool has an excellent graphical interface for handling data exports. After you open the phpMyAdmin tool, click the Export button at the top of the main web page. This produces the interface shown in Figure 4-10.

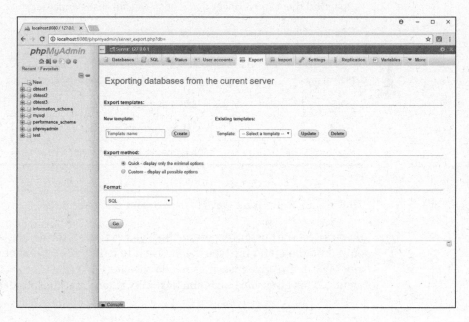

**FIGURE 4-10:**
The phpMyAdmin export web page.

The main export page allows you to choose from two options:

>> A quick export, which exports all the tables from all the databases using the mysqldump default options.

>> A custom export, which allows you to pick and choose the databases and options for the export.

One nice feature about the phpMyAdmin export interface is that it allows you to select the format of the export file from a long list of options, shown in Table 4-1.

**TABLE 4-1** **The phpMyAdmin Export Formats**

| Format | Description |
| --- | --- |
| CodeGen | The NHibernate file format |
| CSV | The comma-separated values format |
| CSV for Microsoft Excel | The CSV format with customizations for Microsoft Excel |
| Microsoft Word 2000 | The Microsoft 2000 Word document |
| JSON | The JavaScript Object Notation format |
| LaTeX | The Lamport TeX format commonly used for academic publications |
| MediaWiki Table | The Wikipedia table format |
| OpenDocument Spreadsheet | The open spreadsheet standard format |
| OpenDocument Text | The open document standard format |
| PDF | The Adobe Portable Document Format |
| PHP array | PHP code to create an array of the data |
| SQL | SQL statements to rebuild the table |
| Texy! | XHTML formatted data |
| YAML | A data serialization format that is human-readable |

That's a lot of different ways to export your database data!

If you select the Custom export method, you can select the databases to export, the output method (and file type if you save it to a file), the format of the output, and any MySQL directives (such as to add the DROP DATABASE or DROP TABLE statements). This gives you maximum flexibility when creating your database backups!

## Restoring your data

Backups are only good if you have the ability to use them to restore the database. Testing out the restore capabilities of your system before you have a catastrophic event is always a good idea.

Each of the MySQL interface methods provides a different way of restoring data from the backup files. This section walks through each of these methods.

## From the command-line interface

To restore a database using the SQL dump file generated by the `mysqldump` utility, just pass the file into the input of the `mysql` command-line tool using the command line redirect symbol (`<`). That looks like this:

```
mysql --user=root --password dbtest1 < dbtest1.sql
```

The MySQL server will process the SQL statements contained in the `dbtest1.sql` file and apply them against the database you specify on the command line. This is a great way to move a database to a new database, either on the same server or on a remote server!

If you opt to save only the table data using either the tab or comma-separated formats, you can read the data into a table by using the `LOAD DATA INFILE` SQL statement:

```
LOAD DATA INFILE filename INTO TABLE table
```

The data fields in the file must match the order in which they appear in the table.

## From Workbench

The MySQL Workbench tool provides a graphical interface for loading the backup file. After you open Workbench, click the Data Import/Restore link in the Management section of the Navigator window pane. Figure 4-11 shows what that window looks like.

In the Import Options section, select either the project folder or the export file that you created with the Export feature. Select the database to use for the import in the Default Target Schema drop-down box.

If you opted to save the backup as a project, you can customize the restore by selecting exactly which objects to restore. If you opted to save the backup as a single file as in the example, you must restore all the objects in the export file.

After you've selected the export file and options, click the Start Import button at the bottom of the window to begin the import process. That makes restoring table data almost simple!

## From phpMyAdmin

Importing data from an export backup using phpMyAdmin is also a fairly simple process. After you open the phpMyAdmin web tool, click the Import button at the top of the web page. This produces the Import Web page, as shown in Figure 4-12.

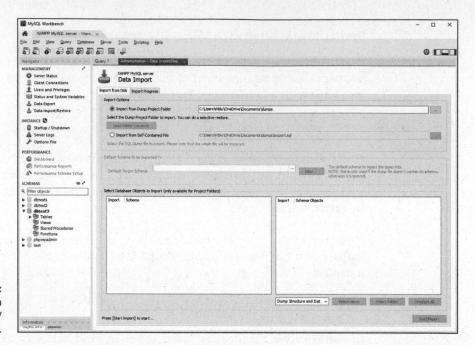

FIGURE 4-11:
The Workbench
Data Import/
Restore window.

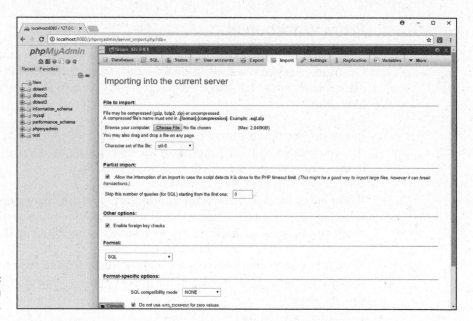

FIGURE 4-12:
The phpMyAdmin
Import web page.

From here, you can browse to find the export file that you generated, along with selecting some options for the import, such as the file format. After you've made your selections, click the Go button at the bottom of the web page to start the import.

IN THIS CHAPTER

» **Examining the PHP database libraries**

» **Connecting to the MySQL server**

» **Submitting SQL queries**

» **Retrieving result set data**

» **Exploring a PHP database application**

Chapter **5**

# Communicating with the Database from PHP Scripts

In the previous chapter, I show you how to insert, delete, and manage data in a MySQL database. Now that you have your content all ready for your application, there's just one more piece to add in the assembly line to complete your dynamic web applications. This chapter explores how you can interact with the MySQL database server from your PHP programs to retrieve the stored data, add new data records, and remove existing data records. This chapter first explores how PHP interacts with databases in general. Then it focuses on the most popular method used for accessing MySQL databases from web applications: the `mysqli` library.

## Database Support in PHP

The PHP programming language doesn't have any functions for accessing databases directly built into the language. However, there are plenty of PHP extension libraries available to help out. The PHP extensions provide additional functionality to the main PHP language by incorporating add-on libraries (see Book 4, Chapter 1).

PHP has a long history of providing library support for accessing different types of databases, making it a popular programming language to use with lots of different database servers. Table 5-1 lists the database server libraries currently available to use with your PHP code.

TABLE 5-1

## PHP Database Extension Libraries

| Library | Description |
|---|---|
| CUBRID | An open-source relational database with object extensions |
| DB++ | A non-SQL-based relational database created by Concept asa |
| dBase | An old proprietary database file format used mostly for microcomputers |
| FireBird/InterBase | A relational database based on the ISO SQL-2003 standard |
| IBM DB2 | A proprietary IBM relational database format |
| Informix | An old relational database format acquired by IBM in 2001 |
| Ingres | An open-source relational database designed for large applications |
| MaxDB | An ANSI SQL-92-compliant relational database used by the SAP software |
| Mongo | An open-source document-oriented database |
| mSQL | A lightweight SQL-based database created by Hughes Technologies |
| MySQL | The open-source MySQL database server |
| OCI8 | The Oracle database server |
| PostgreSQL | An open-source database based on the original Ingres database |
| SQLite | An embeddable database system for small environments |
| SQLite3 | An update to the SQLite database system |
| SQLSRV | The Microsoft SQL database server |
| tokyo_tyrant | An open-source distributed database system |

In addition to the specific database extensions available in PHP, there are also three abstract database interfaces available:

>> **DBA:** A library for accessing Berkeley DB–style database files

>> **ODBC:** A library for interfacing with the Open Database Connectivity (ODBC) standard, originally developed by Microsoft and popular on Windows platforms

>> **PDO:** The PHP Data Objects (PDO) library, which uses a lightweight interface to access different types of databases, based on an installed driver

The benefit of using an abstract database interface in your PHP code is that you can easily change the underlying database your application uses without having to change any of your PHP code. If you use a specific database extension, such as for MySQL, and you need to run your application using a different database server, you need to recode all your database interactions. However, with the abstract database extension you can keep your code and just change the underlying database driver. If you're developing applications for use in multiple environments, this is definitely the way to go.

Because the MySQL database server is the focus of this book, this chapter shows you how to code PHP to interact with a MySQL database using the MySQL-specific database interface. If you decide to use another database server for your applications, you'll be able to apply the same techniques you learn here to the other PHP database libraries.

# Using the mysqli Library

The original MySQL database extension library created for PHP was called *php_ mysql.* It had some limitations, but it was widely popular in developing dynamic web applications across the Internet that used the MySQL database.

As time went on, developers worked on improving the limitations of the php_ mysql library. Eventually, enough changes accumulated to warrant a new library package release. That release was named the *php_mysqli* library (the added *i* stands for "improved"). Starting in PHP version 7, the original php_mysql library has been removed, so it's not recommended that any new application development use it. This section walks through how to use the php_mysqli library to interface your PHP programs to a MySQL database server.

One of the added features of the php_mysqli library is that it supports both procedural language and object-oriented language coding styles. That means you can use the library both as functions in procedural programs and as an object in object-oriented PHP programs.

For the procedural program environment, you just run separate functions for each action. Most of the functions require that you pass the database connection handle along as a parameter. For the object-oriented program environment, you must instantiate a new mysqli object, and then run methods using that object. For each action, you need to interact with the MySQL database. In the following sections, I show you how to use both coding methods.

## Connecting to the database

The first thing you need to do from your PHP code is to establish a connection to the MySQL database server. The connection creates a database session, from which you can submit queries and retrieve result sets.

In the procedural coding method, you establish the connection using the mysqli_connect() function:

```
$con = mysqli_connect(host, user, password, database, port, socket);
```

That's a lot of information to pass for the connection! Fortunately, for most situations, you don't need to include the port or socket values, because those are standard. As you can probably tell from the parameter names, you must specify the host name or IP address of the MySQL server, a userid to log into the server, along with its associated password. The *database* parameter allows you to specify a default database for the session. A typical connection statement would look like this:

```
$con = mysqli_connect("localhost", "user1", "myL0ngP@ssword", "dbtest1");
```

If the connection is successful, the $con variable contains what's called the *connection handle.* You must use it to reference the connection session in some of the other php_mysqli library functions.

If you need to change the default database used in the connection, use the mysqli_select_db() function:

```
mysqli_select_db(handle, database)
```

As you can tell from the function format, for the first parameter you need the connection handle from the original database connection:

```
mysqli_select_db($con, "dbtest2");
```

In object-oriented coding, instead of using the `mysqli_connect()` function, you must instantiate a new instance of the `myslqi` object:

```
$db = new mysqli("localhost", "user1", "myL0ngP@ssword", "dbtest1");
```

The parameters available are the same as for the `mysqli_connect()` function. However, this time the $db variable contains an instance of the `myslqi` object instead of a connection handle.

To select a new default database for the session, you run the `select_db()` method from the $db object you created:

```
$db->select_db("dbtest2");
```

**TIP**

Notice that the names of the procedural functions and object-oriented methods are similar. That holds true for the rest of the functions and methods you'll use in the php_mysqli library, so it's relatively easy to move back and forth between the two coding methods.

**WARNING**

In both the procedural and object-oriented coding methods, you must enter the user ID and password to connect to the database. Unfortunately, you must do that in plain text. This is a bit of a security risk. If anyone has access to your source code, they could gain access to the database. First, make sure the user ID configured on the MySQL server is locked down to a specific host location (don't use a wildcard character for the location). The next step is to move the connection statement to an out-of-the-way place, such as in a separate include file; then use the PHP `include()` function to add it to your programs. That at least limits the visibility of the user ID and password information to a single file. If your server environment permits, you may even be able to hide the include file outside of the `DocumentRoot` folder of your web server.

## Closing the connection

When you open a connection to the MySQL server, the connection remains open for the duration of that program. When the PHP server reaches the end of your PHP code for that web page, it automatically closes the connection.

The MySQL server has a limited number of client connections that it supports (defined by the MySQL configuration file). If you're coding in a high-volume environment that has lots of customers accessing your web application at the same time, it may be crucial that your application releases the MySQL server connection as soon as possible.

If you're working in that type of environment, you can manually close the MySQL server connection as soon as you're done using it to help free up more connections as soon as possible. You do that by using the mysqli_close() function. Just specify the connection handle as the sole parameter:

```
mysqli_close($con);
```

If you're working with object-oriented programming code, just use the close() method on the mysqli instance:

```
$db->close();
```

Again, for most normal situations you don't need to worry about closing the MySQL server connection, it's just nice to know you have that option available if you need it!

## Submitting queries

After you establish a connection to the MySQL server, you can start submitting SQL statements. You can submit any type of statement, just as if you were working from the MySQL command-line interface.

The procedural function you use to submit a query to the MySQL server is the mysqli_query() function. Here's the format:

```
$conresult = mysqli_query(handle, query);
```

The handle parameter is the connection handle created when you connected to the MySQL server. The query parameter is the text SQL statement. Unless you're submitting a very short SQL statement, it has become common practice to store the SQL statement in a variable so as not to make the mysqli_query() statement overly complicated:

```
$query = "SELECT * FROM employees";
$dbresult = mysqli_query($con, $query);
```

The mysqli_query() function returns what's called a *resource handle.* You must store that in a variable to be able to access the data in the result set returned by the query.

In the object-oriented coding world, you use the query() method of the mysqli connection instance to submit SQL statements:

```
$query = "SELECT * FROM employees";
$result = $db->query($query);
```

The query() method returns a result set object, which you must store in a variable to be able to access the data contained in the result set.

**TIP**

The SQL statement that you send to the MySQL doesn't need a semicolon at the end. The semicolon is used by the MySQL command-line interface to indicate the end of the statement. The mysqli_query() function already knows the end of the SQL statement because it will only accept one query per text string. That also helps block SQL-injection types of attacks against your system.

## Retrieving data

If you submit a SQL statement that will return data (such as a SELECT statement), the result set handle returned will point to the data. You can then retrieve the data using other mysqli library functions. There are actually quite a few different ways to retrieve that data using different functions or methods. Table 5-2 lists the different functions and methods available.

**TABLE 5-2** The mysqli Data Retrieval Functions and Methods

| Function | Method | Description |
|---|---|---|
| mysqli_fetch_all | fetch_all() | Retrieves all the data records in the result set as an array |
| mysqli_fetch_array | fetch_array() | Retrieves the current data record in the result set as an array |
| mysqli_fetch_assoc | fetch_assoc() | Retrieves the current data record in the result set as an associative array |
| mysqli_fetch_field_direct() | fetch_field_direct() | Retrieves the metadata for a specific field in a result set |
| mysqli_fetch_field() | fetch_field() | Retrieves the metadata for a single field in a result set |
| mysqli_fetch_fields() | fetch_fields() | Returns the metadata for all the fields in a result set as an array |
| mysqli_fetch_object() | fetch_object() | Retrieves the current data record of a result set as an object |
| mysqli_fetch_row() | fetch_row() | Retrieves the current data record of a result set as a numeric array |
| mysqli_field_seek() | field_seek() | Sets the result set pointer to a specific field in the current data record |
| mysqli_free() | free() | Releases the memory associated with the result set handle |

Communicating with the
Database from PHP Scripts

The mysqli _fetch family of statements retrieves the data records from the result set and places them in an array variable. The type of array variable used depends on the function you use:

>> The mysqli_fetch_array() function creates an associative array, a numeric array, or both, based on the second parameter (MYSQLI_ASSOC, MYSQLI_NUM, or MYSQLI_BOTH).

>> The mysqli_fetch_assoc() function creates an associative array, using the data field names as the array keys.

>> The mysqli_fetch_row() function creates a numeric array, using numeric indexes for each data field (starting at 0, and using the data field order specified in the table or SELECT statement data field).

The fetch statements are also somewhat unique in that they allow you to walk your way through the result set one data record at a time. Each time you call the fetch statement, it returns the data from the current data record in the result set; then it moves a pointer to the next data record in the result set for the next call. When it reaches the end of the result set data, it returns a NULL value, making it ideal to use the fetch statements in a while() loop:

```
$query = "SELECT * FROM employees";
$conresult = mysqli_query($con, $query);
while($row = mysqli_fetch_assoc($conresult)) {
echo "<p>Employee last name: $row['lastname']<br>\n";
    echo "Employee first name: $row['firstname']<br>\n";
    echo "Start date: $row['startdate']<br>\n";
    echo "Salary: $row['salary']</p>\n";
}
```

Or if you're using the object-oriented programming style:

```
$query = "SELECT * FROM employees";
$dbresult = $db->query($query);
while( $row = $dbresult->fetch_assoc()) {
    echo "<p>Employee last name: $row['lastname']<br>\n";
    echo "Employee first name: $row['firstname']<br>\n";
    echo "Start date: $row['startdate']<br>\n";
    echo "Salary: $row['salary']</p>\n";
}
```

The mysqli_fetch_assoc() function returns the data record as an associative array value, which you then store in an array variable. The while loop continues until there are no more data records in the result set; then it drops out so the program can continue.

# Being prepared

You can submit any type of SQL statements using the `mysqli_query()` function, but it's not recommended to use that for submitting `INSERT` statements. All too often, beginning PHP coders retrieve data from an HTML form, place the data directly in an `INSERT` statement string, then submit the string to the MySQL server, like this:

```
$empid = $_POST['employeeid'];
$lname = $_POST['lastname'];
$fname = $_POST['firstname'];
$start = $_POST['startdate'];
$birth = $_POST['birthdate'];
$salary = $_POST['salary'];
$query = "INSERT INTO employees VALUES ($empid, '$lname', '$fname',
   '$start','$birth', $salary)";
$dbresult = $db->query($query);
```

This method works, but it's a dangerous way of inserting data into your database! There's no guarantee that the person using the HTML form will enter the correct data into all the data fields (either by accident or on purpose). There's also no guarantee the data submitted in the form won't contain malicious characters meant to cause issues with the database.

The safer way of submitting data in an `INSERT` statement is to use a *prepared statement,* which defines a template of the query you want to execute on the MySQL server, and then sends the data separate from the template. The MySQL server stores the prepared statement, and then matches the submitted data against the template. This helps filter out malicious data. Plus, it can help speed up executing multiple `INSERT` statements on the server. You just submit one template statement. Then you can apply multiple data statements against the same template.

With a prepared statement, you create the query string as normal, but instead of including data values, you use a question mark as a placeholder for each value, like this:

```
$query = "INSERT INTO employees VALUES (?, ?, ?, ?, ?, ?)";
```

Then you use the `myqli_prepare()` function to submit it:

```
$constmt = mysqli_prepare($con, $query);
```

If you're using the object-oriented coding style, it looks like this:

```
$dbstmt = $db->prepare($query);
```

Now the MySQL server has the prepared statement, but it doesn't have any data to plug into it. To do that you use the `mysqli_stmt_bind_param()` function:

```
mysqli_stmt_bind_param($constmt, "issssi", $empid, $lname, $fname, $start,
    $birth, $salary);
```

The first parameter is the result from the prepared statement you submitted. The second parameter is somewhat odd. It defines the data type of each of the data values as a single character in a string value:

>> b: A blob data type value

>> i: An integer data type value

>> d: A double data type value

>> s: A string data type value

In this example, I define the first data value as an integer, the next four as string values, and the final data value as an integer.

After defining the data types, you just list the values for the data fields, in the order they appear in the prepared statement.

If you're following along in the object-oriented code style, here's how to bind the parameters:

```
$dbstmt->bind_param("isssi", $empid, $lname, $fname, $start, $birth, $salary);
```

After you bind the data values to the prepared statement, there's still one more step — you must execute the prepared statement:

```
mysql_bind_execute($constmt);
```

Or if you're using the object-oriented coding style, it looks like this:

```
$dbstmt->execute();
```

This is what links the data to the template in the MySQL server and processes the statement.

Using prepared statements for INSERT statements is crucial, but you can also use them for submitting SELECT statements if you don't trust the data that you're using in the WHERE clause.

This can be the result of allowing your website visitors to enter text to search for in the database. For example, instead of writing this code:

```php
$empid = $_POST['employeeid'];
$query = "SELECT * FROM employees WHERE employeeid = $empid";
$result = $db->query($query);
$row = $db->fetch_assoc($result);
```

You can use a prepared statement and write it this way:

```php
$empid = $_POST['employeeid'];
$query = "SELECT * FROM employees WHERE empid = ?";
$dbstmt = $db->prepare($query);
$dbstmt->bind_param("i", $empid);
$dbstmt->execute();
$dbstmt->bind_result($empid, $lname, $fname, $start, $birth, $salary);
$dbstmt->fetch();
```

When you submit the SELECT statement using a prepared statement, you must bind the PHP variables for the result set data fields using the bind_result() method (or mysqli_stmt_bind_result() for procedural style coding). Then you can retrieve the data records in the result set using the fetch() method (or mysqli_stmt_fetch() for procedural style coding).

## Checking for errors

Whenever you submit any type of action to the MySQL server, it's always a good idea to ensure that it completed properly before continuing on with your program. There are a couple of different ways to do that.

One method is to test the connection handle or result handle for a NULL value. If the connection or query fails, the handle will be set to NULL:

```php
$con = mysqli_connect("localhost", "user1", "MyL0ngP@ssword", "dbtest1");
if (!$con) {
    echo "Sorry, there was a problem connecting";
    exit;
}
```

Or for procedural-style coding:

```
$db = new mysqli("localhost", "user1", "MyL0ngP@ssword", "dbtest1");
if (!$db) {
    echo "Sorry, there was a problem connecting";
    exit;
}
```

This allows you to halt the program immediately without trying to submit any further statements. The downside is that if the connection fails, the connection statement will generate an ugly PHP error message. If you'd like to suppress the error message, you can precede the code with an ampersand (@), like this:

```
@ $con = mysqli_connect("localhost", "user1", "MyL0ngP@ssword", "dbtest1");
```

Or:

```
@ $db = new mysqli("localhost", "user1", "MyL0ngP@ssword", "dbtest1");
```

The leading ampersand tells PHP to suppress any error output that may be generated from the statement.

The other way of stopping things when the connection fails is to use the PHP die( ) function:

```
@ $con = mysqli_connect("localhost", "user1", "MyL0ngP@ssword", "dbtest1") or
  die("Sorry, something went wrong with the connection");
```

The logical OR statement will only trigger if the connection statement fails, running the die( ) function, which displays the string in the web page output.

Sometimes when you submit queries that fail, it helps to be able to see the exact error message the query generated. You can do that using the mysqli_error( ) function:

```
$conresult = mysqli_query($con, $query)
if (!$conresult) {
    echo mysqli_error($con);
}
```

Or for object-oriented programming:

```
$dbresult = $db->query($query);
if (!$dbresult) {
    echo $db->error();
}
```

The `mysqli_error()` function returns the detailed error message generated by the MySQL server when a submitted SQL statement fails. Often that helps shed some additional light on just what went wrong, and can be invaluable when troubleshooting your SQL code!

**WARNING**

The `mysqli_error()` function is useful for troubleshooting code, but it's also useful for attackers to gain inside information on your database structure. After you're done developing the application code, it's best to remove any `mysqli_error()` functions you have in the code to prevent an attacker from exploiting them.

## Miscellaneous functions

Submitting queries to the MySQL server and retrieving the data records from the result set consists of the bulk of your database requirements, but there are a few more handy functions available in the php_mysqli library that can be useful in your application coding. Table 5-3 lists some of the more common ones that you may want to use.

**TABLE 5-3**

### Additional myslqi Library Functions

| Method | Description |
|---|---|
| autocommit | Turn on or off the autocommit feature in MySQL, which allows you to submit multi-statement transactions |
| change_user | Changes the user account for the session |
| character_set_name | Returns the character set used for the connection |
| commit | Commits a transaction |
| more_results | Checks if there are more query results from a multi-query submission |
| multi_query | Allows you to submit more than one query at a time |
| next_result | Prepares the next data record result from a multi-query |
| real_escape_string | Escapes special characters in a string to make them safe to use in an SQL query |
| rollback | Rolls back the current transaction |
| set_charset | Sets the default character set used for the session |

As you can probably guess, the procedural style names for these methods are the same, just with the `mysqli_` prefix.

The `real_escape_string()` method is useful for cleaning up text input to use in an `INSERT` statement. It places a backslash in front of any character that will cause trouble when sent to the MySQL server. This is especially useful with data that may include single or double quotes.

Though not a method, the `num_rows` property is handy when you just need the number of data records returned in a result set. Because it's a property and not a method, you don't include the parenthesis after it:

```
$query = "SELECT * FROM employees";
$dbresult = $db->query($query);
if ($dbresult->num_rows > 0) {
    echo "There were $dbresult->num_rows data records in the table";
} else {
    echo "Sorry, there weren't any data records returned";
}
```

The procedural style is a little different in that it uses the `num_rows` as a function:

```
if (mysqli_num_rows($conresult) > 0)
```

The `mysqli_num_rows()` function returns the same information, but you just use it as a function instead of a property.

## Putting It All Together

Now that you've seen the basics of using the php_mysqli library to interact with the MySQL server, let's walk through a short web application that does that. First, you need a database with some data. Follow these steps to create that:

1. **Ensure that both the Apache and MySQL servers are running.**

    If you're using XAMPP, start the Control Panel and click the Start buttons for both Apache and MySQL.

2. **Open the MySQL command-line interface.**

    For Windows, open a Command Prompt session and enter these commands:

    ```
    cd \xampp\mysql\bin
    mysql --user=root --password
    ```

For the macOS environment, open a Terminal session and enter these commands:

```
cd /Applications/XAMPP/mysql/bin
./mysql --user=root --password
```

**3.** **Press the Enter key at the MySQL password prompt.**

**4.** **Enter the following statement to create the** apptest1 **database:**

```
MariaDB [(none)]> CREATE DATABASE apptest1;
Query OK, 1 row affected (0.00 sec)
```

**5.** **Enter the following statement to create the** appuser1 **user account:**

```
MariaDB [(none)]> CREATE USER appuser1@localhost IDENTIFIED BY
    "MyL0ngP@ssword";
Query OK, 0 rows affected (0.07 sec)
```

**6.** **Enter the following statement to grant privileges to the** apptest1
**database for the** appuser1 **user account:**

```
MariaDB [(none)]> GRANT SELECT,INSERT,UPDATE,DELETE ON apptest1.*
    -> TO appuser1@localhost;
Query OK, 0 rows affected (0.00 sec)
```

**7.** **Enter the** USE **statement to change the default database to the** apptest1
**database:**

```
MariaDB [(none)]> USE apptest1;
Database changed
```

**8.** **Enter the following statement to create the Bowlers table:**

```
MariaDB [apptest1]> CREATE TABLE bowlers
    -> (bowlerid int primary key,
    -> name varchar(100),
    -> address varchar(200),
    -> phone varchar(20));
Query OK, 0 rows affected (0.28 sec)
```

**9.** **Enter the following statement to create the Games table:**

```
MariaDB [apptest1]> CREATE TABLE games
    -> (gameid int auto_increment primary key,
    -> bowlerid int,
    -> score int);
Query OK, 0 rows affected (0.22 sec)
```

10. **Now you can start entering some data into your tables.**

Here's some sample data for the Bowlers table:

```
MariaDB [apptest1]> INSERT INTO bowlers VALUES
    -> (100, 'Rich', '123 Main St.', '555-1234');
Query OK, 1 row affected (0.08 sec)

MariaDB [apptest1]> INSERT INTO bowlers VALUES
    -> (101, 'Barbara', '123 Main St.', '555-5678');
Query OK, 1 row affected (0.10 sec)

MariaDB [apptest1]> INSERT INTO bowlers VALUES
    -> (102, 'Katie Jane', '567 Oak St.', '555-0123');
Query OK, 1 row affected (0.10 sec)

MariaDB [apptest1]> INSERT INTO bowlers VALUES
    -> (103, 'Jessica', '901 Elm St.', '555-3256');
Query OK, 1 row affected (0.09 sec)
```

11. **Add some data for the Games table for the bowlers:**

```
MariaDB [apptest1]> INSERT INTO games (bowlerid, score) VALUES (100, 110);
Query OK, 1 row affected (0.10 sec)

MariaDB [apptest1]> INSERT INTO games (bowlerid, score) VALUES (100, 115);
Query OK, 1 row affected (0.08 sec)

MariaDB [apptest1]> INSERT INTO games (bowlerid, score) VALUES (100, 105);
Query OK, 1 row affected (0.05 sec)

MariaDB [apptest1]> INSERT INTO games (bowlerid, score) VALUES (101, 110);
Query OK, 1 row affected (0.11 sec)

MariaDB [apptest1]> INSERT INTO games (bowlerid, score) VALUES (101, 112);
Query OK, 1 row affected (0.06 sec)

MariaDB [apptest1]> INSERT INTO games (bowlerid, score) VALUES (101, 130);
Query OK, 1 row affected (0.10 sec)

MariaDB [apptest1]> INSERT INTO games (bowlerid, score) VALUES (102, 115);
Query OK, 1 row affected (0.11 sec)

MariaDB [apptest1]> INSERT INTO games (bowlerid, score) VALUES (102, 125);
Query OK, 1 row affected (0.09 sec)
```

```
MariaDB [apptest1]> INSERT INTO games (bowlerid, score) VALUES (102, 140);
Query OK, 1 row affected (0.08 sec)

MariaDB [apptest1]> INSERT INTO games (bowlerid, score) VALUES (103, 135);
Query OK, 1 row affected (0.08 sec)

MariaDB [apptest1]> INSERT INTO games (bowlerid, score) VALUES (103, 138);
Query OK, 1 row affected (0.09 sec)

MariaDB [apptest1]> INSERT INTO games (bowlerid, score) VALUES (103, 130);
Query OK, 1 row affected (0.08 sec)
```

**12.** Exit the MySQL command-line interface by entering the exit statement:

```
MariaDB [apptest1]> exit;
C:\xampp\mysql\bin>
```

**13.** Close the Command Prompt or Terminal session.

Now that you have some sample data, you can code an application to use the data! Follow these steps to create a simple application that reads the Bowlers table and then calculates the average score for each bowler on your team:

**1.** Open your favorite text editor, program editor, or integrated development environment (IDE) package.

**2.** Enter the following code into the editor window:

```
<!DOCTYPE html>
<html>
<head>
<title>PHP Test Web Page</title>
<style>
table, th, td {
    border: 1px solid black;
    border-collapse: collapse;
    text-align: center;
}
</style>
</head>
<body>
<h1>My Bowling Team</h1>
<CDATAtable>
<tr><th>Bowler</th><th>Games Played</th><th>Average</th></tr>
<?php
$db = new mysqli("localhost", "appuser1", "MyL0ngP@ssword", "apptest1");
```

```
if (!$db) {
    echo "Sorry, I could not connect to the database server";
     exit;
}

$query = "SELECT bowlerid, name FROM bowlers ORDER BY name";
$result = $db->query($query);
while($row = $result->fetch_assoc()) {
    $bowlerid = $row['bowlerid'];
    $name = $row['name'];

    $query2 = "SELECT COUNT(score) AS games, AVG(score) AS average FROM
    games" .
        " WHERE bowlerid = $bowlerid";
    $result2 = $db->query($query2);
    $row2 = $result2->fetch_assoc();
$games = $row2['games'];
    $average = $row2['average'];

    echo "<tr><td>$name</td><td>$games</td><td>$average</td>\n";
}
?>
</CDATAtable>
</body>
</html>
```

3. **Save the file as** phpapptest.php **in the** DocumentRoot **folder for your web server.**

   If you're using XAMPP on Windows, that's c:\xampp\htdocs. For XAMPP on macOS, that's /Applications/XAMPP/htdocs.

4. **Ensure that the Apache and MySQL servers are still running.**

5. **Open your browser and enter the following URL:**

   ```
   http://localhost:8080/phpapptest.php
   ```

   You may need to modify the TCP port in the URL to match your web server.

6. **Observe the output in the web page.**

7. **Open the MySQL command-line interface again and add some new data records.**

   Create a new bowler, along with some new games scores.

**8.** Refresh the browser window and observe the output.

**9.** Stop the Apache and MySQL servers, close out the XAPP Control Panel, and close your browser when you're done.

Figure 5-1 shows the results that you should have seen in your browser window.

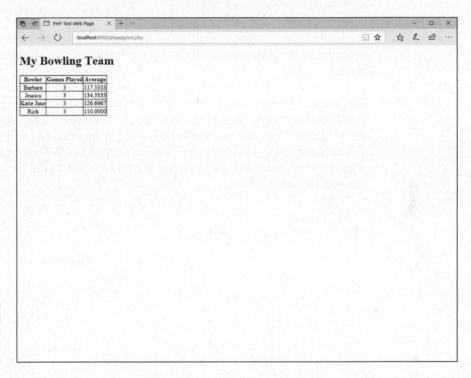

**FIGURE 5-1:**
The output
from the
phpapptest.php
program.

The PHP code first submitted a SELECT statement to retrieve the bowlerid and name data field values for each bowler in the Bowlers table:

```
$query = "SELECT bowlerid, name FROM bowlers ORDER BY name";
```

Then the code iterates through that result set using the fetch_assoc() method:

```
while($row = $result->fetch_assoc()) {
```

For each iteration in the Bowlers table, the code submits another SELECT statement, using the MySQL COUNT() and AVG() built-in functions to determine the number of data records for the bowler, and the average of the score data field values:

```
$query2 = "SELECT COUNT(score) AS games, AVG(score) AS average FROM games" . "
    WHERE bowlerid = $bowlerid";
```

Remember that the dot at the end of the statement is the string concatenation operator, so you can split this long SQL statement into two lines to make it easier to read.

Because this SELECT statement returns only one data record for each bowler, you don't need to iterate through the result set, because there's just one data record in the result set. The code uses the fetch_assoc() function to retrieve the data field values (notice that it uses the alias names assigned to the data fields in the SELECT statement) and uses the echo statement to output the table row HTML code with the embedded data. Fancy!

# 6

# Creating Object-Oriented Programs

# Contents at a Glance

**CHAPTER 1: Designing an Object-Oriented Application** . . . . . . 563

Determining Application Requirements. . . . . . . . . . . . . . . . . . . . . . 563
Creating the Application Database . . . . . . . . . . . . . . . . . . . . . . . . 565
Designing the Application Objects . . . . . . . . . . . . . . . . . . . . . . . . 571
Designing the Application Layout . . . . . . . . . . . . . . . . . . . . . . . . 579
Coding the Website Layout . . . . . . . . . . . . . . . . . . . . . . . . . . . . 582

**CHAPTER 2: Implementing an Object-Oriented Application** . . . . . . . . . . . . . . . . . . . . . . . . . . . . . . . . . . 593

Working with Events . . . . . . . . . . . . . . . . . . . . . . . . . . . . . . . . 593
Bidder Object Events. . . . . . . . . . . . . . . . . . . . . . . . . . . . . . . . 595
Item Object Events . . . . . . . . . . . . . . . . . . . . . . . . . . . . . . . . . 605
Logging Out of a Web Application. . . . . . . . . . . . . . . . . . . . . . . . 614
Testing Web Applications. . . . . . . . . . . . . . . . . . . . . . . . . . . . . 616

**CHAPTER 3: Using AJAX** . . . . . . . . . . . . . . . . . . . . . . . . . . . . . . . . 619

Getting to Know AJAX . . . . . . . . . . . . . . . . . . . . . . . . . . . . . . . 619
Communicating Using JavaScript . . . . . . . . . . . . . . . . . . . . . . . . 621
Using the jQuery AJAX Library . . . . . . . . . . . . . . . . . . . . . . . . . . 629
Transferring Data in AJAX. . . . . . . . . . . . . . . . . . . . . . . . . . . . . 635
Modifying the AuctionHelper Application . . . . . . . . . . . . . . . . . . . 643

**CHAPTER 4: Extending WordPress** . . . . . . . . . . . . . . . . . . . . . . . . . 651

Getting Acquainted with WordPress. . . . . . . . . . . . . . . . . . . . . . . 651
Installing WordPress . . . . . . . . . . . . . . . . . . . . . . . . . . . . . . . . 655
Examining the Dashboard . . . . . . . . . . . . . . . . . . . . . . . . . . . . . 662
Using WordPress . . . . . . . . . . . . . . . . . . . . . . . . . . . . . . . . . . 664
Exploring the World of Plugins . . . . . . . . . . . . . . . . . . . . . . . . . . 669
Creating Your Own Widget. . . . . . . . . . . . . . . . . . . . . . . . . . . . . 674

# Chapter **1**

# Designing an Object-Oriented Application

I f you've been reading through this book in order, the previous five minibooks have walked you through the basics of HTML, CSS, JavaScript, PHP, and the MySQL database server. Now that you've seen all the pieces that are required to create a dynamic web application, this minibook puts them all together to actually create a dynamic web application!

Before you dive too deep into the coding, though, it's a good idea to sit down and map out just what type of application you want to create. This chapter walks you through the process of designing a dynamic web application. First, it shows you how to obtain the functional requirements for the application. It's important to know what you're building before you start building it! Next, the chapter discusses building the database elements required for the application and how to build the PHP objects required to track the data. The chapter finishes by discussing how to design the user interface part of the web application and building the rough template for the application website.

## Determining Application Requirements

The first step to writing a dynamic web application is to define the functional requirements for the application. Many a project has gone awry by not defining exactly what is expected by the customers or users of the application before the coding starts.

For this project, I'm going to task you with creating the AuctionHelper web application to help out at a school silent auction. Silent auctions are popular fundraising events used by many schools and other nonprofit organizations. In a silent auction, items are donated by local businesses to support the organization. The items can be either physical items (such as footballs autographed by famous athletes) or services (such as a free haircut from a local salon). At the auction, the items are presented along with a signup sheet for each item. Bidders are able to walk around the event, making bids on items by writing down their bid on the signup sheet for the appropriate item. (That's the "silent" part of the auction — no auctioneer yelling at you, and you don't have to worry about accidentally raising your hand!) When the event closes, the bidder with the highest bid for an item wins that item.

After talking with the auction event organizers, you've determined a list of requirements that they expect your web application to accomplish:

>> **Track bidder information, such as the bidder name, address, and phone number.** Each bidder is also assigned a unique bidder number by the auction organizers as they register.

>> **Track item information, such as the item name, basic description, and resale price.** Each item is also assigned a unique item number by the auction organizers used to track the item.

>> **Track the winning bid for each item.** There is no need to track individual bids, just the winning bid.

>> **List the items won by a bidder at the end of the event.**

>> **Display the silent auction event totals in real-time for volunteers.**

Based on these functional requirements, you can create a checklist of the individual functions your application must perform. This will help you define what web pages are required, and what PHP code you'll need to create. That checklist looks like this:

>> Create a new bidder.

>> Modify an existing bidder.

>> Delete an existing bidder.

>> List the items won by a bidder.

>> Create a new item.

>> Modify an existing item.

>> Delete an existing item.

>> Assign the winning bidder and price to an item.

You won't be able to use PHP for the last requirement — displaying auction information in real-time. PHP requires that the application users refresh their browsers
to display new information. However, JavaScript can help with that requirement,
so I save that for Chapter 3 in this minibook.

Keep this checklist handy. It'll assist you as you work out both the HTML and PHP
code for the application.

Now that you have a handle on the data requirements for the application, you're
ready to move onto the next step in the design process: working on the database.

# Creating the Application Database

Now that you have a good idea of what the application requirements are, you can
start working out the database design, and create it in your MySQL server. This
section walks through those processes.

## Designing the database

The AuctionHelper application will obviously have some data storage needs. It
will need to store the bidder information, as well as the information on the items
placed in the auction. Without doing a lot of database normalization calculations,
that sounds like you'll need at least two tables.

The Bidders table will contain information about the auction bidders. You'll need
to track the bidder information required by the event organizers, such as the bidder name, address, and phone number, and match that information to a unique
bidder number assigned to each bidder. Table 1-1 shows the data fields and their
associated data types that you'll use for the Bidders table.

Because the application will need to find a specific bidder at checkout time, you'll
want to assign the `bidderid` data field as the primary key for the Bidders table. No
other indexes are required for the application.

The Items table will contain information about the auction items. Again, according to the requirements presented by the event organizers, you'll need data fields

TABLE 1-1

## The Bidders Table Layout

| Data Field | Data Type |
|------------|-----------|
| bidderid | integer |
| lastname | varchar(100) |
| firstname | varchar(100) |
| address | varchar(200) |
| phone | varchar(14) |

to track the name of the item, a brief description of the item, and the resale price of the item. You'll also need to match this information to a unique item number so you can search the database using the item number.

Along with the basic item information, you'll need to include data fields to track the winning `bidderid` number for the item and the winning bid price. Table 1-2 shows the data fields and their associated data types that you'll use for the Items table.

TABLE 1-2

## The Items Table Layout

| Data Field | Data Type |
|------------|-----------|
| itemid | integer |
| name | varchar(100) |
| description | text |
| resaleprice | decimal |
| winbidder | integer |
| winprice | decimal |

Because the event organizers are assigning a unique `itemid` to each item, you can use that as the primary key for the Items table. The `winbidder` data field in the Items table should match an existing `bidderid` value in the Bidders table.

Besides these two tables required to handle the application data, there's one more table that you'll need to create for the application. You'll want your application to be protected — you don't want just anyone using the application to modify information. To do that, you'll need to create a login page where auction volunteers can log in with a user ID and password to access the application. To support that, you'll need to create an Admins table to track the users and their passwords. Table 1-3 shows what the Admins table should look like.

**TABLE 1-3**

## The Admins Table Layout

| Data Field | Data Type |
|------------|-----------|
| userid | varchar(20) |
| name | varchar(100) |
| password | char(64) |

The userid data field is what each volunteer uses to log into the application. The name data field tracks the full name of the volunteer assigned to that user ID. The password data field may be a bit misleading. You're not going to save the password as plain text in the Admins table. Instead, you'll use the MySQL SHA2() function, which uses the SHA-2 encryption standard to create a hash value from the password text:

```
MariaDB [(none)]> select sha2('myL0ngP@ssword', 256);
+------------------------------------------------------------------+
| sha2('myL0ngP@ssword', 256)                                      |
+------------------------------------------------------------------+
| 3cdfa761361762ddedc01ea1428db10a92e327325f490f7f34f1b1b91d994f22 |
+------------------------------------------------------------------+
1 row in set (0.00 sec)

MariaDB [(none)]>
```

Storing the passwords as an encrypted value helps protect the user passwords in case the Admins table becomes compromised by an attacker. The second parameter of the SHA2() function specifies the length of the encryption. As you can see from the output, the 256 generates a 64-byte hash value from the plain text, so you'll need a 64-byte data type field to store the value. The char(64) data type works just fine for that.

To encrypt the password when you store it, you use the SHA2() function directly in the INSERT statement when you add a new user account for the application:

```
INSERT INTO admins VALUES ('rich', 'Rich Blum', SHA2('myL0ngP@ssword',256));
```

**WARNING**

The downside to using the SHA2( ) function is that the values it generates can't be decrypted to determine the original text (that's called a *one-way encryption algorithm*). The only way to check if a password matches the stored value is to encrypt it and then compare the two encrypted values. This also means that if a volunteer forgets his password, there's no way to find out what it was. All you can do is assign a new password to the volunteer.

With your database layout in hand, you're ready to create the database elements in MySQL.

## Creating the database

You can use the MySQL command-line interface (CLI), the MySQL Workbench graphical tool, or the phpMyAdmin web-based tool to create the database and tables required for the application. You'll also need to create an application user account in the MySQL server and grant it privileges to read, modify, and delete data in the tables in the application database.

The following steps show the SQL statements needed to create the database, user account, and tables. You can use whichever MySQL interface you prefer to enter the SQL statements.

**1.** **Log into the MySQL interface of your choice:**

```
C:\Users\rich>cd \xampp\mysql\bin

C:\xampp\mysql\bin>mysql --user=root --password
Enter password:
Welcome to the MariaDB monitor.  Commands end with ; or \g.
Your MariaDB connection id is 2
Server version: 10.1.28-MariaDB mariadb.org binary distribution

Copyright (c) 2000, 2017, Oracle, MariaDB Corporation Ab and others.

Type 'help;' or '\h' for help. Type '\c' to clear the current input
    statement.

MariaDB [(none)]>
```

**2.** **Create the AuctionHelper database named** auction:

```
MariaDB [(none)]> CREATE DATABASE auction;
Query OK, 1 row affected (0.09 sec)

MariaDB [(none)]>
```

3. **Create a MySQL user account named** ah_user **for the AuctionHelper application, and assign it a password of** AuctionHelper:

```
MariaDB [(none)]> CREATE USER 'ah_user'@'localhost'
    -> IDENTIFIED BY 'AuctionHelper';
Query OK, 0 rows affected (0.13 sec)

MariaDB [(none)]>
```

**TIP**

Note that the location for the user account is set to localhost. This assumes the PHP server is running on the same physical server as the MySQL server. If that's not the case in your environment, you'll need to set that value to the host name or IP address of your MySQL server.

4. **Grant the new** ah_user **user account privileges to the** auction **database:**

```
MariaDB [(none)]> GRANT SELECT,UPDATE,INSERT,DELETE
    -> ON auction.* TO 'ah_user'@'localhost';
Query OK, 0 rows affected (0.08 sec)

MariaDB [(none)]>
```

The GRANT statement assigns the specified privileges to all the tables in the auction database, as indicated by the asterisk wildcard character.

5. **Create the Bidders table:**

```
MariaDB [(none)]> USE auction;
Database changed
MariaDB [auction]> CREATE TABLE bidders (
    -> bidderid integer primary key,
    -> lastname varchar(100),
    -> firstname varchar(100),
    -> address varchar(200),
    -> phone varchar(14));
Query OK, 0 rows affected (0.39 sec)

MariaDB [auction]>
```

**REMEMBER**

Don't forget the USE statement to tell MySQL which database the table should go in! For portability, and to prevent typo errors, I prefer to use all lowercase letters for database, table, and data field names. Mixed-case names are supported, but they only work in Linux and Mac environments. Windows ignores uppercase names, which can cause issues when porting code between different servers.

**6.** **Create the Items table:**

```
MariaDB [auction]> CREATE TABLE items (
    -> itemid int primary key,
    -> name varchar(100),
    -> description text,
    -> resaleprice decimal(10,2),
    -> winbidder int,
    -> winprice decimal(10,2));
Query OK, 0 rows affected (0.19 sec)

MariaDB [auction]>
```

**7.** **Create the Admins table:**

```
MariaDB [auction]> CREATE TABLE admins (
    -> userid varchar(20) primary key,
    -> name varchar(100),
    -> password char(64));
Query OK, 0 rows affected (0.23 sec)

MariaDB [auction]>
```

**8.** **Insert a user account into the Admins table to use for testing:**

```
MariaDB [auction]> INSERT INTO admins
    -> VALUES ('rich', 'Rich Blum', SHA2('myL0ngP@ssword', 256));
Query OK, 1 row affected (0.12 sec)

MariaDB [auction]>
```

Note how the password value is created in the INSERT statement. The code uses the SHA2( ) function directly in the value list.

**9.** **Display the tables to ensure that they've been created, and then exit your MySQL tool:**

```
MariaDB [auction]> SHOW TABLES;
+-------------------+
| Tables_in_auction |
+-------------------+
| admins            |
```

```
| bidders          |
| items            |
+------------------+
3 rows in set (0.00 sec)


MariaDB [auction]>
```

That's all there is to it! You now have the database structure for the AuctionHelper application completed.

The next step is to work on creating the PHP objects required to track the data inside the web application. These objects will be the interface between the PHP application and the MySQL database. The next section shows how to do that.

# Designing the Application Objects

Because you've decided to create the AuctionHelper application as an object-oriented application, you'll need to create some PHP objects to represent the data items in the application. This section walks through the process of designing the objects to use for the application, and how to write the PHP code to create them.

## Designing objects

The first step in the process of writing an object-oriented program is to determine the objects that the application needs to do its job. Often you can rely on your work in designing the database to determine the object requirements, too. The Auction-Helper application clearly uses two different types of data objects:

>> Bidders

>> Auction items

It would make sense to create separate objects for each of these data groups to help handle the database tables inside the PHP application. The following two sections walk through defining each of these objects.

## The Bidder object

The Bidder object will track the properties and methods required to interact with bidders in the application. Each data field in the Bidders table will be a separate property in the Bidder object. That produces the following properties:

» bidderid

» lastname

» firstname

» address

» phone

Because the object properties mirror the table data fields, you'll be able to store the application bidder data as a Bidder object and then write that object directly to the database using the Bidder object methods!

The methods that you'll need to create for the Bidder object mirror the functions that the AuctionHelper application needs to accomplish:

» saveBidder: Store the Bidder object data to the Bidders table.

» updateBidder: Modify an existing bidder data record in the Bidders table.

» removeBidder: Delete an existing bidder data record from the Bidders table.

» findBidder: Locate the bidder information in the Bidders table based on a bidderid value.

» getBidders: Retrieve a list of all bidders in the Bidders table.

The last two methods are a little different from the first three. The first three methods operate on an existing instance of the Bidder object. The last two objects retrieve data from the Bidders table and create Bidder objects. Because they don't use an existing Bidder object instance, they're called *static methods*. A static method allows you to call the method directly from the class without having an existing object instance.

Besides these methods, you also need to create a __construct() method to create a new Bidder object, and a __tostring() method so you can easily display the Bidder object information stored in the object as a string value in the application.

## The Item object

The Item object will track the properties and methods required to interact with auction items in the application. Again, this will match the data fields in the Items table, which will require the following properties:

>> itemid

>> name

>> description

>> resaleprice

>> winbidder

>> winprice

The methods required for the Item object mirror the function requirements for the AuctionHelper application:

>> saveItem: Store the Item object data to the Items table.

>> updateItem: Modify an existing data record in the Items table.

>> removeItem: Delete an existing data record in the Items table.

>> findItem: Retrieve a specific data record from the Items table based on the itemid value.

>> getItems: Retrieve all the items from the Items table.

>> getItemsbyBidder: Retrieve all the items with a specific bidderid as the winbidder value from the Items table.

The first three methods require an existing Item object instance, while the last three are static methods that return Item objects.

With these methods, you'll be able to interact with the MySQL database to manage the items for the auction. The next step is to work out the code to implement the methods.

## Coding the objects in PHP

After you've designed what the application objects should look like, you can create the PHP code to define them. Listing 1-1 shows the code to define the Bidder class object.

LISTING 1-1:  **The bidder.php Code for the Bidder Class Object**

```php
<?php
class Bidder {
    public $bidderid;
    public $lastname;
    public $firstname;
    public $address;
    public $phone;

    function __construct($bidderid, $lname, $fname, $address, $phone) {
        $this->bidderid = $bidderid;
        $this->lastname = $lname;
        $this->firstname = $fname;
        $this->address = $address;
        $this->phone = $phone;
    }

    function __toString() {
        $output = "<h2>Bidder Number: $this->bidderid</h2>\n" .
                  "<h2>$this->lastname, $this->firstname</h2>\n" .
                  "<h2>$this->address</h2>\n" .
                  "<h2>$this->phone</h2>\n";
        return $output;
    }

    function saveBidder() {
        $db = new mysqli("localhost", "ah_user", "AuctionHelper", "auction");
        $query = "INSERT INTO bidders VALUES (?, ?, ?, ?, ?)";
        $stmt = $db->prepare($query);
        $stmt->bind_param("issss", $this->bidderid, $this->lastname,
                            $this->firstname, $this->address, $this->phone);
        $result = $stmt->execute();
        $db->close();
        return $result;
    }

    function updateBidder() {
        $db = new mysqli("localhost", "ah_user", "AuctionHelper", "auction");
        $query = "UPDATE bidders SET bidderid = ?, lastname = ?, " .
                 "firstname = ?, address= ?, phone= ? " .
                 "WHERE bidderid = $this->bidderid";
        $stmt = $db->prepare($query);
        $stmt->bind_param("issss", $this->bidderid, $this->lastname,
                            $this->firstname, $this->address, $this->phone);
        $result = $stmt->execute();
        $db->close();
        return $result;
    }
```

```php
    function removeBidder() {
        $db = new mysqli("localhost", "ah_user", "AuctionHelper", "auction");
        $query = "DELETE FROM bidders WHERE bidderid = $this->bidderid";
        $result = $db->query($query);
        $db->close();
        return $result;
    }

    static function getBidders() {
        $db = new mysqli("localhost", "ah_user", "AuctionHelper", "auction");
        $query = "SELECT * FROM bidders";
        $result = $db->query($query);
        if (mysqli_num_rows($result) > 0) {
            $bidders = array();
            while($row = $result->fetch_array(MYSQLI_ASSOC)) {
                $bidder = new Bidder($row['bidderid'],$row['lastname'],
                        $row['firstname'],$row['address'],$row['phone']);
                array_push($bidders, $bidder);
                unset($bidder);
            }
            $db->close();
            return $bidders;
        } else {
            $db->close();
            return NULL;
        }
    }

    static function findBidder($bidderid) {
        $db = new mysqli("localhost", "ah_user", "AuctionHelper", "auction");
        $query = "SELECT * FROM bidders WHERE bidderid = $bidderid";
        $result = $db->query($query);
        $row = $result->fetch_array(MYSQLI_ASSOC);
        if ($row) {
            $bidder = new Bidder($row['bidderid'], $row['lastname'],
                    $row['firstname'], $row['address'], $row['phone']);
            $db->close();
            return $bidder;
        } else {
            $db->close();
            return NULL;
        }
    }
}
?>
```

In Listing 1-1, you should recognize the property and method names from the Bidder object design in the previous section. For each method, you must first connect to the MySQL database using the mysqli object (see Book 5, Chapter 5, for details on how that works). Each method then submits the appropriate SQL statement to interact with the database.

The getBidders() method retrieves multiple data records from the Bidders table. The code uses each data record in the result set to create a separate Bidder object, and then stores each Bidder object instance in the $bidders array. After all the data records have been read from the result set, the method returns the $bidders array back to the calling program.

The findBidder() method requires the bidderid value as a parameter, and then uses that in the SELECT statement to retrieve the specific data record from the Bidders table. If no data record is returned, the method returns a NULL value back to the calling program. If the bidderid value is found, the bidder information is returned as a Bidder object.

The PHP code to create the Item class is shown in Listing 1-2.

**LISTING 1-2:** **The items.php Code for the Item Class Object**

```php
<?php
class Item {
    public $itemid;
    public $name;
    public $description;
    public $resaleprice;
    public $winbidder;
    public $winprice;

    function __construct($itemid, $name, $description, $resaleprice,
                        $winbidder, $winprice) {
        $this->itemid = $itemid;
        $this->name = $name;
        $this->description = $description;
        $this->resaleprice = $resaleprice;
        $this->winbidder = $winbidder;
        $this->winprice = $winprice;
    }

    function __toString() {
        $output = "<h2>Item : $this->itemid</h2>" .
                  "<h2>Name: $this->name</h2>\n";
                  "<h2>Description: $this->description</h2>\n";
```

```
                    "<h2>Resale Price: $this->resaleprice</h2>\n";
                    "<h2>Winning bid: $this->winbid at $this->winprice</h2>\n";
        return $output;
    }

    function saveItem() {
        $db = new mysqli("localhost","ah_user","AuctionHelper","auction");
        $query = "INSERT INTO items VALUES (?, ?, ?, ?, ?, ?)";
        $stmt = $db->prepare($query);
        $stmt->bind_param("issdid", $this->itemid, $this->name,
                          $this->description, $this->resaleprice,
                          $this->winbidder, $this->winprice);
        $result = $stmt->execute();
        $db->close();
        return $result;
    }

    function updateItem() {
        $db = new mysqli("localhost","ah_user","AuctionHelper","auction");
        $query = "UPDATE items SET name= ?, description= ?, resaleprice= ?, " .
                 "winbidder= ?, winprice= ? WHERE itemid = $this->itemid";
        $stmt = $db->prepare($query);
        $stmt->bind_param("ssdid", $this->name, $this->description,
                          $this->resaleprice, $this->winbidder, $this->winprice);
        $result = $stmt->execute();
        $db->close();
        return $result;
    }

    function removeItem() {
        $db = new mysqli("localhost", "ah_user", "AuctionHelper", "auction");
        $query = "DELETE FROM items WHERE itemid = $this->itemid";
        $result = $db->query($query);
        $db->close();
        return $result;
    }

    static function getItems() {
        $db = new mysqli("localhost", "ah_user", "AuctionHelper", "auction");
        $query = "SELECT * FROM items";
        $result = $db->query($query);
        if (mysqli_num_rows($result) > 0) {
            $items = array();
            while($row = $result->fetch_array(MYSQLI_ASSOC)) {
                $item = new Item($row['itemid'], $row['name'],
                                 $row['description'], $row['resaleprice'],
                                 $row['winbidder'], $row['winprice']);
                array_push($items, $item);
            }
```

*(continued)*

LISTING 1-2: *(continued)*

```php
                    $db->close();
                    return $items;
                } else {
                    $db->close();
                    return NULL;
                }
            }


        static function getItemsbyBidder($bidderid) {
            $db = new mysqli("localhost", "ah_user", "AuctionHelper", "auction");
            $query = "SELECT * FROM items WHERE winbidder = $bidderid";
            $result = $db->query($query);
            if (mysqli_num_rows($result) > 0) {
                $items = array();
                while($row = $result->fetch_array(MYSQLI_ASSOC)) {
                    $item = new Item($row['itemid'], $row['name'],
                                    $row['description'], $row['resaleprice'],
                                    $row['winbidder'], $row['winprice']);
                    array_push($items, $item);
                }
                $db->close();
                return $items;
            } else {
                $db->close();
                return NULL;
            }
        }


        static function findItem($itemid) {
            $db = new mysqli("localhost", "ah_user", "AuctionHelper", "auction");
            $query = "SELECT * FROM items WHERE itemid = $itemid";
            $result = $db->query($query);
            $row = $result->fetch_array(MYSQLI_ASSOC);
            if ($row) {
                $item = new Item($row['itemid'], $row['name'], $row['description'],
                    $row['resaleprice'], $row['winbidder'], $row['winprice']);
                $db->close();
                return $item;
            } else {
                $db->close();
                return NULL;
            }
        }
    }
?>
```

In Listing 1-2, you should recognize the properties and methods from the Item object design discussed in the previous section. The getItems() and getItemsbyBidder() methods return the list of items as an array of Item objects, while the findItem() method returns the result as a single Item object (or a NULL value if the item isn't found in the Items table).

Now that you've seen the code, you can create the files. Follow these steps to create the class files for your AuctionHelper web application:

**1.** Open your favorite text editor, program editor, or integrated development environment (IDE) package.

**2.** Enter the code shown in Listing 1-1.

**3.** Create a folder named auction in the DocumentRoot folder for your web server.

If you're using XAMPP in Windows, that's c:\xampp\htdocs. If you're using XAMPP in macOS, that's /Applications/XAMPP/htdocs.

**4.** Save the file as bidder.php in the auction folder you just created in Step 3.

**5.** Open a new tab or window in your editor or IDE package.

**6.** Enter the code shown in Listing 1-2.

**7.** Save the file as item.php in the auction folder.

**8.** Close your editor or IDE package.

**TIP**

Notice that the database connection functions are contained within the Bidder and Item classes. If you prefer to hide that information, you can move the bidder.php and item.php files to an alternate folder outside the DocumentRoot folder. Just make sure the web server user account has access to that folder!

# Designing the Application Layout

I know you're anxious to start coding the application, but before you can dive into the coding you need to create the website design layout first. Knowing what your website should look like ahead of time helps save lots of time of trial-and-error coding! This section discusses some general web page design theory, and then applies that theory to the AuctionHelper application design.

# Designing web page layout

*Web page layout* defines how the web page presents the content you need to display. Displaying content to readers isn't new to the web world — the newspaper and magazine worlds have been struggling with that issue for centuries! If you pick up a copy of your local newspaper, you'll notice that articles aren't just thrown onto the pages haphazardly. There's a specific format to the layout of each newspaper page (yes, even the tabloids have some thought behind them).

The web design world has borrowed many of the concepts from how newspapers organize and display content. One of those borrowed concepts is called *grid theory*. With grid theory, you divide the web page into grids for placing different types of content on the page. You create separate areas in the web page for corporate logos, website navigation menus, advertisements, and of course, the main content. The way you divide the grids on the web page should follow a strict mathematical algorithm that remains constant throughout the entire website, giving the website an organized look.

The most common grid method is called the *golden ratio.* The golden ratio states that to make a page aesthetically pleasing, you should divide it into sections using the golden ratio of 1.62. Applied to a web page layout, that means content sections should be divided into two parts:

>> A main section that takes up two-thirds of the page

>> A supporting section that takes up one-third of the page

Because of this ratio, the layout is also commonly referred to as the *rule of thirds.*

To implement this layout, you divide your web page into three equal columns and three equal rows. If you need finer control over the layout, you can subdivide columns or rows to make smaller sections. After creating the grid, fit the elements of your application into the grid, assigning the more important content to the larger grid areas. Figure 1-1 shows a rough diagram of what this looks like.

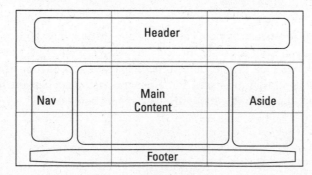

**FIGURE 1-1:**
Sample rule-of-thirds layout.

In the next section, you apply the rule of thirds to the AuctionHelper web application layout.

## The AuctionHelper page layout

For the AuctionHelper application, you'll need five separate sections on each web page:

>> A header area at the top of the web page to display the application title across the top of all pages

>> A footer area at the bottom of the web page to display any copyright or contact information

>> A navigation area on the left side of the web page

>> A real-time data update area on the right-hand side of the web page

>> The main content area in the middle of the web page

Using the grid layout to place things, the basic AuctionHelper website layout is shown in Figure 1-2.

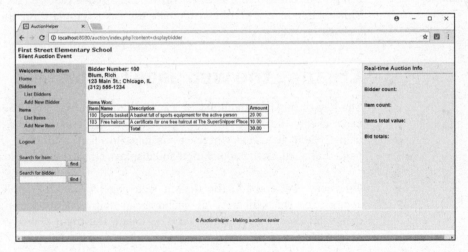

**FIGURE 1-2:**
The basic AuctionHelper web page layout.

The header and footer sections incorporate data that appears on every web page in the application but doesn't need a lot of space. You'll use PHP include files to load a standard header and footer section on each web page without having to code that for every page.

The navigation section provides a way for the application users to find their way around the website. It will display links to the major features in the application, such as adding new bidders or items, listing all the bidders or items, and finding bidders or items.

The real-time information section will be where the JavaScript code does all its work. There won't be any PHP code in this section, but you need to reserve the space for JavaScript to dynamically update the information.

The main section is the main work area to display content that changes from page to page. It'll be used to display a variety of content, including the bidder information, item information, and of course, the items won by a bidder.

Now that you have a plan for the basic website layout, you can start writing some HTML and CSS code to implement it. The next section walks through that process.

# Coding the Website Layout

While you're not quite ready to start coding all the application PHP code yet, you can get started with the basic HTML5 and CSS3 code required for the page layout. This section shows you how to create the basic template for the AuctionHelper website layout.

## Creating the web page template

The key to building dynamic web application is reusability. The more code you can reuse for the different web pages, the less code you need to write! That means using PHP include files wherever possible. However, to do that, you need a main page that anchors the application and displays all the include files.

For most web servers, the default web page for a PHP application is called index.php. This will be your anchor page that controls everything the application displays. Follow these steps to create the main index.php page for the AuctionHelper application.

**1.** Open your editor and enter the following code:

```php
<?php
session_start();
include("bidder.php");
include("item.php");
?>
```

```
<!DOCTYPE html>
<html>
<head>
<title>AuctionHelper</title>
<link rel="stylesheet" type="text/css" href="ah_styles.css">
</head>
<body>
<header>
<?php include("header.inc.php"); ?>
</header>
<section id="container">
<nav>
<?php include("nav.inc.php"); ?>
</nav>
<main>
<?php
if (isset($_REQUEST['content'])) {
    include($_REQUEST['content'] . ".inc.php");
} else {
    include("main.inc.php");
}
?>
</main>
<aside>
<?php include("aside.inc.php"); ?>
</aside>
</section>
<footer>
<?php include("footer.inc.php"); ?>
</footer>
</body>
</html>
```

**2.** **Save the file in the** auction **folder as** index.php.

The index.php code starts out by using the PHP session_start() function to initiate a session. Then it uses the include() function to include the Bidder and Item class code files. Because all the other web pages are based off of this page, this is the only time you need to include these files.

Next you see some standard HTML5 code to build the web page template. The code uses the HTML5 <header>, <nav>, <section>, <main>, <aside>, and <footer> elements to define the different sections of the web page. The <section> element creates a common container to help position the navigation, main, and aside sections. *Remember:* All the actual positioning will happen in the CSS3 style sheet.

The ‹main› section code needs some explaining:

```php
<?php
if (isset($_REQUEST['content'])) {
    include($_REQUEST['content'] . ".inc.php");
} else {
    include("main.inc.php");
}
?>
```

The code checks if an HTML variable/value pair identified by content is set. That's how the application dynamically displays different content in each web page. If the content HTML variable is set, the code uses its value to create the filename to include for the main content area. If it's not set, it uses the main.inc.php file as the default.

For this application, you'll place most of the styling required for the application in an external style sheet file. Follow these steps to create that file:

**1.** **Open your editor and enter the following code:**

```css
body{
    font-family: Arial, sans-serif;
    font-size: 80%;
    color: #333333;
    line-height: 1.166;
    margin: 0px;
    padding: 0px;
}

a{
    color: #006699;
    text-decoration: none;
}

a:link{
    color: #006699;
    text-decoration: none;
}

a:visited{
    color: #006699;
```

```
        text-decoration: none;
}

a:hover{
        color: #006699;
        text-decoration: underline;
}

h1{
        font-family: Verdana, Arial, sans-serif;
        font-size: 120%;
        color: #334d55;
        margin: 0px;
        padding: 0px;
}

h2{
        font-family: Arial, sans-serif;
        font-size: 120%;
        color: #334d55;
        margin: 0px;
        padding: 0px;
}

h3{
        font-family: Arial, sans-serif;
        font-size: 110%;
        color: #334d55;
        margin: 0px;
        padding: 0px;
}

h4{
        font-family: Arial, sans-serif;
        font-size: 100%;
        color: #334d55;
        margin: 0px;
        padding: 0px;
}

header{
        padding: 7px;
        border-bottom: 1px solid #E2EAEF;
```

```css
    height: 40px;
    width: 100%;
}

#container {
    height: 400px;
}

nav {
    padding: 5px;
    border-bottom: 1px solid #E2EAEF;
    border-top: 1px solid #E2EAEF;
    border-right: 1px solid #E2EAEF;
    background-color: #FFE3AA;
    float: left;
    width: 15%;
    height: 100%;
}

main {
    padding: 5px;
    border-top: 1px solid #E2EAEF;
    float: left;
    width: 55%;
    height: 100%;
}
main table {
    padding: 2px;
    border: 1px solid black;
    border-collapse: collapse;
}

main td {
    padding: 2px;
    border: 1px solid black;
    border-collapse: collapse;
}

aside {
    padding: 5px;
    border-top: 1px solid #E2EAEF;
    border-left: 1px solid #E2EAEF;
    background-color: #f3f6f8;
    float: right;
```

```
        width: 15%;
        height: 100%;
    }

    footer {
        clear: both;
        text-align: center;
        padding: 7px;
        border-bottom: 1px solid #E2EAEF;
        border-top: 1px solid #E2EAEF;
        background-color: #f3f6f8;
        width: 100%;
    }
```

**2.** **Save the file in the** auction **folder as** ah_styles.css.

That's a lot of style rules to apply! Don't get too overwhelmed — most of them just apply different aesthetics to the web page layout, such as defining the default fonts and color schemes. There are a few position style rules applied as well, to ensure that the different sections appear in the correct location on the web page.

## Creating the support files

There are four sections of the web page that are common to all pages in the application, each one using a separate include file:

» header.inc.php

» nav.inc.php

» aside.inc.php

» footer.inc.php

Because these files don't change, you can write the code for them now to complete the web page template. Follow these steps:

**1.** **Open your editor and enter this code:**

```
<h1>First Street Elementary School</h1>
<h2>Silent Auction Event</h2>
```

**2.** **Save the file in the** auction **folder as** header.inc.php.

**3.** **Open a new tab or window in your editor and enter this code:**

```
<p>&copy AuctionHelper - Making auctions easier</p>
```

**4.** **Save the file in the** auction **folder as** footer.inc.php.

**5.** **Open a new tab or window in your editor and enter this code:**

```
<h2>Real-time Auction Info</h2>
<hr>
<br>
<br>
<h3>Bidder count: </h3><span id="biddercount"></span>
<br><br>
<h3>Item count: </h3><span id="itemcount"></span>
<br><br>
<h3>Items total value: </h3><span id="itemtotal"></span>
<br><br>
<h3>Bid totals: </h3><span id="bidtotal"></span>
```

**6.** **Save the file in the** auction **folder as** aside.inc.php.

**7.** **Open a new tab or window in your editor and enter this code:**

```
<table width="100%" cellpadding="3">
<tr>
<?php
    if (!isset($_SESSION['login']))
        echo "<td></td>\n";
    else {
        echo "<td><h3>Welcome, {$_SESSION['login']}</h3></td>\n";
 ?>
</tr>
<tr>
<td><a href="index.php"><strong>Home</strong></a></td>
</tr>
<tr>
<td><strong>Bidders</strong></td>
</tr>
<tr>
<td>   <a href="index.php?content=listbidders">
<strong>List Bidders</strong></a></td>
</tr>
<tr>
<td>   <a href="index.php?content=newbidder">
<strong>Add New Bidder</strong></a></td>
```

```
</tr>
<tr>
<td><strong>Items</strong></td>
</tr>
<tr>
<td>   <a href="index.php?content=listitems">
<strong>List Items</strong></a></td>
</tr>
<tr>
<td>   <a href="index.php?content=newitem">
<strong>Add New Item</strong></a></td>
</tr>
<tr><td><hr/></td></tr>
<tr><td><a href="index.php?content=logout">
<strong>Logout</strong></a></td></tr>
<tr>
<td> </td>
</tr>
<tr>
<td>
<form action="index.php" method="post">
<label>Search for item:</label><br>
<input type="text" name="itemid" size="14"/>
<input type="submit" value="find"/>
<input type="hidden" name="content" value="updateitem">
</form>
</td></tr>
<tr>
<td>
<form action="index.php" method="post">
<label>Search for bidder:</label><br>
<input type="text" name="bidderid" size="14"/>
<input type="submit" value="find"/>
<input type="hidden" name="content" value="displaybidder">
</form>
</td></tr>
<?php
}
?>
</table>
```

**8.** Save the file in the auction **folder as** nav.inc.php.

There isn't anything too out of the ordinary in these code files. The nav.inc.php file checks the session cookie named login to determine if the website visitor is logged in or not. If not, it doesn't display the navigation entries. This is a great security feature. Notice that the URLs used in the navigation links all include the content HTML variable and set it to a name that'll be used later on for an include file. The two mini-forms are used for creating search boxes for bidders and items. They also set the content HTML variable, but as a hidden form field that gets passed to the index.php file.

The last piece of the template is the main.inc.php include file. That gets included to create the default main content area. It needs to display a login form if the website visitor isn't logged in. If the website visitor is logged in and goes to the default application web page, it will display some simple information about the application.

Follow these steps to create the main.inc.php include file, along with another helper include file:

**1.** **Open a new tab or window in your editor and enter this code:**

```php
<?php
if (!isset($_SESSION['login'])) {
?>
<h2>Please log in</h2><br>
<form name="login" action="index.php" method="post">
<label>UserID</label>
<input type="text" name="userid" size="10">
<br>
<br>
<label>Password</label>
<input type="password" name="password" size="10">
<br>
<br>
<input type="submit" value="Login">
<input type="hidden" name="content" value="validate">
</form>
<?php
} else {
    echo "<h2>Welcome to AuctionHelper</h2>\n";
    echo "<br><br>\n";
    echo "<p>This program tracks bidder and auction item information</p>\n";
    echo "<p>Please use the links in the navigation window</p>\n";
    echo "<p>Please DO NOT use the browser navigation buttons!</p>\n";
}
```

```
?>
<script language="javascript">
document.login.userid.focus();
document.login.userid.select();
</script>
```

2. **Save the file in the** `auction` **folder as** `main.inc.php`.

3. **Open a new tab or window in your browser and enter this code:**

```php
<?php
$userid = $_POST['userid'];
$password = $_POST['password'];
$query ="SELECT name FROM admins WHERE userid = ? AND password =
    SHA2(?,256)";
$db = new mysqli("localhost", "ah_user", "AuctionHelper", "auction");
$stmt = $db->prepare($query);
$stmt->bind_param("ss", $userid, $password);
$stmt->execute();
$stmt->bind_result($name);
$stmt->fetch();
if (isset($name)) {
    echo "<h2>Welcome to AuctionHelper</h2>\n";
    $_SESSION['login'] = $name;
    header("Location: index.php");
} else {
    echo "<h2>Sorry, login incorrect</h2>\n";
    echo "<a href=\"index.php\">Please try again</a>\n";
}
?>
```

4. **Save the file in the** `auction` **folder as** `validate.inc.php`.

5. **Close your editor window.**

Notice that the `main.inc.php` code has a little JavaScript code section at the bottom. That's a trick that places the cursor in the UserID text box by default when the web page opens! The login form in the `main.inc.php` code passes the login form data to the `validate.inc.php` file. The `validate.inc.php` looks up the login information in the `admins` table, and then sets the `login` session cookie if the login is valid and redirects the browser back to the main `index.php` page.

If you start your Apache web server and open the AuctionHelper application in your browser, you should see the login form, as shown in Figure 1-3.

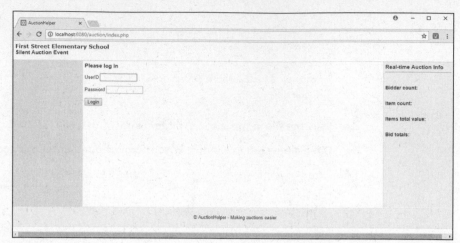

FIGURE 1-3:
The AuctionHelper
login window.

Enter the user ID and password that you stored in the Admins table, and then click the Login button. You should then see the main AuctionHelper window, as shown in Figure 1-4.

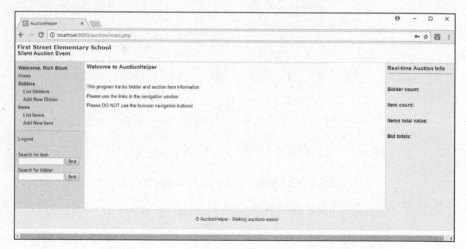

FIGURE 1-4:
The main
AuctionHelper
window.

Congratulations! You've got the start of a dynamic web application!

# Chapter **2**

# Implementing an Object-Oriented Application

I f you've just finished reading through Chapter 1 of this minibook, take a moment and take a deep breath! You did a lot of work preparing the database, PHP objects, and the HTML and CSS templates required for the AuctionHelper application. This chapter walks through how to create the rest of the PHP code required to complete the application. First, it walks through the overall layout of the AuctionHelper application links and buttons, and discusses how to handle the browser events triggered by them. Those are how your application users interact with the website. Then it goes through all the PHP code required to work with the bidder and item objects that you've already created. Finally, the chapter finishes off by discussing how to test out an application to ensure things are working correctly.

## Working with Events

Web-based applications use what's called *event-driven programming.* In event-driven programming, the flow of the program is based on events that the program user generates from the user interface. The program displays the user interface, and then waits and listens for an event to occur. As the program user clicks each link or button on the web page, the application runs different sets of include files to generate the content that it displays in the main web page sections.

Figure 2-1 refreshes your memory on just what the main AuctionHelper web page looks like when the user logs into the application.

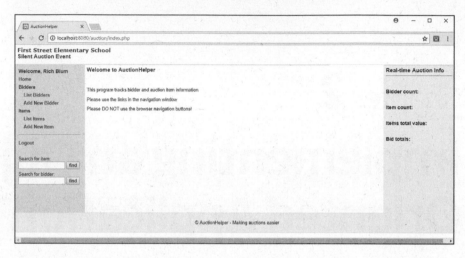

**FIGURE 2-1:**
The main
AuctionHelper
web page.

From the main page, the links and buttons in the navigation area (the section on the left side of the web page) control the application events. There are four links available:

> » List bidders

> » Add new bidder

> » List items

> » Add new item

And below those are two search text boxes:

> » Search for items

> » Search for a specific bidder

Each event, whether a link or a button, creates a new request from the user's browser to the web server, which then passes the index.php file to the PHP server for processing, along with the content HTML variable and value. The following sections discuss how to create the PHP code to handle those events.

# Bidder Object Events

This section walks through the PHP code you need to create to respond to the bidder-oriented events in the navigation menu. This allows you to add, change, and delete bidders, as well as display information about what items a specific bidder has won in the silent auction.

## Listing bidders

When your application user clicks the List Bidders link in the navigation menu (see Figure 2-1), the link URL passes the user's browser to the index.php main file and sets the content HTML variable to a value of listbidders in the link URL:

```
<a href="index.php?content=listbidders">
```

The code in the index.php file tells the PHP server to retrieve the listbidders.inc.php include file for the main content section. You need to create the listbidders.inc.php code file to display a list of the current bidders in the Bidders table.

Follow these steps to create the listbidders.inc.php file:

**1.** Open your favorite text editor, program editor, or integrated development environment (IDE) package.

**2.** Enter the following code:

```php
<?php

echo "<script language=\"javascript\">\n";
echo "function listbox_dblclick() {\n";
echo "document.bidders.displaybidder.click() }\n";
echo "</script>\n";

echo "<script language=\"javascript\">\n";
echo "function button_click(target) {\n";
echo "if(target==0) bidders.action=\"index.php?content=displaybidder\"\n";
echo "if(target==1) bidders.action=\"index.php?content=removebidder\"\n";
echo "if(target==2) bidders.action=\"index.php?content=updatebidder\"\n";
echo "}\n";
echo "</script>\n";

echo "<h2>Select Bidder</h2>\n";
echo "<form name=\"bidders\" method=\"post\">\n";
```

```php
echo "<select ondblclick=\"listbox_dblclick()\" name=\"bidderid\"
    size=\"20\">\n";

$bidders = Bidder::getBidders();
foreach($bidders as $bidder) {
    $bidderid = $bidder->bidderid;
    $name = $bidderid . " - " . $bidder->lastname . ", " . $bidder-
    >firstname;
    echo "<option value=\"$bidderid\">$name</option>\n";
}
echo "</select><br><br>\n";

echo "<input type=\"submit\" onClick=\"button_click(0)\" " .
    "name=\"displaybidder\" value=\"View Bidder\">\n";
echo "<input type=\"submit\" onClick=\"button_click(1)\" " .
    "name=\"deletebidder\" value=\"Delete Bidder\">\n";
echo "<input type=\"submit\" onClick=\"button_click(2)\" " .
    "name=\"updatebidder\" value=\"Update Bidder\">\n";
echo "</form>\n";
?>
```

3. **Save the file in the** auction **folder you created in the** DocumentRoot **folder of your web server as** listbidders.inc.php.

The listbidders.inc.php code generates the web page shown in Figure 2-2.

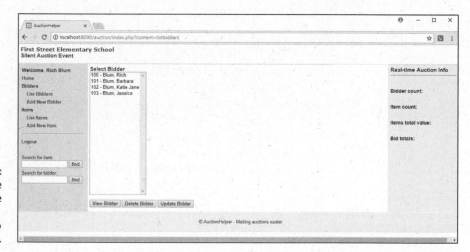

**FIGURE 2-2:**
The web page
generated by the
listbidders.
inc.php
include file.

**TIP**

In Figure 2-2, you'll notice that I placed some bidders into the Bidders table ahead of time so that I could test out the program. It's always a good idea to have some test data on hand so you can see your application working as you build it. You can remove the test data when your application goes live.

The listbidders web page displays a list box of all the bidders in the Bidders table and then three buttons:

>> **View Bidder:** Displays information on the bidder selected in the list box.

>> **Delete Bidder:** Removes the bidder selected in the list box from the Bidders table.

>> **Update Bidder:** Displays a form to update the information in the bidders table for the bidder selected in the list box.

Users trigger events on the web page in two ways: by clicking one of the three buttons, or by double-clicking a bidder in the list box.

In the `listbidder.inc.php` code, the first section of the code defines two JavaScript functions for handling the web page events:

>> `listbox_dblclick()`: Triggers when the application user double-clicks a bidder in the list box. It simulates pressing the View Bidder button, which requests the `index.php` page with the content HTML variable set to `displaybidders`.

>> `button_click()`: Triggers when any of the three buttons is clicked. It dynamically changes the `action` attribute in the `<form>` element to redirect the browser to one of three include files, based on which button the user clicks.

Next, the PHP code creates the `<select>` list box of bidders by calling the `getBidders()` static method from the `Bidder` class. It uses each `Bidder` object returned by the `getBidders()` method to create each entry in the list box.

Finally, the code creates three buttons to view, delete, or update a bidder data record. These buttons use the `button_click()` JavaScript function that was defined. The three buttons redirect three actions to take on a specific bidder entry:

>> The View Bidder button redirects to the `displaybidder.inc.php` include file.

>> The Delete Bidder button redirects to the `removebidder.inc.php` include file.

>> Update Bidder button redirects to the `updatebidder.inc.php` include file.

Now you have three more include files to code! These are described in the following sections.

## Viewing a bidder

When your application user clicks the View Bidder button or double-clicks a bidder from the list box, the code retrieves the `displaybidder.inc.php` include file code, passing the `bidderid` value for the bidder the user selects from the list box. The `displaybidder.inc.php` code displays the bidder data record from the Bidders table and lists any items in the Items table that the bidder has won (where the item `winbidder` value matches the `bidderid` value).

Follow these steps to create the `displaybidder.inc.php` file:

**1.** Open your editor and enter this code:

```php
<?php

if (!isset($_REQUEST['bidderid']) OR (!is_numeric($_REQUEST['bidderid'])))
{
    echo "<h2>You did not select a valid bidderid to view.</h2>\n";
    echo "<a href=\"index.php?content=listbidders\">List bidders</a>\n";
} else
{
    $bidderid = $_REQUEST['bidderid'];
    $bidder = Bidder::findBidder($bidderid);
    if ($bidder) {
        echo $bidder;
        echo "<br><br>\n";
        // List items won
        $items = Item::getItemsbyBidder($bidderid);
        if ($items) {
            echo "<b>Items Won:</b><br>\n";
            echo "<table>\n";
            echo "<tr><td><b>Item</b></td><td><b>Name</b></td>" .
                "<td><b>Description</b></td><td><b>Amount</b></td></tr>\n";
            $itemtotal = 0;
            foreach($items as $item) {
                printf("<tr><td>%s</td>", $item->itemid);
                printf("<td>%s</td>",$item->name);
                printf("<td>%s</td>", $item->description);
                printf("<td>%.2f</td></tr>\n", $item->winprice);
                $itemtotal = $itemtotal + $item->winprice;
            }
            echo "<tr><td/><td/><td><b>Total</b></td>";
            printf("<td><b>%.2f</b></td></tr>\n", $itemtotal);
```

```
            echo "</table>\n";
        } else {
            echo "<h2>There are no items won at this time</h2>\n";
        }
    } else {
        echo "<h2>Sorry, bidder $bidderid not found</h2>\n";
    }
}
?>
```

**2.** **Save the file in the** auction **folder as** displaybidder.inc.php.

The displaybidder.inc.php code generates the web page shown in Figure 2-3.

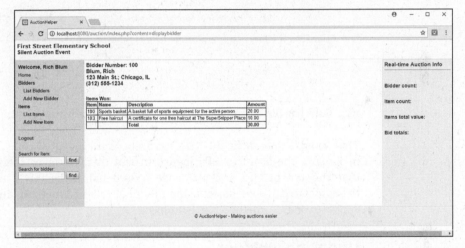

**FIGURE 2-3:**
The web page generated by the displaybidder. inc.php include file.

The displaybidder.inc.php code uses the bidderid value in the findBidder() static method to retrieve the information for the specific bidder. It then uses the bidderid in the getItemsbyBidder() static method from the Items class to retrieve all the items associated with the bidder's bidderid value.

The getItemsbyBidder() method returns the list of matching items as an array of Item objects, so the code uses the foreach statement to iterate through each item and display its properties. That provides all the bidder information in one handy web page, making it a breeze for volunteers to check out bidders at the end of the silent auction!

## Deleting a bidder

When the application user clicks the Delete Bidder button from the bidders list, that triggers the removebidder.inc.php include file. Follow these steps to build that file:

**1.** **Open your editor and enter this code:**

```php
<?php
if (isset($_SESSION['login'])) {
    $bidderid = $_POST['bidderid'];
    $bidder = Bidder::findBidder($bidderid);
    $result = $bidder->removeBidder();
    if ($result)
        echo"<h2>Bidder $bidderid removed</h2>\n";
    else
        echo "<h2>Sorry, problem removing bidder $bidderid</h2>\n";
} else {
    echo "<H2>Please login first</h2>\n";
}
?>
```

**2.** **Save the file in the** auction **folder as** removebidder.inc.php.

That wasn't too difficult! The removebidder.inc.php code first checks to make sure the user is really logged in and then retrieves the bidderid value that the listbidder.inc.php code passed using the POST method. It finds the associated Bidder object using the findBidder() method, and then runs the removeBidder() method for that object.

## Updating a bidder

When the application user clicks the Update Bidder button from the bidders list, that triggers the updatebidder.inc.php file. Follow these steps to build that file:

**1.** **Open your editor and enter this code:**

```php
<?php
$bidderid = $_POST['bidderid'];
$bidder = Bidder::findBidder($bidderid);
if ($bidder) {
    echo "<h2>Update Bidder $bidderid</h2><br>\n";
    echo "<form name=\"bidder\" action=\"index.php\" method=\"post\">\n";
    echo "<table>\n";
    echo "<tr><td>BidderID</td><td>$bidder->bidderid</td></tr>\n";
    echo "<tr><td>Last Name</td><td><input type=\"text\" name=\"lastname\" " .
```

```
        "value=\"$bidder->lastname\"></td></tr>\n";
    echo "<tr><td>First Name</td><td><input type=\"text\" " .
        "name=\"firstname\" value=\"$bidder->firstname\"></td></tr>\n";
    echo "<tr><td>Address</td><td><input type=\"text\" " .
        "name=\"address\" value=\"$bidder->address\"></td></tr>\n";
    echo "<tr><td>Phone</td><td><input type=\"text\" " .
        "name=\"phone\" value=\"$bidder->phone\"></td></tr>\n";
    echo "</CDATAtable><br><br>\n";
    echo "<input type=\"submit\" name=\"answer\" value=\"Update
Bidder\">\n";
    echo "<input type=\"submit\" name=\"answer\" value=\"Cancel\">\n";
    echo "<input type=\"hidden\" name=\"bidderid\"
value=\"$bidderid\">\n";
    echo "<input type=\"hidden\" name=\"content\"
value=\"changebidder\">\n";
    echo "</form>\n";
} else {
    echo "<h2>Sorry, bidder $bidderid not found</h2>\n";
}
?>
<script language="javascript">
document.bidder.lastname.focus();
document.bidder.lastname.select();
</script>
```

2. **Save the file in the** auction **folder as** updatebidder.inc.php.

The updatebidder.inc.php include file generates the web page shown in Figure 2-4.

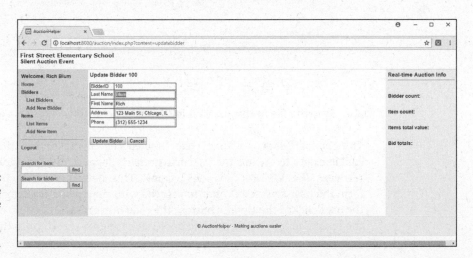

**FIGURE 2-4:**
The web page generated by the updatebidder.inc.php include file.

The updatebidder.inc.php code retrieves the bidder based on the bidderid value and creates a form using the Bidder object properties as the default values for the form text fields. The application user can modify any of the text field values and then click the Update Bidder button to save the changes.

The form calls the changebidder.inc.php file to submit the form data to the MySQL database. Follow these steps to create that file:

**1.** Open your editor and enter this code:

```php
<?php
if (isset($_SESSION['login'])) {
    $bidderid = $_POST['bidderid'];
    $answer = $_POST['answer'];

    if ($answer == "Update Bidder") {
        $bidder = Bidder::findBidder($bidderid);
        $bidder->bidderid = $_POST['bidderid'];
        $bidder->lastname = $_POST['lastname'];
        $bidder->firstname = $_POST['firstname'];
        $bidder->address = $_POST['address'];
        $bidder->phone = $_POST['phone'];
        $result = $bidder->updateBidder();
        if ($result) {
            echo "<h2>Bidder $bidderid updated</h2>\n";
        } else {
            echo "<h2>Problem updating bidder $bidderid</h2>\n";
        }
    } else {
        echo "<h2>Update Canceled for bidder $bidderid</h2>\n";
    }
} else {
    echo "<h2>Please login first</h2>\n";
}
?>
```

**2.** Save the file in the auction folder as changebidder.inc.php.

The changebidder.inc.php code first checks to make sure the login session cookie exists to ensure the user has properly logged into the application. It then retrieves the $_POST['answer'] value. This determines which button in the form the user selected (either to proceed with the update or cancel the update). If the user clicked the Update button, the code retrieves the bidderid value and uses the findBidder() static method to retrieve the data record from the Bidders table.

It then retrieves the rest of the form data using the $_POST[] array variable and updates the Bidder object properties with the new data. Finally, the code uses the updateBidder() method to commit the new values to the database.

## Adding a new bidder

When the application user clicks the navigation link to add a new bidder, that triggers the newbidder.inc.php include file. Follow these steps to build that file:

**1.** **Open your editor and enter this code:**

```
<h2>Enter new bidder information</h2>
<form name="newbidder" action="index.php" method="post">

<CDATAtable cellpadding="1" border="0">
<tr><td>Bidder ID:</td><td><input type="text" name="bidderid" size="4">
</td></tr>
<tr><td>Last name:</td><td><input type="text" name="lastname" size="20">
</td></tr>
<tr><td>First name(s):</td><td><input type="text" name="firstname"
    size="50">
</td></tr>
<tr><td>Address:</td><td><input type="text" name="address" size="75">
</td></tr>
<tr><td>Phone:</td><td><input type="text" name="phone" size="12">
</td></tr>
</CDATAtable><br>
<input type="submit" value="Submit new Bidder">
<input type="hidden" name="content" value="addbidder">
</form>

<script language="javascript">
document.newbidder.bidderid.focus();
document.newbidder.bidderid.select();
</script>
```

**2.** **Save the file in the** auction **folder as** newbidder.inc.php.

The newbidder.inc.php include file generates the web page shown in Figure 2-5.

The newbidder.inc.php code simply creates a form to enter the information for a new bidder.

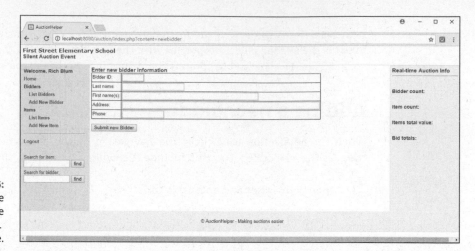

FIGURE 2-5:
The web page
generated by the
newbidder.inc.
php include file.

TIP

The JavaScript code at the end of the newbidder.inc.php file forces the browser to place the cursor in the bidder data field by default. That's a small feature that goes a long way in making your web forms more user-friendly!

When the application user clicks the Submit New Bidder button, it triggers the addbidder.inc.php include file. Follow these steps to create that file:

**1.** **Open your editor and enter this code:**

```php
<?php
if (isset($_SESSION['login'])) {
    $bidderid = $_POST['bidderid'];
    if ((trim($bidderid) == '') OR (!is_numeric($bidderid)))
    {
        echo "<h2>Sorry, you must enter a valid bidder ID number</h2>\n";
    } else
    {
        $lastname = $_POST['lastname'];
        $firstname = $_POST['firstname'];
        $address = $_POST['address'];
        $phone = $_POST['phone'];

        $bidder = new Bidder($bidderid,$lastname,$firstname,$address,$
phone);
        $result = $bidder->saveBidder();
        if ($result)
            echo "<h2>New Bidder #$bidderid successfully added</h2>\n";
        else
            echo "<h2>Sorry, there was a problem adding that bidder
</h2>\n";
```

```
       }
    } else {
        echo "<h2>Please log in first</h2>\n";
    }
    ?>
```

**2.** **Save the file in the** auction **folder as** addbidder.inc.php.

The addbidder.inc.php code first checks to make sure the user is properly logged
in. Then it retrieves the bidderid and makes sure the value isn't empty and
that it's a valid number. It then retrieves the rest of the form data posted by the
newbidder.inc.php form and uses it to create a new Bidder object. Finally, it
uses the saveBidder() method from the Bidder object to store the new bidder
information as a data record in the Bidders table.

## Searching for a bidder

The List Bidders feature allows you to access all the bidders, but if your silent auction event is a success, you may have hundreds of bidders to have to look through
to find a single bidder! To solve that problem, it helps to have a search text box to
find a specific bidder based in the bidderid assigned to the bidder. That's built
into the navigation menu nav.inc.php file with this code:

```
<form action="index.php" method="post">
    <label>Search for bidder:</label><br>
        <input type="text" name="bidderid" size="14" >
        <input type="submit" value="find" >
<input type="hidden" name="content" value="displaybidder">
    </form>
```

When your application user enters a bidderid value into the Bidder search
text box and clicks the find button, the navigation action triggers the
displaybidder.inc.php include file passing the bidderid value. Because it
uses the same displaybidder.inc.php code you've already created for the list
bidders feature, you've already done the coding to complete the bidder search
feature!

# Item Object Events

This section walks through the PHP code you need to respond to the item-oriented
events in the navigation menu. These events allow you to add, change, delete, and
view items tracked for the silent auction.

# Listing items

When your application user clicks the List Items link in the navigation window, it triggers the `listitems.inc.php` include file based on the link URL:

```
<a href="index.php?content=listitems">
```

Just as when you were working with bidders, the `listitems.inc.php` include file code creates a list box with the current Items table data records, along with three buttons to trigger events to view, delete, and update a specific item. Follow these steps to create the `listitems.inc.php` file:

**1.** **Open your editor and enter this code:**

```php
<?php

echo "<script language=\"javascript\">\n";
echo "function listbox_dblclick() {\n";
echo "document.items.updateitem.click() }\n";
echo "</script>\n";

echo "<script language=\"javascript\">\n";
echo "function button_click(target) {\n";
echo "if(target==0) " .
     "document.items.action=\"index.php?content=removeitem\"\n";
echo "if(target==1) " .
     " document.items.action=\"index.php?content=updateitem\"\n";
echo "}\n";
echo "</script>\n";

echo "<h2>Select Item</h2>\n";
echo "<form name=\"items\" method=\"post\">\n";
echo "<select ondblclick=\"listbox_dblclick()\" " .
     "name=\"itemid\" size=\"20\">\n";

$items= Item::getItems();
foreach($items as $item) {
    $itemid = $item->itemid;
    $name = $item->name;
    $option = $itemid . " - " . $name;
    echo "<option value=\"$itemid\">$option</option>\n";
}
echo "</select><br><br>\n";

echo "<input type=\"submit\" onClick=\"button_click(0)\" " .
     "name=\"deleteitem\" value=\"Delete Item\">\n";
```

```
echo "<input type=\"submit\" onClick=\"button_click(1)\" " .
    "name=\"updateitem\" value=\"Update Item\">\n";
echo "</form>\n";

?>
```

2. **Save the file in the** auction **folder as** listitems.inc.php.

The listitems.inc.php code generates the web page shown in Figure 2-6.

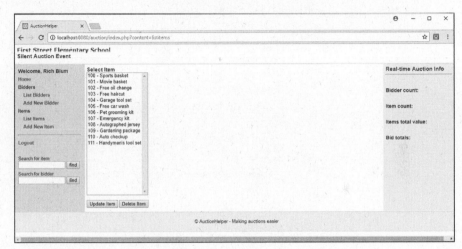

**FIGURE 2-6:**
The web page generated by the listitems.inc. php include file.

You should recognize the similarities with the listbidders.inc.php code. The listitems.inc.php code creates the two JavaScript functions for handling the web page events, displays the items table data records in a list box, and then displays two buttons:

>> **Delete Item:** Removes an item data record from the Items table.

>> **Update Item:** Updates an existing item data record in the Items table.

The form works similar to the listbidders.inc.php code. However, you don't need an event to display an item, because that's not a requirement for the application (see Chapter 1 of this minibook for the application requirements).

If the user double-clicks an item in the list or clicks the Update Item button, that triggers the updateitem.inc.php code. If the user clicks the Delete Item button, that triggers the removeitem.inc.php code. These files are described in the next sections.

## Deleting an item

The `removeitem.inc.php` code works the same way as the `removebidder.inc.php` code does. It retrieves the item ID of the item the user selects in the list box and then uses it to delete the associated data record in the Items table. Follow these steps to create the `removeitem.inc.php` code:

**1.** **Open your editor and enter the following code:**

```php
<?php
if (isset($_SESSION['login'])) {
    $itemid = $_POST['itemid'];
    $item = Item::findItem($itemid);
    $result = $item->removeItem();

    if ($result)
        echo"<h2>Item $itemid removed</h2>\n";
    else
        echo "<h2>Sorry, problem removing item $itemid</h2>\n";
} else {
    echo "<h2>Please login first</h2>\n";
}
?>
```

**2.** **Save the file in the** auction **folder as** `removeitem.inc.php`.

The `removeitem.inc.php` include file code checks to make sure the user is properly logged in. Then it retrieves the `itemid` value passed to it. It uses that `itemid` value in the `findItem()` static method to retrieve the `Item` object and then the `removeItem()` method to remove the item data record from the Items table.

## Updating an item

When the application user either double-clicks an item entry in the list box or selects an entry from the list box and clicks the Update Item button, those events trigger the `updateitem.inc.php` include file. Follow these steps to create that file:

**1.** **Open your editor and enter the following code:**

```php
<?php
if (!isset($_POST['itemid']) OR (!is_numeric($_POST['itemid']))) {
    echo "<h2>You did not select a valid itemid value</h2>\n";
    echo "<a href=\"index.php?content=listitems\">List items</a>\n";
} else {
    $itemid = $_POST['itemid'];
```

```php
    $item = Item::findItem($itemid);
    if ($item) {
        echo "<h2>Update Item $item->itemid</h2><br>\n";
        echo "<form name=\"items\" action=\"index.php\"
method=\"post\">\n";
        echo "<CDATAtable>\n";
        echo "<tr><td>ItemID</td><td>$item->itemid</td></tr>\n";
        echo "<tr><td>Name</td><td><input type=\"text\" name=\"name\" ".
            "value=\"$item->name\"></td></tr>\n";
        echo "<tr><td>Description</td><td><input type=\"text\" ".
            "name=\"description\" value=\"$item->description\"></td>
</tr>\n";
        echo "<tr><td>Resale Price</td><td><input type=\"text\" ".
            "name=\"resaleprice\" value=\"$item->resaleprice\"></td>
</tr>\n";
        echo "<tr><td>Winning Bidder</td><td><input type=\"text\" ".
            "name=\"winbidder\" value=\"$item->winbidder\"></td></tr>\n";
        echo "<tr><td>Winning Price</td><td><input type=\"text\" ".
            "name=\"winprice\" value=\"$item->winprice\"></td></tr>\n";
        echo "</CDATAtable><br><br>\n";
        echo "<input type=\"submit\" name=\"answer\" ".
            "value=\"Update Item\">\n";
        echo "<input type=\"submit\" name=\"answer\" value=\"Cancel\">\n";
        echo "<input type=\"hidden\" name=\"itemid\" value=\"$itemid\">\n";
        echo "<input type=\"hidden\" name=\"content\" value=\
"changeitem\">\n";
        echo "</form>\n";
    } else {
        echo "<h2>Sorry, item $itemid not found</h2>\n";
        echo "<a href=\"index.php?content=listitems\">List items</a>\n";
    }
}
?>
<script language="javascript">
document.items.winbidder.focus();
document.items.winbidder.select();
</script>
```

2. **Save the file in the** auction **folder as** updateitem.inc.php.

The updateitem.inc.php include file generates the web page shown in Figure 2-7.

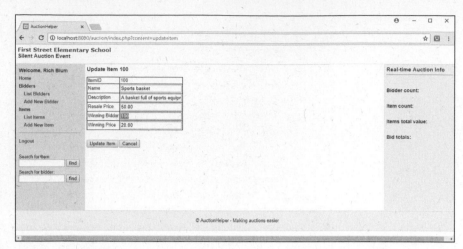

FIGURE 2-7:
The web page
generated by the
updateitem.
inc.php
include file.

The `updateitem.inc.php` code retrieves the `itemid` value passed to it and then uses the `findItem()` static method to retrieve the item's data record from the Items table. It uses the item properties to populate the form, which then allows the user to change any of the item property values.

The last part of the code file adds a JavaScript section to the web page to set the default cursor location for the form. Note, however, that it doesn't set the cursor at the `itemid` data field. Instead, it sets the cursor at the `winbidder` data field:

```
<script language="javascript">
document.items.winbidder.focus();
document.items.winbidder.select();
</script>
```

As the silent auction event ends, the volunteers will need to rush to enter the winning bidder information for each item. This helps out a bit by ensuring the `updateitem` form opens with the cursor in the winning bidder form field so all the volunteers need to do is enter the winning bidder number and the winning bid value!

When the application user clicks the Submit button, the form passes the updated data to the `changeitem.inc.php` include file. Follow these steps to create that file:

1. **Open your editor and enter the following code:**

```
<?php
if (isset($_SESSION['login'])) {
    $itemid = $_POST['itemid'];
    $answer = $_POST['answer'];
```

```
    if ($answer == "Update Item") {
        $item = Item::findItem($itemid);
        $item->itemid = $_POST['itemid'];
        $item->name = $_POST['name'];
        $item->description = $_POST['description'];
        $item->resaleprice = $_POST['resaleprice'];
        $item->winbidder = $_POST['winbidder'];
        $item->winprice = $_POST['winprice'];
        $result = $item->updateItem();
        if ($result) {
            echo "<h2>Item $itemid updated</h2>\n";
        } else {
            echo "<h2>Problem updating item $itemid</h2>\n";
        }
    } else {
        echo "<h2>Update Canceled for item $itemid</h2>\n";
    }
} else {
    echo "<h2>Please login first</h2>\n";
}
?>
```

**2.** **Save the file in the** auction **folder as** changeitem.inc.php.

The changeitem.inc.php code first checks to make sure the user is properly logged in. Then it retrieves the $_POST['answer'] value to determine if the user canceled the update or not. If the user clicked the Update button, the code retrieves the itemid, uses the findItem() static method to retrieve the item's data as an Item object, changes the item's properties using the retrieved form data, and uses the updateItem() method to update the existing data record in the Items table.

## Adding a new item

Are you starting to get the hang of things now? The application is just a series of events, and you just need to create the PHP include files tied to the individual events to perform the task associated with the event. That's the core of dynamic web applications!

When the application user clicks the link to add a new item from the navigation menu (see Figure 2-1), the link points to the main index.php file, setting the content HTML variable to newitem:

```
<a href="index.php?content=newitem">
```

That means you now need to code the `newitem.inc.php` include file. Follow these steps to do that:

**1.** **Open your editor and enter the following code:**

```
<h2>Enter new item information</h2>
<form name="newitem" action="index.php" method="post">

<CDATAtable cellpadding="1" border="0">
<tr><td>Item ID:</td><td><input type="text" name="itemid" size="4">
</td></tr>
<tr><td>Name:</td><td><input type="text" name="name" size="20">
</td></tr>
<tr><td>Description:</td><td><input type="text" name="description"
   size="50">
</td></tr>
<tr><td>Resale Price:</td><td><input type="text" name="resaleprice"
   size="10">
</td></tr>
<tr><td>Winning Bidder:</td><td><input type="text" name="winbidder"
   size="4">
</td></tr>
<tr><td>Winning Price:</td><td><input type="text" name="winprice"
   size="10">
</td></tr>
</table><br>
<input type="submit" value="Submit new Item">
<input type="hidden" name="content" value="additem">
</form>

<script language="javascript">
document.newitem.itemid.focus();
document.newitem.itemid.select();
</script>
```

**2.** **Save the file in the** auction **folder as** `newitem.inc.php`.

The `newitem.inc.php` code generates the web page shown in Figure 2-8.

The `newitem.inc.php` code generates the form that users use to add a new item. When the user clicks the Submit button, that triggers the `additem.inc.php` file. Follow these steps to create that file:

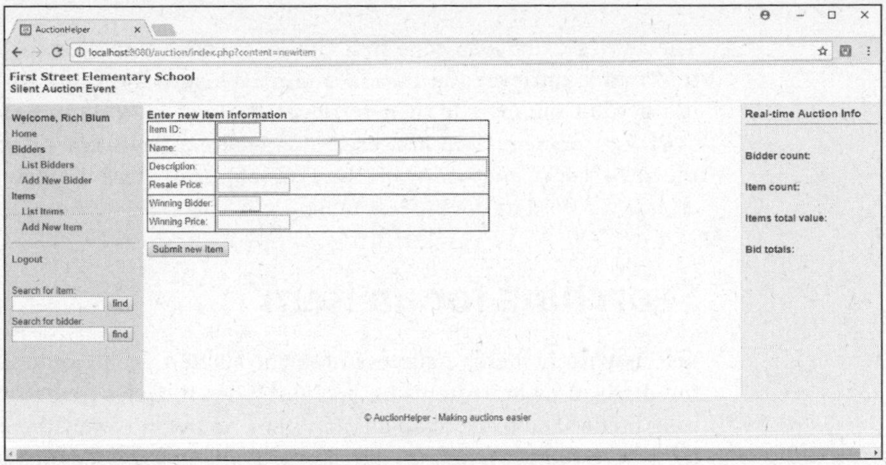

**FIGURE 2-8:**
The web page generated by the `newitem.inc.php` include file.

**1.** Open your editor and enter the following code:

```php
<?php
if (isset($_SESSION['login'])) {
    $itemid = $_POST['itemid'];
    if ((trim($itemid) == '') OR (!is_numeric($itemid)))
    {
        echo "<h2>Sorry, you must enter a valid item ID number</h2>\n";
    } else
    {
        $name = $_POST['name'];
        $description = $_POST['description'];
        $resaleprice = $_POST['resaleprice'];
        $winbidder = $_POST['winbidder'];
        $winprice = $_POST['winprice'];

        $item = new Item($itemid, $name, $description, $resaleprice,
                    $winbidder, $winprice);
        $result = $item->saveItem();
        if ($result)
            echo "<h2>New Item #$itemid successfully added</h2>\n";
        else
            echo "<h2>Sorry, there was a problem adding that item</h2>\n";
    }
} else {
    echo "<h2>Please login first</h2>\n";
}
?>
```

**2.** Save the file in the `auction` folder as `additem.inc.php`.

The `additem.inc.php` code first checks to make sure the user is properly logged in. Then it retrieves the `itemid` and makes sure the value isn't empty and that it's a valid number. It then retrieves the rest of the form data posted by the `newitem.inc.php` form and uses it to create a new `Item` object. Finally, it uses the `saveItem()` method from the `Item` object to store the new item information as a data record in the Bidders table.

## Searching for an item

Just as with bidders, a successful silent auction event could potentially contain hundreds of separate items for auction! When it comes time to assigning the winning bidder and price to an auction item, you won't want the auction volunteers to have to hunt through the list box of items looking for the one item to update. This is where the search box comes in handy.

The navigation section includes the HTML code to create a simple search text box for items:

```
<form action="index.php" method="post">
<label>Search for item:</label><br>
   <input type="text" name="itemid" size="14" >
   <input type="submit" value="find" >
<input type="hidden" name="content" value="updateitem">
</form>
```

The form retrieves the `itemid` value from the text box and sets the `content` HTML variable to `updateitem` to pass to the `index.php` file. This combination passes the `itemid` value to the `updateitem.inc.php` file, which you've already created.

# Logging Out of a Web Application

So far, the application has controlled access to major features (such as adding and updating bidders and items) by checking for the existence of the login session cookie. As long as the volunteer keeps the browser window open, when he or she logs in the session will remain active, and the application will allow the user full control of the data.

The session will end when the browser is closed, but sometimes customers prefer to see an actual Logout feature to ensure that they've properly logged out from the application and that no one can come by later and gain unauthorized access to the application. It's always a good idea to include a logout feature in your dynamic web applications.

In the AuctionHelper program, the Logout link is included as part of the navigation menu:

```
<tr><td><a href="index.php?content=logout">
<strong>Logout</strong></a></td></tr>
```

This link sets the content HTML variable to the value logout, which triggers the index.php file to include the logout.inc.php include file. This is the last file you'll need to create to complete the application! Follow these steps to do that:

**1.** **Open your editor to a new window and enter the following code:**

```php
<?php
if (isset($_SESSION['login']))
{
    unset($_SESSION['login']);
}
header("Location: index.php");

?>
```

**2.** **Save the file in the** auction **folder as** logout.inc.php.

**3.** **You can finally close out your editor — you're done coding for this project!**

The logout.inc.php include file first checks to make sure the login session cookie exists, and if it does, it uses the unset() function to remove it. This doesn't stop the session, but it removes the session cookie the application uses to detect if the user is logged in.

The header() function may take some explanation:

```
header("Location: index.php");
```

The header() PHP function sends an HTTP header message to the browser. The Location message instructs the browser to redirect to the specified URL. In this case, the code redirects the browser back to the index.php file, which causes the browser to repaint the main web page. This time, though, since the login session cookie is gone, the main web page will display the login form.

**WARNING**

The PHP server must send any HTTP messages generated by the header() function before any HTML code. Because this application uses the header() function in an include file, that won't be the case. What allows you to do this is the output_buffer setting in the PHP server. If you enable that setting in the php.ini configuration file, the PHP server buffers all output from the program.

Then it sends all the output in one stream. The output buffer is smart and will rearrange any HTTP messages to the front of the buffer, sending them first.

# Testing Web Applications

Congratulations! If you've been following along with the code in these last two chapters, you've just completed a full-featured dynamic web application to track silent auction data. However, the development work doesn't stop after you've designed the website and created the code. You must ensure that things work correctly before handing the application over to your customer.

That process involves testing. There are generally four levels of testing that you can perform with dynamic web applications. From lowest to highest, they are as follows:

>> **Unit testing:** Perform tests on individual sections of code to ensure that there are no syntax or logic errors.

>> **Integration testing:** Perform tests on passing data between different sections of code to ensure that there is no data mismatch.

>> **System testing:** Perform tests on the entire website to ensure that all the functionality works correctly and nothing is missing.

>> **Acceptance testing:** Your customer tests the website to ensure that it works as he or she specified and that he or she understands the user interface.

In PHP applications, you often perform the unit testing as part of each include file that you create to respond to events. Ensure that when you click a link in the web page, the proper include file triggers and that it performs its job correctly.

When you perform unit testing, watch for PHP warnings as well as errors. Warnings may not adversely affect the outcome of the application, but it's poor programming practice to misuse PHP code, even if it doesn't cause a fatal error.

Integration testing with include files can get somewhat tricky. It's easy to get lost in a sea of include files, even in a small application like AuctionHelper. It often helps to draw a process map, showing which include files are triggered by events and which include files rely on other include files. Figure 2-9 shows a simple process diagram for the include files used in the AuctionHelper application.

**AuctionHelper Processes**

<u>Navigation</u>
nav.inc.php

<u>Bidder Info</u>
(list bidders link) -> listbidders.inc.php (View bidder button) -> displaybidder.inc.php
                 (Delete bidder button) -> removebidder.inc.php
                 (Update bidder button) -> updatebidder.inc.php -> changebidder.inc.php
(Add bidder link) -> newbidder.inc.php -> addbidder.inc.php

<u>Item Info</u>
(List items link) -> listitems.inc.php    (Delete item button) -> removeitem.inc.php
                          (Update item button) -> updateitem.inc.php -> changeitem.inc.php
(Add item link) -> newitem.Inc.php -> additem.inc.php

<u>Searching</u>
(Search for Item) -> updateitem.inc.php -> changeitem.inc.php
(Search for Bidder) -> displaybidder.inc.php

<u>Logout</u>
logout.inc.php

**FIGURE 2-9:**
Process diagram for the AuctionHelper include files.

In situations where a function relies on two separate include files (such as passing new bidder information from the `newbidder.inc.php` include file to the `addbidder.inc.php` include file), integration testing must ensure that all the data values are passed correctly.

System testing requires that you (or better yet, someone else) walk through the entire application from start to finish. Every link and button event must function correctly, producing proper content on the web pages. The system testing often refers back to the original feature requirements that were defined by the customer, ensuring that each of the requirements is met by the applications.

Finally, you're ready to turn your creation over to the customer for acceptance testing. It often helps to have a checklist handy for each of the requirement features, to ensure that the customer doesn't forget to test all the features of the application. If you're also required to create a user guide for the application, this is also a good place to test that out as well!

With all that, there's still one final feature that you haven't implemented from the original requirements. If you remember from Chapter 1 of this minibook, one of the original requirements was to provide real-time statistics for the auction totals. You created an area to display the data, but you didn't actually create the data. That requires some JavaScript tricks that you haven't seen yet, so I saved that for another chapter.

IN THIS CHAPTER

» **Getting acquainted with AJAX**

» **Using JavaScript to communicate**

» **Working with jQuery and AJAX**

» **Using XML to transfer data**

» **Adding AJAX to AuctionHelper**

Chapter **3**

# Using AJAX

The previous two chapters in this minibook walk through the AuctionHelper application, a dynamic web application used to support a silent auction. There is one requirement for that project that I haven't covered yet — the ability to update web pages with real-time data. To do that requires a little more than just PHP or even just JavaScript. It requires using a new technology that combines both languages! This chapter discusses just what that technology is and how to produce dynamic content on a web page without having to reload the web page, a great feature to include in your web applications!

## Getting to Know AJAX

One of the newest technologies to hit dynamic web programming is *Asynchronous JavaScript and XML* (called AJAX). This name doesn't refer to either the household cleaner or the figure in Greek mythology. It also doesn't refer to a new type of programming language.

Instead, AJAX refers to a method of combining several existing web languages and standards to produce dynamic content on a web page. AJAX utilizes the following technologies:

> » **JavaScript:** To communicate with a web server "behind the scenes" in an existing web page in the browser

>> **A server-side programming language:** To retrieve the dynamic content from the application database

>> **Extensible Markup Language (XML):** To safely transfer the dynamic content back to the browser

>> **HTML and CSS:** To place the dynamic content on the web page and assign styles and positioning to it

>> **Document Object Model (DOM):** To reference locations on a web page to place the dynamic content

Trying to picture just how all these piece fit together can be a bit confusing. Figure 3-1 shows a rough diagram of how this all works.

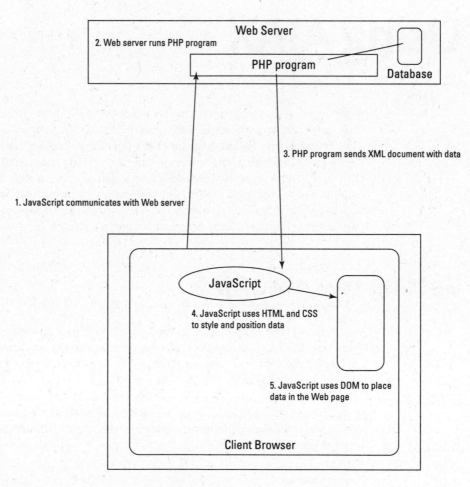

FIGURE 3-1:
The basics
of AJAX.

The first step in AJAX is for JavaScript code embedded within the web page to establish an HTTP connection with a web server to retrieve a specific web page. The web page can be a static HTML file, but more often it utilizes a server-side programming language, such as PHP, to retrieve data from an application database to return to the JavaScript client program.

In AJAX, data retrieved from the server is usually formatted using the XML standard to send back to the browser, although that's not a requirement. Data can be sent using any formatting standard, or even just in plain text. Recently the JavaScript Object Notation (JSON) format has become increasingly popular to use as a method to format data in AJAX implementations.

When the JavaScript code in the browser receives the new data, it uses HTML and CSS to place and style the new content, usually using DOM manipulation to place the data in the existing web page that's displayed in the browser. All this happens behind the scenes of an existing web page while the website visitor is viewing it!

The key to AJAX is the creation of a special JavaScript object that can communicate with web servers. The next section discusses just what that is.

# Communicating Using JavaScript

Allowing JavaScript code to run in a web page and communicate directly with a web server has revolutionized dynamic web applications. This feature actually isn't all that new. Microsoft introduced the feature with the XMLHTTP ActiveX object way back in Internet Explorer version 5.

The XMLHTTP object allowed you to specify a URL to connect to a web server using HTTP and retrieve the web page content that the server returned. Although it's simplistic, this started a revolution that has changed the face of dynamic web applications!

The downside was that Microsoft controlled the standard, and other browsers were reluctant to incorporate it. Soon, though, a JavaScript standard was created to support this feature, called the XMLHttpRequest object. The XMLHttpRequest object does what its awkward names says: It sends an HTTP request to a web server and retrieves the response and creates an XML object. The XMLHttpRequest object quickly became popular and is supported by all the major browsers in use today.

This section walks through the methods and properties available in the XMLHttpRequest object and how to use them to communicate with a web server from your own web pages.

# Considering XMLHttpRequest class methods

The `XMLHttpRequest` object contains several class methods to help you control the interaction between the JavaScript program and the web server. Table 3-1 lists the methods available.

**TABLE 3-1**   **The XMLHttpRequest Class Methods**

| Method | Description |
|---|---|
| abort() | Cancels an existing request that is waiting for a response |
| getAllResponseHeaders() | Retrieves the HTTP header information returned by the web server |
| getResponseHeader() | Retrieves information from a specific HTTP header |
| open(*method*,*url*,*async*,*user*,*pass*) | Opens a connection to the specified web server |
| send(*string*) | Sends a request to the web server |
| setRequestHeader() | Adds HTML variable/value pairs for the request |

There aren't a lot of class methods for the `XMLHttpRequest`, making it not only powerful, but fairly easy to use! After instantiating a new `XMLHttpRequest` object, use the `open()` method to define the connection to the web server and the `send()` method to send the request to the server:

```
var con = new XMLHTTPRequest();
con.open("GET", "myprog.php", true);
con.send();
```

The first parameter of the `open()` method defines the HTTP request type to use — either the `GET` method or the `POST` method. The second parameter defines the URL to send the request to. The third parameter determines if the connection is asynchronous (`true`) or synchronous (`false`).

With a synchronous connection, JavaScript will wait at the `send()` method until it receives a response from the web server. While JavaScript is waiting, the browser won't process any other code or events in the web page. This will make the web page appear frozen, because the user won't be able to click any links or buttons.

With the asynchronous connection type, JavaScript sends the request and then continues on with the rest of the program. When it receives a response from the web server, it triggers a callback function that you define to handle the response (discussed in the next section). This allows the program code to continue operating while it's waiting for the server response, which is a much cleaner experience for the web page viewer.

WARNING

While currently still supported, the synchronous connection type is in the process of being deprecated in the XMLHttpRequest JavaScript standard. It's good practice to just use the asynchronous connection type for your applications, because that doesn't have an adverse effect on the web page user interface.

If you define the HTTP request to use the POST method of sending data, you must place the HTML variable/value data pairs as a parameter in the send() method:

```
con.open("POST", "myprog.php", true);
con.send("id=100&name=rich");
```

If you prefer to use the GET request method, you can include the HTML variable/value data pairs in the URL:

```
con.open("GET", "myprog.php?id=100&name=rich", true);
con.send();
```

Some browsers have a limitation on how long the connection URL can be, so for large amounts of data it's better to use the POST method.

After you send the request, you'll need to retrieve the response from the web server. That requires using a few of the XMLHttpRequest object class properties, discussed next.

WARNING

Due to the potential for abuse, most browsers restrict the URL that the XMLHttpRequest object can connect to. You can only connect to a URL in the same domain as the original web page that loads the object.

## Focusing on XMLHttpRequest class properties

The XMLHttpRequest object contains several class properties that you'll need to know about to handle the HTTP response from the web server. These are shown in Table 3-2.

Using AJAX

**TABLE 3-2**

## The XMLHttpRequest Class Properties

| Property | Description |
|---|---|
| onreadystatechange | Defines a callback function that the browser triggers when the HTTP connection changes state |
| readyState | Contains the connection status of the HTTP connection |
| responseText | Contains the response sent by the web server in text format |
| responseXML | Contains the response sent by the web server in XML format |
| status | Contains the numeric HTTP response code from the web server |
| statusText | Contains the text HTTP response string from the web server |

After you use the send( ) method to send a connection request to a web server, the HTTP connection process works through five connection states, as tracked by the readyState property:

>> **State 0:** The connection has not been initialized.

>> **State 1:** The connection to the server has been established.

>> **State 2:** The server received the HTTP request message.

>> **State 3:** The server is processing the HTTP request.

>> **State 4:** The server sent the response.

As the HTTP connection works through these five connection states, the value contained in the readyState property changes. This causes the function you define in the onreadystatechange property to trigger for each state change. When the readyState property contains a value of 4, the final result from the request is available for processing.

When the readyState property value is 4, you know the communication is complete, but you don't know how it turned out. To determine that, you check the HTTP response returned by the web server using the status property. If the status property contains the 200 numeric HTTP result code, that indicates the connection was successful, and any data returned by the web server is available in the responseText and responseXML properties. If the status property contains some other HTTP result code (such as 403 or 404), that indicates there was an error communicating with the web server.

Because these values are standard, it has become somewhat common practice to start out the onreadystatechange callback function code checking for them:

```
con.onreadystatechange = function() {
    if (this.readyState == 4  && this.status == 200) {
        var result = this.responseText;
    }
};
```

The function only retrieves the data when the connection is complete and has returned valid data. This method of defining the callback function inline is referred to as creating an *anonymous callback function,* because you don't define a name for the function. It only exists inside the onreadystatechange property, so you can't reference it anywhere else in your JavaScript code.

TIP

Although using an anonymous function is a popular way of defining the callback function, you can define the function as a standard named JavaScript function and then reference that function name in the onreadystatechange property.

## Trying out AJAX

Now that you've seen a little about how AJAX works, let's walk through an example of using it. For this example, you write some code that dynamically changes the values in a drop-down box based on a selection in another drop-down box on the web page. Follow these steps to get started:

1.  **Open your favorite text editor, program editor, or integrated development environment (IDE) package.**

2.  **Enter the following code:**

```
<!DOCTYPE html>
<html>
<head>
<title>Car dropdown test</title>
<script language="javascript" type="text/javascript">
function getmodels()
{
    var select = document.getElementById("make");
    var make = select.options[select.selectedIndex].value;
    var URL = "ajaxcars.php?make=" + make;
    var request = new XMLHttpRequest();
    request.open("GET", URL);
    request.onreadystatechange = function() {
        if (request.readyState == 4 && request.status == 200) {
            var models = request.responseText.split(',');
            var model = document.getElementById('model');
```

```
            if (model) {
                model.innerHTML = "";
                for(i = 0; i < models.length; i++) {
                model.innerHTML += "<option value='" + models[i] +
                                "'>" + models[i] + "</option>";
                }
            }
        }
    }
    request.send();
}
</script>
</head>
<body>
<h2>Find your car</h2>
Make:
<select id="make" onchange="getmodels()">
<option value="">Select the make</option>
<option value="buick">Buick</option>
<option value="chevy">Chevy</option>
<option value="dodge">Dodge</option>
<option value="ford">Ford</option>
</select><br><br>

Model:
<select id="model">
<option value="">Select make first</option>
</select>
</body>
</html>
```

3. **Save the file as** ajaxcars1.html **in the** DocumentRoot **area of your web server.**

   For XAMPP on Windows, that's c:\xampp\htdocs; for XAMPP on macOS, that's /Applications/XAMPP/htdocs.

4. **Open a new editor window or tab, and enter the following code:**

```
<?php
$make = $_GET['make'];
switch ($make)
{
    case "buick":
        echo "Enclave,Lacrosse,Regal";
        break;
```

```
        case "chevy":
            echo "Camero,Corvette,Impala";
            break;
        case "dodge":
            echo "Challenger,Charger,Viper";
            break;
        case "ford":
            echo "Fusion,Mustang,Taurus";
    }
?>
```

5. **Save the file as** ajaxcars.php **in the** DocumentRoot **folder of your web server.**

6. **Open your browser and then enter the following URL in the address bar:**

```
http://localhost:8080/ajaxcars1.html
```

*Note:* You may need to use a different port in the URL, depending on your web server configuration.

7. **Make a selection from the Make drop-down box.**

As you make the selection, the options available in the Model drop-down box dynamically change!

The initial web page produced by the ajaxcars1.html file is shown in Figure 3-2.

**FIGURE 3-2:**
The ajaxcars1.
html initial web
page.

## AJAX AND CACHED PAGES

One issue that you may run into when using AJAX in your application is cached web pages. Most web browsers have the ability to cache the response returned by a specific URL. This helps reduce the amount of data the browser must download from the server and speed up the time it takes to load a web page. Unfortunately, caching also applies to the HTTP requests sent by the XMLHttpRequest object. If you use the same URL to retrieve dynamic data from a server-side program, the browser may cache one response and always use that response for the URL. This will cause problems if the data returned by the web server changes.

One way to solve this issue is to create a unique URL for each HTTP request by adding a large random number as a GET variable/value pair:

```
var random = Math.floor(Math.random() * 1000);
var myurl = "myprog.php?x=" + random;
con.open("GET", myurl, true);
```

The random number isn't used by the receiving program. Its sole purpose is to make each HTTP request unique, causing the browser to retrieve the actual data from the web server and not a cached web page.

As you make a selection in the Make drop-down box, the options available in the Model drop-down box dynamically change. After creating the web page layout, the ajaxcars1.html code uses JavaScript to listen for events from the Make drop-down box. When a change is made to a selection, that triggers the getmodels() JavaScript function.

The getmodels() function uses DOM to retrieve the selection made in the select element:

```
var make = select.options[select.selectedIndex].value;
```

Then it passes the selection to the ajaxcars.php program using an XMLHttp Request object:

```
var request = new XMLHttpRequest();
var URL = "ajaxcars.php?make=" + make;
request.open("GET", URL);
```

The ajaxcars.php code returns a simple text string of models, separated by commas, based on the make value it receives. Back at the ajaxcars1.html file, the onreadystatechange callback function retrieves the returned value, converts it into an array, retrieves the `options` DOM object handle for the Models drop-down box, and then uses the `innerHTML` DOM property for the `model` drop-down box to reset and change the options available in the drop-down box. Before your eyes, the drop-down box options change to match the car make you select. Now that's dynamic programming!

# Using the jQuery AJAX Library

Unfortunately, using the `XMLHttpRequest` object is somewhat clunky in JavaScript. There are a lot of parts that you need to have in place and use in the correct order for things to work correctly. The popular jQuery JavaScript library (discussed in Book 3, Chapter 3) comes to our rescue by providing some functions to help simplify using AJAX.

## The jQuery $.ajax() function

The `$.ajax()` function in jQuery allows you to build all the parts for an `XMLHttpRequest` object at one time in one place. Instead of having to break things down into several different methods and properties, you just fill out a series of key/value pairs to submit in your request and process the response:

```
$.ajax({
    type: 'POST',
    url: 'myprog.php',
    data: { id: "100", name: "Rich" },
    dataType: "XML",
    success: function (response) {
        var XMLresult = response;
    },
    error: function(response) {
        console.log('Error: ' + response);
    }
});
```

The key/value pairs defined in the function control just how the request works. Table 3-3 shows the different elements available in the `$.ajax()` function settings.

**TABLE 3-3** The $.ajax() Function Settings

| Settings | Description |
| --- | --- |
| accepts | Defines the MIME data types the request will accept |
| async | Specifies if the connection is synchronous |
| beforeSend | Defines a callback method to trigger before the connection request is sent |
| cache | Prevents the browser from caching the request |
| complete | Defines the callback method to trigger when the connection is complete |
| contents | Defines a regular expression to determine how to parse the response |
| contentType | Defines the Content-type for the data sent to the server |
| context | Defines the DOM context for all callbacks |
| converters | Defines content type converters for the response data |
| crossDomain | Forces a connection to an outside domain |
| data | Sends data to the server in a POST request |
| dataFilter | Defines a function to process raw data in the response |
| dataType | Defines the data type expected in the response |
| error | Defines a callback function to trigger if the connection fails |
| global | Triggers global Ajax event handlers |
| headers | Defines additional HTML header values |
| ifModified | Returns data only if the response has changed since the last request |
| isLocal | Allows the current connection if it uses a local resource (such as a local file) |
| jsonp | Defines a callback function if the connection returns data in JSON format |
| jsonpCallback | Defines the callback function for a JSON request |
| method | Defines the HTTP method used for the request (GET or POST) |
| mimeType | Defines the MIME type used for the response |
| password | Defines the password if required to access the URL |
| processData | Bypasses processing the response data |
| scriptCharset | Sets the charset attribute on the <script> element if the response is a script |
| statusCode | Returns the HTTP status code for the response |

| Settings | Description |
| --- | --- |
| success | Defines a callback function to trigger if the connection succeeds |
| timeout | Sets the time to wait for a response from the server |
| traditional | Uses the traditional AJAX parameter serialization method |
| type | Defines the HTTP request method |
| url | Defines the URL connection string for the request |
| username | Defines the username if required to access the URL |
| xhr | Defines a callback function to create a custom XMLHttpRequest object |
| xhrFields | Defines the field name/value pairs for the XHR object |

Although the $.ajax() function has lots of features that allow you to customize it, most often you'll just need to use a few of them to create a standard connection request and retrieve the response data.

Follow these steps to convert the ajaxcars1.html file to use the $.ajax() function:

1. **Open the** ajaxcars1.html **file you previously created in your editor.**

2. **Modify the code to replace the** XMLHttpRequest **object with the** $.ajax() **function.**

Your final code should look like this:

```
<!DOCTYPE html>
<html>
<head>
<title>Car dropdown test</title>
<script src="jquery-3.2.1.min.js"></script>
<script language="javascript" type="text/javascript">
function getmodels()
{
    var select = document.getElementById("make");
    var make = select.options[select.selectedIndex].value;
    var URL = "ajaxcars.php?make=" + make;
    $.ajax({
        type: "GET",
        url: URL,
        dataType: "text",
```

```
            success: function(response) {
                var models = response.split(',');
                var model = document.getElementById('model');
                if (model) {
                    model.innerHTML = "";
                    for(i = 0; i < models.length; i++) {
                        model.innerHTML += "<option value='" + models[i] +
                                            "'>" + models[i] + "</option>";
                    }
                }
            }
    });
}
</script>
</head>
<body>
<h2>Find your car</h2>
Make:
<select id="make" onchange="getmodels()">
<option value="">Select the make</option>
<option value="buick">Buick</option>
<option value="chevy">Chevy</option>
<option value="dodge">Dodge</option>
<option value="ford">Ford</option>
</select><br><br>

Model:
<select id="model">
<option value="">Select make first</option>
</select>
</body>
</html>
```

3. **Save the file as** `ajaxcars2.html` **in the** `DocumentRoot` **folder for your web server.**

4. **Open your browser and enter the following URL:**

```
http://localhost:8080/ajaxcars2.html
```

5. **Make a selection from the Make drop-down box, and observe the options available in the Model drop-down box.**

The web page generated by the `ajaxcars2.html` file should work exactly the same as the web page generated by the `ajaxcars1.html` file. As you make a selection in the Make drop-down box, the options available in the Models drop-down box dynamically change.

Note that to run the `ajaxcars2.html` file, you need to specify the jQuery library file in a `script` element. If you haven't downloaded that previously while working in Book 3, Chapter 3, you can download the current jQuery library file from `http://jquery.com`.

## The jQuery $.get() function

The `$.ajax()` function helps clean up your code a little bit, but there's still a lot of information you need to enter into the settings for the connection to work. As you create different AJAX applications, you'll notice that many of the settings that you use remain the same from program to program. To help make things easier, the jQuery library contains the `$.get()` function.

The `$.get()` function assumes the common setting values used in the `$.ajax()` function, so that you only need to specify a couple of things:

```
$.get('myprog.php').done(function(response) {
    var result = response;
}).fail(function(response) {
    console.log('Error: ' + response);
});
```

Now that's really making things simple! Follow these steps to modify the `ajaxcars2.html` file to use the `$.get()` jQuery function:

**1.** **Open the** `ajaxcars2.html` **file in your editor.**

**2.** **Modify the code to replace the** `$.ajax()` **function with the** `$.get()` **function.**

Your final code should look like this:

```
<!DOCTYPE html>
<html>
<head>
<title>Car dropdown test</title>
<script src="jquery-3.2.1.min.js"></script>
<script language="javascript" type="text/javascript">
function getmodels()
```

```
{
    var select = document.getElementById("make");
    var make = select.options[select.selectedIndex].value;
    var URL = "ajaxcars.php?make=" + make;
    $.get(URL).done(function(response) {
        var models = response.split(',');
        var model = document.getElementById('model');
        if (model) {
            model.innerHTML = "";
            for(i = 0; i < models.length; i++) {
                model.innerHTML += "<option value='" + models[i] +
                                "'>" + models[i] + "</option>";
            }
        }
    });
}
</script>
</head>
<body>
<h2>Find your car</h2>
Make:
<select id="make" onchange="getmodels()">
<option value="">Select the make</option>
<option value="buick">Buick</option>
<option value="chevy">Chevy</option>
<option value="dodge">Dodge</option>
<option value="ford">Ford</option>
</select><br><br>

Model:
<select id="model">
<option value="">Select make first</option>
</select>
</body>
</html>
```

3. **Save the file as** ajaxcars3.html **in the** DocumentRoot **folder for your web server.**

4. **Open your browser and enter the following URL:**

```
http://localhost:8080/ajaxcars3.html
```

5. **Make a selection in the Make drop-down box and observe the options available in the Model drop-down box.**

With the `$.get()` function, you can focus on the code that handles the response without having to worry about all the settings!

# Transferring Data in AJAX

The `ajaxcars.php` server program used in the previous examples sent the response data back to the client browser as a comma-separated string value. That's fine for small amounts of data, but if your application needs to move large amounts of data that can quickly get confusing.

To help organize the data sent back to the browser, the AJAX standard suggests using the XML markup standard. There are many different data formatting standards you could use, for web developers using XML is a popular choice because it's similar to HTML, so using it isn't too much of a new learning curve. The following sections discuss the XML standard and how to use it in both your PHP and JavaScript code.

## Looking at the XML standard

Similar to HTML, a standard XML document uses element tags to identify each data element in the document. The first element in an XML document identifies the XML standard used. Then that's followed by the actual data elements:

```
<?xml version="1.0" encoding="UTF-8"?>
<car>Dodge</car>
```

Unlike HTML, there are no standard tags used in XML — you can define any tag you want to represent the data in your application! Just as in HTML, you can create levels of data in XML:

```
<?xml version="1.0" encoding="UTF-8"?>
<car>
<make>Dodge</make>
<model>Challenger</model>
</car>
```

Because there are no predefined element names in XML, you can create element names and levels as needed for your application. All the same rules for element names that you're already familiar with in HTML apply to XML:

>> Element names can contain letters, numbers, hyphens, underscores, and periods.

>> Element names are case-sensitive.

>> Element names must start with a letter or underscore.

>> Element names cannot contain spaces.

>> Elements must have a matching close tag.

Just like HTML, XML elements also support attributes:

```
<?xml version="1.0" encoding="UTF-8"?>
<car make="Dodge">
<model>Challenger</model>
</car>
```

The same rules for element names apply to attribute names. You can also define multiple attributes in a single element. Just separate each attribute/value pair with a space. Also, it's important to remember that you must enclose the attribute value in quotes.

One of the benefits of using XML is that finding data in an XML document is a breeze. The XML standard uses the same Document Object Model (DOM) as HTML. You use the XML DOM to reference an individual element or attribute contained anywhere within the XML document.

The following sections explain how to use XML to handle data in PHP and JavaScript.

## Using XML in PHP

You can manually build all the XML elements to create an XML document as a string value in PHP, but there's an easier way to do that! PHP includes the DOMDocument object, which allows you to build an XML document as an object. Often, it's easier to manipulate an object than a string value in the PHP code.

## ELEMENTS OR ATTRIBUTES?

You'll notice that in XML you can specify data as either an element or an attribute within an element. Usually, it doesn't matter which method you use to store your data in the XML document — both methods save the data, and both methods allow you to retrieve the data. For example, you can use all elements:

```
<car>
<make>Dodge</make>
<model>Challenger</model>
</car>
<car>
<make>Ford</make>
<model>Mustang</model>
</car>
```

Or you can use all attributes:

```
<car make="Dodge" model="Challenger"></car>
<car make="Ford" model="Mustang"></car>
```

Or you can mix and match:

```
<car make="Dodge">
<model>Challenger</model>
</car>
<car make="Ford">
<model>Mustang</model>
</car>
```

There are pros and cons to each format. Using the XML DOM, attribute values can be easier to retrieve when you know the element they're associated with. However, having lots of attributes for a single element can get somewhat messy in the document layout. Adding additional attributes isn't as easy as adding new elements. As you design your application, you'll need to decide how to format the XML DOM to handle the data transferred between your PHP and JavaScript programs.

To create a new DOMDocument object, just instantiate the class:

```
$doc = new DOMDocument("1.0");
```

The parameter specifies the XML version number PHP uses to create the document. When you create the object, you use the DOMDocument methods to add elements, attributes, and their values. There are quite a few DOMDocument methods available. Table 3-4 shows the methods that you'll most often use to create an XML document.

**TABLE 3-4** **Popular PHP DOMDocument Methods**

| Method | Description |
| --- | --- |
| appendChild | Adds a new child node to an existing node in the document |
| createAttribute | Creates a new attribute for an existing element |
| createElement | Creates a new element node in the document |
| createTextNode | Creates a text value for an existing element in the document |
| saveXML | Outputs the DOM document in XML format |

As you can see from Table 3-4, it doesn't take all that much code to create an XML document in PHP! Follow these steps to try building an XML document using PHP:

**1.** **Open your editor and enter the following code:**

```php
<?php
$doc = new DOMDocument("1.0");

$carlot = $doc->createElement("carlot");
$carlot = $doc->appendChild($carlot);
$car1 = $doc->createElement("car");
$car1 = $carlot->appendChild($car1);
$make1 = $doc->createAttribute("make");
$make1->value = "Dodge";
$car1->appendChild($make1);
$model1 = $doc->createElement("model", "Challenger");
$model1 = $car1->appendChild($model1);
$model2 = $doc->createElement("model", "Charger");
$model2 = $car1->appendChild($model2);

$car2 = $doc->createElement("car");
$car2 = $carlot->appendChild($car2);
$make2 = $doc->createAttribute("make");
$make2->value = "Ford";
$car2->appendChild($make2);
$model3 = $doc->createElement("model", "Mustang");
$model3 = $car2->appendChild($model3);

$output = $doc->saveXML();
```

```
header("Content-type: application/xml");
echo $output;
?>
```

2. **Save the file as** xmltest.php **in the** DocumentRoot **folder for your web server.**

3. **Open your browser and then enter the following URL in the browser address bar:**

```
http://localhost:8080/xmltest.php
```

4. **View the XML code displayed in the browser window.**

The Content-type HTTP header tells the browser that the document is an XML document and not an HTML document. That causes the browser to parse the text as an XML document and display the contents.

**WARNING**

Setting the Content-type HTTP header is also important when creating an XML document that you pass to the JavaScript XMLHttpRequest object. When JavaScript detects the XML document Content-type, it places the data in the responseXML property instead of the responseText property.

Different browsers display XML files in different formats. Figure 3-3 shows what the output looks like in the Microsoft Edge browser, which does a nice job of formatting the XML document.

**FIGURE 3-3:**
Viewing the XML source code using the Microsoft Edge browser.

The PHP code creates a new DOMDocument object, using the carlot element as the root of the XML tree:

```
$carlot = $doc->createElement("carlot");
$carlot = $doc->appendChild($carlot);
```

It then adds two car elements to the document. The first car element contains an attribute named make, with a value of "Dodge":

```
$car1 = $doc->createElement("car");
$car1 = $carlot->appendChild($car1);
$make1 = $doc->createAttribute("make");
$make1->value = "Dodge";
$car1->appendChild($make1);
```

It also contains two child elements, both named model, with different text values:

```
$model1 = $doc->createElement("model", "Challenger");
$model1 = $car1->appendChild($model1);
$model2 = $doc->createElement("model", "Charger");
$model2 = $car1->appendChild($model2);
```

Notice that you can add the text value associated with the node in the createElement method. If you prefer, you can use the createTextNode method to create the text value separately after you create the element.

**WARNING**

In XML DOM, the text contained within an element is considered a separate node. This is a significant difference from HTML DOM, where the text is part of the element. This can get confusing when you're trying to traverse an XML DOM tree.

Next the PHP code creates another car element with the make attribute set to "Ford". This car element only has one child element, using the model name. The code then appends the model element as a child node of the second car element.

The saveXML() method completes the process by converting the DOMDocument object into an XML document that you can send to the requesting browser using the echo statement.

## Using XML in JavaScript

To read the XML data sent by the PHP server in your JavaScript code, you use the DOMParser object. The DOMParser object creates a DOM tree from the XML document data and provides methods and properties for you to traverse the tree, accessing the elements and attributes it contains.

The `XMLHttpRequest` object uses the `responseXML` property to hold the data sent by the server as an XML `DOMParser` object, so creating the object has already been done for you:

```
var xmldoc = con.responseXML;
```

There aren't a lot of methods and properties that you need to know to get the XML data. You retrieve the XML elements using the `getElementsByTagName()` method:

```
var cars = xmldoc.getElementsByTagName("car");
```

This returns an array of all the `car` elements. You then just iterate through them to examine each element individually:

```
for(i = 0; i < cars.length; i++) {
    make = cars[i].getAttribute("make");
```

The `getAttribute()` method retrieves the value associated with the specified attribute name.

As you retrieve each individual `car` element, you then access each `model` child element from the `car` element using the `getElementsByTagName()` method:

```
var models = cars[i].getElementsByTagName("model");
for (j = 0; j < models.length; j++) {
    var model = models[j].childNodes[0].nodeValue;
```

For each individual `model` element, you need to read the text that it contains. However, with XML, that's a little tricky. Because the XML DOM treats the element text as a separate element node, you need to reference it as a separate node. This is where the `childNodes` property comes in handy. It contains an array of all the child nodes for an element. Because there's only one text node associated with the element, you can retrieve its value using `childNodes[0]` and the `nodeValue` property as shown earlier.

Follow these steps to write a JavaScript program to read the XML document created by the `xmltest.php` program:

**1.** Open your editor and enter the following code:

```
<!DOCTYPE html>
<html>
<head>
<title>XML test</title>
<script language="javascript" type="text/javascript">
```

```
function getcars() {
    var carlist = document.getElementById("carlist");
    carlist.innerHTML = "";
    var URL = "xmltest.php";
    var request = new XMLHttpRequest();
    request.open("GET", "xmltest.php", true);
    request.onreadystatechange = function() {
        if (request.readyState == 4 && request.status == 200) {
            var response = request.responseXML;
            var cars = response.getElementsByTagName("car");
            for(i = 0; i < cars.length; i++) {
                var make = cars[i].getAttribute("make");
                var models = cars[i].getElementsByTagName("model");
                for (j = 0; j < models.length; j++) {
                    var model = models[j].childNodes[0].nodeValue;
                    carlist.innerHTML += make + " " + model + "<br>";
                }
            }
        }
    }
    request.send();
}
</script>
</head>
<body>
<h2>JavaScript XML test</h2>
<p>Cars retrieved from the server:</p>
<div id="carlist"></div>

<p>This is the end of the list</p>
<input type="button" onclick="getcars()" value="Get cars">
</body>
</html>
```

2. **Save the file as** `xmltest.html` **in the** `DocumentRoot` **folder of your web server.**

3. **Open your browser and enter the following URL:**

```
http://localhost:8080/xmltest.html
```

4. **Click the Get Cars button to retrieve the XML document from the** `xmltest.php` **program.**

5. **Observe the changes dynamically made to the web page, and then close the browser when you're done.**

When you run the program and click the Get Cars button, you should see the list of cars defined in the XML document created by the xmltest.php program, as shown in Figure 3-4.

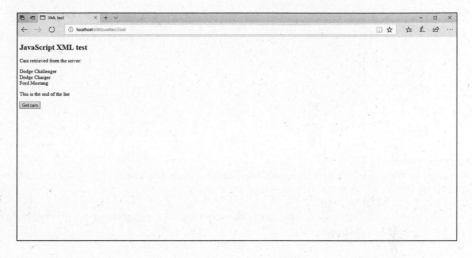

**FIGURE 3-4:**
The output of the
xmltest.html
program.

The JavaScript code uses the XMLHttpRequest object to request the xmltest.php page and then parses the XML document from the responseXML property to retrieve the car makes and models available on the car lot!

Now that you've seen how to use AJAX, the next step is to utilize it in the Auction-Helper program to display the real-time data for the auction. I cover that topic in the next section.

# Modifying the AuctionHelper Application

With your newfound skills in AJAX, you can now tackle the last requirement for the AuctionHelper application! If you remember from Chapter 1 of this minibook, the main layout for the AuctionHelper application contains a separate section to display the real-time data, as shown in Figure 3-5.

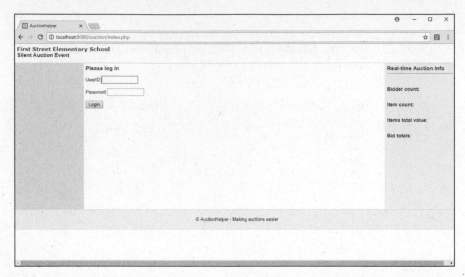

FIGURE 3-5:
The
AuctionHelper
main window.

The `aside.inc.php` code creates four separate `span` elements for the content to display:

» The total number of bidders

» The total number of items

» The total resale value of all the items

» The total current winning bid values

The first step to implement this feature is to create the PHP file that generates the real-time data and returns it as an XML document. Follow these steps to do that:

**1.** Open your editor and enter the following code:

```php
<?php
include("bidder.php");
include("item.php");

$bidders = Bidder::getTotalBidders();
$items = Item::getTotalItems();
$itemtotal = Item::getTotalPrice();
$bidtotal = Item::getTotalBids();

$doc = new DOMDocument("1.0");
$auction = $doc->createElement("auction");
$auction = $doc->appendChild($auction);
```

```
$bidders = $doc->createElement("bidders", $bidders);
$bidders = $auction->appendChild($bidders);

$items = $doc->createElement("items", $items);
$items = $auction->appendChild($items);
$itemtotal = $doc->createElement("itemtotal", $itemtotal);
$itemtotal = $auction->appendChild($itemtotal);
$bidtotal = $doc->createElement("bidtotal", $bidtotal);
$bidtotal = $auction->appendChild($bidtotal);
$output = $doc->saveXML();

header("Content-type: application/xml");
echo $output;
?>
```

2. **Save the file as** `realtime.php` **in the** `auction` **folder in the** `DocumentRoot` **folder for your web server.**

You should recognize the code in the `realtime.php` file. It creates a `DOMDocument` object and then populates it with the data you need. However, notice that I used four new static methods to retrieve the data. You could write the PHP code to directly access the auction database here, but it's better programming practice to let the `Bidder` and `Item` objects do that work for you. That means you'll need to add some code to each of the PHP files that create those objects. Follow these steps to do that:

1. **Open the** `bidder.php` **file from the** `auction` **folder in your editor.**

2. **At the very end of the code after the** `findBidder()` **static method definition (but before the closing bracket) add the following code:**

```
static function getTotalBidders() {
    $db = new mysqli("localhost", "ah_user", "AuctionHelper", "auction");
    $query = "SELECT count(bidderid) FROM bidders";
    $result = $db->query($query);
    $row = $result->fetch_array();
    if ($row) {
        return $row[0];
    } else {
        return NULL;
    }
}
```

3. **Save the file as** bidder.php **in the** auction **folder.**

4. **Open a new tab or window in your editor and then open the** item.php **file from the** auction **folder.**

5. **At the very end of the code after the** findItem() **static method definition (but before the closing bracket), add the following code:**

```php
static function getTotalItems() {
    $db = new mysqli("localhost", "ah_user", "AuctionHelper", "auction");
    $query = "SELECT count(itemid) FROM items";
    $result = $db->query($query);
    $row = $result->fetch_array();
    if ($row) {
        return $row[0];
    } else {
        return NULL;
    }
}

static function getTotalPrice() {
    $db = new mysqli("localhost", "ah_user", "AuctionHelper", "auction");
    $query = "SELECT sum(resaleprice) FROM items";
    $result = $db->query($query);
    $row = $result->fetch_array();
    if ($row) {
        return $row[0];
    } else {
        return NULL;
    }
}

static function getTotalBids() {
    $db = new mysqli("localhost", "ah_user", "AuctionHelper", "auction");
    $query = "SELECT sum(winprice) FROM items";
    $result = $db->query($query);
    $row = $result->fetch_array();
    if ($row) {
        return $row[0];
    } else {
        return NULL;
    }
}
```

**6.** Save the file as item.php **in the** auction **folder.**

Now you have the static class methods created and the code to generate the XML document with the real-time data you need. If you like, you can test that out by opening your browser and entering the following URL:

```
http://localhost:8080/auction/realtime.php
```

You should see the XML document that contains the data you need, as shown in Figure 3-6.

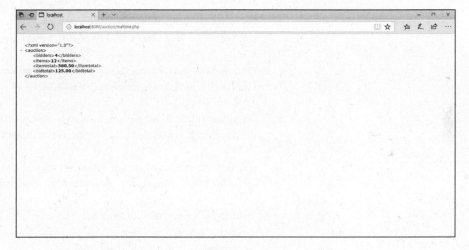

**FIGURE 3-6:**
Displaying the output from the realtime. php file.

The final step is to modify the index.php file to retrieve the data from the realtime.php file at a regular interval and populate the appropriate DOM objects to display the data.

First, you'll need to create the XMLHttpRequest object to retrieve the data and populate the DOM object. Follow these steps to do that:

**1.** Open the index.php **file from the** auction **folder in your editor.**

**2.** Modify the code in the <head> **section to look like this:**

```
<head>
<title>AuctionHelper</title>
<link rel="stylesheet" type="text/css" href="ah_styles.css">
<script language="javascript" type="text/javascript">
function getRealTime() {
    // retrieve the DOM objects to place the content
```

```
        var dombidders = document.getElementById("biddercount");
        var domitems = document.getElementById("itemcount");
        var domitemtotal = document.getElementById("itemtotal");
        var dombidtotal = document.getElementById("bidtotal");
        //send the GET request to retrieve the data
        var request = new XMLHttpRequest();
        request.open("GET", "realtime.php", true);
        request.onreadystatechange = function() {
            if (request.readyState == 4 && request.status == 200) {
                //parse the XML document to get each data element
                var xmldoc = request.responseXML;

                var xmlbidders = xmldoc.getElementsByTagName("bidders")[0];
                var bidders = xmlbidders.childNodes[0].nodeValue;

                var xmlitems = xmldoc.getElementsByTagName("items")[0];
                var items = xmlitems.childNodes[0].nodeValue;

                var xmlitemtotal = xmldoc.getElementsByTagName("itemtotal")[0];
                var itemtotal = xmlitemtotal.childNodes[0].nodeValue;

                var xmlbidtotal = xmldoc.getElementsByTagName("bidtotal")[0];
                var bidtotal = xmlbidtotal.childNodes[0].nodeValue;

                dombidders.innerHTML = bidders;
                domitems.innerHTML = items;
                domitemtotal.innerHTML = itemtotal;
                dombidtotal.innerHTML = bidtotal;
            }
        };
        request.send();
    }
</script>
</head>
```

**3.** **Save the file as** index.php **in the** auction **folder.**

The getRealTime() function uses the XMLHttpRequest object to submit the
request to the realtime.php program and then parses the content received in
the responseXML property. Because each data item is an element with a unique
name, the code uses four separate getElementsByTagName() methods to parse out
each element; then it uses the childNodes[0] property to retrieve the text value
assigned to the element.

However, nothing triggers the getRealTime() function yet. The trick to triggering the function at a regular interval to simulate a real-time update requires the JavaScript setInterval() function:

```
setInterval(function, time);
```

The setInterval() function triggers the function you specify every *time* milliseconds. So to trigger the getRealTime() function every five seconds, you'd write the following:

```
setInterval(getRealTime, 5000);
```

**WARNING**

Be careful when setting how often to fire a trigger to update real-time data. You may be tempted to have it trigger every second, but that could generate a lot of network traffic! Usually retrieving data every five seconds or so is sufficient for most "real-time" environments.

Now the only question is where to place that code! Follow these steps to do that:

**1.** Open the index.php **file from the** auction **folder in your editor.**

**2.** In the ‹aside› **section, modify the code to look like this:**

```
<aside>
<?php include("aside.inc.php"); ?>
<script language="javascript" type="text/javascript">
getRealTime();
setInterval(getRealTime, 5000);
</script>
</aside>
```

**3.** Save the file as index.php **in the** auction **folder.**

And that should do it! The first getRealTime() function triggers when each page loads to display the data and then the setInterval() function triggers the getRealTime() function every five seconds after that. (Notice that you don't use the parentheses when specifying the function name in the setInterval() function.) The new AuctionHelper page is shown in Figure 3-7.

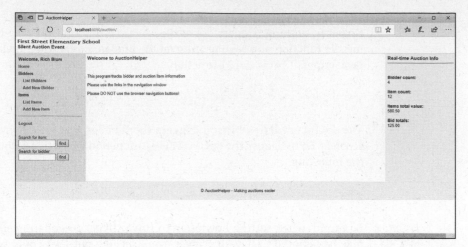

**FIGURE 3-7:**
The AuctionHelper main page with the real-time data added.

You can test this feature by opening two separate browser windows and logging into the AuctionHelper application. In one window, add a new bidder. Then watch the other window update the auction totals automatically!

Congratulations! You've completed the AuctionHelper dynamic web application! That was a lot of code to generate, but you've seen all the parts required to create a full-featured dynamic web application.

# Chapter **4**

# Extending WordPress

*S*ocial media. Two words that have changed the Internet and the world. It's no longer sufficient for a company or organization to just have a standard website presence — it must be plugged into the social media world to interact with customers or donors. Commercial websites such as Facebook and Twitter are all the rage, but there are also many options to create your own social media website. One package that has clearly risen above the rest is the WordPress web application. WordPress provides a standard template for easily creating a blog to express your (or your organization's) views on the Internet. This chapter explains just what WordPress is and how you can leverage the power behind WordPress to create your own custom social media website.

## Getting Acquainted with WordPress

Social interaction with friends, family, customers, or potential customers has become a popular requirement for web applications these days. One such method of interaction is blogging. Blogging allows companies to post information on the latest company business strategies, artists to share their portfolios with anyone on the Internet, or anyone to post articles on his or her personal life. Blogging allows you to engage your audience in conversation, making your website visitors feel more connected to you or your organization.

WordPress incorporates HTML, CSS, JavaScript, and PHP code to provide templates and building blocks for creating your own dynamic web application. You don't have to know anything about any of those languages to get a professional-looking blogging website up and running using WordPress. Just a few clicks of the mouse creates a fancy blogging interface that allows you to post content and your website visitors to find your content and post comments on it.

Over the years, WordPress has expanded its features and capabilities. It's not just a blogging package anymore. You can use WordPress to design more complicated dynamic web applications, easily rivaling the most sophisticated web applications coded by hand. WordPress claims that websites powered by the WordPress software now make up over 25 percent of the total websites on the Internet! It would be foolish for any web developer to ignore the power of WordPress.

As a PHP web developer, don't dismiss WordPress as a tool for those who can't code. You, too, can leverage the power of WordPress to simplify your website development process. Plus, you'll have the ability to customize WordPress with your own PHP code to make your website stand out from others!

This section goes through the basics of WordPress, showing what it can do and describing the different parts that make up the WordPress interface. You'll need to know that before you can start coding with it.

## What WordPress can do for you

WordPress started out life as a simple blogging interface. It created an environment where a blogger could easily enter text to post as a message in a bulletin board style of entry. Each post became an article on the website that was archived in a database; then it could be easily searched and retrieved by website visitors. The website administrator could allow website visitors to post comments on any article if needed. The comments could be open to the public, or the blogger could act as a moderator and approve which comments could stay and which ones would be removed from the website.

From that humble beginning, WordPress morphed into a full *content management system* (CMS). A CMS offers the ability to post and archive any type of content — from simple text articles to pictures to full multi-page documents. The CMS software archives all content posted to the website in the database, making it fully searchable by either the actual content text or by keywords related to the content.

Another great feature of WordPress is the ability to add *plugins.* Plugins provide extended functionality to the core WordPress features. There are plugins for posting calendars for events, listing the most popular posts in your website, accessing archived posts, and even running separate mini web applications inside the main WordPress web page! Plugins are where the real power behind WordPress lies, and that's what you'll focus on as a PHP web developer.

# How to run WordPress

One of the most confusing parts about WordPress is that there are two ways to create a WordPress website:

>> **The WordPress.com commercial website:** This is a standard web-hosting server that offers plans for hosting your own pre-installed WordPress website environment on the Internet using the WordPress servers.

>> **The WordPress.org nonprofit entity:** This group develops and supports the actual open-source WordPress web application software and provides it for you to install on your own web server and run your own WordPress website.

Both methods of running a WordPress website have pros and cons. Obviously, for people who don't happen to have their own data center in their basement, having the ability to have a well-known and respected company host their website is a plus. You can host your WordPress website using the WordPress domain name for free, or you can purchase personal or corporate packages to host your own domain name on the WordPress servers.

The WordPress.com infrastructure ensures almost constant uptime for your website. Another benefit of using the WordPress.com website is that the administrators take care of all the server hardware and software maintenance headaches for you. This allows you to focus on creating and maintaining your WordPress website, instead of worrying about missing a patch for the server that will allow attackers to deface your website or, worse, steal your data.

If you're already running a web server for your company or organization, adding the WordPress application to your existing web server is a breeze. Because WordPress is just a PHP application, you just create a separate folder for your server and copy the WordPress software there to run.

The WordPress.org organization provides the same full-featured WordPress software available on its commercial site free of charge to anyone who wants to run his or her own WordPress website. Just download the WordPress package to your own web server and maintain it yourself. Of course, that means you're responsible for keeping up with updates and patches, both for the web server software and the WordPress software.

**TIP**

A common middle ground is to use a third-party web hosting company, such as GoDaddy (www.godaddy.com), HostGator (www.hostgator.com), or 1&1 (www.1and1.com) to host your website. That way, they're responsible for maintaining the web server hardware and software, but you're responsible for the WordPress software. Many of the major web hosting companies even offer quick install packages for WordPress so you can install it from a single mouse click from the admin website interface!

Extending WordPress

# Parts of a WordPress website

One of the features that makes WordPress so popular is the ability to separate the website content from the website design. You can easily change the look and feel of your website without losing any of the content you've already published. By separating the different features and functions of the website into separate modules, WordPress makes it easy to mix and match just what you want to appear on your website.

There are a few main components in WordPress that provide the overall look and feel of the website:

>> **Themes:** A *theme* is a software bundle that creates the look and feel of the website. Everything that has to do with the website layout, images, and structure are contained within the theme software. Bundling that into a single package allows you to easily change the look and feel of your website without interfering with the content maintained by the CMS.

Each theme package includes only the HTML, CSS, JavaScript, and PHP code required to display content from the database. Each theme package plugs into the overall website interface the same way and interacts with the underlying CMS code the same way. This enables you to change theme packages at any time, often with just a few clicks of the mouse!

>> **Posts and comments:** *Posts* are the articles that you upload to the website to display. Posts can be text, images, or even video clips. You have full control over how posts are visible on the website and how they're archived for future reference.

WordPress provides the option to allow your website visitors to make *comments* on your post. You can open your website to the public for open commenting, but these days that's not a recommended strategy. It's usually best to incorporate a validation process, where you must validate each comment before it displays on your website.

>> **Categories and tags:** *Categories* provide the ability to organize the multitude of posts and comments on your WordPress website. You can divide your website into separate categories and maintain each category as a separate blogging interface. Then you tag each post according to which category (or categories) it belongs to for displaying and searching purposes.

You can add, change, or delete categories within your WordPress website whenever you want, without having any adverse effect on the other categories you maintain. Categories allow you to use your WordPress website to host multiple topics and keep them all separate. That helps you keep your bowling league blog separate from your advanced particle physics blog!

**TIP**

>> **Plugins:** *Plugins* are where the real power of WordPress lies. The plugin feature in WordPress allows anyone to create custom code for just about any type of application to add to a standard WordPress website.

WordPress maintains a public plugin repository, so after you create a plugin, you can share it with the world by uploading it to the repository! There are plugins that support lots of different advanced features, such as filtering posts and comments, displaying event calendars, tracking your website usage, following other websites (such as other bloggers or ecommerce websites), and monitoring RSS news feeds.

Plugins are where your skills as a PHP developer can really shine. This is where you customize your website to stand out from others, by adding special features that no one else has or interfacing with other web applications. Later in this chapter, you explore how to create a plugin by interfacing your WordPress website with the AuctionHelper application later on in this chapter.

# Installing WordPress

As a PHP developer, the best way to get involved with developing plugins for WordPress is to set up a WordPress environment in your own web development environment. That may sound complicated, but it's actually a fairly simple process, thanks to the WordPress developers. This section walks through the steps you need to take to get a full WordPress website up and running in your web environment.

## Downloading the WordPress software

Because the WordPress package is a PHP application, you just need to download the software and install the PHP code into your web server's DocumentRoot folder. Follow these steps to do that:

**1.** **Open your browser and enter the following URL:**

```
http://www.wordpress.org
```

Make sure you go to the .org website and not the .com website.

**2.** **Click the Download WordPress button in the header area of the main web page.**

You're taken to the main download page.

3. **Download the package.**

   If you're developing on a Windows or macOS platform, click the large button that shows the latest version of WordPress. At the time of this writing, you click the Download WordPress 4.9.1 button to download the latest package in .zip file format.

   If you're developing on a Linux platform, click the smaller Download .tar.gz link to download the package as a compressed .tar file to extract on your Linux system.

4. **Extract the files.**

   If you're developing on a Windows or macOS platform, double-click the .zip download package to begin extracting the files. Extract the package into the DocumentRoot folder for your web server. For XAMPP on Windows, that would be the c:\xampp\htdocs folder; for XAMPP on macOS, that would be the /Applications/XAMPP/htdocs folder.

   If you're working on a Linux platform, use the package utility for your distribution to extract the WordPress files from the compressed .tar file.

5. **Close the file extraction window and the browser window.**

This process should create a wordpress folder under the htdocs folder for your web server. That's where all the WordPress files are stored for the application.

Next, you need to configure the WordPress setup for your environment.

## Creating the database objects

WordPress stores just about everything — from configuration settings to content — in a database. You'll need to create that database, and a user account to access it, in your MySQL server.

If you're using a web-hosting company for your web development, follow the instructions it provides to create the database and the user account to access the database.

If you've installed the XAMPP package on your Windows, macOS, or Linux environment for your web development, follow these steps to create the WordPress database and user account:

1. **Ensure that the MySQL server is running and then open the MySQL Console for your XAMPP environment.**

   For XAMPP in Windows, first open a Command Prompt session, and then navigate to the c:\xampp\mysql\bin folder. For XAMPP in macOS, first open a

Terminal session, and then navigate to the /Applications/XAMPP/mysql/ bin folder.

2. **Start the MySQL Console using the** mysql **command.**

For XAMPP in Windows do this:

```
C:\Users\rkblu>cd \xampp\mysql\bin

C:\xampp\mysql\bin>mysql --user=root --password
Enter password:
Welcome to the MariaDB monitor.  Commands end with ; or \g.
Your MariaDB connection id is 2
Server version: 10.1.28-MariaDB mariadb.org binary distribution

Copyright (c) 2000, 2017, Oracle, MariaDB Corporation Ab and others.

Type 'help;' or '\h' for help. Type '\c' to clear the current input
    statement.

MariaDB [(none)]>
```

3. **In the MySQL Console, click the ENTER key at the password prompt to get to the** mysql> **prompt.**

4. **To create a database for WordPress, use the** CREATE DATABASE **command in SQL.**

For your development environment, just call the database wordpress:

```
MariaDB [(none)]> CREATE DATABASE wordpress;
Query OK, 1 row affected (0.00 sec)

MariaDB [(none)]>
```

5. **Create a user account for the WordPress application that has full access to the database you created.**

For the development environment, just call the user account wordpress, and create it using the GRANT command in SQL:

```
MariaDB [(none)]> GRANT ALL on wordpress.* TO 'wordpress'@'localhost'
    -> IDENTIFIED BY 'myL0ngP@ssword';
Query OK, 0 rows affected (0.00 sec)

MariaDB [(none)]>
```

Write down the user account and password you create here. You'll need to use them in the WordPress configuration.

6. **Exit the MySQL Console using the** `exit` **command.**

7. **Exit the Command Prompt or Terminal session using the** `exit` **command.**

With the database and MySQL user account required by WordPress created, you're ready to start configuring the WordPress software.

## Configuring WordPress

The next step in the installation process is to tell WordPress about the database and user account you just created. There are two ways to accomplish that:

>> Manually edit the WordPress configuration file.

>> Run the WordPress setup web application.

WordPress provides a configuration file template as the `wp-config-sample.php` file in the `wordpress` folder. You can manually change the settings for your environment and then save the file as `wp-config.php` in the `wordpress` folder. At a minimum, you'll need to specify the database name, username, and password that you created in MySQL for the WordPress application, as well as the host name where the MySQL server resides. (You use the localhost host name if the MySQL server is on the same physical server as the web server.)

The WordPress setup web application is a web page that produces a standard HTML form interface for you to enter the information required for WordPress to access the database and define instructions for how you'd like it to create the tables for the database. Follow these steps to do that:

1. **Open your browser and go to the following URL:**

   ```
   http://localhost:8080/wordpress/
   ```

2. **Select your preferred language from the list and then click Continue.**

   The next page is a set of instructions about the information you'll need to continue with the configuration.

3. **When you're ready, click the Let's Go button.**

   The next page is a form with the information you'll need to fill out, shown in Figure 4-1.

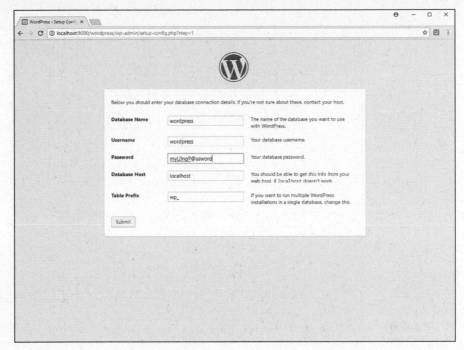

FIGURE 4-1:
The
WordPress
Setup
Configuration
File web page.

4. **Enter** wordpress **for the Database Name and Username fields.**

5. **In the Password field, enter the password you selected (myL0ngP@ssword if you followed the instructions earlier).**

6. **Keep the localhost entry for the Database Host field.**

   The Table Prefix field allows you to place a prefix in front of the WordPress tables so that you can identify them if you need to share a database with other applications. Because you created a separate database for WordPress, this is not needed, but you can keep the wp_ value there if you like.

7. **Click the Submit button to continue.**

   The next page warns you that the installation process will continue (what's up with the application calling us "sparky"?).

8. **Click the Run the Installation button when you're ready to start the process.**

   The first page of the Installation process is shown in Figure 4-2.

9. **Provide a title for your WordPress website.**

   I'm using First Street Elementary School to match my AuctionHelper application title.

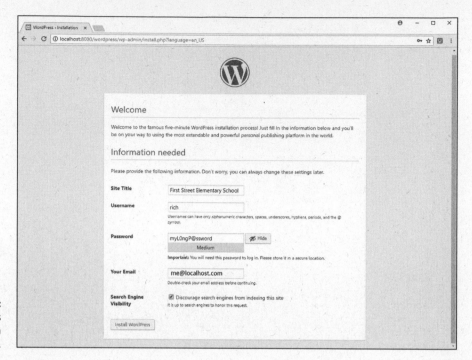

**FIGURE 4-2:**
The WordPress
Installation
web page.

**10.** **Provide a username for the main administrator account on the system.**

I used rich for my website.

**11.** **Provide a password for the administrator account.**

WordPress conveniently provides a suggestion for a strong password for you. If you'd like to test your memory skills, feel free to use it. Otherwise, replace it with something you'll remember (I used myL0ngP@ssword again).

**WARNING**

It's important to remember the username and password you configure here. You'll need it to administer your WordPress website.

**12.** **Enter an email address for the administrator.**

This will be shown as a contact information address in the WordPress website. For your development environment, just enter any email address, but use the correct email address format (I used me@localhost.com).

**13.** **Select the Search Engine Visibility check box if you don't want Search engines to index your WordPress website.**

That creates a file that instructs search engines to not scan the folder. It's up to the individual search engine website whether to honor your request.

**14.** **Click the Install WordPress button to continue the installation process.**

After a few seconds, the installation will complete. Don't click the Login button yet, but keep your browser window open.

After you finish the installation process, your WordPress website is up and running! To test it out, enter the following URL in your browser:

```
http://localhost:8080/wordpress/
```

You'll be greeted with the main WordPress web page, show in Figure 4-3.

The web page uses the default theme for WordPress (for this version it's a stylish picture of a potted houseplant). Notice that the title that you selected for your website appears at the bottom, along with a tagline, that for now is generic. Don't worry — you can change that easily enough!

When you scroll down the web page, the background image is replaced with the content of your website, shown in Figure 4-4.

The left-hand column lists the recent posts (there's a sample post conveniently made for you). Click the post, and you'll get a new web page that shows just the single post, along with any comments made by you or your website visitors associated with that post.

**FIGURE 4-4:**
The main
content area in
the WordPress
web page.

The right-hand column on the main web page contains a few different sections. These features in the sidebar are widgets. You'll be able to customize which widgets appear on your website and where they appear. You'll also be able to modify the posts and comments that appear in the default website. All that happens using the admin dashboard in WordPress.

# Examining the Dashboard

Now that you have a generic WordPress website up and running, you can tweak things to make it look just the way you want. You do that using the WordPress Dashboard.

To get to the Dashboard, click the Login link that appears in the Meta section on the right-hand side of your main WordPress web page, or just enter the following URL:

```
http://localhost:8080/wordpress/wp-admin
```

Both methods produce a login web page. Enter the username or email address that you specified when you configured the website, along with the password you specified, and then click the Login button. The Dashboard web page, shown in Figure 4-5, appears.

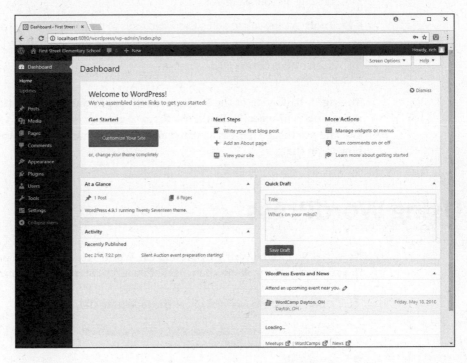

**FIGURE 4-5:**
The WordPress
Dashboard
web page.

The left-hand side of the web page contains a navigation menu for you to select administration options:

>> **Updates:** Notifies you when there's an update to WordPress or any plugins that you can download and install.

>> **Posts:** Allows you to view previous posts and create new posts, categories, and tags.

>> **Media:** Allows you to upload and manage multimedia files such as images and video clips.

>> **Pages:** Manages the web pages that appear in your website.

>> **Comments:** Lists comments and allows you to mark to approve, spam, or delete them.

Extending WordPress

>> **Appearance:** Allows you to manage the look and feel of your website by changing the theme, widgets, menus, and header that appear on the web pages.

>> **Users:** Provides tools to create and manage user accounts for restricting posting on your website.

>> **Tools:** Allows you to add customized tools to help you manage your website.

>> **Settings:** Provides an interface for you to change the configuration settings used by WordPress in your website.

The right-hand side of the Dashboard web page contains widgets to assist you in managing your website. You'll use them to change the look and feel of your website and see those changes as you make them. The next section walks you through how to do that.

# Using WordPress

Now that you know your way around the WordPress Dashboard a little, let's dive in and start making some changes! Follow these steps to customize your website:

1. **Open your browser and enter the following URL:**

   ```
   http://localhost:8080/wordpress/wp-admin
   ```

2. **Log in using the username and password you created in the configuration setup process.**

   The Dashboard web page appears.

3. **In the Dashboard web page, click the Customize Your Site button.**

   The Customize web page, shown in Figure 4-6, appears.

4. **Click the Site Identity menu option in the left-hand navigation window.**

5. **Change the Tagline setting to the text you want to appear.**

   I chose Providing a World-Class Education to All Kids.

   Notice that as you type the text, the text in the picture on the right-hand side of the web page changes. Using this interface you can also change the background image or, if you prefer, upload a video clip to use in the main web page.

**FIGURE 4-6:**
The WordPress
Customize
web page.

6. **Click the left-arrow icon at the top to return to the main Customize web page.**

   Notice that in the Customize web page you can change the colors, media, and menus that appear on the main Home page of your website. We'll skip that for now, though.

7. **Click the Widgets link.**

   You can place widgets either along the sidebar or within one of two footer areas of the web page.

8. **Click the Blog Sidebar link to see the widgets that are currently active in the sidebar.**

   There are three widgets placed there by default:

   - **Find Us:** Text to identify your location
   - **Search:** A search tool for finding posts
   - **About this Site:** Text to identify you or your organization

9. **Click the Find Us link and enter information about the address you want to use for your organization.**

   I just kept the default address for testing.

10. Click the Add a Widget button, and then select the Categories widget from the list.

11. Click the Show Post Counts check box, and then click the Done link.

    The new Categories widget is placed at the bottom of the sidebar list.

12. Click the widget and hold the mouse button down. You can now drag and drop the Categories widget to a new location in the sidebar. Move it to just below the Search widget.

13. Click the X icon to exit the Blog Sidebar section, and then click the X icon to return back to the main Customize web page.

14. Click the Homepage Settings link.

    This web page defines what appears as the main web page for your website. You can use a static web page that remains the same, or you can select to display your posts immediately on the main page.

15. Click the Your Latest Posts radio button so that the latest posts appear on the main page.

16. Click the left-arrow icon at the top of the page to return to the Customize web page.

17. Click the Publish button at the top of the web page to save the changes you've made and make them live on your WordPress website.

18. Click the X icon at the top of the Customize web page to return to the Dashboard web page.

Now that you've been able to change the overall look and feel of your website, the next step is to look at the posts and comments. You'll remember that, by default, WordPress entered a "Hello World" post. To clean up the posts and comments, follow these steps:

1. Navigate to the Dashboard web page for your WordPress website.

2. Click the Posts link in the left-hand navigation menu.

    Figure 4-7 shows the Posts web page, listing the current posts in the database.

3. Hover the mouse pointer over the Hello World! post title.

    A pop-up menu appears under the post title, allowing you to edit, trash, or view the post.

4. Click the Trash option to remove the test post.

    The post is removed, but notice that a warning message appears at the top of the window allowing you to undo the action if needed. There's also now a

Trash category that shows one item in the trash. You can go back to the trash and recover the post at any time (at least until you empty the trash can).

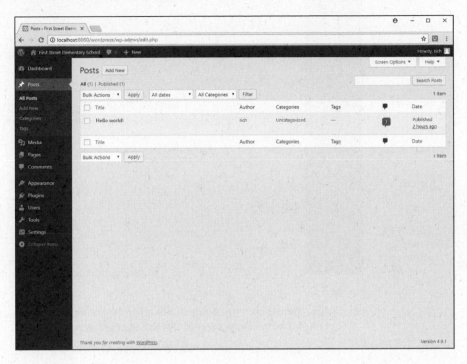

**FIGURE 4-7:**
The WordPress
Posts web page.

5. **Click the Categories submenu option under the Post menu option in the navigation menu.**

   This brings up the Categories web page, shown in Figure 4-8.

   By default there's only one category (named Uncategorized).

6. **In the Add New Category section, add a new category named Silent Auction event.**

7. **For the Slug (what appears in the URL), you can leave the entry blank.**

   WordPress will automatically create the Slug, converting the category name to all lowercase, and inserting dashes for spaces.

8. **In the Description, enter some text to describe the category.**

9. **Click the Add New Category button.**

   Now you're ready to make your first post!

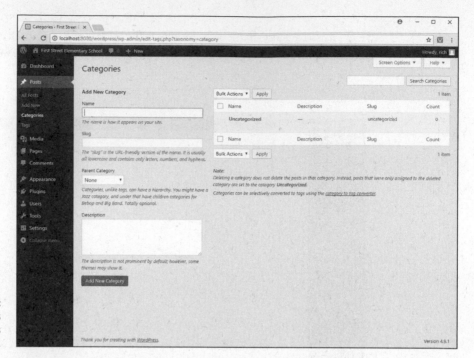

**FIGURE 4-8:**
The WordPress
Categories
web page.

10. **Click the Posts menu entry in the left-hand navigation menu, and then click the Add New button at the top of the Posts web page.**

    This opens the Add New Post web page, shown in Figure 4-9.

11. **Fill in a title for the post and then the text for the post in the Description text area.**

12. **Select the Silent Auction Event category check box in the Categories section.**

13. **In the Publish section on the right-hand side, click the Preview button to see what your post will look like on the web page.**

    This opens a new web page with the post.

14. **Close that browser tab when you're done reviewing it.**

15. **Click the Publish icon to publish the new post.**

16. **Click the Posts link in the navigation menu to make sure your new post published.**

17. **Hover the mouse pointer over the user icon in the upper-right corner of the Dashboard, and then select Logout from the drop-down menu to exit the Dashboard web page.**

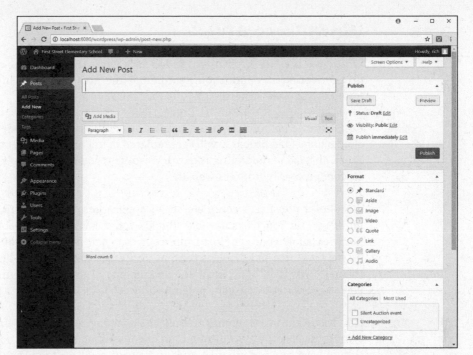

**FIGURE 4-9:**
Adding a
new post in
WordPress.

Now when you enter the main WordPress website address in your browser (`http://localhost:8080/wordpress/`), you'll see your updated creation! To view the activity for a post, click the title of the new post that you made. The post web page shows any comments made for that post and allows others to make new comments. When a site visitor makes a comment, you'll need to go into the Dashboard Comments section to approve the comment before it appears on the post's web page.

**TIP**

There are lots of other features that you'll want to customize for your new website. Everything is accessible from the Dashboard interface, so feel free to peruse the different sections and see all the different things you can do. Plenty of books provide detailed instructions on how to set up and maintain your WordPress website, such as *WordPress All-in-One for Dummies* by Lisa Sabin-Wilson (Wiley).

# Exploring the World of Plugins

WordPress was designed for novice web developers with no knowledge of HTML, CSS, JavaScript, or PHP, but it also has the flexibility of being completely customizable by those who do have those skills (like you!). This section walks through the different methods you have for customizing your WordPress website to add more features using simple PHP coding!

# WordPress APIs

WordPress is a PHP application, and as such, you can view all the code that makes up the WordPress application. Just peruse the files contained in the `wordpress` folder to see what's there.

**TIP**

Resist the temptation to make tweaks or additions to this code. Any code you change may (and probably will) get replaced in the next upgrade version of WordPress. Instead of modifying the core WordPress code files, there's a better way to customize your WordPress website.

WordPress provides a complete set of application programming interface (API) libraries that you use to create plugins for the WordPress website. These API libraries allow your plugin to intercept the code flow in WordPress and modify how it stores and displays content, processes web requests, and even handles themes. This is all done without changing any of the core code in WordPress, so you're guaranteed that your plugins will work in future upgrades to WordPress.

**TIP**

It's important to remember to only make changes in plugins and not the core WordPress code, but WordPress is an open-source project, so if you do see something in the core code that should be changed, feel free to post that in the WordPress developer's forum and offer to make the change in the development code.

Lots of functions are contained within the WordPress API library. These functions are broken into separate library categories to help organize them. Table 4-1 shows the list of the current WordPress API categories.

**TABLE 4-1** ## The WordPress API Library Categories

| Category | Description |
| --- | --- |
| Dashboard widgets | Create new admin widgets for the Dashboard. |
| Database | Intercept database calls. |
| HTTP | Modify HTTP requests and responses. |
| REST | Modify how WordPress responds to HTTP requests. |
| File header | Read and process the header information contained in WordPress files. |
| Filesystem | Read and write files on the WordPress server. |
| Metadata | Retrieve and manipulate metadata of WordPress objects. |
| Options | Store custom options in the WordPress database. |
| Plugin | Write plugins to add functionality to the website. |
| Quicktags | Create additional buttons in the WordPress text editor. |

| Category | Description |
| --- | --- |
| Rewrite | Define or change URL rewrite rules used in WordPress. |
| Settings | Modify the Dashboard Settings interface. |
| Shortcode | Define new tags to use in posts and comments. |
| Theme modification | Alter the modification interface for working with themes. |
| Theme customization | Add controls to the Customize web page for working with themes. |
| Transients | Access cached data in the database. |
| Widgets | Build your own widgets. |
| XML-RPC | Interact with remote clients to pass and retrieve data. |

The WordPress API library functions cover just about any feature that you'd want to modify in your WordPress website. The trick is knowing just which ones to use for which situations. The next section takes a look at that.

# Working with plugins and widgets

The WordPress API library does most of the hard work for you when you're developing new features for WordPress. You just need to know which API library to tap into for your specific application. There are two core API libraries that you'll mainly work with to add new features to your WordPress applications:

>> The Plugins API library

>> The Widget API library

The following sections describe how to use each of these libraries.

## Plugins

The Plugins API library provides hooks into the content data and the processes that handle it within the WordPress application. You can tap into these hooks to modify the data or process at any step as WordPress processes data and creates the resulting web page.

There are two types of hooks into WordPress for plugins:

>> **Filters:** Filters are hooks that intercept data as it traverses the different stages within the WordPress application. After you intercept the data, you can modify, delete, or add to it before passing it on to the next step in the process. This gives you a great amount of power over the data in the application!

>> **Actions:** Actions are hooks that intercept the processes within WordPress and allow you to alter the process action. For example, you can hook into the commenting action in WordPress so that when a site visitor submits a comment, WordPress calls your plugin, which can send you an email notification.

TIP

When you write a plugin, you have to follow specific rules for the format of your code and which API functions you call:

>> Your plugin files must be stored in the wp-content/plugins folder in the wordpress folder structure.

>> If your plugin requires just a single file, name the file the same as your plugin name. If your plugin requires multiple files, create a folder in the plugins folder with your plugin name, and then place the plugin files in there. If you use the folder method, the main program file must be named init.php.

>> Start your PHP code with a comment section that identifies important information about the plugin. This is called the *header metadata*. WordPress uses the header metadata to provide information about your plugin to users. At a minimum, you must specify the Name and Description of the plugin in the header:

```php
<?php
/*
Plugin Name: My Plugin
Description: My clever plugin for WordPress
/*
```

>> After you define your function code, use the add_filter() or add_action() functions to hook your plugin into WordPress.

Inside your plugin, the code that you write must follow standard PHP coding practices. Listing 4-1 shows an example of an action plugin.

**LISTING 4-1:** **A Sample Action Plugin**

```php
<?php
/*
Name: My Comment Mailer
Description: Email me when someone makes a comment
function my_comment_mailer($comment_ID) {
    $myaddress = "me@localhost.com";
    $message = "Comment $comment_ID just posted to my website";
```

```
        mail($myaddress, "Comment on website", $message);
        return $comment_ID;
}
add_action('comment_post', 'my_comment_mailer');
?>
```

The `my_comment_mailer()` function name that you create must be unique within WordPress, so be careful to not use too generic of a function name.

Most action and filter hooks pass data into your plugin function, so usually you'll need to provide a parameter variable to accept the incoming data, even if you don't use it. The `add_action()` function specifies the WordPress hook to tap into to trigger your function, and the name of your function to call when the hook is triggered in WordPress.

**TIP**

When you create a plugin, it appears in the Plugins page in the Dashboard. You must activate your plugin using that interface before it will work.

## Widgets

The Widgets API works similar to the Plugins API. Widgets are a special type of plugin. They follow the same rules as when you write a filter or action plugin, but instead of creating a simple function, you must create your widget as a class that inherits the `WP_Widget` class:

```
class mywidget extends WP_Widget {
```

By inheriting the `WP_Widget` class, your widget automatically gets all the features and functions available for all widgets. You need to create a constructor method to accept the parent class methods:

```
function mywidget() {
    parent::WP_Widget(false, "mywidget");
}
```

Following that, you create the code to generate the output that appears in the web page area assigned to the widget (usually located in the sidebar, but you can also place widgets in the footer area). This code uses a special function named `widget()`:

```
function widget($args, $instance) {
    echo "Welcome to my first widget!<br>\n";
}
```

Extending WordPress

The WordPress hook passes any arguments required for the widget to run, along with an array of any options the widget saved in the WordPress database.

If your widget needs to have customized options, you can specify them in a `form()` method within the widget class. WordPress will display the output of the `form()` method in the Widget manager so your widget users can add their custom options. You then define the `update()` method to save those options in the WordPress database.

Finally, you need to register your widget in WordPress by defining the `register_widget()` method, and using it in the `add_action()` method:

```
function register_mywidget{} {
    register_widget('mywidget');
}
add_action('widgets_init', 'register_mywidget');
```

After you've created the code for your widget, you need to activate it in the Plugins area of the Dashboard. Then you can go to the Appearance area and add your new widget to the web page.

# Creating Your Own Widget

Now that you've seen how plugins (and specifically, widgets) are made, you're ready to create one of your own! This section walks through creating a sidebar widget that will display the current totals from the AuctionHelper database — the total number of bidders, the total number of donated items, and the total resale price of the times.

## Coding the widget

The first step is to create the code for the AuctionHelper widget. The widget must follow the standard WordPress plugin coding rules. As a widget, it needs to inherit the `WP_Widget` class. You'll then need to create a constructor method to reference the parent object, a `widget()` method that contains the code to create what we want to see on the web page, and the method to register the widget as a widget plugin.

Follow these steps to build the code for the AuctionHelper widget:

**1.** Open your favorite text editor, program editor, or integrated development environment (IDE) package.

2. **Enter the following code:**

```php
<?php
/*
Plugin Name: AuctionHelper
Description: Retrieve real-time data from AuctionHelper
*/

class AuctionHelper extends WP_Widget {
    function AuctionHelper() {
        parent::WP_Widget(false, "AuctionHelper");
    }

    function widget($args, $instance) {
        $db = new mysqli("localhost", "ah_user", "AuctionHelper",
    "auction");
        $query = "SELECT count(bidderid) FROM bidders";
        $result = $db->query($query);
        $row = $result->fetch_array();
        $bidders = $row[0];

        $query = "SELECT count(itemid) FROM items";
        $result = $db->query($query);
        $row = $result->fetch_array();
        $items = $row[0];

        $query = "SELECT sum(resaleprice) FROM items";
        $result = $db->query($query);
        $row = $result->fetch_array();
        $totprice = $row[0];

        echo "<h2>Auction Totals</h2><hr>\n";
        echo "Registered bidders: $bidders<br>\n";
        echo "Total Items: $items<br>\n";
        echo "Items resale value: $$totprice<br>\n";
        echo "<hr><br>\n";
    }
}

function register_AuctionHelper() {
    register_widget('AuctionHelper');
}

add_action("widgets_init", "register_AuctionHelper");
?>
```

3.  **Open File Explorer for Windows or Finder for Mac and navigate to the** wordpress **folder under the** htdocs **folder in your web server.**

4.  **Double-click the** wp-content **folder, and then double-click the** plugins **folder.**

5.  **Create a new folder here named** AuctionHelper.

6.  **Back in your editor, save the file in the new** AuctionHelper **folder as** init.php.

7.  **Open a new tab in your editor, and enter the following code:**

```php
<?php
    //dummy file
?>
```

8.  **Save the file in the** AuctionHelper **folder as** index.php.

You should recognize the code for the widget() method. It uses the php_mysqli library functions to query the auction MySQL database to get the bidder and item information and then stores that information in PHP variables. After retrieving the necessary data, the code uses echo statements to display the information. What you display from the widget() method will be what appears in the sidebar area of the WordPress website.

TIP

The index.php file is an empty dummy file. It helps prevent an attacker from navigating directly to the plugin folder and being able to list the files located there. If you specify a folder in the URL, the web server will automatically serve the index.php file to the browser. If the index.php file is not there, the browser will display a listing of the files in the folder.

Now that you've built the widget, you need to get it active in your WordPress website.

## Activating the widget plugin

Before you can use the AuctionHelper widget that you just coded, you need to let WordPress know that it can be used. Follow these steps:

1.  **Open your browser and enter the following URL:**

```
http://localhost:8080/wordpress/wp-admin
```

2.  **Log into WordPress using the username and password you created during the installation process.**

3. **Click the Plugins menu option in the left-hand navigation menu of the Dashboard.**

   Your AuctionHelper widget plugin should appear in the list of plugins, as shown in Figure 4-10.

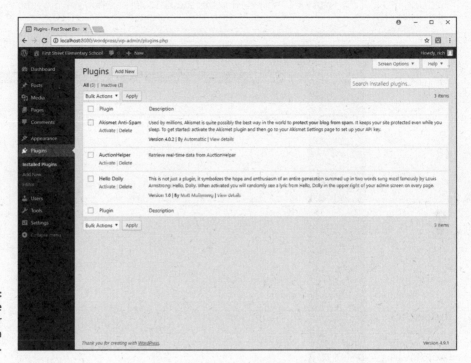

**FIGURE 4-10:**
Activating the
AuctionHelper
plugin in
WordPress.

4. **Click the Activate link under the AuctionHelper plugin.**

   A message appears at the top of the web page letting you know that the plugin has activated.

Now that the AuctionHelper widget is activated, it's ready for use in your WordPress website. The final step is to add it to the sidebar.

## Adding the widget

With the AuctionHelper widget plugin activated, it should now appear in the list of widgets in the Customize page. Follow these steps to add the AuctionHelper widget to your web page:

1. **Click the Appearance link in the left-hand navigation menu of the Dashboard, and then select the Widgets menu entry that appears under the Appearance link.**

You'll see the AuctionHelper widget appear in the list of widgets on the right-hand side of the web page.

2. **Drag and drop the AuctionHelper widget to the blog sidebar area, positioning it at the top of the list.**

   Figure 4-11 shows what this should look like when you drop the widget.

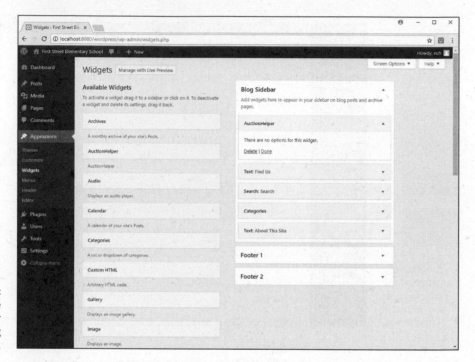

**FIGURE 4-11:**
Adding the
AuctionHelper
widget to the blog
sidebar.

3. **Click the Done link in the AuctionHelper widget area to complete the process.**

4. **Log out from the Dashboard.**

Congratulations! You've just created and installed your first WordPress widget. Yes, that's really all there is to it! Now for the moment of truth — testing your widget. Open your browser and enter the WordPress URL:

```
http://localhost:8080/wordpress
```

Scroll down to display the content of your website. At the top of the sidebar section, you should see the Auction Total area, created by your widget! This is shown in Figure 4-12.

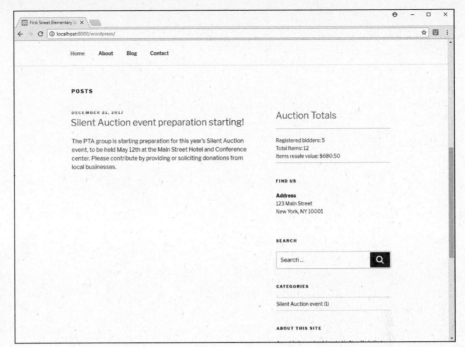

FIGURE 4-12:
The result of
adding the
AuctionHelper
widget to the
WordPress
website.

You should see the values current for your AuctionHelper database appear in your WordPress sidebar. To make sure things really are working, jump back into your AuctionHelper application and add an item or two. Then jump back into your WordPress website, refresh the page, and make sure the changes appear. How cool is that?

This just covers a bit of the power you have at your fingertips when working with WordPress and creating your own plugins. Now with your new skills you can add just about any type of feature or application to a WordPress website to impress your boss or customers!

# 7

# Using PHP Frameworks

# Contents at a Glance

**CHAPTER 1: The MVC Method** ................................... 683

Getting Acquainted with MVC ............................. 683

Comparing MVC to Other Web Models .................... 691

Seeing How MVC Fits into N-Tier Theory .................. 693

Implementing MVC ........................................ 694

**CHAPTER 2: Selecting a Framework** ......................... 695

Getting to Know PHP Frameworks ........................ 695

Knowing Why You Should Use a Framework ............... 702

Focusing on Popular PHP Frameworks .................... 704

Looking At Micro Frameworks............................. 710

**CHAPTER 3: Creating an Application Using Frameworks** .... 715

Building the Template.................................... 715

Creating an Application Scaffold .......................... 721

Modifying the Application Scaffold ....................... 725

# Chapter **1**

# The MVC Method

I n Book 6, I walk you through how to create a complete dynamic web application using object-oriented PHP programming techniques. But there's more than one way to design and program an object-oriented PHP application. There are, in fact, many different theories on just how best to design and code your dynamic web applications with PHP, all with their own pros and cons. This chapter walks you through one of the more popular methods for designing object-oriented web applications and compares it to some other methods available.

## Getting Acquainted with MVC

If you've been spending any time reading articles, books, or even discussion group posts about PHP programming, you've come across the term *MVC*. The acronym stands for *model–view–controller*, which is a method of splitting your object-oriented program code into multiple parts to make it easier to code and implement in an object-oriented environment.

This section first describes how MVC works and then digs deeper into each of the separate components that make up an MVC application.

# Exploring the MVC method

The MVC method of programming actually predates the web programming world by quite a bit. It was designed in the early days of graphical desktop programming as a way to help organize applications that required lots of coding to support user interaction. Instead of intertwining the display code inside the application code, developers decided early on it was best to try to separate those features into separate components.

The MVC method divides a graphical application into three basic components:

>> **The model:** One or more classes that interact with the application data and implement the coding logic required to store and manipulate application data

>> **The view:** A class that displays the application data in the graphical environment

>> **The controller:** A class that listens for user input and passes the input to the appropriate model class methods for processing

Web application programming has many similarities to desktop graphical application programming, so many web developers have adopted the MVC method for creating object-oriented web applications.

Most MVC experts agree on the three basic components of the application, but there are several different theories on how they should interact with one another. Before your eyes start glazing over hearing the word *theory*, let me just show you the most popular interpretation of MVC theory, as shown in Figure 1-1.

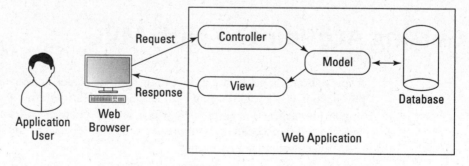

**FIGURE 1-1:**
A basic MVC
theory diagram.

Most MVC experts agree that the controller component is the "front door" to your application. The controller's job is to be the traffic cop of the application, shuttling user requests to the correct model class method to interact with the requested data — whether that's inserting new data, updating existing data, or just listing the existing data (or some subset of the data). The model class methods do the actual work to produce the data required to support the user request and then pass the result to the view.

The view's job is to organize the result of the request into a visual output. That visual output could be as simple as a notice that the operation was successful, or as complex as displaying a full report of requested data elements. Whatever the result of the request, it's the view's job to communicate it to the application user.

You can probably start to see how the MVC method can easily fit into your dynamic web applications. Web applications receive requests from client browsers requesting some type of data operation, and then need to display the requested data back to the client browser in the form of a web page. Being able to split these functions into separate components can be handy.

This feature is attractive in large development environments where it's easier to separate the different coding requirements between development groups. With the MVC programming method, you can allow your best HTML and CSS programmers to focus on the view code, while your best PHP and SQL coders can focus on the model and controller code.

This also means that you can have multiple development groups working on the application code at the same time, without causing problems for each other. With different groups simultaneously writing code, the application may get done quicker than with other object-oriented approaches.

Of course, with all coding methods, there are downsides, and that's certainly the case with the MVC method of application development. One of the biggest complaints you'll see regarding applications developed using the MVC method is that they can be somewhat difficult to understand and troubleshoot.

Breaking code up into separate components can make trying to follow the application code more complicated. As a client makes a request for data, multiple class files get involved with the process. Instead of being able to trace the execution of a single application file, you'll find yourself having to dig through several different smaller application files, looking for the one bug that's causing the issue.

Yet another complaint about the MVC method is that it can be somewhat hard to implement in a programming environment. It can take time and practice incorporating the MVC programming method into an application, time that most web application developers don't have. Fortunately, there are tools available to help out with that, which I cover in Chapter 2 of this minibook.

# Digging into the MVC components

Now that you've seen the high-level overview of just what MVC is, let's take a look at the internals required for the individual components. This section goes a little more in depth into what each of the MVC components does.

## The model

The model component of the MVC method is where the majority of the PHP application coding takes place. Its job is to provide a common interface between the application and any data that the application requires.

Of course these days, most web applications use some type of database system to store the application data (such as the MySQL server in the application example). The model code sits between the application and the database tables. Any access to the data must go through the model code.

Most MVC model implementations use a technique called *object-relational mapping* (ORM) to provide this interface. The ORM class is responsible for handling the methods for all interaction with the underlying table:

>> Creating new data records

>> Reading existing data records

>> Updating existing data records

>> Deleting existing data records

The combination of the create, read, update, and delete methods are commonly referred to as CRUD. Besides the four CRUD methods, the model class often contains additional methods for any type of data manipulation that are required to support the application.

There are two different approaches to how the ORM interacts with the data used in an application:

>> **Relational data method:** In the relational data method, you create a model class for each table contained in the application database. For example, in the AuctionHelper application discussed in Book 6, which contains a Bidders table and an Items table, you'd need to create a model class for the Bidders table and a second model class for the Items table. The model classes use standard SQL to interact with the data contained in the tables. Figure 1-2 demonstrates this method.

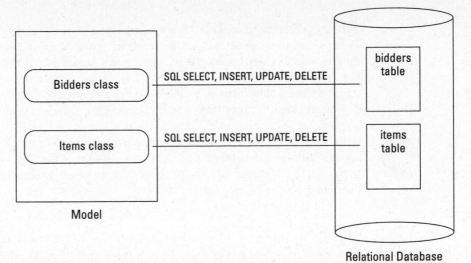

**FIGURE 1-2:** The relational data method model.

>> **Object-oriented data method:** The object-oriented data method takes a slightly different approach to interfacing the application to the underlying database tables. Instead of using a relational database method, this uses an *object-oriented database management system* (OODBMS), which stored data as objects instead of tables. Because the data is stored as objects, the model class objects can more easily map directly to the database objects. Figure 1-3 demonstrates the object-oriented data method.

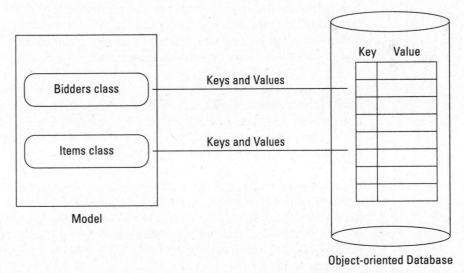

**FIGURE 1-3:** The object-oriented data method model.

With an OODBMS, related data is automatically grouped together in the database as keys and their associated values, such as the bidders as keys and the items they've won as their values. There is no formal separation of the data into tables like in the relational database method. By grouping these objects together, you create a virtual object that is quicker to query and retrieve the information by just submitting keys to the database and retrieving the associated values.

TIP

With the growing popularity of OODBMS theory, a few different OODBMS database servers have been developed. Currently, the popular OODBMS server is the NoSQL server project. It stores data as XML files that can be easily added and appended as the data grows in an application.

## The view

The view component is responsible for all the output from the application. It takes the raw data provided by the model component and formats it in a way that's visually pleasing to the application user. For our web applications, the view component is where all the HTML and CSS code resides.

The view component code is often placed into a folder area in the application, with different files responsible for creating different features of the application. This completely separates the view code from the model and component code in the application.

In the AuctionHelper application, I chose not to implement a separate view component, but instead placed the code to display the application data directly in the files that controlled the data. This requires mixing the PHP, HTML, CSS, and even JavaScript code into the same files. That's fine if you're writing your own application, but it can get confusing if you're working in a programming environment that divides the modules up between separate programming groups.

One area where having a separate code component to handle the view comes in handy is when working with mobile devices. These days, it may not be sufficient to write your application solely to display web pages for a normal desktop browser environment. With the popularity of mobile devices, your application may need to be usable (and readable) in both the desktop and mobile environments.

That may require that you create different sets of CSS styles (and sometimes even different sets of HTML code) for different display environments. Mobile devices have a much smaller display area and need some extra consideration to ensure your website visitors can interact properly with the application. Trying to maintain two separate code bases can get confusing, especially if you're embedding the view code within your application.

Isolating the code required to generate the display output into a separate component makes it easier to incorporate multiple code for multiple devices — one set of view code for desktop browsers and another set for mobile devices. Figure 1-4 demonstrates how this works.

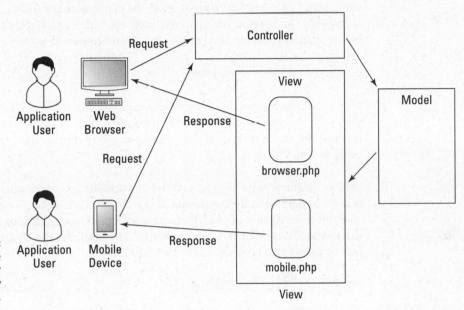

**FIGURE 1-4:**
Using multiple view modules for different display environments.

Two devices submit the same HTTP request to the controller, which forwards both requests to the model. The model sends the same responses to the view, but the view processes the responses differently.

**TIP**

Both CSS3 and JavaScript provide ways for you to detect the device monitor size and determine whether the website visitor is viewing the application on a mobile device or desktop browser. In CSS3, the `max-width` property in the `@media` rule allows the browser to select which CSS rules to apply based on the size of the browser window. For JavaScript, you can use the `screen.width` global property to determine the viewing area size.

## The controller

The controller accepts requests from the application user and sends them to the components required to satisfy the request. That means being able to communicate between all the model classes, as well as the view files required to display the data.

The controller uses *routing* to determine which model class method to run based on the client browser's request. Routing maps the specific HTTP GET or POST request received from a client browser to a specific model class method.

In the AuctionHelper application, I did that by setting the HTML content variable/value pair. The index.php code acted as the application controller, directing which include file to display as the main web page content. So, to display the details of the bidder with a bidderid value of 100, the client browser sent the following request:

```
index.php?content=showbidder&id=100
```

The index.php code in the AuctionHelper application retrieved the content HTML variable/value pair and then used that value to include the showbidder.inc.php include file, which then used the id value of 100 to display the appropriate bidder information.

MVC controllers use a similar method but utilize the *rewrite rules* feature of web servers to help clean up the format of the request URL. Rewrite rules allow you to customize the format of the URL to pass information in a cleaner-looking format than what the standard GET method uses. For example, the URL request to show information for bidder 100 might look like this:

```
index.php/bidders/show/100
```

The web server parses the URL to set the HTML variable/value pairs. Then the controller routing rules direct the application to call the show method of the bidders model class and pass it the bidderid value of 100.

**TIP**

Search engine optimization (SEO) is the process of designing your application to make it easier for Internet search engines (such as Google) to find and catalog your website pages. Web server rewrite rules can play a crucial role in helping add to your search engine visibility, as many search engines won't scan websites with URLs that contain long lists of variable/value pairs. By parsing out the URL data automatically, you can trim off quite a bit of length in your URLs, making them more SEO-friendly!

## Communicating in MVC

In the MVC method, because you must divide all the functions of your web application into separate components, communication between the components becomes crucial. Each component must know when and how to communicate information to the other components for the application to function correctly.

Earlier, Figure 1-1 showed the classical MVC communication method. There were five separate steps for communicating with a website visitor's request:

1. The controller receives the request from the website visitor's browser.

2. The controller passes the request to the appropriate class method in the model component.

3. The model class method performs the appropriate action with the data based on the request.

4. The model class method passes any resulting data or status to the view.

5. The view sends a response back to the website visitor with the data, formatted appropriately for the visitor's display device.

That all seems organized and proper, but there are some holes in this process that can cause issues in the application:

>> **The controller is responsible for handling the client request but is not responsible for returning the response.** If any special communication is required for the session (such as an encryption key or session ID), the view must get that information from the controller.

>> **The model is responsible for retrieving the data required to satisfy the request, but the view is responsible for the format in which the data appears in the display.** This can make common web page features such as paging through long result sets of data on multiple web pages more complex. Paging through data is usually more easily handled with SQL directives in the model code rather than PHP in the view code. This means the view and the model must communicate information between each other as well.

>> **The view must have knowledge of the client browser's environment to format the data to display properly on the client device.** This may require communication between the view and the controller that initiated the session.

Because of little issues like these, many MVC implementations violate the strict MVC method rules and implement communication between the different component classes. This helps eliminate issues within the application and provide a smoother interface for the website visitor.

# Comparing MVC to Other Web Models

As you might guess, the MVC method is not the only theory available for creating object-oriented web applications. This section explores a couple of other popular methods that you may encounter as you explore the world of object-oriented web applications: the MVP method and the MVVM method.

## The MVP method

The *model–view–presenter* (MVP) method is another popular method of creating object-oriented web applications. At first, its name may sound a bit redundant — the presenter sounds as if it's doing the same job as the view.

The MVP method takes a more linear approach to the process of handling client requests, as shown in Figure 1-5.

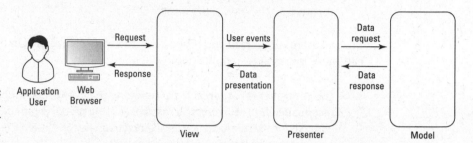

**FIGURE 1-5:**
The model–
view–presenter
method.

In the MVP method, the view handles both the request and response parts of the process, taking on the MVC controller's function of communicating with the client.

The presenter acts as the middleman between the model and the view. It interprets the client requests and calls the appropriate model class methods. After the model processes the request and generates the appropriate response, it sends the response to the presenter, which passes it to the view to format for display.

As you can see, the MVP method basically splits the controller jobs from the MVC method between the view and presenter modules, making things a little more streamlined. This helps eliminate some of the communication issues presented in the MVC method.

## The MVVM method

The *model–view–viewmodel* (MVVM) method is similar to the MVP method, but with a slight twist, as shown in Figure 1-6.

The viewmodel acts as a middleman between the view and the model, similar to the presenter module in MVP. But unlike the MVP presenter module, the viewmodel doesn't manipulate the data — it just provides an interface between the view and the model.

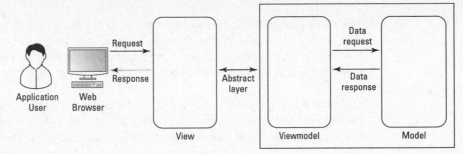

FIGURE 1-6:
FIGURE 1-6:
The model–
view–viewmodel
method.

The viewmodel creates an abstract layer between the graphical environment of the view and the data–centric environment of the model. This abstract layer allows the programmers working on the view code to provide an interface to the data in the model without having to know the details of the underlying data or how the model handles it.

This data abstraction helps the development process, because the user interface often changes more frequently than the underlying data. The graphical designers can make changes without worrying about messing up the database designers.

# Seeing How MVC Fits into N-Tier Theory

If you've been doing any type of web application development in a large–scale environment, you've probably heard of or even used the *multitier architecture* (often called *n-tier*) approach to web applications. With *n*–tier architecture, developers divide a web application into separate physical servers, based on functionality, as shown in Figure 1-7.

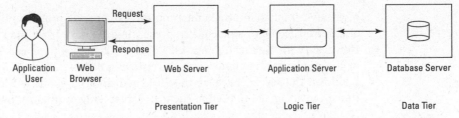

FIGURE 1-7:
The *n*-tier theory
architecture.

The *n*–tier architecture layout often consists of three physical servers:

>> A web server that interacts with client browsers (called the *presentation tier*)

>> An application server that runs the server-side application code (called the *logic tier*)

>> A database server that stores the application data (called the *data tier*)

The main goal of the $n$-tier architecture is to divide the separate functions of a web application into separate physical servers. This action helps prevent server bottlenecks and makes it easier to both expand individual servers as needed to support application load or share server resources between web applications.

The web–application–database layout of the $n$-tier architecture sounds a lot like the model–view–controller model of MVC, but there's a difference. It's important to remember that the $n$-tier architecture refers to the physical server environment of the application and not the application software. The MVC method represents a method of dividing the software requirements of a web application, regardless of the underlying hardware.

The $n$-tier architecture can support any type of software application method, and your MVC application can run in any type of server environment. It's certainly possible to implement your MVC application in an $n$-tier server environment, but you can just as easily run it within a standard one-server web environment.

# Implementing MVC

In the AuctionHelper application, you use PHP code on the server and HTML, CSS, and JavaScript code on the client to create the application. The first question that often comes to mind when considering the MVC programming method is "Where is that implemented?"

The MVC method isn't necessarily a client-side or server-side programming paradigm. There are parts of the MVC method that work in either side of the web application environment. Trying to figure out which parts fit where can be somewhat of a challenge.

Most MVC implementations focus on the server-side programming environment and leave the client-side code to presenting the data from the view component. However, with Ajax technology (see Book 6, Chapter 3), you can implement parts of the model in the client as well, retrieving data as needed from the database tables on the server. Because this book is primarily about writing PHP applications, I focus on using MVC in the PHP server-side programming code.

Fortunately, there are many tools available to help you utilize MVC concepts within your PHP applications. The next chapter discusses the use of these programming tools.

# Chapter 2

# Selecting a Framework

As you write larger web applications, you'll find yourself having to write lots of the same code within your projects. Much of the code for performing standard web application functions, such as displaying data from a table and inserting new data into the table, is fairly customary and can be repetitive. Before you fall asleep writing your PHP programs, there's a solution you should try. There are some tools available that help write the repetitive code for you, as well as provide some extra utilities for making the code you do need to write easier to handle. This chapter introduces the concept of using a programming framework tool to assist you in your web application development. If you create a lot of web applications, it's well worth the effort to become familiar with these tools.

## Getting to Know PHP Frameworks

A *PHP framework* is not a special server to use for your applications, nor is it another programming language you need to code in. PHP framework packages are a combination of code files, library files, and utility scripts that help you kick-start your web application development by automatically generating some of the tedious code required to implement a web application for you. This helps you focus on writing the application-specific code required for your web application to work.

Frameworks provide the templates you use to create your web application. Just like the framework of a house remains hidden, supporting the drywall, roof, and outside brick, a programming framework creates template files that remains hidden but that you use to build your application on. You're still responsible for creating the code to produce the final product, but much of the underlying coding work has been done for you!

With framework tools, often you just need to point the tool to your database tables, and it'll automatically generate the HTML, CSS, JavaScript, and PHP code required to create the web pages that interact with those tables. That can be a huge time saver for you (as opposed to having to hand-code those features yourself).

You may be wondering just how a program can generate program code that would create a web application. Well, the answer lies in the MVC method. In Chapter 1 of this minibook, I introduce you to the concept of the model–view–controller method of developing web applications. That's the key behind most framework packages.

By sticking to a strict rule set for splitting up features in the application based on the MVC, the framework packages generate the model code to interface with your tables, the view code to display the data, and the controller code used to direct browser requests to the correct class methods. These files become the templates that you use to build the rest of your application.

Most PHP framework packages use the MVC method to generate application code, but they vary in the features they offer and how you use them. The following sections walk through some of the different features you'll find in PHP framework packages.

## Convention over configuration

One feature that makes using framework packages simpler to use is imposing a specific file-naming convention for files in the application. In an MVC application, there are lots of different model files, controller files, and of course, lots and lots of different view files used to complete the application. Trying to organize all these files so that they make sense can be a nightmare.

One solution is to use a standard configuration file. In a configuration file, you must specify which controller class file handles which browser request. After the controller handles the request, it needs to know which model class file it should use to interact with the requested data.

Finally, when the controller code retrieves the data, it needs to know which view file it should use to display the data it retrieved from the model. As you can probably guess, trying to use a configuration file to define all that would be somewhat difficult.

Instead of trying to define all those actions in a configuration file, most framework packages have incorporated a file-naming convention. The phrase *convention over configuration* is commonly used in framework circles. It means to stick with file-naming conventions to direct the controller actions, instead of trying to use configuration files to direct everything (there may still be some configuration files, such as to define the connection information for the database).

The convention defines strict rules on what filenames you should use within the application. This way each component can assume the name of the corresponding file it needs to interact with. The application knows which controller, model, and view files to use based solely on their filenames. This is demonstrated in Figure 2-1.

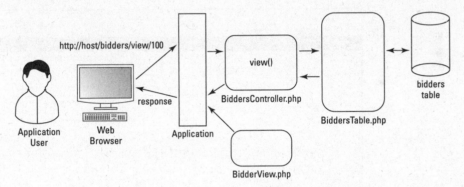

**FIGURE 2-1:**
Using a file-naming convention to handle web requests.

In the example shown in Figure 2-1, when your browser submits a request to view a data record contained in the Bidders table, the application calls the `view()` method defined in the controller file named `BiddersController.php`. When the controller `view()` method needs to access data from the Bidders table, it uses the model class file named `BiddersTable.php`. After retrieving the data field values for the data record, the `view()` controller method uses the view file named `BidderView.php` to display the data in the web page.

Notice the flow of the application and how each part of the flow incorporates the name of the object it's handling, as well as the name of the action it's performing. By incorporating a file-naming convention, framework packages don't need to define configuration settings for all that interaction — the framework packages handle all that for you!

# Scaffolding

As I mention earlier in this chapter, lots of the coding you write to interact with tables ends up looking the same. Just about every web application needs to create, read, update, and delete data records in database tables (see Chapter 1 of this minibook for more on the CRUD acronym). These functions have become so commonplace in web applications that most framework packages have the ability to write that code for you!

*Scaffolding* is the process of framework package scripts inspecting the data fields defined in a table and automatically generating the controller, model, and view code files required to perform all the CRUD operations with the table data. If your application uses multiple database tables, you can perform the scaffolding operation on each table, automatically generating the files to interact with all the tables. Figure 2-2 shows an example of a CRUD interface generated from scaffolding code.

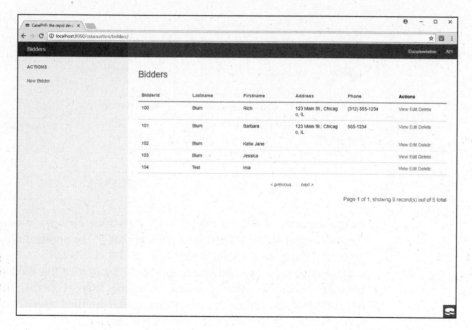

**FIGURE 2-2:**
A CRUD interface generated by the CakePHP framework package.

Just as in construction work, the scaffolding isn't the final product — it's there to help you build the final product. After the framework package generates the scaffolding code, you can easily modify things to fit your particular application environment, including adding any styling required for your web pages.

Another great feature of scaffolding is that you're not stuck with the code the scaffolding process generates. If something doesn't quite fit within your application, it's easy to tweak the generated code to just the way you want things. By splitting the functions into the model, view, and controller components, it's easier to find just what you need to change.

# Routing

Dynamic web applications require lots of interaction with the client browser. As the website visitor clicks links or pushes buttons, URLs are generated that the browser uses to request more information from the application.

Those interactions require different URLs to pass information back and forth between the client browser and the application. Just trying to keep track of all the different URLs required for an application can be a fulltime job.

*Routing* helps that process by defining the rules for directing the controller on how to handle each URL received from client browsers. Most framework packages incorporate a specific routing rule set for handling URLs received from browsers:

```
http://hostname/classname/methodname/data
```

The URL specifies the name of the controller class that should handle the request, along with the name of the class method within the class that processes the request. Any data required for the function is added as a third element. Figure 2-3 demonstrates how this works with the `view()` method from the `Bidders` class.

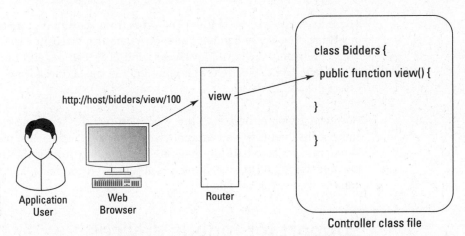

**FIGURE 2-3:**
Using routing to direct client requests.

Routing is yet another example of the convention over configuration feature found in frameworks. By sticking to a standard routing convention, you can easily add new features to the application and ensure that they're handled correctly by the controllers.

TIP

Besides the standard routing, most framework packages allow you to define your own custom routing paths as you incorporate additional features in the framework. This gives you full flexibility in using both automatic and custom request routing within your application if needed.

## Helper methods

All framework packages allow you to code using standard HTML, CSS, JavaScript, and PHP, but most of them also provide a code library to help make creating the application a little easier.

These additional library functions are referred to as *helper methods* within the framework. You can choose to use them, or continue coding using HTML, CSS, JavaScript, and PHP. However, the helper methods often can save you time and effort in your coding.

Just as the jQuery library methods help simplify complex JavaScript features (see Book 3, Chapter 3), the framework helper methods help simplify complex HTML, CSS, and PHP code. For example, in CakePHP, the `link()` helper method generates an `<a href>` tag based on the controller and method names you supply to it. That makes it easier than trying to write out the URLs in an `<a href>` tag as you go along.

## Form validation

These days, receiving data in HTML forms from website visitors can be a dangerous thing. The key to handling unknown data from website visitors is validation. There are plenty of HTML, JavaScript, and PHP features and functions available to validate data to ensure that it's not only in the correct format but also safe to insert in your database.

However, trying to utilize all the validation features available can be somewhat complicated and time consuming trying to write. Fortunately, most PHP framework packages automatically generate the necessary form validation code for you, to some degree. All you need to do is define the form fields, and their data types and the framework code do the rest!

## Support for mobile devices

No longer can you write a single web application and expect it to satisfy customers using it from a desktop or laptop device with a large monitor *and* customers using it from a mobile device with a small display.

Instead, you often have to write multiple versions of the application presentation code, checking for the size of the browser's viewing area and sending the proper styles to size things appropriately. This is one place where the MVC programming method comes in handy. With that setup, you only need to worry about duplicating the view code, so you can keep the controller and model codes the same.

This is also another place where framework packages can come to your rescue. Instead of having to write multiple versions of your web pages, some framework packages provide the ability to automatically scale the presentation features to fit the viewing area used by each individual website visitor.

## Templates

Sometimes I think the worst feeling for a programmer is when you have to generate a great-looking web application and you're staring at an empty editor window. Just trying to get that first bit of code written to support the web pages can be a hurdle.

This is yet another place where framework packages can come to the rescue. The framework scripts can automatically generate basic code templates that you can use for the base of your website design layout. Then you just need to apply those templates to every web page in the application. This helps you create a consistent look and feel for your application. It also saves you from having to come up with all that code yourself!

## Unit testing

Software bugs are the bane of web programmers. Having to deal with software bugs after you've released a web application to the public or, even worse, to a paying customer is a hassle. Software bugs ruin the application's (any maybe your) reputation and can drive potential visitors to other websites. The key to reducing software bugs is testing.

However, trying to test an application during development can be confusing, because different parts of the application may rely on other parts being completed. Often, you find yourself in a circular situation where you're constantly waiting for another part of the application to become complete before you can test any of the parts.

Framework packages have incorporated a feature called *unit testing* to help with that problem. Unit testing provides simple tests based on the expected input and output of an individual operation within the application. With unit testing, you can determine if a part of the application is working correctly based on the expected input, and the output you expect it to produce based on that input. There's no need for the other parts of the web application — everything is self-contained within the unit testing environment.

By not having to rely on other parts of the application, unit testing allows you to compartmentalize your testing process, and helps ensure each individual feature within a web application is performing correctly before you try to put them all together.

# Knowing Why You Should Use a Framework

If you're a seasoned PHP developer, you may be thinking you don't need any help with developing your web applications. That may be true, but there are other reasons for incorporating a framework package in your web development tools. Here are some of the common reasons even professional web developers are turning to framework packages:

>> **Organization:** PHP frameworks force you to organize your application code into a specific file and folder structure. This not only helps with the development process, but is also handy when you're trying to troubleshoot an application that you may have written years ago. Knowing just where to look to find a specific function makes all the difference in finding bugs and updating features.

>> **Speed of development:** PHP frameworks help cut down application development time by stubbing out the code blocks for you, giving you a boost to your development. Just having the code files present and filling in the required methods can help with the process of creating code.

>> **Helper methods:** Even if you don't use the scaffolding features in the framework packages, just having the library of helper methods available to simplify your code can greatly increase your development speed. Instead of having to hand-code long HTML code blocks, you can just insert a simple helper method and provide a few options.

>> **Database integration:** Integration with the underlying database is also a key to using frameworks. If you must create web applications that run in multiple environments, you may need to support multiple types of database servers. Most framework packages use a simple configuration file to define the location and type of server that the database uses. Changing the underlying

database server is a simple matter of changing that configuration file — no code needs to be changed!

>> **Reusable code:** Adhering to the same coding templates and patterns makes it easier to use the same controllers, models, or even views in multiple applications.

>> **Consistent look and feel:** Along the same lines as reusable code, using the same application templates allows you to maintain a consistent look and feel within an application, as well as between applications if you want.

>> **Testing:** Using the unit testing features of a framework package is a huge benefit to finding software bugs before you release your web applications. The unit testing abilities of most framework packages makes it easy to test each component individually to ensure they meet your expectations.

>> **Community:** Each framework package has its own community of developers, working together to both improve package features and support those who have questions using those features.

Using a framework package may not be for everyone, but it doesn't hurt to give one or two a try and see how they could help with your web development environment. To help with that, the following section discusses five of the most popular PHP framework packages to help give you an idea of which ones to try.

## FRAMEWORKS AND PACKAGE MANAGEMENT

Framework packages are nothing more than a bundle of code files, but many of them utilize the Composer package manager for installation. The Composer package manager provides a standard format for bundling software files and library files for distribution and installation. It's also good for tracking file dependencies, so upgrading an installed package is a breeze.

If you're familiar with Linux package managers such as yum or apt-get, you'll notice that Composer is a bit different. Instead of using a central database to track installed packages, Composer merely downloads and installs the package from a software repository into a folder on your workstation or server. This makes it ideal for installing different framework packages for different applications on your web server.

Before you can install most PHP framework packages, you'll need to install the Composer package manager. You can find it at the main Composer website (https://getcomposer.org). Click the Download button for instructions on how to download and install Composer on your workstation or server environment.

# Focusing on Popular PHP Frameworks

Now that you've seen what frameworks are and what they can do, you're ready to take a look at some of the more popular PHP framework packages. In this section, I review five of the most popular options:

>> CakePHP

>> CodeIgniter

>> Laravel

>> Symfony

>> Zend Framework

Each of these packages is currently supported and has its own following within the PHP developer community. Choosing a framework package is a lot like buying a car — different people have different needs and tastes that play into just which framework package they prefer to use. Don't hesitate to give a couple of them a try before you decide on which one to use for your development work.

## CakePHP

The CakePHP framework package (www.cakephp.org) was developed during the height of the Ruby on Rails framework craze and supports many of the same features. The Ruby on Rails framework uses the Ruby programming language as the server-side web language and was one of the early pioneers in developing web applications using the MVC method.

CakePHP followed that pattern and is highly MVC oriented. It structures the web applications it develops into specific controller, model, and view components. That makes it easier to follow along with the code, and interject your own code when necessary.

When you peruse through the CakePHP website, you'll find that it has lots of documentation, tutorials, and forum support. Here are some of the benefits you'll find in CakePHP:

>> Built-in authentication helpers

>> Enhanced form validation to protect against SQL injections, cross-site scripting attacks, and form tampering

>> The ability to use scaffolding to generate one or all components of the MVC application

>> Its own `find()` method for creating complex SQL queries with just a little input from you

>> Heavy reliance on convention over configuration for most framework features

CakePHP uses the Composer package manager to download and install the template files needed to create an application framework. Just navigate to the `DocumentRoot` folder for your web server and enter the following command:

```
composer create-project --prefer-dist cakephp/app appname
```

The *appname* parameter is the name for your application. This command downloads all the controller, model, and view template files necessary to use CakePHP in your application. Figure 2-4 shows the initial web page generated from a CakePHP install.

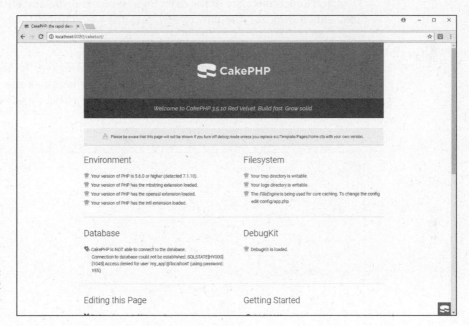

**FIGURE 2-4:** The default CakePHP framework web page.

If you're looking for a full-featured framework package that follows MVC conventions, CakePHP is a great tool to consider.

## CodeIgniter

The CodeIgniter framework package (www.codeigniter.com) was another early entrant into the PHP framework world. It supports full MVC compatibility, but you can also write an application framework by only defining controllers with no model or view components. This can make CodeIgniter easier to use to quickly develop smaller web applications.

CodeIgniter is known as one of the easier-to-learn frameworks (and is often recommended for beginners). It produces framework code that is known for its speed. Here are some of the other features that make CodeIgniter popular:

>> No configuration is required for simple web applications.

>> There's a large set of library methods to help with complex coding.

>> You can create high-performance websites with little overhead.

CodeIgniter is one of the few PHP framework packages that doesn't use the Composer package manager to install the package (at least at the time of this writing). To install CodeIgniter, go to the main CodeIgniter website and click the Download link. This downloads the latest version of the CodeIgniter framework files as a single zip file.

Extract the zip file into a folder under the DocumentRoot folder for your web server to start your application development. This becomes the folder for your new application. Figure 2-5 shows the main web page that appears from the basic installation.

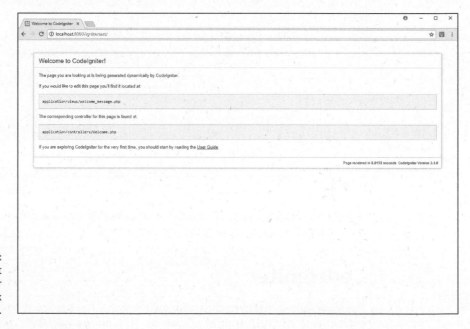

**FIGURE 2-5:**
The default
CodeIgniter
framework
web page.

If you're looking to just test-drive a PHP framework package to get a feel for how they work, CodeIgniter is certainly one of the easier packages to install and play around with.

## Laravel

The Laravel PHP framework package (`www.laravel.com`) has quickly become the most popular package among PHP developers. It has a wide array of features and capabilities for producing sophisticated web applications. It can be a bit complex to install and configure, but the features that the Laravel framework provides can make it worth it. Here are some of the features included in Laravel:

>> Routing using the common REST principles

>> An advanced object-relational mapping (ORM) database interface modeler

>> An advanced query builder for simplifying submitting queries to the database

>> Database seeding for creating data records for testing

>> Pagination for large data result sets included automatically

>> Includes its own package bundling system for handling library files

>> Version control for database schemas

>> Class file auto loading for increased performance

>> Automatic form validation

The Laravel package uses the Composer package manager for installation:

```
composer create-project --prefer-dist laravel/laravel appname
```

The front door" to your Laravel application is actually in the folder named `public`. You need to point your web server `DocumentRoot` setting to this folder, or you need to include it in your URLs:

```
http://localhost:8080/laraveltest/public
```

Figure 2-6 shows the default Laravel application web page.

**TECHNICAL STUFF**

Laravel provides a package called Homestead that is a complete prebuilt web development environment running on a virtual machine. It uses the Vagrant configuration management tool to build the virtual machine environment that can run in VirtualBox, Hyper-V, Docker, or VMware. Simply download and install VirtualBox, Vagrant, and Homestead, and you'll have a complete Ubuntu Linux server with a Laravel development environment up and running in a virtual server environment!

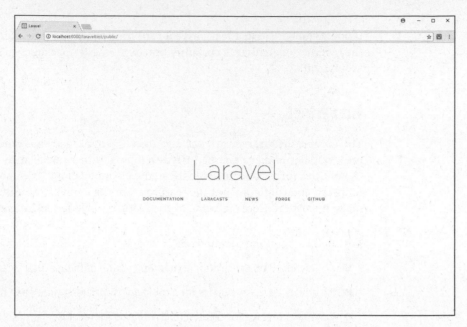

**FIGURE 2-6:**
The default
Laravel
framework
web page.

## Symfony

The Symfony project is primarily a bundle of PHP libraries that provide lots and lots of useful features for creating dynamic web applications. The libraries include tools for authentication, form creation and validation, routing, and building page templates.

The Symfony libraries have become extremely popular, used by many high-profile PHP applications, such as the Drupal content management system. In fact, many of the other framework packages use them in their own code!

You can combine the Symfony libraries into a framework environment to generate your own web applications. Symfony uses the Composer package manager, so you can easily install the framework and test it out:

```
composer create-project --prefer-dist symphony/skeleton appname
```

When you run the default Symfony web page from the skeleton (see Figure 2-7), it provides a link that points you to a guide for building your frameworks using the Symfony libraries.

One downside to Symfony is that it uses the older YAML-style configuration files to define just about everything. YAML is a markup language that was popular for a while in configuration files, but it can be somewhat confusing for beginners.

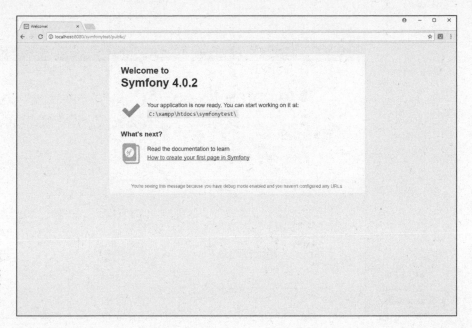

**FIGURE 2-7:**
The default
Symfony
framework
web page.

# Zend Framework

By far the most popular professional PHP framework package has been Zend Framework (`https://framework.zend.com`). Zend specializes in PHP development and is the corporate sponsor for the PHP open-source project. It's no stranger to advanced PHP development and support.

The Zend Framework is a full-featured framework package that uses the MVC model for the framework structure. You can install the Zend Framework MVC template using Composer:

```
composer create-project --prefer-dist zendframework/skeleton-application appname
```

Figure 2-8 shows the default web page generated by the Zend Framework skeleton code.

The Zend Framework skeleton application produces the file and folder structure that you need to start your application. It provides some level of scaffolding for you to use with the zf tool. You use that to create individual controller, model, and view scaffolding files for an application based on the application database.

The Zend Framework package provides lots of high-end features for PHP development, and is highly respected in professional PHP development circles. It can be somewhat complicated to start out with, but when you get the hang of things, you can create some pretty amazing websites with it!

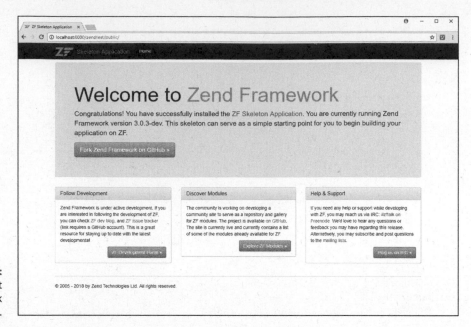

**FIGURE 2-8:**
The default
Zend Framework
web page.

# Looking At Micro Frameworks

After test-driving a couple of the PHP framework packages, you may find that you don't need that much support for your PHP development. You're not alone in that, which has spurred another type of framework package: the micro-framework.

*Micro-frameworks* are framework packages that don't include all the fancy helper methods and library utilities that the big framework packages include. They do, however, produce great bare-bones framework code for you to build your web applications from. This is ideal if you're just looking for a little help and organization for your web application.

This section walks you through a few popular micro-framework packages to give you an idea of what they have to offer.

## Lumen

The Lumen framework package (https://lumen.laravel.com) is a micro-framework supported by Laravel. It eliminates many of the fancy features that the Laravel framework provides and leaves you with just the bare-bones necessities to build an MVC application framework.

You can install a Lumen framework using Composer:

```
composer create-project --prefer-dist laravel/lumen appname
```

You'll get an idea of just how bare-bones Lumen is by opening the default web page that it generates with the skeleton files, shown in Figure 2-9.

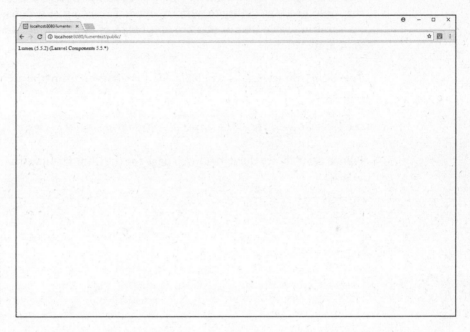

**FIGURE 2-9:**
The default
Lumen
framework
web page.

That's about as bare-bones as you can get! Lumen is great if you're looking for just a little help with your web development, without committing to a large framework package. It has a small footprint, which doesn't add much overhead to your application performance.

## Slim

The Slim framework package (www.slimframework.com) is quite possibly the smallest of the micro-framework packages, but it has a reputation for being the fastest. Here are the core features of Slim:

» URL routing that maps URLs to function callbacks and has the ability to perform pattern matching on URLs so that you don't need to specify all the possible URLs used in your application

>> Middleware you use to build your application code around specific URL requests from clients

>> The ability to dissect HTTP messages, statuses, and cookies within your code

>> Interoperability with other PHP libraries and tools

The URL routing feature makes Slim a good framework to use for static websites that only need the ability to perform dynamic routing of web pages. You just set up a routing table that directs browser requests to the proper static Web page in your application.

The Slim framework is available for installation from the Composer package manager:

```
composer create-project --prefer-dist slim/slim-skeleton appname
```

Figure 2-10 shows the default web page for the Slim framework.

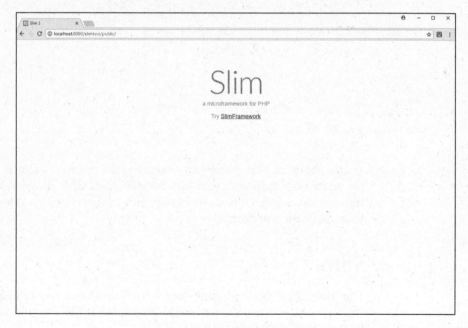

**FIGURE 2-10:**
The default
Slim framework
web page.

The Slim framework package offers some interesting features for non-PHP applications to use and may be worth looking into if you still maintain any static websites.

# Yii

The Yii framework package (`https://yiiframework.org`) is a simple PHP framework that provides all the standard MVC components for your application. There aren't a lot of bells and whistles in the Yii package, but it can do a lot of the basic coding work for you.

There are two versions of the framework that you can install: basic and advanced. To install an advanced skeleton, use this command from Composer:

```
composer create-project --prefer-dist yiisoft/yii2-app-advanced appname
```

The Yii framework doesn't produce a default framework page — it's up to you to create the pages you need for your application. It uses the `gii` tool (which you need to install separately) to generate simple scaffolding files for your application.

# Chapter **3**

# Creating an Application Using Frameworks

The previous chapter introduces some of the various framework packages available for PHP programming. Using a framework package can help simplify your web application development efforts, but you have to follow the framework rules. This chapter dives into creating a simple application using CakePHP so you can get a feel for just how frameworks operate, and how you can add your own PHP touches to the code they generate.

## Building the Template

The CakePHP framework package creates a lot of the behind-the-scenes code for your application for you. That allows you to focus more on what's important: the code that does all the application-specific work.

TIP

For this demo, I walk you through re-creating some of the basic features from the AuctionHelper application introduced in Book 6. If you aren't familiar with that project, take a few minutes to jump back and skim through Book 6, Chapter 1, to get an idea of just what the AuctionHelper program does. I'll be here when you get back.

Before you can start writing any code for the new application, you need to allow CakePHP to generate the application template for you. It's amazing how much code CakePHP can do for you, and it would be a shame to not utilize all that power in your application. This section walks through how to start out a new project using the CakePHP framework.

## Initializing the application

It's important to remember that working with framework packages isn't like installing a server, where you install the software once and use it multiple times. Framework packages generate specific code for each single application, so each time you create a new application, you need to reinstall the framework package just for that application.

Fortunately, as discussed in Chapter 2 of this minibook, CakePHP uses the popular Composer package management system to manage your code. That makes installing an up-to-date CakePHP framework code easy. Follow these steps to do that for your application:

1. **Open a command-line tool for your operating system environment.**

   For Windows, use the Command Prompt window. For macOS, use the Terminal utility. For Linux environments, you can either use a virtual command-line terminal or launch a graphical command-line utility from your graphical desktop.

2. **Navigate to the** DocumentRoot **folder for your web server.**

   Use the cd command-line command to change to the htdocs folder for your web server. If you're using the XAMPP server in Windows, that's the c:\xampp\ htdocs folder. For the XAMPP server in macOS, that's the /Applications/ XAMPP/htdocs folder. So for Windows, use:

   ```
   C:\Users\rkblu> cd \xampp\htdocs
   C:\xampp\htdocs>
   ```

   Or for macOS use:

   ```
   /usrs/rblum> cd /Applications/XAMPP/htdocs
   /Applications/XAMPP/htdocs>
   ```

3. **Run the Composer program from the command prompt, specifying the** create-project **option; for the name of the application, use** cakeauction:

```
C:\xampp\htdocs> composer create-project --prefer-dist cakephp/app
   cakeauction
Installing cakephp/app (3.5.1)
  - Installing cakephp/app (3.5.1): Loading from cache
Created project in cakeauction
Loading composer repositories with package information
Updating dependencies (including require-dev)
Package operations: 47 installs, 0 updates, 0 removals
...
Generating autoload files
> Cake\Composer\Installer\PluginInstaller::postAutoloadDump
> App\Console\Installer::postInstall
Created `config/app.php` file
Created `C:\xampp\htdocs\cakeauction/tmp/cache/views` directory
Set Folder Permissions ? (Default to Y) [Y,n]? y
Updated Security.salt value in config/app.php

C:\xampp\htdocs>
```

TIP

If you don't have the Composer program installed, go to https://getcomposer.org and follow the instructions to download and install it on your workstation.

**4.** **Close the command prompt window by typing** exit.

The Composer utility retrieves the current CakePHP framework template files from its software repository and copies them into the cakeauction folder structure on your workstation. At the end of the process, it asks if you would like it to set the folder security permissions for you. If you answer yes, Composer will modify the folder properties so the web server can access the application.

When the process completes, you have a full CakePHP application template installed in the cakeauction folder. You may not realize it, but there's a complete web page infrastructure built into the template files. You can test that out yourself by starting your web server environment, opening your browser, and then going to the following URL:

```
http://localhost:8080/cakeauction
```

You should see the main CakePHP template web page, shown in Figure 3-1.

The web page code checks your web server environment to ensure that it's compatible with running CakePHP code. You should see green icons for all the Environment and Filesystem checks that CakePHP performs on your system.

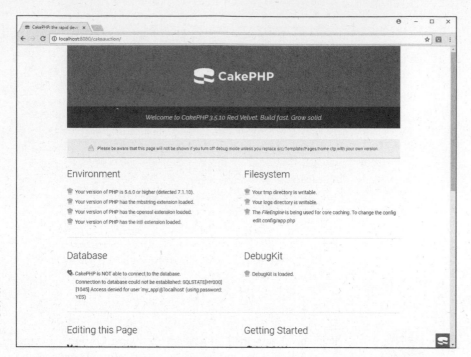

**FIGURE 3-1:**
The generic
CakePHP
application
web page.

If any of the Environment or Filesystem icons is red, that will be a potential problem down the road. It's best to make the necessary modifications to your web environment now to satisfy the CakePHP requirements before you start out with any coding. At this point in the process, the icon for the Database check icon will be red, because you haven't told CakePHP how to access your database yet.

## Exploring the files and folders

With the core CakePHP template files installed for the application, you can do some snooping around to see just what was installed. Open your system's File Manager tool and navigate to the `cakeauction` folder that the install process created.

In that folder, you should see several folders and a few files. There are three folders that are of particular interest:

>> `bin`: Contains the `cake` utility that helps you manage the CakePHP environment.

>> `config`: Contains the few configuration files required by CakePHP to operate properly in your server environment

>> `src`: Contains the source code files for your web application

The `src` folder is the main area for the application code files. This is where you'll be spending most of your time coding. If you take a quick peek in this folder, you'll see the subfolders `Controller`, `Model`, `Template`, and `View`.

This is a clue that, indeed, the CakePHP template is using the MVC method (see Chapter 1 in this minibook) to design and lay out the application program files. The code for the different MVC components resides in each of these folders. That is a great help in keeping the application code organized and being able to quickly find the files you need to modify.

## Defining the database environment

Before you can start working with the template code, you need to tell CakePHP where to find the database for your application. You do that in the `app.php` configuration file, located in the `config` folder in the application template. Follow these steps to change the `app.php` file to recognize your application database:

1. **Open your favorite text editor, program editor, or integrated development environment (IDE) editor package.**

2. **Choose File⇨Open to navigate to the** `app.php` **file in the** `cakeauction/config` **folder, contained within the application template.**

3. **Scroll through the** `app.php` **file until you see the** `Datasources` **section of the file.**

   It should contain the following lines:

   ```
   'className' => 'Cake\Database\Connection',
   'driver' => 'Cake\Database\Driver\Mysql',
   'persistent' => false,
   'host' => 'localhost',
   //'port' => 'non_standard_port_number',
   'username' => 'my_app',
   'password' => 'secret',
   'database' => 'my_app',
   'encoding' => 'utf8',
   'timezone' => 'UTC',
   'flags' => [],
   'cacheMetadata' => true,
   'log' => false,
   ```

**4.** **Modify the database configuration for your MySQL server environment.**

If you follow the instructions in Book 6, Chapter 1, for the AuctionHelper application, enter these changes in the app.php code:

```
'className' => 'Cake\Database\Connection',
'driver' => 'Cake\Database\Driver\Mysql',
'persistent' => false,
'host' => 'localhost',
//'port' => 'non_standard_port_number',
'username' => 'ah_user',
'password' => 'AuctionHelper',
'database' => 'auction',
'encoding' => 'utf8',
'timezone' => 'UTC',
'flags' => [],
'cacheMetadata' => true,
'log' => false,
```

**5.** **Save the** app.php **file changes and exit your editor.**

Now if you run the application's main web page again, you should see the Database icon turn green, indicating that the CakePHP application can connect to the MySQL server and access the auction database where your application data resides.

This creates the basic CakePHP application template. If you prefer to create your own application code on your own, you can start building your model, view, and controller files now. If you'd like to take advantage of the CakePHP scaffolding features, continue to the next section.

WARNING

If you skipped working out the AuctionHelper application in Book 6, Chapter 1, turn back to that chapter and go through the steps to create the auction database, the Bidders and Items tables within the database, and the ah_user MySQL user account to access the database. You'll need those items to work out this demonstration.

TIP

The default configuration template that CakePHP creates assumes that you're using the MySQL database server, but it also supports other database servers. Consult the CakePHP documentation to see what other drivers are available for accessing data on other database servers.

# Creating an Application Scaffold

The real power behind framework packages is the amount of code they can generate for you, saving you from having to hand-code the boring stuff. That power comes in the scaffolding code. Most framework packages provide some level of scaffolding code support, but the scaffolding code generated by CakePHP is pretty amazing! This section walks you through the steps to create the scaffolding code for the auction application.

## Installing the scaffolding

The CakePHP package has the ability to create scaffolding code for one part of the application or all the parts of the application. How much code CakePHP generates for you is completely up to you. If you just need some help creating the CRUD methods for your tables, you can tell CakePHP to just create the model scaffolding. If you need some help creating a controller to start out your application, you can tell CakePHP to just create the controller scaffolding. *Remember:* The choice of how much help you want is up to you!

CakePHP doesn't generate the scaffolding code automatically when you install the template files, but you can easily generate it yourself. CakePHP uses the bake utility (cute name, isn't it?) to generate the scaffolding code for your application. You run the bake utility from within the cake utility, which is contained in the bin template folder:

```
C:\xampp\htdocs\cakeauction>bin\cake bake
The following commands can be used to generate skeleton code for your application.

Available bake commands:

- all
- behavior
- cell
- component
- controller
- fixture
- form
- helper
- mailer
- middleware
- migration
- migration_diff
- migration_snapshot
- model
```

```
- plugin
- seed
- shell
- shell_helper
- task
- template
- test

By using `cake bake [name]` you can invoke a specific bake task.

C:\xampp\htdocs\cakeauction>
```

There are a lot of options available in the bake utility. You can bake just the model code, just the controller code, or everything you need for your application. The all option allows CakePHP to generate scaffolding code for a complete web application that provides CRUD features for the table you specify.

Follow these steps to create a simple CRUD application for the Bidders table in the auction database:

**1.** **Open the command-line utility in your OS, and navigate to the** cakeauction **folder for your project:**

```
C:\users/rblu> cd \xampp\htdocs\cakeauction
C:\xampp\htdocs\cakeauction>
```

**2.** **Run the** bake **utility to generate all scaffolding for the** Bidders **table:**

```
C:\xampp\htdocs\cakeauction>bin\cake bake all bidders
Bake All

----------------------------------------------------------------

One moment while associations are detected.
...
Bake All complete.

C:\xampp\htdocs\cakeauction>
```

**3.** **Ensure that the Apache and MySQL servers are running, and then open your browser; in the address bar enter the following URL:**

```
http://localhost:8080/cakeauction/bidders/
```

Peruse through the application a bit to see what functionality is there by default.

**4.** Repeat Step 2 to run the bake **utility for the Items table:**

```
C:\xampp\htdocs\cakeauction>bin/cake bake all items
```

**5.** In your browser address bar, enter the following URL:

```
http://localhost:8080/cakeauction/items/
```

You just created a complete web application with just one command! (Okay, maybe CakePHP helped a bit.) Figure 3-2 shows the main web page that's generated for the Bidders table scaffolding.

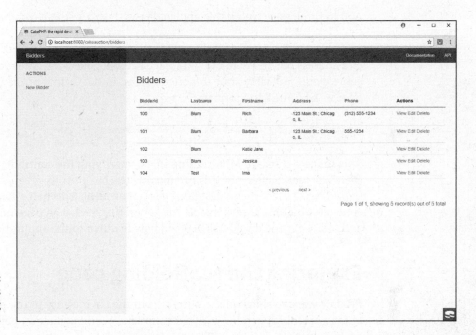

**FIGURE 3-2:**
The main Bidders
scaffolding
web page.

When you go to the web page that the items scaffolding generated, you'll see the same layout and features, but with the Items table data.

The scaffolding creates a complete data management website for each of the database tables. Just take a look at all the features "baked into" this simple application:

» The main web page displays the data field values for each of the data records contained in the Bidders or Items tables.

» The main web page incorporates content paging, so if there are lots of data records, you can view them one page at a time.

>> You can sort the output based on any data field by clicking the data field name at the top of the column.

>> The action icons allow you to perform functions on an individual data record. You can

- View the complete data record.

- Edit the data record values.

- Delete the data record.

>> You can add a new data record using the New link in the navigation bar.

And to think you created this application with just a single command!

As you click the different links within the application, take a look at your browser's address bar and note the URL that each link generates. After you move around some, you'll probably start to notice a trend in the format of the URLs. The URLs all use the same basic format:

```
http://localhost:8080/cakeauction/controller/method/data
```

This follows standard MVC routing rules, specifying the controller and method in the URL (see Chapter 1 of this minibook). The bake utility creates the basic routing rules as part of the scaffolding code in CakePHP. This helps you identify which controller method is responsible for generating each web page in the application and easily expand on that as you add new features to the application.

## Exploring the scaffolding code

I didn't want to show all the output from the bake utility in the preceding steps, but if you still happen to have your command prompt window open, you can scroll back through the output. The output from the bake utility shows all the files that the scaffolding process creates. You can also open your File Manager utility and peruse through the src template folder to see the changes added to the file structure.

In the Controllers folder, two new files have been added: BiddersController. php and ItemsController.php. As you can guess, they contain the class definitions for the bidders controller and the items controller. As you can tell from these filenames, CakePHP is big on the convention versus configuration part of frameworks. The filenames directly correspond to the function of the code they contain.

If you open either of the controller files in your text editor, you'll see they each define the following methods:

- ❯❯ index: Generates the listing on the main web page.

- ❯❯ view: Displays the details for a specific data record.

- ❯❯ add: Displays a form to enter a new data record, and then retrieves the form data and saves it in the table.

- ❯❯ edit: Displays a form with the data from an existing data record, and then retrieves the form data and updates the existing data record.

- ❯❯ delete: Prompts the visitor to confirm the deleting request, and then removes the data record from the table.

These are the default methods required to implement the CRUD features in the application. Now, take a look at the src/Template folder. Notice that it contains a Bidders subfolder and an Items subfolder. Double-click one of the folders to see what's inside.

Inside the Bidders and Items template subfolders are the files required to display the output from the controller methods. You should see four files in the folders:

- ❯❯ add.ctp: The template file for the add controller method

- ❯❯ edit.ctp: The template file for the edit controller method

- ❯❯ index.ctp: The template file for the index controller method

- ❯❯ view.ctp: The template file for the view controller method

This is yet another place where the convention over configuration part of the framework kicks in. CakePHP knows when the controller method runs to use the template file with the same name to control the view output.

# Modifying the Application Scaffold

You have a pretty cool web application created, just by using the standard CakePHP scaffolding code, but now it's time to add your own touch to the application. If you remember, the original AuctionHelper application was required to be able to list the items won by a bidder. The scaffolding application doesn't provide that feature, so you need to add it yourself.

Adding the new feature is a multistep process:

» **You'll need to add a link somewhere in the application that allows the website visitor to launch the new feature web page to view the bidder's won items.** It would make sense to add this link to the listing of bidders, so that you can select the link for the appropriate bidder.

» **You'll need to add a controller method to handle the new feature.** The controller method will need to receive the bidderid value for the bidder selected back in the bidder listing, and be able to query the items model to retrieve the items table data records that match the bidderid.

» **You'll need to modify the items model class to add a method to perform the specialized search function.** It'll need to receive the bidderid value, and then return an array of items data records with the matching winbidder data value.

» **You'll need to create a new view template file to display the bidderid, along with the list of items the bidder won.** Being able to total the winning bid amounts so the bidder knows how much to pay would also be a nice feature to have.

That seems like a lot of steps required for adding a single feature to the application. Don't worry, though. With CakePHP, you won't have to do much coding. The following sections walk you through each step.

## Adding a new feature link

The first step in adding the new feature web page in the application is to create a link to it in the existing application. Your website visitors will need some way of getting to the new feature within the existing application structure.

The bidders scaffold code that CakePHP created already lists each bidder data record contained in the Bidders table, along with a set of action links for performing actions for the bidder. That's a perfect place for you to plug in a link to the web page that lists the items won by the bidder.

The page code that generates the Bidders main page is located in the src/ Template/Bidders folder and contained in the index.ctp template file.

If you open that file in your editor, you'll see the code that CakePHP uses to generate the bidders listing. The action links are created in this section of the code:

```
<td class="actions">
  <?= $this->Html->link(__('View'), ['action' => 'view', $bidder->bidderid]) ?>
  <?= $this->Html->link(__('Edit'), ['action' => 'edit', $bidder->bidderid]) ?>
  <?= $this->Form->postLink(__('Delete'), ['action' => 'delete',
  $bidder->bidderid], ['confirm' => __('Are you sure you want to delete # {0}?',
  $bidder->bidderid)]) ?>
</td>
```

The link() method is a CakePHP helper method that creates HTML links for you, based on the controller and method you supply. If you omit the controller value, the link() method assumes to use the same controller that generated the web page. (*Remember:* The controller name is embedded in the URL.)

To add a new link, you need to come up with a new method name for the feature. I give it the name listItemsWon(). Because you're listing items, the new feature should be part of the items controller.

Follow these steps to add that link to the application code:

1. **Open your favorite editor and navigate to the** cakeauction/src/ Template/Bidders **folder in the** DocumentRoot **folder for your web server.**

2. **Select the** index.ctp **file to open in the editor.**

3. **Before the lines that create the View, Edit, and Delete links (but after the** <td> **line), add this code:**

```
<?= $this->Html->link(__('Items'), ['controller' => 'items','action' =>
    'listItemsWon', $bidder->bidderid]) ?>
```

4. **Save the updated file as** index.ctp.

If you open your browser and go to the bidders main page as before, you should now see your new link appear in the action links, as shown in Figure 3-3.

The new Items link appears in the actions, just as you planned. However, if you click the Items link you'll get an error message, shown in Figure 3-4.

The error message is telling you that the link requested the listItemsWon() method from the ItemsController class, which doesn't exist yet. The error message was even nice enough to show you the file that needs to be updated and the basic code needed to implement the method. That's exactly what you do in the next section.

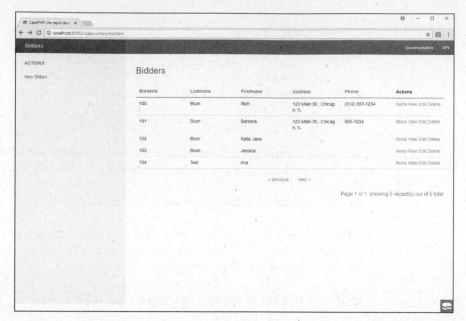

**FIGURE 3-3:**
The new link
in the bidders
action links.

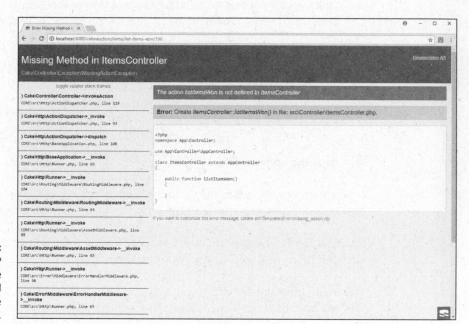

**FIGURE 3-4:**
The CakePHP
error message
generated
by clicking the
new link.

## Creating the controller code

Now that you have a way for your website visitors to access the new feature, you need to start writing the code to implement it. Don't worry — that part isn't all that hard, thanks to the help that CakePHP provides for you.

As shown in the previous section, the next step in the process is to write the listItemsWon() method for the ItemsController.php file. Follow these steps to do that:

**1.** **Open your favorite editor and navigate to the** ItemsController.php **file, located in the** cakeauction/src/Controllers **folder in the** DocumentRoot **folder of your web server.**

**2.** **Scroll down through the existing methods contained within the** ItemsController.php **file until you get to the bottom of the file.**

**3.** **Before the closing bracket, add the** listItemsWon() **method code:**

```php
public function listItemsWon($id = null)
{
    $bidderid = $this->request->getParam('pass');
    $items = $this->Items->find('winbidder', ['winbidder' => $bidderid]);
    $this->set(['items' => $items, 'winbidder' => $bidderid]);
}
```

**4.** **Save the updated file as** ItemsController.php.

Thanks yet again to CakePHP, the entire listItemsWon() method consists of only three lines of code! The first line uses the getParam() helper function to retrieve the bidderid value passed from the URL that the link() helper method created.

The second line uses the find() method of the Items model to submit a SQL search to the database server. The find() method is a huge benefit of the CakePHP framework package. Instead of your having to hand-code SQL statements to retrieve data, the find() method does most of the work for you. You just need to specify the data field and value to match in the search.

Finally, the last line of code uses the special set() method. This method triggers the call for the view template and passes data to the template code to display. In this statement, I pass both the array of items data records that's returned from the find() method, along with the bidderid value.

If you click the Items link for a bidder now, you'll be passed to the controller method that you just created, but you'll still be somewhat disappointed with the results, as shown in Figure 3-5.

The listItemsWon() controller method uses the find() model method but specifies for it to find a winbidder data field instead of the primary key of the table. Because that's a custom operation, you need to create a custom method to support it. Thanks to the convention rules of CakePHP, you know that you'll need to create a findWinbidder() method in the model class for the items table. That's up next on the to-do list.

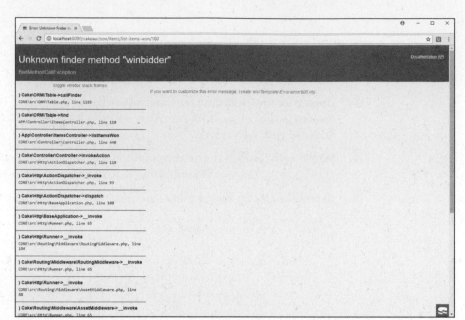

**FIGURE 3-5:**
The find error message from the application.

## Modifying the model code

You're almost there — just a couple more code files to modify to implement the new feature! As the previous section discusses, in this step you need to create a custom `find()` method in the `items` table model class to find the `winbidder` data values that match the `bidderid` value passed from the link URL.

As you may have guessed by now, you'll find the model class files in the `src/Model/Table` folder. (Are you starting to get the hang of the MVC file layout yet?) When you peek in that folder, you'll see the `ItemsTable.php` file. That's where you add any custom model methods your application needs for the `items` table.

Follow these steps to continue on with the update:

**1.** **Open your browser and navigate to the** `cakeauction/src/Model/Table` **folder and open the** `ItemsTable.php` **file.**

**2.** **Scroll down to the bottom of the file, and just before the closing bracket, add the following code:**

```
public function findWinbidder(Query $query, array $options)
{
    $items = $this->find()->select(['itemid', 'name','description',
    'winprice']);
```

```
$items->where(['Items.winbidder IN' => $options['winbidder']]);
    return $items->group(['Items.itemid']);
}
```

**3.** **Save the updated file as** `ItemsTable.php`.

Yes, another method with just three lines of code — I love frameworks! The first line of code calls the `find()` method from the `Item` model's parent class. The `find()` method allows you to build a `SELECT` query statement piece by piece.

The first piece is to provide the list of data fields you want the query to return. The result of the `find()` method is an array of the matching data records returned from the table. The code stores that result in the `$items` variable.

The second added line continues to further define the `find()` results by using the `where()` method. The `where()` method is similar to using a SQL `WHERE` clause, but it has some additional features, such as using the `IN` operator as shown in this code. This is needed because the options passed to the controller appear as an array object. The `IN` operator allows you to match the data field against an array of values.

Finally, the last line of code uses the `group()` method to order the resulting data records based on the `itemid` value. The `$items` variable contains the final result from the search, which is then returned back to the controller.

Okay, another step completed! If you click the `Item` action link for a bidder, you get further along in the process, but you still get an error message, shown in Figure 3-6.

The convention rules strike again! According to the error message, the `listItems Won()` controller method is looking for a view file named `list_items_won.ctp` to use to display the results. You'll tackle that final piece of the puzzle in the next section.

## Painting a view

You're almost there! Can you see the finish line ahead? Before you cross it, let me recap to remind you what you've accomplished. So far you've created

>> A new link in the bidder index view template file using the `link()` helper method to pass the website visitor to a controller method to list all the items won by a bidder

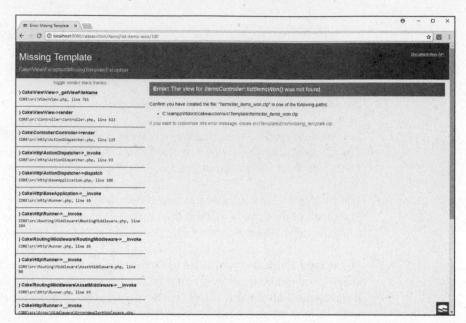

FIGURE 3-6:
The missing
template error
message.

>> A new method in the `ItemsController.php` controller file to process the link
request and request the data from the items model

>> A new method in the `ItemsTable.php` model file to find the data records in
the Items table that match the `winbidder` data field value to the selected
`bidderid` value

That was quite a bit, but then again, it didn't require all that much coding on your
part — CakePHP did most of the work for you.

The last step to get the new feature working in the web application is to create the
view template file to display all the results. CakePHP stores the view template files
in the `src/Template` folder. Each controller has its own subfolder, so you need to
work in the `Items` subfolder.

If you remember from Figure 3-6, CakePHP is trying to help you out by telling
you just what template file you need to create: `list_items_won.ctp`. Follow these
steps to do that:

**1.** Open your favorite editor, and enter the following code:

```
<div class="items view large-9 medium-8 columns content">
<?php echo "<h3>Items won by Bidder $winbidder[0]</h3>\n"; ?>
<section>
```

```php
<?php $total = 0; ?>
<table>
<tr><th>ItemID</th><th>Name</th><th>Description</th><th>Winning Bid
    </th></tr>
<?php foreach ($items as $item): ?>
    <?php $total = $total + $item->winprice; ?>
    <?php echo "<tr><td>$item->itemid</td><td>$item->name</td>" ?>
    <?php echo "<td>$item->description</td><td>$item->winprice</td>
    </tr>\n"; ?>
<?php endforeach; ?>
<?php echo "<tr><td/><td/><td>Total</td><td>$total</td>\n"; ?>
</table>
<?= $this->Html->link(__('Return to Bidders list'),['controller' =>
    'bidders', 'action' => 'index']) ?>
</section>
</div>
```

2. **Save the file as** list_items_won.ctp **in the** cakeauction/src/Template/
   Items **folder, under the** DocumentRoot **folder for your web server.**

The template code uses a mixture of HTML and PHP code to retrieve and display the data values. I copied the <div> class from the index.ctp template for the bidders controller so that the new page would have the same look and feel as the rest of the pages in the scaffolding application. The PHP code should look somewhat familiar to you — it's just a matter of retrieving the class properties that contain the data values for each item data record and plugging them into an HTML table.

I added a local variable named $total to track the total amount of the winning bids and then display that at the bottom of the table. Also, after the table I threw in a link() helper method to create a link that allows the website visitor to jump back to the main page of the bidders controller, listing the bidder data records.

Now for the moment of truth. Open your browser, and enter the following URL:

```
http://localhost:8080/cakeauction/bidders/
```

You should see the listing of data records from the Bidders table as before. Now when you click the Items link for a bidder that you know has won items, you should see the items appear in the template output web page that you just defined, shown in Figure 3-7.

Congratulations! You've just written your first modification to a CakePHP framework project!

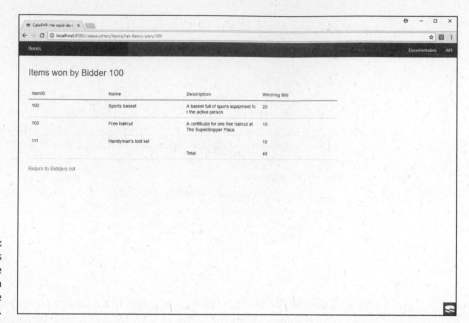

**FIGURE 3-7:**
The final results of adding the items won feature to the scaffolding code.

**TIP**

You're not stuck with the web page layout and styling used by the CakePHP scaffolding for your projects. You can override any part of the scaffolding application with your own code — creating your own Web page layout and applying your own CSS styles.

# Index

## Special Characters

" (double quote), 384
' (single quote), 385
− operator, 317
.NET 4.5, 471
/ operator, 317
:: (double colon symbol), 106
; (semicolon symbol), 91
\. command shortcut, 469
|| operator, 319
+ operator, 317
++ (incrementor operator), 208, 220
= (assignment operator), 204, 211
== (equal-to operator), 210
== operator, 327
=== operator, 327
−> symbol, 398
¢ (cent symbol), 91
© (copyright symbol), 91
° (degree symbol), 91
! operator, 319
!= operator, 327
!== operator, 327
# (hash symbol), 91, 105
#storemap value, 183
$( ) function, 247
$_COOKIE[] array variable, 426–427
$_FILES[] array variable, 373
$_GET[] array variable, 340, 342, 380, 381
$_POST[] array variable, 344, 359, 380, 381, 603
$_POST['age'] array variable, 344–345
$_POST['answer'] value, 602, 611
$_POST['fname'] array variable, 386
$_SESSION[] array variable, 431
$_SESSION['cart'] session cookie, 437
$admin variable, 380
$age variable, 326

$.ajax( ) function, 629–633
$bidders array, 576
$con variable, 544
$count variable, 333
$counter variable, 318
$db object, 545
$description property, 402
$favs variable, 336
$fname variable, 379, 388
$food variable, 336
$.get( ) function, 633–635
$inventory property, 397
$items variable, 731
$key variable, 336
$myfamily[0] value, 316
$onsale property, 406
$ounces property, 418
$price property, 402
$price variable value, 327
$prod1 instance, 408
$prod1 object, 398
$prod1->inventory property, 398
$prod2 instance, 401
$result variable, 320
$salary variable, 315
$(this) object, 279
$this variable, 397
$today variable, 367–368
$total variable, 318
$value variable, 335
$value1 variable, 311, 338
$value2 variable, 311
% operator, 317
% unit of measurement, 115
& (ampersand), 91, 384
&& operator, 319
&gt; code, 356, 384

&lt; code, 356, 384

* operator, 317

? (Ternary operator), 211

?> tag, 305–306

@ (ampersand), 552

@font-face rule, 168, 169–170

@media command, 170–172

@media rule, 689

~__clone( ) method, 408

~_construct( ) method, 406

< (command line redirect symbol), 539

< (less than), 385

< operator, 327

<% tag, 306

<= operator, 327

<> operator, 327

> operator, 327, 385

> prompt, 468

>= operator, 327

# Numbers

000webhost, 32

1 type, 94

1&1, 32, 653

1px border property value, 122

# A

a code, 365

A code, 365

<a href> tag, 700

A type, 94

a type, 94

<a> tag, 9, 87

AAC (Apple audio coding), 187

abbr elements, 86

abort( ) method, 622

abs function, 362

absolute address, 89

absolute keywords, 115

absolute positioning method, 128–130

absolute units of measurement, 114

acceptance testing, 616

accept-charset attribute, 136

accepts setting, 630

access control list (ACL), 457

accessor magic methods, 403–406

ACID (atomicity, consistency, isolation, durability) compliant database, 459–461

ACL (access control list), 457

acos function, 363

acosh function, 364

action attribute, 136, 343, 347

action parameter statement, 503

actions, 672

active pseudo-classes, 108, 109

Active Server Pages (ASP) style tag, 306

Active Server Pages (ASP).NET, 22–23

activeElement property, 227

ADD COLUMN name action, 503

ADD constraint action, 503

add method, 725

add_action( ) function, 672, 673, 674

add_filter( ) function, 672

addbidder.inc.php file, 604–605, 617

addClass( ) function, 279

.addClass(class) function, 257

add.ctp folder, 725

--add-drop-database export, 533

--add-drop-table export, 533

.addEventListener( ) function, 275–276

AddHandler directive, 43

additem.inc.php code, 614

additional styles, 75

address property, 572

addslashes function, 355, 356

administration tools, 465–476

Adobe Dreamweaver, 52

Adobe Flash Player, 10

Adobe Photoshop, 183, 369

advanced framework, 713

advanced queries, 527–531

.after( ) function, 260

AFTER DELETE trigger, 463

AFTER INSERT trigger, 463

after pseudo-element, 107

AFTER UPDATE trigger, 463
age variable, 205–206
AJAX (Asynchronous JavaScript and XML)
  AuctionHelper application, 643–650
  cached pages and, 628
  data, transferring in, 635–643
  files and, 244
  JavaScript, communicating using, 621–629
  jQuery AJAX library, using, 629–635
  overview, 619–621
ajaxcars1.html file, 628, 631–633
ajaxcars.php code, 628
alert( ) function, 201, 210, 223, 248, 269, 284
alert( ) pop-up box, 378
alert error level, 43
aliases, 531
all media type, 173
ALL privileges, 482
--all-databases export, 533
all-in-one packages, 31, 38, 470, 473
alt attribute, 178
ALTER COLUMN name MODIFY action, 503
ALTER privileges, 482
ALTER ROUTINE privileges, 482
ALTER TABLE statement, 501, 503–504
altering, 640
Amazon Web Services (AWS), 32
American National Standards Institute. See ANSI
  (American National Standards Institute)
American Standard Code for Information Interchange
  (ASCII), 90
ampersand (&), 91, 384
ampersand (@), 552
anchor element, 87
anchors property, 227
and operator, 319
AND operator, 529
.animate( ) function, 261
animation, 261
anonymous function, 251, 625
ANSI (American National Standards Institute), 452
ANSI SQL89, 452
ANSI SQL-92-compliant relational database, 542

any-hover attribute, 173
any-pointer attribute, 173
Apache Friends organization, 38
Apache packages, 33, 37
Apache web server, 22
  configurations, 41
  customizing, 41–44
  error levels, 43–44
  installing, 34–36
  pros of, 28
API (application programming interface), 455, 670
appearance, 664
.append( ) function, 260
appendChild method, 232, 638
.appendTo( ) function, 260
Apple audio coding (AAC), 187
Apple Numbers, 97
Apple Pages, 53
application data, 693
application presentation code, writing versions
  of, 701
application programming interface (API), 455, 670
application scaffold
  creating, 721–725
  modifying, 725–731
applications, creating using frameworks, 715–720
appname parameter, 705
app.php file, 719
apptest1 database, 555
appuser1 user account, 555
<area> tag, 182
arithmetic operators, 317–318
arithmetic shortcuts, 318–319
array( ) function, 315
array variables, grouping data values and, 315–316
article element, 78
ASCII (American Standard Code for Information
  Interchange), 90
<aside> element, 78, 134, 583
aside.inc.php file, 587–588, 644
asin function, 363
asinh function, 364
ASP (Active Server Pages) style tag, 306

asp_tags setting, 306

aspect-ratio attribute, 173

ASP.NET, 22–23

assign statement, 311

assignment operator (=), 204, 211

associative array, 316, 437, 548

associative array key, 426, 432

async setting, 630

asynchronous (true) connection, 622

Asynchronous JavaScript and XML (AJAX), 643–650

atan function, 363

atanh function, 364

atomicity, 459–460

atomicity, consistency, isolation, durability (ACID) compliant database, 459–461

.attr( ) function, 253

attribute values, 637

attributes, 14, 73–75, 253, 637

attributes property, 230

.au audio file, 187

auction database, 676, 720, 722

auction information, 565

AuctionHelper application, 565, 569, 643–650, 686

AuctionHelper page, designing, 581–582

AuctionHelper widget, 675, 715

audio

    formats for, 350

    playing, 185–190

Audio Video Interleave (AVI), 191

<audio> tag, 188, 189

authentication, 350

authentication helpers, 704

autocommit method, 553

autocomplete attribute, 136

autocomplete property, 239

autofocus property, 239, 240

autoload feature, 410

autoplay attribute, 189, 193

AVG( ) functions, 560

AVI (Audio Video Interleave), 191

.avi video formats, 192

AWS (Amazon Web Services), 32

Axmark, David, 454

Azure, 32

# B

B code, 365

b data type value, 550

b elements, 85, 86

background-color property, 116, 124, 231–232

backups, performing, 532–538

bake utility, 721–724

banana value, 316

bare-bones framework code, 710

base table, 501–503

basedir setting, 45

basic framework, 713

basic functions, 513

basic hosting packages, 23

basic layout, 1

.before( ) function, 260

BEFORE DELETE trigger, 463

BEFORE INSERT trigger, 463

before pseudo-element, 107

BEFORE UPDATE trigger, 463

beforeSend setting, 630

Berners-Lee, Tim, 8

beta statistical values, 364

Bidder class, 579, 597

bidder information, 564, 565

Bidder objects, 572, 595–605, 645

bidder. php file, 579

bidderid data field, 565–566

bidderid property, 572

bidderid value, 566, 576, 602, 605, 690, 726, 729–730

bidder.php file, 645–646

bidders

    adding and updating, 614

    deleting, 600

    listing, 595–596

    new, adding, 603–605

    searching for, 605

    updating, 600–603

    viewing, 596–599

Bidders class, 699

bidders controller, 724

bidders scaffold code, 726

Bidders sub-folder, 725
Bidders template, 725
BiddersController.php folder, 724
BiddersTable.php file, 697
bin folder, 718, 721
binary data, 136, 463
binary large object (BLOB), 463–464
bind_result( ) method, 551
birthdate data field, 504–505
bit rate, 187
Bitnami, 38–39
black border property value, 122
Blackhole, 456
_blank attribute, 87
BLOB (binary large object), 463–464
blob data type value, 550
block element, 259
block statements, 62
block-level elements, 85
blockquote element, 83–84
blogging, 651–652
blur( ) event, 277
blur( ) method, 232
blur parameter, 167
body element, 76, 201–203
body object, 224–225
body property, 227
<body> tag, 267
bold text, 9
bool data type, 451
Boolean operators, 208–209, 319–320
Boolean value, 141, 392, 463
border element section, 120
border images, 157–159
border style property, 182
border-bottom property, 122
border-collapse property, 122
border-image property, 160
border-image-outset property, 161
border-image-repeat property, 161
border-image-slice property, 161
border-image-source property, 161
border-image-width property, 161

border-radius property, 158, 159
borders, 16, 121–122
bowlerid data field values, 559
Bowlers table, 556–557, 560
box model, 119–121
box shadows, 167–168
box-shadow property, 167
<br> element, 74, 84, 355, 356
Break control icon, 292
Break on New Worker control icon, 292
break statement, 212
Breakpoints pane, 291
Brown, Barry, 364
browser (web clients), 10–11
browser debuggers, 67–69
built-in web servers, 29
bulleted lists, 92
button form field element, 138, 145
button input field type, 145
button_click( ) function, 596, 597
buttons, 145–146, 270–272
buttontest.html file, 271
buyProduct( ) method, 397, 398, 401, 405–406, 418

## C

c code, 365
\C command shortcut, 468
C programming language, 455
C#.NET, 23, 28
C++ programming language, 455
cache setting, 630
cached pages, AJAX and, 628
cakeauction folder, 716–718
cakeauction/config folder, 719
CakePHP framework, 704–705, 715–717
CakePHP template, 719, 720
Call Stack pane, 291
calling the function, 221
carlot element, 640, 641
carrot value, 316
cart session cookie, 437, 438
carttest.php file, 441

`carttest.php` program, 440

cascading style rules, 111–112

Cascading Style Sheets (CSS), 15–17
- classes, 257–259
- issues, 67
- objects, 256–257

Cascading Style Sheets (CSS1), 16, 79, 152
- client browser and, 152
- HTML and, 620
- styling, 79

Cascading Style Sheets, first version (CSS1), 16

Cascading Style Sheets, second version (CSS2), 16–17, 171

Cascading Style Sheets, third version (CSS3)
- advanced
  - border images, using, 157–159
  - color gradients, 164–166
  - corners, rounding, 157–159
  - CSS3, 157–159
  - fonts, creating, 168–170
  - media queries, handling, 170–175
  - overview, 157
  - shadows, adding, 166–168
- box model, 119–121
- elements, positioning, 125–134
- overview, 16, 103
- styling
  - overview, 103–104
  - positioning and, 79
  - rules of, 104–112
  - tables, 121–125
  - text, 112–119

case code, 330

case statements, 212, 215

case values, 331

case-insensitive mode, 494

case-sensitive comparisons, 494

`catch( )` function, 296

catch code block, 295, 297, 298

categories, 654

CDN (content delivery network), 245, 246–247

`ceil` function, 362

cells, 97, 124

cent symbol (¢), 91

CentOS, 33, 35–36

CentOS7 system, 36

central processing unit (CPU), 285

centralized data management, 304

centralized programming language, 304

certificate authority, 42

CGI (Common Gateway Interface) scripting, 22

ch unit of measurement, 115

`change( )` event, 277

`change_user` method, 553

`changebidder.inc.php` file, 602

Changed field, 517

`changeit( )` function, 235, 273, 288, 289, 293, 294

`changeitem.inc.php` file, 610–611

`changeme( )` function, 231

`char(64)` data type, 567

character entity reference, 91

character number, 91

character sets, 90–91, 494

character strings, 463

`character_set_name` method, 553

characters, 90–92

`characterSet` property, 227

character-to-number mapping scheme. *See* character set

charset command, 468

charsets, 476

`char(x)` data type, 451

check boxes, 141–142, 240–241

checkbox input type, 140

checkbox object, 240, 241

checked attribute, 142, 143

checked property, 240

checked pseudo-classes, 109

child class, 414

child elements, 640

`child objects`, 224–225

`childNodes` property, 230

`childNodes[0]` value, 641

`children` property, 230

chi-square statistical values, 364

`chop` function, 355

chunk_split function, 356
ci collation, 494
circle shape value, 182
cite elements, 86
class attribute, 104–106
class keyword, 396
classes
  defining, 396–397
  extending, 414–418
  loading, 409–414
classList property, 230
className property, 230
cleaner format, 212
CLI (command line interface)
  data
    adding, 514–517
    modifying and deleting, 517–519
  data backups using, 533–534
  databases, creating using, 492–495
  JavaScript code and, 289
  tables and
    base tables, defining, 501–503
    features, adding, 503–505
    overview, 500–501
  tools, using, 466–470
  user account, creating from, 477–478
click( ) event, 277
.click( ) function, 251
click( ) method, 232
clickable region (hotspot), 182
client browsers, 20, 693
client errors, 12
client tool, 467–470
client-side code, 694
client-side data validation, 380–381
client-side programming, 18–25
clone keyword, 407
cloneNode method, 232
close( ) method, 546
closest–corner location, 165
closest–side location, 165
closing tag, 74
cloud environment, 32

cm absolute units of measurement, 114
CMS (content management system), 304, 652
code completion, 64
code elements, 86
code files, 695, 703
code formatting, 64
code sections, marking and collapsing, 63
CodeGen, 538
CodeIgniter framework, 705–707
cold backup, 532
collapse value, 122
collations, character sets and, 494
color attribute, 173
color gradients, 164–165
color input element type, 150
color names, 116
color parameter, 167
color property, 116, 124
color scheme, changing, 116–119
color1 direction, 164
color2 direction, 164
color–index attribute, 173
colors
  looking at, 162–163
  semitransparent, 17
  text, 14, 16
colortest.html code, 120
colortest.html file, 120
cols attribute, 146, 240
colspan attributes, 100–101
columns, 97–99, 514
command line interface (CLI), 492–495, 500–505, 514–519, 533–534
command line redirect symbol (<), 539
command-line tool, 33
comma-separated spreadsheet format, 532
comma-separated string values, 635
comma-separated values (CSV), 456, 514, 538
comment tags, 80
comments, 654, 663
commercial server, 31
commit and rollback system, 459
commit method, 553

commit phase, 459

Common Gateway Interface (CGI) scripting, 22

community, 703

comparison operator, 210–211, 326

complete setting, 630

Composer, 703, 707, 717

compression, 186–187, 350

concatenation operator, 320

condition, 217

condition parameter, 334

conditional statements, 209–216

config folder, 718, 719

configuration files, 696, 708

configuration options, 41, 44

connect command, 468

CONNECT request, 11

connection handle, 544

consistency, 460

Console, 287–290

console.log( ) function, 289, 294

__construct( ) keyword, 415

__construct( ) method, 572

constructor magic method, 406, 673

contains(object) method, 232

content delivery network (CDN), 245, 246–247

content element section, 119

content management system (CMS), 304, 652

content variable, 341, 383, 584, 590, 595, 611, 615

content variable/value pair, 690

contents setting, 630

Content–type HTTP header, 639

contentType setting, 630

context setting, 630

Continue control icon, 292

controller code, 729–730

controller method, 689–690

Controllers folder, 719, 724

controls attribute, 189, 193

convention over configuration, 696–697, 705

converters setting, 630

cookie property, 227

Cookie statement, 423

cookies, PHP and, 424–430

cookietest2.php, 428

cookietest3.php, 430

copyright symbol (©), 91

core server settings, 45

corners, rounding, 157–159

cos function, 363

cosh function, 364

cosine, 363

COUNT( ) function, 560

counter variable, 208, 212, 220

counter++; variable, 208

CPU (central processing unit), 285

crash recovery, 460

CREATE DATABASE command, 657

CREATE DATABASE statement, 492, 493–494, 496

CREATE privileges, 482

CREATE ROUTINE privileges, 483

CREATE statement, 501, 515–516

CREATE TABLE statement, 500–501, 507

CREATE TABLESPACE privileges, 483

CREATE TEMPORARY TABLES privileges, 483

CREATE USER privileges, 483

CREATE USER statement, 477, 481

createAttribute method, 638

createElement( ) method, 227, 638

create–project option, 716

Create-Read-Update-Delete (CRUD), 686, 698

createTextNode( ) method, 227, 638

crit error level, 43

crossDomain setting, 630

crossorigin attribute, 246

Cross-Platform, Apache, MariaDB, PHP, and Perl (XAMPP), 38–42, 47–49, 354, 470, 474, 656

cross-site scripting (XSS), 376–379, 704

CRUD (Create-Read-Update-Delete), 686, 698

cryptography, 350

cs collation, 494

CSS (Cascading Style Sheets), 15–17

  classes, 257–259

  issues, 67

  objects, 256–257

.css( ) function, 254, 256
CSS1 (Cascading Style Sheets), 16, 79, 152
  client browser and, 152
  HTML and, 620
  styling, 79
CSS1 (Cascading Style Sheets, first version), 16
CSS2 (Cascading Style Sheets, second version), 16–17, 171
CSS3 (Cascading Style Sheets, third version)
  advanced
    border images, using, 157–159
    color gradients, 164–166
    corners, rounding, 157–159
    CSS3, 157–159
    fonts, creating, 168–170
    media queries, handling, 170–175
    overview, 157
    shadows, adding, 166–168
  box model, 119–121
  elements, positioning, 125–134
  overview, 16, 103
  styling
    overview, 103–104
    positioning and, 79
    rules of, 104–112
    tables, 121–125
    text, 112–119
CSS3 For Dummies (Mueller), 112
CSV (comma-separated values), 456, 514, 538
CUBRID library, 542
Cumulative Distributions Functions, Inverses, and Other parameters (DCDFLIB), 364
cursive font, 113
custom export, 537
customerid data field, 529, 530
customerid value, 491, 528–529
Customers table, 449–450, 458, 490

**D**
d code, 365
D code, 365
\d command shortcut, 468
d data type value, 554
dashboard widgets category, 670

dashed border, 122
data
  adding, 514–517
  arrays of, 206–207
  binary, 464
  in databases
    backups, performing, 532–538
    restoring, 538–540
    searching for, 524–531
    using, 513–524
  inserting, 685
  invalid, 380–382
  managing, 489–492
  output, 525–527
  overview, 204–205
  replacing, 250–254
  retrieving, 547–549, 554–560
  sanitizing, 384–389
  short-term storage of, 419
  string, 387
  transferring in AJAX, 635–643
  types, 205–206
  validating, 389–394
data constraints, 500
data dictionary, 447
data export, 532
data fields, 450, 514
data format, 391–394
data lists, 149–150
data normalization, 449
data operation, 685
data permissions, 457
data records, 450, 514, 686
data setting, 630
data spoofing, 379–380
data table definition, 500
data tier, 693
data types, 155–156, 312–315, 389–391
data validation, 25, 154–156
data values, 204, 315–316
data variable, 248
database category, 670
database engine, 446

database management system (DBMS)
  features of, 455
  isolation and, 460
  purpose of, 445–449
  views, querying using, 462
database objects, 656–658
database parameter, 544
database server, 30–31
databases
  backups, 532–538
  connecting to, 544–545, 554–560
  creating, 492–500, 571
  data constraints, 451–452
  data types, 451
  environment, 719–720
  features, 30
  high-end, 25
  integration, 702–703
  managing data in, 489–492
  name, 658
  normalization, 490
  overview, 445–449, 489, 513
  password, 658
  PHP scripts, communicating from
    database support, 541–543
    MySQL library, using, 544–553, 554–560
    overview, 541
  relational, 449–450
  restoring data, 538–540
  searching for data, 524–531
  software options, 25–26
  SQL, 452–454
  support, 541–543
  tables, building
    CLI, using, 500–505
    overview, 500
    phpMyAdmin tool, using, 508–512
    Workbench tool, using, 505–508
  username, 658
  using data, 513–524
--databases export, 533
data-centric environment, 692
datadir setting, 45

datafield statement, 517
datafields parameter, 453
dataFilter setting, 630
datalist element, 138, 149
Datasources section, 719
dataType setting, 630
date( ) function, 365, 367–368
date data type, 451
date functions, 365–369
date input element type, 150
dates, 365–369
datetime data type, 150, 451
datetime-local input element type, 150
date.timezone default setting and value, 48
DB++ library, 542
DBA (DB-style database files), 543
dBase library, 542
dblclick( ) event, 277
DBMS (database management system), 446–447, 455, 460, 462
DB-style database files (DBA), 543
dbtest1 database, 494, 501, 534
dbtest1.sql file, 534, 539
dbtest2 database, 505, 508, 535
dbtest3 database, 509, 512
DCDFLIB (Cumulative Distributions Functions, Inverses, and Other parameters), 364
dd two-sided element, 95
Debian-based Linux distributions, 33–34
debug error level, 43
debug log level, 44
Debugger, 290–295
debugger statement, 291
decimal data types, 566
declarations, 104
decrementor operations, 319
default applications, 57
default collation, 494
default configuration settings, 28
default file extensions, avoiding, 54–55
default shape value, 182
default statement, 212, 331
default styles, 111

default value, 145
defaultChecked property, 240
defaultValue property, 239, 240
deg2rad( ) function, 363, 364
degree symbol (°), 91
del elements, 86
DELETE keyword, 453
delete method, 725
DELETE statement, 495, 505, 514, 518, 519
delimiter command, 468
Delphi, 23
departmentcode 5 department, 527
DESC keyword, 526
DESCRIBE SQL statement, 514
description data field, 566
description lists, 95–96
description property, 408, 415, 573
descriptors, 170
desktop.css external style sheet, 175
__destruct( ) method, 407
destructor magic methods, 407
Developer Tools, 285–290
dfn elements, 86
dialog boxes, 19
dialog bubbles, 159
die( ) function, 552
digital audio formats, 186–188
digital video formats, 191–192
direction parameter, 164
directives, 41
disabled attribute, 139, 146, 239, 240
disabled pseudo-classes, 109
display property, 198, 259
display_errors setting, 48, 324
displaybidder.inc.php file, 597, 598–599, 605
distribution software packages, 36
div element, 78, 79
dl element, 95
Docker, 707
<!DOCTYPE> tag, 75, 77, 425, 431
document object, 226, 229
Document Object Model. See DOM
document structure, 73–81

document.body object, 231
documentElement property, 227
documentMode property, 227
document.property format, 226
DocumentRoot folder, 77, 90, 117, 245, 382, 383, 545, 706
documents, 8–9
document-viewing software, 8
document.write( ) function, 229
Dodge value, 640
DOM (Document Object Model), 259–260, 268, 620, 628, 636
    form data
        check boxes, 240–241
        overview, 235–238
        radio buttons, 241
        text areas, 239–240
        text boxes, 238–239
    JavaScript code and
        object methods, 232–233
        object properties, 229–232
        overview, 223–224
DOM (Document Object Model) Explorer, 285–287
DOM (Document Object Model) tree, 224–229, 235–238, 249, 309
domain property, 227
Domain=site attribute, 423
DOMDocument object, 636, 637, 640, 645
DOMParser object, 640, 641
domproperties.html code, 231
domtest.html file, 228
dotted border, 122
double border, 122
double colon symbol (::), 106
double data type value, 550
double parameter, 385
double quote ("), 384
double up-arrow icon, 289
double-write buffering, 460
do.while statement, 333
Dreamweaver application, 52
DROP (Drop the Database) link, 500
DROP COLUMN name action, 503

DROP constraint action, 503
DROP DATABASE statement, 533, 538
DROP keyword, 453
DROP privileges, 483
DROP statement, 495, 518
DROP TABLE statement, 505, 533, 538
Drop the Database (DROP) link, 500
drop-down lists, 147–149
Drupal content management system, 708
dt two-sided element, 95
dump folder, 536
durability, 461
dynamic data typing, 205
dynamic features, 1
dynamic web applications, 26, 29, 295, 376, 419,
    651, 685
dynamic web pages, 17–25

# E

e code, 365
\e command shortcut, 468
E symbol, 318
e symbol, 318
E_ALL & E_DEPRECATED setting, 48
E_ALL setting, 48
E_COMPILE_ERROR setting, 48
E_COMPILE_WARNING setting, 48
E_CORE_ERROR setting, 48
E_CORE_WARNING setting, 48
E_DEPRECATED setting, 48
E_ERROR setting, 48
E_NOTICE setting, 48
E_PARSE setting, 48
E_RECOVERABLE_ERROR setting, 48
E_STRICT setting, 48
E_USER_DEPRECATED setting, 48
E_USER_ERROR setting, 48
E_USER_NOTICE setting, 48
E_USER_WARNING setting, 48
E_WARNING setting, 48
easier-to-learn frameworks, 706
ebidder.inc.php file, 600

e-book version, 2–3
echo statement
  class objects and, 414
  displaying code, 676
  example, 408–409
  inventory properties, displaying, 401
  new-line characters and, 310
  outputting code, 560
  PHP program and, 325
  text, injecting, 307
  values, displaying, 336
Eclipse, 66–67
Eclipse PDT (Eclipse PHP Development Tool), 65
ECMAScript 2017 (eighth version), 20
ECMAScript standard, 20
edit command, 468
edit method, 725
edit.ctp folder, 725
ego command, 468
eighth version (ECMAScript 2017), 20
element names, 636
element tag, 15, 74
element type, 105
elements. *See also names of specific elements*
  attributes or, 637
  defined, 73–75, 206
  finding
    DOM tree, 235–238
    overview, 233, 247–250
    pointers, 235
  HTML5
    breaks, 84–85
    headings, 81–82
    overview, 81
    text groupings, 82–84
  positioning, 128–134
ellipses. *See dialog bubbles*
elliptical radial gradient, 166
else statement, 212, 295, 328, 394
elseif statement, 328–330
em elements, 86, 115, 287
email input type, 150, 152
embed element, 186

embedded audio, 185–186

Embedded OpenType front file formats, 169

embedded program code, 18

embeds property, 227

emerg error level, 43

employeeid data field, 490–491, 506

Employees table, 449–450, 490–492

employees table, 515

.empty( ) function, 260

empty pseudo-classes, 109

emulation, 286

enabled pseudo-classes, 109

encodeURI( ) function, 296

encoding parameter, 385

encryption key, 691

encryptions, 42

enctype attribute, 136, 144

endless loop, 216, 332

engines, 476

ENT_COMPAT flag, 385

ENT_DISALLOWED flag, 385

ENT_HTML401 flag, 385

ENT_HTML5 flag, 385

ENT_IGNORE flag, 385

ENT_NOQUOTES flag, 385

ENT_QUOTES flag, 385

ENT_SUBSTITUTE flag, 385

ENT_XHTML flag, 385

ENT_XML1 flag, 385

Environment icon, 718

equal-to operator (==), 210

error messages, 43–44

Error object, 296

error setting, 43, 630

error_reporting setting, 48

ErrorLog directive, 44

errors
  avoiding, 295–299
  browser Developer Tools, 285–290
  catching, 295
  checking for, 551–560
  identifying, 283–285
  tracking, 43–44
eval( ) function, 296

EvalError error, 296

event functions, 276–280

event handler, 280–282

event listeners, 275–276

event parameter, 280

EVENT privileges, 483

event-driven Personal Home Page (PHP)
  form data, processing, 343–348
  links, using, 339–343
  overview, 339

event-driven programming, 264, 593–594

events
  bidder object, 595–605
  defining, 263–266
  item object, 606–614
  JavaScript and
    event listeners, 275–276
    keystrokes, listening for, 273–275
    mouse events, listening for, 269–273
    overview, 267
    web page, loading and unloading, 267–269
  jQuery and, 276–282

ex unit of measurement, 115

Excel application, 97

Exception Control control icon, 292

EXECUTE privileges, 483

exit command, 468, 658

exp function, 363

expire parameter, 425

expires=datetime attribute, 423

explode function, 356

expm1 function, 363

exponents, calculating, 362–363

expression, 212

Expression Web package, 51

Extensible Hypertext Markup Language (XHTML), 10, 74, 77, 538

Extensible Markup Language (XML), 291, 351, 620, 636–643, 687–688

extensions, 16, 349–354

extensions.php file, 352

external JavaScript files, 203

external style sheet method, 110

external style sheets, 15, 111

# F

F code, 365

f statistical values, 364

F12 key, 284

fact variable, 221

factest.php program, 338

factorial( ) function, 221, 338–339

factorial.html code, 219

false (synchronous) connection, 622

false value, 210, 240

FALSE value, 326, 328, 332, 333, 345, 360

false value, 406

fantasy font, 113

farthest–corner location, 165

farthest–side location, 165

feature link, adding, 726–728

feature parameter, 173

Fedora, 33, 35–36

fetch( ) method, 551

fetch statements, 548

fetch_all( ) method, 547

fetch_array( ) method, 547

fetch_assoc( ) method, 559, 560

fetch_field( ) method, 547

fetch_field_direct( ) method, 547

fetch_fields( ) method, 547

fetch_object( ) method, 547

fetch_row( ) method, 547

ffa500 value, 116

ffetch_assoc( ) method, 547

field_seek( ) method, 547

fieldlist parameter, 514, 516, 525, 529

fieldset element, 140–141

‹figcaption› element, 183, 184

figure element, 183

file access, unauthorized, 382–383

file data input type, 372

file extensions, 54–57

file header category, 670

file input type, 144

file management, 64

FILE privileges, 483

file server, 28

File Transfer Protocol (FTP), 7

file upload, 144–145

filename, 90

files

  Ajax and, 244

  folders and, 718–719

filesystem category, 670

Filesystem icon, 718

filter parameter, 280, 387

FILTER_SANITIZE_EMAIL option, 387

FILTER_SANITIZE_ENCODED option, 387

FILTER_SANITIZE_FULL_SPECIAL_CHARS option, 387

FILTER_SANITIZE_MAGIC_QUOTES option, 387

FILTER_SANITIZE_NUMBER_FLOAT option, 387

FILTER_SANITIZE_NUMBER_INT option, 387, 389

FILTER_SANITIZE_SPECIAL_CHARS option, 387

FILTER_SANITIZE_STRING option, 387

FILTER_SANITIZE_STRIPPED option, 387

FILTER_SANITIZE_URL option, 387

FILTER_UNSAFE_RAW option, 387

FILTER_VALIDATE_BOOLEAN option, 392

FILTER_VALIDATE_EMAIL option, 392

FILTER_VALIDATE_FLOAT option, 392

FILTER_VALIDATE_INT option, 392

FILTER_VALIDATE_IP option, 392

FILTER_VALIDATE_MAC option, 392

FILTER_VALIDATE_REGEXP option, 392

FILTER_VALIDATE_URL option, 392

filter_var( ) function, 384, 386–389

filters, 671

finally code block, 298

finally statement, 297

find( ) method, 705, 729–730, 731

findBidder( ) method, 572, 600, 602

findBidders( ) method, 576

findItem method, 573, 579, 608, 611, 646

findtest.html code, 235

findWinbidder( ) method, 729

FireBird/InterBase library, 542

first normal form, 490–491

firstChild property, 230, 235–237

first–child pseudo-classes, 108, 109

first–letter pseudo-element, 106, 107

first-line pseudo-element, 107
firstname data field, 526, 566
firstname property, 572
first-of-type pseudo-classes, 109
first-rate server-side programming language, 23
fixed positioning method, 130
fixed-length character strings, 463
flags parameters, 387
Flash, 10, 186, 191
flat files, 446
float data type, 451
float property, 131, 134
floating elements, 130–134
floating point numbers, 312, 463
floor function, 362
flow control statements, 209
.flv video formats, 192
fmod function, 362
focus( ) event, 277
focus( ) method, 232
focus pseudo-classes, 109
focusin( ) event, 277
focusout( ) event, 277
folders, files and, 718–719
font files, 168–169
font-family property, 170
fontlist value, 113
fonts
    creating, 168–170
    setting, 112–116
    text, 14, 16
    web, 17
fontsize property, 114
font-stretch descriptors, 170
font-style descriptors, 170
font-weight descriptors, 170
<footer> element, 583
footer.inc.php file, 587–588
for encrypted connections (https), 90
for statement, 333–334, 437
Ford attribute, 640
foreach statement, 334–336, 359, 437–438, 440, 599
foreign keys, 501
form( ) method, 674

Form Editor, 521–522
form fields, 73–74, 137–138
form property, 239, 241
form tampering, 704
form validation, 704, 707
form values, 253–254
<form> element, 136, 145, 146, 343, 596
format parameter, 365
formatting features, 9
formatting text, 85–86
forms property, 227
forms validation, 700
formtest.html file, 347
four values, 161
four-color scheme, 163
fps (frames per second), 191
frame rate, 190
frames, 87, 190
frames per second (fps), 191
frameworks
    application scaffold
        creating, 721–725
        modifying, 725–731
    creating applications using, 715
    package management and, 703
    selecting, 695–713
free( ) method, 547
free-for-all of methods, 185
FROM clause, 528
fruit value, 316
FTP (File Transfer Protocol), 7
full applications, 2
full-featured framework package, 709
functions
    building, 336–339
    callbacks for, 712
    creating, 221
    date and time, 365–369
    image-handling, 369–374
    logarithmic, 363
    math, 361–364
    miscellaneous, 553–560
    overview, 220
    using, 222

## G

G code, 366

g code, 366

\G command shortcut, 468

\g command shortcut, 468

gamma statistical values, 364

Generalized Markup Language (GML), 9

generic font group, 113

GET, POST, Cookies, and System variables (GPCS) default settings and value, 49

__get( ) method, 403

GET method, 340, 343, 379, 380, 622–623, 690

GET request, 11, 340, 422

GET variable, 383, 628

getAllResponseHeaders( ) method, 622

getAttribute( ) method, 232, 641

getBidders( ) method, 572, 576, 597

getElementByClassName( ) function, 247

getElementById( ) function, 233–235, 247, 288, 289, 292

getElementByTagName( ) function, 247

getElementsByClassName(class) method, 227, 232

getElementsByTagName( ) method, 641, 648

getElementsByTagname(tag) method, 227, 232

getItems methods, 573, 579

getItemsbyBidder( ) method, 573, 579, 600

getmodels( ) function, 628

getParam( ) helper function, 729

getrandmax( ) function, 362

getRealTime( ) function, 648–649

getResponseHeader( ) method, 622

getters, 403

gii tool, 713

GIMP (GNU Image Manipulation Program), 183, 369

global setting, 630

GML (Generalized Markup Language), 9

GNOME editor, 60

GNU Image Manipulation Program (GIMP), 183, 369

go command, 468

GoDaddy, 32, 653

golden ratio, 580

Google Cloud Platform, 32

gotkey( ) function, 274

GPCS (GET, POST, Cookies, and System variables) default settings and value, 49

GRANT command, 657

GRANT OPTION privileges, 483

GRANT statement, 482

graphical desktop programming, 684

graphical desktop tools, 52

gray boxes (sidebars), 2

greater than (>), 385

grid attribute, 173

grid theory, 580

group( ) method, 731

## H

H code, 366

h code, 366

\h command shortcut, 468

h elements, 81

<h1> element, 9, 14–15, 82, 105, 118, 167

<h2> element, 82

handle parameter, 546

hasAttributes( ) method, 232

hasChildNodes( ) method, 232

.hasClass( ) function, 257, 258

hasFocus( ) method, 227

hash symbol (#), 91, 105

head element, 76, 200–201

head object, 224–225

head property, 227

HEAD request, 11

<header> element, 78, 583

header.inc.php file, 587

headers setting, 630

headings, 9, 14, 81–82

height attribute, 173, 178, 193, 194

help command, 468

helper methods, 700, 702

helper programs, 2

here value, 235
hgroup element, 82
hidden fields, 143–144
hidden input type, 144
.hide( ) function, 259
high-end database environments, 25
higher-level rule, 15
high-strength, low alloy (HSLA), 117, 163
HKEY_LOCAL_MACHINE/Software/PHP registry
  hive, 46
Homestead, 707
host, 90
--host parameter, 468
HostGator, 32, 653
hot backup, 532
hotspot (clickable region), 182
hover( ) event, 277
hover( ) function, 278
hover attribute, 173
hover pseudo-classes, 108, 109
hover.html file, 288
hovertest.html file, 273, 293
hr element, 84
href attribute, 87, 88, 89, 181, 183, 343
HSL (hue, saturation, and lightness) method, 117,
  162–163
hsl( ) format, 163
HSLA (high-strength, low alloy), 117, 163
htdocs folder, 42, 656, 676
HTML (Hypertext Markup Language). See also HTML5
  client browser and, 152
  CSS and, 620
  defined, 9
  forms, 25
  programming codes, embedding, 23
  retrieving documents, 10–13
  styling documents, 14
  troubleshooting issues, 67
  using, 252–253
  versions, 10
  .html( ) function, 252
html element, 76

.html file, 43, 307
html object, 224
<html> element, 76, 426
HTML5 (Hypertext Markup Language version 5.0).
    See also PHP
  characters, 90–92
  CSS3 and, 17
  document structure
    attributes, 73–75
    document type, 75
    elements, 73–75
    overview, 73
    page definition, 76–78
    page sections, 78–81
  elements of
    breaks, 84–85
    headings, 81–82
    overview, 81
    text groupings, 82–84
  lists
    description, 95–96
    ordered, 93–95
    overview, 92
    unordered, 92–93
  multimedia and
    audio, playing, 185–190
    images, 177–185
    overview, 177
    streamers, getting help from, 194
    videos, watching, 190–194
  overview, 73
  popularity of, 10
  tables, building
    headings, 99–101
    overview, 96–97
    rows and columns, 97–99
  tags, 73–75
  text, marking
    formatting, 85–86
    hypertext, using, 86–90
    overview, 85

HTML5 (Hypertext Markup Language version 5.0) forms
  data validation, 154–156
  defining, 135–138
  drop-down lists, using, 147–149
  enhancing
    data lists, 149–150
    input fields, additional, 150–154
    overview, 149
  images
    figures and captions, 183–184
    overview, 183
    picture element, 184–185
  input fields, using
    buttons, 145–146
    check boxes, 141–142
    file upload, 144–145
    hidden fields, 143–144
    overview, 138
    password entry, 140
    radio buttons, 142–143
    text boxes, 138–140
  overview, 135
  text area, adding, 146–147
HTML5h1 element, 74
htmlentities function, 355
htmlspecialchars( ) function, 355, 356, 384–386, 387
HTTP (Hypertext Transfer Protocol), 10, 28
http (unencrypted connections), 90
HTTP category, 670
HTTP cookies, 420–424, 712
HTTP GET method, 137
HTTP messages, 712
HTTP PUT method, 137
HTTP statuses, 712
httpd.conf file, 41, 306
HttpOnly attribute, 423
HttpOnly cookie, 421, 425
https (for encrypted connections), 90
hue, saturation, and lightness (HSL) method, 117, 162–163
human language, 350
hyperbolic functions, 364
hyperlink, 87–89, 182

hypertext, 8, 86–90
hypertext link, 181
Hypertext Markup Language. See HTML
Hypertext Transfer Protocol (HTTP), 10, 28
Hyper-V, 707
hyphens, 636
hypot function, 363

# I

i code, 366
I code, 366
i data type value, 550
i elements, 85
i type, 94
I type, 94
IBM DB2 library, 542
id attribute, 79, 89, 105, 140, 150, 237, 247
id property, 230
identifier, 453
IDEs (integrated development environments), 64–67, 77, 117
if statement, 210–211, 326–327
if.else statement, 295, 394
ifModified setting, 630
iframe element, 194
<iframe> tag, 194
if.then condition, 297
IIS (Internet Information Services), 22, 28
image copyresampled( ) function, 373
image maps, 182–183
image processing, 350
imagechar function, 370
imagecolorallocate( ) function, 369
imageconvert.php code, 373
imagecopyresampled( ) function, 371
imagecreatefromstring( ) function, 373
imagecreatetruecolor( ) function, 369
imagedestroy( ) function, 370
imagefilledrectangle function, 370
image-handling functions, 369–374
imagejpeg( ) function, 370, 373
imageline function, 370
imagerectangle function, 370

images
  adding, 52
  HTML5 image additions
    figures and captions, 183–184
    overview, 183
    picture element, 184–185
  image maps, 182–183
  linking, 181–182
  overview, 177
  placing, 178
  styling, 179–181
images property, 227
imagestring function, 370
imageSX( ) function, 373
imageSY( ) function, 373
imageupload.html file, 372
img element, 178
<img> tag, 178, 181–185, 373
implode function, 356
in absolute units of measurement, 114
IN operator, 731
in text, 273
include( ) function, 320–323, 339, 382, 409, 545
Include directive, 41
.inc.php file extension, 410
incrementor operations, 319
incrementor operator (++), 208, 220
index, 206
index controller method, 725
index method, 725
INDEX privileges, 483
index table, 492
index variable, 220
index.ctp folder, 725
index.ctp template file, 726
indexed sequential access method (ISAM), 454
index.html default web page, 90
index.php file, 65, 382, 582–583, 590, 591, 594, 595,
    676, 690
informational messages, 11
Informix library, 542
Ingres library, 542
inheritance, 414
IniFilePath registry key name, 46
initializing applications, 716–718

inline. See text-level elements
inline style sheet method, 110
inline styling, 14, 75
INNER JOIN join type, 529
innerHTML DOM object, 629
innerHTML object, 235
innerHTML property, 230, 235, 237, 239, 274
innochecksum tool, 466
InnoDB storage engine, 45–46, 456, 458, 461
innodb_data_file_path setting, 45–46
innodb_data_home_dir setting, 45
input element, 154
input fields
  buttons, 145–146
  check boxes, 141–142
  file upload, 144–145
  hidden fields, 143–144
  overview, 138
  password entry, 140
  radio buttons, 142–143
  text boxes, 138–140
input fields, additional, 150–154
input form field, 155
input form field element, 138
input interfaces, 135
<input> tag, 149, 150
inputtypestest.html web page, 151
in-range pseudo-classes, 109
ins elements, 86
INSERT keyword, 453
INSERT privileges, 483
INSERT statement, 514, 515, 549, 551, 554,
    567, 570
.insertAfter( ) function, 260
.insertBefore( ) function, 232, 260
inset keyword, 168
instantiate, 397
int data type, 451
intdiv function, 362
integer data types, 550, 566
integers, 463
integrated development environments (IDEs), 64–67,
    77, 117
integration testing, 616
integrity attribute, 246

intermediate property, 241

internal style sheets, 110, 111

internal styling, 14

Internet. *See* World Wide Web

Internet Information Services (IIS), 22, 28

interoperability, 712

interpreted programming languages, 23, 349

invalid pseudo-class, 109, 155

inventory property, 397, 405, 415

inverted-colors attribute, 173

is null data constraint, 451

is_bool( ) function, 360, 389

is_finite function, 362

is_float( ) function, 360, 389

is_infinite function, 362

is_int( ) function, 360, 389

is_nan( ) function, 362

is_null( ) function, 360, 389

is_numeric( ) function, 389, 391

is_numeric function, 360

is_string( ) function, 389

ISAM (indexed sequential access method), 454

isLocal setting, 630

ISO (Organization of International Standards), 9, 367

isolation, 460–461

isset( ) function, 345, 347, 427

italic text, 9

Item action link, 731

Item class, 576, 579

item information, 564

Item object, 573, 579, 599, 645

  adding items, 611–614

  deleting items, 607–608

  listing items, 606–607

  overview, 606

  searching for items, 614

  updating items, 608–611

item1 variable, 237

item2 variable, 237

itemid data field, 566

itemid property, 573

itemid value, 611, 614

item.php file, 579

items

  adding, 611–614

  deleting, 607–608

  listing, 606–607

  searching for, 614

  updating, 608–611

items controller, 724

Items sub-folder, 725

items table, 729

Items template, 725

ItemsController class, 727

ItemsController.php file, 724, 729, 732

ItemsTable.php file, 730, 732


## J

j code, 366

J#.NET, 23

Java Development Kit (JDK), 63, 66

Java programming language, 22

Java Runtime Environment (JRE), 63, 66

Java Server Pages (JSP), 22

Java Server Pages.Active Server Pages (JSP.ASP) programs, 22

JavaScript

  AJAX, communicating with using, 623–629

  basics of, 203–209

  CLI and, 289

  client browser and, 152

  defined, 19–20

  DOM and

    DOM tree, 224–229

    object methods, 232–233

    object properties, 229–232

    overview, 223–224

  DOM form data

    check boxes, 240–241

    overview, 235–238

    radio buttons, 241

    text areas, 239–240

    text boxes, 238–239

  downloading code, 20

  elements, finding, 233–238

  embedding code, 199

events and
  event listeners, 275–276
  keystrokes, listening for, 273–275
  mouse events, listening for, 269–273
  overview, 267
  web page, loading and unloading, 267–269
functions of, 20, 220–222
issues, troubleshooting, 67
jQuery and, 263–266
language of, 23
overview, 197, 223
program editor, free, 61
program flow, controlling
  conditional statements, 209–216
  loops, 216–220
  overview, 209
reasons for using, 197–1998
troubleshooting programs, 283–289
using in XML, 640–643
web pages, creating using, 696
JavaScript Object Notation (JSON), 538, 620
JDK (Java Development Kit), 63, 66
jEdit, 63–64
jhovertest.html file, 279
jkeytest.html file, 281
joins, 529–531
jointype parameter, 529
JPEG image type, 178
jQuery
  animation, using, 261
  DOM, changing, 259
  elements, finding, 247–250
  events, and, 276–282
  functions of, 247
  JavaScript and, 263–266
  language of, 20–21
  overview, 243–244
  replacing, 250–254
  styles, changing, 254–259
  website for, 244
jQuery( ) function, 247
jQuery AJAX library, 629–635
jQuery library, 244–247
jquery2.html file, 251

jquery4.html file, 257, 258, 261
jquery5.html file, 259
jquery6.html file, 261
JRE (Java Runtime Environment), 63, 66
.js file, 203
JSON (JavaScript Object Notation), 538, 620
jsonp setting, 630
jsonpCallback setting, 630
JSP (Java Server Pages), 22
JSP.ASP (Java Server Pages.Active Server Pages)
    programs, 22

**K**

kbd elements, 86
KDE (K Desktop Environment) editor, 60–61
key topics, 1
keydown( ) event, 277
keygen form field element, 138
keypress( ) event, 277
keystrokes, listening for, 265, 273–275
keytest.html code, 280
keyup( ) event, 277
keywords, 452–453

**L**

L code, 366
l code, 366
14z_decompress tool, 466
label element, 139
LAMP (Linux, Apache, MySQL, and Perl), 35, 474
Lamport TeX (LaTeX), 538
lang(language) pseudo-classes, 109
Laplace statistical values, 364
Laravel package, 707
large absolute keywords, 115
larger relative keywords, 115
large-scale database environments, 30
largestring, 360
Larsson, Allan, 454
lastChild property, 230, 236
last-child pseudo-classes, 108, 109
lastModified property, 227
lastname data field, 505, 566

lastname property, 572

last-of-type pseudo-classes, 109

LaTeX (Lamport TeX), 538

latin1 character set, 494

latin1_general_ci collation, 494

latin1_general_cs collation, 494

Lavato, James, 364

layout
  coding
    overview, 582
    support files, creating, 587–592
    web page template, creating, 582–587
  designing, 579–581

lcfirst function, 355

LEFT JOIN join type, 529, 530

left position value, 131

left property, 128, 130

length property, 207, 274

Lerdorf, Rasmus, 29

less than (<), 385

li object, 237

<li> element, 92, 93

library files, downloading to server, 245–246

licensing restrictions, 187

lighthttpd server, 28

light-level attribute, 173

LIMIT modifier, 454

line numbering, 54, 61

linear gradients, 164–165

linear-gradient( ) function, 164

link( ) method, 700, 727, 729, 733

link pseudo-classes, 108, 109

<link> tag, 15, 110, 175

links, 594

links property, 227

linktest2.php file, 341, 342

linktest.html web page, 341

Linux, Apache, MySQL, and Perl (LAMP), 35, 474

Linux environment, 33–36, 42, 60–61, 188, 466, 493

Linux Mint, 33

Linux package managers, 703

liquid layout, 134

list attribute, 150, 239

list_items_won.ctp file, 731, 732

listbidder.inc.php code, 596

listbidders value, 595

listbidders.inc.php file, 595–596, 607

listbox_dblclick( ) function, 596

Listen directive, 42

listitems.inc.php file, 606–607

listItemsWon( ) method, 727, 729

lists
  description, 95–96
  ordered, 93–95
  overview, 92
  unordered, 92–93

literals, 453

LOAD DATA INFILE statement, 539

LoadModule directive, 43

loads, 268

loadtest.html file, 268

localhost host name, 658

Location message, 615

LOCK TABLES privileges, 483

locking, 460–461

--lock-tables export, 533

log function, 363

log1p function, 363

log10 function, 363

logarithmic functions, 363

LogFormat directive, 44

logic control
  else statement, 328
  elseif statement, 328–330
  if statement, 326–327
  overview, 325
  switch statement, 330–331

logic tier, 693

logical operations, 320

login session cookie, 590, 591

logistic statistical values, 364

LogLevel directive, 44

logout value, 615

logout.inc.php file, 615

logs, calculating exponents and, 362–363

long-term data storage, 419

loop attribute, 189, 193

looping
  foreach statement, 334–336
  overview, 331
  for statement, 333–334
  while statement, 331–333
lower-level rule, 15
low-level detailed message, 43
ltrim function, 355
Lumen frameworks, 710–711

# M

m code, 366
M code, 366
Mac, Apache, MySQL, and PHP (MAMP), 37, 38, 44, 474
Mac environments, 33, 36–37, 466, 493
macOS, 57–59
magic class methods
  accessor, 403–406
  constructor, 406
  destructor, 407
  mutator, 401–402
  objects, 408–409
  overview, 401
&lt;main&gt; element, 583, 584
main.inc.php file, 584, 590, 591
maintenance features, 30
make attribute, 640
make value, 628
MAMP (Mac, Apache, MySQL, and PHP), 37, 38, 44, 474
margins, 16, 120
MariaDB, 31, 36, 470
mark elements, 86
markup languages, 9, 75
math functions, 361–364
math operators, 207–208
matrix(a,b,c,d,e,f) effect, 179
max attributes, 151
max function, 362
max_execution_time default settings and value, 49
Max-Age=number attribute, 423
max-aspect-ratio attribute, 173
max-color attribute, 173
max-color-index attribute, 173

MaxDB library, 542
max-device-aspect-ratio attribute, 173
max-device-height attribute, 173
max-device-width attribute, 173
max-height attribute, 173
maxLength property, 239
max-monochrome attribute, 173
max-resolution attribute, 173
max-width attribute, 174
max-width property, 689
.mdb file, 447
media, 663
media queries, handling
  @media command, using, 171–172
  multiple style sheets, applying, 175
  overview, 170–171, 172–175
media support, 17
MediaWiki Table, 538
medium absolute keywords, 115
members, 396
memory_limit default settings and values, 49
menus, adding, 52
message property, 296
&lt;meta&gt; tag, 91
metadata, in header, 672
metadata category, 670
method attribute, 136, 137, 343, 630
micro-frameworks, 710–713
Microsoft Active Server Pages (ASP).NET, 22–23
Microsoft Azure, 32
Microsoft developers, 22
Microsoft Excel, 97
Microsoft Expression Web package, 51
Microsoft .NET 4.5, 471
Microsoft SQL Server, 25
Microsoft Windows
  running, 53–57
  server environments, 28
Microsoft Windows Servers, 25
MIDI (Musical Instrument Digital Interface), 187
MIME (Multimedia Internet Mail Extension), 186, 189, 351
mimeType setting, 630
min attribute, 151

min function, 362

min–aspect–ratio attribute, 174

min–color attribute, 174

min–color–index attribute, 174

min–device–aspect–ratio attribute, 174

min–device–height attribute, 174

min–device–width attribute, 174

min–height attribute, 174

minified files, 244

min–monochrome attribute, 174

min–resolution attribute, 174

min–width attribute, 174

miscellaneous functions, 553, 554–560

mixed–case names, 569

mm absolute units of measurement, 114

mobile devices, support for, 700–701

model code, 731

model element, 640

model method, 686–688

Model sub-folder, 719

model–view–controller method. See MVC method

model–view–presenter (MVP) method, 692

model–view–viewmodel (MVVM) method, 692–693

modifiers, 453

mom-and-pop web-hosting companies, 33

money_format function, 355

Mongo library, 542

monochrome attribute, 174

monospace font, 113

month input element type, 151

more_results method, 553

Motion Picture Experts (MP3), 187, 189

Motion Pictures Expert Group (MPEG), 192

Motion Pictures Expert Group updated version (MPEG-4), 192

mouse events
  listening for, 269–273
  watching, 264–265

mousedown( ) event, 277

mouseenter( ) event, 277

mouseleave( ) event, 277

mousemove( ) event, 277

mouseout( ) event, 277

mouseover( ) event, 277

mouseup( ) event, 277

.mov video formats, 192

Mozilla Foundation developers' website, 162

.mp3 audio format, 187, 188

.mp4 video format, 187, 192

mSQL library, 542

multi_query method, 553

multimedia, HTML5 and
  audio, playing, 185–190
  images, 177–185
  overview, 177
  streamers, getting help from, 194
  videos, watching, 190–194

multimedia clips, 52, 74

multimedia content, 10

Multimedia Internet Mail Extension (MIME), 186, 189, 351

multipart/form–data value, 145

multiple attribute, 149

multiple style sheets, applying, 175

multiple tables, querying from, 527–529

multi-server clustering, 30

multi-threading, 455

multitier architecture. See n-tier

multiuser databases, 460

Musical Instrument Digital Interface (MIDI), 187

mutator magic methods, 401–402

muted attribute, 189, 193, 194

MVC (model–view–controller) method
  communicating in, 690–691
  components of, 686–690
  implementing, 694
  n-tier and, 693–694
  other web models, comparing, 691–693
  overview, 683–685

MVP (model–view–presenter) method, 692

MVVM (model–view–viewmodel) method, 692–693

my_comment_mailer( ) function, 673

mybadmain.php program, 323

my.cnf filename, 44

myfont font family name, 170

myfont.woff font file, 170

my.ini filename, 44

MyISAM storage engine, 454–455, 456

myisam_ftdump tool, 466
myisamchk tool, 466
myisamlog tool, 466
myisampack tool, 466
mypage.html file, 339
mypage.php file, 343
MySQL
  administration tools
    command line, 466–470
    overview, 465–466
    phpMyAdmin tool, 474–476
    Workbench tool, 470–474
  data permissions, 457
  databases, 449–454
  features of, 458–464
  overview, 445
  pros of, 26
  storage engine, 456
  user accounts, managing
    creating, 477–481
    overview, 477
    user privileges, 481–488
  utilities, 532
MySQL AB, 31
MySQL cloud server, 31
MySQL Cluster Carrier Grade Edition, 30
mysql command, 467, 468, 470, 478, 657
mysql command-line tool, 539
MySQL Community Edition, 30, 31
MySQL Console, 656
MySQL Enterprise Edition, 30
MySQL library
  connection, closing, 545–546
  data, retrieving, 547–549
  database, connecting to, 544–545
  errors, checking for, 551–553
  example, 554–560
  functions, miscellaneous, 553
  overview, 544
  prepared statement, 549–551
  queries, submitting, 546–547
MySQL packages, installing, 37
mysql program, 469
MySQL server

customizing, 46
database, creating, 656
installing and running, 36
MariaDB and, 31
options for, 31
versions of, 30
MySQL server package, 33–36
MySQL Standard Edition, 30
mysql tool, 466
mysql> prompt, 657
mysqladmin tool, 466
mysqlbinlog tool, 467
mysqlcheck tool, 467
mysqld tool, 466
mysqld_multi tool, 466
mysqld_safe tool, 466
mysqldump export options, 535
mysqldump utility, 467, 533, 534, 539
mysqldumpslow tool, 467
mysqli instance, 546
mysqli object, 543, 545, 576
mysqli_ connect( ) function, 544, 545
mysqli_ prefix, 554
mysqli_ select_db( ) function, 544
MYSQLI_ASSOC parameter, 548
MYSQLI_BOTH parameter, 548
mysqli_close( ) function, 546
mysqli_error( ) function, 552–553
mysqli_fetch_all function, 547
mysqli_fetch_array( ) function, 547, 548
mysqli_fetch_assoc( ) function, 548
mysqli_fetch_assoc function, 547
mysqli_fetch_field( ) function, 547
mysqli_fetch_field_direct( ) function, 547
mysqli_fetch_object( ) function, 547
mysqli_fetch_row( ) function, 547, 548
mysqli_field_seek( ) function, 547
mysqli_free( ) function, 547
MYSQLI_NUM parameter, 548
mysqli_num_rows( ) function, 554
mysqli_query( ) function, 546, 547, 549
mysqli_stmt_bind_param( ) function, 550
mysqli_stmt_bind_result( ) method, 551
mysqli_stmt_fetch( ) method, 551

mysqlimport tool, 467
MySQL/PHP packages, 32
mysqlpump tool, 467
mysql.server tool, 466
mysqlsh tool, 467
mysqlshow tool, 467
mysqlslap tool, 467

## N

n code, 366
\n command shortcut, 310, 315, 469
name attribute, 136, 139, 140, 146, 182, 343, 344
name data field, 559, 566, 567
name property, 239, 241, 296
NATURAL INNER JOIN join type, 530
NATURAL keyword, 530
<nav> element, 78, 134, 583
nav.inc.php file, 587, 589–590, 605
Netbeans, 65–66
new attribute, 287
newbidder.inc.php file, 603–605, 617
newimage.jpg file, 373
newitem variable, 611
newitem.inc.php file, 612, 614
new-line characters, 309–310
next_result method, 553
nextSibling property, 230, 235–238
nginx server, 28
nl2br( ) function, 355, 356
Node.js library, 23
nodeName property, 230
nodeType property, 230
nodeValue property, 230, 641
none element, 259
none position value, 131
non-PHP applications, 712
nopager command, 469
normal forms, 490
normal statistical values, 364
NOT NULL data constraint, 504–505, 509, 516–517
NOT operator, 48
notee command, 469

Notepad, 53–54
Notepad++, 62
notice error level, 43
not(selector) pseudo-classes, 109
novalidate attribute, 136
nowarning command, 469
nth-child pseudo-class, 124
nth-child(n) pseudo-classes, 109
nth-last-child(n) pseudo-classes, 109
nth-of-type(n) pseudo-classes, 109
n-tier, MVC and, 693–694
NULL characters, 355
NULL startdate value, 517
NULL value, 425, 551, 576, 579
num_rows property, 554
number input element type, 151
number theory, 361–362
number variable, 221
number_format function, 355
numbered lists. See ordered lists
numbers, 205
Numbers application, 97
numeric array, 315–316, 548
numeric character reference, 91

## O

0 code, 366
o code, 366
object instance, creating, 397–401
object methods, 232–233
object properties, 229–232
object-oriented application
  database, creating, 571
  events
    bidder object, 595–605
    item object, 606–614
  layout
    coding, 582–587, 588–592
    designing, 579–582
  logging out of, 614–616
  objects
    coding in PHP, 573–579
    designing, 571–573

overview, 563, 593

programming, event-driven, 593–594

requirements for, 563–565

testing, 616–617

object-oriented data method, 687

object-oriented database management system (OODBMS), 687–688

object-oriented programming (OOP)

basics of, 395–401

classes

extending, 414–418

loading, 409–414

magic class methods

accessor, 403–406

constructor, 406

destructor, 407

mutator, 401–402

objects, 408–409

overview, 401

overview, 395

splitting, 683

writing, process of, 571

object-relational mapping (ORM), 686, 707

objects

coding in PHP, 574–579

copying, 408

defined, 207

designing

Bidder object, 572

Item object, 573

overview, 571

displaying, 408–409

objects list, 482

OCI8 (Oracle database server), 542

OCI8 library, 542

ODBC (Open Database Connectivity), 543

offsetx parameter, 167

offsety parameter, 167

.ogg audio file, 187

Ogg Theora, 192

.ogg video format, 192

Ogg Vorbis, 187–189

ol element, 93

on( ) function, 280

ON condition clause, 529

on part, 276

onafterprint event, 266

onbeforeprint event, 266

onbeforeunload event, 266, 269

onclick attribute, 145, 251

onclick event, 265, 270, 276

oncontextmenu event, 265

ondblclick event, 265

one value, 161

onerror event, 266

one-sided elements, 74

one-way encryption algorithm, 568

onhaschange event, 266

onkeydown event, 265

onkeypress event, 265

onkeyup event, 265, 273

online material, 3–4

onload event, 266, 267, 268, 269

only–child pseudo-classes, 109

only–of–type pseudo-classes, 109

onmessage event, 266

onmousedown event, 265

onmouseenter event, 265

onmouseleave event, 265

onmousemove event, 264, 265

onmouseout event, 265, 272, 273

onmouseover event, 265, 272, 273, 293, 294

onmouseup event, 265

onoffline event, 266

ononline event, 266

onpagehide event, 266

onpageshow event, 266

onpopstate event, 266

onreadystatechange callback function, 628

onreadystatechange property, 624–625

onresize event, 266

onsale property, 415

onscroll event, 266

onstorage event, 266

onunload event, 266, 267, 269

OODBMS (object-oriented database management system), 687–688

OOP (object-oriented programming). *See* object-oriented programming

ooptest1.php file, 400

ooptest3.php file, 413

ooptest4.php code, 418

opacity, 117

opacity value, 117

open( ) method, 622

Open Database Connectivity (ODBC), 543

OpenDocument Spreadsheet, 538

OpenDocument Text, 538

opening tag, 74

open(method,url,async,user,pass) method, 622

open-source community, 29, 31

open-source library, 364

open-source packages, 37

OpenType front file formats, 169

operating system (OS), 22, 28

operators, 207–209, 317–320

<option> element, 149

optional pseudo-classes, 109

options category, 670

options DOM object, 629

OPTIONS request, 11

or operators, 319

OR statement, 552

Oracle

acquisition of by Sun, 65

cloud service, providing, 31

features of, 25

MySQL package and, 470

website for, 63

Oracle Cloud Platform, 32

Oracle database server (OCI8), 542

ORDER BY clause, 526

ORDER BY modifier, 454

ordered lists, 93–95

orderid value, 491, 528–529

Orders table, 449–450, 458

organization, 702

Organization of International Standards (ISO), 9, 367

orientation attribute, 174

ORM (object-relational mapping), 686, 707

OS (operating system), 22, 28

out text, 273

outer joins, 529

out-of-range pseudo-classes, 109

output, displaying, 307–309

output data, 525–527

output form field element, 138

output variable, 274

output_buffer setting, 425, 615

outputs, styles for, 16

overflow-inline attribute, 174

overloading, 401

overriding, 401

**P**

\p command shortcut, 469

\P command shortcut, 469

<p> element, 83, 105, 118, 225, 235

package management, frameworks and, 703

padding element section, 119

padding property, 124

page definition, 76–78

page sections, 78–81

pager command, 469

pages, 663

Pages application, 53

pagination, 707

parent class, 414–415, 673

parent div element, 134

parent:: keyword, 415

_parent attribute, 87

parentNode property, 230

parseinput.html file, 357, 358

parseoutput.php file, 358, 359

password data field, 567

password entry, 140

--password export, 533

password input field, 140

--password parameter, 468

password setting, 630

PATCH request, 11

Path=path attribute, 423

pattern matching, 712

pattern property, 239

pc absolute units of measurement, 114

PCRE (Perl Compatible Regular Expressions), 361

PDF (Portable Document Format), 538

PDO (PHP Data Objects), 543

PECL (PHP Extension Community Library), 354

percentages, 287

Perl, 22, 23, 38

Perl Compatible Regular Expressions (PCRE), 361

perror tool, 467

persistent attack, 379

persistent cookie, 421–422, 425–426, 431

persistent data, storing, 419–424

Personal Home Page (PHP). See PHP

phone data field, 566

Phone Numbers table, 491

phone property, 572

Photoshop, 183, 369

PHP (Personal Home Page), 29

  behavior of, 350

  benefits of, 303–304

  code for, 61, 305–306, 696

  coding objects in, 573–579

  files, including, 320–324

  OOP

    basics of, 395–401

    classes, 409–418

    magic class methods, 401–409

    overview, 395

  operators, using, 317–320

  overview, 23, 303

  pages, 306–307

  program flow, controlling

    event-driven PHP, using, 339–348

    functions, building, 336–339

    logic control, using, 325–331

    looping, 331–336

    overview, 325

  quotes and, 314

  scripts, communicating with databases from, 541–544

  security

    cross-site scripting, 376–379

    data, invalid, 380–382

    data spoofing, 379–380

    file access, unauthorized, 382–383

    overview, 375–376

    solutions, 384–394

  sessions and, 430–436

  tools, 29

  using in XML, 636–640

  variables, using, 310–317

  versions, 29

  web pages, adding, 305–310

PHP Data Objects (PDO), 543

PHP Extension Community Library (PECL), 354

.php file, 306, 307, 309, 341

PHP framework

  convention, 696–697

  form validation, 700

  helper methods, 700

  mobile devices, support for, 700–701

  overview, 695–696

  routing, 699–700

  scaffolding, 698–699

  templates, 701

  unit testing, 701–702

PHP libraries

  extensions, using, 349–354

  functions

    date and time, 365–369

    image-handling, 369–374

    math, 361–364

    text, 354–361

  overview, 349–350

PHP packages, 36–37

PHP server, 29–30, 36, 43

<?php tag, 305–306, 309, 431

php_gd2 extension, 369, 371

php_mysqli library, 543, 545, 554

php_name format, 353

phpdatatest.php program, 313

phpinfo( ) function, 47, 351, 352, 353

php.ini configuration file, 615

php.ini file, 46, 47, 48, 353, 354, 379

PHPIniDir directive, 46

phpmyadmin database, 484, 488

phpMyAdmin tool, 474–481, 497–500, 508–512, 522–524, 536–540

PHPRC system environment variable name, 46

PHPSESSID value, 433, 435

phptest.php file, 308, 309

pi function, 362

<picture> tag, 185

pixels, 158–159

placeholder attribute, 154–155, 239

plugin category, 670

plugins, 185, 476, 652, 654, 671–673

Plugins API library, 671

pointer attribute, 174

pointers, 235, 272–273

Poisson statistical values, 364

poly shape value, 182

popular framework, focusing on, 704–710

pop-up messages, 19

Portable Document Format (PDF), 538

Portable Operating System Interface for UniX (POSIX), 361

position property, 128

positioning properties, 128

POSIX (Portable Operating System Interface for UniX), 361

POST data, 344

POST method, 347, 379, 600, 622–623, 690

POST request, 11

poster attribute, 193

PostgreSQL library, 26, 542

posts, 654, 663

pound symbol (#), 91, 105

pow( ) function, 363

preload attribute, 189, 193

pre-loaded packages, 38

premade servers, 37–40

prepare phase, 459

prepared statement, 549–551, 554–560

.prepend( ) function, 260

.prependTo( ) function, 260

presentation tier, 693

previousSibling property, 230, 236

price property, 415

primary key, 451, 490, 500

print command, 469

print media type, 173

private keyword, 397

private visibility, 401, 402, 416

privileges list, 482

procedural programming, 264

procedural style coding, 551

PROCESS privileges, 483

processData setting, 630

Product class, 397, 398, 405, 406, 408–409, 413

productid value, 491

Product.inc.php file, 413

Products table, 449–450, 458, 490

program editors, 61–64

program execution, 64

program flow
  controlling
    conditional statements, 209–216
    event-driven PHP, using, 339–348
    functions, building, 336–339
    logic control, using, 325–331
    looping, 331–336
    loops, 216–220
  defined, 325
  overview, 209

programming languages
  interpreted, 23, 349
  providing APIs, 455
  server-side, 28

project management, 64

prompt( ) function, 215, 219, 223, 235

prompt command, 469

properties, 254–256

proprietary codes, 9

proprietary software plug-ins, 10

proprietary word-processing packages, 7, 9

protected keyword, 397

protected visibility, 414, 415

protocol format, 90

PROXY privileges, 483

pseudo-class, 104, 107–110

pseudo-elements, 104, 106–107

pt absolute units of measurement, 114

public class methods, 415
public keyword, 397
push( ) method, 207
PUT request, 11
putonsale( ) method, 414
px absolute units of measurement, 114
Python, 22, 23

# Q

\q command shortcut, 468, 469
q elements, 86
queries
  advanced, 527–531
  defined, 453
  submitting, 546–547, 554–560
query( ) method, 546–547
query parameter, 546
Query1 panel, 474
quick export, 537
quicktags category, 670
QuickTime, 186, 192
quirks mode, 75
quit command, 469
quotes, PHP and, 314

# R

r code, 366
\r command shortcut, 468
\R command shortcut, 469
.ra audio file, 187
rad2deg function, 363
radial gradients, 165–166
radial-gradient( ) function, 165
radio buttons, 142–143, 241
radio input type, 142
radius value, 158
rand( ) function, 329, 336, 362
range input element type, 151
RangeError error, 296
readonly attribute, 110, 146
readOnly property, 239
read–only pseudo-classes, 109

read/write database cluster, 30
read–write pseudo-classes, 110
ready( ) event, 277
.ready( ) function, 249
readyState property, 624
real_escape_string method, 553, 554
RealAudio, 186, 187
real-time information, 582
realtime.php file, 645, 648
RealVideo, 192
rect shape value, 182
recursive acronym, 23
Red, Green, and Blue (RGB) hexadecimal values, 116, 162
Red Green Blue Alpha (RGBA), 117
Red Hat, 33, 35, 36
redirection, 11
ReferenceError error, 296
REFERENCES privileges, 483
reflected attack, 378
register_ globals setting, 379, 380
register_widget( ) method, 674
regular expressions, 361
rehash command, 469
related documents, linking, 8
relational data method, 686
relational databases, 449–450
relative address, 89
relative keywords, 115
relative positioning method, 130
relative units of measurement, 114, 115
RELOAD privileges, 483
rem unit of measurement, 115
.remove( ) function, 260
removeAttribute(attr) method, 232
removeBidder method, 572
removebidder.inc.php file, 597, 600
removeChild(object) method, 232
.removeClass(class) function, 257
.removeEventListener( ) function, 276
removeItem methods, 573
removeitem.inc.php code, 607–608
RENAME COLUMN old TO new action, 503
RENAME TO new action, 503

repeat parameter, 161

replaceChild(object) method, 232

REPLICATION CLIENT privileges, 483

REPLICATION SLAVE privileges, 483

require( ) function, 323–324

required attribute, 155, 239, 241

required pseudo-classes, 110

resaleprice property, 566, 573

reset field, 145

reset input field type, 145

resize( ) event, 277

resolution attribute, 174

resource handle, 546

responseText property, 624

responseXML property, 624, 639, 641, 643, 648

REST category, 670

REST principles, 707

restock( ) method, 415, 418

result set, 525

result variable, 222

return statement, 221, 337, 408

reusable code, 703

reversed attribute, 94

rewrite category, 671

rewrite rules, 690

RGB (Red, Green, and Blue) hexadecimal values, 116, 162

rgb( ) function, 117, 162

RGBA (red green blue alpha), 117

rich text files (.rtf), 57

RIGHT JOIN join type, 529, 530

right position value, 131

.rm video formats, 192

rollback method, 553

root pseudo-classes, 110

root user account, 34, 36, 457, 475, 477

rotate(angle) effect, 179

round parameter, 161

routing, 690, 699–700

routing table, 712

row-level locking, 461

rows, columns and, 97–99

rows attribute, 146

Rows matched field, 517

rows property, 240

rowspan attributes, 100

RSS news feeds, 655

.rtf (rich text files), 57

rtrim function, 355

rule of thirds, 580

rules, styling, 104–112

Run to Cursor control icon, 292

## S

S code, 366

s code, 366

\s command shortcut, 469

s data type value, 550

SameSite cookie type, 421

SameSite=setting attribute, 423

samp elements, 86

sample resolution, 186–187

sampling rate, 186–187

sans-serif font, 113

SAP (Systems Applications and Products ) software, 542

saveBidder( ) method, 572, 605

saveItem( ) method, 573, 614

saveXML( ) method, 638, 640

scaffolding, 698–699, 721–725

Scalable Vector Graphics (SVG) front file formats, 169

scale(x,y) effect, 179

scaleX(x) effect, 179

scaleY(y) effect, 179

scan attribute, 174

Scintilla, SciTE and, 62–63

screen media type, 173

screen.width global property, 689

script element, 199

script pane, 291

<script> element, 203, 245–246, 305–306, 378, 388

scriptCharset setting, 630

scriptheadtest.html code, 200

scripting attribute, 174

scripting language, 19

scroll( ) event, 277

scrollbars, 23

search engine optimization (SEO), 690

search input element type, 151

second normal form, 491

<section> element, 78, 134, 583

Secure attribute, 423

Secure cookie type, 421, 425

select( ) event, 277

select closing tags, 147

select element, 147

select form field element, 138

SELECT format, 525

SELECT keyword, 453

select opening tags, 147

SELECT statements
  aliases and, 531, 560
  Bowlers and, 559
  building, 731
  clauses, adding, 526–527
  example, 547–548
  format of, 525
  join, using, 529
  submitting, 551
  testing, 530
  verifying mistakes using, 518

select_db( ) method, 545

<select> list box, 597

<select> tag, 148, 149

selection pseudo-element, 107

selector, 104, 254, 280

_self attribute, 87

self-signed certificate, 42

semicolon symbol (;), 91

semitransparent colors, 17

send( ) method, 622–623

send(string) method, 622

SEO (search engine optimization), 690

series, 312

serif font, 113

server default values, 498

server environment, 33–37

server-side application code, 693

server-side data validation, 381–382

server-side programming, 18, 21–25, 28, 320, 620

service support levels, 32

Session cookie type, 421

session cookies, 421–435

session data, 431–436

session ID, 691

session_destroy( ) function, 436

session_start( ) function, 431, 436, 583

session_unset( ) function, 436

sessions
  defined, 420
  overview, 419
  persistent data, storing, 419–424
  PHP and, 436–442
  shopping carts and, 436–442

sessiontest1.php web page, 433

sessiontest2.php file, 435

sessiontest2.php web page, 433

set( ) method, 729

__set( ) mutator method, 402

Set Next Statement control icon, 292

set_charset method, 553

setAttribute(attr) method, 232

setcookie( ) function, 424, 425, 426

Set-Cookie statement, 422

setInterval( ) function, 649

setRequestHeader( ) method, 622

setters, 401

setting values, 44

settings category, 671

SGML (Standard Generalized Markup Language), 9

SHA2( ) function, 567–568, 570

shadows, adding, 166–168

shape parameter, 165

Shockwave Flash, 187

shopping carts, sessions and, 436–442

short open tag, 306

short_open_tag default settings and values, 49

shortcode category, 671

short-term data storage, 419

.show( ) function, 259

SHOW CHARACTER SET statement, 494

SHOW COLLATION statement, 494

SHOW CREATE DATABASE statement, 493–494

SHOW CREATE TABLE statement, 505, 514

SHOW CREATE TABLES statement, 502

SHOW DATABASES statement, 483, 493

SHOW GRANTS statement, 484

Show Next Statement control icon, 292

SHOW TABLES statement, 502

SHOW VIEW privileges, 483

showbidder.inc.php file, 690

SHUTDOWN privileges, 483

side1 variable, 208

side2 variable, 208

sidebars (gray boxes), 2

sin function, 363

single quote ('), 385

sinh function, 364

site visitors, 25

size attribute, 139, 148

size keyword, 114

size parameter, 165

size property, 239

skew(x,y) effect, 179

skewX(x) effect, 179

skewY(y) effect, 179

slice value, 160

slide bars, 23

Slim files, 244

Slim frameworks, 711–712

Slug, 667

small absolute keywords, 115

small elements, 86

smaller relative keywords, 115

SND (SouND), 187

.snd audio file, 187

social media, 651

Social Security numbers (SSNs), 140

socket files, 45

socket setting, 45

Soda class, 414, 418

software, downloading, 655–656

software bugs, 701

solid border property value, 122, 124

SouND (SND), 187

source code packages, 33

source command, 469

<source> tag, 188, 189

space parameter, 161

special characters, 91–92

special margins, 9

special styling, 79

specific file-naming convention, 696

specific font name, 113

specific URL, 628

speech media type, 173

speed of development, 702

spl_autoload_register( ) function, 410

spot variable, 237

spread value, 168

SQL (Structured Query Language), 452–454
  injections, 382, 704
  statements, 532

SQL CREATE TABLE statement, 510

SQL Server, 25

SQL Wizard, 520

sql_mode value, 516

SQLite library, 542

SQLite3 library, 542

SQLSRV library, 542

sqrt function, 362

Squarespace, 52

src attribute, 178, 186, 189, 194, 203

src folder, 718–719

SRI (Subresource Integrity), 246

SSNs (Social Security numbers), 140

standard anchor element, 185

Standard Generalized Markup Language (SGML), 9

standard network communication channel (TCP port 80), 10

start attribute, 94

startdate data field, 491

startdate index table, 492

startdate values, 492

state variable, 293

statement1 parameter, 334

statement1 statement, 217

statement2 parameter, 334

statement2 statement, 217

`static` positioning method, 130
static web pages, 17, 25, 32, 43, 666
static websites, 712
statistical functions, 364
statistical values, 364
statistics, tracking, 364
`status` command, 469
`status` property, 624
`statusCode` setting, 630
`statusText` property, 624
Step Into control icon, 292
Step Out control icon, 292
Step Over control icon, 292
storage engine, 456
stored procedures, 461–463
`storemapname` attribute, 183
storing content, 25–26
`str_getcsv( )` function, 356, 357, 359
`str_replace` function, 355
`str_split` function, 356
`str_word_count` function, 360
`strcasecmp` function, 360
`strcmp` function, 360
streamers, 194
`stretch` parameter, 161
STRICT_ALL_TABLES value, 516
string data, 387, 550
string operators, 320
string values
  altering, 354–356
  assigning, 314
  comma-separated, 635
  merging, 320
  objects and, 636
  quotes and, 270
  searching, 360–361
  splitting, 356–359
  testing, 209, 359
  valid, testing, 391
strings, 205
`strip_tags` function, 355, 356
`strlen` function, 360
`strncmp` function, 360

`strong` elements, 86
`strtolower` function, 355
`strtotime( )` function, 367–369
`strtoupper` function, 355
Structured Query Language. *See* SQL
`style` attribute, 75, 110, 111, 178
style definition, 14
style features, 16
style levels, 15
style object, 256
`style` property, 230
style sheets, 14–16
`<style>` tag, 110
styling
  changing styles, 254–259
  CSS standards, 16–17
  overview, 14–16, 103–104
  rules of, 104–112
  tables, 121–125
  text, 112–119
`sub` elements, 86
`submit( )` event, 277
`submit` form field element, 138
`submit` input, 145, 146
Subresource Integrity (SRI), 246
substring, 360
`success` setting, 631
Sun Microsystems, 31, 65, 66
`sup` elements, 86
SUPER privileges, 483
`Supercookie` cookie type, 421
support files, 587–592
SVG (Scalable Vector Graphics) front file formats, 169
`.swf` audio file, 187
`switch` statement, 213–216, 330–331
`switchtest.html` code, 215
Symfony framework, 708–709
synchronous (`false`) connection, 622
syntax error marking, 61
`SyntaxError` error, 296
system testing, 616
`systemctl` utility, 35
Systems Applications and Products (SAP)
    software, 542

# T

t code, 366

T code, 366

\T command shortcut, 469

\t command shortcut, 469

t statistical values, 364

t1 alias, 531

t2 alias, 531

--tab export, 533

table alias, 531

table data, 123–125

table element, 95, 122

table features, 503–505

table header (th) elements, 99, 100, 122, 124

table headings, 99–101

<table> element, 96

table1 parameter, 529

table2 parameter, 529

table-level locking, 461

tables, 96–101, 121–125, 449–450, 500–512

tags, 9, 73–75, 654

tan function, 363

tanh function, 364

.tar file, 656

target attribute, 87, 136

target pseudo-classes, 110

.tar.gz link, 656

TCP port 80 (standard network communication channel), 10

td element, 97, 99, 122

<td> element, 97, 100

tee command, 469

tel input element type, 151, 153

Template sub-folder, 719

template-based sites. *See* web-hosting sites

templates, 701, 715–720

Ternary operator (?), 211

test variable, 204

text, 85–90, 112–119, 250–252

  alignment, 16

  colors, 14, 16

  fonts, 14, 16, 354–361

  shadows, 166–167

  size, 14, 16

.text( ) function, 250, 252

text areas, 146–147, 239–240

text attribute value, 139

text boxes, 138–140, 238–239

text codes, 9

text data type, 451, 566

text editors

  Linux, 60–61

  macOS, 57–59

  Windows, 52–57

text values, 640

text-align property, 124

textarea object, 239–240

<textarea> element, 138, 147, 281, 344

text-based browser, 178

text-based document-formatting system, 8

text-based interactive interface. *See* command line interface (CLI)

textbox input element, 238

textbox object, 239

textbox properties, 239

TextEdit, 57–59

text-level elements, 85

text-shadow style property, 167

Texy! 538

th (table header) elements, 99, 100, 122, 124

theme customization category, 671

theme modification category, 671

themes, 654

third normal form, 491–492

third-party cookies, 421–422

third-party web hosting company, 653

three-color scheme, 163

three-digit status codes, 11–13

throw statement, 296, 297

time( ) function, 425

time elements, 86

time functions, date and, 365–369

time input element type, 151

time milliseconds, 649

timeout setting, 631

Times New Roman font, 113

timestamps, 367–368

title object. *See also* child objects

title property, 227

<title> tag, 246

tmpdir setting, 45

to bottom direction, 164

to right direction, 164

to top direction, 164

.toggleClass(class) function, 257

tokyo_tyrant library, 542

tools
  browser debuggers, 67–69
  graphical desktop tools, 52
  integrated development environments, 64–67
  overview, 51, 53
  program editors, 61–64
  text editors, 53–57, 58–61
  web-hosting sites, 52–53
  word processors, 53

top property, 128, 130

_top attribute, 87

topics, key, 1

toString( ) method, 232

__toString( ) method, 408–409, 418, 572

tr element, 97, 122

<tr> element, 97

TRACE request, 11

traditional setting, 631

transactions, 458–459

transform property, 179

transients category, 671

translate(x,y) effect, 179

translateX(x) effect, 179

translateY(y) effect, 179

TRIGGER privileges, 483

triggers, 463

trigonometric functions, 363–364

trim( ) function, 355, 359

true (asynchronous) connection, 622

true value, 210, 240

TRUE value, 326, 345, 360, 361, 389, 392, 394

TrueType front file formats, 169

try code block, 295, 296, 298

try.catch statement, 295, 296, 297

tuple, 514

two values, 161

two-color scheme, 163

two-sided elements, 74

.txt file, 55, 60

type attribute, 94, 139, 173, 189, 239, 241, 631

TypeError error, 296

typetest.php file, 390–391, 393

## U

U code, 366

\u command shortcut, 469

Ubuntu, 33–34, 707

ucfirst function, 355

ul element, 92, 237

uncompressed files, 244

undefined value, 204

underscores, 636

unencrypted connections (http), 90

Unicode, 90

Uniform Resource Identifier (URI), 13

Uniform Resource Locator (URL), 89, 678, 711–712

uninterruptable power supply (UPS), 461

unit testing, 616, 701–702

Unix systems, 22, 466, 493

unordered lists, 92–93

unset( ) function, 407, 436, 438, 615

update( ) method, 674

UPDATE keyword, 453

UPDATE privileges, 483

UPDATE statement, 514, 517, 518

updateBidder( ) method, 572, 603

updatebidder.inc.php file, 597, 601–602

update-frequency attribute, 174

updateItem( ) method, 573, 610, 611, 614

updateitem.inc.php code, 607, 608

updates, 663

UPS (uninterruptable power supply), 461

URI (Uniform Resource Identifier), 13

URIError error, 296

URL (Uniform Resource Locator), 89, 678, 711–712

url( ) function, 160

url input element type, 151

URL property, 227

url setting, 631

USAGE privileges, 483, 484

use command, 469

USE statement, 501, 555, 569

usemap attribute, 182

--user export, 533

--user parameter, 468

user privileges, 481-488

user@location combinations, 477

user1 user account, 478, 484, 486

user2 user account, 486

userid data field, 567

username setting, 631

users, 664

USING keyword, 530

utf8 character set, 91-92, 494

utility scripts, 695

## V

Vagrant, 707

.val( ) function, 253, 254

valid pseudo-class, 110, 155

valid state, 460

validate.inc.php file, 591

value attribute, 139, 144, 238, 254, 344

value property, 239, 241, 274

value3 variable, 208-209

valuelist data values, 514, 516

values, 74

var statement, 204

varchar data type, 451, 506, 566

variable-length character strings, 463

variables, 204, 310-316

variables_order default settings and value, 49

variable/value data pairs, 623, 690

veggie value, 316

vertical-align property, 124

vh unit of measurement, 115

video element, 192

<video> tag, 193

videos, 190-194

view( ) method, 697, 699

view component, 694

view controller method, 725

view methods, 688-689, 725

View sub-folder, 719

view.ctp folder, 725

views, 461-462

VirtualBox, 707

visited pseudo-classes, 108, 110

Visual Basic.NET, 23, 28

Visual C++ 2015 Redistributable, 471

visual output, 685

vmax unit of measurement, 115

vmin unit of measurement, 115

VMware, 707

vw unit of measurement, 115

## W

W code, 366

w code, 366

\W command shortcut, 469

\w command shortcut, 469

W3C (World Wide Web Consortium), 9

walkingtest.html code, 237

WAMP (Windows, Apache, MySQL, and PHP), 37

Wampserver, 38

warn error level, 43

warning value, 106

warnings command, 469

watch pane, 291

WAV (Waveform Audio), 187, 189

.wav audio file, 187

web applications, dynamic, 23, 295, 376, 419, 651, 685

web browser, 8

web clients, 10-11

web development environment, 27, 33, 51-69

web folder location, 41-42

web fonts, 17, 113, 169-170

web models, comparing MVC with, 691-693

Web Open Font Format (WOFF) front file formats, 169

web pages

adding, 305-310

content, changing, 198

creating

HTML documents, retrieving, 10-13

markup languages, 9

overview, 7–8
styling, 14–17
World Wide Web and, 8
designing, 580–581
dynamic, 17–25
JavaScript code, including in, 199–203
loading and unloading, 267–269
overview, 1
paying attention to, 266
static
hosting, 32
information, changing, 25
loading, 43
manual changes, 17
styles, changing, 198
template for, 582–587
videos, adding to, 192–194
Wikipedia, 32
web programming
overview, 7
storing content, 25–26
web pages, creating
dynamic, 17–25
HTML documents, retrieving, 10–13
markup languages, 9
overview, 7–8
styling, 14–17
World Wide Web and, 8
web scripting language, 18
web servers
adjustments, making, 41–49
client requests, responding, 11–13
options for, 31–40
overview, 27
requirements for, 27–31
software package, 10
web-hosting, 23
web-hosting companies, 23, 26, 30–33
web-hosting sites, 52–53
WebM video, 191, 192
. webm video formats, 192
website visitors, 28
websites, customizing

overview, 664–669
plugins, 671–673
widgets, 673–674
WordPress APIs, 670–671
Weebly, 52
week input element type, 151
Weinbull distributions statistical values, 364
welcome( ) function, 267
what you see is what you get (WYSIWYG) method, 52, 53
where( ) method, 731
WHERE clause, 517, 518, 526–527, 529, 531, 731
while( ) loop, 548
while statement, 331–333, 437
white space, 80
Widenius, Michael, 454
widget( ) function, 673, 675, 676
Widget API library, 671
widgets, 662, 673–679
widgets category, 671
width attribute, 174, 178, 186, 193, 194
width style property, 127
Wikipedia web page, 32
winbidder data field, 566, 573, 598, 610, 730
Windows, 36–37, 53–57, 466, 493
Windows, Apache, MySQL, and PHP (WAMP), 37
Windows servers, 25, 28
winprice data field, 566, 573
. wmv video format, 192
WOFF (Web Open Font Format) front file formats, 169
word processors, 53
word wrap, 54
WordPress
dashboard, examining, 662–664
installing, 655–662
overview, 651–652
running, 653
website
customizing, 664–674
parts of, 654–655
widgets, creating, 674–679
WordPress All-in-One for Dummies (Sabin-Wilson), 669
wordpress folder, 656, 672, 676

wordpress user account, 657, 658

WordPress.com commercial website, 653

WordPress.org nonprofit entity, 653

word-processing software packages, 53

Workbench tool, 470–474, 478–479, 495–497, 505–508, 519–522, 535–539

World Wide Web Consortium (W3C), 9

WP_Widget class, 673, 675

wp-config.php file, 658

wp-content folder, 676

wp-content/plugins folder, 672

wrap property, 240

write( ) method, 228–229, 232

writeln(text) method, 227

write(text) method, 227

WYSIWYG (what you see is what you get) method, 52, 53

# X

XAMPP (Cross-Platform, Apache, MariaDB, PHP, and Perl), 38–42, 47–49, 354, 470, 474, 656

xhr setting, 631

xhrFields setting, 631

XHTML (Extensible Hypertext Markup Language), 10, 74, 77, 538

x-large absolute keywords, 115

XML (Extensible Markup Language), 291, 351, 620, 635–643, 687–688

XML DOM, 636, 637

XMLHTTP ActiveX object, 621

XMLHTTP object, 620

XMLHttpRequest class
methods, 622–623
properties, 623–625

XMLHttpRequest object, 621–623, 628–629, 639, 641

XML–RPC category, 671

xmltest.php page, 643

xmltest.php program, 641

xor operators, 319

x-small absolute keywords, 115

XSS (cross-site scripting), 376–379, 704

xx-large absolute keywords, 115

xx-small absolute keywords, 115

# Y

Y code, 366

y code, 366

YAML (YAML Ain't Markup Language), 538, 708

Yii frameworks, 713

# Z

z code, 366

Z code, 366

Zend Framework, 29, 709–710

zf tool, 709

.zip file format, 656

zlib_decompress tool, 467

## About the Author

Richard Blum has been a network and systems administrator for more than 30 years for a large government organization. During this time, he has had the opportunity to support Microsoft, Unix, and Linux servers, and write support programs in C/C++, Java, Unix/Linux shell scripts, PHP, and the .NET platform. Rich is also an instructor for a worldwide online course provider, with more than ten years of experience teaching PHP, JavaScript, HTML5, and CSS3 programming courses, as well as a Linux administration course in an adult continuing education environment used by community colleges. Rich also volunteers for nonprofit organizations doing computer and audiovisual support. When he's not busy being a computer nerd, Rich enjoys his time helping out at his church Friendship Bible Study and English as a Second Language groups, and spending time with his wife, Barbara, and two daughters, Katie Jane and Jessica.

## Dedication

To all the students, readers, and coworkers who have forced me to continue learning new things by asking questions. Never stop asking questions!

"Great are the works of the LORD, studied by all who delight in them."

—Psalm 111:2 (ESV)

## Author's Acknowledgments

First, all praise and glory go to God, who through His Son makes all things possible and gives us the gift of eternal life.

Many thanks go to the great team at John Wiley & Sons for their help and guidance throughout the development of this book. Special thanks to Steve Hayes for offering me the opportunity to work on this project and to Elizabeth Kuball for helping keep me focused and the project on track. Also, many thanks to Jack Shepler, the technical editor. This book is a true team effort, and I've had an excellent team to work with. I'd also like to thank Carole Jelen at Waterside Productions for helping arrange this gig for me. You've been a great friend for many years!

Finally, I'd like to thank my parents, Mike and Joyce Blum, for constantly stressing education over goofing off, and my wife, Barbara, and two daughters, Katie Jane and Jessica, for their love and support when I was being grumpy while working on this project.

## Publisher's Acknowledgments

**Executive Editor:** Steven Hayes
**Project Editor:** Elizabeth Kuball
**Copy Editor:** Elizabeth Kuball
**Technical Editor:** Jack Shepler

**Production Editor:** Vasanth Koilraj
**Cover Image:** © hxdyl/Shutterstock